Owin   t,
and n   1-
plex,   ?s
bring: 'e
introc   ;s
Europ
In   al
appro   :o
fascis   s,
offeri   1t
defini   t.
The tl   :

- (n
  ɛ
- (1,
  r
- (g
  f

This Reader provides a sample of authoritative works that have revolutionized the field in the past two decades, supplemented by recent challenging reinterpretations of key aspects of fascism. Chapters include works by: Zeev Sternhell, George L. Mosse, Stanley G. Payne, Roger Griffin, Roger Eatwell, Robert O. Paxton, Michael Mann, Aristotle A. Kallis, Ian Kershaw, Emilio Gentile, Richard Steigmann-Gall, and Constantin Iordachi.

Each extract also has an introduction and annotations to guide the student through the complex arguments. This Reader is the perfect informative introduction to debates on comparative fascist studies.

Constantin Iordachi is Associate Professor of History at the Central European University, Budapest. His publications include: *Charisma, Politics and Violence: The Legion of the "Archangel Michael" in Inter-war Romania* (2004) and *Citizenship, Nation and State-Building: The Integration of Northern Dobrogea in Romania, 1878–1913* (2002).

REWRITING HISTORIES
Edited by Jack R. Censer

COMPARATIVE FASCIST STUDIES

New perspectives

Edited by Constantin Iordachi

Taylor & Francis Group

LONDON AND NEW YORK

First published 2010
by Routledge
2 Park Square, Milton Park, Abingdon, Oxon OX14 4RN

Simultaneously published in the USA and Canada
by Routledge
270 Madison Ave, New York, NY 10016

*Routledge is an imprint of the Taylor & Francis Group,
an informa business*

Typeset in Times New Roman by
Book Now Ltd, London

Printed and bound in Great Britain by
CPI Antony Rowe, Chippenham, Wiltshire

British Library Cataloguing in Publication Data
A catalogue record for this book is available from the British Library

Library of Congress Cataloging in Publication Data
Comparative fascist studies: new perspectives / edited by Constantin Iordachi.
p. cm.—(Rewriting histories)
1. Fascism—Europe—History—20th century. 2. Europe—Politics and government—
1918–1945. 3. Fascism—Study and teaching (Higher) 4. Fascism—Cross-cultural
studies. 5. Europe—Politics and government—1918–1945—Study and teaching
(Higher) 6. Transnationalism—Study and teaching (Higher) I. Iordachi, Constantin.
D726.5.C66 2009
320.53'3094—dc22
2008054219

ISBN10: 0–415–46221–5 (hbk)
ISBN10: 0–415–46222–3 (pbk)

ISBN13: 978–0–415–46221–1 (hbk)
ISBN13: 978–0–415–46222–8 (pbk)

CONTENTS

SERIES EDITOR'S PREFACE

Rewriting history, or revisionism, has always followed closely in the wake of history writing. In their efforts to re-evaluate the past, professional as well as amateur scholars have followed many approaches, most commonly as empiricists, uncovering new information to challenge earlier .accounts. Historians have also revised previous versions by adopting new perspectives, usually fortified by new research, which overturn received views.

Even though rewriting is constantly taking place, historians' attitudes towards using new interpretations have been anything but settled. For most, the validity of revisionism lies in providing a stronger, more convincing account that better captures the objective truth of the matter. Although such historians might agree that we never finally arrive at the 'truth', they believe it does exist and over time may be better approximated. At the other extreme stand scholars who believe that each generation or even each cultural group or subgroup necessarily regards the past differently, each creating for itself a more usable history. Although these latter scholars do not reject the possibility of demonstrating empirically that some contentions are better than others, they focus upon generating new views based upon different life experiences. Different truths exist for different groups. Surely such an understanding, by emphasizing subjectivity, further encourages rewriting history. Between these two groups are those historians who wish to borrow from both sides. This third group, while accepting that every congeries of individuals sees matters differently, still wishes somewhat contradictorily to fashion a broader history that incorporates both of these particular visions. Revisionists who stress empiricism fall into the first of the three camps, while others spread out across the board.

Today the rewriting of history seems to have accelerated to a blinding speed as a consequence of the evolution of revisionism. A variety of approaches has emerged. A major factor in this process has been the enormous increase in the number of researchers. This explosion has reinforced and enabled the retesting of many assertions. Significant ideological shifts have also played a major part in the growth of revisionism. First, the crisis of Marxism, culminating in the events in Eastern Europe in 1989, has given rise to doubts about explicitly Marxist accounts. Such doubts have spilled over into the entire field of social history which has been a dominant subfield of the discipline for several decades. Focusing on society and its class divisions implied that these are the most important elements in historical analysis. Because Marxism was built on the same claim, the whole basis of social history has been questioned, despite the very many studies that directly had little to do with Marxism. Disillusionment with social history simultaneously opened the door to cultural and linguistic approaches largely developed in anthropology and literature. Multiculturalism and feminism further generated revisionism. By claiming that scholars had, wittingly or not, operated from a white European/American male point of view, newer researchers argued that other approaches had been neglected or misunderstood. Not surprisingly, these last historians are the most likely to envision each subgroup rewriting its own usable history, while other scholars incline towards revisionism as part of the search for some stable truth.

Rewriting Histories will make these new approaches available to the student population. Often new scholarly debates take place in the scattered issues of journals which are sometimes difficult to find. Furthermore, in these first interactions, historians tend to address one another, leaving out the evidence that would make their arguments more accessible to the uninitiated. This series of books will collect in one place a strong group of the major articles in selected fields, adding notes and introductions conducive to improved understanding. Editors will select articles containing substantial historical data, so that students – at least those who approach the subject as an objective phenomenon – can advance not only their comprehension of debated points but also their grasp of substantive aspects of the subject.

Few fields are more vexed than that of fascism. First, despite an ocean of empirical research on the details of individual countries, relatively little research crosses national boundaries. Nonetheless, the scholarly community, as well as the public, uses the generic term of fascism in a way that suggests it possesses clear characteristics. This volume reminds us that no consensus exists on this subject. In fact, a collection on comparative fascism must be more about the debates on the definition of this political ideology than a selection of articles disputing one or another of the characteristics of fascist states. This book makes a very important contribution by drawing together and contextualizing the massive discussion that does exist concerning the traits of fascism as it has evolved and changed since its beginning with Mussolini's seizure of power in Italy in the early 1920s. It also takes up the relationship of fascism to totalitarianism and communism. Through its exhaustive introduction and its articles, this volume provides an enormously useful guide to past debates and now a solid ground from which to pursue more comparative empirical studies.

ACKNOWLEDGEMENTS

We are grateful to all those who have granted us permission to reproduce the extracts listed below. While every effort has been made to trace and acknowledge ownership of copyright material used in this volume, the publishers will be glad to make suitable arrangements with any copyright holders whom it has not been possible to contact.

Zeev Sternhell. "Fascism," in D. Miller, ed., *The Blackwell Encyclopedia of Political Thought* (Oxford: Basil Blackwell, 1987), pp. 148–151.

George L. Mosse. "Toward a General Theory of Fascism," in *The Fascist Revolution: Toward a General Theory of Fascism* (New York: Howard Fertig, 1999), pp. 1–44, 200–205.

Stanley G. Payne. "Introduction. Fascism: A Working Definition," in *A History of Fascism, 1919–1945* (Routledge © 1995 The Board of Regents of the University of Wisconsin System), pp. 3–19. Reproduced by permission of Taylor and Francis Books UK and by permission of The University of Wisconsin Press.

Roger Griffin. "General Introduction" in Roger Griffin (ed.) *Fascism* (Oxford: Oxford University Press, 1995), pp. 1–12. By permission of Oxford University Press and the author.

Roger Griffin. "The Primacy of Culture: The Current Growth (or Manufacture) of Consensus within Fascist Studies," reproduced with permission from *the Journal of Contemporary History* 37 (2002): 21–43. © Sage Publications Ltd 2002, by permission of Sage Publications Ltd and the author.

Roger Eatwell. "The Nature of 'Generic Fascism': the 'Fascist Minimum' and the 'Fascist Matrix'", first published as Eatwell, R. (2003). Zur Natur des "generischen Faschismus." Das "faschistische Minimum" und die "faschistische Matrix," in U. Backes (ed.) *Rechtsextreme Ideologien im 20 und 21 Jahrhundert*. Cologne: Boehlau, pp. 93–122, (3-412-03703-6). Reproduced by permission of the publisher and the author.

ACKNOWLEDGEMENTS

Robert O. Paxton. "The Five Stages of Fascism," *The Journal of Modern History*, 70 (1998), The University of Chicago Press, 1: 1-23.

Michael Mann. "A Sociology of Fascist Movements," and "Conclusion: Fascists, Dead and Alive," in *Fascists* (Cambridge: Cambridge University Press, 2005), pp. 1–5, 13–17; 23–30; 353–365, by permission of the publisher and the author.

Aristotle A. Kallis. "The 'Regime-Model' of Fascism: A Typology," *European History Quarterly,* 30: 77–107. © Sage Publications Ltd, 2000, by permission of Sage Publications Ltd and the author.

Ian Kershaw. "Hitler and the Uniqueness of Nazism," *Journal of Contemporary History,* 39 (2): 239–254. © Sage Publications Ltd, 2004, by permission of Sage Publications Ltd and the author.

Emilio Gentile. "The Sacralisation of Politics: Definitions, Interpretations and Reflections on the Question of Secular Religion and Totalitarianism," *Totalitarian Movements and Political Religions*, 1 (Summer 2000) 1: 18–55. Taylor & Francis Ltd, http://www.informaworld.com, reprinted by permission of the publisher and the author.

Roger Griffin. "Cloister or Cluster? The Implications of Emilio Gentile's Ecumenical Theory of Political Religion for the Study of Extremism," *Totalitarian Movements and Political Religions*, 6 (June 2005) 1: 41–43, 51–52. Taylor & Francis Ltd, http://www.informaworld.com, reprinted by permission of the publisher and the author.

Richard Steigmann-Gall. "Nazism and the Revival of Political Religion Theory," *Totalitarian Movements and Political Religions*, 5 (2004) 3: 376–396. Taylor & Francis Ltd, http://www.informaworld.com, reprinted by permission of the publisher and the author.

THE STRUCTURE OF THE VOLUME

The collection is structured in introduction and three main parts, corresponding to distinct methods and levels of comparison employed in fascist studies. They focus on: 1) debates over ideal-types models of generic fascism used as instruments of comparison and evaluation of historical case studies; 2) cross-national and trans-national empirical comparisons of historical examples of fascism, measured against each-other or against theoretical models of generic fascism; and 3) debates over totalitarianism and political religions related to the study of fascist movements and regimes.

The first part of the volume, entitled "Defining Generic Fascism: A New Consensus?" concentrates on attempts at constructing dominant ideal-type models of generic fascism and the academic debates they have generated. The first major departure from the "hegemony" of Marxist theory of fascism was the study of fascist ideology understood as a coherent and comprehensive set of propositions and not simply as a "messy mixture." In order to document this breakthrough in the study of fascism, the part opens with a short encyclopedia entry on the main features of the fascist ideology authored by Zeev Sternhell. His article focuses mainly on the roots of the fascist ideology in France and Italy, and the fascist synthesis of both rightist and leftist political themes, such as the idea of organic nationalism and the socialist reaction again materialism. The part continues with a seminal article written by George L. Mosse, who examines the main features of the fascist ideology and culture and, on the basis of his extensive and decades-long comparative work, proposes a general theory of fascism. The work of Sternhell and Mosse, among others, have set the foundation for the elaboration of sophisticated theoretical models of generic fascism, the most influential being those elaborated by Emilio Gentile, Stanley G. Payne, Roger Griffin and Roger Eatwell. In the third chapter, Stanley G. Payne puts forward a descriptive model and a typology of interwar fascist movements and regimes, and arrives at a "retrodictive" theory of fascism. In the fourth chapter, Roger Griffin summarizes the main features of his widely-employed ideal-type model of generic fascism. In a second short excerpt, Griffin presents his model as the nucleus of an incipient consensus in fascist studies over the definition of generic fascism. In the last chapter of the first part, Roger Eatwell presents his own model of generic fascism, underscoring the importance of ideology but defining the core of fascism as "a flexible 'matrix'" rather than as an essentialist and static minimum. Although the theoretical models of generic fascism presented in the first part are in many ways divergent, the selection allows the reader to grasp the nature of the theoretical and methodological debates over generic fascism. It also documents the research convergence emerging in fascist studies, around the core culturalist paradigms put forward by Sternhell, Mosse, Gentile, Payne, Griffin and Eatwell.

The second part of the volume, entitled "Historical Fascism: Cross- and Trans-National Comparisons," shifts the attention from theoretical models of generic fascism to comparative analyses of *historical or existing fascism*, offering authoritative comparative surveys of European fascism or trans-national comparative perspectives. The first article, authored by Robert O. Paxton, a reputed historian of Vichy France, challenges ideal-type models of generic fascism pleading for comparative works on historical fascism, approached in view of its main stages of development. The excerpts from Michael Mann's recent book on fascism offer comparative sociological insights into the social basis of European fascism and a systematic reflection on the origins and rise of fascist movements in various European regions, supplemented by an in-depth analysis of five case studies of major fascist movements. In the third article, Aristotle Kallis redirects the research agenda from the fascist ideology and movements to the neglected history of fascist regimes. He identifies a series of factors that shaped the outlook of fascist regimes and proposes a typology in view of their main features and evolution. The part ends with a case study on the uniqueness of Nazism by Ian Kershaw. The second part thus familiarizes the readers with alternative typologies of fascism in view of the history of interwar fascist movements and regimes.

The third part of the volume explores academic controversies surrounding the issue of fascism as a form of totalitarianism and the recent debates over civil and political religions. The part opens with an article by Emilio Gentile, in which the author advances a comprehensive framework for analyzing "the sacralization of politics." In order to assess the applicability of the concept of political religion to concrete case studies, the third part continues with two critically minded articles by Richard Steigmann-Gall and Constantin Iordachi focusing on Nazi Germany and the Romanian Iron Guard, respectively. Arguing in favour of empirically-grounded surveys on the social basis of fascism, Steigmann-Gall rejects the political religion theory and questions its validity for the case of Nazi Germany. Iordachi highlights the link between nineteenth century Romantic religious revival, militarism, and the sacralization of politics on the one hand, and the emergence of fascism in Romania, on the other. On this basis, he provides a wider reflection on the religious roots of charismatic forms of nationalism in European discourses of palingenesis, and argues for the inclusion of Central European allegedly "peripheral" or "minor" movements into mainstream fascist studies.

COMPARATIVE FASCIST STUDIES

An introduction

Constantin Iordachi

Fascism continues to be one of the most intriguing and most debated radical political phenomena of the twentieth century. The reasons for this continued scholarly interest lie primarily in fascism's complexity, its vast mass appeal, the fanaticism it instilled in its followers, and in its tremendous political impact, with strong reverberations in contemporary politics. Although, with the exception of Germany and Italy, fascists almost invariably failed to gain full political power, their ideas, new style of politics, and concerted assault on the established parliamentary regimes and international order shaped politics in inter-war Europe, the period being euphemistically dubbed 'the era of fascism' (Nolte 1963). The influence of fascism extends nevertheless well beyond the inter-war period. On the one hand, its ideological roots go back to the Enlightenment, Romanticism, and the intellectual and political atmosphere of the turn of the nineteenth century. On the other hand, the legacy of fascism had a strong impact on post-1945 politics and has resurfaced with vigour in the post-Cold War world, prompting scholars to speak of 'neo-fascism' (Gregor 2006).

In addition to the paramount political importance and continuous relevance of fascism, the on-going interest in the history of fascism has been also amplified by the major difficulties social scientists have encountered in their efforts to capture the 'nature' or 'essence' of this contested political phenomenon. These difficulties have mainly to do with the international character of fascism and its multiple aspects and dimensions. The concept of fascism can refer to a trans-national ideology, to a set of related political movements, and to a set of related political regimes in inter-war Europe and, arguably, even beyond these geographical and temporal confines. Each aspect of the triad *ideology–movement–regime* has its own history and diachronic evolution, and can be analysed separately, by means of distinct methodologies.

A product of a long-term gestation finally crystallized by the Great War, the *fascist ideology* was highly eclectic, a mixture of both rightist and leftist

1

ingredients in a 'new key'. As a 'latecomer' in European politics (Linz 1976), fascism proposed a 'Third Way' – conceived as an alternative to both liberal democracy and revolutionary socialism – an original synthesis of socialism, right-wing conservatism, and integral nationalism, most often coupled with anti-Semitism and pseudo-scientific social Darwinist discourses on racial regeneration. As a revolutionary form of nationalism, fascism promoted concomitantly a 'regressive' and 'futurist' political utopia, appropriating and redefining Romantic symbols, rites, and rituals while proposing at the same time an alternative totalitarian society based on the creation of the 'new men' through spiritual regeneration, new forms of socialization and education, corporatism, and a new style of charismatic leadership.

As a novel type of political *movement*, fascism was a product of post-World War I mass politics. Its evolution exhibited a peculiar combination of grass-roots vitality, on the one hand, and weakness and vulnerability in the face of authoritarian rule, on the other. Fascist movements thrived in unconsolidated multiparty political regimes, evolving soon as the main challenge to constitutional, liberal political orders, but proved at the same time highly vulnerable to political repression from above. Their vitality was rarely conducive to the establishment of consolidated *regimes*. This led to an underlying paradox: while fascist movements existed in almost all European countries as well as in other regions of the world, there are only two examples of independent, long-lasting, and fully consolidated *fascist regimes*, namely Mussolini's Italy and Hitler's Nazi Germany. In Nazi satellite countries or occupied territories during World War II such as Vichy France, Slovakia, Croatia, Hungary, Romania, and Ukraine, short-lived fascist governments depended either on German support or on the collaboration of factions of the old elites, resulting in puppet regimes or hybrid military-fascist dictatorships.

The multifarious character of fascism as a historical phenomenon accounts for the sharp academic debates in the field. The study of these debates is essential to understanding fascism: as Ernst Mandel pertinently pointed out, 'The history of fascism is at the same time the history of the theoretical analysis of fascism' (1971: 9). More generally, these academic debates are also important for grasping the emergence and main features of mass politics in the twentieth century, as they touch upon fundamental issues connected to the nature of modern politics and societies. Indeed, one cannot become a comprehensively trained historian of the modern period without an in-depth familiarity with the academic debates over fascism and related themes, such as radical politics and totalitarianism.

This endeavour poses, nevertheless, several underlying challenges. First, the literature on fascism is enormous. Because no individual researcher can fully cover such a vast, heterogeneous, fragmented and linguistically diverse literature, it becomes evident that textbooks, works of synthesis, and issue-oriented collections of studies on fascism are essential to the dissemination of research results to a larger audience. Although the available offer is apparently very large, such collections are either unavoidably outdated by the highly dynamic rhythm of research in the field (necessitating regular reappraisals), or forcefully address only certain issues or specialized segments of the public and should thus be treated as complementary rather than overlapping (Weber 1964; Laqueur and Mosse 1966; Woolf 1968, 1969; Laqueur 1976; Larson *et al*. 1980; Griffin, 1991, 1995, 1998; Blinkhorn 2000; Davies and Lynch 2002; Passmore 2002; Kallis 2002; Morgan 2003; Griffin *et al*. 2006).

The second, inter-related, challenge is the issue of *selection*: no compilation of texts can do full justice to the extraordinary richness and diversity of the academic literature on fascism. Since the body of existing literature is so vast, the current volume intends neither to provide an exhaustive overview of the evolution of this field of study over time, nor to fully illustrate the extremely large spectrum of available theories of fascism, which would be a self-defeating task for such a small volume. Instead, the volume is centred on *comparative fascist studies*. It aims to provide students of fascism with a theoretically minded and informative introduction to the recent debates on comparative fascism, by means of a sample of some of the most influential works that have revolutionized fascist studies in the past decades, supplemented by a couple of new challenging reinterpretations of key aspects of inter-war European fascism. Needless to say, this selection is not meant to reduce the vast literature on fascism to a handful of authors. My choice is motivated by the fact that most of the articles included in this collection offer rich historical overviews as well as comprehensive theoretical frameworks, thus enabling further original empirical work on historical case studies. Moreover, most of these works have received considerable international attention, informing meaningful academic debates in the field of comparative fascism. They also include ample (critical as well as appreciative) cross-references to each other, thus providing a window into the academic dialogue and the process of scholarly cross-fertilization in this field of study.

This introduction is made up of two main parts. The first section explicates the main levels and methods of comparison employed in fascist studies, contextualizing the debates presented in the volume and providing ample bibliographical references. The second section surveys comparative treatments of fascism and communism as forms of totalitarianism and political religions, and evaluates their impact on fascist studies. The conclusion critically assesses the state of the art in the field of comparative fascist studies and identifies new avenues of research based on a combination of geographical, temporal, and analytical criteria.

Fascist studies and the comparative method

As an analytical concept, fascism is inherently comparative. That is because fascism was a European-wide, and – according to many authors – even global phenomenon. The moment a given scholar uses the word fascism to refer not to a movement or regime in inter-war Italy but to a generic or universal phenomenon, he or she engages in an exercise in comparative history. (In order to differentiate between the two, scholars spell Italian *F*ascism with a capital 'F', reserving *f*ascism spelled with a lower case 'f' for the idea of generic or universal fascism). Given the transnational character of fascism, the comparative method is indispensable to fascism studies, enabling students to identify similarities and differences among historical examples of fascism, and thus to account for those common or entangled dimensions at a pan-European or global level, the *tertium comparationis* of fascism serving as the basis for comparison.

The basic premise of comparative fascist studies is that, although fascist movements and regimes took specific or even original forms in different countries, they were shaped by common trans-national conditions, were animated by a common ideology, and shared a sum of common features in terms of their organization, style of politics, social composition, and political evolution. Comparison is indispensable in understanding what fascist movements and regimes had in common within their own 'class', on the one hand, and what differentiates them from other types of political movements and regimes in the twentieth century, on the other. Certainly, this is not to say that comparison is, in itself, a panacea of knowledge; as every methodological tool, the comparative method is a kind of 'empty vessel'; it is up to the researcher to devise the most appropriate comparative frameworks for his work and 'endow them with meaning' (Seigel 2005: 71). Consequently, a clear understanding of the heuristic advantages and limitations in the application of comparative method to the field of fascist studies is essential in assisting scholars in their efforts to critically evaluate the explanatory problems associated with fascism.

In order to study fascism comparatively, one needs to insert historical case studies within a unified theoretical framework. How can such a comparative framework be built? What would it entail? Any comparative framework needs to necessarily specify the following elements: (1) the aim of the comparison, the working hypothesis to be tested, and the method employed to this end; (2) the objects and units of comparisons; and (3) the employment of a diachronic or a synchronic perspective (Haupt and Kocka 2004: 26–27, 37). These stages are common to research in comparative fascist studies, as well, yet the diversity and heterogeneous nature of fascism as a historical phenomenon pose additional challenges to comparatists.

The first stage in the elaboration of a comparative framework for studying fascism is to define the premises of the investigation, identifying and clarifying the concepts to be employed. As Stain Ugelvik Larsen pertinently pointed out, students of fascism need to differentiate between a *definition* of fascism, meaning a conceptual understanding, and an *explanation* of fascism, meaning a theory of the causes and conditions of the emergence of fascism (2001: 713). In other words, they need to differentiate analytically between 'what a phenomenon *is* from what makes, or brings, it into *being*' (ibid.: 713). Students of fascism also need to differentiate between fascism as a dependent variable illuminating 'the "causes" which *produced* fascism as a political movement and as a regime', and fascism as an independent variable, illuminating 'the *effects* fascism had as a movement/regime upon the societies concerned' (ibid.: 713).

The second stage is to define the scope and nature of the investigation and, as a function of that, to select the most appropriate methods, objects and units of comparison. What forms of comparison are possible in fascist studies? Since comparison does not consist of a fixed methodology that can be indiscriminately applied to empirical case studies, many forms of comparison can be employed, at various analytical, geographical, or temporal levels, as a function of the aims of the respective research. They depend on the (inter-)disciplinary methodological tool-kits available to researchers, but also on their own imagination and creativity. For exemplification, let me review some of the most widely and routinely employed forms of comparison: if we want to arrive at a definition of generic fascism, we either build an ideal-type model of fascism which can then be tested on historical case studies, or provide a descriptive definition of fascism, based on commonalities derived through comparative observation of historical cases. If we want to understand the ideological origins of fascism, we need to compare products of fascist ideologues in various countries and at different moments in time. If we want to understand the social origins and composition of fascist movements, we need to compare social contexts and patterns of membership in those states where fascist movements developed. But we might also employ a 'contrast comparison', and measure these cases against countries where fascist movements failed to develop, in order to understand 'what was missing' there. If we want to grasp the common features of fascist regimes, we might compare their ideological goals, their political-institutional features, their evolution and performance in government, etc. If we want to understand the main features of fascism as a distinct type of modern politics, then we also need to compare fascist ideology, movements, and regimes, on the one hand, with other types of ideologies, movements, and regimes, such as liberal or communist, on the other. As a political ideology and practice, fascism is inserted into two larger taxonomies: that of the right, involving comparisons to forms of conservative-authoritarian nationalism, within the larger family *of inter-war authoritarianism*; and that of totalitarian movements and regimes, where fascism is lumped together with communism and contrasted with liberal democracy, as its ideological arch-enemy.

Since there is no one predetermined, ready-made comparative framework for the study of fascism, the *objects and units* of comparison are equally diverse: their selection is intimately related to the purpose of the comparison, depending on the problem being addressed and the explanatory hypothesis employed. From an analytical perspective, most forms and units of comparison could be successfully justified. One should nevertheless compare what is comparable. Peter H. Merkl emphasized the importance of identifying compatible units of comparison in fascist studies, arguing that we cannot compare 'a platonic essence called "German fascism" with another essence called "French fascism"' or 'a Fascist regime with a fascist book'. But 'we can compare fascist persons, groups, organizations, regimes, or policies, as long as we first establish some equivalency among the units of our comparison' (1980: 753).

What are the possible outcomes of comparison in fascist studies? A function of the analytical goals set by researchers, comparative analyses of fascism can result in theoretical models of generic fascism, in descriptive definitions of inter-war historical fascism, in general theories identifying the structural conditions or mutual causation for the emergence and evolution of fascist movements, or in typologies of existing fascist movements and regimes based on their similarities and differences. In addition, comparisons can be diachronic, in the sense that they can aim at tracing the origins and evolution of certain processes in time, such as the roots of fascist ideology, or synchronic, in the sense that they can aim at examining contemporary or trans-epochal cases of fascism. The following section provides a brief overview of the evolution of comparative fascist studies as a distinct sub-field of historical inquiry, emphasizing the main research dilemmas and the various methodological strategies employed to solve them.

Comparative fascist studies: research stages, approaches, debates

Comparative fascist studies have a long but protracted and non-linear history. One can distinguish several stages in the evolution of this sub-field of study, shaped by radically different political contexts, and characterized by distinct interdisciplinary influences and analytical focuses (for overviews, see Gregor 1974, 1997; de Felice 1977; Gentile 1986, 2000, 2004; Griffin 1995, 2002a, 2002b, 2004, 2005a, 2005b; Kallis 2002, 2004; Umland 2005).

The first stage of comparative fascist studies occurred during the inter-war period, being stimulated by the establishment and consolidation of fascist regimes in Italy (1922–43), and Germany (1933–45), and by the emergence of similar right-wing movements in various European countries. Incipient research on the fascist phenomenon originated from a wide variety of political positions, ranging from conservative, Catholic, liberal, social-democrat, and communist. One can distinguish three major – and by now 'classic' – interpretations of fascism as: (1) a symptom of a moral crisis in European society; (2) an expression of belated and largely peculiar patterns of nation- and state-building and economic development in Italy and Germany; and (3) the Marxist view of fascism as the last stage of development of the capitalism system in crisis (de Felice 1977: 14–54). In addition to these, there was also a number of minor interpretations, such as the 'Catholic' and the 'totalitarian', each of them with a long-lasting influence on the scholarship of fascism (ibid.).

By and large, inter-war research on fascism was confined within the Marxist-Leninist historiographic 'camp'. After a brief period of puzzlement with the advent of a novel political phenomenon that challenged their classical scheme of history which posited a direct teleological transition from capitalism to socialism, Marxist-Leninist thinkers were the first to put forward a general theory of fascism explaining its ideological roots, the structural and social-political conditions favouring the emergence of fascist movements, the evolution of these movements over time, their social composition, the main features of fascist regimes and their domestic and foreign policy. This theory was crystallized mostly during Cominform meetings and elaborated on, with various accents, by prominent theoreticians such as Leon Trotsky (1944), Georgi Dimitrov (1935, 1967, 2002), Rajani Palme Dutt (1934), Palmiro Togliati (2004), and Antonio Gramsci (see Fabio-Liguori 2004), among others.

For Marxists, fascism did not bring about an end to the capitalist system, but was the last stage of capitalist class rule, 'a *substitution* of one state form of class domination of the bourgeoisie – bourgeois democracy – by another form – open terrorist dictatorship' (Dimitrov 1935). The essence of the new regime was the close relationship between the fascist government and big business, an idea synthesized by Dimitrov in a catchy phrase that was to become the main cliché associated with the Marxist position: 'Fascism is the power of finance capital itself.' According to this interpretation, fascism had no genuine mass appeal; its popularity was based on demagogy and deceiving, capitalizing on the masses' 'most urgent needs and demands' but also on 'their sense of justice and sometimes even on their revolutionary traditions'. The fascist regime was a form of 'political gangsterism, a system of provocation and torture', based on 'social demagogy, corruption and active white terror'. In foreign policy, fascism acted as 'the spearhead of international counter-revolution, as the chief instigator of imperialist war' (ibid.).

These major similarities among fascist movements and regimes did not exclude differences. Marxist thinkers were the first to comment on the 'variety of fascism' in Europe: In Dimitrov's words, 'The development of fascism, and the fascist dictatorship itself, assume *different forms* in different countries, according to historical, social and economic conditions and to the national peculiarities, and the international position of the given country.' Dimitrov even advanced an incipient typology of fascist movements and regimes; this included Nazi Germany, regarded as 'the most reactionary' form of fascism. After June 1941, in the Soviet official historiography, Nazi Germany was constantly referred to as fascist. Often, the Marxist historiography stretched the concept of fascism to also embrace conservative authoritarian regimes, such as Horthy's regime in Hungary or Pilsudski's regime in Poland.

Building on these initial positions, the Marxist historiography on fascism has since been extremely prolific, but has also become very heterogeneous. One can distinguish markedly different schools of Marxist thought, among which I mention selectively Austrian, British, German, Italian, and the distinct Soviet and East European branches of Marxism. Especially after World War II, new generations of Marxist thinkers questioned the main tenets of the inter-war Stalinist dogma on fascism and put forward neo-Marxist interpretations (for overviews, see Poulantzas 1974; Beetham 1983; Gregor 2000). The innovative work of the British Marxist historian Timothy M. Mason stands out in this respect. While focusing on the social origins of National Socialism and its antithetical relation to the working class, Mason departed from Dimitrov's view that fascism was simply a tool of big business. Arguing for the 'primacy of politics', he pointed out that fascist governments were autonomous in their decision-making from capitalist interests (1968, 1977). He also pleaded for the comparative study of fascism, especially of Nazi Germany and Fascist Italy (1991, 1995).

While contributing important aspects to the comparative study of fascist movements and regimes in terms of their social origins, membership, and political evolution, Marxist interpretations have often remained marred by ideological presuppositions and a rigid schema of history that led almost invariably to predictable results and clichés even in the most sophisticated works. They continued to stress the statist, dictatorial dimension of fascist regimes, paying less attention to the nationalist, populist and revolutionary character of the fascist movements on which these regimes were built. In addition, the unilateral emphasis on material interests and economic 'base' made Marxist thinkers less receptive to the idea of a specific fascist ideology and culture that could account for fascism's mass appeal.

Studying fascism 'from the inside out': toward non-Marxist comparative approaches

After a period of stagnation in the first post-war decades, the comparative study of fascism outside the Marxist camp was boosted in the mid-1960s, in distinct academic settings, by several pioneering scholars from North America and Western Europe: Ernst Nolte, a German historian with a research interest in fascism and communism; Eugen Weber, a reputed historian of modern Europe, with a focus on France and Romania; and Walter Lacquer and George L. Mosse, two prominent cultural historians, founders of the *Journal of Contemporary History*. Their work was continued by sociologist Juan J. Linz and historian Stanley Payne in the USA, and by historian Renzo de Felice in Italy, among others. Together, these scholars set the basis of comparative fascism as a distinct field of study. Their work was to have a long-lasting influence on fascist studies, inspiring three related but nevertheless distinct directions of research: (1) the emphasis on a distinct ideology and culture responsible for fascism's genuine mass appeal; (2) the comparative historical analysis of fascist movements and regimes, and (3) the debate over arriving at a consensual theoretical model of 'generic' fascism.

In 1963, Ernst Nolte published his magisterial *Der Faschismus in seiner Epoche* (translated into English as *The Three Faces of Fascism*, 1966). Employing Edmund Husserl's phenomenological method, Nolte advanced a comparative historical analysis of three movements: the French *Action Française*, German Nazism, and Italian Fascism. Nolte treated Italian Fascism and German National Socialism as compatible phenomena, approaching them not in terms of mutual influences but in view of the structural European conditions which produced them. The inclusion of *Action Française* in this comparison came as a surprise, since routinely this organization, established in 1898, is not classified as fascist but as conservative nationalist (Weber 1962). Nolte assigned a particular importance to this case study. In his view, the origins of the Italian Fascism and German National Socialism were 'simultaneous and entirely independent'; overall, the two phenomena displayed 'as many differences as similarities'. It was the *Action Française* that provided the 'missing link' between the Italian Fascism and German National Socialism (1966: 26, 275–276). Using a

Hegelian dialectics, Nolte argued that *Action Française* was the thesis, the Italian fascism the antithesis, and the German National Socialism the synthesis of the two movements (Maier 1988: 85–87).

On the basis of this triadic sample of case studies, Nolte arrived at a concise generic definition of fascism as a rejection of modernity based on a set of negations: anti-liberalism, anti-capitalism, anti-bourgeois, and most importantly, anti-communism:

> Fascism is anti-Marxism which seeks to destroy the enemy by the evolvement of a radically opposed and yet related ideology and by the use of almost identical and yet typically modified methods, always, however, within the unyielding framework of national self-assertion and autonomy.
>
> (1966: 20–21)

To these, he later added a set of 'positive' characteristics of fascist movements, most importantly the leadership principle and the emergence of a militarized party (1968b: 385). In his subsequent work, doubting that generic fascism constitutes, in itself, 'a suitable subject for research and expertise', Nolte subsumed his analysis of fascism to the concept of totalitarianism, and redirected his research toward the comparison between fascism and communism, mostly in their most peculiar historical incarnations as National Socialism and Stalinism, respectively (1977/1982). Yet, his pioneering approach was to have a lasting impact on fascist studies.

In 1964, almost concomitantly with Nolte, Eugen Weber published one of the first works in the emerging field of comparative fascist studies, suggestively entitled *Varieties of Fascism*. The book provided a comprehensive overview of the history of fascism in Europe. Weber employed concomitantly a synchronic as well as a diachronic perspective. First, he approached comparatively the history of inter-war fascist movements, attempting 'to note some of their similarities and differences'. Second, Weber studied fascist ideology from a long-term perspective, paying attention to the coagulation of a set of fascist myths, in close connection with the evolution of nationalism, anti-liberalism, socialism, and racism. Third, aiming at a new type of objectivity by 'taking Fascists and National Socialists at their words' (1964: 3), Weber proposed a close reading of fascist texts, providing a sample of primary sources on eight countries.

The aim of Weber's comparative approach was to arrive at a 'new classification' of the inter-war radical-right movements, based on their ideology and not on their history or political practice. To this end, Weber differentiated between conservative nationalism oriented toward the maintenance of the existing social-political status quo, and the radical right oriented toward anti-systemic revolutionary change. In regard to the latter trend, Weber noted major differences between a fascist and a national-social(ist) streams of thought. The fascist stream emerged first and foremost in Italy. The national-socialist stream, based on an uneven combination of nationalism with socialism, developed predominantly in Austria, Germany and France. Weber thus arrived at *two analytical models* of the radical right, distinguishing between fascism, which was 'pragmatically activist' and oriented toward action, and National Socialism, which was in his view more 'theoretically motivated', at least at the level of ideology if not in practice (ibid.: 142, 143).

Another pioneering comparative endeavour in fascist studies was the first issue of the *Journal of Contemporary History* (1966) edited by Walter Lacquer and George L. Mosse and devoted – quite tellingly – to fascism. In his introduction to the thematic issue, Mosse pleaded for the revitalization of the research agenda of fascist studies by liberating it from the almost exclusive focus on Germany and from the prevailing tendency to define fascism in 'negative terms'. Mosse emphasized the importance of the comparative method in the study of fascism, pointing out that 'if we want to get close to the essence of the fascist revolution we must analyze it on a European-wide scale' and recommended looking not only for differences and variations but also for 'what these movements had in common': 'Fascism lacked a common founder, but all over Europe it sprang out of a common set of problems and proposed a common solution to them' (1966: 4). Although research on fascism remained focused on inter-war Europe, in general, and on Nazi Germany and Fascist Italy, in particular, the editors of the thematic journal issue affirmed the global character of fascism, arguing that 'a discussion of fascism that does not draw attention to fascist, proto- or semi-fascist movements outside Europe, would be incomplete' ('Editorial Note', 1966b: v). Mosse also identified a set of innovative research themes that were to revitalize fascist studies in the decades to come. His scholarly vision on fascism, detailed in numerous books and articles, came close to a general theory of fascism (see his seminal article in Chapter 2 of this volume).

The first fully elaborate theoretically minded and historically informed framework of comparative fascist studies, stemming from the analytical tradition of comparative sociology, was advanced in 1976 by Juan J. Linz. Rejecting the view that Italian Fascism and German National Socialism were unique and largely divergent political phenomena, or that fascist parties in Central and Eastern Europe were simply offspring of the two 'core' foreign movements, Linz persuasively argued that 'there is such a phenomenon as fascism, making its appearance in many countries, not only in Europe' (1976: 10). He employed a multilayered approach to fascism aimed at providing: a theory of the emergence, social origins, and compositions of fascist movements; a typology of existing fascist movements; and an ideal-type of fascism, in view of the negative as well as the positive features of its ideology.

First, Linz pointed out that fascism was a latecomer on the political scene, a fact that explains 'the essential anti-character of its ideology and appeal'. This anti-orientation allow fascism to define its identity in contrast, but paradoxically, to also incorporate elements of what it rejected and create a new synthesis, accounting for the heterogeneous character of its mass support. Second, Linz argued that the inter-war fascist movements and regimes exhibited common characteristics in European as well as non-European countries that were not the result of diffusion or imitation but *of common conditions*. Third, Linz pleaded for 'a comparative sociological historical analysis' of fascism that would reveal their similarities and differences. In his view, the variations between inter-war fascist movements and regimes were not due to ideological differences, but 'to the particular historical national situation in which they were born, the political space already occupied before the arrival of those latecomers, and some distinctive social structural problems of the different societies' (1976: 10). Concerning the *social basis of fascism*, following Otto Krichheimer, Linz defined fascist movements as socially heterogeneous catch-all parties. The actual social basis of fascist movements nevertheless depends 'on the particular historical constellation of social and political forces in each country' (ibid.: 5). Fourth, on this basis, Linz pleaded for the elaboration of an ideal-type definition of fascism which, 'with some deviations would fit the variety of move-ments around the world' (ibid.: 10). In building an ideal-type model, Linz opted for a multi-dimensional typological definition of fascism, even if he acknowledged that 'some dimensions might be more central to one or another of them'. His one-page multi-dimensional definition of fascism takes into account ideological, social-structural, and historical factors. It deals with the 'anti' character of fascism as well as with its positive appeal and the intellectual and emotional needs it satisfied (ibid.: 12–13). Linz's multilayered approach was pregnant with major future directions of research in the field.

From synergy to entropy: fascist studies in search of consensus

The wave of pioneering non-Marxist works during late 1960s and the 1970s stirred a renewed interest in fascism, giving birth to a bourgeoning industry (Carsten 1967; Woolf 1968, 1969; Greene 1968; Weiss 1969; Ledeen 1972; Laqueur 1976). Fascist studies greatly expanded their temporal boundaries, exploring the origins of fascism in a long-term diachronic perspective going back to the Enlightenment and the French Revolution and covering the evolution of (neo)fascism in the post-1945 period, as well. They also inflated their spatial borders, going beyond the original focus on Germany and Italy to tackle related political movements in non-Western and even non-European areas. Although routinely claiming to approach fascism as a general, pan-European phenomenon, early anthologies of European fascism focused mostly on Italy, Germany, France, Spain, Portugal, Great Britain, and the Low Countries. It was only in the 1960s and 1970s that overviews on European fascism included chapters on fascist movements in Central and Eastern Europe, soon followed by pioneering monographs on single fascist movements in countries such as Slovakia, Hungary, Yugoslavia, Romania, Poland, the Ukraine, Bulgaria or Russia. Other works extended the study of fascism to non-European countries, mostly in South Africa, Chile, Brazil, Japan or the United States. The great expansion of fascist studies went hand in hand with the broadening of inter-disciplinary studies. Fascist studies became a major field of experimentation with new themes of academic inquiry, such as the emergence and main feature of fascist ideology, the fascist culture, the social origins of fascism, the leader cult, fascism and modernization, etc.

Paradoxically, however, the extraordinary proliferation of fascist studies seemed to bring more confusion than light to the field, throwing it into a state of perpetual crisis. First, attempts at producing a 'grand theory' of fascism did not produce satisfactory results. For example, contrary to naïve expectations, research on the social composition of various fascist movements in Europe was not cumulative; it did not add to a comprehensive picture, but resulted into a puzzle of disparate data, bringing to the fore more questions than definite answers. It soon became apparent that, since there were so many factors at work in the emergence and evolution of fascist movements (or 'analytical variables' in the specialized jargon of comparative studies), no general or universal theory of fascism could gain absolute validity.

Second, instead of leading to an alternative grand theory of fascism, the departure from the Marxist 'unifascist theory' opened the field to a plethora of 'single-variable' theories of fascism, all claiming to have discovered the most important causal factor explaining its emergence and evolution. In a critical review of the state of the art in the field of fascist studies published in 1980, Larson and Hagtvet identified no less than eleven distinct theories of fascism, corresponding to as many sub-fields of research:

1 Fascism as the product of a 'daemonic Fuhrer personality. . . .
2 Fascism as a result of Europe's *moral disease.* . . .
3 Fascism as a product of a particular developmental sequence confined to Germany and Italy. . . .
4 Marxist theories: Fascism as a product of capitalist society and expression of anti-proletarian hysteria. . . .
5 Fascism as a manifestation of totalitarianism, which holds that there is an essential similarity between communist and fascist dictatorships. . . .
6 Fascism as a 'revolt against transcendence'. . . .
7 Fascism as the outgrowth of the social structure. . . .
8 Fascism as a particular stage in broader processes of modernization. . . .
9 Fascism as an *aesthetic* aberration. . . .
10 Fascism as the product of a pathological *cultural tradition.* . . .
11 Fascism as the expression of a specifically European syndrome of *counter-revolution.* . . .

(Hagtvet and Kühnl 1980: 29–29)

Third, the wealth of new comparative studies did not bring a breakthrough in the conceptual understanding of fascism. Most studies of fascism were empirically oriented and operated with an implicit definition of fascism, thus contributing little to the general understanding of the phenomenon. They set the emphasis on uniqueness rather than similarities in the nature of fascist movements and regimes, thus undermining the basis of comparison. At the same time, the few theoretic comparative treatments of fascism were generally divorced from empirical evidence; their treatments of fascism did not refer to case studies at all, but resembled a 'semantic debate about labels' (Payne 1979).

Fourth, the expansion of the research on fascism to new case studies and geographical areas brought to the forefront the issue of the typological classification of varieties of fascism, a very difficult task given the great number of historical examples and the multiple analytical levels at which their history could be approached. The typological approach to fascism was pioneered by Ernst Nolte. Although he advanced a generic definition of fascism, Nolte doubted that a general and unified history of fascism could ever be written. Instead, he recommended a typological approach as 'more promising and appropriate' since 'it offers empirical material unlimited scope for verification' (1966: 459). Using multiple poles of differentiation (such as authoritarian or totalitarian features, nationalist or socialist features, particular or universal tendencies), Nolte classified inter-war fascist movements along four main positions: the 'not-yet-fascist' or pre-fascist movements as the lower pole; early fascist movements as the 'first point of the inner area'; 'normal fascism' occupying a central position; and radical fascist movements in the upper pole (ibid.: 459–461). Following Nolte, other students of fascism classified fascist movements in view of their chronology. Taking as the main measuring stick the history of European fascism between the wars, they distinguished between proto- or pre-fascism, early fascism, inter-war fascism, and post-1945 neo-fascism. Others took into account regional patterns of development, thus operating with a combination of a field of study (fascism) and traditions of area studies. Merkl, for example, advanced a left–right regional-political classification of fascist movements, arguing that 'the left and left-center patterns seem to predominate in the West and South, while centrist fascist and center-right combinations are more typical of Central and Northern Europe, including Belgium and the Netherlands' (1980: 780). Still other students used regional labels to stand not as geographical denominations but for distinct analytical types of fascism, thus moving form typologies to *topologies* of fascism. Arguing that regional differences are more salient than common features or other criteria of differentiations, they distinguished between 'Western European fascism', 'East European fascism', 'Southern European fascism', 'Mediterranean fascism', or 'Latin fascism' (the latter focusing on France, Italy, Spain and Portugal), and 'Third World fascism' in developing countries (Kedward 1971; Vago 1976; Payne, 1976; Chomsky and Herman 1979). Once established as distinct types, the integration of these regional forms of fascisms into mainstream theories became difficult. The scholarly controversies concerning the nature of fascism in non-Western areas are a case in point: in line with the ideologically charged Cold War division of Europe into the 'first', Western world, and the 'second', Eastern world, fascism in Central and Eastern Europe was distinguished from its 'Western' counterpart and exoticized as 'the most deviant sector of the fascist universe' (Merkl 1980: 780). Stefan Woolf offered a synthetic articulation of this position: while acknowledging that fascism in Europe emerged under similar historical conditions generated by the Great War, Woolf argued that 'central and eastern European fascism remained distinct from that of the west', as a 'reactionary', 'conspiratorial', and abortive 'clear-cut version of fascism' (1969: 4). The division of historical fascism into distinct regional types further undermined theories of generic fascism, contributing to the prevailing fragmentation in fascist studies.

No wonder, therefore, that the debate on the conceptual definition of fascism became a 'dialogue of the deaf' in which parties perpetuated their self-fulfilling prophecies without listening to the other sides. Exasperated by the lack of convergence in fascist studies, numerous scholars proposed to drop the concept of fascism altogether as an imprecise, excessively politicized and ultimately meaningless term. Other scholars retained the term but restricted its application to Mussolini's Italy, where the fascist phenomenon originated, arguing that to apply the term outside Italy would be a conceptual overstretch. The thesis of the uniqueness of Italian Fascism was reinforced, on the German side, by those scholars who denied any structural similarities between Italian Fascism and German National Socialism, searching instead for theories better suited to Germany's peculiar historical experience. In one of the first and most comprehensive works on the origins and evolution of the Nazi regime, Karl Dietriech Bracher, for example, regarded the course of the Radical Right in Germany as 'a special case in international history', 'unique in its realization', despite possible comparisons (1970: 608). Bracher acknowledged the paramount importance of comparative history and argued for the need to employ a dual, European and national, perspective in approaching fascism. But he also highlighted the insurmountable difficulties in trying to arrive at a 'generalized' and 'undifferentiated' concept of fascism', arguing that radical nationalist movements in inter-war Europe 'were the product of specific national conditions that are not readily comparable or exportable' (ibid.: 605). In the long run, such views divorced the study of National Socialism from the field of comparative fascist studies and led to idiosyncratic theories of National Socialism tailored exclusively on the history of Germany. The most articulate yet controversial expression of this view was the thesis of the German *Sonderweg* or special path to modernity, the idea that Germany departed from the Western European 'normative' pattern of development and experienced a specific *malaise* that culminated in National Socialism (Wehler 1985; Kocka 1988, 1999; for critical evaluations, see Blackbourn and Eley 1984; Evans 1987).

The most poignant refutation of the concept of fascism was advanced by Gilbert Allardyce (1979). Reminding scholars that 'Only individual things are real; everything abstracted from them, whether concepts or universals, exists solely in the mind', Allardyce argued unequivocally that 'There is no such thing as fascism. There are only the men and movements that we call by that name' (ibid.: 369). In order to free fascist studies from 'the tyranny of concepts', Allardyce battled against three understandings of fascism prevailing in the literature of the time: (1) fascism as a generic concept; (2) fascism as a political ideology; and (3) fascism as a personality type. On the basis of a thorough critical review of the existing literature, Allardyce concluded that students of fascist faced an inescapable dilemma: they had to either define fascism comprehensively or acknowledge their inability to explain it, and do away with the term. From a position of cognitive scepticism, Allardyce doubted that 'A satisfactory comparative international model of fascism can ever be built, simply because fascist movements were too mixed, diverse, and exceptional.' He therefore proposed that fascism should be 'de-modelled, de-ideologised, de-mystified, de-escalated, and ultimately declassified as a generic concept' (ibid.: 378).

However pertinent, Allardyce's criticism did not offer a solution to the dilemma; taken to its logical consequences, his recommendation would have pushed fascist studies into the dead end of studying fascism disparately as a set of unrelated movements. Yet, although amply discussed, Allardyce's article did not inhibit research on generic fascism; on the contrary, it occasioned fruitful methodological debates over the nature of fascism.

Rescuing the concept of fascism: from grand theories to the 'fascist minimum'

In the 1980s and 1990s, a new generation of scholars gradually brought the debates over the conceptual understanding of fascism to a new level of analytical sophistication. Unlike previous attempts to produce unified grand narratives or 'all-embracing' theories of fascism, in the new stage the search for the common ground of fascism movements and regimes was animated by a compulsion for reductive logic (Tannenbaum 1972: 3): scholars of fascism limited their endeavour to producing more flexible theoretical models encompassing only the 'main features' or 'essence' of the phenomenon, the so-called 'fascist minimum'. This approach was pioneered by Ernst Nolte who advanced the first concise definition of fascism (1963; 1968b). Although his interpretation of fascism remained idiosyncratic, Nolte was a trendsetter, opening up an important direction of research that was to become dominant in the decades to come: the search for the lowest common denominator of fascist movements expressed in a concise one-sentence definition.

To understand the scholarly debates over the 'fascist minimum', one should first reflect on the epistemological status of concepts in general, and on that of the concept of fascism, in particular. A concept is an abstract idea denoting a concrete object or phenomenon by means of both a term that labels or designates it, and an 'explanatory' model implicitly or explicitly attached to that label. The label has to be distinct and unambiguous, since an expansion in the number of denotations a concept takes decreases its basic connotations, leading to confusion in meanings. As an intellectual, theoretical construct, the explanatory model 'simplifies reality in order to emphasize the recurrent, the general and the typical' (Burke 2005: 28). Its role is to cover, in a comprehensive manner, all the necessary and sufficient features, patterns, and relations which indisputably characterize the given object or phenomenon. In this sense, concepts are universal or generic: as abstract models, they overlook the differences among the objects or phenomena in their particular class in favour of common features, characteristics or functions. Concepts are thus able to serve as building blocks of scientific theories: they assist researches in *identifying* the particular object or phenomenon under investigation, in *understanding* its nature and particular features and, on this basis, in *differentiating* between objects in that particular class and other dissimilar objects.

The concept of fascism could not fulfil its basic epistemological functions due to a combination of reasons. First, the polysemantic label used to designate the phenomenon was abused, excessively politicized and thus devalued in colloquial and scholarly usages. Fascism has two distinct but inter-related etymological roots in Latin and modern Italian language. The word fascism resembles the Latin word *fasces*, which denotes a bundle of rods around an axe carried out by Roman *Lictors* and symbolizing the juridical authority of the magistrates but also the unity and strength of the community. The term fascism also derives from the Italian word *fascio* (plural *fasci*), meaning 'bundle' or 'union'. During the nineteenth century, the word *fascio* was used by groups of political activists of various – socialist or nationalist – orientations, such as the *Fasci Siciliani* (1895–1896). This tradition of activism was emulated during World War I and the first post-war years by a new type of radical nationalists, organized in *fasci di combatimento* (bands or leagues of combat), such as the one organized by Benito Mussolini in 1919 in Milano. Later, this self-referential label was appropriated by the *Partito Nazionale Fascista* (National Fascist Party, NFP), established in 1921. The two meanings of fascism were soon conflated in the NFP propaganda, which capitalized both on the word fascism's connotation of grass-roots political activism, unity and strength, and on the symbolic link with ancient Rome, exploited by the propagandistic revival of the cult of the Lictors (Gentile 1993). Since the 1920s, the term 'fascism' and its derivates have permeated political languages, becoming a highly abused concept. 'Fascist' has been used as a noun, to refer to the members of fascist parties, to their votes or followers; as an adjective, to refer to a set of radical political ideas, to persons or groups who shared those ideas, or to political regimes organized according to certain ideological or organizational principles. The term fascist generated also a new verb, 'to fascisize', which denotes the process of adoption of fascist convictions and ideas by individuals or groups, their enrolment in fascist parties, or their taking part in fascist institutions of indoctrination and common socialization. Outside the academic realm, in public or political discourses, fascism was used to refer not only to those inter-war politicians sharing a certain set of political ideas (however those ideas were defined or understood), but indiscriminately employed to discredit political enemies of various radical political orientations.

Second, the explanatory model associated with the label became a matter of continuous debate and contestation. Fascism thus turned into an 'essentially contested' concept: there was an imperious need to go 'back to the basics' and to reconstruct the meaning of the concept in a scholarly manner, by rebuilding the explanatory model associated to the label. Yet, how could such a theoretical model of fascism be built? Moreover, how could fascism's cluster of traits or attributes best be represented? The issue generated a heated international debate, been approached by students of fascism from various angles, reflecting their ideological convictions, their disciplinary training, their theoretical assumptions and methodological choices, and the main features of the historical case studies most closely related to their research. Students of fascism have employed two main research strategies: the *inductive-observational* versus the *deductive-abstract* methods, which correspond, by and large, to a cleavage between historians' and political scientists' approaches to fascism. The proponents of the *inductive method* start from the history of inter-war fascism and, on the basis of empirical research of case studies, derive a set of general common features of fascism. The proponents of the *deductive method* start from a theoretical model of fascism which is then used as a measuring stick against existing case studies. These different methodological choices resulted in distinct analytical models of fascism. Through retroductive reasoning, scholars who employ the inductive method arrive at a 'descriptive definition' or an 'average model' of fascism, most often expressed through a list of common characteristics. Scholars who employ the deductive method build an ideal type of fascism made up of as few but essential set of axioms as possible, identifying the 'core' of fascism.

The two analytical models take into consideration different elements of fascism. The descriptive definition refers to all manifestations of fascism: ideological values, the organizational aspect of fascist movements, and the main features of fascist regimes. The ideal-type model limits the discussion to the fascist 'ideological minimum', on the count that peculiar features related to the history of fascist movements cannot be part of a definition of fascism. Finally, the proponents of the first, inductive method treat fascism as a synchronic-epochal phenomenon, anchoring the discussion on the inter-war period. The proponents of the second, deductive method treat fascism as a generic-diachronic phenomenon, detaching its definition from particular historical examples and extending its relevance in time and space to cover a global phenomenon of the modern age.

In an effort to contextualize the articles included in this volume, the following section reviews, from a relational perspective, the theoretical models of fascism authored by Emilio Gentile, Stanley Payne, Roger Griffin, Roger Eatwell, Michael Mann, Zeev Sternhell and Aristotle Kallis, to supplement the more in-depth descriptions of their work and articles advanced in individual chapter introductions. The emphasis will be on the methodological strategies employed to build a model of generic fascism as: a comprehensive descriptive definition of average characteristics (Gentile), a tripartite typology of features (Payne), an ideological core (Griffin), an ideological core supplemented by sociological features (Mann), a series of processes (Paxton), or an ideological matrix (Eatwell). In the end, I present the contours of a new, incipient debate in fascist studies along two would-be dominant paradigms.

A descriptive definition of fascism as a set of characteristics

The first reaction to the conceptual confusion prevalent in fascist studies in the 1970s was to deny that fascism existed as a generic phenomenon and to provide instead an all-encompassing definition of fascism on the basis of its inter-war historical characteristics.

The most articulated, historically-informed criticism against 'political science' models of generic fascism was put forward in Italy by two prominent, innovative and prolific historians, Renzo de Felice (1929–96) and Emilio Gentile. De Felice was first to provide a novel interpretation of the history of Italian fascism that challenged the main tenets of Marxist historiography prevalent at the time (1975, 1976; on the controversy surrounding the latter book, see Ledeen 1976). Pointing to the complexity of fascism as a historical phenomenon, de Felice differentiated between the 'fascism-movement', defined as a genuinely revolutionary force, and the 'fascism-regime', seen as an expression of the totalitarianism of the left, with roots in the Enlightenment. He underscored the complementary but also tense relations between the two, marked by the uneasy subordination of the movement to the regime. He also emphasized the strong middle-class support for fascism in Italy, and the role Mussolini's charisma played in forging a large consensus in society (de Felice and Fermi 1961; de Felice 1965–97). His thesis generated heated political debates over fascism between the left and the right in Italy, con-tributing to the development of this field of study.

De Felice also actively participated in the international dialogue on fascism, and introduced and popularized scholarly debates on fascism to the Italian public (1969; 1977). An adept of historicist approaches valuing the societal context extracted from ample documentary evidence at the expense of generalization and abstractization (Gentile 1997), de Felice criticized the tendency to define fascism in view of a rigid theoretical model 'attempting to encompass all forms of fas-cism' on the grounds that such approaches 'obliterate a realistic view of the prob-lem' (1977: 8). De Felice acknowledged the existence of a minimal common denominator of various fascist movements and regimes, but argued that it can only consist of few general features, such as: (1) a set of common historical roots and socio-political conditions generated by the Great War and the Great Depression; (2) a set of ideological characteristics; and (3) a twofold typology made up of countries where fascist movements emerged, and countries where these movements developed into political regimes. De Felice denied the possibil-ity of arriving at 'a definition of the Fascist phenomenon except through such a broad typology' (ibid.: 12), arguing that to expand this minimal common denom-inator to other aspects of fascism 'would be as difficult as it is distorting' (ibid.: 11). Moreover, he pointed out that the heuristic value of this typology is limited, since it can only serve as a negative comparison, in the sense that 'it prevents an almost unlimited expansion of the Fascist model to include historical reality which has nothing to do with it' (ibid.: 12). On this basis, de Felice denied the existence of generic fascism and restricted the use of the term to inter-war Europe, contesting the fascist nature of non-European or post-1945 movements (ibid.: 10–11).

Following on the path opened by de Felice, Emilio Gentile also criticized the approach on generic fascism on the count that it often results into an 'elastic', unstable definition of fascism, which enlarges or shrinks itself in time and space to either define a global phenomenon or an exclusively European phenomenon (2002: 59). In his work, Gentile went far beyond Felice's incipient typological definition to produce a comprehensive and meticulously documented definition of fascism as a form of totalitarianism and sacralization of politics culminating in a new political religion. Building on insights provided by Hannah Arendt, Gentile advanced a new understanding of totalitarianism to denote not only a political regime based on terror, but also a political movement with an integral view of politics, oriented toward the creation of the 'new man'. In his view, the complex nature and novelty of fascism as a historical phenomenon cannot be reduced to its ideological dimension; its definition should thus take into account social and institutional factors, as well. To this end, Gentile elaborated in ten points, a fully-fledged descriptive definition of fascism which refers to three analytical dimensions: (1) fascism as a specific *ideology*, having its own specific culture, civil ethic, and view of politics; (2) fascism as a heterogeneous *mass movement* dominated by elements of the middle class and organized in a paramilitary structure; and (3) fascism as *a political regime* made up of a single-party state, a repressive police apparatus, a corporatist organization of society, and an imperialist foreign policy (1992: 198; 2002: 71–73; see Payne, Chapter 3 in this volume, pp. 111–112, n. 6). More recently, in line with the new trend of providing a concise definition of fascism, Gentile contracted this ten-point description into a one-sentence definition:

> Fascism is a modern political phenomenon, which is nationalistic and revolutionary, anti-liberal and anti-Marxist, organised in the form of a militia party, with a totalitarian conception of politics and the State, with an ideology based on myth; virile and antihedonistic, it is sacralised in a political religion affirming the absolute primacy of the nation understood as an ethnically homogeneous organic community, hierarchically organised into a corporative State, with a bellicose mission to achieve grandeur, power and conquest with the ultimate aim of creating a new order and a new civilisation.
>
> (2004: 329)

The definition reiterates the cultural, institutional, and organizational aspects of fascism, couching them in a theoretical framework centred on the concepts of the sacralization of politics, totalitarianism and the development of political religions.

From a descriptive definition to a typology of historical fascism

The American historian Stanley Payne pursued a similar, inductive analytical direction of research to that of de Felice and Gentile, but arrived ultimately at different, even if related, results. In several innovative works on fascism, Payne advanced a 'descriptive' model of generic fascism, a comprehensive typology of historical fascist movements, and a 'retrodictive' theory of fascism (1980a; 1980b; 1995).

Payne argued for a new understanding of the 'fascist minimum' as a 'pluralistic categorization'. In his view, de Felice's model of 'fascist minimum' was unsatisfactory, since it was 'both complex and vague' (1978: 129). But he also criticized concise definitions of the ideological core of fascism (of the type advanced by Griffin 1991, see below) as being too general and reductionist and thus having a limited heuristic utility. For Payne, the complexity of fascism can only be defined as a 'multiform hypothetical category' and captured by a 'complex typology'. To this end, he elaborated a working model of fascism made up of a *tripartite descriptive typology* pertaining to: (1) ideology; (2) style of politics; and (3) principles for the organization of the movement, the regime, and the society at large. This inductive typology is not understood as a reified category but as 'a wide-spectrum description'. Payne also supplemented this descriptive typology with a single-sentence definition. In his view, fascism was

a form of revolutionary ultra-nationalism for national rebirth that is based on a primarily vitalist philosophy, is structured on extreme elitism, mass mobilization, and the *Führerprinzip*, positively values violence as end as well as means and tends to normatize war and/or the military virtues.

(1980: 14a)

Payne treated fascism as concomitantly a 'generic and comparative phenomenon', an approach which places him in-between historical and political science approaches to fascism (1995: 4). He employed the term 'generic' only in a 'tentative sense', on the count that models of generic fascism are useful to the extent they underline 'the historical uniqueness of fascism' in relation to the other two faces of inter-war authoritarian nationalism, namely the conservative right and the radical right; yet they cannot fully explain the history and main features of individual movements, which can be done only by marrying theoretical models with empirical research. The uniqueness of fascism should not be overestimated; however, for Payne, fascism is *not* a distinct 'genus' of political movements but a major type of revolutionary mass movement, as part of a larger taxonomy of related phenomena that include anarchism, socialism, Leninism, and populism (ibid.: 465).

While operating with a heuristic definition of generic fascism as a unitary analytical category, in his empirical work Payne also advanced a typology of forms of historical fascism. He criticized 'the reduction of all putative fascism to one single generic phenomenon of absolutely common identity' as 'distortive and inaccurate'; but he also rejected the 'radically nominalist approach which insists that all [fascisms] ... were inherently different', on the ground that it overlooks 'distinctive similarities' (1980b: 195). Based on thorough research, Payne differentiated among five main 'varieties' or sub-types of historical fascism: (1) 'paradigmatic' Italian fascism and its direct derivates; (2) 'radical' German National

Socialism and its derivates; (3) Spanish Falangism; (4) Romanian Legionary or Iron Guard movement; and (5) Szalasi's Hungarist or Arrow Cross movement. Payne's *A History of Fascism, 1914–1945* (1995), is acknowledged to date as the most comprehensive history of inter-war fascism, aptly combining theory with case-study methodology.

From the fascist minimum to an ideal-type of generic fascist ideology: a new consensus?

At the beginning of the 1990, when the debate on the fascist minimum seem to be dominated by comparativist historians, there was a remarkable revival of the theory of generic fascism in a new and more developed form. The new wave of interest was mostly due to Roger Griffin's book *The Nature of Fascism* (1991). Griffin noted the extraordinary proliferation of idiosyncratic models of fascism but also the 'limited success' these models reached in forging a consensus in the field. He attributed the relative failure of these models to the fact that they combined history with theory in an ambiguous way and were too broad to serve as flexible and easy-to-use analytical tools.

Griffin set out to offer a way out of the 'conceptual labyrinth' (1991: 5) of fascist studies by reviving the idea of generic fascism but paving the way toward a new conceptual definition of the fascist minimum. His view on fascism is indebted to a long tradition of reasoning, initiated by Nolte and Linz and continued by Mosse, Sternhell and Payne, among others. While incorporating key empirical and methodological gains in fascist studies, Griffin's analytical model of fascism rests, nevertheless, on distinct methodological choices.

First, Griffin treated the concept of fascism as an ideal-type, serving as a 'valuable heuristic and taxonomic device'. He argued, however, that ideal-types are not definitive taxonomic categories, but only 'tentative conceptual frameworks' (ibid.: 11). Second, in building an ideal-type of generic fascism, Griffin focused exclusively on the fascist *ideology*, leaving aside issues of style and organization of fascist movements and regimes as irrelevant to a conceptual understanding of fascism. Third, Griffin criticized the descriptive definitions of the type put forward by Gentile and Payne as 'a sort of check-list which is somewhat cumbersome as a conceptual framework'. Instead, following political science approaches to ideology authored by Connolly (1976) and Freeden (1986), Griffin concentrated on core values in defining the fascist ideology (1991: 13). This 'generic ideological core' model does not exclude major differences among fascist movements. But, in Griffin's terminology, these differences should be seen as 'permutations' of the common core rather than as disparate phenomena. For this reason, Griffin did not engage with the individual histories of fascism that would 'degenerate into a series of potted histories' and an inflation of historiographical details at the expense of conceptual clarifications (ibid.: 20). In his book, he deals with the history of fascism in Germany and Italy only in order to illuminate the dynamics of these paradigmatic fascist movements and regimes. Fourth, the ideological core of fascism is defined in a concise single-sentence definition, which has the advantage of 'succinctness and manageability' over more knotty typologies: 'Fascism is a genus of political ideology whose mythic core in its various permutations is a palingenetic form of populist ultra-nationalism' (ibid.: 26). Fifth, the new definition of generic fascism is intended to serve as a basis of an incipient consensus in the field, on the count that 'the time is ripe for a new theory of the fascist minimum' (ibid.: 13).

Griffin's (1991) book invigorated the international debate on fascism. His new ideal-type model of generic fascism became a 'mandatory' reference in the field, obliging scholars of fascism to spell out their position vis-à-vis his model and to reposition or reconsider their own offer. A full treatment of this grand debate – which resulted in a plethora of book reviews, review essays, polemical articles, thematic journal issues or edited volumes – is beyond the limited scope of this Introduction. In the following, I provide nevertheless a sample of reactions focusing mostly on the authors included in this volume, in an effort to illustrate the spectrum of opinions advanced in the debate and their impact on arriving at a new 'negotiated' definition of generic fascism.

On the one side of the debate were those scholars who either contested the heuristic usefulness of ideal-type models of generic fascism or openly rejected Griffin's model on various grounds (see Walter Lacquer, A. James Gregor, Michael Burleigh, David D. Roberts, Jan Kershaw, Robert Paxton, etc.). Walter Lacquer, for example, argued that the use of the generic term fascism is 'problematic' in relation to historical fascism, mostly since it obliterates the difference between National Socialism and Italian Fascism (1996: 6). Lacquer acknowledged that Griffin's one-sentence definition of fascism 'might be difficult to improve', yet he criticized it on the ground that 'it still covers movements that are not really fascist and omits others that are' (1996: 9). He doubted that it is possible to arrive at an ideal and fully consensual definition of generic fascism 'covering every aspect of the phenomenon' (ibid.: 9).

Robert Paxton contested the validity of ideal-typical models of fascist minimum on the grounds that they treat fascism in a static manner and isolate this phenomenon from its concrete social, political and cultural contexts (1998). To correct these fallacies, Paxton emphasized the imperious need to study fascism in motion, to differentiate among various stages in the evolution of fascism, to place its various manifestations in their historical milieus, and to compare them in time and space. In *The Anatomy of Fascism*, Paxton proposed a new methodological strategy for approaching fascism 'as a series of processes' rather than 'as the expression of some fixed essence' (2004: 219). Paxton argued that fascists can be better understood in view of their actions rather than their words or ideology. In order to account for the fascists' political behaviour, he identified a set of 'visceral feelings' or 'mobilizing passions' that animated the deeds of fascists (2004: 15). In his conclusions, while refraining from producing a theoretical model of fascism resembling the ones he criticized, Paxton advanced a synthetic definition:

Fascism may be defined as a form of political behaviour marked by obsessive preoccupation with community decline, humiliation, or victimhood and by compensatory cults of unity energy, and purity, in which a mass-based party of committed nationalists militants, working in uneasy but effective collaboration with traditional elite groups, abandons democratic liberties and pursues with redemptive violence and without ethical or legal restraints goals of internal cleansing and external expansion.

(2004: 218)

This definition resonates with the one proposed by Griffin in its stress on fascists' central obsession with decadence and redemption. To this central dimension of the fascist ideology, Paxton added nevertheless additional elements, underscoring the mass character of fascist movements and the role played by violence in attaining their goals of cleansing the nation and expanding its territory.

Another articulated critique of models of generic fascism centred solely on ideology was put forward by Michael Mann, from the perspective of comparative sociology. In *Fascists* (2004), Mann disapproved of Griffin's approach on the grounds that it completely overlooks issues connected with the social composition of fascism movements, their structure and organization of power. He also contended that Griffin's definition obscured fascism's drive to political violence and destruction in favour of its 'positive' core values of rebirth and regeneration, and neglected the vital connection between fascism, as a form of nationalism, and the institutional framework of the nation-state (ibid.: 12). To overcome these pitfalls, Mann advanced his own definition of generic fascism, rivalling in conciseness that of Griffin but more comprehensive in its scope: 'Fascism is the pursuit of a transcendent and cleansing nation-statism through paramilitarism' (ibid.: 13). This definition associates with fascism a set of additional analytical concepts: *nationalism, statism, transcendence, cleansing,* and *paramilitarism,* amply discussed in Mann's work.

On the other side of the debate were those scholars who accepted the methodological foundations of Griffin's theoretical model of fascism but expressed their minor or more substantive reservations in regard to the actual definition of the mythical core of fascism or the analytical strategy employed to represent it, advancing instead their own counter-models. Stanley Payne acclaimed Griffin's essential contribution to fascist studies. He also agreed with the core of his definition but pointed out that the myth of rebirth is not a sufficient component of the fascist ideology, since it is also shared by non-fascist nationalist or socialist movements. He concluded that Griffin's minimal approach 'cannot define certain of the central characteristics fundamental to a definition of fascism', among which Payne underscores militarism and the *Führerprinzip* (1995: 5; Payne, in Griffin *et al.* 2006: 175–178).

Roger Eatwell agreed that fascism 'can be best described in view of its ideology', but doubted that the fascist synthesis can be captured by a Weberian ideal-typical model of the kind proposed by Griffin. In his view, to reduce the complexity of fascist ideology and its various forms of manifestations to a single core means to unavoidably essentialize its nature. To overcome this limitation, Eatwell proposed an alternative, 'spectral-syncretic' model representing the fascist ideological minimum not as a static core but as a 'matrix' made up of a cluster of central themes that can coagulate in multiple and original combinations. Methodologically, this approach combines a 'one sentence definition' with 'a four-point core set of annotations'. Eatwell defined fascism as:

> An ideology that strives to forge social rebirth based on a holistic-national radical Third Way, though in practice fascism has tended to stress style, especially action and the charismatic leader, more than detailed programme, and to engage in a Manichaean demonisation of its enemies.
>
> (1996)

This succinct definition was supplemented by four themes constituting the basis of the 'core fascist worldview': (1) Nationalism; (2) Holism; (3) Radicalism; and (4) the Third Way. Although it sets the emphasis on ideology, this definition also accounts for fascism's political style, organization, and charismatic leadership.

In a monograph on fascism in Russia, Stephen D. Shenfield praised Griffin's approach as 'influential and illuminating' (2001: 17), but he also criticized Griffin's definition as too narrow since it leaves out forms of historical fascism on the fringes of Europe. Shenfield proposed an alternative definition of fascism which includes authoritarian (rather than totalitarian or revolutionary) movements oriented toward the restoration of 'pre-modern patriarchal values' (ibid.: 17). Kevin Passmore also adhered to the new consensus but regarded it as a point of departure rather than the end result of the scholarly effort to define fascism. He doubted that palingenetic nationalism was the ideological core from which all the other features of fascism sprang, arguing that such a claim is 'essentialist and effectively reifies the concept of fascism' (Passmore, in Griffin *et al.* 2006: 352). Passmore also disagreed with Griffin's relegation of certain features of inter-war fascist to secondary importance (2002: 25). Instead, he proposed his own, 'full' descriptive definition of fascism that accounts for a plurality of ideological values and practices (ibid.: 31).

In numerous polemical answers or overviews of the recent literature in the field, Roger Griffin claimed the existence of a *de facto* consensus in fascist studies around his definition of fascism, arguing that even those scholars who openly distance themselves from his ideal-type model agree in fact implicitly, if not explicitly, that the idea of rebirth and regeneration constitutes the core of fascist ideology. Approved by many prominent scholars of fascism but also contested by others (for samples of both categories, see Roberts *et al.* 2002; Griffin *et al.* 2006), this controversial claim appears accurate if considered in the broad terms in which it was conceived. In the light of the divergences highlighted above, the new consensus in recent fascist studies can be better understood as a loose *convergence* around a culturalist approach and agenda of research – most aptly synthesized by Griffin's heuristic model – rather than as a complete, in-detail agreement over a particular definition of generic fascism. In addition, this convergence has been so far limited, by and large, to scholarship produced in the Anglophone world. With few exceptions, German and Austrian scholarship on fascism has proved rather reticent in employing models of generic fascism, while scholars in Central and Eastern Europe have only recently joined this debate.

The emerging research convergence over a culturalist approach to fascism underscores the merits of the international scholarly dialogue in identifying common grounds that can serve as a new foundation in fascist studies. The interaction and cross-fertilization among various research traditions and viewpoints have been multidirectional. In this respect, it is equally important to note that, in response to criticism and in view of new research in the field, Griffin re-worked his definition of fascism, thus re(de)fining the basis of the would-be consensus in the field. While his first concise definition of fascism referred exclusively to its ideological core (1991), discarding issues of style and organization as irrelevant to a conceptual definition of fascism, his second variant made reference to the mass support of fascist movements as well (1998). His third variant reconfirmed the ideological core of fascism but referred to fascism as an ideology, set of movements and also *regimes* (2002a: 24, n. 15; see also this volume, p. 132). In his most recent book, *Modernism and Fascism* (2007), Griffin further enlarged his concise definition, enriching it with new elements. First, he elevated fascism from the rank of a political 'genus' to that of a 'species'. Second, he redefined fascism as a revolutionary form of political *modernism* that originated in the early twentieth century. Third, while reiterating the palingenetic core of fascism, Griffin specified the nature of the fascist regeneration as 'national and ethnic', thus underscoring the centrality of the nation in the fascist ideology. Fourth, Griffin also mentioned the fight against degeneration by means of ethnic cleansing and exclusion of unwanted ethnic or racial categories, an aspect omitted in his first definition which only focused on the positive values of the fascist ideology. Finally, Griffin expanded his definition into a one-page description; in keeping with the tradition, he also concisely summarized his up-to-date view on fascism:

> Fascism is a form of programmatic modernism that seeks to conquer political power in order to realize a totalizing vision of national or ethnic rebirth. Its ultimate end is to overcome the decadence that has destroyed a sense of communal belonging and drained modernity of meaning and transcendence and usher in a new era of cultural homogeneity and health.
>
> (Griffin 2007)

This new definition is (re)centred on the key concepts of modernism, totalitarianism, and transcendence, being thus in line with the recent rejuvenation of the totalitarian approach in fascist studies; to the palingenetic ideological core of fascism, it also adds institutional and organizational aspects, resulting into a more comprehensive model.

Generic fascism vs. historical fascism: toward a new clash of paradigms?

More recently, there have been attempts to overcome the fixation with arriving at a consensual ideal-typical definition of fascism and to instead refashion the lines of controversies along methodological lines. The main cleavage is between those scholars who treat fascism as an epochal phenomenon confined to inter-war Europe and those scholars who treat fascism as a generic or universal phenomenon and approach it from a diachronic perspective.

The first explicit distinction between the two alternative framework of interpreting fascism was advanced by Zeev Sternhell, who, in a new introduction to his work *Neither Right nor Left*, argued for the existence of two distinct forms of fascism: an ideological one, (which was referred to as 'Fascism A'), and a historical or concrete form of inter-war fascism, (which was referred to as 'Fascism B') (Sternhell 2000: 80–82; for earlier editions, see 1983, 1987). A similar line of reasoning was pursued, from a markedly different perspective, by Robert Paxton, who, in an article on the usage of the comparative method in fascist studies (1998, see this volume) pointed out the complexities of fascism's historical forms of manifestations and its evolution from an ideology to a set of movements and then political regimes – and argued that fascism's distinct stages of development should be analyzed by means of distinct methodological tools. Following the path opened by Sternhell and Paxton, in a recent programmatic article, Aristotle Kallis identified an emerging 'paradigmatic clash' between two main analytical frameworks for the study of fascism:

> one, that is rooted in the history of ideas and cultural trends, that deals with fascism as a coherent, diachronic intellectual system, regardless of its subsequent adaptations and distortions in practice; the other, that is derived from the specific experience of inter-war fascism, with a heavy emphasis on examining the political choices that movements and regimes made.
>
> (2004: 10)

In order to consolidate the second, less-developed approach, in his recent work, Kallis focuses on the neglected issue of fascism in power, and elaborates a typology of fascist regimes to be added to the existing studies of fascism ideology and typologies of fascist movements (see Kallis 2000, Chapter 9 in this volume).

Are these two analytical frameworks of analysing fascism mutually exclusive? Commenting on Sternhell's 'two-stage, bifocal view on fascism', Griffin acknowledged its 'considerable heuristic potential as a properly elaborated theory' for the development of fascist studies but pointed out that the relationship between the two forms of fascism and their overall analytical implications is not clearly spelled out. Griffin sees the two frameworks as mutually exclusive: yet he also posited that, in order to successfully challenge the ideological-diachronic paradigm, the proponents of the epochal view on fascism are still to articulate their view in a systematic manner (2002b: 33). Kallis agreed that 'there are simply too many fascisms around', the existence of rival paradigms leading to 'conceptual confusion and methodological incongruity'. He argues, however, that this 'persistent definitional dichotomy' should be resolved 'not through the declared victory of one over the other, but through a heightened awareness of the current absence of a methodological/conceptual common ground and the need to reclaim one' (2004: 33, 25). In other words, the way out of the new methodological dilemma is to engage in a genuine dialogue in fascist studies over key theoretical and methodological issues involving the relationship between the theory and the history of fascism, and between the fascist ideology and its various forms of implementation.

This author would argue that the plurality of 'paradigms' and frameworks of interpretations is neither problematic nor anomalous. Unlike in the legal realm, where there can exist only one single legal definition of an offence at a given point in time, in scholarship, 'paradigms' do exist side by side. They serve different analytic purposes, depending on the question being posed and the research problem under investigation. Indeed, the two approaches to fascism rest on different methodological foundations: One is deductive, since it starts from theoretical assumptions and premises to arrive at a definition of fascism, the other is inductive, since it extracts such a definition from an empirical investigation of existing case studies. Yet the two approaches fulfil different roles: one provides an ideal-type of generic fascism, the other a historical account and descriptive definition of historical fascism. These approaches are complementary and, to a certain extent, even interdependent. On the one hand, the ideal-type definition of fascism is first and foremost an instrument of comparison, most useful when tested against existing case studies in order to both fine-tune our conceptual understanding but also enhance our knowledge of historical fascism. Treating ideal-types of fascism as a goal in themselves leads to a sterile 'scholastic' or 'manierist' debate over attaining 'the perfect' theoretical definition, inappropriately divorced from, and thus often irrelevant to, historical research. On the other hand, the approach that rests on an empirical examination of existing fascisms cannot be conducted without an *a priori* conceptual understanding of fascism that informs the selection of case studies and the organization of research. For these reasons, the two research frameworks should be treated as complementary rather than mutually exclusive.

Fascism and communism as (uni)totalitarianism: comparative approaches

In parallel with the evolution of the field of comparative fascism, studies of fascism and communism under the common conceptual banner of (uni)totalitarianism have emerged during the time as a major dimension of academic inquiry which, given its importance, requires special treatment. Although the association of fascism with communism is routinely regarded as an ideological product of the Cold War, the comparison originated in fact in the inter-war period, being applied to the study of Fascist Italy, Nazi Germany, and the Soviet Union. During the Cold War, the totalitarian thesis had a disruptive effect on comparative fascist studies, rivalling theories of generic fascism as an explanatory paradigm for the inter-war extreme right. On the one hand, numerous scholars doubted that Fascist Italy – the original locus of both the concept and the first debates on totalitarianism – was a totalitarian state and thus kept it out of the debate. On the other, the application of the concept of totalitarianism to the study of Nazi Germany and the routine comparison with Stalinist Russia, isolated, implicitly or explicitly, the historiography of Nazi Germany from the field of comparative fascist studies (on the relevance of the totalitarian approach for the study of Nazi Germany, see Sauer 1967; Kershaw 1989: 18–41). The end of the Cold War rejuvenated comparative studies on totalitarianism, due to a combination of factors. First, the collapse of the communist system brought a historical period to a close, making possible comparative historical retrospectives of totalitarian regimes during the 'short twentieth century' (1917–91). Second, freed from political taboos, scholars in Central and Eastern Europe have applied the totalitarian approach to the study of their countries' recent communist past, giving birth to a rich (even if uneven and at times uncritical) literature. Third, outside of the academic realm, the concept of totalitarianism served as a major propaganda tool of delegitimizing the communist past and of creating consensus for the consolidation of a new democratic order, being therefore placed at the centre of charged political debates. Fourth, the rise of fundamentalist movements around the world redirected the study on totalitarianism toward the topic of *political religions*, with a strong impact on fascist and communist studies.

Just like the term 'fascism', totalitarianism is an 'essentially contested concept', with a long and highly politicized history. Etymologically, the word derives its meaning from the stem 'total' and its derivates, such as 'totality'. Since its inception, totalitarianism has been a polysemous term, being invested with a set of positive as well as highly negative connotations (Losurdo 2004). Positively, totalitarianism was employed to refer to the pretence of new religions or political ideologies to provide solutions to the challenges posed by modern society and to restore the 'totality' of human nature by bringing about the salvation and emancipation of the humanity through radical social engineering and spiritual rebirth. Negatively, it refers to the attempt of modern illiberal political movements and regimes to abolish civil and political rights and institute a system of total control and domination over the lives of the citizens.

Historically, the concept of totalitarianism is almost as old as that of fascism, to which it was closely associated. The term was coined in Italy in early 1920s to denounce the Fascist 'total' monopoly of power as opposed to the previous pluralistic, multi-partly political regime (Gleason 1995: 14). The term was soon appropriated by the Italian fascists, who were attracted by its extremist as well as modern political connotations, and extensively employed it with the sense of 'wild radicalism', 'possessed will', or 'ferocity' (1995: 14). After the post-1925 consolidation of the fascist regime in Italy, the term was further theoretized by Benito Mussolini and Giovanni Gentile (2002) and invested with a new meaning, denoting the intent of the Fascist state to control every sphere of the human life. In Germany, the term totalitarianism was borrowed in the early 1930s by Nazi ideologues from the Italian political debates. It was used to both describe and legitimize the dismantlement of the institutional structure of the Weimar Republic and its replacement with a dictatorial regime, a process euphemistically referred to in the Nazi political vocabulary as 'synchronization' (*Gleichschaltung*). With the consolidation of the Nazi rule, the term totalitarianism was soon abandoned in favour of the specific vocabulary of racial utopia that dominated the official Nazi political language. The main objection against the term totalitarianism was its 'static' connotations which could not accurately describe the political dynamism of the new regime.

The concept of totalitarianism had thus a passing history in the official fascist political discourse. Soon, however, the concept migrated from political to academic discourses. The 'totalitarian thesis' was first elaborated in early to mid-1930s in the United Kingdom and the United States and stressed the similarities between Nazism and Stalinism as dictatorial regimes and as the greatest threats to liberal democracies (Halberstam 1998). Originally applied to Fascist Italy and Nazi Germany, the concept of totalitarianism was thus extended to the study of the Stalinist Russia as well, commonly labelled 'Red Fascism' (Adler and Paterson 1970). This gave birth to the theory of uni-totalitarianism based on the idea that the Fascist, Nazi, and Bolshevik regimes shared a common set of characteristics as an expression of a new *totalitarian* form of government (for a critical evaluation of this theory, see Groth 1964). One can identify, by and large, four major comparative approaches to the study of fascism and communism put forward during the time: (1) structural models of fascism and communism as 'generic' totalitarian regimes; (2) comparative inquiries into the similarities and differences among historical case studies of totalitarian regimes; (3) historical-genetic theories of totalitarianism focusing on the common intellectual origins of fascist and communist ideologies; and (4) fascism and communism as totalitarian 'political religions'. The following section discusses these major approaches, in an effort to evaluate their relevance and implications for the field of fascist studies.

The uni-totalitarian model: structural approaches to fascism and communism

Structural comparative approaches to fascism and communism advance a common theoretical framework for the analysis of totalitarianism political regimes of the twentieth century, notwithstanding the obvious fact that these regimes were otherwise very different in their other social, economic, or cultural aspects. The most influential analytical models of totalitarianism were put forward by Hannah Arendt in *The Origins of Totalitarianism* (1951), and by Carl J. Friedrich and

Zbigniew Brzezinski in *Totalitarian Dictatorship and Autocracy* (1956). Published at a short interval one after the other and reedited numerous times, these books shaped public and scholarly views on totalitarianism during the Cold War. The two books proposed different methodological approaches: Arendt's 'developmental' model explores mostly the origins of totalitarianism as a political trend; Friedrich and Brzezinski's 'operational' or 'functional' model explains the main features and the functioning of totalitarian *regimes*. Yet both approaches are compatible in their emphasis on issues of coercion, repression, and terror in defining the nature of totalitarianism, and can even be seen as complementary in their analytical and chronological emphases.

Arendt approached the origins of totalitarianism from the perspective of the emergence of mass politics, and focused mainly on the psychological and sociological conditions under which totalitarian movements and regimes emerged. Her main thesis is that the disintegration of the bourgeois society of the nineteenth century resulted in the transformation of classes into masses, the elimination of all forms of group solidarity, and the 'atomization' and 'extreme individualization' of society, thus creating the conditions for the emergence of inter-war totalitarian movements.

Arendt defined totalitarian movements as a new type of 'mass organizations of atomized, isolated individuals', having as a main goal the creation of a distinct, self-contained, and fully indoctrinated society (1951: 323). Totalitarian movements which managed to conquer the political power attempted to establish totalitarian regimes, defined by Arendt as a new type of rule striving for 'total' and 'permanent domination of each single individual in each and every sphere of life' (ibid.: 326). The 'essence' of the new type of regime was institutionalized terror, while the main instrument of terror was the Secret Police. To implement their utopian ideological goals, totalitarian regimes adopt innovative means of 'dominating and terrorising human beings from within' (ibid.: 325). By means of totalitarian indoctrination and absolute terror in concentration camps, they aim 'to destroy the essence of man' and to fabricate the 'inanimate men', as a new kind of human species (ibid.: 438).

In her historical analysis, Arendt used the term totalitarianism 'sparingly and prudently'. She argued that, although there were many genuinely totalitarian movements in inter-war Europe, most of them 'failed' in traditional one-party dictatorships. Only two political regimes in history could be classified as totalitarian: Nazi Germany (1938–45) and Soviet Russia (1928–41, and 1945–53). By discussing Stalinist Russia and Nazi Germany under a common theoretical framework, Arendt provides a powerful articulation of the theory of uni-totalitarianism. Her comparative analysis is, however, largely uneven. Her definition of totalitarianism is tailored to Nazi Germany, of which she had direct experience and extensive scholarly knowledge. Her views on the nature of communist regimes are less informed, due to the lack of access to archival sources, and to the fact that, at the time of her writing, the Soviet-types regimes in Eastern Europe and South-East Asia were 'in the making' and thus difficult to classify.

Arendt's book explored the origins of totalitarian movements and their evolution into totalitarian political regimes, but devoted less attention to the actual functioning of those regimes. This gap was soon filled by Friedrich and Brzezinski (1956) who advanced an analytical model for the study of totalitarian regimes. Friedrich and Brzezinski emphasized the common elements but also the differences between traditional autocracies and modern totalitarian regimes, the latter being defined as autocracies 'based on modern technology and mass legitimization'. The novelty of totalitarian regimes was their technologically conditioned forms of organization and methods of rule. In order to explain the main features of totalitarian regimes, Friedrich and Brzezinski identified six underlying features of what they called the 'totalitarian syndrome' or 'model', but which they also ambitiously qualified as a 'general, descriptive theory' of totalitarianism:

1   An official ideology, consisting of an official body of doctrine covering all vital aspects of man's existence, to which everyone living in that society is supposed to adhere at least passively.
2   A single mass party consisting of a relatively small percentage of the total population (up to 10 percent),organized in strictly hierarchical, oligarchic manner, usually under a single leader.
3   A technologically conditioned near-complete monopoly of control ... of all means of effective armed combat.
4   A similar technologically conditioned near-complete monopoly of control ... of all means of effective mass communication, such as the press, radio, motion pictures, and so on.
5   A system of terrorist police control ... characteristically directed not only against demonstrable 'enemies' of the regime, but against arbitrarily selected classes of the population.
6   A centrally directed economy.

(ibid.: 10–11)

Friedrich and Brzezinski argued that this cluster of 'intertwined and mutually supportive' traits should only be considered together, as an 'organic' system (2nd edn, 1965: 21). In the spirit of the uni-totalitarian theory, they also argued that these traits characterized all fascist as well as communist regimes, which were all 'basically alike', not 'wholly alike', yet 'sufficiently alike to class them together' (ibid.: 21). Among them, the two authors listed Soviet Russia since 1917 to the time of their writing, Fascist Italy (1925–43), Nazi Germany (1933–45), and post-1945 East European and Asian communist regimes.

This descriptive model soon became the standard view on totalitarianism, the received wisdom of the Cold War, widely cited in scholarly or even public discussions on totalitarian regimes. During the time, however, the explanatory value of this analytical model was questioned on numerous counts. The first criticism was that this model lacked both an elaborated theoretical framework to support it, and a 'connotative' definition of totalitarianism. Defining totalitarian regimes by means of a set of characteristics was 'an attempt to convey the meaning of an automobile solely by a description of its parts'; the result was 'an encyclopaedia of totalitarian politics' rather than a theory of totalitarianism (Burrowes 1969: 283, 288). Other scholars doubted that politics can be visualized in terms of a static 'model', arguing that such an analytical construct fails to capture the dynamic nature and evolution of totalitarian regimes. Finally, others argued that this political science model of totalitarian regimes placed too much stress on the nature of the political regime, its official ideology and leader, at the expense of deeper economic and social structures in fascist and communist societies (Groth 1964: 888–901).

More recently, political scientists made concerted efforts to put forward a more comprehensive definition of totalitarian regimes; to account not only for the similarities but also for the marked differences between the outlook and main features of fascist and communist regimes; and to insert them into a more sophisticated taxonomy of political regimes. The transition from the uni-totalitarian theory to the more elaborate field of comparative politics is best exemplified by the work of the political scientist Juan J. Linz, spanning several decades (1975; 1997). In his most recent work on the topic, Linz departed from the simplistic dichotomy between democratic versus totalitarian regimes to also include various forms of authoritarian and dictatorial regimes and thus arrive at a complex taxonomy of political regimes (2000).

Comparing historical case studies: Nazi Germany, Stalinist Russia, Fascist Italy

Initiated mostly by political scientists, the totalitarian approach has also stimulated comparative historical analyses of dictatorial regimes of the twentieth century, in an effort to identify in concrete details their common characteristics but also their differences. Most comparative works on the history of totalitarian regimes have routinely focused on the case studies of Nazi Germany and Stalinist Russia, the regimes considered the closest historical incarnations of an ideal-typical totalitarian regime, and only to a lesser extent on the comparison between Fascist Italy and Nazi Germany (Bessel 1996; Kallis 2000; Knox 2000, 2007). How useful is the concept of totalitarianism for the comparative historical study of fascist and communist regimes? Some comparativists fully insert their historical analysis into the conceptual framework of the totalitarian paradigm. As Viktor Zaslavsky argued: 'It is undoubtedly possible to compare Nazism and Stalinism while completely rejecting the category of "totalitarianism" but ... the results of such research are too often shallow and banal' (2003: 11). Other comparative historians reject the totalitarian approach as ideologically charged, searching instead for more politically neutral and methodologically viable alternatives. In their Introduction to a comparative collective volume on Nazi Germany and Stalinist Russia, Jan Kershaw and Moshe Lewin explore the 'common historical ground' in the evolution of the two dictatorships. Instead of only looking for sameness, they accounted for striking communalities as well as 'crucial differences' in the totalitarian aspects of the two societies. On the basis of a set of historically informed essays focusing on the cult of the leader, war machines, and the afterlife of these regimes in the historical memory in Germany and Soviet Union, Kershaw and Lewin concluded that 'the Nazi and Stalin regimes are *essentially different* despite their superficial similarities' (1997: 19). Their conclusion refutes the main claim of the uni-totalitarian approach that fascism and communism are 'basically alike'.

Fascist Italy has generally been left out of historical or typological comparative surveys of totalitarian regimes of the twentieth century, on the count that Mussolini failed to build a fully-fledged totalitarian political regime. Arendt, for example, argued that Fascist Italy was only a dictatorship and one-party regime. The reason for this evolution was the relatively small size of the country, which lacked human resources to sustain a totalitarian regime; the evidence for it was the lack of mass terror in Fascist Italy, illustrated by the 'surprisingly' small numbers of death sentences executed against political enemies (1951: 308–309). De Felice characterized Italian fascism as a regime of 'imperfect totalitarianism', since it lacked key instruments of totalitarian rule, such as an omnipotent, centralized state, an all-embracing fascist party, and a system of concentration camps (1969). Similarly, Alexander de Grand treated the Italian fascist regime as a form of 'failed totalitarianism'. He argued that between 1926 and 1933, Mussolini conducted a policy of 'parcelling out of the state into separate fiefdoms', allowing not only the survival of autonomous centre of power in the Italian society, such as the monarchy, the Catholic Church, the traditional bureaucracy, the army, and the economic elites, but also guaranteeing their corporate rights and privileges. This regime of 'fiefdoms and hyphenated fascism' resulted in the 'fractionalization of the state', considerably restricting Mussolini's room to manoeuvre in domestic policy. Mussolini's continuous dependence on traditional elites and his neglect of the Fascist Party explain his inability to mobilize the masses and drive the regime into a totalitarian direction. This failure led the regime into the political crisis of 1933–40. It was only after the 1940 close alliance with Germany and the political radicalization generated by the war that the first genuine totalitarian regime traits appeared in Italy, but they remained ultimately unfulfilled (de Grand 1991). Linz characterized Italian fascism as a form of 'arrested totalitarianism' (2000: 7). In contrast to these views, a handful of authors, most notably Emilio Gentile, argued that, even if allegedly unfulfilled at the level of state organization, the drive toward totalitarianism in inter-war Italy was genuine and should not be dismissed on the count that it was not fully implemented (1986).

Common historical origins: historical-genetic theories of fascism and communism

Historical-genetic theories of totalitarianism underscore both the common intellectual origins of fascist and communist ideologies and the multiple interactions between these two ideologies, the movements and regimes they inspired. The proponents of this approach argue that fascism and communism have a 'common date of birth', which is traced back to the eighteenth-century Enlightenment, to the cataclysm of the French Revolution and its aftermath (1789–1815), to the Romantic age in the first half of the nineteenth century, or to last quarter of the nineteenth century and the intellectual ferment of the turn of the nineteenth to the twentieth centuries. The proponents of the 'totalitarian model' and 'historical-genetic' approaches generally take a critical stance against each other: due to their different analytical and chronological emphases, the two approaches should be nevertheless seen as complementary.

A first genealogical view on the common origins of fascist and communist ideologies focuses on their relation to the intellectual matrix of the Enlightenment. Some scholars argue that both fascism and communism are legal heirs of the Enlightenment, and therefore of modernity (Bauman 1991). Other scholars see communism as grounded in modernism or humanism, but regard fascism as an essentially anti-modern phenomenon (Žižek 2002, 2005). A minority of scholars argue that both ideologies should be viewed as anti-modern reactions against the Enlightenment project. Still others point to fascists' ambivalent relationship with modernity, seeing it as a manifestation of the 'dark side of modernity' (Mann 2004: 365).

A second genealogical view on the common origins of fascism and communism focuses on the role of the French Revolution in crystallizing radical modern political ideologies (Mosse 1989). In a path-breaking trilogy, the Israeli political scientist Jacob L. Talmon distinguished between two main ideological trends originating from the political matrix of the French Revolution: liberal versus totalitarian messianic democracies (1960; 1970; 1979). Concerning the second trend, Talmon further distinguished between the 'totalitarianism of the right', based on glorifying the collective entity of the state, the nation, or the race, which culminated in fascism, and the 'totalitarianism of the left', since it proclaims the goodness and perfectibility of the human nature, which culminated in communism (1970: 6–7; 1991).

A third genealogical view argues that fascism and communism were not only related but also *mutually inter-dependent* collectivist revolts against liberalism. A. James Gregor regarded fascism as a left-wing rather than right-wing ideology; in view of the common intellectual roots and multiple cross-contaminations, he characterized the relationship between fascism and Bolshevism as 'curvilinear', and described the two phenomena as 'the faces of Janus' (2000: 128–148). Other historians credit World War I with a decisive role in the crystallization of fascism and communism as major political movements. In a polemical dialogue, two prominent historians, François Furet and Ernst Nolte, value the historico-genetic approach as being 'more convincing', 'of greater interpretative force', and 'more interesting than the structural comparison of Hitlerian and Stalinian totalitarianism' (Furet and Nolte 2001: 33) but interpreted differently the relationship between fascism and communism. Speculating on the fact that the Bolshevik Revolution (1917) preceded the advent to power of the Nazi Party in Germany (1933), Nolte argued that 'Fascism was born as a defensive reaction against communism' (1977), a view encapsulated in the catchy phrase 'Without-Marxism-there-is-no-fascism' (1965: 21). In his view, Marxism was 'an original movement, the product of very old roots', while fascism was 'a reaction *of a secondary order*, artificial in large part, based on postulates' (2001: 25). On this basis, Nolte established a 'causal nexus' between the Gulag system in the USSR and the Nazi Holocaust, seeing the second as a defensive reaction to the first (2001: 27). This controversial thesis stirred a heated debate in Germany over the uniqueness of the Holocaust and the place of Nazism in German and European history, called the *Historikerstreit* (the 'Historians' quarrel', 1986–89). The controversy started with a polemical exchange between Nolte and Jürgen Habermas, and was soon joined by prominent German and foreign scholars (*Historikerstreit* 1993; for a critical evaluation, see Evans 1989). During the debate, Nolte's view on Nazism as a mere defensive reaction against Bolshevism was denounced as an attempt to shift the blame for the war and thus exculpate the Nazis of responsibility for their atrocities.

Furet acknowledged the common intellectual 'matrix' of communism and fascism, arguing that 'the only serious way to approach these two original ideologies and political movements is to take them together as the two faces of an acute crisis of liberal democracy' (1999). Yet he rejected 'simplistic interpretations through linear causality' contending instead that fascism and communism were in a *dialectical relationship*, marked by 'mutual endangering and reinforcing' (Furet and Nolte 2001: 2). Furet also objected against the relegation of fascism to a secondary role, as a 'purely reactive, anti-Bolshevik' movement (ibid.: 35). Fascism was not a counterrevolutionary but a genuinely revolutionary movement which proved potent enough to take the European Right out of its political impasse (ibid.: 62). Both ideologies, fascist and communist, were related yet distinct attempts to solve 'the political deficit' of modern democracy by integrating the masses in novel political regimes.

Fascism and communism as totalitarian political religions

In the past two decades, the comparison between fascism and communism as similar and inter-related *totalitarian* ideologies, movements, and regimes has been relaunched, mostly in connection with debates over the issue of political religions. The concept of political religion has a long history, closely interlinked with the kindred concepts of fascism and totalitarianism. It was coined for the first time in inter-war critiques of fascism advanced by Protestant and Catholic intellectuals and theologians such as Luigi Sturzo, Adolf Keller, Paul Tillich, Gerhard Leibholz, and – most importantly – by the German political philosopher (later US émigré) Eric Voegelin, the first scholars to place political religions at the centre of his research (1938; 1952; 1998; 1999a; 1999b). At its origins, the concept referred to the anti-Christian character of totalitarian regimes and their concerted campaign of subverting established churches while taking over some of the main functions of traditional religions. A similar critique, but from the position of liberalism, was advanced by the French philosopher and political scientist Raymond Aron, who – as early as 1939 – denounced the totalizing quest and anti-Enlightenment nature of totalitarian political or secular religion (*religion politique* or *religion séculière*) (1965). After World War II, the emergence of political religions was valued as an important feature of totalitarian regimes in the work of Friederich and Brezinski (1956), Bracher (1970) or Waldemar Gurian (1964), but this dimension remained largely unexplored. A related debate was generated in late 1960s, in a different context, by the American sociologist Robert Bellah, who argued for the renewal of the bonds of *civil religion* as a way out of the moral-political crisis of the American society (1967).

In fascist studies, interest in political religions was mainly stimulated by the emergence and exponential expansion of Holocaust studies as a distinct field of research (Maier 2007: 5). The inquiry into the causes that led to the Holocaust prompted scholars to re-evaluate the role of fascist rites and rituals in accounting for the 'fascination with the evil' exercised over large segments of the population. Two main approaches to the emotional appeal of fascism can be distinguished: one explores the process of 'nationalization of the masses' and the aesthetization of modern politics, the other the process of sacralization of politics and the emergence of political religions.

The first approach was pioneered by George Mosse, who, in *The Nationalization of the Masses*, underscored the intimate relationship between German Romantic nationalism and Nazism, pointing out that 'what we call fascist style was in reality the climax of a "new politics" based upon the emerging eighteenth-century idea of popular sovereignty' (1991: 1). The essence of the new style of politics was the aestheticization of politics, 'the force which linked myths, symbols, and the feeling of the masses'. He also emphasized the organic link between fascism and Romantic nationalism, which made symbols the essence of the new politics. Mosse acknowledged the quasi-religious character of nationalism but defined it as a 'secular religion', or a substitute of tradition religion. His innovative approach, and the related rich literature on the relationship between power and its representations, inspired a distinct field of study focusing on the aestheticization of politics in fascist and communist regimes (on fascist Italy, see Berezin 1997; Falasca-Zamponi 2000a; 2000b).

The second approach was mainly brought to the forefront by the Italian scholar Emilio Gentile, who developed a new, well-structured theoretical framework for the study of fascism, based on the conceptual triad of the sacralization of politics, totalitarianism, and the emergence of political religion (see this volume, pp. 257–289). The translation of Gentile's works into English (1990; 1996; 2000; 2006) resuscitated interest in the issue of political religions, resulting in a plethora of monographs, edited works, thematic issues or even specialized journals, such as *Totalitarian Movements and Political Religions* (Maier 1995; Burrin 1997; Ley and Schoeps 1997; Ley 1997; Maier and Schafer 1997; Huttner 1999; Blinkhorn 2004; Griffin 2005b).

Most analysts treat the rise of political religions as a phenomenon characteristic of the twentieth century. Nevertheless, in order to study the intellectual and political origins of modern political religions they go back in time to the Enlightenment and the French and American Revolutions. Few historians argue for the continued relevance of political religions in the twenty-first century, focusing mostly on contemporary Islamic fundamentalist movements (Payne 2005), while others doubt it (Gentile 2000). Empirical works on political religions concentrate mostly on revolutionary France, the United States (Richey and Jones 1974; Wimberley 1976; Albanese 1976: Hughey 1983; Schieder 1987; Gentile 2006; 2008); on the paradigmatic cases of Soviet Russia (Griffin 2002; Shorten, 2003; Riegel 2005); on Nazi Germany (Lübbe, 1995; Ley and Schoeps 1997; Bärsch 1999; Burleigh, 2000; Vondung 2005) and Fascist Italy (Gentile 1996); on inter-war fascist movements (Durham 2004; Linehan 2004); Kemalist Turkey (Mateescu 2006); Asian or Eastern European communism, and nationalist movements in developing countries (Apter 1963), often in comparative perspective. More recently, two rich syntheses authored by Michael Burleigh integrate the emergence of political religions into the large framework of the intersection between religion and politics, also covering the related phenomena of secularization, Church responses and the politicization of religions, religious politics and religions political visions from the Enlightenment to present-day religious fundamentalism (2005; 2007).

The political religion approach stirred several substantive theoretical, methodological, and historical debates. The first, most general, debate concerns the relationship between fascism and established churches, an issue which touches upon the history of religion but also upon key aspects of our understanding of mass political mobilization and legitimization of power. Due to the great number of variables involved in this relationship, their hybrid nature, and their multiple intellectual genealogies, approaches to this issue are of a bewildering variety. Scholars point to the politicization of established religions, the syncretism between the Christian religious tradition and fascist ideology leading to 'pseudo-religions', the collaboration between established churches and fascist movements resulting in forms of clerical fascism, new 'civil', 'national' or 'secular' religions that evolved in parallel to established religions, or – in the culmination of this trend – the emergence of totalitarian political religions based on the sacralization of politics.

The second, related, debate concerns the meaning of the term religion in the concept of 'political religion'. Can the distinct worldviews of totalitarian movements and regimes, their ritual practice and the fanaticism they instilled in their followers be defined as religions? If yes, what type of religiosity they entail? Generally, three main methodological approaches to religion can be delineated, generically called transcendental, gnostic, and functional. The transcendental approach employs a traditional understanding of religion as a belief in a supernatural God (for an example, see Stark 2003). Scholars who adopt this view reject the concept of political religion, arguing that the sacralization of secular entities in politics cannot and should not be qualified as 'religion'. The *gnostic* approach to religion was advanced by Eric Voegelin precisely in order to account for the emergence of modern political religions. According to his phenomenological interpretation, totalitarian regimes are forms of gnosticism based on a set of philosophical teachings which serve as foundation of modern political cults aimed at bringing salvation to human communities through esoteric ritual or practice (1999b). Voegelin's pioneering work provided an invaluable source of inspiration for scholars working on political religions; yet, today his approach is often either marginalized as too idiosyncratic or is openly rejected by many scholars (Griffin 1991). The *functional* approach rests on Emile Durkheim's understanding of religion as stemming not from a belief in a transcendental God but from the sacralization of collective beliefs and practices. As Durkheim put it: 'If religion generates everything that is essential in society, this is because the idea of society is the soul of religion' (2001: 314). The Durkheimian approach informs most proponents of the secular religion thesis; yet its application to modern political religions is not free of terminological or methodological controversies. Many scholars acknowledge the important role played by the 'sacred' in modern politics but object to the usage of the word 'religion' to denote what are essentially political phenomena. Hans Maier, for example, accepts the term only for the lack of better alternatives (2007: 15). Originally, Payne rejected the term 'political', claiming that fascist movements strove in fact to create new 'civil religions', within a 'post-Christian, postreligious, secular, and immanent frame of reference' (1995: 9). More recently, he endorses a heuristic approach to political religions (2006). Eatwell criticized the political religion approach for overemphasizing culture and form over belief and function' (2003: 147). Arguing that fascism was a political ideology and not a religion, he agrees with the political religion thesis only insofar it is treated as a heuristic approach (2003: 162).

The third debate concerns the relationship between totalitarianism and political religions. Generally, scholars who contest the heuristic value of the concept of totalitarianism also reject the political religion approach; those who employ the totalitarian model tend to adopt the concept of political religion as its corollary. In the latter approach, the two concepts reinforce each other as complementary: the structural model of totalitarianism focuses on the political-institutional system of domination and organized terror, while the political religion thesis highlights psychological technologies of totalitarian rule and their strong affinities with religion, at the level of both ideology and practice. Political religions emerge in the context of totalitarian movements or regimes, as instruments of both sacralizing and institutionalizing totalizing ideologies. How central are political religions for the functioning of totalitarian movements or regimes? Gentile sees them as subsumed to the larger phenomenon of the sacralization of politics, and thus arguably of a secondary importance to that (2004). While building on Gentile's framework, Griffin invests political religion with an even greater importance, arguing that it 'lies at the heart of the totalitarian project' (2002a: 29). In contrast, proponents of the aestheticization of politics approach contend that, while useful, the concept of political religion is unable to cover the full range of cultural policies of fascist regimes (Falasca-Zamponi 2000b: 198).

It may well be that, due to their far–reaching implications, the debates over the political religion approach will never be 'resolved' (Gentile 2000: 31). Yet, these debates have had a positive impact on fascist studies, since they challenged the neat dichotomy between the 'secular' and the 'religious', demanding instead a redefinition of the multiple meanings attached to contested concepts such as 'religion' and 'secularization', and the nature of the 'sacred' or the 'holy' in the modern period.

Transnational entanglements and transfers: recent trends in comparative fascist studies

To conclude, what is the state of the art in comparative fascist studies? In 2001, Stein Ugelvig Larsen, a leading figure in the field, lamented that 'the longstanding debate about the definition of fascism has been frustrating', reflecting 'the apparent inability of academics to come up with either a clear definition or a comprehensive explanatory theory' (2001: 711). Yet, despite countless passionate debates that degenerated at times in a dialogue of the deaf, the field of comparative fascist studies does *not* resemble 'the remains of a battlefield littered with abandoned or burned-out wrecks' (Knox, cited in Payne 1995: 487). As this volume also illustrates, after decades of accumulated research and sophisticated methodological gains, we do know much more about fascism today than we did several decades ago. Surely, given the epistemological nature of knowledge in humanities and social sciences, the debate over fascism will never be resolved in absolute terms. The multitude of discourses and methods in the field of comparative fascist studies notwithstanding, there are signs of convergence and synergy, if not in the form of a single, 'illusionary' grand consensus (Bauerkämper 2006), at least around several loosely defined clusters of approaches. These clusters are not mutually exclusive but complementary. Plurality in comparative fascist studies is here to stay, but international debates will continue to carry the field ahead.

One can discern several new trends or directions in fascist studies. First, there is an opening toward multi- and inter-disciplinarity. To be sure, fascist studies have always been interdisciplinary, their subject matter providing 'an ideal meeting ground for historians, political scientists, sociologists and economists' (Woolf 1968: 4–5). More recently, the field has been joined by anthropologists, gender historians, art historians, linguists, and students of biomedicine and biopolitics, among others. Inter-disciplinarity brings with itself both a broadening and a deepening of the research agenda in the field. It enables students of fascism to revisit old themes from novel perspectives, and to tackle previously unexplored topics of research by means of new methods. Consider, for example, the positive impact of gender history on fascist studies: it makes it possible for researchers to account, from a relational perspective, for the formation of fascists' masculine but also feminine identities; to explore the role of women in fascist movements and their own experiences and perceptions; and to understand gender relations and family policies under fascist regimes (Theweleit 1987–89; de Grazia, 1992; Spackman 1996; Durham 1998; Sigmund 2000; Gottlieb 2000; 2004; Richmond 2003). Equally important, the critical and culturally-oriented methodologies associated with gender studies inspired new approaches to fascism. They underscored the fact that the issue of gender permeates all social phenomena and should not be marginalized as a mere 'appendix' to mainstream research.

Although comparative fascist studies have had their own research tradition and internal dynamic, they have also followed wider research trends in the humanities and social sciences, being deeply influenced by the social, linguistic, cultural and anthropological turns. These changes are illustrated by new interdisciplinary approaches to fascism as totalitarianism, which depart from rigid political science regime-models to focus instead on the fascists' cultural-anthropological revolution aimed at creating a new type of human being. Nowadays, students of fascism explore a richness of new themes, such as the fascist ideology, political languages, and culture; the circulation of fascist ideas and printed artefacts; totalitarian technologies of domination and rule; demographic, eugenic, racial or other aspects of the biopolitics of fascist regimes; fascist rites and rituals and their relation to established religions or new forms of political religions, etc. There is also a renewed interest in the interplay between social and cultural history resulting in studies of micro-history, everyday life, and forms of education and socialization in the context of totalitarian fascist movements and regimes.

Second, fascist studies have recently benefited from an injection of new methods of approaching global, continental, or regional history from trans-national perspectives, such as world history, shared or entangled history, *histoire croisée* and the history of transfers (Kaelble and Schriewer 2003; Lepenies 2003; Cohen and O'Connor 2004; Werner and Zimmermann 2006). New approaches re-evaluate critically 'classical' comparative methods and shift the focus of research from variable-dependent methodology and causal reasoning to multiple levels of interaction, placing the emphasis on processes of reciprocal perceptions, asymmetric mutual influences, and entanglements among inter-related historical actors. These approaches are able to revitalize comparative fascist studies, illuminating aspects that have not been subject to systematic research – such as the international character of fascism, and the interaction, entanglements, exchange of ideas, and dissemination of political and ideological models among fascists, – thus revealing previously unknown intellectual genealogies or connections (Schieder 1996; Orlow 2003; Reichardt and Nolzen, 2005).

Third, the new approaches and angles of comparison also challenge students of fascism to revisit their units, objects, and levels of analysis. As a generic phenomenon, fascism can be understood only from an integrated perspective that takes into account national as well as sub-national and trans-national dimensions. Its study involves an analysis of the national context as well as of the international circulation of ideas across countries. So far, comparative historians of fascism have mostly concentrated on 'holistic' national case studies. Surely, the concentration on national units of analysis makes sense for numerous research questions, such as patterns of nation- and state-building, the nature of political regimes, the evolution of national institutions, electoral results, processes of elite formation, or the social composition and stratification of fascist movements and regimes. Yet, the national context is less relevant for other types of questions, such as European wartime experiences or the trans-national circulation of ideas. For such topics, a unilateral focus on national contexts obscures rather than illuminates, trapping scholars in attributing pseudo-local causes to international phenomena.

Fourth, these new trends in writing history from integrated global or European perspectives challenge historians of fascism to incorporate non-Western fascist movements and regimes into a unified perspective. Too often, comparative analyses of fascism have been tributary to politicized symbolic geographies as politicized ways of mentally mapping and classifying historical regions. Scholars of fascism have often tended to compare geographical regions or topographical categories rather than specific actors, institutions, or problems. They have also employed *rigid* and *totalizing* definitions of regions stemming from the Cold War ideological divisions of the world. By employing analytical categories such as 'Western European', 'Eastern European', or 'Third World' fascisms, they fell into the trap of reifying geographical labels into historical types. On the one, they operate with the image of a unified and homogenous West, thus succumbing to 'Occidentalism, an attitude informed by 'typified' or 'stylized images of the West' (Carrier 1995). On the other hand, they employ the over-generalizing Cold War notion of 'Eastern European fascism' to refer to movements as diverse as those in Hungary, Slovakia, Croatia, Romania, Bulgaria, the Baltic states or Russia, thus running the danger of 'essentializing' or 'Orientalizing' these phenomena (on the concept of Orientalism, see Said 1979; on the invention of 'Eastern Europe', see Wolff 1994; on 'imagining the Balkans', see Todorova 1997).

Recent studies have integrated various fascist movements and regimes in Central and Eastern Europe more firmly into mainstream fascist studies (Payne 1995; Mann 2004; Iordachi 2004), and developed theoretical models of generic fascism that account for the evolution of non-European fascism, as well (Larsen 2001). This effort is not meant to elevate non-Western radical movements to the level of generic fascism or to pride 'underdeveloped' regions with their 'genuine' fascism, but to highlight the fact that, as a universal phenomenon, fascism was concomitantly generated in various societal settings. Even if uneven, the circulation of fascist ideas, practices, and activists from/to various historical regions was not one-directional but a truly transnational and multiple-way process. Consider, for example, the transfer of certain anti-Semitic ideas and practices from Central and Eastern Europe to Western Europe and vice versa, the contribution of numerous German émigrés from Russia to the doctrine and practice of National Socialism, and the influence some 'minor' fascist movements in inter-war Central Europe exercised upon their neighbours, such as the Romanian Iron Guard upon Polish, Ukrainian and Hungarian fascists, or even upon neo-fascists in Italy. The new wave of critical comparative works promotes new transnational perspectives and angles of research, stimulating the further evolution of fascist studies in novel directions.

BIBLIOGRAPHY

Adamson, Walter L. (1980) 'Gramsci's interpretation of fascism', *Journal of the History of Ideas*, 41(4): 615–633.

Adler, Les K. and Paterson, Thomas G. (1970) 'Red Fascism: The Merger of Nazi Germany and Soviet Russia in the American Image of Totalitarianism, 1930's–1950s', *The American Historical Review*, 75: 1046–1064.

Albanese, Catherine L. (1976) *Sons of the Fathers: The Civil Religion of the American Revolution*. Philadelphia, PA: Temple University Press.

Allardyce, Gilbert (1979) 'What Fascism Is Not: Thoughts on the Deflation of a Concept', *The American Historical Review*, 84(2): 367–388.

Apter, David A. (1963) 'Political Religion in the New Nations', in Clifford Geertz (ed.) *Old Society and New States: The Quest for Modernity in Asia and Africa*. New York: Free Press, pp. 57–103.

Arendt, Hannah (1951) *The Origins of Totalitarianism*. New York: Harcourt Brace Jovanovich.

Aron, Raymond (1965) *Démocratie et totalitarisme*. Paris: Gallimard; English edn: *Democracy and Totalitarianism*. London: Weidenfeld and Nicholson, 1968.

Bärsch, Claus-Ekkehard (1999) *Die politische Religion des Nationalsozialismus*. Munich: Wilhelm Fink.

Bauerkämper, Arnd (2006) 'A New Consensus? Recent Research on Fascism in Europe, 1918–1945', *History Compass*, 4(3): 536–566.

Bauman, Zygmunt (1991) *Modernity and the Holocaust*. Ithaca, NY: Cornell University Press.

Beetham, David (1983) *Marxism in Face of Fascism*. Manchester: Manchester University Press.

Bellah, Robert (1967) 'Civil Religion in America', *Daedalus*, 97(1): 1–21.

Berezin, Mabel (1997) *Making the Fascist Self: The Political Culture of Interwar*. Ithaca, NY: Cornell University Press.

Bessel, Richard (ed.) (1996) *Fascist Italy and Nazi Germany: Comparisons and Contrasts*. New York: Cambridge University Press.

Blackbourn, David and Eley, Geoff (1984) *The Peculiarities of German History: Bourgeois Society and Politics in Nineteenth-century Germany*. Oxford: Oxford University Press.

Blinkhorn, Martin (2000) *Fascism and the Right in Europe, 1919–1945*. Harlow: Longman.

Blinkhorn, Martin (2004) 'Afterthoughts, Route Maps and Landscapes: Historians, "Fascist Studies" and the Study of Fascism', *Totalitarian Movements and Political Religions*, 5(3): 507–526.

Bracher, Karl Dietrich (1970) *The German Dictatorship: The Origins, Structures, and Effects of National Socialism*. New York: Praeger.

Burke, Peter (2005) *History and Social Theory*. Ithaca, NY: Cornell University Press.

Burleigh, Michael (2000) *The Third Reich: A New History*. New York: Hill and Wang.

Burleigh, Michael (2005) *Earthly Powers: The Clash of Religion and Politics in Europe from the French Revolution to the Great War*. New York: HarperCollins.

Burleigh, Michael (2007) *Sacred Causes: The Clash of Religion and Politics from the Great War to the War on Terror*. New York: HarperCollins.

Burrin, Phillipe (1997) 'Political Religion: The Relevance of a Concept', *History and Theory*, 9(1–2): 321–349.

Burrowes, Robert (1969) 'Totalitarianism: The Revised Standard Version', *World Politics*, 21(2): 272–294.

Carrier, James G. (ed.) (1995) *Occidentalism: Images of the West*. Oxford: Clarendon Press.

Carsten, F.L. (1967) *The Rise of Fascism*. Berkeley, CA: University of California Press.

Chomsky, Noam and Herman, Edward S. (1979) *The Washington Connection and Third World Fascism*. Boston: South End Press.

Cohen, Deborah and O'Connor, Maura (eds) (2004) *Comparison and History: Europe in Cross-National Perspective*. New York: Routledge.

Connolly, W.E. (1976) *The Term of Political Discourse*. Lexington, DC: Heath.

Davies, Peter and Lynch, Derek (2002) *The Routledge Companion to Fascism and the Far Right*. New York: Routledge.

de Felice, Renzo (ed.) (1965–1997) *Mussolini*, 8 vols. Torino: Einaudi.

de Felice, Renzo (1969) *Le interpretazioni del fascismo*. Roma: Laterza. English edn: *Interpretations of Fascism*, trans. B. H. Everett. Cambridge, MA: Harvard University Press, 1977.

de Felice, Renzo (ed.) (1970) *Il Fascismo: le interpretazioni dei contemporanei e degli storici*. Roma: Laterza.

de Felice, Renzo (1975) *Intervista sul fascismo, a cura di Michael A. Ledeen*. Bari: Laterza; English edn: *Fascism: An Informal Introduction to its Theory and Practice, an Interview with Michael A. Ledeen*. New Brunswick, NJ: Transaction Books, 1976.

de Felice, Renzo (ed.) (1976) *Antologia sul fascismo*, 2 vols. Rome: Laterza.

de Felice, Renzo and Fermi, Laura (1961) *Mussolini*. Chicago: University of Chicago Press.

de Grazia, Victoria (1992) *How Fascism Ruled Women: Italy, 1922–1945*. Berkeley, CA: University of California Press.

Dimitrov, Georgi (1935) 'The Fascist Offensive and the Tasks of the Communist International in the Struggle of the Working Class against Fascism', Main Report delivered at the Seventh World Congress of the Communist International, August 2, 1935. Available at: http://www.marxists.org/reference/archive/dimitrov/works/1935/08_02.htm

Dimitrov, Georgi (1967) *Selected Works*, 2 vols. Sofia: Foreign Languages Press.

Dimitrov, Georgi (2002) *Against Fascism and War*. New York: International Publisher.

Durham, Martin (1998) *Women and Fascism*. London: Routledge.

Durham, Martin (2004) 'The Upward Path: Palingenesis, Political Religion and the National Alliance', *Totalitarian Movements and Political Religions*, 5(3): 454–468.

Durkheim, Emile (2001) *The Elementary Forms of Religious Life*. Oxford: Oxford University Press.

Dutt, Rajani Palme (1934) *Fascism and Social Revolution*. New York: International Press.

Eatwell, Roger (1996) 'On Defining the "Fascist Minimum": The Centrality of Ideology', *Journal of Political Ideologies*, 1(3): 303–319.

Eatwell, Roger (2003) 'Reflections on Fascism and Religion', *Totalitarian Movements and Political Religion*, 4(3): 145–166.

Evans, Richard J. (1987) *Rethinking German History: Nineteenth-century Germany and the Origins of the Third Reich*. London: HarperCollins.

Evans, Richard J. (1989) *In Hitler's Shadow: West German Historians and the Attempt to Escape the Nazi Past*. New York: Pantheon.

Fabio-Liguori, Frosini (ed.) (2004) *Le parole di Gramsci. Per un lessico dei Quaderni del carcere*. Rome: Carocci.

Falasca-Zamponi, Simonetta (2000a) 'The Sacralization of Politics in Fascist Italy', *History of Religions*, 40: 4.

Falasca-Zamponi, Simonetta (2000b) *Fascist Spectacle: The Aesthetics of Power in Mussolini's Italy*. Berkeley, CA: University of California Press.

Freeden, Michael (1986) *Liberalism Divided: A Study in British Political Thought 1914–1939*. Oxford: Oxford University Press.

Friedrich, Carl J. (ed.) (1964) *Totalitarianism*. New York: Grosset & Dunlap.

Friedrich, Carl J. and Brzezinski, Zbigniew K. (1956) *Totalitarian Dictatorship and Autocracy*. Cambridge, MA: Harvard University Press.

Furet, François (1999) *The Passing of an Illusion: The Idea of Communism in the Twentieth Century*. Chicago: University of Chicago Press.

Furet, François and Nolte, Ernst (2001) *Fascism and Communism*. Lincoln, NE: University of Nebraska Press.

Gentile, Emilio (1986) 'Fascism in Italian Historiography: In Search of an Individual Historical Identity', *Journal of Contemporary History*, 21: 179–208.

Gentile, Emilio (1990) 'Fascism as Political Religion', *Journal of Contemporary History*, 25(2–3): 229–251.

Gentile, Emilio (1992) 'Fascismo', in *Enciclopedia italiana di scienze, lettere ed arti, 1979–1992*, V Appendice. Rome: Istituto della Enciclopedia Italiana.

Gentile, Emilio (1993) *Il culto del littorio: la sacralizzazione della politica nell'Italia fascista*. Rome: Laterza.

Gentile, Emilio (1996) *The Sacralization of Politics in Fascist Italy*. Cambridge, MA: Harvard University Press.

Gentile, Emilio (1997) 'Renzo de Felice: A Tribute', *Journal of Contemporary History*, 32(2): 139–151.

Gentile, Emilio (2000) 'The Sacralisation of Politics: Definitions, Interpretations and Reflections on the Question of Secular Religion and Totalitarianism', *Totalitarian Movements and Political Religion*, 1(1): 18–55.

Gentile, Emilio (2002) *Fascismo. Storia e Interpretatione*. Roma: Laterza.

Gentile, Emilio (2004) 'Fascism, Totalitarianism and Political Religion: Definitions and Critical Reflections on Criticism of an Interpretation', *Totalitarian Movements and Political Religions*, 5(3): 326–375.

Gentile, Emilio (2006) *Politics as Religion*. Princeton, NJ: Princeton University Press.

Gentile, Emilio (2008) *God's Democracy: American Religion after September 11*. Westport, CT: Praeger.

Gentile, Giovanni (2002) *Origins and Doctrine of Fascism*. New Brunswick, NJ: Transaction.

Gleason, Abbott (1995) *Totalitarianism: The Inner History of the Cold War*. New York: Oxford University Press.

Gottlieb, Julie V. (2000) *Feminine Fascism: Women in Britain's Fascist Movement, 1923–45*. London: I. B. Tauris.

Gottlieb, Julie V. (2004) 'Women and British Fascism Revisited: Gender, the Far-Right, and Resistance', *Journal of Women's History*, 16(3): 108–123.

Grand, Alexander de (1991) 'Cracks in the Façade: The Failure of Fascist Totalitarianism in Italy, 1935–9', *European History Quarterly*, 21: 515–535.

Greene, Nathaniel (ed.) (1968) *Fascism: An Anthology*. New York: Crowell.

Gregor, A. James (1974) *Interpretations of Fascism*. Morristown, NJ, General Learning Press; New edn: New Brunswick, NJ: Transaction, 1997.

Gregor, A. James (1979) *Young Mussolini and the Intellectual Origins of Fascism*. Berkeley, CA: University of California Press.

Gregor, A. James (2000) *The Faces of Janus: Marxism and Fascism in the Twentieth Century*. New Haven, CT: Yale University Press.

Gregor, A. James (2006) *The Search for Neofascism: The Use and Abuse of Social Science*. Cambridge: Cambridge University Press.

Griffin, Roger (1991) *The Nature of Fascism*. New York: St. Martin's Press.

Griffin, Roger (ed.) (1995) *Fascism*. Oxford: Oxford University Press.

Griffin, Roger (ed.) (1998) *International Fascism: Theories, Cases, and the New Consensus*. London: Arnold.

Griffin, Roger (2002a) 'The Palingenetic Political Community: Rethinking the Legitimization of Totalitarian Regimes in Inter-War Europe', *Totalitarian Movements and Political Religions*, 3(3): 24–43.

Griffin, Roger (2002b) 'The Primacy of Culture: The Current Growth (or Manufacture) of Consensus within Fascist Studies', *The Journal of Contemporary History*, 37(1): 21–43.

Griffin, Roger (2004) 'Introduction: God's Counterfeiters? Investigating the Triad of Fascism, Totalitarianism, and (Political) Religion', *Totalitarian Movements and Political Religions*, 5(3): 291–326.

Griffin, Roger (2005a) 'Cloister or Cluster? The Implications of Emilio Gentile's Ecumenical Theory of Political Religion for the Study of Extremism', *Totalitarian Movements and Political Religions*, 6(1): 33–52.

Griffin, Roger (ed.) (2005b) *Fascism, Totalitarianism and Political Religion*. London: Routledge.

Griffin, Roger (2007) *Modernism and Fascism: The Sense of a Beginning under Mussolini and Hitler*. Houndsmill: Palgrave Macmillan.

Griffin, Roger, Loh, Werner and Umland, Andreas (eds) (2006) *Fascism Past and Present, West and East: An International Debate on Concepts and Cases in the Comparative Study of the Extreme Right*. Stuttgart: Ibidem-Verlag.

Groth, Alexander J. (1964) 'The "isms" in Totalitarianism', *The American Political Science Review*, 58: 888–901.

Gurian, Waldemar (1964) 'Totalitarianism as Political Religion', in C. Friedrich, ed., *Totalitarianism*, New York: Grosset & Dunlap, pp. 119–129.

Hagtvet, Bernt and Kühnl, Reinhard (1980) 'Contemporary Approaches to Fascism: A Survey of Paradigms', in S.U. Larson, B. Hagtvet and J.P. Myklebust (eds) *Who Were the Fascists? Social Roots of European Fascists*. Bergen: Universitetsforlaget, pp. 26–51.

Halberstam, Michael (1998) 'Totalitarianism as a Problem for the Modern Conception of Politics', *Political Theory*, 26(4): 459–488.

Haupt, Heinz-Gerhard and Kocka, Jürgen (2004) 'Comparative History: Methods, Aims, Problems', in Deborah Cohen and Maura O'Connor (eds) *Comparison and History: Europe in Cross-National Perspective*. New York: Routledge, pp. 23–39.

Historikerstreit (1993) *Forever in the Shadow of Hitler? Original Documents of the Historikerstreit, the Controversy Concerning the Singularity of the Holocaust*. Atlantic Highlands, NJ: Humanities Press.

Hughey, Michael W. (1983) *Civil Religion and Moral Order: Theoretical and Historical Dimensions*. Westport, CT: Greenwood Press.

Huttner, Markus (1999) *Totalitarismus und säkulare Religionen: Zur Frügeschichte totalitarismuskritischer Begriffs- und Theoriebildung in Großbritannien*. Bonn: Bouvier.

Iordachi, Constantin (2004) *Charisma, Politics and Violence: The Legion of "Archangel Michael" in Inter-war Romania*. Trondheim: Trondheim Studies on East European Cultures and Societies.

Kaelble, Hartmut and Schriewer, J. (eds) (2003) *Vergleich und Transfer. Komparatistik in den Sozial-, Geschichts- und Kulturwissenschaften*. Frankfurt/Main: Campus.

Kallis, Aristotle A. (2000) *Fascist Ideology: Territory and Expansionism in Italy and Germany, 1922–1945*. London: Routledge.

Kallis, Aristotle A. (2002) *Fascism: A Reader – Historians and Interpretations of Fascism*. London: Routledge.

Kallis, Aristotle A. (2004) 'Studying Fascism in Epochal and Diachronic Terms: Ideological Production, Political Experience and the Quest for "Consensus",' *European History Quarterly*, 34(1): 9–42.

Kedward, H. R. (1971) *Fascism in Western Europe, 1900–45*. New York: New York University Press.

Kershaw, Ian (1989) *The Nazi Dictatorship: Problems and Perspectives of Interpretation*. London: E. Arnold.

Kershaw, Ian and Lewin, Moshe (eds) (1997) *Nazism and Stalinism: Dictatorships in Comparison*. Cambridge: Cambridge University Press.

Knox, MacGregor (2000) *Common Destiny: Dictatorship, Foreign Policy, and War in Fascist Italy and Nazi Germany*. Cambridge: Cambridge University Press.

Knox, MacGregor (2007) *To the Threshold of Power, 1922/33: Origins and Dynamics of the Fascist and National Socialist Dictatorships*. Cambridge: Cambridge University Press.

Kocka, Jürgen (1988) 'German History before Hitler: The Debate about the German Sonderweg', *Journal of Contemporary History*, 23: 3–16.

Kocka, Jürgen (1999) 'Asymmetrical Historical Comparison: The Case of the German Sonderweg', *History and Theory*, 38(1): 40–50.

Laqueur, Walter (ed.) (1976) *Fascism: A Reader's Guide. Analyses, Interpretations, Bibliography*. Berkeley, CA: University of California Press.

Laqueur, Walter (ed.) (1996) *Fascism: Past, Present, Future*, New York: Oxford University Press.

Laqueur, Walter and Mosse, George L. (eds) (1966) *International Fascism, 1920–1945*. New York: Harper & Row.

Larsen, Stein Ugelvik (2001) 'Was There Fascism Outside Europe? Diffusion from Europe and Domestic Impulses', in Stein Ugelvik Larsen (ed.) *Fascism Outside Europe*. Boulder Social Science Monographs, Distributed by Columbia University Press, New York, pp. 705–818.

Larson, Stein Ugelvik, Hagtvet, Bernt, and Myklebust, Jan Petter (eds) (1980) *Who Were the Fascists? Social Roots of European Fascists*. Bergen: Universitetsforlaget.

Ledeen, Michael (1972) *Universal Fascism: The Theory and Practice of the Fascist International, 1928–1936*. New York: H. Fertig.

Ledeen, Michael A. (1976) 'Renzo de Felice and the Controversy over Italian Fascism', *Journal of Contemporary History*, 11(4): 269–283.

Lepenies, Wolf (ed.) (2003) *Entangled Histories and Negotiated Universals*. Frankfurt/ Main: Campus.

Ley, Michael (1997) *Apokalypse und Moderne: Aufsäze zu politischen Religionen*. Vienna: Sonderzahl.

Ley, Michael and Schoeps, Julius H. (1997) *Der Nationalsozialismus als politische Religion*. Bodenheim b. Mainz: Philo Verlagsgesellschaft.

Linehan, Thomas (2004) 'The British Union of Fascists as a Totalitarian Movement and Political Religion', *Totalitarian Movements and Political Religions*, 5(3): 397–418.

Linz, Juan J. (1975) 'Totalitarian and Authoritarian Regimes', in F.I. Greenstein and N.W. Polsby (eds) *Handbook of Political Science: Macropolitical Theory*, vol. 3. Reading, MA: Addison-Wesley, pp. 175–411.

Linz, Juan J. (1976) 'Some Notes toward a Comparative Study of Fascism in Sociological Historical Perspective', in Walter Laqueur (ed.) *Fascism: A Reader's Guide. Analyses, Interpretations, Bibliography.* Berkeley, CA: University of California Press, pp. 2–103.

Linz, Juan J. (1980) 'Political Space and Fascism as a Late-Comer', in S.U. Larson, B. Hagtvet and J.P. Myklebust (eds) *Who Were the Fascists? Social Roots of European Fascists.* Bergen: Universitetsforlaget, pp. 153–189.

Linz, Juan J. (1997) 'Totalitarianism and Authoritarianism: My Recollections on the Development of Comparative Politics', in Alfons Söllner, Ralf Walkenhaus, and Karin Wieland (eds) *Totalitarismus: eine Ideengeschichte des 20. Jahrhunderts.* Berlin: Academie Verlag, pp. 141–157.

Linz, Juan J. (2000) *Totalitarian and Authoritarian Regimes.* Boulder, CO: Lynne Rienner.

Losurdo, Domenico (2004) 'Towards a Critique of the Category of Totalitarianism', *Historical Materialism*, 12(2): 25–55.

Lübbe, Hermann (1995) *Heilserwartung und Terror: Politische Religionen des 20. Jahrhunderts.* Düsseldorf: Patmos.

Maier, Charles (1988) *The Unmasterable Past.* Cambridge, MA: Harvard University Press.

Maier, Hans (1995) *Politische Religionen: die totalitaren Regime und das Christentum.* Freiburg im Breisgau: Herder Spektrum.

Maier, Hans (2004) *Totalitarianism and Political Religions*, Vol. 1: *Concepts for the comparison of dictatorships.* London: Routledge.

Maier, Hans (2007) 'Political Religion: A Concept and its Limitations', *Totalitarian Movements and Political Religions*, 1: 5–16.

Maier, Hans, and Bruhn, Jodi (2007) *Totalitarianism and Political Religions*, Vol. 3: *Concepts for the Comparison of Dictatorships: Theory and History of Interpretation.* London: Routledge.

Maier, Hans and Schäfer, Michael (eds) (1997) *Totalitarismus und Politische Religionen. Konzepte des Diktaturvergleichs*, 3 vols. Paderborn.

Mandel, Ernest (1971) 'Introduction', in Leon Trotsky, *The Struggle Against Fascism in Germany.* New York: Pathfinder Press.

Mann, Michael (2004) *Fascists.* Cambridge: Cambridge University Press.

Mason, Timothy M. (1968) 'Primacy of Politics: Politics and Economics in National Socialist Germany', in S.J. Woolf (ed.) *The Nature of Fascism.* New York: Random House, pp. 165–195.

Mason, Timothy M. (1977) 'National Socialism and the German Working Class, 1925– May 1933', *New German Critique*, 11: 49–93.

Mason, Timothy M. (1991) 'Whatever Happened to "Fascism"?', *Radical History Review*, 49: 89–98.

Mason, Timothy M. (1995) *Nazism, Fascism, and the Working Class.* Cambridge: Cambridge University Press.

Mateescu, Dragoş (2006) 'Kemalism in the Era of Totalitarianism: A Conceptual Analysis', *Turkish Studies*, 7(2): 225–241.

Merkl, Peter H. (1980) 'Comparing Fascists Movements', in Stein Ugelvik Larson, Bernt Hagtvet and Jan Petter Myklebust (eds) (1980) *Who Were the Fascists? Social Roots of European Fascists.* Bergen: Universitetsforlaget, pp. 752–783.

Morgan, Philip (2003) *Fascism in Europe, 1919–1945.* London: Routledge.

Mosse, George L. (1966) 'Introduction: The Genesis of Fascism', *Journal of Contemporary History*, 1(1): 14–26.

Mosse, George L. (1989) 'Fascism and the French Revolution', *Journal of Contemporary History*, 224: 5–26.

Mosse, George L. (1991) *The Nationalization of the Masses: Political Symbolism and Mass Movements in Germany from the Napoleonic Wars through the Third Reich*. Ithaca, NY: Cornell University Press.

Nolte, Ernst (1963) *Der Faschismus in seiner Epoche: die Action française, der italienische Faschismus, der Nationalsozialismus*. München: R. Piper; English edn: *Three Faces of Fascism: Action Française, Italian Fascism, National Socialism*. New York: Holt, Rinehart and Winston, 1965.

Nolte, Ernst (1968a) *Der Faschismus. Von Mussolini zu Hitler. Texte, Bilder und Dokumente*. München: Desch.

Nolte, Ernst (1968b) *Die faschistischen Bewegungen. Die Krise des liberalen System und die Entwicklung der Faschismen*. München: Deutscher Taschenbuch Verlag.

Nolte, Ernst (1977) *Marxismus, Faschismus, kalter Krieg: Vorträge und Aufsätze, 1964–1976*. Stuttgart: Deutsche Verlags-Anstalt. English edn: *Marxism, Fascism, Cold War*. Atlantic Highlands, NJ: Humanities Press, 1982.

Orlow, Dietrich (2003) 'Fascists among Themselves: Some Observations on West European Politics in the 1930s', *European Review*, 11(3): 245–266.

Otto, Rudolf (1923) *The Idea of the Holy*. Oxford: Oxford University Press.

Passmore, Kevin (2002) *Fascism: A Very Short Introduction*. Oxford: Oxford University Press.

Paxton, Robert O. (1998) 'The Five Stages of Fascism', *The Journal of Modern History*, 70(1); 1–23.

Paxton, Robert O. (2004) *The Anatomy of Fascism*. London: Allen Lane.

Payne, Stanley G. (1976) 'Fascism in Eastern Europe', in Walter Laqueur (ed.) *Fascism: A Reader's Guide. Analyses, Interpretations, Bibliography*. Berkeley, CA: University of California Press, pp. 295–311.

Payne, Stanley G. (1978) 'Interpretations of Fascism', *Political Science Quarterly*, 93(1): 129.

Payne, Stanley G. (1979) '[What Fascism Is Not: Thoughts on the Deflation of a Concept]: Comment', *The American Historical Review*, 84(2): 389–394.

Payne, Stanley G. (1980a) 'The Concept of Fascism', in Stein Ugelvik Larson, Bernt Hagtvet and Jan Petter Myklebust (eds) (1980) *Who Were the Fascists? Social Roots of European Fascists*. Bergen: Universitetsforlaget, pp. 14–25.

Payne, Stanley G. (1980b) *Fascism: Comparison and Definition*. Madison, WI: University of Wisconsin Press.

Payne, Stanley G. (1995) *A History of Fascism, 1914–1945*. Madison, WI: University of Wisconsin Press.

Payne, Stanley G. (2005) 'On the Heuristic Value of the Concept of Political Religion and its Application', *Totalitarian Movements and Political Religions*, 6(2): 163–174.

Poulantzas, Nicos (1974) *Fascism and Dictatorship*. London: New Left Books.

Reichardt, Sven and Nolzen, Armin (eds) (2005) *Faschismus in Italien und Deutschland. Studien zu Transfer und Vergleich*. Göttingen: Wallstein Verlag.

Richey, R.E. and Jones, D.G. (eds) (1974) *American Civil Religion*. New York: Free Press.

Richmond, Kathleen (2003) *Women and Spanish Fascism: The Women's Section of the Falange, 1934–1959*. London: Routledge.

Riegel, Klaus-Georg (2005) 'Marxism-Leninism as a Political Religion', *Totalitarian Movements and Political Religions*, 6(1): 97–126.

Roberts, David D., De Grand, Alexander, Antliff, Mark and Linehan, Thomas (2002) 'Comments on Roger Griffin, "The Primacy of Culture",' *Journal of Contemporary History*, 37(2): 259–274.

Said, Edward (1979) *Orientalism*. New York: Vintage Books.

Sauer, Wolfgang (1967) 'National Socialism: Totalitarianism or Fascism?', *The American Historical Review*, 73: 404–424.

Schieder, Rolf (1987) *Civil Religion. Die religiöse Dimension der politischen Kultur*. Gütersloh: G. Mohn.

Schieder, Wolfgang (1996) 'Das italienische Experiment. Der Faschismus als Vorbild in der Krise der Weimarer Republik', *Historische Zeitschrift*, 262: 73–125.

Seigel, Micol (2005) 'Beyond Compare: Comparative Method after the Transnational Turn', *Radical History Review*, 91: 62–90.

Shenfield, Stephen D. (2001) *Russian Fascism: Traditions, Tendencies, and Movements*. Armonk, NY: M.E. Sharpe.

Shorten, Richard (2003) 'The Enlightenment, Communism and Political Religion: Reflections on a Misleading Trajectory', *Journal of Political Ideologies*, 8(1); 13–38.

Sigmund, Anna Maria (2000) *Women of the Third Reich*. Richmond Hill, Ont: NDE Publishing.

Spackman, Barbara (1996) *Fascist Virilities: Rhetoric, Ideology, and Social Fantasy in Italy*. Minneapolis: University of Minnesota Press.

Stark, Rodney (2003) *For the Glory of God: How Monotheism led to Reformations, Witch-Hunts and the End of Slavery*. Princeton, NJ: Princeton University Press.

Sternhell, Zeev (1983) *Ni Droite, Ni Gauche: L'ideologie fasciste en France*. Paris: Editions du Seuil; Bruxelles: Complex, 1987, 2000. English edn: *Neither Right Nor Left: Fascist Ideology in France*. Princeton, NJ: Princeton University Press, 1996.

Talmon, Jacob L. (1960) *Political Messianism: The Romantic Phase*. New York: Praeger.

Talmon, Jacob L. (1970) *The Origins of Totalitarian Democracy*. New York: Norton.

Talmon, Jacob L. (1979) *Romanticism and Revolt: Europe 1815–1848*. New York: Norton.

Talmon, Jacob L. (1991) *The Myth of the Nation and the Vision of Revolution: Ideological Polarisation in the Twentieth Century*. New Brunswick, NJ: Transaction.

Tannenbaum, Edward R. (1972) *The Fascist Experience: Italian Society and Culture, 1922–1945*. New York: Basic Books.

Theweleit, Klaus (1987–1989) *Male Fantasies*, 2 vols. Minneapolis: University of Minnesota Press.

Todorova, Maria (1997) *Imagining the Balkans*. New York: Oxford University Press.

Trotsky, Leon (1944) *Fascism: What it Is – How to Fight it*. New York: Pioneer.

Umland, Andreas (2004) 'Concepts of Fascism in Contemporary Russia and the West', *Political Studies Review*, 3: 34–49.

Vago, Bela (1976) 'Fascism in Eastern Europe', in Walter Laqueur (ed.) *Fascism: A Reader's Guide. Analyses, Interpretations, Bibliography*. Berkeley, CA: University of California Press, pp. 229–253.

Voegelin, Eric (1938) *Die Politische Religionen*. Vienna: Bermann-Fischen Verlag. English edn: *The Political Religions*. Lewiston, NY: E. Mellen Press, 1986.

Voegelin, Eric (1952) *The New Science of Politics*. Chicago: University of Chicago Press.

Voegelin, Eric (1998) *Religion and the Rise of Modernity*. Columbia, MO: University of Missouri Press.

Voegelin, Eric (1999a) *Hitler and the Germans*. Columbia, MO: University of Missouri Press.

Voegelin, Eric (1999b) *Collected Works*, vol. 5: *Modernity without Restraint*. Columbia, MO: University of Missouri Press.

Vondung, Klaus (2005) 'National Socialism as a Political Religion: Potentials and Limits of an Analytical Concept', *Totalitarian Movements and Political Religions*, 6(1): 87–95.

Weber, Eugen (1962) *Action Française: Royalism and Reaction in Twentieth Century France*. Stanford, CA: Stanford University Press.

Weber, Eugen (1964) *Varieties of Fascism: Doctrines of Revolution in the Twentieth Century*. Princeton, NJ: Van Nostrand.

Wehler, Hans-Ulrich (1985) *The German Empire, 1871–1918*. Providence, RI: Berg.

Weiss, John (ed.) (1969) *Nazis and Fascists in Europe, 1918–1945*. Chicago: Quadrangle Books.

Werner, Michael and Zimmermann, Bénédicte (2006) 'Beyond Comparison: *Histoire Croisée* and the Challenge of Reflexivity', *History and Theory*, 45: 30–50.

Wimberley, R. C. (1976) 'Testing the Civil Religion Hypothesis', *Sociological Analysis*, 37: 341–352.

Wolff, Larry (1994) *Inventing Eastern Europe: The Map of Civilization on the Mind of the Enlightenment*. Stanford, CA: Stanford University Press.

Woolf, S. J. (ed.) (1968) *The Nature of Fascism*. New York: Random House.

Woolf, S. J. (ed.) (1969) *European Fascism*. New York: Vintage Books.

Zaslavsky, Viktor (2003) 'The Post-Soviet Stage in the Study of Totalitarianism. New Trends and Methodological Tendencies', *Russian Social Science Review*, 44(5): 4–31.

Žižek, Slavoj (2002) *Did Somebody Say Totalitarianism? Five Interventions in the (Mis)Use of a Notion*. New York: Verso.

Žižek, Slavoj (2005) 'The Two Totalitarianisms', *London Review of Books*, 17 March.

Part I

DEFINING GENERIC FASCISM

A new consensus?

1

FASCISM

Zeev Sternhell

The Israeli historian and political scientist Zeev Sternhell has emerged, in the past decades, as a leading scholarly authority on the rise and main features of the fascist ideology. Sternhell treats fascism as a pan-European phenomenon that existed at three distinct levels: as an ideology, as a movement, and as a regime. Following the research path opened by his professor and mentor, Jacob L. Talmon (see Sternhell 1996), in several path-breaking works Sternhell explored the intellectual origins of the fascist ideology, with an emphasis on France (1972; 1978; 1986; 1994; 1996) and also Italy, supplemented by a synthetic, European-wide perspective (2000).

This encyclopaedia entry summarizes Sternhell's approach to fascism, offering an introduction to the main arguments developed in his major works. Sternhell regards interwar fascist ideology as a result of a long-term synthesis of several pre-World War I ideological trends, filtered by the intellectual revolt of the turn of the century and then crystallized and implemented in political practice during the Great War. The fascist ideology originated as a reaction against the political culture of the eighteenth-century Enlightenment and the French Revolution. It was the original outcome of the amalgamation of two main intellectual/political trends in the context of what Sternhell calls the "Franco-Italian cultural complex" (Sternhell with Sznajder and Ashéri 1944: 4): (a) the transformation of nationalism into a coherent political theory by the French political thinkers and activists Maurice Barrès (1862–1923) and Charles Maurras (1868–1952), the leader of Action Française, and the Italian writer, journalist and nationalist activist Enrico Corradini (1865–1931), founder of the Italian Nationalist Association (Associazione Nazionalista Italiana); and (b) the reformulation of Marxism undertaken by the "New School" initiated by Georges Sorel (1847–1922), and continued by the German sociologist Robert Michels (1876–1936), and by Italian revolutionary syndicalists such as Arturo Labriola (1873–1959), Sergio Nanunzio, Paolo Orano, and Benito Mussolini (1883–1945). In addition, fascism borrowed massively from Social Darwinism, the anti-Cartesian and anti-Kantian philosophy of the French philosopher Henri Bergson (1859–1941) and of the German philosopher Friedrich Nietzsche (1844–1900), the social psychology of the French Gustav LeBon (1841–1931) and the sociology of the Italian Vilfredo Pareto (1848–1923). The fascist ideological synthesis resulted ultimately into an "organic, tribal, exclusive nationalism based on biological determinism." This novel synthesis was complete before World War I: As "a veritable laboratory in which ideas were put into practice," the upheaval of the Great War facilitated nevertheless the emergence of fascism as a significant mass movement in the interwar period.

In his work, Sternhell introduced or substantiated several major innovations in fascist studies. First, he dated back the origins of fascist ideology to the late 1880s, grounding them in the "great ideological laboratory of the Belle Époque" (Sternhell 1986: 29). In a controversial fashion, he also argued that the gestation of fascism as a historical phenomenon was complete, in its essential characteristics, well before the Great War, backed by "a solid conceptual framework" (1986: 1). Second, Sternhell attached paramount importance to France as an intellectual laboratory where the fascist ideology was born, twenty years before the emergence of a similar political trend in Italy (ibid.: 29). Given its ideological "richness" and its high intellectual standard, French fascist literature exercised a considerable influence abroad (ibid.: 6, 7, 27–29). Although French fascism was conspicuously weak and failed to conquer the political power, in Sternhell's view, it came, nevertheless, the "closest to the ideal, the 'idea' of fascism in the Weberian sense of the term" (ibid.: 26–27). Third, he emphasized the revolutionary character of fascism, bringing about "a national, moral and psychological revolution." Fascism promoted a "new civilization" founded on the idea of an organic community transcending class barriers and on the moral unity of the nation as a supreme category of political practice. Fourth, he underlines the conflictual nature of fascism, as a culmination of a two-century-old anti-Enlightenment revolt against liberalism, bourgeois materialism, and Marxism. But Sternhell also convincingly argued that the fascist ideology cannot be reduced to its negations or rejections. Fifthly, he also stressed the left-wing intellectual and political origins of fascism, which cannot be understood without the socialist revolt against materialism that took place at the turn of the century in France and Italy. Finally, Sternhell regarded fascism as a paradigmatic manifestation of totalitarianism in terms of both ideology and practice and explored, in his recent works, the comparison between fascism and communism (Avineri and Sternhell 2003). It is important to note that, while adhering to the theory of the generic nature of fascism, Sternhell did not include National Socialism into the interwar family of fascists, but saw it as a unique phenomenon mostly in view of its racism (Sternhell 1994: 4–5).

BIBLIOGRAPHY

Avineri, Shlomo and Sternhell, Zeev, eds. (2003). *Europe's Century of Discontent: The Legacies of Fascism, Nazism, and Communism* (Jerusalem: Hebrew University Magnes Press).

Sternhell, Zeev, ed. (1972). *Maurice Barrès et le nationalisme français*. Préf. de Raoul Girardet (Paris: A. Colin).

Sternhell, Zeev (1978). *La droite révolutionnaire: 1885–1914. Les origines françaises du fascisme* (Paris: Editions du Seuil).

Sternhell, Zeev (1986). *Neither Right Nor Left: Fascist Ideology in France*, trans. David Maisel (Berkeley, CA: University of California Press). New edition (Princeton, NJ: Princeton University Press, 1996). Original edition: *Ni Droite, Ni Gauche: L'idéologie fasciste en France* (Paris: Editions du Seuil, 1983). Second edition (Bruxelles: Complexe, 1987); Third edition (Bruxelles: Complexe, 2000).

Sternhell, Zeev, with Mario Sznajder and Maria Ashéri (1994). *The Birth of Fascist Ideology: From Cultural Rebellion to Political Revolution* (Princeton, NJ: Princeton University Press). Original edition: *Naissance de l'idéologie fasciste* (Paris: Fayard 1989).

Sternhell, Zeev, ed. (1996). *The Intellectual Revolt against Liberal Democracy, 1870–1945: International Conference in Memory of Jacob L. Talmon* (Jerusalem: Israel Academy of Sciences and Humanities).

Sternhell, Zeev (2000). "Fascism: Reflections on the Fate of Ideas in Twentieth Century History," *Journal of Political Ideologies*, 5(2): 139–162.

*   *   *

fascism. Of all the major ideologies of the twentieth century, fascism was the only one to come into being together with the century itself. It was a synthesis of organic NATIONALISM and anti-Marxist SOCIALISM, a revolutionary movement based on a rejection of liberalism, democracy and Marxism. In its essential character, fascist ideology was a rejection of materialism – liberalism, democracy and Marxism being regarded simply as different aspects of the same materialist evil. It was this revolt against materialism which, from the beginning of the century, allowed a convergence of anti-liberal and anti-bourgeois nationalism and a variety of socialism which, while rejecting Marxism, remained revolutionary. This form of socialism was also, by definition, anti-liberal and anti-bourgeois, and its opposition to historical materialism made it the natural ally of radical nationalism. The fascist synthesis symbolized the rejection of a political culture inherited from the eighteenth century and the French Revolution, and it aimed at laying the foundations of a new civilization. Only a new communal and anti-individualistic civilization was deemed capable of assuring the permanence of a human collectivity in which all strata and all classes of society would be perfectly integrated, and the natural framework for such a harmonious, organic collectivity was held to be the nation – a nation enjoying a moral unity which liberalism and Marxism, both agents of warfare and disunity, could never provide.

An organic, tribal, exclusive nationalism based on biological determinism was a translation into political terms of the intellectual revolution of the turn of the century. With BARRÈS, MAURRAS and Corradini (who created the idea of the 'proletarian nation'), nationalism became a coherent political theory. It converged quite naturally with the second element in the fascist equation: the revision of

Marxism undertaken at the beginning of the century by Georges SOREL and the theoreticians of Italian revolutionary SYNDICALISM. If one fails to take into account this initially socialistic revolt against materialism, fascist ideology can hardly be understood. Intellectually, it was greatly influenced by SOCIAL DARWINISM, by the anti-Cartesian and anti-Kantian philosophy of Bergson and NIETZSCHE, by the psychology of Le Bon and the sociology of PARETO. Its immediate context was the enormous changes which were taking place in the capitalist economy, in bourgeois society and in the life of the working class – changes which ran quite contrary to Marxist expectations.

Sorel replaced the rationalistic, Hegelian foundations of Marxism with anti-materialist, voluntarist, vitalist elements. This form of socialism was a philosophy of action based on intuition, and the cult of energy and *élan*, activism and heroism. To activate the masses, thought Sorel, one did not require reasoning but myths, systems of images which strike the imagination. When it became obvious that the myth of the general strike and proletarian violence was ineffective because the proletariat was incapable of fulfilling its role as a revolutionary factor, the Sorelians had no option but to abandon Marxism and to replace the proletariat with the great rising force: the nation as a whole. One arrived in this way at a socialism for all, embodying a new idea of revolution – a national, moral and psychological revolution, the only kind of revolution which does not bear the characteristics of class struggle. This was the real contribution of Sorel and the revolutionary syndicalists and non-conformists of France and Italy to fascism.

Among these were the theoreticians of revolutionary syndicalism such as Arturo Labriola, Robert MICHELS, Sergio Panunzio and Paolo Orano, and their fellow-traveller Benito Mussolini. The connection between Mussolini and the revolutionary syndicalists was already very strong in 1902 and, throughout the period prior to the first world war, Mussolini's development took place under their shadow. In 1914 Mussolini and the revolutionary syndicalists together with Corradini's nationalists constituted the spearhead of the interventionist movement: the synthesis of a radical nationalism and a new type of socialism thus became a political reality. During the war, revolutionary syndicalism turned into national syndicalism and then into fascism.

In the sphere of political theory, this synthesis was already clearly expressed around the years 1910–12 in such publications as *Les Cahiers du Cercle Proudhon* in France, and above all *La Lupa* in Italy. The nationalists and revolutionary syndicalists wished to replace the mercantile civilization of their day with a civilization of monks and warriors, a warlike, virile and heroic civilization in which a sense of sacrifice would replace bourgeois hedonism and egoism. This new world would be created by an elite conscious of its duties which alone would be capable of leading the masses, who in turn were only a herd, to battle.

These constitutive elements of the fascist ideology, elaborated previous to August 1914, reappeared in an almost identical form in the 1920s and 1930s both in Italy and elsewhere: among the French fascists who had come from the right such as Georges Valois, Robert Brasillach and Pierre Drieu La Rochelle, and former French socialists and communists such as Marcel Deat or Jacques Doriot. Other examples were Jose Antonio Primo de Rivera in Spain, Léon Degrelle in Belgium and Corneliu Zelia Codreanu in Rumania.

From this perspective, it is clear that fascism was a pan-European phenomenon, and it existed on three levels – as an ideology, as a political movement, and as a form of government. From the point of view of the history of ideas, the first world war was not the watershed it appears to have been in so many other areas. Fascism did not belong only to the inter-war era but to that whole period of history which began with the modernization of the European continent at the end of the nineteenth century. The intellectual revolution of the turn of the century, the entry of the masses into politics, produced fascism as a system of thought, as a sensibility, as an attitude to the essential problems of civilization. The first world war and the economic crisis of the 1930s produced the sociological and psychological conditions necessary to the construction of the fascist movement, but they did not produce fascist ideology.

The war did, however, contribute to the final crystallization of fascist ideology, not only because it provided a proof of the capacity of nationalism to mobilize the masses, but because it displayed the tremendous power of the modern state. It revealed quite new possibilities of economic planning, and of mobilizing the national economy as well as private property in the service of the state. The state was regarded as the expression of national unity and its might depended on the spiritual unanimity of the masses, but at the same time the state was the guardian of this unity which it fostered with every means possible. The war revealed how great the capacity of the individual for sacrifice could be, how superficial was the idea of internationalism, and how easily all strata of society could be mobilized in the service of the state. It demonstrated the importance of unity of command, of authority, of leadership, of moral mobilization, of the education of the masses, and of propaganda as an instrument of power. Above all, it had shown how easily democratic liberties can be suspended and a quasi-dictatorship gain acceptance.

The fascists felt that in many respects the war had proved the validity of the ideas expressed by Sorel, Michels, Pareto and Le Bon, namely, that the masses need a myth, they only want to obey, and democracy is merely a smokescreen. The first world war, the first total war in history, was a laboratory in which the ideas they put forward throughout the first decade of the century proved themselves in practice. Thus the fascism of the 1930s, as found in the writings of Gentile and Mussolini, José Antonio and Oswald Mosley, Léon Degrelle and Drieu La Rochelle, was made up both of the theoretical contribution of the pre-war nationalists and syndicalists, and of the experience of the war.

Basic to the political philosophy of fascism was a conception of the individual as a social animal. For Gentile the human individual is not an atom; in every respect man is a political animal. In so far as man is outside the organization of society with its system of reciprocal rules and obligations, he has no significant freedom. Ultimately, for Gentile and Mussolini, man has existence only in so far as he is sustained and determined by the community.

Fascist thought did not stop there, however, but went on to develop a conception of liberty that in Mussolini's terminology was 'the liberty of the state and of the individual within the state'. This is the reason why, according to Alfredo Rocco, Mussolini's minister of justice, individual rights were only recognized in so far as they were implied in the rights of the state. It was by way of such arguments that fascism arrived at the concepts of the new man and the new society so admirably characterized by the French fascist Marcel Deat: 'the total man in the total society, with no clashes, no prostration, no anarchy'. Fascism was a vision of a coherent and reunited people, and it was for this reason that it placed such emphasis on march-pasts, parades and uniforms on a whole communal liturgy where deliberation and discussion were supplanted by songs and torches, by the cult of physical strength, violence and brutality. This unity found its most perfect expression in the quasi-sacred figure of the leader. The cult of a leader who embodied the spirit, will, and virtues of the people, and who was identified with the nation, was the keystone of the fascist liturgy. Gentile was quite correct when he defined fascism as a revolt against POSITIVISM.

Preserving the integrity of the nation and solving the social question means destroying the dictatorship of money. Wild capitalism must be replaced by the classic tools of national solidarity: a controlled economy and corporate organization topped by a strong state, a decision-making apparatus that represents the victory of politics over economics. The fascist state, creator of all political and social life and of all spiritual values, would of course be the undisputed master of the economy and of social relations.

The reform of the relations of power was the cornerstone of the fascist revolution. The most striking aspect of that moral and political revolution was TOTALITARIANISM. 'Ours will be a totalitarian state in the service of the fatherland's integrity,' said José Antonio. Innumerable passages in an identical vein are to be found throughout fascist literature. Totalitarianism is the very essence of fascism, and fascism is without question the purest example of a totalitarian ideology. Setting out as it did to create a new civilization, a new type of human being and a totally new way of life, fascism could not conceive of any sphere of human activity remaining immune from intervention by the state. 'We are, in other words, a state which controls all forces acting in nature. We control political forces, we control moral forces, we control economic forces …,' Mussolini wrote, and, 'everything in the state, nothing against the state, nothing outside the state' (p. 40). For Mussolini and Gentile the fascist state is a conscious entity and has a will of its own – for this reason, it can be described as 'ethical'. Not only does the existence of the state imply the subordination of the individual's rights, but the state asserts the right to be 'a state which necessarily transforms the people even in their physical aspects' (p. 39). Outside the state, 'no human or spiritual values can exist, much less have value'; 'no individuals or groups (political parties, cultural associations, economic unions, social classes) outside the state' (p. 11).

The concrete consequences of such a conception of political power and the physical and moral repression it would engender are not hard to imagine. Here we see how communist and fascist totalitarianisms differ: whereas the Stalinist dictatorship could never be described as an application of the Marxist theory of the state, fascist terror was doctrine put into practice in the most methodical way. Fascism constitutes one of the best examples of the unity of thought and action.

READING

Gentile, G.: 'The philosophic basis of fascism'. In *Readings on Fascism and National Socialism*. Denver, Col.: Swallow, n.d.

Gregor, A.J.: *Young Mussolini and the Intellectual Origins of Fascism*. Berkeley and Los Angeles: University of California Press, 1979.

Hamilton, A.: *The Appeal of Fascism: a study of intellectuals and fascism 1919–1945*. New York: Macmillan, 1971.

Laqueur, W. ed.: *Fascism: a Readers' Guide; analyses, interpretations, bibliography*. Harmondsworth: Penguin, 1979.

Lyttelton, A. ed.: *Italian Fascisms from Pareto to Gentile*. London: Cape, 1973.

Mosse, G.L.: *Masses and Man*. New York: Howard Fertig, 1980.

Mussolini, B.: *Fascism: Doctrine and Institutions*. New York: Howard Fertig, 1968.

Nolte, E.: *Three Faces of Fascism: Action française, Italian Fascism, National Socialism*. New York: New American Library, 1969.

Payne, S.G.: *Fascism: Comparison and Definition*. Madison: University of Wisconsin Press, 1980.

Primo de Rivera, J.A.: *Selected Writings*, ed. and intro. H. Thomas. London: Cape, 1972.

Rocco, A.: *La dottrina politica del fascismo*. Rome: Aurora, 1925.

Sternhell, Z.: *Neither Right nor Left: fascist ideology in France*. Berkeley and Los Angeles: University of California Press, 1986.

Turner, H.A. Jr. ed.: *Reappraisals of Fascism*. New York: New Viewpoints, 1975.

Weber, E.: *Varieties of Fascism*. New York: Van Nostrand, 1966.

2

TOWARD A GENERAL THEORY
OF FASCISM

George L. Mosse

A multifarious, prolific, and highly original historian, with a remarkable but tumultuous life (see his autobiography Confronting History, *2000), George L. Mosse (1918–1999) was for several decades a major pioneer in the emerging field of comparative fascist studies. In twenty-five books and numerous articles, he pushed the frontiers of our knowledge of the modern Western civilization in general, and the history of Germany in particular, to new, previously unexplored, territories, with a focus on the origins and history of Nazism (1964; 1966), anti-Semitism (1970), racism (1978), European fascism (1979), nationalism and related themes such as mass politics and the creation of secular religions (1975, 1980), the cult of the fallen soldier (1990), sexuality (1985), masculinity (1996), etc.*

Convinced that the gates to understanding the nature of fascism can be opened not by a single-factor explanation but by multiple keys, in accounting for the powerful mass appeal of fascism Mosse departed from an exclusive concentration on social and economic factors prevalent in the historiography of his time. Instead, in line with the cultural turn that transformed research in the humanities since the 1970s, Mosse explored the culture of fascism. To be sure, Mosse did not completely discard the role economic interests played in the rise of fascism. However, arguing that "Class analysis . . . cannot really capture the essence of fascism" (1999: x), Mosse explained the appeal of fascism primarily in views of its system of beliefs and the powerful emotions it generated across various strata of society. In line with the first wave of academic interest in comparative fascism, Mosse advanced three main innovations in fascist studies.

First, Mosse treated fascism as primarily a cultural movement. His concept of culture was not confined solely to the history of ideas, but referred, in his own words, "to life seen as a whole—a totality" (ibid.: xi). For Mosse, the totality of the fascist culture was larger than the worldview proposed by "traditional" political ideologies. In order to reconstruct the fascist totalizing worldview and way of life, Mosse focused on fascists' cultural perceptions in their given social and political contexts. He believed a cultural interpretation of fascism allows historians "to penetrate the fascist self-understanding." Mosse's main goal was to understand fascism "on its own terms" and "from the inside out," by exploring the way fascism "saw itself" (ibid.: x).

Second, Mosse treated fascism as a form of nationalism, defined as "collective self-understanding through a belief system" (ibid.: xii). Mosse acknowledged the heterogeneous character of the fascist ideological synthesis, and even went as far as to call fascism a "scavenger" in view of the fact that it co-opted disparate ideas from ideologies as far apart as Romanticism, liberalism, socialism, and Social Darwinism, borrowed largely from the rites and rituals of established religions, and made ample use of modern technology. Mosse also paid particularly attention to racism, which he regarded as a distinct worldview, and not simply a derivate of nationalism or fascism (1979). He pointed out that racism was, nevertheless, often closely associated with nationalism, giving the latter "additional substance." Ultimately, Mosse argued that the variegated fascist collage did not result in an eclectic hodgepodge of ideas, but they were integrated into "a coherent attitude toward life through the basic fascist nationalist myth" (1999: 23).

Third, Mosse defined fascism as a revolutionary movement of change. In doing so, he challenged the view that genuine political revolutions were confined only to the left side of the political spectrum, pointing out the numerous attempts in modern history to implement a right-wing revolution though "a forceful reordering of society in the light of a projected utopia." The right-wing revolutionary tradition was based on the fin-de-siècle rebellion of the youth as enhanced by the experience of World War I and the social upheaval it generated.

The comparison of fascist ideology, movements and regimes in various European countries stood at the very heart of Mosse's approach to fascism. His theory of fascism was inductive, in the sense that it was derived from a comprehensive comparison of the main common features of Nazi Germany and Fascist Italy, supplemented at times by examples drawn from other case studies of fascism developed in Spain, Hungary, Romania, France or Belgium. In line with his cultural approach to fascism, Mosse argued that comparison should focus upon an "analysis of cultural similarities and differences" (ibid.: 12). Although Mosse carefully documented striking differences among various fascist movements and regimes (primarily between Nazi Germany and Fascist Italy), he ultimately stresses similarities at the expense of differences, the latter being treated as "matters of degree, not absolutes." Critically evaluating the state of the art in comparative fascist studies, Mosse called for more detailed comparisons between, for example, Mussolini's regime and that of Franco, or between Mussolini's and Hitler's personalities and styles of leadership. Mosse also tested the heuristic value of the concept of totalitarianism in comparing fascism and communism, a discussion that has direct relevance for the debates included in Part III of this volume.

The Fascist Revolution *(1999) summarizes Mosse's "general theory of fascism" as a right-wing revolutionary movement of change based on its own nationalistic system of belief. Made up of essays written over a period of thirty-five years (1964–1999), the collection offers a* kaleidoscope *of neglected but essential fascist themes, among which the most important are the intellectual origins of fascism, fascist culture, aestheticism and the avant garde, fascist leadership and community, the occult, sexuality, etc. The present essay is the core and most synthetic chapter of the volume; originally published in 1979, the essay was extensively revised for the 1999 edition. It is important to note that Mosse's approach to fascism shares many elements in common with the recent trend in fascist studies to treat fascist ideology in a "culturalist key." While Mosse had conducted research along these lines since 1964, his compatibility and even convergence with what Roger Griffin calls the "new consensus" increased in the 1990s by numerous cross-references to, and (mutual) influences from, the work of Stanley Payne, Emilio Gentile, and Roger Griffin, among others (below, see also Griffin's laudatory comments on Mosse's work).*

BIBLIOGRAPHY

Mosse, George L. (1964). *The Crisis of German Ideology: Intellectual Origins of the Third Reich* (New York: Grosset and Dunlap).

Mosse, George L. ed. (1966). *Nazi Culture: Intellectual, Cultural and Social Life in the Third Reich* (New York: Schocken Books).

Mosse, George L. (1970). *Germans and Jews: The Right, the Left, and the Search for a "Third Force" in Pre-Nazi Germany* (New York: H. Fertig).

Mosse, George L. (1975). *The Nationalization of the Masses: Political Symbolism and Mass Movements in Germany from the Napoleonic Wars through the Third Reich* (New York: H. Fertig).

Mosse, George L. (1978). *Toward the Final Solution: A History of European Racism* (New York: H. Fertig).

Mosse, George L. ed. (1979). *International Fascism: New Thoughts and New Approaches* (London: Sage Publications).

Mosse, George L. (1980). *Masses and Man: Nationalist and Fascist Perceptions of Reality* (New York: H. Fertig).

Mosse, George L. (1985). *Nationalism and Sexuality: Respectability and Abnormal Sexuality in Modern Europe* (New York: H. Fertig).

Mosse, George L. (1990). *Fallen Soldiers: Reshaping the Memory of the World Wars* (New York: Oxford University Press).

Mosse, George L. (1996). *The Image of Man: The Creation of Modern Masculinity* (New York: Oxford University Press).

Mosse, George L. (1999). *The Fascist Revolution: Toward a General Theory of Fascism* (New York: H. Fertig).

Mosse, George L. (2000). *Confronting History: A Memoir* (Madison, WI: University of Wisconsin Press).

* * *

In our century two revolutionary movements have made their mark upon Europe: that originally springing from Marxism, and the fascist revolution. The various forms of Marxism have occupied historians and political scientists for many decades, while the study of fascism was late catching up. Even so, because of the war and the fascist record in power, fascism has remained synonymous with oppression and domination; it is alleged that it was without ideas of its own, but merely a reaction against other more progressive movements such as liberalism or socialism. Earlier scholarship concerning fascism has more often than not been used as an occasion to fight contemporary polemical battles.

In a justified reaction against stereotyping, recent scholarship has been suspicious of general theories of fascism. As many local and regional studies show, while on one level fascism may have presented a kaleidoscope of contradictory attitudes, nevertheless these attitudes were based upon some common assumptions. We shall attempt to bring together some of the principal building blocks for such common assumptions—there seem to be enough of them to construct at least a provisional dwelling. Germany and Italy will dominate the discussion, as the experience of European fascism was largely dominated by Italian fascism and German National Socialism. The word "fascism" will be used without qualification when both these movements are meant. From time to time I shall also refer to various other fascisms in Europe, but only specifically or as subsidiary examples.

We can best develop a general theory of fascism through a critique of past attempts to accomplish this task. Some historians have seen an integral connection between bolshevism and fascism. Both were totalitarian régimes and, as such, dictatorships based upon the exclusive claim to leadership by one political party.[1] Although such an equation was often politically motivated, it was not, as its opponents claimed, merely a child of the cold war.

Both movements were based on the ideal, however distorted, of popular sovereignty. This meant the rejection of parliamentary government and representative institutions on behalf of a democracy of the masses in which the people would in theory directly govern themselves. The leader symbolized the people; he expressed the "general will"—but such a democracy meant that, instead of representative assemblies, a new secular religion mediated between people and leaders, providing, at the same time, an instrument of social control over the masses. It was expressed on the public level through official ceremonies, festivals, and not least, the use of political imagery, and on a private level through control over all aspects of life by the dictates of the single political party. This system was common in various degrees to fascist and bolshevist movements.

The danger inherent in subsuming both systems under the concept of totalitarianism is that it may serve to disguise real differences, not only between bolshevism and fascism but also between the different forms of fascism themselves. Moreover, the contention that these theories really compare fascism not with the early, more experimental years of bolshevism, but with Stalinism instead seems justified. Indeed, totalitarianism as a static concept often veils the development of both fascism and bolshevism. In Soviet Russia, for example, the kind of public

63

ceremonies and festivals that mark the fascist political style were tried early in the régime but then dropped, and not resumed until after the Second World War, when they came to fulfill the same functions as they had for fascism earlier. In 1966, *Pravda* wrote that rallies, ceremonial processions, speeches, and music gave emotional strength to the political commitment of the people.[2] Fascism, too, did not remain static, although even some critics of totalitarian theory apparently see it as unchanging. There is, for example, a difference between fascism as a political movement and as a government in power.

Theories of totalitarianism have also placed undue emphasis upon the supposedly monolithic leadership cult. Here again, this was introduced into the Soviet Union by Stalin rather than at first by Lenin. Even within fascism, the cult of the leader varied: Piero Melograni has written on how the cult of "Il Duce" and fascism were not identical, and that it was "Mussolinianism" which won the people's allegiance.[3] In Germany there is no discernible difference between Hitlerism and National Socialism.

More serious is the contention, common to most theories of totalitarianism, that the leader manipulates the masses through propaganda and terror: that free volition is incompatible with totalitarian practice.[4] The term "propaganda," always used in this context, leads to a serious misunderstanding of the fascist conception of politics and its essentially organic and religious nature. In times of crisis such politics provided many millions of people with a more meaningful involvement than representative parliamentary government—largely because it was not itself a new phenomenon, but instead based upon an older and still lively tradition of direct democracy, which had always opposed European parliaments.

Even the widespread notion that fascism ruled through terror must be modified; rather, it was built at first upon a popular consensus. Tangible successes, the ability to compromise and to go slow, combined with the responsive chord struck by fascist culture, integrated Italians and Germans into this consensus which undoubtedly was more solid in Germany than Italy. Hitler, after all, shared a volkish faith with many of his fellow Germans, especially in times of crisis, and his tangible successes in domestic and foreign policy up to the Second World War were much more spectacular than Mussolini's achievements.

Terror increased with the continued survival of the régimes, for disillusionment with fascism in power could easily lead to unrest. By the time many earlier fellow travelers woke up to fascist reality, it was too late to resist, except by martyrdom. Mass popular consensus during the first years of fascism in power allowed it to develop a secret police—outside and above regular channels and procedures[5] — as well as the special courts needed to reinforce its actions. This was easier in the Soviet Union since the revolution had destroyed the old legal framework; while in Germany and Italy traditional safeguards paradoxically continued to exist and even to be used side by side with arbitrary action. In Germany, judges freed some concentration camp inmates as late as 1936.

Terror must not then be treated as a static concept, but as something that develops in intensity. Moreover, there was a great deal of disharmony and disunity on the local level in its application. Manpower in Germany, for example, was scarce and the secret police depended in large part on plentiful private denunciations.[6] Not only must historical development be taken into account, but also the existence and extent of a popular consensus, which, although differing in scope in the so-called totalitarian nations, did exist at some time in each of them.

Despite all these caveats, both bolshevists and fascists reached back into the anti-parliamentary and anti-pluralistic traditions of the nineteenth century in order to face the collapse of social, economic, and political structures in their nations during and after the First World War. So-called totalitarianism was new only as a form of legitimate government: it derived from a long tradition; otherwise it would not have received such immediate mass support. Beginning its modern history with the French Revolution, that tradition continued to inform both the nationalism and the quest for social justice of the nineteenth century. Even if Jacob Talmon's concept of "totalitarian democracy" rests, as some have claimed, upon a misreading of the Enlightenment,[7] men like Robespierre and Saint-Just shared in such misconceptions. Rousseau's "general will," his exaltation of "the people," was bent by the Jacobins into a dictatorship in which the people worshipped themselves through public festivals and symbols (such as the Goddess of Reason), where traditional religious enthusiasm was first transferred to civic rites.[8]

The distinction between private and public life was eradicated, just as totalitarian régimes would later attempt to abolish such differences. Public allegiance through active participation in the national cults or party organizations, was the road to survival, and as, for example, the Jacobins used dress as an outward sign of true inner allegiance (the revolutionary cap and trousers instead of breeches), so fascists and bolshevists integrated various dress codes into their systems. Nationalist movements during the nineteenth century carried on these traditions, even if at times they attempted to compromise with liberal values. The workers' movement, though most of it was in fact wedded to parliamentary democracy, also stressed outward symbols of unity as in the serried ranks and Sunday dress of May Day parades, massed flags, and the clenched fist salute. Italy was less influenced by this legacy, but it also played a part in the fight for national unity. At the turn of the century, the radical Left and the radical Right were apt to demand control of the whole man, not just a political piece of him.

Bolshevism and fascism attempted to mobilize the masses, to substitute modern mass politics for pluralistic and parliamentary government. Indeed, parliamentary government found it difficult to cope with the crises of the postwar world, and abdicated without a struggle, not only in Germany and Italy but also in Portugal and, where it had existed immediately after the war, in the nations of eastern Europe. The fascists helped the demise of parliamentary government, but that it succumbed so readily points to deep inherent structural and ideological problems—and, indeed, few representative governments have withstood the pressures of modern economic, political, and social crises, especially when these coincided with unsatisfied national aspirations and defeat in war.[9] Wherever during the interwar years one-party governments came to power, they merely toppled régimes ripe for the picking; this holds good for Russia as well as for Germany and Italy. But unlike bolshevism, fascism never had to fight a proper civil war on its road to power: Mussolini marched on Rome in the comfort of a railway carriage, and Hitler simply presented himself to the German president. Certainly, representative government and liberal politics allowed individual freedom to breathe and prosper, but the new post First World War political movements cannot be condemned without taking the collapse of existing parliaments and social structures into account. We must not look at a historical movement mainly from the viewpoint of our political predilections, lest we falsify historical necessity.

If some historians have used the model of totalitarianism in order to analyze fascism, others, and they are in the majority, have used the model of the "good revolution."[10] The French, American, and especially the Russian revolutions, so it is said, led to the progress of mankind, while fascism was an attempt to stop the clock, to maintain old privilege against the demands of the new classes as represented by the proletariat. In reality, fascism was itself a revolution, seizing power by using twentieth-century methods of mass mobilization and control, and replacing an old with a new élite. (In this sense, National Socialism brought about a more fundamental change than Italian fascism, where new and traditional élites co-existed to a greater extent.) Economic policy was subordinated to the political goals of fascism, but in Germany, at least, this did not preclude nationalization (as for example, the huge Hermann Goering Steel Works). By and large, however, fascism worked hand in hand with the larger industrial enterprises. Fascism, as Stanley Payne, writing the most authoritative history of fascism sees it, was a radical force seeking to create a new social order.[11]

Yet a one-sided emphasis either upon economic factors or upon the proletariat obscures our view of the revolutionary side of fascism. Fascism condemned the French Revolution but was also, at least in its beginnings, a direct descendant of the Jacobin-political style.[12] Above all, the fascist revolution saw itself as a "Third Force," rejecting both "materialistic Marxism" and "finance capitalism" in the capitalist and materialist present. This was the revolutionary tradition within which fascism worked. But it was not alone in such an aim; in the postwar world, many left-wing intellectuals rejected both Marxist orthodoxy and capitalism. Unlike the fascists, however, they sought to transcend both by emphasis on the triumphant goodness of man once capitalism was abolished.

Fascism retreated instead into the nationalist mystique. But here, once more, it followed a precedent. French socialists of the mid-nineteenth century, and men like Édouard Drumont toward the end of the century, had combined opposition to finance capitalism and the advocacy of greater social equality with an impassioned nationalism. They were National Socialists long before the small German Workers' Party took this name. Such National Socialism was in the air as a "Third Force" in the last decades of the nineteenth century, when Marxism was to be reckoned with and capitalist development seemed accompanied by a soulless positivism in a world where only material values counted. There were early national socialist movements in France (in which former leaders of the Paris

Commune, with their Jacobin traditions, joined, but also some anarchists and bourgeois *bien-pensants*), in Bohemia, and even in Germany, advocated at the turn of the century by the Hessian Peasants' League led by Otto Boeckel.[13]

In Italy, argument for the "Third Force" resulted from the First World War—the struggle to get Italy to intervene in this war, and the subsequent war experience seemed to transcend vested interests and political parties.[14] There was indeed a similar reaction among a good many veterans in Germany (but not in France, which had won the war and successfully weathered postwar upheaval). Yet in Italy, unlike Germany, the "war experience" carried revolutionary implications. Mussolini was joined in this hope by students and by revolutionary syndicalists who wanted to abolish the existing social and economic order so that the nation could be regenerated through the searing experience of war. After the war as "revolutionary veterans" they appealed both to the revolutionary spirit and to a sense of Italy's historic national mission. It is typical that when the local Fascist Party was founded in 1920 in Ferrara, it was a youth group called the "Third Italy" which took the initiative.[15] In Germany and Italy—nations plunged into crisis by the war—and also among many political groups of other nations, the "Third Force" became an alternative revolution to Marxism, a retreat into the organic community of the nation when the world seemed to be dominated on the one hand by the mysterious power of money and on the other by the Marxist conspiracy.[16]

Yet this "Third Force" became ever less revolutionary and more nationalistic as fascists and Nazis strove for power. Mussolini broke with the revolutionary syndicalists early on and tamed his youth organization but stayed with the Futurists, whose revolutionary ardor took the fast sports car as its model rather than the nationalization of production. Hitler got rid of social revolutionaries like Otto Strasser who wanted to challenge property relationships, however slightly. Yet we must not limit our gaze to property relationships or the naked play of power and interest; such issues alone do not motivate men. It was the strength of fascism everywhere that it appeared to transcend these concerns, gave people a meaningful sense of political participation (though, of course, in reality they did not participate at all), and sheltered them within the national community against the menace of rapid change and the all too swift passage of time. At the same time it gave them hope through projecting a utopia, taking advantage of apocalyptic longings.

National Socialism was able to contain the revolutionary impetus better than Italian fascism because in Germany the very term "Third Force" was fraught with mystical and millenarian meaning. The mythos of the "Third Force" became a part of the mythos of the "Third Reich," carrying on a Germanic messianic tradition that had no real equivalent in Catholic Italy. The prophecy by Joachim of Flora about the future "Third Age," which would be a kingdom of the spirit—the biblical millennium—had become an essential ingredient of German Protestantism, as had the three mystical kingdoms of Paracelsus: that of God, the planets, and the Earth. The German mystics such as Jakob Böhme believed that man, by overcoming his baser self and seeking harmony within nature, could rise from Earth to the kingdom of God—an important emphasis on "becoming" or joining the eternal spirit of the race rather than "being"; on the quest for the "genuine" as exemplified first by nature and, later, by the "Volk" itself.[17]

Moeller van den Bruck, whose book *The Third Reich* (1923) was originally entitled *The Third Way*, brought this tradition up to date for a defeated nation: the Germanic mission would transcend all the contradictions inherent in modern life, including Germany's defeat in war; Germans must struggle continually toward utopia, which he equated with the German Reich of the future. To be sure, Moeller was pragmatic in his demand for political action, his advocacy of the corporate state, and his desire to institute a planned economy (hence his praise of Lenin's new economic policy).[18] Yet he also retained the traditional elements that were so much a part of this kind of revolution, calling for the maintenance of state authority, preferably that of a monarchy, as well as of the family structure.

However, for Moeller the pragmatic was always subsumed under the messianic. The arrival of the "Third Reich" would automatically solve all outstanding problems. Such a belief was part of the "Third Force" in Germany: the purified national community of the future would end all present difficulties and anxieties, social inequalities and economic crises. Man would then "overcome" the dialectic of earthly life. Small wonder that the Nazis enthusiastically annexed the fairy tale and folk legend to their cause. However, this vision of the future was rooted in the past— it was the traditional fairy tale which the Nazis used in creating their emphasis upon the modern Volk. Precedent was always an integral part of the Nazi ideology, and of Italian fascism too—as when in the fourth year of Mussolini's government the ancient monuments of Rome were restored. For Mussolini, however, history was never more than a platform from which to jump into an ill-defined future.

Hitler and Goebbels's obsession with history reached a climax at the moment of defeat: in 1945, they clung to memories of Frederick the Great, who had been saved from certain defeat by the opportune death of the Czarina Elizabeth, as well as remembering the victory of Rome over Carthage.[19] Utopia and traditionalism were linked, a point to which we shall return when discussing the new fascist man.

Ernst Bloch called this urge to "overcome"—the mystical and millenarian dynamic—the "hidden revolution" essential to the realization of the true socialist revolution.[20] Men must hope before they can act. National Socialism claimed to represent this "inner dynamic," though it was always careful to state that the "Third Reich" stood at the threshold of fulfillment and that a period of struggle and suffering must precede eventual salvation. And indeed, in the end, this revolutionary tradition did transfer a religious enthusiasm to secular government.

While few would deny that in order to understand communism or bolshevism we have to comprehend their revolutionary tradition, fascism has often been discussed as if it had no such tradition. The revolutionary appeal of fascism is easy to underestimate in our own time; the object has been to de-mystify, and a new positivism has captured the historical imagination.

The fascist revolution built upon a deep bedrock of popular piety and, especially in Germany, upon a millenarianism that was apt to come to the fore in times of crisis. More about this tradition will be said in the chapter below on the occult origins of National Socialism. The myths and symbols of nationalism were superimposed upon those of Christianity—not only in the rhythms of public rites and ceremonies (even the Duce's famed dialogues with the masses from his balcony are related to Christian "responses")—but also in the appeal to apocalyptic and millenarian thought. Such appeals can be found in the very vocabulary of Nazi leaders. Their language grew out of Christianity as we mentioned in the introduction; it was, after all, a language of faith. In 1935, for example, at Munich's *Feldherrnhalle*, where his *putsch* of 1923 had resulted in a bloody fiasco, Hitler called those who had fallen earlier "my apostles," and proclaimed that "with the Third Reich you have risen from the dead." Many other examples spring to mind, as when the leader of the Labor Front, Robert Ley, asserted that "we have found the road to eternity." The whole vocabulary of blood and soil was filled with Christian liturgical and religious meaning—the "blood" itself, the "martyrdom," the "incarnation."[21]

Moreover, historians have recently found that in the past, millenarianism was not simply a protest by the poor against the rich, but a belief shared by most classes;[22] not inherently psychotic, but a normal strain of popular piety running through the nineteenth century and into twentieth-century Europe, and common to all nations. This background was vital for the cross-class appeal of National Socialism, and perhaps, despite a different emphasis, for Italian fascism as well: the "new man," for whom all fascism yearned, was certainly easily integrated into such popular piety as it became transformed into political thought.

The "Third Force" in Italy did not directly build upon a mystical tradition, though it existed there as well as in Germany. Rather than referring to Savonarola, for example, Giovanni Gentile the important fascist philosopher saw in the fascist state a Hegelian synthesis, which resolved all contradictions. In consequence, German idealism was more important in Italian fascism, derived from Gentile, than in National Socialism, though some Nazi philosophers used Hegel to prove that Hitler had ended the dialectic of history. After the Concordat of 1929, Italian fascism, seeking to rival the Church, became increasingly the religion of the state. The will to believe was emphasized, and the Italian anti-rational tradition was searched for precedents.[23] Yet when all was said and done, such efforts were sporadic, and some leading fascists retained their skepticism about "*romanità*" or civil religions.

While the "Third Force" is vital for understanding fascism, its importance should not be exaggerated. For fascism, it was always "the experience" that counted, and not appeals to the intellect. In a play by Hans Johst, written in 1934, the young Leo Schlageter, about to fight against the French occupation of the Ruhr Valley after the First World War, facing his socialist father speaks these lines:

Son:	The young people don't pay much attention to these old slogans anymore ... the class struggle is dying out.
Father:	So ... and what do you live on then?
Son:	The Volk Community ...
Father:	And that's a slogan ...?
Son:	No, it's an experience![24]

It was an organic view of the world, which was supposed to take in the whole man and thus end his alienation. A fundamental redefinition is involved in such a view of man and his place in the world. "Politics," wrote the Italian fascist Giuseppe Bottai, "is an attitude toward life itself,"[25] and this phrase is repeated word for word in National Socialist literature. Horia Sima, one of Codreanu's successors in the leadership of the Romanian Iron Guard, summed it up: "We must cease to separate the spiritual from the political man. All history is a commentary upon the life of the spirit."[26] When fascists spoke of culture, they meant a proper attitude toward life: encompassing the ability to accept a faith, the work ethic, and discipline, but also receptivity to art and the appreciation of the native landscape.[27] The true community was symbolized by factors opposed to materialism, by art and literature, the symbols of the past and the stereotypes of the present. The National Socialist emphasis upon myth, symbol, literature and art is indeed common to all fascism.

If, then, fascism saw itself as a cultural movement, any comparative study must be based upon an analysis of cultural similarities and differences. Social and economic programs varied widely, not only between different fascisms but within each fascist movement. Some historians and political scientists have stumbled over this fact; for them, culture defined as "attitudes toward life" is no substitute for neatly coherent systems of political thought. They believe, as mentioned in our introduction, that fascism was devoid of intellectual substance, a mere reflection of movements which depend upon well-constructed ideologies. This has led many of them to underestimate fascism, to see it as a temporary response to crises, vanishing when normality is restored (though Italian fascism, with its twenty years in power, is surely more than a "temporary response"). In reality, fascism was based upon a strong and unique revolutionary tradition, fired by the emphasis on youth and the war experience; it was able to create a mass consensus that was finally broken only by a lost war.

Fascism was a movement of youth, not only in the sense that it covered a definite span of time but also in its membership. The *fin de siècle* had seen a rebellion of the young against society, parents, and school; they longed for a new sense of community. These youths were of bourgeois background, and their dominant concern for several generations had been with national unity rather than with social and economic change—for which they felt little need. Thus they were quite prepared to have their urge to revolt directed into national channels, on behalf of a community which seemed to them one of the "soul" and not an artificial creation. Such were the young who streamed not only into the earlier German Youth Movement but also into the *fasci* and the S.A., and who made up the cadres of other fascist movements. Returned from the war, they wanted to prolong the camaraderie of the trenches or if they were too young to have fought, repeat an experience which had been idealized in retrospect. Fascism offered them this chance. It is well to note in this connection that the early fascists were a new grouping, not yet bureaucratized, and that their supposed open-endedness made them appear more dynamic than rival political parties. The leaders, too, were young by the standards of that age—Mussolini became prime minister at thirty-nine; Hitler attained the chancellorship at forty-four.

Youth symbolized vigor and action; ideology was joined to fact. Fascist heroes and martyrs died at an early age in order to enter the pantheon, and symbolic representations of youth expressed the ideal type in artistic form. This was the classical ideal of beauty, which had become the manly stereotype. There must have been many who, like Albert Speer's mother, voted for the Nazis because they were young and clean-cut. The hero of the Italian novel *Generazione* (*Generations*, 1930), by Adolfo Baiocchi, finds his way from communism to fascism. His final conversion comes when he sees his former comrades, now unattractive, dirty, and disheveled, taken away by the police after an unsuccessful attempt at revolution: "These are the men of the future?" Similarly in the Nazi film *Hitler-Junge Quex* (1933), the communists were slovenly and disheveled while the Hitler Youth were clean-cut, true and respectable men. Monuments to the soldiers who fell in the First World War often represented young Siegfrieds or Greek youths. Indeed, this stereotype was reinforced by the war when the cult of youth joined the cult of the nation.

The war became a symbol of youth in its activism, its optimism, and its heroic sacrifice. For Germans, the Battle of Langemarck (November, 1914), where members of the German Youth Movement were mowed down in thousands, came to stand for the sacrifice of heroic youth. The flower of the nation, so the myth tells us, went singing to their death. One writer, Rudolf Binding, asserted that through this sacrifice only German youth had the right to symbolize national renewal among the youth of the world.[28]

Benito Mussolini also declared himself the spokesman of a youth that had shown its mettle in war. While Hitler promised to erase the "shame of Versailles," Mussolini wanted to complete Italy's "mutilated" victory in the Great War. Both took up the slogan of the young and old nations which gained currency after the war, as a reassertion of the defeated against the victors.

Fascism thus built upon the war experience, which, in different ways, had shaped the outlook of Mussolini and Hitler themselves toward the world: the former moving from a Nietzschean rather than a Marxist socialism to ideals of nationalism and struggle; the latter deepening his ever present racist world view. Above all, for millions of their contemporaries the war was the most profound experience of their lives. While a very few became pacifists, many more attempted to confront the mass death they had witnessed by elevating it into myth. Both in Germany and Italy the myth of the war experience—the glory of the struggle, the legacy of the martyrs, the camaraderie of the trenches—defeated any resolve never to have war again. France, the victorious and satisfied nation, saw the rise of powerful veterans' movements which proclaimed an end to all war;[29] but in Germany and Italy such movements proclaimed the coming resurrection of the fatherland.

The Left in Germany and Italy, as in all other nations, had difficulty in coming to grips with this war experience, shared though it was by their own members.

71

Social Democrats and communists sometimes paraded in their old uniforms (but without decorations), and founded self-defense and paramilitary organizations, like the *Reichsbanner* in Germany (which was supposed to defend the Republic). But in the last resort the Left was halfhearted about all this, and its didactic and cosmopolitan heritage, as well as its pacifist traditions, proved stronger. The communists, while they were ready to discard this past, found it impossible to redirect loyalty away from the fatherland and toward the Red Army.[30] To this day, few historians have investigated the Left's confrontation with the war experience, perhaps in itself a comment on the continued underestimation of this myth as a political force. Here was a political void readily occupied by the fascists.

The war experience aided fascism in another, more indirect manner. The front-line soldiers had become immune to the horrors of war, mass death, wounded and mutilated comrades. They had faced such unparalleled experiences either with stoicism or with a sense of sacrifice—war had given meaning to their dull and routine lives. Indeed, the war experience, despite all its horrors, catered to the longing for the exceptional, the escape from the treadmill of everyday life and its responsibilities. The political liturgy of fascism with its countless festivals catered to the same dream of excitement, of taking part in meaningful action. Typical was the expression, often repeated during the war, that death in battle had made life worthwhile.

Whatever the actual attitudes of the front-line soldiers during the war, their war experience later took on the appearance of myth, concretized through countless war cemeteries and memorials. The cult of the fallen soldier was central to the myth of the war experience in defeated Germany and Italy, and the dead were used to spur on the living to ever greater efforts of revenge. Mussolini put it succinctly: "A people which deifies its fallen can never be beaten." It was said that Hitler offered up his conquests on the altar of the war dead.[31] The horrors of war became part of an as yet incomplete struggle for national and personal fulfillment.

The acceptance of war was aided by new techniques of communication, which tended to trivialize mass death by making it a familiar part of an organized and channelled experience shared by thousands. For example, the battlefields of France and Flanders were among the tourist attractions organized by Thomas Cook and Sons. The massed and impersonal military cemeteries were faced by an equally impersonal mass of tourists, who could buy souvenir shells, helmets, and decorations. Still more important, the First World War was also the first war in the era of photography. During the war, postcards, films, and newsreels showed happy and healthy soldiers, and emphasized their work of destroying farms, towns, and churches rather than the dead and wounded. After the war, tourists could photo-graph the trenches, but what had once been experienced in these trenches was now for the most part tidied up and surrounded by flowers and shrubs.

Most people, however, were familiar with the face of war through the count-less picture books that appeared after 1918. The illustrations and photographs of the peaceful dead or wounded were presented as a part of a glorious struggle, a desirable sacrifice that would reap its deserved reward. One such book, typical of the genre, called the war both horrible and yet a purveyor of aesthetic values. Arms were depicted as symbols of the highest human accomplishment, armed conflict as the overcoming of self in the service of collective ideals and values.[32] Horror pictures were transcended, suffused with ideals of sacredness and sacrifice; the dead and mangled corpses of soldiers were by association equated with the body of Christ in the service not of individual, but of national salvation.

Through this dual process of trivialization and transcendence, the war experience served the purposes alike of the dynamic of fascism and of the movement's brutality. Death and suffering lost their sting; the martyrs continued to live as a spiritual part of the nation while exhorting it to regenerate itself and to destroy its enemies.

Joseph Goebbels's definition of the nature of a revolutionary, written in 1945 when Germany faced defeat, is typical of the process of brutalization begun by the First World War. The Nazis, in common with all fascists, had always condemned half-measures as typically bourgeois and anti-revolutionary. Goebbels now defined as "revolutionary" those who would accept no compromise in executing a scorched earth policy, or in shooting shirkers and deserters. Refusal to carry out such actions marked the worn-out old bourgeois.[33] During the desperate years of the Republic of Salò, Mussolini also resorted to brutal measures, even at times threatening to execute pupils who refused to attend school.[34] There is little doubt that the myth of the war experience made fascist brutality more acceptable and fascism itself more attractive. Here was none of the ambivalence, shared by socialists and liberals, toward what millions must have regarded—if they survived—as a great experience, and perhaps, as we have mentioned, even the high point of their otherwise uneventful lives.

The crucial role which the war experience played in National Socialism is well enough known. The war was "a lovely dream" and a "miracle of achievement," as one Nazi children's book put it. Any death in war was a hero's death and thus the true fulfillment of life.[35] There was no doubt here about the "greatness and necessity of war."[36] In Mussolini's hands, this myth had even greater force because of the absence of a truly coherent volkish ideology in Italy. The fascist struggle was a continuation of the war experience. But here, as in Germany, the glorification of struggle was linked to wartime camaraderie and put forward as a method to end class divisions within the nation. "Not class war but class solidarity" reigned in the face of death, wrote an Italian fascist who had been a syndicalist up to the last months of the war; it was not a conflict between potentates or capitalists but a necessity for the defense of the people. Historical materialism was dead.[37]

The *élan* of the battlefield was transformed into activism at home. The *fasci* and the German storm troopers regarded their postwar world as an enemy, which as patriotic shock troops they must destroy. Indeed, the leaders of these formations were in large part former front-line officers: Roehm, the head of the S.A.; Codreanu, founder of the Iron Guard; De Bono in Italy and Szalasi in Hungary— to give only a few examples. But this activism was tamed by the "magic" of the leadership of which Gustave Le Bon had written toward the end of the nineteenth century. Among the returned veterans it was even more easily controllable, for they desperately sought comradeship and leadership, not only because of the war experience but also to counteract their sense of isolation within a nation that had not lived up to their expectations.

The revolutionary tradition of the "Third Force" contained ingredients essential to this taming process: stress upon the national past and the mystical community of the nation; emphasis upon that middle-class respectability which proved essential for political success. The cult element to which we referred earlier gave it direction by channeling attention toward the eternal verities, which must never be forgotten. Activism there must be, enthusiasm was essential; the leader, aided by fascist methods of self-representation would direct it into the proper channels.

Here the liturgical element must be mentioned again, for the "eternal verities" were purveyed and reinforced through the endless repetition of slogans, choruses, symbols, and participation in group and mass ceremonies. These were the techniques that went into the taming of the revolution and that made fascism a new religion annexing rites long familiar through centuries of religious observance. Fascist mass meetings seemed something new, and so they were in the technology used and the *mise-en-scène*, but they also contained predominantly traditional elements in the technique of mass participation as well as in ideology.

To be sure, this process did not always work. The youthful enthusiasm that reigned at the outset of the movement was apt to be disappointed with its course. Italy, where fascism lasted longest, provides the best example, for the danger point came with the second fascist generation. There, the young men of the "class of '35" wanted to return to the beginnings of the movement, to its activism and its war on alienation—in short, to construct the fascist utopia. By 1936, they had formed a resistance movement within Italian fascism, which stressed that "open-endedness" the revolution had at first seemed to promise: to go to "the limits of fascism where all possibilities are open."[38] Similar signs can be discerned as Nazism developed, but here the SS managed to capture the activist spirit. Had it not been for the Second World War, Hitler might well have had difficulty with the SS, which thought of itself as an activist and spartan élite. But then fascism never had a chance to grow old except in Italy; given the ingredients that went into the revolution, old age might have presented the movement with a severe crisis.

But in the last resort taming was always combined with activism, traditionalism inevitably went hand in hand with a nostalgic revolution. Both Hitler and Mussolini disliked drawing up party programs, for this smacked of "dogmatism." Fascism stressed "movement"—Hitler called his party a *"Bewegung,"* and Mussolini for some time favored Marinetti's Futurism as an artistic and literary form that stressed both movement and struggle. All European fascisms gave the impression that the movement was open-ended, a continuous Nietzschean ecstasy. But in reality definite limits were provided to this activism by the emphasis upon nationalism, sometimes upon racism, and by the longing for a restoration of traditional morality. The only variety of fascism of which this is not wholly true is to be found among the intellectuals in France. There a man like Drieu La Rochelle continued to exalt the "provisional"—the idea that all existing reality can be destroyed in one moment.[39] Elsewhere that reality was "eternal," and activism was directed into destroying the existing order so that the eternal verity of Volk or nation could triumph, and with it the restoration of traditional morality.

The traditionalism of the fascist movement coincided with existing society's most basic moral values. This was to be a respectable revolution. When Hans Naumann spoke at the Nazi book-burning in 1933, he exalted activism; the more books burned the better. But he ended his speech by stressing the traditional bonds of family and Volk. Giuseppe Bottai, too, had called for a "spiritual renewal," and, in Belgium, the leading Rexist Jean Denis held that without a moral revolution there could be no revolution at all.[40] Some fascisms defined the moral revolution within the context of a traditional Christianity: this is true of the Belgian Rexist movement, for example, as well as of the Romanian Iron Guard. The Nazis substituted racism for religion, but once more, the morality was that shared with the rest of respectable society.

Almost all analyses of fascism have been preoccupied with the crucial support it received from the bourgeoisie. However, the Marxist model, based upon the function of each class in the process of production, is much too narrow to account for the general support of fascism. A common ethos united businessmen, government officials, and the intellectual professions that made up the bourgeoisie.[41] They were concerned about their status, access to education, and opportunity for advancement. At the same time they saw their world as resting upon the pillars of respectability: hard work, self-discipline, and good manners—always exemplified in a stereotyped ideal of male beauty which the Nazis annexed as one of their prime symbols.[42] The so-called middle-class morality, which had come to dominate Europe since the end of the eighteenth century, gave them security in a competitive world. Moreover, toward the end of the nineteenth century, the very structure of this world was challenged through the youthful revolt against accepted manners and morals by some schoolboys, bohemians, radicals, and the cultural avant garde.

Nationalism annexed this world of respectability, as did racism in central and eastern Europe, promising to protect it and to restore its purity against all challengers. This explains the puritanism of National Socialism, its emphasis upon chastity, the family, good manners, and the banishment of women from public life. However, there is no evidence that the workers did not also share such longings: the workers' culture did not oppose the virtues of the bourgeois consensus, it had co-opted the standards of respectability long ago. There was no repeating the brief relaxation of normative manners and morals that occurred in the years following the October Revolution in Russia.

Thomas Childers has supplied much evidence concerning the amorphous nature of the Nazi electorate. The Nazis, in the end, capitalized on the resentment felt by all classes, including the working class.[43] Italian fascism, Renzo De Felice has told us, was in large part an expression of the emerging, mobile middle classes, the bourgeois who were already an important social force and were now attempting to acquire political power.[44] This is exactly the opposite of the Bonapartist analysis, once so popular among the Left, which adapts to fascism Karl Marx's discussion of the dictatorship of Napoleon III. The middle class gave up political power, so the argument runs, in order to keep their social and economic power.

As a matter of fact, in Italy, and also in other European fascist movements, some important leaders came from the Left: for the most part they were syndicalists inspired by the war and the activism promised by the movement. Jacques Doriot, the only really significant leader of French fascism, traveled from the militant Left to fascism—a road, as Gilbert Allardyce has shown, not so different from that of Mussolini earlier. Doriot wanted a greater dynamic within French communism, and was impatient with party bureaucracy and discipline. As a fascist, he advocated "a revolution in France with French materials."[45] Nationalism became the refuge for such frustrated revolutionaries. National Socialism did not, by and large, attract former leaders of the Left. German Social Democrats and communists were too disciplined to desert so easily; moreover, they formed an almost self-contained subculture, whose comfort was not readily rejected. Revolutionary traditions, lively in Italy and France, easily became fossilized dogma in Germany.

Fascism thus attracted a motley crowd of followers from different backgrounds and of all classes, even though the bourgeoisie provided the backbone of the movement and most of the leaders. Rather than renewed attempts to show that fascism could not attract the working class, at best a partial truth, the very diversity of such support needs analysis. Most large-scale business and industrial enterprise, as we now know, did not support the Nazis before their seizure of power, and indeed looked upon them as potential radicals.[46] The Hitler government of 1933, which they did support, was at first a coalition in which conservatives predominated. When, six months later, the conservatives left the cabinet, industrialists compromised with Hitler, just as the Industrial Alliance in Italy came to support Mussolini. But even so, the primacy of fascist politics over economics remains a fact: the myth pushed economic interests into a subservient position. Until the very end, Adolf Hitler believed that a political confession of faith was the prerequisite for all action. From his experience in the First World War, he drew the lesson that man's world view was primary in determining his fate.[47] It was the fascist myth which had cross-class appeal, and which, together with the very tangible successes of the régimes, made possible the consensus upon which they were at first based.

Fascist movements seems to have been most successful in mobilizing the lower classes in underdeveloped European countries where the middle class was small and isolated. Spain provides one example in the West, and it is true of the Iron Guard as well as of the Hungarian fascist movement in eastern Europe. To be sure, in those countries the bourgeoisie was not as strong as elsewhere; but another factor is of greater importance in explaining the fascist appeal to the laboring and peasant classes. Here, for the first time, was a movement which tried to bring these segments of society into political participation, for in such nations Marxist movements were strictly prohibited. The stress upon an end to alienation, the ideal of the organic community, brought dividends—for the exclusion of workers and peasants from society had been so total that purely economic considerations did not provide the sole or perhaps even the principal reason for joining.

The fascist myth was based upon the national mystique, its own revolutionary and dynamic traditions, which we have discussed, and the continuation of the war experience in peacetime. It also encompassed remnants of previous ideologies and political attitudes, many of them paradoxically hostile to fascist traditions. It was a scavenger which attempted to co-opt all that had appealed to people in the nineteenth- and twentieth-century past: romanticism, liberalism, and socialism, as well as Darwinism and modern technology. Too little attention has been paid to this co-optation; it has been subsumed under the so-called eclecticism of fascism. But in reality all these fragments of the past were integrated into a coherent attitude toward life through the basic fascist nationalist myth.

The romantic tradition infused the national mystique, but it was also present in the literature and art supported by the fascists, especially by the Nazis. It had supplied the framework for a popular culture that had changed little during the preceding century. Adventure, danger, and romantic love were the constant themes, but always combined with the virtues we have mentioned: hard work, sexual purity, in short the respectability at the core of normative morality. Here the novels of Karl May in Germany, with a circulation of half a million by 1913 and 18 million by 1938, are typical. They were set in faraway places—the American plains or the Orient—and combined a romantic setting with the defense of good against evil, bodily purity, law and order, against those who would destroy them. Interestingly enough, many Nazis wanted to ban May's stories because he exalted the American Indian race and pleaded for tolerance and understanding between peoples. Hitler, however, had his novels distributed to the armed forces during the Second World War. He once said that Karl May had opened his eyes to the world, and this was true of many millions of German youth. The virtues which American Indian heroes defended against evil European trappers were precisely those the Nazis also promised to defend. They called themselves tolerant—but the tolerance and compassion that fill May's novels would come about only after Hitler had won his battles, and eliminated the "intolerant" Jewish world conspiracy.[48]

Unfortunately, we have seen no detailed analysis of similar novels popular in the Italy of the 1920s and 1930s.[49] But both National Socialism and Italian fascism used the phrase "romantic realism" to describe realistic character portrayal within a romantic setting.[50] In Italy, such realism was expressed through the strictness of classical form. Thus Francesco Sapori could summarize these aspirations: "Live romantically, as well as according to the classical idea. Long live Italy!"[51] Sapori was a member of the "Novocento" (Twentieth Century) group of writers and artists who wanted to create a native Italian style that was both natural and neoclassical. Though inspired by Mussolini's friend (and mistress) Margherita Sarfatti, it was but one of several competing cultural groups in fascist Italy. "Magic realism" was their formula, created by the writer Massimo Bontempelli.

Such romantic realism had already informed popular literature in the past, and provided a mystical and sentimental dimension even while proclaiming a clarity of purpose everyone could understand. Painters like Casorati in fascist Italy or Adolf Ziegler in Germany (Hitler's own favorite) provided corresponding examples in the visual arts.

Admittedly, here as elsewhere "magic realism" exemplified only one trend in Italy, while in Germany it was officially approved and furthered. But even in Germany non-approved literature could be obtained, at least until the war broke out. Parallels can also be drawn between Italian and German architecture under fascism, though in Italy even a party building could still reflect avant-garde style. (In Germany, among non-representational buildings and even in military barracks, the otherwise condemned Bauhaus style often surfaced.) The athletic stadium, "Forum Mussolini," was praised for the same "simplicity of style," the hard lines, displayed by the Nazi Nuremberg Stadium. The plea that architectural material must be genuine and subordinated to that "divine harmony" which reflected the Italian spirit was duplicated in Germany.[52]

Romanticism was integrated into fascism all the more easily because it had always provided the major inspiration for nationalist thought. "Magic realism" stood side by side with the romanticized view of the past: whether it was the ancient Germans who had defeated the Roman Legions, or those Roman ruins that were now bathed nightly in a romantic light, the kind of illumination so attractive to Italian fascism. Differences between the two political styles existed. The liturgy was not quite as all-embracing in Italy as in Germany; and the regime was less concerned with the total control over culture. There was some truth to the contention that the Italian fascist dictatorship was an innovative force in the arts which could persist into the 1930s,[53] but in Germany no such assertion was ever possible except in the first years of the regime when some leaders like Goebbels patronized the Expressionists until Hitler himself put a stop to it. However, for such nationalist movements, these differences are matters of degree, not absolutes. Some of the differences may relate to the fact that Mussolini was a journalist, never really comfortable with the visual expressions of fascism, while Hitler thought of himself as an architect and was not truly interested in the written word.

Liberal ideas were interwoven with romanticism. Middle-class manners and morals would lead to success (the Cinderellas of popular literature were models of respectability). But as there was no real Horatio Alger tradition in Europe, it was the "pure heart" that counted and made possible Cinderella's progress from kitchen to ballroom. Moreover, fascists everywhere believed in the threat posed by degeneration which the liberal Max Nordau had popularized during the last decade of the nineteenth century.

Nordau saw the moderns in art and literature as literally sick people, maintaining that their lack of clarity, inability to uphold moral standards, and absence of self-discipline all sprang from the degeneration of their physical organism. The Nazis, of course, illustrated their opposition to artistic modernism by the exhibition of "degenerate art," and Hitler and Mussolini prided themselves on the supposed clarity of their rhetoric. Fascism deprived the concept of degeneration of its original foundations: clinical observation linked to a universe ruled by scientific laws. But this was typical of such annexations—the popular and traditional superstructure was absorbed but now set upon racial or nationalist foundation.

The concept of degeneration had provided the foil to the liberal's concept of clarity, decency, and natural laws. Fascism also took over the ideals of tolerance and freedom, changing both to fit its model. Tolerance, as mentioned earlier, was claimed by fascists in antithesis to their supposedly intolerant enemies, while freedom was placed within the community. To be tolerant meant not tolerating those who opposed ascism: individual liberty was possible only within the collectivity. Here once more, concepts that had become part and parcel of established patterns of thought were not rejected (as so many historians have claimed) but instead co-opted—fascism would bring about ideals with which people were comfortable, but only on its own terms.

Socialism was also emasculated. The hatred of capitalism was directed against finance capitalism only. At first glance, the opposition to the bourgeoisie seemed shared equally between Nazis and socialists, as both thundered against the moribund bourgeois era. However, fascism cut away the class basis of socialist opposition to the bourgeoisie and substituted the war between generations. "Bourgeois" no longer meant a class of exploiters, but the old and worn out, those who lacked a vibrant dynamic. The setting of the young against the old was a theme which, as we saw earlier, fascism co-opted from the *fin de siècle* and then transferred from people to nations. Thus young nations with their dynamic fascist youth confronted the old nations with their ancient pot-bellied parliamentarians. This was the fascist "class struggle," and here the socialist vocabulary was employed. In this, the Italian fascists went beyond the National Socialists. Fascist students exalted the Latin, Roman, fascist revolution at the expense of the fat and pacifist bourgeois. Indeed, in Italy the lower middle class (never clearly defined) was constantly berated as being incapable of grasping the myths of nationalism and war, and as lacking any power of social interaction. It is perhaps ironic that certain Italian fascists saw their adversary as precisely that lower middle class which, according to some modern historians, constituted the most important social basis of fascism. This anti-bourgeois rhetoric was undoubtedly also part of the resentment that fascist leaders, usually from modest backgrounds, felt against so-called established society.

Fascists not only borrowed socialist rhetoric, they also made use of some rituals provided by working-class meetings: the massed flags, and the color red, for example. Moreover, some of the socialist workers' cultural and sports organizations were adapted to fascist ends. The liturgy was for the most part based on nationalist precedent from the previous century, but, with typical eclecticism, useful socialist examples were also appropriated.[54]

Fascism absorbed important parts of well-established ideologies like romanticism, liberalism, or socialism; but it was also not afraid to annex modern technology if this could be embedded within fascist myths. Indeed, the dictators were singularly perceptive in their appreciation of technological advance.

Both Hitler and Mussolini had a passion for speed—aircraft and powerful cars provided one outlet for their activism. Hitler was the first German politician to use an airplane in order to make campaign appearances throughout Germany on the same day. Use of the latest technology was immediately linked to Nazi ideology: Hitler literally dropping from the sky, Hitler by his personal courage helping to pilot his plane throughout an awesome storm (this story with its obvious biblical analogy was required reading in Third Reich schools). But Mussolini shared this passion, and in both régimes air aces like Hermann Goering or Italo Balbo had a special status and were surrounded by an aura of adventure and daring.

Anson Rabinbach has shown how technology was used to improve modes of production in Germany, how the program known as the "Beauty of Labor" turned fear of the machine into a glorification of technology through emphasis on efficiency and volkish aesthetics.[55] The newest technology was annexed to an ideology that looked to the past in order to determine the future.

Little is as yet known of how Italian fascism absorbed and used traditional modes of thought as well as the newest technology. In fact, the Italian Nationalist Association (founded in 1910), which was to be Mussolini's partner in fascist rule, combined emphasis upon industrial growth and modern technology with the nationalist mystique.[56] Nationalism, and even volkish thought, were not necessarily opposed to modernization, provided it was made to serve the ideology of the régime, which in turn justified it. That is why, for example, the Nazis supported modern technology and industrial planning, but opposed modern physics as a "Jewish science"—pragmatism was accepted, but any science resting on an abstract theoretical base had to be examined for racial purity.

Italian fascism had no such anti-scientific bias. There, for example, the physicist and Nobel Laureate Enrico Fermi flourished during the 1930s until the proclamation of the racial laws. In Germany, Volkish thought transformed the scientist into a provincial. Films in the Third Reich, for example, praised the faithful family physician, and favorably contrasted this avuncular type to a many-sided scientist like Rudolf Virchow. For all that, Germany as well as Italy integrated technology into fascism, using it to praise and further modernization as well as to enhance the political liturgy (as in Albert Speer's dome of light in mass festivals, borrowed from the anti-aircraft batteries of the defense establishment).[57]

Within its basic presuppositions of revolution, nationalism, and the war experience, fascism contained two rhythms: the amoeba-like absorption of ideas from the mainstream of popular thought and culture, countered by the urge toward activism and its taming. Both were set within the nationalist myth, and all together provided the proper attitude toward life. Fascism attempted to cater to everything people held dear, to give new meaning to daily routine and to offer salvation without risk. The fact that Adolf Hitler shared in popular tastes and longings, that in this sense he was a man of the people, was one vital ingredient of his success.

Mussolini entertained intellectual pretensions that Hitler never claimed, nor did he share the tastes of the people, perhaps because in Italy popular culture was diversified in a nation with stronger regional traditions and ties than Germany.

The frequent contention that fascist culture diverged from the mainstream of European culture cannot be upheld; on the contrary, it absorbed most of what had the greatest mass appeal in the past. In fact, it positioned itself much more in this mainstream than socialism, which tried to educate and elevate the tastes of the worker. Fascism made no such attempt: it accepted the common man's preferences and went on to direct them to its own ends. Moreover, the lack of original ideas was not a disadvantage, as many historians have implied, for originality does not necessarily lead to success in an age of democratic mass politics. The synthesis which fascism attempted between activism and order, revolution and the absorption of past traditions, proved singularly successful. To be sure, Marxism, conservatism, and liberalism made original contributions to European thought, but they underwent a long period of gestation, and by the time they became politically important movements, they had founded their own traditions. Fascism, appearing as a political force only after the First World War, had no time to create a tradition for itself: like Hitler, it was in a hurry, confronted with an old order that seemed about to fall. Those who did not strike at once were sure to be overtaken by other radicals of the Left or Right.

Yet fascism would never have worked without the tangible successes achieved by fascist régimes; social and economic factors are not to be ignored and we shall return to them later. But the preeminence of the cultural factors already discussed is certainly the other half of the dialectic. Without them, the ways in which the men and women of those times were motivated cannot be properly understood.

What, then, of the fascist utopia? It was certainly a part of the fascist myth. The fairy tale would come true once the enemies had been defeated. The happy ending was assured. But first men must "overcome"—the mystical ingredient of National Socialism was strong here; and in Italy, the ideal of continuing the wartime sacrifice was stressed. The happy end would bring about the "new Rome" or the Third German Empire, infused with middle-class virtues, a combination of the ancient past and the nineteenth-century bourgeois ideal. The new, fascist man would usher in this utopia—and he already existed, exemplified by the Führer and the Duce. Eventually, it was implied, all Germans or Italians would approach their example.

The new fascist man provided the ideal stereotype for all fascist movements. He was, naturally masculine: fascism represented itself as a society of males, re-enforced by the struggle for national unity that had created fellowships such as "Young Italy," or the German fraternities and gymnastic societies. Moreover, the cult of masculinity of the *fin de siècle*, which Nietzsche himself so well exemplified, contributed its influence. More immediately, a male society continued into the peace the wartime camaraderie of the trenches, that myth of the war experience so important in all of fascism. The masculine ideal did not remain abstract, but was personified in ideals of male strength and beauty.

Such an ideal may be vague, as in a children's book where the Duce is described as being as beautiful as the sun, as good as the light, and as strong as the hurricane.[58] It is less vague in sculptures of the Duce as a Renaissance prince or, more often, as the emperor Augustus. In addition, the innumerable pictures of the Duce harvesting, running, boxing—often bare-chested—projected a strong and invulnerable masculinity. Yet such stereotypes were not all-pervasive in Italy; they were all but absent even at such events as the exhibition honoring the tenth anniversary of the March on Rome (1933).[59] The inner characteristics of this new man were expressed through the strength and harmony of his body: athletic, persevering, in control of his passions, filled with self-denial and the spirit of sacrifice. At the same time, the new fascist man must be energetic, courageous, and spartan.[60] The ideal fascist was the very opposite of muddleheaded, talkative, intellectualizing liberals and socialists—the exhausted, tired old men of the old order. Indeed, Italian fascism's dream of an age-old masculine ideal has not vanished from our own time.

Germany shared such ideals of the male society and the new fascist man, but much more consistently. This gave the Nazi utopia quite a different direction from that of Italy. Volkish thought had always advocated the ideal of the "Bund" of males; the German Youth Movement reinforced the link between the fellowship of men and the national mystique, while the war completed the task. Mussolini might talk about the war and the continuing struggle, but right-wing Germans believed that a new race of men had already emerged from the war—energy come alive, as Ernst Jünger put it; lithe, muscular bodies, angular faces, and eyes hardened by the horrors they had seen.[61] Here the inner nature of the new race was immediately connected with its outward features. Whenever Adolf Hitler talked about the "new German," he wasted little time on the inner self of the Aryan but instead defined him immediately through an ideal of beauty—"*Rank und Schlank*" (slim and tall) was his phrase.[62] There was never any doubt about how the ideal German looked, and it is impossible to imagine a Nazi exposition without the presence of this stereotype.

Racism made the difference. It gave to volkish thought a dimension which Italian fascism lacked. To be sure, as we shall see later, an effort was made to introduce this dimension into Italy with the Racial Laws of 1938, but these were by and large less successful as far as the stereotype was concerned. The Aryan myth had from its beginning in the eighteenth century linked the inward to the outward man, and combined scientific pretensions with an aesthetic theory that saw in Greek sculpture the ideal of male beauty.[63] Indeed, while the nude male was commonplace in German volkish art (see Chapter Ten [*sic*]), the female was usually veiled: the modest and chaste bearer of the children of the race had to be hidden from public view.

Was the fascist man then tied to the past or was he the creator of new values? Renzo De Felice has seen here one of the chief differences between Italian fascism and German National Socialism. For the Germans, the man of the future had always existed, even in the past, for the race was eternal, like the trunk of a tree, while the ideal man of Italian fascism created new values.[64] If we look at the famous definition of fascism given by Mussolini and Giovanni Gentile in the *Encyclopedia Italiana* (1932), the new "fascist man" is, on the one hand, set within the Italian patriotic tradition, and, on the other, supposed to live a superior life unconstrained by space and time. He must sacrifice his personal interests and realize that it is his spirituality which gives him human values. But his spirituality must be informed by history, meaning Italian traditions and national memories. Such an apparent paradox of standing within and yet soaring above tradition accompanied most discussions of the new fascist man in Italy. Man must proceed to ever higher forms of consciousness, culture must not crystallize, and yet the great Italian authors of the past must be studied ("These are germs which can fructify our spirit and give us spontaneity").[65] The Universal Roman Exhibition of 1942 illustrated such principles concretely. Indeed, the new Rome built for this exhibition (*Rome Eure*) was supposed to transmit its heritage to its own day, as shown by the effort to imitate all the Italian architectural styles of the past: Roman, Renaissance, and Baroque. But the exhibition was also supposed to be a signpost for the future. These diverse intentions were symbolized by the completion of the archaeological excavations of Ostia Antiqua (Roman Ostia), creating access to it by means of an Autostrada, and as the catalogue tells us, thus making the new Rome encompass the old,[66] except that by 1942 what was supposed to be unique had been tamed into an historical eclecticism.

In fact, the new fascist man in Italy ignored history no more than his Nazi counterpart.[67] The cult of the Roman past was pervasive; it determined the fascist stereotype wherever we do find it. But this past remained, at least until the final years of the régime, a jumping-off point for the ideal fascist man of the future. Tradition informed his consciousness, but he himself had to rise beyond it without losing sight of his starting point. Such a flexible attitude toward the ideal reflected the greater openness of Italian fascism to the new in both art and literature. This utopia was willing to leave the door to the future halfway open, while in Germany it was shut tight. The difference reflects the grouping of Italian fascism for an ideology, its greater emphasis upon struggle and energy, its syndicalist and Futurist elements.

The new German incorporated the eternal values of the race, summarized in a frequently used admonition: "You yourself represent a thousand years of the future and a thousand years of the past."[68] The SS, the most dynamic of all party organizations, fits into this picture. True, an official SS publication tells us that the SS man should never be a conformist, and every SS generation should improve upon its predecessors. Yet the maxim that "history is human fate" meant emphasis upon racial ancestry, that the accomplishments of the past dominated the present and determined the future.[69]

Was this ideal man then to be stripped of his individuality? Was individuality not a part of the fascist utopia? For liberal democracy and for social democracy, the final goal of all social organization was the good of the individual. Did fascism really change this goal? To do so, it would have to eradicate one of the deepest utopian traditions. But it was the pattern of fascism to annex and bend to its purpose, rather than change concepts deeply rooted in the national consciousness, and individualism was not exempted from this pattern, being at the same time retained and redefined. In contrast to unlimited economic and social competition, setting man against man, the ideal of an organic community had taken root in the previous century. The German Youth Movement had thought of itself as such a community, voluntarily joined but based upon shared origins. The ideal of the "*équipe*" played a similar role among French fascist intellectuals, a team spirit grounded in a common world view, exalted by the young male writers grounded around the fascist newspaper *Je Suis Partout* (see Chapter Nine [*sic*]). It was the camaraderie of trench life, which, as we have mentioned repeatedly, many men had actually experienced, and which for others had become a myth that seemed to provide the model for the ideal society. To be sure, they had been conscripted, but this awkward fact was ignored as veterans thought back to comradeship under fire, when each man had had to subjugate his will to that of the others in his unit in order to survive.

Fascism could all the more easily co-opt this idea of community since nationalism had always advocated it: individualism is only possible when men voluntarily join together on the basis of a common origin, attitude, and purpose. Fascism dropped the voluntary aspect, of course, but only as a temporary measure. Education was directed to help the young understand that "*Credere, Obedire e Combattere*" on behalf of the national community was the true fulfillment of individualism.[70] The prospectus of the élite Nazi school at Feldafing sums up this redefinition of individualism: "He who can do what he wants is not free, but he is free who does what he should. He who feels himself without chains is not free, but enslaved to his passions."[71]

Individualism under fascism then meant self-fulfillment while sheltering within the collectivity, having the best of both worlds. It is therefore mistaken to characterize fascism simply as anti-individualist, for this ignores the longing for a true community in which the like-minded joined together, each through his own power of will. The French fascist intellectuals, merely a coterie out of power, could as we have seen praise the provisional, yet for all this Nietzschean exaltation, one of their number, Robert Brasillach, not only found refuge in an "inner fatherland" but also saw in his beloved Paris a collection of small villages in which he could be at home.[72] Between the wars the young men in the Latin Quarter wanted to be original and spontaneous, while longing for an end to intellectual anarchy.[73] Fascism gave them the means to do all that and still remain sheltered by the national community.

These French fascists expressed an *élan* typical of fascism as a movement out of power, though even here the dynamic had to be tamed. Fascism in power, as we saw earlier, was often a disappointment to the young fascist activists. Although it kept much of the earlier rhetoric, once in power it inevitably became the Establishment. Indeed, Stanley Payne's suggestion that at that point the differences between fascism and the reaction become less marked seems close to the facts, if not to the professed ideology.[74] The reactionaries, men like Francisco Franco, based themselves on the traditional hierarchies, on the status quo and, as often as not, took as their ideology the Christianity of the Catholic Church. The fascist revolutionary base, the dynamic nationalist attitudes, and the prominent rhythms were lacking. However, before the relationship between fascism and the reaction can be redefined, more detailed comparison is needed between, for example, the various stages of Mussolini's government and the evolution of Franco's rule in Spain. Here, once again, the particular national histories of those countries are of great importance.

Although national differences culminated in the distinctions between the "new fascist man" of Italy and of Germany, all fascism essentially went back to the anti-parliamentary tradition of the nineteenth century in order to redefine popular participation in politics. Both such participation and individual liberty were supposedly part of a collective experience. It must not be forgotten that, in the last resort, all fascisms were nationalisms, sharing the cult of national symbols and myths as well as the preoccupation with mythical national origins. Himmler sent an expedition to Tibet in order to discover Aryan origins, while other young Germans searched for the original Aryans in Scandinavia, closer to home. The Italian fascist Foreign Ministry sponsored archaeological expeditions to revive the idea of the Roman Empire,[75] while Mussolini restored Rome's ancient ruins, saying that the city was Italian fascism's eternal symbol. The Museum of Classical Antiquity, named after the Duce, was situated in the Campodoglio, in the heart of ancient Rome. Nationalism meant emphasis upon origins and continuity, however much the Italian fascist man was supposed to be a man of the future.

Racism and anti-Semitism were not a necessary component of fascism, and certainly not of those parts of the movement that looked for their model to Italy, where until 1936, racism was not part of official doctrine. Léon Degrelle, the leader of the Belgian Rexists, at one time explicitly repudiated that racism which he was later to embrace wholeheartedly (to become Hitler's favorite foreign National Socialist). What, he asked, is the "true race"—the Belgian, the Flemand, or the Walloon? From the Flemish side, the fascist newspaper *De Daad* inveighed against race hatred and called upon "upright Jews" to repudiate the Marxists in their midst.[76]

Even Dutch National Socialism under Anton Andriaan Mussert did not at first appeal to racism and kept silent about the Jews, an attitude the German Nazis were later to find incomprehensible. The French fascist group around the newspaper *Je Suis Partout* did go in for anti-Semitism, but even here the Germans were accused of exaggerating the racial issue, for good relations were possible with a foreign people like the Jews.[77] This state of affairs did not last. By 1936 Mussolini had embraced racism and though, as we mentioned, racism was not really successful in Italy, Mussolini himself first used it in 1936 against blacks during the Ethiopian war, and then through the racial laws of 1938 against the Jews. We shall never know whether Mussolini himself became a convinced racist, but he did increase the severity in the draft of the racial laws which had been submitted to him.[78] The proclamation of these laws was not solely due to German influence, though much of their content, and their method had to be imported from the north. Rather, Mussolini may have embraced racism out of opportunism (in the Ethiopian war it lay readily at hand), or to give fascism a clearly defined enemy like the Jews in order to reinvigorate his ageing movement, to give a new cause to a young generation becoming disillusioned with his revolution.

It was only in central and eastern Europe that racism was from the beginning an integral part of fascist ideology. In eastern Europe, the masses of Jewry were to be found still living under quasi-ghetto conditions. They were a distinctive part of the population and vulnerable to attack. Jews prayed differently, dressed differently, and spoke a different language (Yiddish). Even if some were assimilated, enough non-assimilated Jews remained to demonstrate the clash of cultures that underlay much of the anti-Semitism in the region. Moreover, in underdeveloped countries like Romania or Hungary the Jews had become *the* middle class, forming a vulnerable entity within the nation as that class which seemed to exploit the rest of the population through its commercial activities. No wonder the Romanian Iron Guard, in appealing to the nationalism of the peasants, became violently anti-Semitic and even racist despite their Christian orientation—for they had begun as the "Legion of the Archangel Michael."

From the 1880s on, a great part of East European Jewry began to emigrate into the neighboring countries, predominantly Germany and Austria. The account in *Mein Kampf* of how sharply Hitler reacted to the sight of such strangers in pre-war Vienna may well have been typical. However that may be, the facts of the situation in that part of Europe gave fascism an enemy who could be singled out as symbolizing the forces that must be overcome. Hitler built upon the so-called "Jewish question," and until the late 1930s this led to a further differentiation between National Socialism and western or southern fascism. For Hitler, unlike Mussolini, the enemy was not just a vague liberalism or Marxism; he was physically embodied by the Jews who supposedly had created liberalism and Marxism, and who were the sworn enemies of all nations. Building on the central European tradition of a racist-oriented nationalism, he could give to the enemy of his world view a concrete and human shape.

We have discussed Italian fascism and National Socialism as placing their emphasis upon culture. Both Mussolini and Hitler attempted to epitomize their movements, to provide in their own persons living symbols and an integrative force. Discussing the movements without the leaders is rather like describing the body without the soul. Astute politicians that they were, neither could have succeeded without an instinct for the tastes, wishes, and longings of their people; both ended states of near civil war which they themselves had largely created, managing to provide economic stability and success in foreign policy. Hitler's success was the more spectacular. Between 1933 and 1936, he led Germany from the depths of a depression to full employment. Rearmament played only a limited role in this economic revival, traditional investments and public works were more important. Hitler was instrumental in the building of a powerful army, and his successes in foreign policy need no further comment. It is true, as Sebastian Haffner wrote in one of the most insightful biographies of Hitler, that by 1938 he had converted even those who had earlier voted against him by the sheer weight of his political and economic success.[79] But here again such consensus, in the last resort, rested upon shared myths and aspirations which, because of this achievement, seemed nearer realization.

Mussolini could at first claim equal success. The population had reason to be satisfied. If in Italy the Duce had not restored work to 6 million unemployed or torn up the Treaty of Versailles, he had brought order and a certain dynamic to a government that had been inert and corrupt. Moreover, Italy avoided most of the European depression. Even conservatives, who did not want a fascist revolution, could be content with the quality of life. However, by 1938, under the pressure of the unpopular German alliance and then an unpopular Ethiopian war, Mussolini maintained a consensus only with difficulty.

Like many other historians, Sebastian Haffner fails to recognize Hitler's success as a politician in the age of the masses using the new style of politics based upon traditional emotions and myths. He therefore easily distinguishes between Hitler and a German people who, in his view, merely responded to the Führer's tangible gains. In fact, to the contrary, just because the desires of the people coincided so largely with those of the régime, the new political style won their acclaim. Gustave Le Bon, in his book *The Crowd* (1895), had stressed that successful leadership must genuinely share the myths of the people—and both Hitler and Mussolini were his disciples.[80]

We know that real wages fell in Germany and that the Italian workers and peasants did not materially benefit from the fascist régime. But it would seem that, to many of them, this mattered less than the gain in status. Those who have tried to prove otherwise apparently believe that material interests alone determine men's actions. Hitler and Mussolini knew that what mattered was how people would perceive their position: myth is always more important as a persuader than the sober analysis of reality.

Moreover, people, and not just material forces, do make history—not just the leader himself but also the likes and dislikes, wishes and, above all, the perceptions of the followers. Whenever he took an action which might upset many Germans, Hitler tried—successfully—to appear to be the pushed rather than the pusher. The staging of the local riots that preceded all new steps in his Jewish policy are a good example. His tactic of making an aggressive move in foreign policy and then proclaiming it as his very last, confused friend and foe alike. Mussolini's policies until the mid-1930s were more modest, but he too combined gestures with patience, moving slowly in order to accomplish his ends. Yet Mussolini came to power much earlier than Hitler, and his achievement, as we have seen, was in minimizing the economic depression Hitler had to overcome. Speaking of the fascist consensus in Italy, Renzo De Felice puts it graphically: "The country was thinking more about the evils that fascism had avoided than whether it brought true benefits."[81] There was a difference between the consensus in Italy and in Germany, even though the two dictators' approaches to politics and their successful emphasis upon the myths that determine human perceptions were similar.

The desired end was different also. Mussolini's long-range objectives were traditional: to create an empire built upon the example of ancient Rome. Hitler's long-range goals of racial domination were not traditional. A wide gulf divided Adolf Hitler, the provincial whose exposure to the far-out racist sects of Vienna provided his intellectual awakening, and Mussolini, who emerged from the conflicts within international socialism. Mussolini confessed himself to be influenced by some of the masters of European thought—such men as Gustave Le Bon, Georges Sorel, William James, and Vilfredo Pareto—while Hitler, also a pupil of Le Bon, was mainly taken with the thoughts of obscure racist sectarians like Lanz von Liebenfels, Alfred Schuler, or Dietrich Eckart, who but for their disciple's success would have remained deservedly unknown. From one perspective Mussolini may be called a man of the world, and Adolf Hitler a true believer, a member of an obscure racist-theosophical sect. But then this man who believed in secret sciences, Aryan mythologies, and battles between the powers of light and darkness, through his political genius turned such ideas into the policies of a powerful nation. Hitler's goal was both the acquisition of a traditional empire— "*Lebensraum*"—and the enslavement of the Slavs to the superior race as well as the extermination of the mentally and physically handicapped, the gypsies and above all the Jews. His devotion to genocide summarized the difference between Germany where the Volkish tradition of nationalism triumphed, and Italy with its more humanitarian nationalism of the *Risorgimento*.

Because of his ideological commitment, Hitler showed a tenacity that was absent in Mussolini. This is exemplified on one level by comparing Mussolini, the bon vivant and womanizer, with Hitler, the lonely, spartan figure. But on a more important level, it may have meant, as Sebastian Haffner states, that Hitler, knowing the war was lost, would nevertheless continue the conflict so that he could kill as many Jews as possible before the inevitable end. Hundreds of thousands of Germans died so that Hitler could, at the last moment, kill hundreds of thousands of Jews.[82]

Mussolini was cynical about the potentialities of his own people, and even came to despise them toward the end of his rule. But while Hitler felt himself in the end betrayed by the German people, for the most part he thought in apocalyptic terms. Every action had to contribute to a "final end": indeed, Hitler himself believed in finite time—it was during the short span of his own life, he was fond of remarking, that the Aryan must triumph over Jew and find his *Lebensraum*. The German occult tradition asserted itself, as we saw when discussing the "Third Way," not mediated by Jakob Böhme but by an obscure and bizarre racism.[83]

Haffner's speculation as to why Hitler kept on fighting fits better into our picture of the Führer than the usual interpretation (adopted by all other biographers as the sole explanation), that in the end he became a captive of his own myth of invincibility. It is quite possible that Hitler lost contact with reality at some point shortly before the end of the war; however, the Hitler who emerges from Joseph

Goebbels' Diaries does not seem to have lost control, though perhaps he realized earlier than anyone else that the war was lost.[84] To be sure, Hitler and Mussolini became isolated during the course of the war, but the consistency of Hitler's whole life makes the tenacity of his end believable as well. Mussolini changed, whereas Hitler from the end of the First World War onward remained locked in his unchanging world view.

Any comparison of Hitler and Mussolini becomes difficult because of the absence of works on Hitler that in historical detail and powerful analysis correspond to Renzo De Felice's monument biography of Benito Mussolini. Admittedly, Mussolini had no Auschwitz and, unlike Germany, Italy had an important anti-fascist movement. The Duce also showed more human dimensions than the Führer. Yet the materials for a large-scale biography of Hitler exist, and are certainly as extensive as the resources that made De Felice's biography possible. But in spite of the availability of such documentation, up to now each recent biography of Hitler has merely added minor facts, without any new interpretations of note. To be sure, psychohistorians have begun to analyze the record of Hitler's life in an attempt to find new insights. Yet it is difficult to accept their contention that his mother's death by cancer determined the structure of his entire life, or that the hallucinations of Hitler, the temporarily blinded soldier, led to his hatred of the Jews. Scholarship has not really advanced much beyond Alan Bullock's pioneering work of 1952 *Hitler, A Study in Tyranny*. German historians, even of the younger generation, have for the most part avoided the figure of the Führer and concentrated instead upon the more impersonal causes of National Socialism. The biographies of Hitler which do exist have for the most part been written by those outside the historical profession. Yet to write about National Socialism while omitting to confront Adolf Hitler, who was at the heart of it, means shirking a true confrontation with the past.

The building blocks for a general theory of fascism now seem to lie before us. Fascism was everywhere an "attitude toward life," based upon a national mystique which might vary from nation to nation. It was also a revolution, attempting to find a "Third Way" between Marxism and capitalism, but still emphasizing ideology over economic change, the "revolution of the spirit" of which Mussolini spoke, or Hitler's "German revolution." However, fascism encouraged activism, the fight against the existing order of things. Both in Germany and Italy, fascism's chance at power came during conditions of near civil war. But this activism had to be tamed, fascism had to become respectable for activism was in conflict with the general desire for law and order, with those middle-class virtues that fascism promised to protect against the dissolving spirit of modernity. Fascism in power was also sometimes constrained by a head of state who continued to represent the old order and who could not be ignored. While Hitler was freed from this constraint by President von Hindenburg's death in 1934, Mussolini always had to report to King Victor Emmanuel. The main dilemma, however, which faced fascism was that activism had to exist side by side with the effort to tame it and to keep it under control. This was one of the chief problems faced by Hitler and Mussolini before their rise to power and in the early years of their rule.

Fascism could create a consensus because it annexed and focused those hopes and longings that informed diverse political and intellectual movements of the previous century. Like a scavenger, fascism scooped up scraps of romanticism, liberalism, the new technology, and even socialism, to say nothing of a wide variety of other movements lingering from the nineteenth into the twentieth century. But it threw over all these the mantle of a community conceived as sharing a national past, present, and future—a community that was not enforced but presumably "natural," or "genuine," with its own organic strength and life, analogous to nature. The tree became the favorite symbol; but the native landscape or the ruins of the past were also singled out as exemplifying on one level the national community, a human collectivity represented by the Fascist Party.

Fascism with its glorification of war and struggle needed enemies and some of these we have mentioned already. Foreign nations considered hostile were not close or tangible enough, thus internal enemies were essential. Racism as we saw focused upon tangible enemies like the Jews or Gypsies, but fascism in general also provided a category of "asocials," men and women who were said to be without any sense of community. The so-called asocials were homeless people like the beggars or vagabonds, the mentally impaired and so-called sexual deviants. They were not usually of an inferior race, but as aryans or good Italians were thought to undermine the nation or race, to lead it into degeneration. These enemies could, at times, be reformed, but in Germany if they resisted they too were doomed. Indeed, German homosexuals, for example, were classified as either merely shamming when they could perhaps be saved, or hereditary and must be exterminated.

These were, of course, precisely those members of the population whom normative society had always deplored and pushed to the margins of existence. Here again fascism trod on familiar ground with, in the case of Germany, one all important difference: in the quest for utopia the asocials were to be killed, exterminated, a procedure which settled, respectable society rejected. Indeed, the Nazis felt that the extermination process had to be kept a dark secret. The belief in racism made the difference here between prison, being an outcast and death. Whether it focused upon its enemies or attempted to inculcate its attitude towards life, basically fascism invented nothing new, but pushed already present hopes, fears and prejudices to their logical conclusions.

Support for fascism was not built merely upon appeal to vested interests. Social and economic factors, to be sure, proved crucial in the collapse after the First World War, and in the Great Depression, while the social and economic successes of fascism gave body to fascist theories. But—and this seems equally crucial—political choices are determined by people's actual perception of their situation, their hopes and longings, the utopia toward which they strive. The fascist "attitude toward life" was suffused by cultural factors through which, as we have attempted to show, the movement presented itself;

it was the only mass movement between the wars that could claim to have a largely cross-class following.

In the end, it is not likely that Europe will repeat the fascist or the National Socialist experience. However, the fragments of our Western cultural and ideological past which fascism used for its own purposes still lie ready to be formed into a new synthesis, even if in a different way. Most ominously, nationalism, the basic force that made fascism possible in the first place, not only remains but is growing in strength—still the principal integrative force among peoples and nations. Those ideals of mass politics upon which fascism built its political style are very much alive, for ours is still a visual age to which the "new politics" of fascism were so well attuned. The method used to appeal to the masses (or public opinion as it is called today), if not the form or content, is in our time, for example, reflected in the public relations industry[85] and refined through the use of television as an instrument of politics. Symbols and myth are still used today though no longer in order to project a single and official attitude, but instead a wide variety of attitudes towards life. The danger of successful appeals to authoritarianism is always present, however changed from earlier forms or from its present worldwide manifestations.

Speculations about the future depend upon an accurate analysis of the past. This chapter is meant to provide a general framework for a discussion of fascism, in the hope of leading us closer to that historical reality without which we cannot understand the past or the present.

NOTES

1 The best recent discussion of fascism and totalitarian doctrine is Karl-Dietrich Bracher, *Zeitgeschichtliche Kontroversen um Faschismus, Totalitarismus, Demokratie* (Munich, 1976).

2 Aryeh L. Unger, *The Totalitarian Party: Party and People in Nazi Germany and Soviet Russia* (Cambridge, 1974), 189, 202.

3 Piero Melograni, "The Cult of the Duce in Mussolini's Italy," *Journal of Contemporary History*, Vol. 77 (1976), 223–225.

4 Aryeh L. Unger, op. cit., 1, 264.

5 Cf. George L. Mosse, ed., *Police Forces in History* (London and Beverly Hills, 1975).

6 I am grateful to Eric Johnson for letting me see part of his soon to be published crucial new research on the Gestapo.

7 See J. L. Talmon, *The Rise of Totalitarian Democracy* (Boston, 1952); and the criticism in George L. Mosse, "Political Style and Political Theory," *Confronting the Nation* (Hanover and London, 1993), Chapter 4.

8 Mona Ozouf, *La Fête révolutionnaire 1789–1799* (Paris, 1976), 22.

9 For a more thorough discussion of the point, see George L. Mosse, *The Nationalization of the Masses* (New York, 1975, 1999), and the unjustly forgotten Harold J. Laski, *Reflections on the Revolution of Our Time* (New York, 1943), not for his analysis of fascism but for the weakness of parliamentary government.

10 The term "good revolution" is by Karl Dietrich Bracher, op. cit., 68.

11 Stanley Payne, *A History of Fascism 1914–1945*, *passim*.

12 Renzo De Felice, *Fascism* (New Brunswick, N.J., 1976), 24.

13 Zeev Sternhell, *La Droite révolutionnaire 1885–1914* (Paris, 1978), *passim*; George L. Mosse, *Toward the Final Solution*, Chapter 10.

14 I.e. Emilio Gentile, *Le origini dell'ideologia Fascista* (Rome/Bari, 1975), 76ff.

15 Renzo De Felice, *Mussolini il rivoluzionario* (Turin, 1965), 591; Paolo Nello, *L'Avanguardismo Giovannile alle origini del fascismo* (Rome, 1978), 26–27.

16 George L. Mosse, *Germans and Jews: The Right, the Left, and the Search for a "Third Force" in Pre-Nazi Germany* (New York, 1970), Chapter 1.

17 See Chapter 6.

18 Otto-Ernst Schüddekopf, *Linke Leute von Rechts* (Stuttgart, 1960), 84.

19 Joseph Goebbels, *Tagebücher 1945* (Hamburg, 1976), 55, 69–70.

20 Ernst Bloch, *Thomas Münzer als Theologe der Revolution* (Munich, 1921), 295.

21 Victor Klemperer, *LTI; Notizbuch eines Philologen* (Berlin, 1947), 116–118.

22 I.e. Clarke Garrett, *Respectable Folly: Millenarians and the French Revolution in France and England* (Baltimore, 1975), 8.

23 Paolo Nello, review of Daniele Marchesini, "La scuola dei gerarchi," *Storia contemporanea* (September, 1977), 586.

24 Quoted in George L. Mosse, ed., *Nazi Culture* (New York, 1966), 116.

25 Giuseppe Bottai, *Il Fascismo e l'Italia Nuova* (Rome, 1923), 19.

26 Horia Sima, *Destinée du Nationalisme* (Paris, n.d.), 19.

27 These qualities are taken from *Voor Volk en Vaderland, De Strijd der Nationaalsocialistische Bewegung 14. December 1931–Mei 1941*, ed. C. Van Geelkerken (n.p., 1941), 315.

28 The remarks on the First World War are taken from George L. Mosse, *Fallen Soldiers: Shaping the Memory of the World Wars* (New York, 1990), Chapters 4, 5; see also his *The Image of Man*, Chapter 6.

29 Antoine Prost, *Les Anciens Combattants et la Société Française*, 3 vols. (Paris, 1978).

30 See George L. Mosse, "La sinistra europea e l'esperienza della guerra," *Rivoluzionee Reazione in Europa (1917–1924)*, Convegno storico internazionale—Perugia, 1978 (Florence, 1978), Vol. II, 151–167.

31 Mussolini quoted in Umberto Silva, *Kunst und Ideologie des Faschismus* (Frankfurt-am-Main, 1975), 108. For Hitler, see *Die Fahne Hoch!* (1932), 14; also George L. Mosse, *Fallen Soldiers*, *passim*.

32 Alfred Steinitzer and Wilhelm Michel, *Der Krieg in Bildern* (Munich, 1922), 97; *Der Weltkrieg im Bild* (Berlin-Oldenburg, 1926), Preface.

33 Goebbels, op. cit., 28.

34 Teresa Maria Mazzatosta, "Educazionee scuola nella Repubblica Sociale Italiana," *Storia contemporanea* (February 1978), 67.

35 Peter Hasubeck, *Das Deutsche Lesebuch in der Zeit des National-sozialismus* (Hanover, 1972), 77, 79.

36 Ernst Jünger, ed., *Das Antlitz des Weltkrieges* (Berlin, 1930), Preface.

37 Oldo Marinelli, quoted in Emilio Gentile, *Le Origini del'Ideologia Fascista* (Rome, 1974), 92.

38 Ruggero Zangrandi, *Il lungo viaggio* (Milan, 1948); for a discussion of this revolt of youth, see Michael Ledeen, *Universal Fascism* (New York, 1972), *passim*.

39 Drieu La Rochelle, *Socialisme Fasciste* (Paris, 1943), 72.

40 For Hans Naumann's speech, see Hildegard Brenner, *Die Kunstpolitik des Nationalsozialismus* (Hamburg, 1963), 188; Bottai, op. cit., 18 ff; and Jean Denis, *Principes Rexistes* (Brussels, 1936), 17.

41 Hugh Seton-Watson, *Nations and States* (Boulder, Colo., 1977), 420, 421.

42 I.e. George L. Mosse, *The Image of Man*, Chapter 8.

43 Charles S. Maier, "Some Recent Studies of Fascism," *Journal of Modern History* (September 1976), 509; and Thomas Childers, "The Social Bases of the National Socialist Vote," in *International Fascism*, ed. George L. Mosse (London, 1979), 161–189.

44 Renzo De Felice, *Fascism* (New Brunswick, N.J., 1976), 46.

45 Gilbert D. Allardyce, "The Political Transition of Jacques Doriot," in *International Fascism*, ed. George L. Mosse, 287.

46 Henry A. Turner, Jr., "Big Business and the Rise of Hitler," in *Nazism and the Third Reich*, ed. Henry A. Turner, Jr. (New York, 1972), 93.

47 I.e. George L. Mosse, *Nazi Culture*, Chapter 1.

48 I.e. George L. Mosse, *Masses and Man* (New York, 1980), Chapter 3.

49 A list of popular novels under fascism·will be found in Carlo Bordoni, *Cultura e propaganda nell'Italia fascista* (Messina-Florence, 1974), 85, but without any analysis of their individual content. However, see Pasquale Falco, *Letteratura Populare Fascista* (Cosenza, 1984), which is disappointing.

50 *Storia d'Italia*, ed. Ruggiero Romano and Corrado Vivanti (Turin, 1973), 1526; George L. Mosse, *The Nationalization of the Masses*, 194.

51 Francesco Sapori, *L'Arte e il Duce* (Milan, 1932), 141.

52 Ibid., 123 ff.

53 Adrian Lyttleton, *The Seizure of Power: Fascism in Italy 1919–1929* (London, 1973), 389; Emilio Gentile, *The Sacralization of Politics in Fascist Italy, passim*.

54 George L. Mosse, *The Nationalization of the Masses*, Chapter 7; for the liturgy of Italian fascism, see Emilio Gentile, *The Sacralization of Politics, passim*.

55 Anson G. Rabinbach, "The Aesthetics of Production in the Third Reich," *International Fascism*, ed. George L. Mosse (London, 1979), 189–223.

56 Adrian Lyttleton, op. cit., 19.

57 Oral communication, Albert Speer to George L. Mosse, June, 1974.

58 Schkem Gremigni, *Duce d'Italia* (Milan, 1927), 116.

59 E.g., *Ausstellung der Faschistischen Revolution, erste Zehnjahrfeier des Marsches auf Rom* (1933). Typically enough, the official poster for the exhibition featured soldiers from the First World War.

60 Donino Roncará, *Saggi sull'Educazione Fascista* (Bologna, 1938), 61; George L. Mosse, *The Image of Man*, Chapter 8.

61 Ernst Jünger, *Der Kampf als inneres Erlebnis* (Berlin, 1933), 32 ff.

62 I.e. Hitler at the Reichsparteitag, 1935, *Adolf Hitler an seine Jugend* (Munich, 1940), n.p.

63 See George L. Mosse, *Toward the Final Solution*, Chapter 2.

64 Renzo de Felice, *Fascism*, 56.

65 Domino Roncará, op. cit., 55, 58.

66 *Esposizione Universale di Roma*, MCMXLII, XX E.F. (1942), 83, 88.

67 Giuseppe Bottia wrote that fascism was an intellectual revolution concerned with the problem of its origins—*Pagine di Critica Fascista (1915–1926)* (Florence, n.d.), 322.

68 *Führer Blätter der Hitler-Jugend* (1935), 10.

69 *Lehrplan für Sechsmonatige Schulung* (SS, Hauptamt IV, n.d., n.p.), 25, 79.

70 Typically enough, the newsletter of a Nazi elite school repeated this phrase in Italian, commenting that these ideals were shared by German and Italian youth—*Reichsschule der NSDAP Feldafing* (1940–41), 73.

71 *Ibid.* (1939–40), 17.

72 I.e. Robert Brasillach, *Le Marchand d'Oiseaux* (Paris, 1936), *passim*.

73 Charles Beuchat, "Le Quartier Latin aux temps du jeune Brasillach," *Hommages à Robert Brasillach* (Lausanne, 1965), 78.

74 Stanley G. Payne, "Fascism in Western Europe," in *Fascism: A Reader's Guide*, ed. Walter Laqueur (London, 1976), 303.

75 Sapori, *op. cit.*, 15ff; George L. Mosse, *Toward the Final Solution*, 42–43.

76 *Rex*, 23 (September 1938); *De Daad*, 2 (September 1933).

77 *Je Suis Partout*, April 18, 1938.

78 Michele Sarfatti, *Mussolini contro gli ebrei* (Turin, 1994), especially 6 ff, 29.

79 Sebastian Haffner, *Anmerkungen zu Hitler* (Munich, 1978), 43.

80 George L. Mosse, *Nationalization of the Masses*, 12, 202.

81 Renzo de Felice, *Fascism*, 65.

82 Sebastian Haffner, op. cit., 154 ff.

83 See Chapter 6; also George L. Mosse, *Toward the Final Solution*, Chapters 7, 18.

84 See also Percy Ernst Schramm, *Hitler als militärischer Führer* (Frankfurt-am-Main, 1965), *passim*.

85 I.e. Stuart Ewen, *P.R.! A Social History of Spin* (New York, 1996), *passim*.

3

FASCISM
A working definition

Stanley G. Payne

A reputed historian of Franco's Spain (1961; 1967; 1973; 1987, 1999, 2004), the American scholar Stanley Payne has earned in the past three decades the unchallenged reputation of being the leading comparative historian of interwar fascism. Payne's working definition of fascism was first advanced in a book chapter (Payne, 1980a), and soon reiterated and expanded on in a full-size book that advanced a comparative taxonomy of European fascism (1980b). In a new book published in 1995, Payne reworked his model of fascism in the light of new research in the field, and added to it a much-needed comparative narrative account of the history of interwar fascism. That book—the Introduction of which is included below—remains the most comprehensive theoretically-minded comparative treatment of the history of interwar fascism available to date.

Building on the insights put forward by his mentors, George Mosse and Juan Linz, and on the ten-point definition advanced by Emilio Gentile in 1992 (see below note 6), Payne has elaborated a working model of fascism made up of a tripartite descriptive typology pertaining to: (1) the fascist ideology and goals (such as idealist, vitalist, voluntarist philosophy and the creation of a new nationalist state based on multiclass national economic structure); (2) the fascist negations (anti-fascism, anti-communism, and anti-conservatorism); and (3) the style of organization (such as "authoritarian, charismatic, personal style of command"). In its first version (1980a), this model emphasized the fascist negations; in the current 1995 edition, the positive fascist characteristics take pre-eminence over "negations;" in addition, Payne pays more attention to the fascist culture, the mythical structure of the fascist ideology, and its relation to religion.

Payne's model of fascism is inductive, in the sense that it is derived from the study of the history and main features of interwar European fascism, and not from general theoretical principles. His working definition does not involve a sublimation or exaggeration of the main traits of fascism, but a typological classification of its existing, historical features. Payne's model of fascism is thus a comparative taxonomy of generic fascism or, in his own words, "a general inventory of the common characteristics of fascist movements," and not an ideal-typical model of its essence. Since some of these characteristics are not exclusively fascist but are shared by other types of contemporary political movements, in evaluating the (non-)fascist nature of historical movements, researchers have to confront them with the whole set of characteristics, in their entirety. Payne emphasizes the unavoidable analytical limits of theoretical models of generic fascism: the similarities of fascist movements do not exclude original characteristics of various national manifestations.

This theoretical model of fascism is meant to serve as "an analytical device for purposes of comparative analysis" (ibid. 6). Payne applies it to provide a comparative overview of the history of fascist movements in interwar Europe and in some non-European context. His narrative history of fascist movements employs a long-term perspective: it begins with the origins of fascist ideology in the turn-of-the-century intellectual movements, continues with a discussion of major centers for the elaboration of the fascist ideology and of few examples of proto-fascism, and accounts for the strong impact of World War I on the emergence of fascism. Fascist movements and regimes are divided into several categories: Italian Fascism and German National-Socialism, which are treated extensively in separate chapters given their originality, their political importance, and the influence they exercised outside the borders of the two countries; and fascism in other European countries, divided into major and minor movements. In the category of major movements, Payne places fascist organizations in Austria, Romania, Hungary and Spain, on the count that these movements originated in the 1920s, exhibited a considerable mass appeal, and even managed to establish fascist or quasi-fascist regimes. In the category of minor or abortive fascist movements, Payne places various fascist organizations in France, the Low Countries, Great Britain, Scandinavia, Switzerland, Czechoslovakia, Finland, Portugal, Greece, Poland, Bulgaria, the Baltic States, and Yugoslavia. His analysis of fascism outside Europe focuses on Japan, China, South Africa, Latin America, the United States, and the Middle East.

On the basis of this historical overview, in the second part of his book, Payne advances a retrodictive theory of fascism, referring to the specific interwar constellation of cultural, political, social, economic and international historical factors necessary for the emergence of fascism as a significant mass movement. Fascism was a mass phenomenon in the new states created in the 1860 and 1870s, such as Germany, Italy, Austria, Hungary and Romania, which exhibited an unconsolidated democracy and went through a crisis of identity and international status. In these countries, fascism manifested with vigor as the most original and radical revolutionary form of nationalism. Although it profoundly marked interwar Europe, fascism nevertheless failed to obtain political dominance and to attain genuine world significance. Moreover, since the constellation of historical factors responsible for the accession of fascism cannot repeat itself, Payne asserts that interwar fascism is over as a historical phenomenon; the cultural residue of fascism can, however, still give birth to novel forms of authoritarian nationalism.

BIBLIOGRAPHY

Payne, Stanley G. (1961). *Falange: A History of Spanish Fascism* (Stanford, CA: Stanford University Press).

Payne, Stanley G. (1967). *Franco's Spain* (New York: Crowell).

Payne, Stanley G. (1973). *A History of Spain and Portugal*, 2 vols. (Madison, WI: University of Wisconsin Press).

Payne, Stanley G. (1980a). "The Concept of Fascism," in Stein Ugelvik Larson, Bernt Hagtvet, and Jan Petter Myklebust (eds.), *Who Were the Fascists? Social Roots of European Fascists* (Bergen: Universitetsforlaget), 14–25.

Payne, Stanley G. (1980b). *Fascism: Comparison and Definition* (Madison, WI: University of Wisconsin Press).

Payne, Stanley G. (1987). *The Franco Regime, 1936–1975* (Madison, WI: University of Wisconsin Press).

Payne, Stanley G. (1995). *A History of Fascism, 1914–1945* (Madison, WI: The University of Wisconsin Press).

Payne, Stanley G. (1999). *Fascism in Spain, 1923–1977* (Madison, WI: University of Wisconsin Press).

Payne, Stanley G. (2004). *The Spanish Civil War, the Soviet Union, and Communism* (New Haven, CT: Yale University Press).

* * *

At the end of the twentieth century *fascism* remains probably the vaguest of the major political terms. This may stem from the fact that the word itself contains no explicit political reference, however abstract, as do *democracy, liberalism, socialism,* and *communism.* To say that the Italian *fascio* (Latin *fasces,* French *faisceau,* Spanish *haz*) means "bundle" or "union" does not tell us much.[1] Moreover, the term has probably been used more by its opponents than by its proponents, the former having been responsible for the generalization of the adjective on an international level, as early as 1923. *Fascist* has been one of the most frequently invoked political pejoratives, normally intended to connote "violent," "brutal," "repressive," or "dictatorial." Yet if *fascism* means no more than that, then Communist regimes, for example, would probably have to be categorized as among the most fascist, depriving the word of any useful specificity.

Definition in fact bedeviled the original Italian Fascists from the beginning.[2] The problem is compounded by the fact that whereas nearly all Communist parties and regimes have preferred to call themselves Communist, most of the movements in interwar Europe commonly termed fascist did not in fact use the name for themselves. The dilemmas of definition and categorization which arise are so severe that it is not surprising that some scholars prefer to call putative fascist movements by their individual names alone without applying the categorical adjective. Still others deny that any such general phenomenon as fascism—as distinct from Mussolini's own Italian movement—ever existed. Finally, the great majority of the hundreds of authors of works on fascism or individual fascist movements make little or no effort to define the term and simply assume that their readers will understand and presumably agree with the approach, whatever that may be.

This book argues that it is useful to treat fascism as a general type or generic phenomenon for heuristic and analytic purposes, just as other categories of political forces are so treated. As Arthur L. Stinchcombe has observed, "Whenever a large number of variables go together, so that specific values of one are always associated with specific values of another, the creation of typologies, or sets of type-concepts, such as the chemical elements, is scientifically useful."[3] Like all general types and concepts in political analysis, generic fascism is an abstraction which never existed in pure empirical form but constitutes a conceptual device which serves to clarify the analysis of individual political phenomena.

If fascism is to be studied as a generic and comparative phenomenon, it has first to be identified through some sort of working description. Such a definition must be derived from empirical study of the classic interwar European movements. It must be developed as a theoretical construct or an ideal type, for all general political concepts are broadly based abstractions. Thus no single movement of the group under observation would necessarily be found to have announced a program or self-description couched in the exact terms of this definition. Nor would such a hypothetical definition be intended to imply that the individual goals and characteristics identified were necessarily in every case unique to fascist movements, for most items might be found in one or more other species of political movements. The contention would be, rather, that *taken as a whole* the definition would describe what all fascist movements had in common without trying to describe the additional unique characteristics of each individual group. Finally, for reasons to be discussed later, the definition might refer only to interwar European fascist movements and not to a presumed category of fascist regimes or systems.

Any definition of common characteristics of fascist movements must be used with great care, for fascist movements differed from each other as significantly as they held notable new features in common. A general inventory of their distinctive characteristics is therefore useful, not as a full and complete definition of such movements in and of themselves, but only as an indication of the chief characteristics that they shared which distinguish them (in most respects, but not absolutely) from other kinds of political forces.

The problems involved in reaching an inductive set of characteristics may be illustrated by reference to the six-point "fascist minimum" postulated by Ernst Nolte, who helped to initiate the "fascism debate" of the 1960s and 1970s.[4] It consists of a set of negatives, a central organizational feature, a doctrine of leadership, and a basic structural goal, expressed as follows: anti-Marxism, antiliberalism, anticonservatism, the leadership principle, a party army, and the aim of totalitarianism. This typology is helpful as far as it goes and correctly states the fascist negations, yet it does not describe the positive content of fascist philosophy and values and makes no concrete reference to economic goals.

More recently, Roger Griffin has sought to achieve elegance, parsimony, and precision through the definition of fascism as "a genus of political ideology whose mythic core in its various permutations is a palingenetic form of populist ultra-nationalism."[5] This once more is accurate and useful, referring tersely to the cross-class populist appeal of fascist politics and its grounding in ultranationalism. Fascist ideology was certainly "palingenetic"; that is, it emphasized above all the rebirth of the national spirit, culture, and society. Yet leftist, moderate, conservative, and extreme right-wing nationalisms are also frequently "palingenetic," for the rebirth and re-creation of the nation are goals fundamental to many different forms of nationalism. Similarly, there have been nonfascist populist revolutionary forms of nationalism, such as that of the MNR in Bolivia in 1952, that were also palingenetic, so that the qualification of "populist" does not serve adequately to restrict and to specify. Finally, as we shall see, Griffin's definition—while admirably succinct—cannot describe certain of the central characteristics fundamental to a definition of fascism.

Indeed, the uniqueness and complexity of fascism cannot be adequately described without recourse to a relatively complex typology, however laudable the principle of parsimony may be. Thus in his authoritative article on *fascismo* for the new *Enciclopedia Italiana* (1992), Emilio Gentile presents the "constituent elements for an orientative definition of fascism" in a dense list of ten complex points.[6]

The common characteristics of fascist movements were grounded in specific philosophical and moral beliefs, a new orientation in political culture and ideology,

Table I.1 Typological description of fascism

A. *Ideology and goals:*
Espousal of an idealist, vitalist, and voluntaristic philosophy, normally involving the attempt to realize a new modern, self-determined, and secular culture
Creation of a new nationalist authoritarian state not based on traditional principles or models
Organization of a new highly regulated, multiclass, integrated national economic structure, whether called national corporatist, national socialist, or national syndicalist
Positive evaluation and use of, or willingness to use, violence and war
The goal of empire, expansion, or a radical change in the nation's relationship with other powers

B. *The fascist negations:*
Antiliberalism
Anticommunism
Anticonservatism (though with the understanding that fascist groups were willing to undertake temporary alliances with other sectors, most commonly with the right)

C. *Style and organization:*
Attempted mass mobilization with militarization of political relationships and style and with the goal of a mass party militia
Emphasis on aesthetic structure of meetings, symbols, and political liturgy, stressing emotional and mystical aspects
Extreme stress on the masculine principle and male dominance, while espousing a strongly organic view of society
Exaltation of youth above other phases of life, emphasizing the conflict of generations, at least in effecting the initial political transformation
Specific tendency toward an authoritarian, charismatic, personal style of command, whether or not the command is to some degree initially elective

---

generally common political goals, a distinctive set of negations, common aspects of style and somewhat novel modes of organization—always with notable differences in the specific character of these new forms and ideas among the various movements. To arrive at a criterial definition applicable to all the interwar fascist movements sensu stricto, it becomes necessary therefore to identify common points of ideology and goals, the fascist negations, and also special common features of style and organization.[7] The descriptive typology in Table I.1 is suggested merely as an analytic device for purposes of comparative analysis and definition. It does not propose to establish a rigidly reified category but a wide-spectrum description that can identify a variety of differing allegedly fascist movements while still setting them apart as a group from other kinds of revolutionary or nationalist movements. Individual movements might then be understood to have also possessed further doctrines, characteristics, and goals of major importance to them that did not necessarily contradict the common features but were added to them or went beyond them. Similarly, an individual movement might differ somewhat with regard to one or two individual criteria but nonetheless conform generally to the overall description or ideal type.

The term *fascist* is used not merely for the sake of convention but because the Italian movement was the first significant force to exhibit those characteristics as a new type and was for a long time the most influential. It constituted the type whose ideas and goals were the most readily generalized, particularly when contrasted with racial National Socialism.

It has often been held that fascism had no coherent doctrine or ideology, since there was no single canonical or seminal source and since major aspects of fascist ideas were contradictory and nonrationalist. Yet fascist movements did possess basic philosophies that were eclectic in character and in fact, as Roger Eatwell has pointed out, represented a kind of synthesis of concepts from varied sources.[8] Griffin reminds us that all ideology contains basic contradictions and nonrational or irrational elements, usually tending toward utopias that cannot ever be realized in practice. Fascist ideology was more eclectic and nonrational than some others, but these qualities did not prevent its birth and limited development.

The extreme nationalism of each fascist movement inevitably produced certain distinct or idiosyncratic features in each group, so that every fascist organization tended to differ more from its fellows in other countries than, for example, any given Communist party in comparison with other Communist groups. Different national emphases did not, however, blur a common physiognomy based on the common fascist beliefs and values.

Fascist ideology, unlike that of most of the right, was in most cases secular but, unlike the ideology of the left and to some extent of liberals, was based on vitalism and idealism and the rejection of economic determinism, whether of Manchester or Marx. The goal of metaphysical idealism and vitalism was the creation of a new man, a new style of culture that achieved both physical and artistic excellence and that prized courage, daring, and the overcoming of previously established limits in the growth of a superior new culture which engaged the whole man. Fascism was not, however, nihilistic, as many critics charged. Rather, it rejected many established values—whether of left, right, or center—and was willing to engage in acts of wholesale destruction, sometimes involving the most ghastly mass murder, as "creative destruction" to usher in a new utopia of its making, just as Communists murdered millions in the name of an egalitarian utopia.

Fascist ideas have often been said to stem from opposition to the Enlightenment or the "ideas of 1789," when in fact they were a direct by-product of aspects of the Enlightenment, derived specifically from the modern, secular, Promethean concepts of the eighteenth century. The essential divergence of fascist ideas from certain aspects of modern culture lay more precisely in the fascist rejection of rationalism, materialism, and egalitarianism—replaced by philosophical vitalism and idealism and the metaphysics of the will, all of which are also intrinsically modern. Fascists aspired to recover what they considered the true sense of the natural and of human nature (themselves originally eighteenth-century concepts) in opposition to the reductionist culture of modern materialism and prudential egotism.

Fascists strongly reflected the preoccupation with decadence in society and culture that had been growing since the mid-nineteenth century. They believed that decadence could only be overcome through a revolutionary new culture led by new elites, who would replace the old elites of liberalism and conservatism and of the left.

The free man of developed will and determination would be self-assertive like few before him, but he would also be able to transvalue and go beyond himself and would not hesitate to sacrifice himself for the sake of those ideals. Such modern formulations rejected nineteenth-century materialism but did not represent anything that could be called a reversion to the traditional moral and spiritual values of the Western world before the eighteenth century. They represented a specific effort to achieve a modern, normally atheistic or agnostic form of transcendance and not, in Nolte's words, any "resistance to transcendance." Griffin has aptly observed that fascist doctrine encouraged self-assertion and self-transcendance at the same time.

One key modality in which fascist movements seemed to parallel certain religious groups was the projection of a sense of messianic mission, typical of utopian revolutionary movements. Each had the goal of realizing a new status and mode of being for its nation, but the fascist ambitions typically paralleled those of other secular revolutionary movements in functioning within an immanent, this-worldly framework, rather than the otherworldly transcendance of religious groups.

Fundamental to fascism was the effort to create a new "civic religion" of the movement and of its structure as a state. This would build a system of all-encompassing myths that would incorporate both the fascist elite and their followers and would bind together the nation in a new common faith and loyalty. Such civic religion would displace preceding structures of belief and relegate supernatural religion to a secondary role, or to none at all.

This orientation has sometimes been called political religion, but, though there were specific examples of religious or would-be "Christian fascists," fascism basically presupposed a post-Christian, postreligious, secular, and immanent frame of reference. Its own myth of secular transcendance could earn adherents only in the absence or weakness of traditional concepts of spiritual and otherworldly transcendance, for fascism sought to re-create nonrationalist myth structures for those who had lost or rejected a traditional mythic framework. Ideologically and politically, fascism could be successful only to the extent that such a situation existed.

Fascists were even more vague about the shape of their ultimate utopia than were members of most other revolutionary groups, because their reliance on vitalism and dynamism produced a mode of "permanent revolution" that almost by definition could take no simple, clear final form. They sought nothing so seemingly clear-cut as the classless society of Marxists or the stateless society of anarchists but rather an expansive nationalism built of dynamic tension ever seeking new expression. This generated an inherent irrationality that was itself one of the greatest handicaps, if not the greatest, that fascist movements had to overcome.

Much of the confusion surrounding interpretation of the fascist movements stems from the fact that only in a very few instances did they succeed in passing to the stage of governmental participation and only in the case of Germany did a regime in power succeed in carrying out the broader implications of a fascist doctrine, and even then incompletely. It is thus difficult to generalize about fascist systems or the fascist doctrine of the state, since even the Italian variant was seriously compromised. All that can be established with clarity is that fascist aspirations concerning the state were not limited to traditional models such as monarchy, mere personal dictatorship, or even corporatism but posited a radical new secular system, authoritarian and normally republican. Yet to specify the full aim of totalitarianism, as has Nolte, seems unwarranted, for, unlike Leninism, fascist movements never projected a state doctrine with sufficient centralization and bureaucratization to make possible complete totalitarianism. In its original Italian meaning, the sense of the term was more circumscribed. This problem will be treated in greater detail in subsequent chapters.

Least clear within fascist ideology was the issue of economic structure and goals, but in fact all fascist movements generally agreed on a basic orientation toward economics. This subordinated economic issues to the state and to the greater well-being of the nation, while retaining the basic principle of private property, held inherent to the freedom and spontaneity of the individual personality, as well as certain natural instincts of competitiveness. Most fascist movements espoused corporatism, beginning with the Italian prototype, but the most radical and developed form of fascism, German National Socialism, explicitly rejected formal corporatism (in part because of the pluralism inherent in it). The frequent contention of Marxist writers that the aim of fascist movements was to prevent economic changes in class relationships is not borne out by the movements themselves, but since no fascist movement ever fully completed the elaboration of a fascist economic system, the point remains theoretical. What fascist movements had in common was the aim of a new functional relationship for the social and economic systems, eliminating the autonomy (or, in some proposals, the existence) of large-scale capitalism and major industry, altering the nature of social status, and creating a new communal or reciprocal productive relationship through new priorities, ideals, and extensive governmental control and regulation. The goal of accelerated economic modernization was often espoused, though in some movements this aspect was muted.

Equally if not more important was the positive evaluation of violence and struggle in fascist doctrine. All revolutionary mass movements have initiated and practiced violence to a greater or lesser degree, and it is probably impossible to carry violence to greater lengths than have some Leninist regimes, practitioners of, in the words of one Old Bolshevik, "infinite compulsion." The only unique feature of the fascist relationship to violence was the theoretical evaluation by many fascist movements that violence possessed a certain positive and therapeutic value in and of itself, that a certain amount of continuing violent struggle, along the lines of Sorelianism and extreme Social Darwinism, was necessary for the health of national society.

Fascism is usually said to have been expansionist and imperialist by definition, but this is not clear from a reading of diverse fascist programs. Most were indeed imperialist, but all types of political movements and systems have produced imperialist policies, while several fascist movements had little interest in or even rejected new imperial ambitions. Those which appeared in satisfied national or imperialist states were generally defensive rather than aggressive. All, however, sought a new order in foreign affairs, a new relationship or set of alliances with respect to contemporary states and forces, and a new status for their nations in Europe and the world. Some were frankly oriented toward war, while others merely prized military values but projected no plans for aggression abroad. The latter sometimes sought a place of cultural hegemony or other nonmilitary forms of leadership.

Though fascism generally represented the most extreme form of modern European nationalism, fascist ideology was not necessarily racist in the Nazi sense of mystical, intra-European Nordic racism, nor even necessarily anti-Semitic. Fascist nationalists were all racists only in the general sense of considering blacks or non-Europeans inferior, but they could not espouse Germanicism because most of the movements were not Germanic. Similarly, the Italian and most western European movements were not initially—or in some cases ever—particularly anti-Jewish. All fascist movements were nonetheless highly ethnicist as well as extremely nationalist, and thus they held the potential for espousing doctrines of inherent collective superiority for their nations that could form a functional parallel to categorical racism.

The nature of the fascist negations is clear enough. As "latecomers" (in Linz's phrase), the post-World War I radical nationalist movements that we call fascist had to open new political and ideological space for themselves, and they were unique in their hostility to all the main currents, left, right, and center. This was complicated, however, by the need to find allies in the drive for power. Since such movements emerged mostly in countries with established parliamentary systems and sometimes relied disproportionately on the middle classes, there was no question of their coming to power through coups d'état or revolutionary civil wars, as have Leninist regimes. Though Fascists in Italy established a short-lived tactical alliance with the right center and in Portugal with the anarchist left, their most common allies lay on the right, particularly on the radical authoritarian right, and Italian Fascism as a fully coherent entity became partly defined by its merger with one of the most radical of all right authoritarian movements in Europe, the Italian Nationalist Association (ANI). Such alliances sometimes necessitated tactical, structural, and programmatic concessions. The only two fascist leaders who actually rose to power, Hitler and Mussolini, began their governments as multiparty coalitions, and Mussolini, despite the subsequent creation of a one-party state, never fully escaped the pluralist compromise with which he had begun. Moreover, since the doctrines of the authoritarian right were usually more precise, clear, and articulate—and often more practical—than those of the fascists, the capacity of the former for ideological and programmatic influence was considerable. Nonetheless, the ideas and goals of fascists differed in fundamental respects from those of the new authoritarian right, and the intention to transcend right-wing conservatism was firmly held, though not always clearly realized in practice.

Most fascist movements did not achieve true mass mobilization, but it was nonetheless characteristic that such was their goal, for they always sought to transcend the elitist parliamentary cliquishness of poorly mobilized liberal groups or the sectarian exclusiveness and reliance on elite manipulation often found in the authoritarian right. Together with the drive for mass mobilization went one of the most characteristic features of fascism, its attempt to militarize politics to an unprecedented degree. This was done by making militia groups central to the movement's organization and by using military insignia and terminology in reenforcing the sense of nationalism and constant struggle. Party militia were not invented by fascists but by nineteenth-century liberals (in countries such as Spain and Portugal) and later by the extreme left and radical right (such as Action Française). In interwar Spain the predominant "shirt movements" practicing violence were those of the revolutionary left. The initial wave of central European fascism, however, was disproportionately based on World War I veterans and their military ethos. In general, the party militia played a greater role and were developed to a greater extent among fascists than among leftist groups or the radical right.

The novel atmosphere of fascist meetings struck many observers during the 1920s and 1930s. All mass movements employ symbols and various emotive effects, and it might be difficult to establish that the symbolic structure of fascist meetings was entirely different from that of other revolutionary groups. What seemed clearly distinct, however, was the great emphasis on meetings, marches, visual symbols, and ceremonial or liturgical rituals, given a centrality and function in fascist activity which went beyond that found in the left revolutionary movements. The goal was to envelop the participant in a mystique and community of ritual that appealed to the aesthetic and the spiritual sense as well as the political.

This has aptly been called theatrical politics, but it went beyond mere spectacle toward the creation of a normative aesthetics, a cult of artistic and political beauty that built upon the broad diffusion of aesthetic forms and concepts in much of nineteenth-century society to create a "politics of beauty" and a new visual framework for public life. More than any other new force of the early twentieth century, fascism responded to the contemporary era as above all a "visual age" to be dominated by a visual culture. This relied on stereotypes of form and beauty drawn from neoclassical concepts as well as key modern images of the nineteenth and early twentieth centuries. Standard motifs included the representation of male and female bodies as the epitome of the real and the natural, almost always in poses that emphasized the dynamic and muscular, even though normally balanced by a posture of discipline and self-control.[9]

Another fundamental characteristic was extreme insistence on what is now termed male chauvinism and the tendency to exaggerate the masculine principle in almost every aspect of activity. All political forces in the era of fascism were overwhelmingly led by and made up of men, and those that paid lip service to women's equality in fact seem to have had little interest in it. Only fascists, however, made a perpetual fetish of the virility of their movement and its program and style, stemming no doubt from the fascist militarization of politics and need for constant struggle. Like that of many rightist and also some leftist groups, the fascist notion of society was organic and always made a place for women, but in that relationship the rights of the male were to enjoy predominance.[10] Griffin has termed this fascist reality a "radical misogyny or flight from the feminine, manifesting itself in a pathological fear of being engulfed by anything in external reality associated with softness, with dissolution, or the uncontrollable."[11] No other kind of movement expressed such complete horror at the slightest suggestion of androgyny.

Nearly all revolutionary movements make a special appeal to young people and are disproportionately based on young activists. By the 1920s even moderate parliamentary parties had begun to form their own young people's sections. Fascist exaltation of youth was unique, however, in that it not only made a special appeal to them but also exalted youth over all other generations, without exception, and to a greater degree than any other force based itself on generational conflict. This no doubt stemmed in part from the lateness of fascism and the identification of the established forces, including much of the left, with leaders and members from the older, prewar generation. It also stemmed in part from the organic concept of the nation and of youth as its new life force, and from the predominance of youth in struggle and militarization. The fascist cult of daring, action, and the will to a new ideal was inherently attuned to youth, who could respond in a way impossible for older, feebler, and more experienced and prudent, or more materialistic, audiences.

Finally, we can agree with Gaetano Mosca, Vilfredo Pareto, and Roberto Michels that nearly all parties and movements depend on elites and leadership but some recognize the fact more explicitly and carry it to greater lengths. The most unique feature of fascism in this regard was the way in which it combined populism and elitism. The appeal to the entire people and nation, together with the attempt to incorporate the masses in both structure and myth, was accompanied by a strong formal emphasis on the role and function of an elite, which was held to be both uniquely fascist and indispensable to any achievement.

Strong authoritarian leadership and the cult of the leader's personality are obviously in no way restricted to fascist movements. Most of them began on the basis of elective leadership—elected at least by the party elite—and this was true even of the National Socialists. There was nonetheless a general tendency to exalt leadership, hierarchy, and subordination, so that all fascist movements came to espouse variants of a *Führerprinzip*, deferring to the creative function of leadership more than to prior ideology or a bureaucratized party line.

If these fundamental characteristics are to be synthesized into a more succinct definition, fascism may be defined as "a form of revolutionary ultra-nationalism for national rebirth that is based on a primarily vitalist philosophy, is structured on extreme elitism, mass mobilization, and the *Führerprinzip*, positively values violence as end as well as means and tends to normatize war and/or the military virtues."[12]

Three faces of authoritarian nationalism

Comparative analysis of fascist-type movements has been rendered more complex, and often more confused, by a common tendency to identify these movements with more conservative and rightist forms of authoritarian nationalism in the interwar period and after. The fascist movements represented the most extreme expression of modern European nationalism, yet they were not synonymous with all authoritarian nationalist groups. The latter were pluriform and highly diverse, and in their typology they extended well beyond or fell well short of fascism, diverging from it in fundamental ways.

The confusion between fascist movements in particular and authoritarian nationalist groups in general stems from the fact that the heyday of fascism coincided with a general era of political authoritarianism that on the eve of World War II had in one form or another seized control of the political institutions of most European countries. It would be grossly inaccurate to argue that this process proceeded independent of fascism, but neither was it merely synonymous with fascism.

It thus becomes crucial for purposes of comparative analysis to distinguish clearly between fascist movements per se and the nonfascist (or sometimes protofascist) authoritarian right. During the early twentieth century there emerged a cluster of new rightist and conservative authoritarian forces in European politics that rejected moderate nineteenth-century conservatism and simple old-fashioned reaction in favor of a more modern, technically proficient authoritarian system distinct from both leftist revolution and fascist radicalism. These forces of the new right may in turn be divided into elements of the radical right and the more conservative authoritarian right.[13] (For suggested examples, see Table I.2.)

The new right authoritarian groups combated many of the same things that fascists opposed (especially liberalism and Marxism) and did espouse some of the same goals. Moreover, there were numerous instances of tactical alliances—usually temporary and circumstantial—between fascists and right authoritarians, and sometimes even cases of outright fusion, especially between fascists and the radical right, who always stood rather closer to fascists than did the more moderate and conservative authoritarian right. Hence contemporaries tended to lump the phenomena together, and this has been reenforced by subsequent historians and commentators who tend to identify fascist groups with the category of the right or extreme right.[14] Yet to do so is correct only insofar as the intention is to separate all authoritarian forces opposed to both liberalism and Marxism and to assign them the arbitrary label of *fascism* while ignoring the basic differences between them. It is a little like identifying Stalinism and Rooseveltian democracy because both were opposed to Hitlerism, Japanese militarism, and western European colonialism.

Fascism, the radical right, and the conservative authoritarian right differed among themselves in a variety of ways. In philosophy, the conservative authoritarian right,

Table I.2 Three faces of authoritarian nationalism

Country	Fascists	Radical Right	Conservative Right
Germany	NSDAP	Hugenburg, Papen, Stahlhelm	Hindenburg, Brüning, Schleicher
Italy	PNF	ANI	Sonnino, Salandra
Austria	NSDAP	Heimwehr	Christian Socials, Fatherland Front
Belgium	late Rex, Verdinaso, Légion Nationale		early Rex, VNV
Estonia		Veterans' League	Päts
France	Faisceau, Francistes, PPF, RNP	AF, Jeunesses Pat., Solidarité Française	Croix de Feu, Vichy
Hungary	Arrow Cross, National Socialists	"Right Radicals"	Horthy, National Union Party
Latvia	Thunder Cross		Ulmanis
Lithuania	Iron Wolf	Tautininkai	Smetona
Poland	Falanga, OZN	National Radicals	Pilsudski, BBWR
Portugal	National Syndicalists	Integralists	Salazar/UN
Romania	Iron Guard	National Christians	Carolists
South Africa	Greyshirts	Ossewabrandwag	National Union
Spain	Falange	Carlists, Renovación Española	CEDA
Yugoslavia	Ustasa	Zbor, Orjuna	Alexander, Stojadinovic

and in many instances also the radical right, based themselves upon religion more than upon any new cultural mystique such as vitalism, nonrationalism, or secular neoidealism. Hence the "new man" of the authoritarian right was grounded on and to some extent limited by the precepts and values of traditional religion, or more specifically the conservative interpretations thereof. The Sorelianism and Nietzscheanism of core fascists were repudiated in favor of a more practical, rational, and schematic approach.

If fascists and conservative authoritarians often stood at nearly opposite poles culturally and philosophically, various elements of the radical right tended to span the entire spectrum. Some radical right groups, as in Spain, were just as conservative culturally and as formally religious as was the conservative authoritarian right. Others, primarily in central Europe, tended increasingly to embrace vitalist and biological doctrines not significantly different from those of core fascists. Still others, in France and elsewhere, adopted a rigidly rationalistic position quite different from the nonrationalism and vitalism of the fascists, while trying to adopt in a merely formalistic guise a political framework of religiosity.

The conservative authoritarian right was only anticonservative in the very limited sense of having partly broken with the parliamentary forms of moderate parliamentary conservatism. It wished, however, to avoid radical breaks in legal continuity, if at all possible, and normally proposed only a partial transformation of the system in a more authoritarian direction. The radical right, by contrast, wished to destroy the existing political system of liberalism root and branch. Even the radical right, however, hesitated to embrace totally radical and novel forms of authoritarianism and normally harkened back to a reorganized monarchism or an eclectic neo-Catholic corporatism or some combination thereof. Both the radical and the conservative authoritarian right tempered their espousal of elitism and strong leadership by invoking traditional legitimacies to a considerable degree. The conservative authoritarian right preferred to avoid novelty as much as possible in forming new elites, as in dictatorship, while the radical right was willing to go further on both points, but not so far as the fascists.

The conservative authoritarian right usually, though not always, drew a clear distinction between itself and fascism, whereas the radical right sometimes chose deliberately to blur such differences. In the fascist vertigo that afflicted so much of European nationalism in the 1930s, however, even some sectors of the conservative authoritarian right adopted certain of the trappings of fascism, though they neither desired nor would have been able to reproduce all the characteristics of generic fascism.

Though the conservative authoritarian right was sometimes slow to grasp the notion of mass politics, it sometimes managed to exceed the fascists in mobilizing mass support, drawing on broad strata of rural and lower-middle-class people. The radical right was normally the weakest of all three sectors in popular appeal, for it could not compete with the fascists in a quasirevolutionary cross-class mobilization campaign and could not hope for the backing of the broad groups of more moderate elements who sometimes supported the conservative authoritarian right. To an even greater degree than the latter, the radical right had to rely on elite elements of established society and institutions (no matter how much they wished to change political institutions), and their tactics were aimed at manipulation of the power structure more than at political conquest from outside that would draw on popular support.

Thus the radical right often made a special effort to use the military system for political purposes, and if worst came to worst it was willing to accept outright praetorianism—rule by the military—though mostly in accordance with radical right principles. The fascists were the weakest of these forces in generating support among the military, for the conservative authoritarian right might in moments of crisis expect even more military assistance than could the radical right, since its legalism and populism could more easily invoke principles of legal continuity, discipline, and popular approval. Consequently efforts by both the conservative authoritarian right and the radical right to organize their own militia usually stopped short of paramilitary competition with the armed forces. By contrast, fascists sought only the neutrality or in some cases the partial support of the military while rejecting genuine praetorianism, realizing full well that military rule per se precluded fascist rule and that fascist militarization generated a sort of revolutionary competition with the army. Hitler was able to make his power complete only after he had gained total dominance over the military.

When, conversely, the new system was led by a general—Franco, Pétain, Antonescu—the fascist movements were relegated to a subordinate and eventually insignificant role. Mussolini, by contrast, developed a syncretic or polycratic system which recognized broad military autonomy while limiting that of the party.

Contrary to a common assertion, economic development was a major goal of groups in all three categories, though there were exceptions (perhaps most notably the early Portuguese Estado Novo). The fascists, as the most "modernizing" of these sectors, gave modern development greater priority (again with some exceptions), though depending on national variations, some radical right and conservative authoritarian groups also gave it major priority. Right radicals and conservative authoritarians almost without exception became corporatists in formal doctrines of political economy, but the fascists were less explicit and in general less schematic.

One of the major differences between fascists and the two rightist sectors concerned social policy. Though all three sectors advocated social unity and economic harmony, for most groups of the radical and conservative authoritarian right this tended to mean freezing much of the status quo. The question of fascism and revolution will be taken up later, but suffice it to say here that the fascists were in general more interested in changing class and status relationships in society and in using more radical forms of authoritarianism to achieve that goal. The rightist sectors were simply more rightist—that is, concerned to preserve more of the existing structure of society with as little alteration as possible, except for promoting limited new rightist elites and weakening the organized proletariat.

The conservative authoritarian right was in general less likely to advocate an aggressive form of imperialism, for that in turn would imply more drastic domestic policies and incur new risks of the kind that such movements were primarily designed to avoid. The same, however, could not necessarily be said of the radical right, whose radicalism and promilitaristic stance often embraced aggressive expansion. Indeed, elements of the radical right were frequently more imperialistic than the moderate or "leftist" (social revolutionary) elements within fascism.

As a broad generalization, then, the groups of the new conservative authoritarian right were simply more moderate and generally more conservative on every issue than were the fascists. Though it had taken over some of the public aesthetics, choreography, and external trappings of fascism by the mid-1930s, the conservative authoritarian right in its style emphasized direct conservative and legal continuity, and its symbolic overtones were more recognizably traditional.

The radical right, on the other hand, often differed from fascism, not by being more moderate, but simply by being more rightist. That is, it was tied more to the existing elites and structure for support, however demogogic its propaganda may have sounded, and was unwilling to accept fully the cross-class mass mobilization and implied social, economic, and cultural change demanded by fascism. It sought a radically distinct political regime with radically distinct content, but it sought to avoid major social changes and any cultural revolution (as distinct from radical cultural reform). In some respects, with regard to violence, militarism, and imperialism, however, the radical right was almost as extreme as were the fascists (and sometimes, with regard to individual aspects, even more so). Such differences will be more easily understood in the concrete examples to be discussed in the chapters that follow.

NOTES

1 One of the first German works on Italian Fascism, by the Social Democrat Fritz Schotthöfer, aptly observed that "Fascism has a name that tells us nothing about the spirit and goals of the movement. A fascio is a union, a league; Fascists are unionists and Fascism a league-type organization [Bündlertum]." Schotthöfer, *Il Fascio. Sinn und Wirklichkeit des italienischen Fascismus* (Frankfurt, 1924), 64. For further discussion of the problem, see the chapter "Was ist Faschismus: politischer Kampfbegriff oder wissenschaftliche Theorie?" in W. Wippermann, *Faschismustheorien* (Darmstadt, 1989), 1–10.

2 In this study the names of the Italian Fascist Party and its immediate antecedents, members, and components will be capitalized, while the terms *fascism* and *fascist* used in a broader and more generic sense will not.

3 A. L. Stinchcombe, *Constructing Social Theories* (New York, 1968), 43.

4 E. Nolte, *Die Krise des liberalen Systems und die faschistischen Bewegungen* (Munich, 1968), 385.

5 R. Griffin, *The Nature of Fascism* (London, 1991), 44. This is the best work on the comparative analysis of fascism to appear in the past decade.

6 Gentile defines *fascismo* as follows:

"1 a mass movement with multiclass membership in which prevail, among the leaders and militants, the middle sectors, in large part new to political activity, organized as a party militia, that bases its identity not on social hierarchy or class origin but on the sense of comradeship, believes itself invested with a mission of national regeneration, considers itself in a state of war against political adversaries and aims at conquering a monopoly of political power by using terror, parliamentary tactics, and deals with leading groups, to create a new regime that destroys parliamentary democracy;

"2 an 'anti-ideological' and pragmatic ideology that proclaims itself antimaterialist, anti-individualist, antiliberal, antidemocratic, anti-Marxist, is populist and anticapitalist in tendency, expresses itself aesthetically more than theoretically by means of a new political style and by myths, rites, and symbols as a lay religion designed to acculturate, socialize, and integrate the faith of the masses with the goal of creating a 'new man';

"3 a culture founded on mystical thought and the tragic and activist sense of life conceived as the manifestation of the will to power, on the myth of youth as artificer of history, and on the exaltation of the militarization of politics as the model of life and collective activity;

"4 a totalitarian conception of the primacy of politics, conceived as an integrating experience to carry out the fusion of the individual and the masses in the organic and mystical unity of the nation as an ethnic and moral community, adopting measures of discrimination and persecution against those considered to be outside this community either as enemies of the regime or members of races considered inferior or otherwise dangerous for the integrity of the nation;

"5 a civil ethic founded on total dedication to the national community, on discipline, virility, comradeship, and the warrior spirit;

"6 a single state party that has the task of providing for the armed defense of the regime, selecting its directing cadres, and organizing the masses within the state in a process of permanent mobilization of emotion and faith;

"7 a police apparatus that prevents, controls, and represses dissidence and opposition, even by using organized terror;

"8 a political system organized by a hierarchy of functions named from the top and crowned by the figure of the 'leader,' invested with a sacred charisma, who commands, directs, and coordinates the activities of the party and the regime;

"9 a corporative organization of the economy that suppresses trade union liberty, broadens the sphere of state intervention, and seeks to achieve, by principles of technocracy and solidarity, the collaboration of the 'productive sectors' under the control of the regime, to achieve its goals of power, yet preserving private property and class divisions;

"10 a foreign policy inspired by the myth of national power and greatness, with the goal of imperialist expansion." (Quoted with the kind permission of Professor Gentile.)

7 The idea of a tripartite definition was first suggested to me by Juan J. Linz at a conference in Bergen, Norway, in June 1974. The specific content is my own.

8 R. Eatwell, "Towards a New Model of Generic Fascism," *Journal of Theoretical Politics* 4:1 (April 1992): 1–68; *idem*, "Fascism," in *Contemporary Political Ideologies*, ed. R. Eatwell and A. Wright (London, 1993), 169–91.

9 Here I am drawing particularly on George L. Mosse's unpublished paper "Fascist Aesthetics and Society: Some Considerations" (1993).

10 The term *organic* will be used in this study in a general sense to refer to concepts of society in which its various sectors are held to bear a structured relationship to each other that serves to define and delimit their roles and rights, taking precedence over the identities and rights of individuals.

11 Griffin, *Nature of Fascism* 198.

12 A different but noncontradictory and partially parallel approach may be found in Eatwell's "Towards a New Model of Generic Fascism."

13 These analytic distinctions bear some analogy to Arno J. Mayer's differentiation of the counterrevolutionary, reactionary, and conservative in his *Dynamics of Counterrevolution in Europe, 1870–1956* (New York, 1971). Yet as will be seen below, my criterial definitions differ considerably in content from Mayer's.

14 For example, J. Weiss, *The Fascist Tradition* (New York, 1967). In a somewhat similar vein, Otto-Ernst Schüddekopf's *Fascism* (New York, 1973), which is distinguished primarily for being one of the best illustrated of the volumes attempting to provide a general treatment of fascism, also tends to lump various fascist and right authoritarian movements and regimes together.

4

FASCISM

General introduction

Roger Griffin

A theoretically-sophisticated, highly innovative and prolific scholar, the British political scientist Roger Griffin has been in the past two decades at the very centre of major debates in the field of comparative fascist studies. His approach builds on the fruitful analytical tradition initiated by Juan Linz and continued by E. Weber, Z. Sternhell, S. Payne, J. A. Gregor and G. Mosse, among others, bringing it to new conclusions in a subtle and original manner. Griffin's path-breaking theory of fascism put forward in his monumental monograph The Nature of Fascism *(1991) has been highly influential, being accepted by numerous scholars as the basis of a new emerging consensus in the field.*

This article—which originally served as an introduction to an edited collection of primary sources on fascism (1995) to accompany and support the theoretical framework advanced in The Nature of Fascism—*concisely summarizes Griffin's ideal-type model of generic fascism. In his 1991 monograph, Griffin pleaded for a more open framework of analyzing fascism recognizing "the primacy of culture" over politics, the revolutionary nature of fascism, and its genuine mass appeal based on the mobilizing myth of national rebirth, suggestively called "the palingenetic myth". He shared with previous approaches the treatment of fascism as an ideal-type, the effort to arrive at a concise definition of the fascist ideological minimum, the insertion of fascism into a larger political taxonomy as a distinct "genus," and the central importance assigned to the comparison between the theoretical model of generic fascism and historical case studies. Pointing out, in line with Linz, that fascism "cannot be given an absolute definition by social scientists because it is an ideal type" (1991: 26), Griffin adopted a Weberian ideal-type methodology to define the nature of fascism. On this basis, Griffin criticized the typological definition of fascism put forward by Payne (1980) as a confusing "checklist" of characteristics, and employed a different methodological strategy for building a heuristically useful ideal-type of generic fascism. Adopting Georges*

Sorel's theory of political myth, Griffin argued that fascism can be defined "in terms not of a common ideological component, but of a common mythic core." On this basis, Griffin advanced a new, flexible yet substantive, ideal-type model of the fascist minimum, conveyed by means of a one-sentence definition: "Fascism is a genus of political ideology whose mythic core in its various permutations is a palingenetic form of populist ultra-nationalism" (1991: 26).

This composite definition combines two central components of the fascist ideology: the palingenetic myth of rebirth and regeneration defined as "the vision of a revolutionary new order which supplies the affective power of an ideology" (ibid.: 35); and fascism as "ultra-nationalism," referring to a form of nationalism that explicitly rejects liberal institutions and the humanist legacy of the Enlightenment (ibid.: 37). The contested term populist refers here to "political forces which . . . depend on 'people power' as the basis of their legitimacy" (ibid.: 37).

To the ideological core of fascism, Griffin added a sum of "corollary"—but not definitional—components of fascism (that is, of secondary or tertiary importance), concisely discussed below, such as: its anti-liberal and anti-conservative character; the fact that it tends to operate with a charismatic form of politics; anti-rationalism; racism; internationalism; eclecticism; the heterogeneity of its social support; and the drive toward totalitarianism striving "to create the "total state" with the aim of carrying out a comprehensive scheme of social engineering."

Griffin's conceptual framework of analyzing fascism as a "cultural revolution in nationalist key" concisely captures core common elements of the culturalist research agendas put forward by prominent scholars of fascism in the last decades, thus serving as a potential basis for a new scholarly consensus on generic fascism. The claim that a "new consensus" is emerging in fascist studies was first made by Roger Griffin in the introduction to an edited reader on fascism (1998). In a second, more elaborated review essay on the topic entitled "The Primacy of Culture" (originally published in 2002 and included as Chapter 5 in this volume in an abridged version that leaves out the lengthy historiographical overview), Griffin reiterates his claim, arguing that, in the four years that had passed since his 1998 article, "the evidence of the emergence of a consensual approach to fascism within Anglophone academia has grown rather than faded" (p. 26). To substantiate his argument, Griffin cited in favor of the new consensus not only those scholars who openly and explicitly adopt his theoretical model of generic fascism, but even those scholars who have independently arrived at similar conclusions, or those who, while explicitly opposing Griffin's theoretical model, have in fact reached related or largely compatible conclusions. Certainly, Griffin is well aware that, given the essentially contested nature of the concept of generic fascism, the incipient scholarly consensus is bound to remain minimal and partial, being "virtual rather than actual, its postulation programmatic rather than empirical" (2002: 39). Yet, the new framework of analyzing fascism can lead to a deeper convergence in fascist studies, equilibrating the balance between theoretical works and empirical investigations, and between the attention paid to "core" case studies as opposed to "marginal" ones.

Scholarly reactions to Griffin's model of generic fascism and programmatic agenda of the new consensus cover a large spectrum of opinions, from enthusiastic approval and full adoption to partial alignment, skepticism or open criticism (for a sample of such views, see the Introduction). It is nevertheless undeniable that Griffin's theory of fascism has exerted a paramount influence over the way generic fascism is currently understood and researched.

BIBLIOGRAPHY

Griffin, Roger (1991). *The Nature of Fascism* (New York: St. Martin's Press).
Griffin, Roger (1995). *Fascism* (Oxford: Oxford University Press).
Griffin, Roger (1998). "Introduction," in Roger Griffin, ed. *International Fascism: Theories, Cases, and the New Consensus* (Oxford: Oxford University Press).

*   *   *

This volume in the Oxford Reader series is designed to make available in English a wide selection of texts written by fascist thinkers, ideologues, and propagandists both inside and outside Europe before and after the Second World War. To my knowledge it is the first ever attempt to produce a comprehensive anthology of fascist texts. Why should this be?

One reason is the dubious nature of the exercise itself. To have a Reader in Ethics or Ecology raises no eyebrows, because both subjects are generally associated with potentially positive, life-asserting areas of human endeavour which encompass a rich variety of different arguments and insights from authors ancient and modern. On the other hand, fascism is very much a product of the modern age. (Throughout the notes to the texts I capitalize Mussolini's Fascism, though both upper and lower case were used by contemporaries, and use lower-case 'fascism' to refer to the generic phenomenon. The corresponding adjectives are 'Fascist' and 'fascist' respectively.) Moreover, it is identified with a whole range of forces which crush any genuine human creativity of word or deed: totalitarianism, brainwashing, state terror, social engineering, fanaticism, orchestrated violence, blind obedience. A Reader devoted to fascism might thus be construed as endowing with a bogus aura of serious theoretical content, and even dignity, something which is best regarded as a perversion of the human mind and spirit. Yet there is no reason in principle why primary sources relating to negative aspects of the human condition should be any less worthy of scholarly or general interest than positive ones, a point underlined by the fact that one of the companion volumes in the Oxford Readers series is devoted to war. Moreover, with fascism back in the headlines as a phenomenon in the ascendant, it is arguably high time to renew rather than suspend attempts to come to grips with the ideas and mind-set which lie behind it.

A second argument against such a Reader is the chronic lack of consensus among specialists about what constitutes the 'fascist minimum', that is, the lowest common denominator of defining features to be found in all manifestations of fascism. This is bound up with another unresolved issue, namely whether fascism possesses anything resembling a coherent ideology. Many would be tempted to agree with the historian Hugh Trevor-Roper's verdict that fascist ideology is at bottom no more than 'an ill-sorted hodge-podge of ideas' (Woolf 1981: 20). More recently the social scientist Stephen Turner conceded that:

> The puzzle of fascism remains, half a century after the conclusion of the war against the fascist regimes. [...] No sociology of the interwar era grasped fascism fully or produced an unambiguously 'correct' political recipe for dealing with it. The continuing dispute over the character of fascism and the interwar 'fascist' regimes suggests that these are inappropriately high standards for social science. But the failure to meet them indicates that the pretensions to political wisdom of social science are inappropriate as well.
>
> (Turner and Käsler 1992: 11–12)

Fortunately for me, and, I hope, for the reader, I was able to accept Oxford University Press's invitation to prepare this volume without compromising deep-seated convictions about the nature of fascism, convictions which make an anthology of excerpts from primary sources not just feasible but highly desirable. Indeed, in the book which staked my own claim to provide a more cogent and useful definition of fascism than previous ones, I declared that a 'regrettable lacuna in this text is an appendix providing extensive and wide-ranging samples of fascist ideology, both inter-and post-war, to illustrate the highly nuanced and varied permutations that the same core of ideas can generate' (Griffin 1993: 20).

The background to such a remark is the central importance which my theory attributes to the role of ideology in the definition and dynamics of fascism. I am one of a minority of academics concerned with generic fascism who take its ideas seriously as a key to understanding the characteristic policies, institutions, and style of its politics (though it should be stressed that other members of this fairly exclusive 'club', such as Ernst Nolte, Zeev Sternhell, Stanley Payne, George Mosse, Emilio Gentile, James Gregor, and Roger Eatwell, are far from seeing eye to eye on what these ideas actually are). Moreover, my approach happens to be restrictive enough to exclude many ultra-right movements and regimes, but inclusive enough to encompass phenomena from outside Europe, as well as treating post-war fascism as a prolific source of important variations on the inter-war models. This makes the range of phenomena sampled in this book strictly delimited while being richly variegated.

What are the essentials of this approach? To summarize the elaborate methodological argument put forward in *The Nature of Fascism*, it starts by assuming that there can be no objective definition of fascism, since, like all generic concepts in the human sciences, 'fascism' is at bottom an ideal type. In other words, it ultimately results from an act of idealizing abstraction which produces an artificially tidy model of the kinship that exists within a group of phenomena which, despite their differences, are sensed to have certain features in common. The assumption that some such ideal-typical common denominator exists arguably lies at the basis of all Readers in political thought, be it liberalism, anarchism, socialism, communism, ecologism, feminism, conservatism, or any other 'ism'. To turn fascism into a taxonomic term which can be used in scientific enquiry is to select certain attributes of phenomena associated with fascism as definitional or essential (thereby relegating others to being secondary or peripheral), and assemble these in sterile laboratory conditions into a schematic conceptual model. As Max Weber, who pioneered 'ideal type' theory, recognized, such a model is essentially a utopia, since it cannot correspond exactly to anything in empirical reality, which is always irreducibly complex, 'messy', and unique. Definitions of generic terms can thus never be 'true' to reality, but they can be more or less useful in investigating it ('heuristically useful') when applied as conceptual tools of analysis. The continuing debate over what constitutes fascism merely indicates that no academic consensus has so far grown up about which of the many available ideal types of it is the most useful (see Griffin 1993: 8–22).

The second premiss of my approach is that it is possible to define fascism, or identify the 'fascist minimum', in terms not of a common ideological component, but of a common mythic core. This suggests that it is just as misguided to seek to establish that there is a common denominator between all forms of fascism at the level of articulated ideas as to deny fascism any coherent ideological content. The coherence exists not at the surface level of specific, verbalized 'ideas', but at the structural level of the core myth which underlies them, serving as a matrix which determines which types of thought are selected in certain national cultures and how they are arranged into a political ideology, whether at the level of theory, policies, propaganda, culture, or of semiotic 'behaviour', such as the use of symbols or the enactment of ritual. The term 'myth' here draws attention, not to the utopianism, irrationalism, or sheer madness of the claim it makes to interpret contemporary reality, but to its power to unleash strong affective energies through the evocative force of the image or vision of reality it contains for those susceptible to it. This generic mythic image, laden with potential mobilizing, and even mass-mobilizing, force, may, like any psychological matrix or archetype (such as the Hero, or Paradise), take on a wide variety of surface formulations according to the particular cultural and historical context in which it is expressed.

The mythic core that forms the basis of my ideal type of generic fascism is the vision of the (perceived) crisis of the nation as betokening the birth-pangs of a new order. It crystallizes in the image of the national community, once purged and rejuvenated, rising phoenix-like from the ashes of a morally bankrupt state system and the decadent culture associated with it. I was drawn to exploring the heuristic value of this ideal type as a result of noticing recurrent references in Fascist texts to the alleged decay of the 'old Italy' (its senility, decadence, sickness, decline, disintegration, collapse, debilitation, etc.) and the urgent need for its rebirth (reawakening, regeneration, health, revival, rejuvenation, invigoration, etc.) in a 'new' Italy. Such *topoi* bore an uncanny resemblance to the slogans of other 'putative' fascist movements, such as the Nazis' cry of 'Germany awake', the British Union of Fascists' campaign for a 'Greater Britain', or the Romanian Iron Guard's call for the appearance of *omul nou*, the New Man.

The idea that a 'nation' is an entity which can 'decay' and be 'regenerated' implies something diametrically opposed to what liberals understand by it. It connotes an organism with its own life-cycle, collective psyche, and communal destiny, embracing in principle the whole people (not just its ruling élites), and in practice all those who ethnically or culturally are 'natural' members of it, and are not contaminated by forces hostile to nationhood. In this way of conceiving the nation—sometimes referred to by academics as 'integral nationalism', 'hypernationalism' or 'illiberal nationalism'—it becomes a higher reality transcending the individual's life, which only acquires meaning and value in so far as it contributes directly to the whole organism's well-being. Extensive study of the primary sources of Fascism and of other fascisms convinced me that at the core of its mentality was the *idée fixe* of devoting, and, if necessary sacrificing, individual existence to the struggle against the forces of degeneration which had seemingly brought the nation low, and of helping relaunch it towards greatness and glory. The fascist felt he (and it generally was a 'he') had been fatefully born at a watershed between national decline and national regeneration, a feeling that alchemically converted all pessimism and cultural despair into a manic sense of purpose and optimism. He knew himself to be one of the 'chosen' of an otherwise lost generation. His task it was to prepare the ground for the new breed of man, the *homo fascistus*, who would instinctively form part of the revitalized national community without having first to purge himself of the selfish reflexes inculcated by a civilization sapped by egotism and materialism.

Within fascist studies the recurrent obsession with national rebirth and the need for a 'new man' seemed to have been frequently noted without being recognized as a candidate for the 'fascist minimum'. A deliberate exercise in 'idealizing abstraction' turned this theme into fascism's sole necessary definitional trait. To sum up the mythic core in a single concept involved resuscitating what is an obscure and obsolescent word in English, 'palingenesis' (meaning rebirth), and coining the expression 'palingenetic ultra-nationalism'. The premise of this Reader is thus that generic fascism can be defined in terms of this expression, or to repeat the formula expounded at length elsewhere (Griffin 1993: 2): *Fascism is a genus of political ideology whose mythic core in its various permutations is a palingenetic form of populist ultra-nationalism.* From this assumption about the matrix of fascist ideology, a number of features of generic fascism follow which have a profound bearing on how it operates in practice both as an opposition movement and as a regime.

1. *Fascism is anti-liberal.* Fascism's call for the regeneration of the national community through a heroic struggle against its alleged enemies and the forces undermining it involves the radical rejection of liberalism in all its aspects:

pluralism, tolerance, individualism, gradualism, pacifism, parliamentary democracy, the separation of powers, the doctrine of 'natural rights', egalitarianism, the rectilinear theory of progress, the open society, cosmopolitanism, one-worldism, etc. The important proviso to this aspect of fascist movements is that, though they oppose parliamentary democracy and their policies would in practice inevitably lead to its destruction, they may well choose to operate tactically as democratic, electoral parties. Indeed, they may go to considerable lengths to camouflage the extent of their hostility to liberalism through euphemism and dishonesty, reserving their rhetoric of destruction of the 'system' and of revolution for the initiated.

2. *Fascism is anti-conservative.* The centrality to fascism of a myth of the nation's regeneration within a new order implies a rejection of illiberal conservative politics (for example, an absolutist system in which sovereignty is invested in a hereditary monarchy or oligarchy), as well as of liberal and authoritarian conservative solutions to the current crisis which imply a restoration of law and order that does not involve social renewal. In other words, in the context of fascism 'rebirth' means 'new birth', a 'new order', one which might draw inspiration from the past but does not seek to turn the clock back. However, two factors have obscured fascism's revolutionary, forward-looking thrust. First, in order to achieve power in the inter-war period fascism was forced to ally itself or collude with conservative forces (the army, Civil Service, Church, industrialists, reactionary bourgeois, etc.) on the basis of common enemies (such as communism, cosmopolitanism) and common priorities (such as law and order, the family).

Second, fascist ideologues frequently attach great importance to allegedly glorious epochs in the nation's past and the heroes which embody them. They do so not out of nostalgia, but to remind the people of the nation's 'true' nature and its destiny to rise once more to historical greatness. In *The Eighteenth Brumaire of Louis Bonaparte* Marx expressed an insight into the readiness of Napoleon III's regime to use myths based on the past to enlist popular support for the Second Empire which is equally pertinent to fascism. He saw that the 'awakening of the dead [...] served the purpose of glorifying the new struggles, not parodying the old; of magnifying the given task in imagination, not fleeing from its solution in reality; of finding once more the spirit of revolution, not making a ghost walk around again'.

3. *Fascism tends to operate as a charismatic form of politics.* Since, to use Weberian terminology, fascism rejects both the traditional politics of the *ancien régime* and the legal-rational politics of liberalism and socialism, it follows that it is predisposed to function as a *charismatic* form of politics. This does not necessarily involve the epitome of such politics, the leader cult. Historically, some forms of fascism (for example Valois's *Le Faisceau*) have opted for a technocratic, managerial model of the planned society, while others (for example, the French New Right) focus exclusively on the battle for cultural hegemony of ideas which would form the basis of a new order. In practice, though, there has been a marked tendency for fascist movements not to be containable within the framework of conventional

party politics and to take the form of cadre or mass 'movements' with strong liturgical or cultic elements overtly appealing to highly charged collective emotions rather than to the individual's capacity for reasoned judgement.

All political ideologies are prone to assume a charismatic aspect when they operate as revolutionary forces—liberalism did, for example, in the French Revolution. It is significant, though, that fascism *remained* a charismatic form of politics in the two cases where it managed to install itself in power. Symptoms of this trait are the 'oceanic assemblies' and all-pervasive *littorio* (the *fasces*, or axe and rods carried as a symbol of power by lictors in ancient Rome) in the New Italy, and the Nuremberg rallies and the omnipresent *Hakenkreuz* (swastika) in the Third Reich. Both Fascism and Nazism as regimes were characterized by the centrality of the leader cult, the celebration of public over private space and time, and the constant attempt to use social engineering to regiment people into organizations with an ethos of activism and enthusiasm.

Such phenomena have often led specialists to use religious terminology in the analysis of fascism, claiming that it is a 'secular', 'civic', 'lay', or 'political' religion, replete with 'millenarian' or 'eschatological' energies. Such phrases are in order only so long as it is borne in mind that fascism sets out to operate on human society through human agency and within human history. It thus lacks a genuine metaphysical dimension and is the utter antithesis and destroyer of all genuine religious faith. Its compulsive use of the religious language of sacrifice, belief, resurrection, redemption, spirit, and its attacks on scepticism, doubt, materialism, consumerism, hedonism as the signs of moral decay are to be understood as the hallmarks of a modern political ideology seeking to offer a panacea to the malaise and anomie of contemporary society. They do not signify a literal regression to an earlier age of religious certainties (in which the nation as the focus of populist energies and the concept of the State as the creator of the ideal society did not exist).

4. *Fascism is anti-rational*. Consistent with its tendentially charismatic nature is fascism's frequent repudiation of rationalism and its overt celebration of myth. It is not so much irrational as anti-rational, seeing the most distinctive human faculty not in the reason celebrated in the Enlightenment, humanist, and positivist tradition, but in the capacity to be inspired to heroic action and self-sacrifice through the power of belief, myth, symbols, and *idées-forces* such as the nation, the leader, identity, or the regeneration of history. It should be stressed that fascism's anti-rationalism has not prevented it from producing a vast amount of highly articulate ideological writings, some of them displaying great erudition and theoretical verve, nor from turning selected components of the Western philosophical and scientific traditions into grist for its own mill.

5. *Fascist 'socialism'*. If it is the core mobilizing myth of the imminent (or, under a regime, ongoing) rebirth of the nation that forms the definitional core of fascism, it follows that the various fascist negations (anti-communism, anti-liberalism, etc.) are corollaries of this 'positive' belief, not definitional components. The same myth

explains the recurrent claim by fascist ideologues that their vision of the new order is far from anti-socialist. Clearly it axiomatically rejects the internationalism and materialism of Marxism, but may well present the rejuvenation of the national community as transcending class conflict, destroying traditional hierarchy, expunging parasitism, rewarding all productive members of the new nation, and harnessing the energies of capitalism and technology in a new order in which they cease to be exploitative and enslaving. Indeed, in the inter-war period, when Bolsheviks were confident that their cause represented the next stage of human progress, many fascists made the counter-claim that their solution to the crisis of civilization embodied the only 'true' socialism, an assertion often associated with a commitment to corporatist economics, national syndicalism, and a high degree of state planning.

6. *Fascism's link to totalitarianism.* Also implicit in fascism's mythic core is the drive towards totalitarianism. For from being driven by nihilism or barbarism, the convinced fascist is a utopian, conceiving the homogeneous, perfectly co-ordinated national community as a total solution to the problems of modern society. Yet any attempt to expunge all decadence necessarily leads to the creation of a highly centralized 'total' State with draconian powers to carry out a comprehensive scheme of social engineering. This will involve massive exercises in regimenting people's lives, and the creation of an elaborate machinery for manufacturing consensus through propaganda and indoctrination combined with repression and terror directed against alleged enemies, both internal and external, of the new order.

In this way any regime's attempt to realize the fascist utopia would lead in practice to an Orwellian dystopia, though the actual scale of destruction and atrocities it caused would vary considerably according to how the ideal 'national community' was conceived and the degree of co-operation in the general public and crucial areas of State power that it could count on. As a result the 'totalitarian State' in Italy became a grim travesty of what Mussolini intended, namely a new order in which the individual's life was to be infused with moral purpose and heroism by becoming symbiotically linked to that of the State. The term thus acquired instead its chilling post-war connotations. It is worth remembering, however, that modern society is intrinsically and irreducibly heterogeneous, and that no 'totalitarian' regime, fascist or not, has ever managed to stamp out elements of pluralism and polycentrism, no matter what lengths it has gone to.

Fortunately for humanity only two fascist movements have been in a position to attempt to implement their total solutions to society's alleged woes, namely Fascism and Nazism. All others have so far in one way or another been marginalized, emasculated, or crushed, though in the inter-war period some conservative authoritarian regimes (such as Franco's Spain or Antonescu's Romania) temporarily incorporated fascist movements, a ploy used by the Third Reich in several of its puppet states (for example, Norway and Hungary).

7. *The heterogeneity of fascism's social support.* The sociological implication of this ideal type of fascism is that it has no specific class basis in its support. If the

middle classes were over-represented in the membership of Fascism and Nazism, this is because specific socio-political conditions made a significant percentage of them more susceptible to a palingenetic form of ultra-nationalism than to a palingenetic form of Marxism or liberalism. There is nothing in principle which precludes an employed or unemployed member of the working classes or an aristocrat, a city-dweller or a peasant, a graduate, or someone 'educationally challenged' from being susceptible to fascist myth. Nor is the fascist mentality exclusively the domain of men or the young, though its stress on heroism and the need for a new élite easily lends itself to militarism and hence to male chauvinism, especially when heroism is associated with physical courage, violence, war, and imperialism.

8. *Fascist racism*. By its nature fascism is racist, since all ultra-nationalisms are racist in their celebration of the alleged virtues and greatness of an organically conceived nation or culture. However, fascist ultra-nationalism does not necessarily involve biological or Social Darwinian concepts of race leading to eugenics, euthanasia, and attempted genocide. Nor does it necessarily involve anti-Semitism, or hatred directed against any particular group perceived as culturally or genetically different, or simply 'internal enemies' of the nation (such as Roma/Gypsies, Muslims, Hungarians, homosexuals, blacks). Obviously, if such elements of 'heterophobia' (fear and hatred of those felt to be 'different') are already present in the particular political culture of the nation where fascism arises, it is more than likely that they will be incorporated into its myth of national decadence and hence into the policies for creating the new order.

Fascism is also intrinsically anti-cosmopolitan, axiomatically rejecting as decadent the liberal vision of the multi-cultural, multi-religious, multi-racial society. However, this does not necessarily lead to a call for other races to be persecuted *per se*, but may express itself 'merely' in a campaign of propaganda and violence against their presence as 'immigrants' who have abandoned their 'natural' homeland. This type of fascism thus tends to produce an *apartheid* mentality calling for ethnically pure nation states, for 'foreigners' to go back, or be returned, to 'where they belong', and a vitriolic hatred of 'mixed marriages' and cultural 'bastardization'.

9. *Fascist internationalism*. Fascism, though anti-internationalist in the sense of regarding national distinctiveness and identity as primordial values, is quite capable of generating its own form of universalism or internationalism by fostering a kindred spirit and bond with fascists in other countries engaged in an equivalent struggle for their own nation's palingenesis, often against common enemies (for example, liberals, communists, and, if they are white supremacists, non-white races). In Europe this may well lead to a sense of fighting for a common European homeland on the basis of Europe's alleged cultural, historical, or even genetic unity in contrast to non-Christian, non-Indo-European/Aryan peoples (for instance, Muslims, 'Asian' Soviet or Chinese communists) or degenerate ones (citizens of the USA or the 'Third World'). Within such a Europe, national or ethnic identities would, according to the fascist blueprint, be strengthened, not

diluted. (The practical impossibility of realizing such a scheme does not worry fascists, since the nebulousness and impracticality of all their long-term goals are crucial to the mythic power they exert.)

10. *Fascist eclecticism.* Perhaps the most important corollary of our ideal type for the purposes of this Reader, however, is its suggestion that fascism pre-exists any particular externalization in the form of articulated or concretized thought. Inevitably each fascism will be made in the image or imagining of a particular national culture, but even within the same movement or party its most influential ideologues will inevitably represent a wide range of ideas and theories sometimes quite incompatible with each other *except at the level of a shared mythic core of palingenetic ultra-nationalism.* Fascism is thus inherently syncretic, bringing heterogeneous currents of ideas into a loose alliance united only by the common struggle for a new order. As a result there is in fascist thought a recurrent element of (and sometimes declared intention of) synthesis. This befits a latecomer to the European political scene which not only had to fight for its own political space against rival modern ideologies (liberalism, conservatism, socialism, communism), but legitimate itself ideologically in a culture teeming with well-established ideas and thinkers. What conditions the content and thrust of fascist eclecticism is the myth of national rebirth.

It is worth adding that, in its self-creation through synthesis, fascist ideology can draw just as easily on right-wing forms of thought (such as mutations of Christianity, racism, élitist and decadent aesthetics, Nietzscheanism, occultism, forms of illiberalism, integral nationalism, etc.) as on forms of left-wing thought (for example, derivatives of anti-materialist or utopian socialism, such as syndicalism). It is also implicit in what has been said that fascism is not necessarily confined to inter-war Europe, but can flourish wherever the stability of Western-style liberal democracy is threatened by a particular conjuncture of destabilizing forces (see Griffin 1993: ch. 8).

If read in the light of the above considerations, many of the excerpts of fascist writings assembled in this volume will not appear simply as isolated samples of an aberrant genus of political thought. They should cumulatively acquire a deeper resonance as different products of the same ideological matrix as permutations of the same rationale for a war of 'creative destruction' to be waged against a particular status quo. Within the shell of their utopianism lies the seed of a totalitarian nightmare for all those who in one way or other are not deemed to belong within the regenerated national community or fit into the new order. Whether their author is a lone dreamer, the mouthpiece of a purely 'cultural' think-tank, the spokesman of an activist paramilitary movement, the propagandist of a campaigning electoral party, the policy-maker of an organization within a fascist regime, or the charismatic leader himself, he is giving specific form to the latent mythic core which defines fascism and determines its various attributes in historical reality.

It is this mythic core which accounts for the sharp distinction which this volume implicitly draws between the fascist regimes in Italy and Germany bent on creating a revolutionary new social and ethical order on the basis of mass mobilization, and the many authoritarian right-wing regimes which have been spawned by the twentieth century whose fundamental aim is the reactionary one of using mechanisms of intensive social engineering and repression to maintain the social status quo. Many military dictatorships fit into this latter category, and are characterized by an absence of genuine ideology or myth of renewal: when they have recourse to a leader cult, appeal to populist nationalist sentiment or stress traditional family or religious values, it is simply to manufacture consensus and conceal and ideological vacuum. In the inter-war period, however, a number of authoritarian regimes consciously adopted some of the trappings and style of Fascism or Nazism to generate an illusion of national rejuvenation while resolutely resisting any populist pressures to change the system from below. Examples are Salazar's Portugal, Franco's Spain, Pétain's 'Vichy' France, Dollfuss's Austria, Horthy's Hungary, Antonescu's Romania, Vargas's Brazil, and Tōjō's Japan. The creation of a single-party state, the founding of a youth movement or a 'shirted' militia, and the rhetoric of national reawakening do not in themselves constitute fascism unless they are associated with a core ideology of rebirth which is as anti-conservative as it is anti-liberal or anti-Bolshevik whatever compromises it has had to make with existing élites and institutions to achieve and retain power in practice. Such regimes I have termed elsewhere 'para-fascist' (Griffin 1993: 120–4). They have been ignored in this volume as a source of original texts.

[...]

A few further points might usefully be made here before readers embark on, or dip into, the texts which follow. It is in the nature of the exercise of assembling such an anthology that it can only scratch the surface of fascism as a textual phenomenon, and that it has both a degree of Anglophone and Anglocentric bias (particularly evident in Parts IV and V) in the materials selected. What is less self-evident is that a fundamental editorial decision has been made to sample as many forms of fascism as possible rather than offer a few lengthy specimens of it. This has meant a series of heavily cropped snapshots to illustrate fascism's extraordinarily protean quality rather than some more detailed portraits. Even so, countless smaller movements have been left out of the album, ranging from insignificant ones, like the Fascist Brown Shirts in Canada, to much more important ones like the Dutch National Socialists led by Mussert, eventually nominal head of state under the Nazis. I would urge readers who want to go into more depth than this volume permits to study any full-length primary source(s) available to them, hopefully with renewed curiousity and a sharpened eye for the typical features of its 'discourse'. (Incidentally, I would be grateful to receive samples of primary sources relating to fascisms I have omitted.)

On a quite different tack, I would like to emphasize that this is an academic work, not a journalistic one. It necessarily involves operating a particular ideal type of the term 'fascist' as a taxonomic category of political analysis. As such it is not being used as a term of personal abuse, nor does the selection of a particular passage imply its author's guilt by association for the suffering inflicted on millions of people as a result of the policies pursued by the two fascist regimes half a century ago, nor for the acts of criminality and violence carried out by contemporary fascist movements committed to racist or terrorist violence. The subject under investigation here is 'fascism' as a political myth and an ideology, not the 'fascist' as a personality type or historical actor. Clearly there is a causal connection between the two, but the connection is not immediate or simple. In particular, there are numerous cases of modern ideologues who produce texts which my ideal type identifies as fascist, but who stay aloof from paramilitary or mass movements and repudiate violence, seeing culture, not the streets or parliament, as the prime arena in which the battle for national, European, or Aryan regeneration is to be fought. They would be likely to resent their ideas being categorized as fascist, whatever the structural links between their ideas and the mythic matrix I have identified. Moreover, it is quite possible to contribute to some of the newer discourses of fascism, such as revisionism or the New Right, without harbouring any sympathy with organized fascism at all, but simply by having written works which can be cited as mitigating circumstances for the atrocities committed by Nazism, or as theoretical justification for the rejection of egalitarian ideals.

By now the reader should be assured that this anthology has no 'revisionist' intent of euphemizing fascism, let alone vindicating it. To grant fascism full ideological status, to claim that the well-springs of fascism are idealism and the longing for a new and better age, or to defend its compatibility with modernity is not to rehabilitate it. In a sense, assembling this volume has been like preparing scores of laboratory slides to exhibit different species of the same genus of disease for the benefit of those concerned by the damage it can wreak or engaged in the search for a cure. If fascists were to peruse this volume I trust they would have no difficulty alighting on passages which chime in with their diagnosis of the ills of contemporary society, but that they would find that the accompanying notes smack unpleasantly of the decadent liberal values which they reject. The 'true' readers are all those who want to understand better the fascist syndrome in order to inoculate themselves, and even others, against it.

As I write in the summer of 1994, 'post-fascist' politicians have recently been elected to the new Italian Government and to the European Parliament, while radically fascist sentiments are being openly expressed by the publicity machine of Vladimir Zhirinovky, who according to some Pundits might just conceivably become the next Russian president. Meanwhile, all over the world groups of population are retrenching into their ethnic or cultural identity, many in a spirit of radical intolerance of the equivalent identity of others. I would like to think that by the time these lines are read this volume will have lost rather than increased its relevance, so that it can be seen as a companion to historical studies rather than to current affairs. But this is probably to indulge in wishful thinking. A close causal relationship exists in modern societies between political and economic crises and the growth of ultra-nationalism. Given the structural forces now generating such crises in various parts of the globe, I fear that not many years will pass before this selection requires an appendix of new passages to bring it up to date, or someone is commissioned to compile an anthology entirely devoted to contemporary forms of rebirth ultra-nationalism. This may be the first Reader in fascism. It is a sign of the times that it seems destined not to be the last.

REFERENCES

Griffin, R.D. (1993) *The Nature of Fascism*, London: Routledge.
Turner, S. and Käsler, D. (eds) (1992) *Sociology Responds to Fascism*, London: Routledge.
Woolf, S.J. (ed.) (1981) *European Fascism*, London: Weidenfeld and Nicolson.

5

THE PRIMACY OF CULTURE

The current growth (or manufacture) of consensus within fascist studies

Roger Griffin

[...]

The claim which I made in 1998 that a 'new consensus' in fascist studies was finally emerging about the nature of fascism as a revolutionary form of ultra-nationalism[15] was thus dubious in more than one respect. First, it was if anything the reformulation of an 'old' consensus on the basis of the area of significant overlap between a group of rival theories which had never quite crystallized into a fully articulated common position when it should have (the early 1980s). Second, being as yet unrecognized, the consensus which I posited in 1998 was virtual rather than actual, its postulation programmatic rather than empirical. It was more like a conciliatory 'offer' made during protracted negotiations than a closing 'deal'. Third, sufficient salient differences in approach exist between the members of the 'club'[16] and enough theorists are reticent about joining it[17] or sceptical about the whole notion of defining fascism,[18] as to make the notion of 'consensus' spurious to any onlookers more concerned to highlight division than unity. Fourth, it is in the nature of the liberal human sciences, which are inveterately individualistic and pluralistic despite the countervailing coercive powers of 'schools of thought' and sheer modishness, that any consensus that exists about fundamental aspects of generic phenomena can only be fragmentary, temporary and 'heuristic'. No matter how empirically substantiated, agreement within an academic discipline on a particular definition, which is at bottom merely a conceptual construct, is conventional, and will inevitably wax and wane.[19] Indeed, the life-cycle of paradigms could be seen curiously to mirror microcosmically the one which Spengler reads into entire cultures. Finally, the imagined community of scholars who make up the putative consensus on fascism is far from evenly spread in global terms, being largely restricted to anglophone areas of the social sciences (themselves isolated ivory towers with respect to 'common sense' usage even in their own countries). Key countries such as Italy, Germany, France, the former Soviet Empire (notably Russia), not to mention partially Europeanized academic institutions in the Far East (notably Japan) and in Latin America, have developed a high degree of intellectual autarky in conceptualizing fascism. This apparently places a prohibitively high excise duty on the ruminations of a handful of US, British, Scandinavian and Israeli scholars to the point where the 'models' they produce are treated like luxury imports. It would seem that the world's citadels of learning (mercifully) have a built-in traditionalism in the humanities which immunizes them more effectively from the ravages of cultural globalization than if they were part of more commercialized sectors of cultural production, such as the entertainment industry.

Thus the fact that my duplicitous thesis concerning the emergence of a 'new consensus', which set out to foster the very process of convergence it claimed to discover objectively, met with the approval of none other than the USA's doyen of fascist studies himself, Stanley Payne,[20] would be unlikely to cut much ice with many non-anglophone experts. Nor, for that matter, with any anglophone ones who nurture their own pet theory in a harsh climate where social Darwinian laws have condemned most definitions of fascism to perish of exposure (or lack of it) before they could inspire any concrete empirical research by others.[21] Moreover, serious scholars are likely to be underwhelmed by the fact that in 2000 Microsoft's *Encarta Reference Suite* adopted a version of the 'consensus' definition of fascism to replace Robert Soucy's more traditional theory (used for the 1999 edition) which denied it any genuine revolutionary dimension, even if this may boost its currency among a new generation of anglophone and anglophile cyberscholars. There are thus no grounds for a triumphalist sense that some new paradigm in fascist studies is sweeping all before it, transforming dark to light and dissent to harmony wherever the magic formulas 'holistic third-way nationalism' or 'palingenetic ultra-nationalism' are uttered. In any case, such a mood would imply that hubris and territorial ambition had taken over from the spirit of collaboration and openness to doubt which should always prevail in the humanities.

Yet it is the contention of this article, probably no less tendentious and programmatic than my introduction to *International Fascism*, that in the four years since I postulated its existence, the evidence for the emergence of a consensual approach to fascism within anglophone academia has grown rather than faded.

[…]

The contours of a particular scenario for the future of fascist studies can now be discerned within the portrait of their present state as I have (so partially) drawn it. It is one which would have been unthinkable in the days of ritual breast-beating about the unresolvable fascist conundrum, and is certainly just as open to criticism and scepticism as the idea of an 'emergent consensus' which it subsumes. It predicts a period of increasing convergence and cross-fertilization between comparative fascist studies carried out within the broad framework of the new consensus (constantly evolving and refining itself until its heuristic value is exhausted) and the study of specific aspects of the revolution which particular fascisms planned/plan (as a movement) or undertook (as a regime) in the field of political, social, artistic and intellectual culture, enriched as much by anthropological and psycho-historical insights as by ones drawn from conventional political science and history.

In his incisive critique of Sternhell in the pages of this journal, David Roberts has argued that a key to understanding fascism is to recognize 'the exciting sense of possibility among the creators of fascism, the sense that Italians ... could create a wholly new form of state buttressed by a whole new political culture'. He also issued a timely warning against reducing this culture to unbridled irrationalism, charismatic politics and myth.

> We can find ritual and rhetoric, virility and the body, but we can also find, in written texts, serious rethinking of the Hegelian ethical state for a mass age, serious discussion of the scope for new forms of education, serious reassessment of the legacy of Giuseppe Mazzini in light of the outcomes of Marxism.[59]

If theories of generic fascism can retain a healthy empirical sense of the extraordinary heterogeneity of the genus, while empirical studies of it can be informed by a sophisticated concept of cultural revolution, then the 1990s could come to be looked on as the decade when fascist studies finally came of age. It was a decade which hosted an exciting process of symbiosis between political science and history resulting in a multifaceted but concerted effort by the academic community to unlock the mysteries of fascism and to exorcize its spells. It would signal the symbolic triumph of humanism over one of the more virulent modern ideologies bent on destroying it.

In short, this article aims to foster a healthy dialectic between the 'nomothetic' and the 'idiographic', between the conceptual framework of cultural revolution in nationalist key provided by the new consensus and specific case-studies in the welter of specific theories, policies, measures, organizational structures and institutions embraced or created by fascist movements or the two fascist regimes to bring about the nation's rebirth. The fruits of such a dialectic applied both in 'macro' comparative investigations and 'micro' case-studies could definitively transform fascist studies from the unsightly tangle of conflicting positions which they were once widely perceived to be, into an exemplary source of academic insights into the ideological and political dynamics of contemporary history under the impact of modernity.[60] Thanks to the transformation, the study of fascism would be profoundly humanized. Its experts would no longer be able to get away with focusing on leaders, élites, propaganda, social engineering and national Sonderwege, or with revelling in abstruse hermeneutic model-building, but would, in the words of one commentator, 'have to rush everywhere they get the slightest whiff of human flesh'.[61] Some interesting examples of just such a tendency are already appearing, both on fascist regimes and abortive fascist movements.[62]

The jewels in the crown of the miniature cultural empire created through the growing hegemony of the consensus would be 'native' historians of fascism, most of whom continue to reconstruct events relating to fascism in their country oblivious of how insights drawn from generic fascist studies might enrich their analyses. There are encouraging signs that such a process of assimilation is already in train. Notoriously, Sternhell has made a sustained onslaught on the insular citadels of French historiography in which conventionally the very existence of significant currents of indigenous fascism was denied. More discretely, the study of Salazar and Portuguese fascism has been authoritatively brought into step by Antonio Costa-Pinto,[63] while Spain is gradually being opened up to the realization that 'Franquismo' is not equatable with 'fascismo', not just by foreigner experts such as Sheelagh Eastwood and Stanley Payne,[64] but by homegrown scholars such as Wahnón and Mellón.[65] Elsewhere, Russian neo-fascism is already being interpreted by a convert to the new consensus, Andreas Umland.[66]

Yet in Italy historians are only now being sensitized to current anglophone theories of generic fascism by a few indigenous scholars, notably Emilio Gentile and Alessandro Campi.[67] Even more out on a limb, Wolfgang Wippermann is one of the only notable non-Marxist scholars in Germany to have persistently staked his reputation on the value of the concept of generic fascism to historians of the Third Reich, even if his own theory continues to diverge considerably from the consensus. Hopefully, the extraordinary international success of Ian Kershaw's magisterial biography of Hitler, which makes constant reference to the importance of the myth of national rebirth and renewal to the dramatic increase in Hitler's charismatic powers in the run-up to the 'seizure of power',[68] will persuade German academics to be more open to the new consensus on the definition of generic fascism[69] (even if Kershaw himself never refers to it and studiously avoids the term 'palingenetic'). It would remove another anomaly if US scholars working on the contemporary extreme right also became more alive to its heuristic value in their taxonomies and ideological analyses.[70]

It is by now all too obvious that this article has been less a neutral evaluation of the contention that a new consensus is emerging in fascist studies than a bid to lend a hand in the manufacture of that consensus. But if the scenario I have sketched out proves to be more than a piece of self-indulgent wishful thinking (of a markedly palingenetic bent), it would suggest that what Bosworth calls the 'culturalist school' is here to stay. Indeed, the fertility which it is already displaying as a heuristic framework for empirical studies in comparative fascism lends a certain poignancy to the question which Tim Mason, so keen to locate the nazi dictatorship in a wider context, used for the title of the essay cited earlier, 'Whatever happened to fascism?', which was published in 1991, the very year that the second wave of fascist studies symbolically began. Whether he would have been sufficiently impressed by the answers now being given to overcome his Marxist leanings and accept the notion that what he took to be the 'primacy of politics over economics' was actually the 'primacy of culture over politics'[71] is another matter.

In the defiantly major key of Nietzschean *Lebensbejahung*, the scenario I have sketched here would also throw into relief the full significance of George Mosse's last book, *The Fascist Revolution*, a collection of seminal essays on the centrality of culture to the fascist revolution written over a period of 35 years (the earliest actually preceding by four years the English edition of Nolte's less than seminal contribution). His introduction contains a number of assertions which would once have been considered heretical, but can now be seen as providing authoritative signposts to the future of fascist studies. Here is just one example:

> Fascism considered as a cultural movement means seeing fascism as it saw itself and as its followers saw it, to attempt to understand the movement in its own terms. Only then, when we have grasped fascism from the inside out, can we truly judge its appeal and its power. ... The cultural interpretation of fascism opens up a means to penetrate fascist self-understanding, and such empathy is crucial in order to grasp how people saw the movement, something which cannot be ignored or evaluated merely in retrospect.[72]

I believe that this work could well come to be seen as one of the most significant ever published on generic fascism in this, the formative phase of its study. It would then serve as a fitting monument to an academic who combined historiographical range and depth with methodological and conceptual adventurousness to a degree which should serve as a lesson to all of us left to labour in the same field. There would also be more than a touch of irony in the fact that when that first issue of the *JCH* came out all those years ago, one of its two founding editors had already unwittingly and modestly alighted upon the ideal type of fascism which was to prove empirically the most heuristically valuable of all.

Mosse's own contribution to that issue way back in 1966 is, in this respect, a harbinger of things to come. In reconstructing 'the genesis of fascism' he offers the reader a typically cogent, lucid, and wide-ranging account of the central importance to its initial impact of being identified with the myth of the new man, the cult of youth and an organic view of the world. People turned to it, he explains, because of the prospect which it held out of putting an end to *anomie* and alienation by restoring a sense of belonging and rejuvenating the life of the spirit, thereby bringing about the moral rebirth of society. Nor has Mosse any hesitation in spelling out the vital inference to be drawn from these salient features of fascism as a distinctive form of modern politics. They meant that it was not economics or even politics which provided the focal point of its revolutionary mission. Instead, 'cultural expressions of the true community moved to the forefront as symbols of the new society'.[73]

NOTES

[...]

15 I summarized the area of common ground (consensus) on the fascist minimum in the introduction to *International Fascism. Theories, Causes, and the New Consensus* (London 1998), 14. This definition is cited in Stanley Payne's review article,

'Historical Fascism and the Radical Right', *Journal of Contemporary History*, 35, 1 (January 2000), 110. In the light of the present article I would now modify it to read: 'Fascism is a genus of modern politics which aspires to bring about a total revolution in the political and social culture of a particular national or ethnic community. While extremely heterogeneous in the specific ideology of its many permutations, in its social support, in the form of organization it adopts as an anti-systemic movement, and in the type of political system, regime, or homeland it aims to create, generic fascism draws its internal cohesion and affective driving force from a core myth that a period of perceived decadence and degeneracy is imminently or eventually to give way to one of rebirth and rejuvenation in a post-liberal new order.'

16 See the essay by Roger Eatwell, 'On Defining the Fascist Minimum: The Centrality of Ideology', *Journal of Political Ideologies* 1, 3 (October 1996), who, despite his criticisms of Payne and myself, is still very much a member of the 'club', as is demonstrated by his basic definition of the fascist minimum as a form of 'holistic third-way nationalism' in *Fascism*, op. cit., 11.

17 We shall return to the particular misgivings of Gregor and Paxton later.

18 E.g. John Whittam, *Fascist Italy* (London 1995), 1.

19 See Thomas Burger, *Max Weber's Theory of Concept Formation, History, Laws, and Ideal Types* (Durham, NC 1976), esp. 127–9.

20 Payne, 'Historical Fascism and the Radical Right', op. cit., 109–11.

21 E.g. Paul Hayes, *Fascism* (London 1973); A.J. Gregor, *Italian Fascism and Developmental Dictatorship* (Princeton, NJ 1979); Neil O'Sullivan's *Fascism* (London and Melbourne 1983); Peter Brooker, *Faces of Fraternalism: Nazi Germany, Fascist Italy, and Imperial Japan* (Oxford 1991); and more recently Walter Laqueur, *Fascism. Past, Present, and Future* (New York 1996).

[…]

59 David Roberts, 'How Not to Think about Fascism and Ideology, Intellectual Antecedents and Historical Meaning', *Journal of Contemporary History*, 35, 2 (April 2000), 208.

60 'Modernity under the New Order: The Fascist Project for Managing the Future', Thamesman Publications (Oxford Brookes School of Business imprint), 1994. Downloadable at: http://www.brookes.ac.uk/schools/humanities/staff/moderni.txt

61 Sergio Luzarro, 'The Political Culture of Fascist Italy', *Contemporary European History*, 8, 2 (1999), 334.

62 E.g. Philip Coupland, 'The Blackshirted Utopians', *Journal of Contemporary History*, 33, 2 (April 1998), 255–72; Charles Burdett, 'Journeys to Other Spaces of Fascist Italy', *Modern Italy*, 5, 1 (2000), 7–23.

63 António Costa-Pinto, *Salazar's Dictatorship and European Fascism. Problems of Interpretation* (New York 1995); *The Blue Shirts. Portuguese Fascists and the New State* (New York 2000).

64 Sheelagh Eastwood, *Spanish Fascism in the Franco Era: Falanga Española de las JONS* (New York 1988); Stanley Payne, *Fascism in Spain 1923–1977* (Madison, WI 1999).

65 Sultana Wahnón, 'The Theatre Aesthetics of the Falange', in G. Berghaus (ed.), *Fascism and Theatre* (Oxford 1996). A forthcoming book also informed by the new consensus is Joan Mellón (ed.), *Orden, Jerarquía y Comunidad. Fascismos, Autoritarismos y Neofascismos en la Europa Contemporánea* (Madrid, forthcoming).

66 Andreas Umland, *Vladimir Zhirinovskii in Russian Politics: Three Approaches to the Emergence of the Liberal-Democratic Party of Russia, 1990–1993*, unpublished DPhil dissertation, Freie Universität Berlin (1998); idem, "Wladimir Shirinowskij in der russischen Politik: Einige Hintergründe des Aufstiegs der Liberal-Demokratischen Partei Rußlands", *Osteuropa*, 44, 12 (1994), 1117–31; *idem*, "The Post-Soviet Russian Extreme Right", *Problems of Post-Communism*, 44, 4 (1997), 53–61. Stephen D. Shenfield, *Russian Fascism: Traditions, Tendencies, and Movements* (New York 2001) also uses a modified version of the new consensus in his investigation.

67 Alessandro Campi is editor of the series *Fascismo/Fascismi* which is publishing a series of non-Italian publications on generic fascism as part of an attempt to introduce Italian scholars to approaches to the subject of which they have to date remained generally (blissfully?) unaware. A significant book in this series promises to be Alessandro Campi (ed.), *Il fascismo e i suoi interpreti* (Rome 2001) with essays by many of the 'major players', Italian and foreign, in the field. Meanwhile, Emilio Gentile has produced for the recent volume *Le religioni della politica fra democrazie e totalitarismi* (Roma, Bari 2000), a seminal redefinition of totalitarianism in terms of the sacralization of politics and the attempt to realize a palingenetic vision of the 'new man' which he specifically applies to generic fascism. It has appeared in English as 'The Sacralization of Politics: Definition, Interpretations and Reflections on the Question of Secular Religion and Totalitarianism', *Totalitarian Movements and Political Religions*, 1, 1 (Summer 2000).

68 Ian Kershaw, Hitler (London 1998), vol. 1: Hubris, *passim*.

69 Wippermann is perhaps academia's most faithful follower of fascism: his *Faschismustheorien* (Darmstadt), which was first published in 1972, reached its seventh revised edition in 1997, and he also produced *Europäischer Faschismus im Vergleich, 1922–1982* (Frankfurt 1983). He was recently involved in an impressive initiative in spreading the word further, namely an issue of *Ethik und Sozialwissenschaft*, 11, 2 (2000), 289–334, edited by Werner Loh. It was devoted to the question of generic fascism and is due to appear in book form as W. Wippermann and W. Loh (eds), *'Faschismus' Kontrovers* (Paderborn forthcoming). Conceived as a forum discussion, it featured an article by Wippermann making the case for the term fascism to be more widely used in the non-Marxist generic sense which he gives it (based on the premise that the Italian fascist regime can be construed as the 'real type' of generic fascism), followed by responses from thirteen German political scientists and historians as well as two Americans (Peter Fritzsche, Stanley Payne) and one 'Brit' (R. Griffin).

70 It is a curious paradox that, while it was US academics who pioneered the original drive towards conceptual sophistication in fascist studies, many of their most productive colleagues have yet to recognize the relevance of an ideal type of fascism which stresses its palingenetic thrust in such murky areas as neo-nazism, the 'new' Ku Klux Klan, and new forms of the pagan and religious right. See, for example, Jeffrey Kaplan and Leonard Weinberg, *The Emergence of a Euro-American Radical Right* (New Brunswick, NJ 1998); Jeffrey Kaplan, *Radical Religion in America. Millennarian Movements from the Far Right to the Children of Noah* (Syracuse, NY 1997).

71 Tim Mason, 'The Primacy of Politics. Politics and Economics in National Socialist Germany', in S. Woolf (ed.), *The Nature of Fascism* (London 1968), 165–95.

72 George L. Mosse, *The Fascist Revolution* (New York 1999), x.

73 George L. Mosse, 'The Genesis of Fascism', *Journal of Contemporary History*, 1, 1 (January 1966), 19–20.

6

THE NATURE OF 'GENERIC FASCISM'

The 'fascist minimum' and the 'fascist matrix'

Roger Eatwell*

In the past two decades the British academic Roger Eatwell has been a prominent theoretician of generic fascism (1992; 1996; 1999) and a major historian of comparative fascism in Western Europe (1997). Exposing major shortcomings of four dominant approaches to fascism, namely fascism as an incoherent form of nihilism; fascism as a specific national form; fascism as a European epochal movement; and fascism as a universal concept, in his first major article (1992) Eatwell attempts to "move on" by developing a new model of fascism that would eliminate the prevailing confusion between a concept of fascist ideology (meaning "classification and semantic refinement") and a theory of fascist social support (involving "the testing of hypotheses on concrete case studies").

The starting point of Eatwell's approach is the remark that "the vast literature on fascism adopts a socio-economic approach to the problem of definition." These approaches add important elements to the understanding of the social base and appeal of fascism; yet, while focusing on the "suprastructures" of fascism movements and regimes, they largely ignored "superstructural" features, such as the ideology of fascism. Eatwell acknowledged that "it is useful to distinguish between fascism as a regime, a movement, and an ideology"; however, in line with the "political approach" to fascism developed by major scholars of fascism, he reiterated the primacy of ideology in understanding generic fascism. In his view, the most heuristically useful model of fascism is that which explains its ideology, while providing at the same time the best insights into its history.

Methodologically, Eatwell argues that, given the nature of the fascist ideological syncretism that indiscriminately combined rightist as well as leftist ideas, Weberian ideal-type models cannot capture the main features of fascism, no matter how elaborate and comprehensive they would be. In order to overcome this shortcoming, Eatwell advances his own conceptual model of the "fascism minimum" combining a "one sentence definition"—of the kind provided by Payne and Griffin—with "a four-point core set of annotations" (or synthesis) derived from the study of "primarily European fascism," and suggestively called the "fascist matrix." First, Eatwell's concisely defines fascism as: "An ideology that strives to forge social rebirth based on a holistic-national radical Third Way, though in practice fascism has tended to stress style, especially action and the charismatic leader, more than detailed programme, and to engage in a Manichaean demonisation of its enemies" (1996). This definition incorporates the fascist ideological core underscored by Griffin (the palingenetic drive, defined by Eatwell as social rebirth), but adds to it the idea of fascist synthesis resulting in a "holistic-national Third Way." The definition also attempts to link the ideological core of fascism with the political practice, alluding to the multiple tensions between the fascist ideology, on the one hand, and fascist style, actions and the dominance of the charismatic leadership, on the other. To underscore this point, in his most recent writings, Eatwell proposed a new model of charisma that departs from the Weberian ideal-type to also account for the economic interests of the followers (2006).

Second, Eatwell advances a "spectral-syncretic model" of fascist ideology based on four major themes of generic fascism: (1) natural history, referring to the Fascist general philosophy of history, synthesizing natural and historical arguments about human nature, expressed mainly in campaigns for the creation of the "new man;" (2) geopolitics, referring to the relation between the basic fascist unit (the community, the nation, the race) and larger temporal and spatial units; (3) political economy, referring to the underlying principles behind the fascist economic policy, of which the most important were corporatism, the emphasis on a strong (would-be totalitarian) state, and the idea of economic autarchy; and (4) leadership, activism, party and propaganda, referring to fascist activism as a form of permanent revolution, ideas about the role of the fascist party, hierarchy, collective or charismatic leadership (1992). Fascism's syncretic ideology is crucial to understanding its rise and support.

Eatwell emphasizes the fact that this series of core themes of fascism did not produce a unique set of conclusions in each country that developed fascism, but varied over time and space, balancing between conservative and left-wing visions of the "new man;" between commitment to science and anti-rationalism and vitalism; between Christian faith and the heroism of Classical thought; and between respect for private property of the right and the welfare-ism of the left (1992: 189).

Eatwell's model of fascist ideology as a set of synthesis accommodates a large diachronic as well as synchronic perspective. First, while incorporating Paxton's central insight about the changing nature of fascism over time, Eatwell departs from what he calls "a rigid understanding of fascism stages" to provide "a spectral-syncretic distillation of different phases of fascism" (1992: 174). Second, Eatwell attempts to de-essentialize European interwar fascism, by treating fascism as a genuinely generic phenomenon, including non-European movements such as the Brazilian Integralists, Franco's Spain, Perón's Argentina (but not Pinochet's Chile).

Eatwell's interpretative model ultimately aims to shed light on the mass appeal and political trajectory of fascist movements and on the central policies employed by fascist regimes. Therefore, in a major monograph on fascism (1997), Eatwell tests his model of fascism on the "world of real politics." Based on a comparative sample of four Western European countries (Germany, Italy, France and Britain), Eatwell explores the social appeal of fascism, the importance of national traditions and the role of leadership in accounting for national differences in fascist political programs and trajectory. Eatwell also deals comprehensively with the phenomenon of "neo-fascism" in the four countries since the 1980s.

In this recent article (not previously published in English), Eatwell fine-tunes his theoretical model of generic fascism in view of recent research on the topic. While reiterating the basic premises of his approach, Eatwell redefines his spectral-syncretic model around three core fascist themes: (1) the quest for a new man; (2) the reborn nation; and (3) a new state. Eatwell also underscores a set of ideological sub-themes which corresponds to recent fruitful research directions in fascist studies: the new elite, women and fascism, myths, science, race, the State, leadership, totalitarianism, religion, and the economy. Together, these themes and sub-themes constitute the flexible "matrix" of fascism, each movement forging its own synthesis out of the existing local national tradition and priorities.

BIBLIOGRAPHY

Eatwell, Roger (1992). "Towards a New Model of Generic Fascism," *Journal of Theoretical Politics*, 4: 2, 161–194.

Eatwell, Roger (1996). "On Defining the 'Fascist Minimum': The Centrality of Ideology," *Journal of Political Ideologies*, 1: 3, 303–319.

Eatwell, Roger (1997). *Fascism: A History* (New York: Penguin Books).

Eatwell, Roger (2006). "The Concept and Theory of Charismatic Leadership," *Totalitarian Movements and Political Religions*, 7: 2, 141–156.

Eatwell, Roger (2003). "Reflections on Fascism and Religion," *Totalitarian Movements and Political Religion*, 4: 3, 145–166.

* * *

Introduction

Writing in the late 1980s, Tim Mason lamented 'Whatever Happened to Fascism?'[1] Mason was not referring to the disappearance of the 'f' word from current discourse (to this day, 'fascism' remains a commonplace in popular demonology). Nor was he mourning a dearth of academic books about fascism. Rather, Mason was referring to the decline of the academic view that inter-war Europe was characterised by an explosion of 'fascist' movements and regimes. Outside the Marxisant left (where fascism continues to be viewed as the dictatorship of capitalism in crisis), conventional wisdom had come to hold that 'fascisms' differed notably. Many scholars even held that what had previously been seen as the two core exemplars, Italian Fascism and German National Socialism, were in fact not members of the same party family.[2] Among political historians, one crucial difference was found in the allegedly more formal nature of the Italian Fascist state compared to the mercurial and murderous Nazi regime. Even more commonly, the argument held that the Nazism's virulent racism made it *sui generis*.[3]

Yet by the late 1990s, Roger Griffin could claim that there was a 'new consensus' about the nature of 'generic fascism'.[4] At the turn of the decade, Griffin had set out to delineate a version of what Ernst Nolte in the 1960s had termed the 'fascist minimum'. This involved setting out a brief definition, based mainly on an empathetic reading of fascist doctrine and propaganda. This had led Nolte to see fascism as: 'anti-Marxism seeking to destroy the enemy by the development of a radically opposed yet related ideology ... within the unyielding framework of national self-assertion and autonomy'. At a deeper level, Nolte held that the core of fascism was to be found in its 'resistance to transcendence' (by which he meant hostility to liberalism's and socialism's a priori vision of a 'new man', radically uprooted from tradition).[5] Subsequently, Nolte added a list-form minimum, seeing fascism in terms of: i) anti-Marxism; ii) anti-liberalism; iii) the Führer principle; iv) the paramilitary party; v) the tendency to anti-conservatism; and vi) the aim of totalitarianism.[6] By the 1980s, partly in an attempt to give the 'minimum' more analytical purchase, Nolte was increasingly stressing the anti-Marxist dimension – in particular, by claiming that Nazism was a mirror of the horrors of Soviet communism (an assertion which led to a bitter '*Historikerstreit*' in Germany, as critics held that Nolte was trying to relativise rather than explain the course of Nazi history – especially the Holocaust).[7]

Griffin's 1990s' one sentence minimum held that:

> Fascism is a genus of political ideology whose mythic core in its various permutations is a palingenetic form of populist ultra-nationalism.[8]

Gone was Nolte's focus on what Stanley Payne, in an elegant tripartite re-working of the list approach, has termed fascism's 'negations' (Payne identified the other two definitional dimensions as lying in fascism's style and organisation, and its ideology and goals).[9] Instead, Griffin's line was closer to that of two other pioneers of the empathetic approach – namely, Emilio Gentile and George Mosse.[10] Griffin portrayed fascism as a revolutionary alternative form of modernity, whose mythical goal was the rebirth/palingenesis[11] of a 'new man' after a period of decadence. By 1998, Griffin was claiming that a growing number of scholars were employing the empathetic approach, including the core of his fascist minimum.[12]

However, the claim that a 'new consensus' has emerged is overstated. Many historians continue to ignore the generic fascism debate, or dismiss it as being of little or no use by way of historical explanation. This seems to be particularly true of historians who focus on understanding Nazism's turbulent trajectory.[13]

Griffin's work has unquestionably had an impact on scholars of generic fascism,[14] and on some who have found it fruitful in specific fields, for instance the study of fascist art.[15] But Griffin has his critics even within the growing field of generic fascist studies. In a forthcoming work, David Baker will argue that there are at least two other 'consensi': first, the liberal historiographical approach which rejects the overdetermining elements in any conceptual framework, and secondly variations on the developmental dictatorship school.[16] A new work by Kevin Passmore sees Griffin's approach as essentially a reworking of the totalitarian model.[17] Whilst this is misleading in the sense that Griffin is little concerned with refining regime typology, his approach clearly has affinities with mass society theory, which emphasises the role of anomie leading to a quest for new community, culminating in the mass mobilising-state.[18] Indeed, in recent writings Griffin has sought to counter the criticism that his Weberian 'ideal-type' was simply a typological abstraction by joining the camp of those who argue that crisis and trauma led people to worship a new 'political religion'.[19]

I have already argued that there are serious dangers in over-stressing fascism's affective, rather than its more rational economic and other appeals. It is true that fascism often employed the iconography and language of religion, such as hagiographic processions and the terminology of 'rebirth'. But in part this was a propagandistic attempt to exploit existing sentiments, or to counter the religious mythology of the left. Most fascists did not seek to replace existing religions, at least in the foreseeable future. I have also argued that the rise of fascism was linked to an attempt to delineate a serious nationalist ideology, and that fascism should be defined essentially as an ideology – just like liberalism or socialism.[20] Put another way, fascism can be seen as a collective body of thought about issues such as human nature, and the organisation of economic and political life.[21] Within this fascist ideology, a partly left-influenced productivist economics dimension was crucial – a point which has been underlined by two other pioneers of the empathetic ideological approach – A.J. Gregor and Zeev Sternhell (though neither admit Nazism into the fascist Pantheon on account of its racism).[22] As a result, I have argued that a more comprehensive one-sentence definition holds that fascism is:

> An ideology that strives to forge social rebirth based on a *holistic-national radical Third Way*, though in practice fascism has tended to stress style, especially action and the charismatic leader, more than detailed programme, and to engage in a Manichean demonisation of its enemies.[23]

However, whilst ideal type fascist 'minima' are important as categorising devices, they raise a major methodological problem in relation to fascism. Some critics argue that fascism was not essentially ideological – that it was opportunistic and that action and policy were very context dependent.[24] Others, most notably Robert Paxton, have argued that fascism changed dramatically through time.[25] For example, Italian fascism began with a programme which owed much to the left, but by the turn of the 1930s it was more clearly on the right and had signed a Concordat with the Catholic church, yet aspects of the Salò Republic during 1943–5 can be seen as an attempt to return to Fascism's radical roots. Moreover, themes featured in various definitional 'minima' exerted very different appeals even in the same country at the same time. Thus in Weimar Germany, 'anti-Marxism' could invoke a philosophical hostility to materialism on the part of intellectuals, but on the streets it appealed to members of the working class who resented left-wing clientelism,[26] while in the salons and boardrooms of the bourgeoisie the concern was more to defend privilege and property rights against the rising tide of the left.

Therefore, I argue in this paper that the 'fascist minimum' needs to be supplemented by what I call the 'fascist matrix'. Instead of seeking to offer a relatively brief definition focusing on specific keywords, the term 'matrix' highlights the need to contrast the different ways in which fascists could interpret three partly overlapping key themes. The first theme in the fascist matrix is the quest for a 'new man', which has been central to most of the empathetic school's attempts to distinguish fascism from the reactionary and reformist right.[27] Second and third are the fascist goals of forging a new sense of nation and state. These themes lay at the very heart of thinking among most key fascist ideologues, and are neatly captured by Georges Valois, who was shortly afterwards to found the French *Faisceau*, when he wrote in 1919: 'You want to reformulate the state, restore the nation? You need to appeal to the power of the spirit'.[28]

To be more precise, at the heart of fascist thinking was the creation of a new elite of men, who would forge a holistic nation and build a new third way state. However, there were notable differences among fascists about the new man, the nation and state. Fascism more than any other ideology has fuzzy edges, overlapping at times both the conservative right and even the left. Part of the problem involved in neatly delineating fascism stems from the fact that in practice it was at times opportunistic – and where it achieved power, it in turn attracted many opportunists. More fundamentally, fascism is elusive because it sought radical syntheses of ideas.[29] This point was put well by Sir Oswald Mosley, the leader of the British Union of fascists in the 1930s, when he wrote: 'In this new synthesis of Fascism we find that we take the great principle of stability supported by authority, by order, by discipline, which has been the attribute of the Right, and we marry it to the principle of progress, of dynamic change, which we take from the Left.'[30] The point of the matrix is to highlight that instead of simply prioritising key words like 'new man', 'nation' or 'state', we need to ask how fascists conceived such terms, including what they were defined against. The matrix also shows that syntheses could produce conclusions which tended more to the left or more to the right – for example, in relation to the interests of workers versus employers.

Moreover, the matrix points to the need to break away from a purely history of ideas approach. Differences about themes such as the 'new man' cannot be understood simply in philosophical terms. It is necessary to contextualise the situations

139

in which particular ideas emerged and exerted a popular appeal. For example, nationalism in 1920s' Germany was evidently likely to have a more expansionary and militarist side than nationalism in Britain at the same time; radical nationalism was also likely to exert a more popular appeal. It must be stressed that the evidence about the exact motives as to why the masses turned to fascism in some countries remains relatively weak, especially outside Germany.[31] Nevertheless, any model of fascism clearly needs to suggest not just to why intellectuals and activists turned to the movement, but also why it could in some countries attract widespread support. An advantage of the matrix is that it points away from what might be termed 'one dimensional man' views of behaviour. People turned to fascism for a variety of reasons, including affective ones, economic ones and community norms.[32]

In the pages that follow, I seek to delineate the main inter-war sub-themes within this matrix and to explore their parameters. As the broad goal of this chapter is to refine the debate about generic fascism, I do not engage in specific national debates, such as to what extent Franco's Spain or Salazar's Portugal can be considered fascist.[33] And whilst the matrix is potentially both diachronic and synchronic, I do not discuss the issue of whether fascist ideology existed before the First World War,[34] nor consider how fascists have adapted doctrine since the end of the Second World War.[35] Ultimately, (though constraints on space prevent me developing the arguments, especially the second) I seek to argue that:

1   The homogenising-static problems of minimum approaches are over-stated, and the matrix further reduces the dangers.
2   The fascist matrix is not simply a definitional abstraction – the matrix can offer insights into concrete historical situations, including the dynamics of Nazism.

1. The new man

In the mid-1930s Cornelius Codreanu, wrote that: 'This country is dying because of a lack of men not programmes ... We do not need to create new programmes, but new men.'[36] The quote is misleading in the sense that, whilst the Iron Guard exhibited a mystical Orthodox religiosity, it did have a programme of agricultural and wider socio-economic reform. But Codreanu's emphasis on the creation of a 'new man' was central to fascist thinking. Some idea of the type of new man sought by fascists can be gauged from Mussolini, who wrote in the 1930s that: 'From beneath the ruins of liberal, socialist, and democratic doctrines, Fascism extracts those elements which are still vital ... supercede[s] socialism and supercede[s] liberalism ... create[s] a new synthesis ... Man is integral, he is political, he is economic, he is religious, he is saint, he is warrior.'[37]

But what was 'integral' fascist new man to be like? Was he something totally new, in the way in which the Bolsheviks dreamed of writing a new mentality on to the *tabula rasa* of both men and women in the post-1917 Soviet Union? Or was new man in many ways a restoration of the old? Whilst fascist leaders like Hitler and Mussolini (unlike more authoritarian-conservative politicians such as Charles Maurras and the Action Française)[38] never suggested the restoration of any form of *ancien régime*, at times there was a clear admiration of the past. For instance, Fascist developed a cult of ancient Rome (*Romanità*), although in its more popular manifestations the theme was also clearly deployed for propagandistic reasons. To the extent that there is a strong linking strand in the new man theme it is typified by Alfred Rosenberg's argument that the key lay in the emergence of a new elite which would manufacture a blend of the old and the new.[39]

1.i. New elite

Arguably the primary concern of fascist intellectuals was the creation of a new type of elite. Symptomatically, Hitler argued: 'Isn't every deed of genius in this world a visible protest of genius against the inertia of the mass?'[40] He argued that the parliamentary system sinned against the laws of nature, which demonstrated the importance of a dynamic aristocracy.[41] Fascists identified parliamentary elites with a series of failings. They preached a false egalitarianism, but at the same time political parties divided rather than united society. Party elites – even on the left – increasingly came from the bourgeois class, which was primarily concerned with short-term commercialism, though without providing leaders who could prevent disasters like the great depression which struck in 1929. At worst, they combined decadence with corruption.

The origins of this elitism were several. In Germany, Social Darwinism, with its emphasis on hierarchy and struggle, was unquestionably important. In Italy, elite theorists such as Roberto Michels (who was to become a supporter of Fascism) exerted a greater appeal. More generally, *fin de siècle* new ideas in psychology and philosophy about the power of the irrational and need for vitalist leadership began to pervade part of the intellectual scene. Nietzsche, especially his concepts of superman and the will, was particularly important in several continental countries: the young journalist-Mussolini even wrote admiringly about Nietzsche.[42]

Mussolini after 1918 talked of the need for a new young 'trenchocracy', a young elite which had been forged in war. This points to the crucial way in which the First World War turned diverse proto-fascist strands into a more concrete ideology. Valois provides a particularly interesting commentary on this, writing that war had given its participants an understanding of the nature of man that years of school had failed to achieve. According to Valois, the outbreak of hostilities in 1914 had placed people in an equal state of nature, and natural hierarchies had quickly emerged. In particular, war had underlined the importance of the great leader, who could rally morale.[43] However, war helped undermine faith in old elites, who had sent wave after wave to their deaths in pursuit of the 'knockout blow'. Disillusionment was especially strong in the defeated countries and in Italy, where, for nationalists at least, war had culminated in a 'mutilated victory'. Max Weber brought the word 'charisma' into the social science vocabulary only after the war, but the experience of 1914–18 and its traumatic aftermath in some countries unquestionably heightened the thirst for a great new leader. In Germany in particular after the battle of Langemarck in 1914, there was a widespread celebration of war and sacrifice for the reborn nation, linked to a longing for the emergence of a great leader.

1.ii. Martial man

An important strand in fascist new man thinking was concerned with the need to fight war, which was seen as endemic in the international system (partly as a result of a reading of history in which nation or race replaced the Marxist motor of class). The proto-fascist Maurice Barrès coined in the late nineteenth century the epitaph for the grave of bourgeois, decadent, individualist man: 'born a man, died a grocer'. Barrès sought to create a French nation which could avenge the humiliating military defeat suffered at the hands of Prussia in 1870. Influenced by Japan's defeat of Russia in 1905, the Italian Nationalist Enrico Corradini wrote of the need to create a Bushido type ethic in order to help liberate Italy, which he saw as 'the proletarian nation par excellence, suffocated in a world dominated by the high-handedness and greed of capitalist and plutocratic nations.'[44] After 1917, the emergence of the USSR created another powerful potential enemy for many countries, especially in Eastern Europe. Some fascists celebrated the impact of violence and/or war more in terms of its impact on individuals. Violence was seen as a central act of (young male) bonding in fascist paramilitary groups, which themselves were viewed as part of the new elite – especially the SS. The violence of early Nazism and Fascism in turn provided these movements with a litany of martyrs, designed in part to inspire others to reject the comfortable bourgeois life.

However, war was also seen as pointing to lessons which could be used in economic organisation. The 'conservative-revolutionary' Ernst Jünger celebrated war as creating 'blood socialism', a community of the trenches which counteracted the alienating nature of bourgeois society.[45] Jünger saw this as laying the basis of a new form of economic world in which 'neither work nor labour will exist in any sense that we have known.'[46] The silver Death's Head symbol popularly associated with the Nazis was worn before 1914 by the aristocratic cavalry, but during the war it was adopted by elite 'Stormtroops' which included all classes. The Death's Head and Stormtroopers after 1918 were, therefore, symbols of both militarism and a new egalitarian-elitism.

Moreover, paramilitary organisation and the immediate post-1918 violence began on the left rather than with fascism. It is true that the left tended to see violence as instrumental rather than as self-actualising. But not all fascists positively valued violence and/or war. This was especially true in countries, such as Britain, which had no territorial aspirations after 1918. To a lesser extent it was also true in France, although here there were fears about German *revanchisme* which helped encourage martial values in the Faisceau and the more-debatably fascist

Croix de Feu.[47] Valois did not so much celebrate war as derive lessons from it: for example, he wrote about the emergence of a sense of fraternity in his battalion, where men had used the egalitarian-familiar 'tu' form of address. Drieu La Rochelle argued that the romance of war had gone in an age of the machine gun, high explosive and mass death. He suggested cultivating the aesthetics of the body and sport as a way of preserving a healthy race, capable of fighting if necessary: politics became an extension of his artistic concerns, which sought to synthesise classicism with surrealism.[48]

1.iii. Women

The term 'new man' is especially appropriate for fascism in the sense that it was very much a male-dominant ethic and its iconography was often highly masculine too. Party membership was also largely masculine (although this would have been true of most parties at this time, even on the left).

Women were mainly conceived in terms of their childbearing capacity, not least to provide new soldiers, and the need to tend their men folk.[49] In Italy, there were even financial rewards for mothers of large families. However, the tendency in fascist thought to celebrate the important role played by women was something not typical of conservative thought. Hitler, for example, stated in 1934 that: 'in my State the mother is the most important citizen.'[50] Moreover, in the British fascist movement, women were given tasks which were not stereotypical female ones, including undertaking 'special patrols'. More generally, women, especially young ones, were given a public role under fascism: they could join organisations, parade in the streets, engage in public sporting activities. They could even adopt leadership roles within their own sphere. It is worth adding that in Nazi Germany, a small number of women achieved prominent positions. For the best known, Leni Riefenstahl, sexual attraction on the part of some Nazi leaders, most notably Josef Goebbels, may have played a part. Nevertheless, but some Nazis seem to have accepted that it was possible for women to display exceptional talents in a male world. These factors seem to have been a factor in attracting many women to fascism in an economically depressed inter-war world where there were few opportunities for women to pursue fulfilling careers. Indeed, by 1932 more women were voting Nazi than men.

Nevertheless, it is important to stress that whilst fascism made women more visible, in general it did not tolerate independent women's organisations in the way that most modern forms of conservatism did. Ideologically, the range of options open to women (of the right racial stock) was very limited.[51]

1.iv. 'Mass' man

Views on the nature of 'mass' new man could vary notably among fascists. One strand of fascist thinking was largely contemptuous of the masses, and saw new man largely in terms of being socialised into accepting elite authority. An extreme example of such thinking was Julius Evola, who held that Italian Fascism was too democratic in that it sought mass support rather than the cultivation of a warrior priesthood, which would manipulate the masses through myths. Although Hitler came to pursue, albeit equivocally, the parliamentary road to power, he certainly did not eulogise the wisdom of the masses. Indeed, he wrote in *Mein Kampf* of the 'mob' needing a leader to make them understand.[52] These were hardly 'populist' views in what is arguably the most common sense of the word – namely, celebrating the wisdom of the people (though Hitler can be seen as populist in another sense – namely, through the way in which he portrayed himself as the representative of a new elite which had risen from the people). There were other sides to the fascist view of mass man. For instance, Walter Darré espoused a kind of back to the land populism in Germany, where man would discover himself in the simple life. However, Darré's blood and soil views were in many ways atypical of leading Nazis in that they were essentially anti-modern.

More typically, fascists placed emphasis on integrating man through a form of manipulated activism in both the political and economic spheres (interestingly, Darré's main intellectual point of contact with other leading Nazis was a highly Manichaean world view, but unlike many of the others, Darré did not see this in part in terms of mass manipulation). People were encouraged to join the (single) party and linked organisations, such as youth ones. They were encouraged to attend mass celebrations, which unquestionably had a quasi-religious appeal for some. Fascism consciously adopted the language, metaphors and images of Christianity – for instance, opening scenes of Leni Riefenstahl's film of the 1934 Nuremberg rally, *Triumph of the Will*, in which the shadow of the plane carrying Hitler forms a cross which 'blesses' a column of supporters marching to the rally, and in which back-lighting gives Hitler a halo-effect as he steps down from the plane (or is it a Norse-god chariot?). But in a reversal of the aphorism that 'man cannot live by bread alone', there was also significant emphasis in the Nazi and Fascist regimes on workplace linked organisation which had a modernist, consumerist side. The Dopolavoro and German copy, the KdF, organised events such as mass holidays, for example to the island of Rügen, which had the largest hotel in the world in 1939.

Professional sport too became a form of popular control. This could involve an extension of the collective fervour of mass party meetings – for instance, the choreography and crowd reactions of international football matches when Germany or Italy were playing. But state-subsidised sport could also provide more individualised and even commercially-related pleasures, such as motor sport in which Alfa Romeos, Mercedes and Auto Unions vied for dominance – and national prestige – on Europe's circuits.

2. Nation

Nationalism was central to fascist thought. Hitler wrote in *Mein Kampf* that his dream was: '*A Germanic State of the German Nation.*'[53] Later, he planned with his court architect, Albert Speer, the rebuilding of Berlin as a capital fit for a new Thousand Year Reich. Mosley wrote in the early 1930s, thinking more of economic recovery than empire, that: 'We are essentially a national movement, and if our policy could be summarised in two words, they would be "Britain First".'[54]

But how did fascists conceive the nation? Mussolini frequently talked of completing the work of the *Risorgimento*, underlining the way in which Italian Fascists believed that much work was to be done to create Italians. Giovanni Papini, later to become a leading Fascist intellectual, put the point crudely when he wrote that Italy: 'had been shit dragged kicking and screaming towards unification by a daring minority, and shit it remained throughout fifty years of unification.'[55] On the other hand, the Nazis tended to see the nation as founded on a primordial *Volksgeist* and in blood. Nevertheless, there were notable similarities between the various forms of fascist nationalism. All were essentially holistic, stressing the pre-eminence of group over the individual or locality (features of conservative and/or liberal nationalism). Moreover, the centrality of the concept of decadence to fascism underlines the way in which even the Nazis could not take the nation for granted. It needed to be re-forged, bringing the liberal-bourgeoisie and the 'Marxists' (who included the Social Democrats, the largest party of the early Weimar Republic, as well as the relatively large Communist Party) back into the German national community.

2.i. Myths

A key feature in fascist nationalism was what might be termed mythical thought. Mussolini in particular derived from the syndicalist theorist, Georges Sorel, the idea of the motivating myth – a simple slogan that was meant to take on a psychological reality and condition action. Other notable thinkers whose work inspired an interest in political myth were Gustav Le Bon and Sigmund Freud. For the syndicalists before 1914 the great myth was that of the revolutionary general strike. After the masses flocked to the colours at the start of the Great War, the myth of the nation became increasingly attractive as capable of both uniting the people and inspiring ever-greater fighting and productive efforts (whereas most socialism was essentially concerned with re-distribution, the syndicalists stressed the need to create an economy which could compete with capitalist production). Wartime propaganda which helped inspire both hatred and national sacrifice also influenced some who were to become leading fascists. Both Hitler and Goebbels were particularly impressed by British efforts in this sphere (British 'fair play' totally disappeared during 1914–18 in efforts to damn the 'Beastly Hun' as capable of the most evil atrocities, such as the mass rape of nuns and bayoneting babies).

However, fascist myths were not designed simply to mobilise people for production or war. Often neglected are exemplar or identity myths. Wagnerian tales of Kingdoms of the Gods and other worlds could have a martial side. But they were also about the deeply rooted identities of Germans in primeval forests and *völkisch* communities. The cult of *Romanità* told Italians that they were not a divided, mongrel nation, but the proud descendants of ancient Rome. Such myths were also about more everyday behaviour – for example, the importance of: great leaders, authority, fulfilling one's duty, and the dangers of decadence and miscegenation. In a world of declining traditional authority, especially religion, some fascists saw such myths as an important form of social indoctrination.

Nevertheless, it is important not to over-state the role of mythology in fascism. Whilst there is no doubt that Mussolini was fascinated by the power of myth, several of the leading syndicalists who came over to fascism saw the key task as the construction of a 'synthesis' to produce a rational, stable new order.[56] Arguably two of the key theorists of the Fascist state in practice also had little or no interest in myths – namely, the Nationalist Alfredo Rocco and Giovanni Gentile (the latter co-wrote with Mussolini the entry on fascism in the 1932 *Enciclopedia Italiania*). Rocco was an academic lawyer by profession, and his main concern was constructing the legal basis of the Corporate State. Gentile was a neo-idealist philosopher, concerned to build a totalitarian 'ethical state'. Turning to Germany, Hitler did not see the nation as a myth in the sense that modern theorists of nationalism talk about an 'imagined community' or the 'invention of tradition'.[57] Hitler saw the German race as an historical reality, whose existence was supported by modern science.

2.ii. Science

Mythology was also relatively unimportant in British fascism: Mosley was critical of Oswald Spengler's vision of the decline of the West because he argued that modern science could help revive western economies and help them face the challenge of the rise of new states such as Japan. Mosley also saw modern science as the key to helping the poorest, arguing: 'I think we must all agree that it would be possible, by sane organisation of the world, with the power of modern science and of industry to produce, to solve once and for all the poverty problem.'[58] In Germany, aspirations for national *Lebensraum* were also closely linked to the new science of geopolitics, associated in particular with Karl Haushofer. This portrayed the world as divided into natural spheres, which should be controlled by great powers. Carving the world up into such spheres of interest was seen as legitimate both for productive development and as ultimately likely to reduce the risks of war by removing grey zones. Behind these grand visions of German *Lebensraum* lay a small army of demographers, statisticians and others who provided the bureaucratic-rational basis for the Holocaust by euphemising a language of death in pursuit of solving rural over-population, or dealing with unproductive labour.[59]

The belief that some nations were fitted to rule over others was reinforced by nineteenth century science. For example, Rosenberg in *The Mythos* wrote that: 'The emergence in the nineteenth century of Darwinism and Positivism constituted the first powerful, though still wholly materialistic, protest against the lifeless and suffocating ideas of the humanist and Christian traditions.'[60] However, it is important not to overstate the impact of developments such as Social Darwinism on fascist thought in general. Some saw it as too biologically reductionist, as involving too unidimensional a view of man. Many fascists, like Drieu La Rochelle, held a more syncretic view. This held that humans belong to a natural order which is governed by scientific laws, including innate inequalities and the naturalness of aggression. But Drieu also held that humans, especially a talented elite, were to some extent free to impose their will and secure change.

2.iii. Race

It is impossible to separate a discussion of science and nationalism from race. It is not necessary to go to the extreme of damning virtually all Germans as anti-semitic to see that racial science held considerable prestige in Germany even before the Nazis came to power.[61] This helps explain the appeal of exterminationist anti-semitism to doctors and others steeped in eugenics, though it is important to note other factors too, including a German Christian tradition of demonising the Jews. However, in general, the 'ordinary' Germans who took part in the shootings of Jews do not seem to have seen this as part of millenarian quest to renew the nation. Rather, extensive propaganda seems to have simply inured them to the fate of Jews.[62] Especially during wartime, this may have been reinforced by the Manichaean conspiracy theory form of anti-semitism, epitomised in the closing scenes of the propaganda film *The Eternal Jew* (1940), in which it was claimed that: 'This is no religion … this is a conspiracy against all non-Jews, of a cunning, unhealthy, contaminated race' (the film was distributed widely in cinemas, including a version for children and women which edited out graphic scenes of kosher killings).

Nazi racism, culminating in the Holocaust, is arguably the key reason why some scholars have sought to distinguish between Nazism and fascism. It is, therefore, important to note that Hitler's biological-conspiracy form of anti-semitism was by no means the most common one within the Nazi leadership, nor was anti-semitism in general central to the Nazis' early appeal.[63] Anti-semitism was linked to a variety of concerns, such as hostility to liberalism, cosmopolitanism, finance capitalism, and Marxism. Dietrich Eckhart saw Jewishness essentially in terms of a materialistic bent, which exists to some extent in everyone. Goebbels even spoke of the 'rubbish of race materialism' and regarded Himmler as 'in many ways mad' – though he was happy enough to use anti-semitism when it suited his purposes, such as at the time of *Kristallnacht* in 1938.[64] Speer seems to have had little time for anti-semitism intellectually, but the charismatic power of Hitler and the drive for personal self-advancement, seems to pushed moral scruples to the back of his mind.

It is also important to stress that Italian Fascism was in its own way racist. It is true that Gentile found biological racism and anti-semitism abhorrent. And Mussolini for many years had a Jewish mistress, and Jews were prominent in the Fascist Party until 1938, when Mussolini introduced Nuremberg style laws. But it is a mistake to portray Mussolini's extensive colonial ambitions as nothing more than mimicry of what many other European states had achieved generations before.[65] This misses the point that international norms for behaviour were changing. It also misses the point that in the 1930s Mussolini wrote the preface to an Italian edition to a book by Richard Korherr (who was to be Himmler's chief statistician during the war) in which he claimed: 'the whole White race, the Western race, can be submerged by other coloured races which are multiplying at a rate unknown in our race.'[66] Mussolini may not have hated other races, but he shared the geopolitical racism characteristic of fascism. Moreover, there were some Fascist leaders, like Roberto Farinacci, who were anti-semitic. More important in determining policy was a body of Italian scientific opinion. Although racial science was never as strong in Italy as in Germany, it helped produce an intellectual climate in which apartheid and mass killings of Africans, as happened in Ethiopia after 1935, seemed defensible (Italian racial science was much less concerned about Jews).

2.iv. Europe

Although it is important not to overstress this dimension, it is also worth nothing that there was an element of Europeanism in some forms of fascism. Mussolini's reference to the threat from coloured peoples cited above clearly referred to a threat to more than just Italian values. Some fascists in other countries saw Italy as trying to set up a form of fascist international. For instance, a leading member of the British Union of Fascists (BUF), W.E.D. Allen, approvingly wrote that: 'Signor Mussolini appears to aim at an ultimate Pan-European association based on the concepts of Fascism rather than at a literal revival of Roman territorial glories.'[67] The sense of collective threat to Europe can be found even more clearly in relation to the attitudes of some fascists to the USSR. It is vital not to be taken in by the post-war self-justification of Waffen-SS leaders and fighters, like Léon Degrelle,[68] but there was a side to fascism which genuinely portrayed itself as a crusade against Bolshevism.

A key idea of the conservative revolutionaries in the 1920s was the quest for European Imperium, not understood in terms of conquest but in terms of an overarching understanding which would allow different peoples to pursue their own life style, whilst at the same time being linked through a sense of being one. Such Europeanism was sometimes linked to race, but it could also be linked to economic concerns. Nazi economists sometimes sought inspiration in Friedrich List, whose support for autarchy had increasingly become linked to the need to unite Europe against the Anglo-American challenge. Drieu La Rochelle and several other key intellectuals within the Parti Populaire Française (PPF), such as Alfred Fabre-Luce in his journal *Pamphlet*, similarly saw 'Europe' very much in terms of creating a new non-liberal economic order. Another important dimension of this new Europeanism was belief in rule by technicians and in the need for a break with the corrupt and divisive national parliamentary politics, which had very much been a feature of post-1870 France. Here Europe was being invoked to redress the failings of the nation.

3. The state

A third key theme in fascist thought was the state. Mussolini, for instance, wrote that 'The Fascist conception of the State is all-embracing; outside of it no human or spiritual values can exist, much less have value ... The Fascist State is ... a unique and original creation. It is not reactionary but revolutionary.'[69] For Mussolini, the goal was a positively valued 'totalitarian' state, which would transcend divisions and closely link people and government (a notable contrast to the use of the term 'totalitarianism' after 1945, where it became synonymous with pseudo-mobilisation of the masses, and police-state enforced conformity). Reference to the state was also common in Nazi thought, though terms like 'totalitarianism' or 'total state' were less frequently used (Goebbels was a notable exception). Moreover, support for a strong state was not necessarily associated with dictatorship. Henri De Man wrote of a new conception of nationalism in which the state reflected the expression of the will of a people. The point was put even more clearly by some of the intellectuals in the PPF, such as Drieu La Rochelle.[70] They saw positive affinities between fascism and Jacobinism, especially in their linking of an activist style of politics with the strong state.[71]

Discussing fascist views of the state is difficult for a variety of reasons. One concerns the fact that the term 'state' can refer to a historical entity or a philosophical ideal. It is possible to find fascist statements which are critical of the state, but these tend to refer to the first context. The Nazis were highly critical of the Weimar state, which they saw as colonised by political opponents and unadventurous elites. The impossibility of removing all such state employees in 1933 meant that hostility to the state in this sense did not end with the establishment of a dictatorship. It is also important to remember that the main fascist regimes lasted only a relatively short period of time. In the case of the Nazis, six out of twelve years was spent fighting a war which had led by 1941–2 to massive territorial gains and which involved the marshaling of vast resources. Predictably, the result at times was bureaucratic chaos, with divisions between party and state, and even within the Nazi Party. But this does not mean that Nazism should be seen as an 'anti-state',[72] or that it differed significantly in philosophical terms from fascism. There were notable differences between the two core regimes, but it is also possible to identify important linkages too – not least in their quest for a new economic order.

3.i. Leadership

Central to fascist thinking about the state was the need for strong leadership. Even Valois, who is generally accepted to have been notably uncharismatic, argued that: 'In order to be great, strong, prosperous, a nation needs leaders', something which he held was unlikely to emerge in the liberal state which was designed to produce mediocrity.[73] Some fascist leaders stressed that leadership could be collective. Valois was one. Mosley (although the dominant figure in his party), was another writing that: 'Modern organisation is too vast and too complex to rest on any individual alone, however gifted'.[74] Codreanu humbly titled himself 'Captain', while Anton Mussert – not inaccurately – referred to himself as 'first among equals'. On the other hand, some fascist leaders, especially Hitler and Mussolini, sought to portray themselves as characterised by a special sense of mission to save the nation and possessed of remarkable powers.

However, this does not mean that their image of style of governing was identical. Although Hitler in the early years of the Nazi Party sometimes played on the corporal-everyman image, he increasingly sought to diffuse a more god-like aura and Nazi propaganda focused on the Führer.[75] In the early years of Fascism, the local *ras* were arguably more central to campaigning that Mussolini. Later the Duce's image was different. Mussolini was often pictured engaged in sporting activities, even in swimsuit; although Hitler was often pictured in uniform, machismo was arguably less central to his image. In daily life, Hitler tended to indolence and formal Cabinet meetings had ended by 1937. Although Hitler took a significant interest in foreign and later military policy, on major policies – such as the launching of the Holocaust – it is not clear exactly how the Führer was involved. In contrast, Mussolini was hard working and regularly attended formal meetings, including bi-weekly visits to the king.

Nevertheless, this should not be taken to mean that Hitler was, paradoxically, a 'weak dictator'. Whilst he may not have taken part in the detailed planning of many major policies, there seems little doubt that those around him believed that they were 'working towards the Führer'.[76] Although it is very debatable whether Hitler exerted true mass charismatic appeal, there seems no doubt that he exerted considerable affective power over a coterie within the Nazi Party until near the very end.[77] Mussolini too is typically portrayed as exerting charismatic appeal.[78] But this seems to have been more limited both within the party and among the public at large. Indeed, unlike Hitler, the Italian dictator was overthrown as the war began to turn against the Axis powers (only to be rescued and restored in the 1943–5 Salò Republic on Hitler's orders – in part, a mark of fraternity to his fellow fascist).

3.ii. Totalitarianism

Giovanni Gentile set the philosophy of the totalitarian state out most clearly. He did not defend unbridled dictatorship. Rather, his 'ethical state' involved a critique of the liberal night watchman state and its moral pluralism in which subjectivist relativism reigned over moral certainties. For Gentile, the state was essentially a teacher – notable difference compared to Mussolini, who was more skeptical of the masses and for whom the strong state was necessary to back up fascist mythology.

Fascists like Gentile believed that the liberal state allowed many of its members to live in abject poverty, whereas the ethical state sought to care for those who were considered part of the true community. As José Antonio Primo de Rivera sarcastically wrote in 1933: 'You are free to work as you wish ... [but] we are rich, we offer you whatever conditions that please us; as free citizens, you are not obliged to accept them if you do not want to; but as poor citizens, if you do not accept them you will die of hunger, surrounded of course by the utmost liberal dignity.'[79] However, it is important to reiterate that the two core fascist states sought to imbue their people with strong national consciousness, and to be prepared to die in war. They were therefore both warfare and welfare states.

In practice, the Fascist state was notably less than totalitarian, conceding significant power especially to the church and business (the monarchy and army too retained some independence, and were crucial to overthrowing Mussolini). Nazism was more totalitarian in the sense that it rapidly came to exert greater control over major businesses such as I.G. Farben (the largest company in Europe until it was overtaken in 1938–9 by the tentacles of the Herman Göring Works' empire). Nazism was also helped notably in its *Gleichschaltung* by its penetration of the Protestant church, including the appointment of a Reich Bishop (a development helped by the fact that authoritarian, nationalist and even anti-semitic views were deeply entrenched in major parts of the Protestant churches; the German and Austrian Catholic churches also had notable anti-semitic strands, but did not see themselves as politically-national churches in the way that some Protestants did). However, there was notably greater similarity between Nazism and Fascism than is normally accepted at the more philosophical level. Whilst some Fascists did not seek a highly authoritarian, repressive state, there was a strong tendency to reject a central aspect of the Western political tradition dating back to Aristotle and especially the Enlightenment – namely the distinction between state and civil society. A similar point could be made about the Nazis. Whilst there were differences over the exact nature of the state, there was no disagreement over whether there should exist centers of pluralist power which could threaten the national interest. Thus the *Märzgefallen* 'Crown Jurist' of the early Nazi regime, Carl Schmitt, was concerned with retaining a semblance of the traditional state in the sense of keeping a clearly codified legal structure which could regulate civil society, whereas Hitler preferred vague 'legal' concepts such as the 'people's' or 'Führer's will'. But central to Schmitt's thought was a friend–enemy dichotomy which meant that there could be no basis of compromise with those who did not support the basic goals of the state.

3.iii. Religion

The issue of whether fascism sought to create a new religion is a crucial one, not least as several recent works have portrayed fascism as a 'political religion'.[80] As has already been noted, there is no question that many forms of fascism adopted aspects of the discourse and iconography of religion. However, this was a characteristic of other ideologies – not least socialism. In both pre-1914 Germany and Italy, socialism spawned spawned quasi-religious festivals and processions, complete with their own martyrology. Mussolini came from Emilia-Romagna, where socialism took on notably religious forms. Pictures of the Ferdinand Lassale, the founder of the Social Democratic Party, adorned workers' homes in Germany. Although August Babel criticized this cult, his picture in turn came to be carried regularly in processions by workers.[81] Indeed, theorists such as Corradini saw fascist mythology as necessary propaganda to free the working class of socialist myths. The issue is therefore not so much one of analysing form, as of considering fundamental doctrinal intention and social function and penetration.

There seems no doubt that fascists differed over the issue of whether existing religions needed replacing by a new fascist religion. Several leading Nazis, such as Rosenberg, were willing to attack not just church authority but also Christian doctrine and church pronouncements on specific policy. This included Catholic opposition to sterilization, and later to the 'euthanasia' programme. However, according to Degrelle, Hitler thought that religion did not need attacking directly as this would provoke a dangerous response. Moreover, it would gradually fade away under the dual impact of science undermining its mysticism and consumerism alleviating its appeal to the poor.[82] Albert Speer, who was far closer to Hitler, has written that Hitler believed that the church was indispensable and that any attempt to replace the church by party ideological would lead to a relapse into the mysticism of the Middle Ages.[83] The latter seems to have been Hitler's basic position and that of most Nazis. Some Fascists like Mussolini began as rabid anticlericals, but in general there was no Fascist desire either for direct confrontation with the Catholic Church. Indeed, in 1936, Mussolini suggested to Hans Frank, the Nazi Justice Minister, that relations with the Catholic Church in Germany should be improved. Although this comment needs to be considered within the context of Mussolini's desire to help improve the image of the Nazis within Italy, in order to help forge the Axis,[84] it is interesting to note that Mussolini added that a separation between church and state was crucial, as this provided the state with more freedom. In the case of the Iron Guard, the movement actively promoted Orthodoxy and its meetings were regularly attended by priests. Arguably its greatest intellectual supporter, Mircea Eliade, wrote in 1937 that: 'the supreme target of the Legionary revolution, is, as the Captain has said, *the salvation of the people*, the reconciliation of the Romanian people with God.'[85] Another of the most sophisticated theorists of fascism, Valois, was a practicing Catholic.

It is, therefore, misleading to argue that generic fascist involved the question to establish a political religion. If there was a common strand it was more syncretism, of *Gleichschaltung*. Put another way, there was an attempt to remove conflict between the pronouncements of the church and state. However, even here the parties trod carefully. For example, after an initially flurry of activity, including the appointment of a Reich Bishop, the Nazis largely dropped their efforts to create a united 'national' Protestant church, realizing that many within the church were hostile to overt political commitments – a view which was strong even among some nationalists.[86]

There are also dangers in becoming carried away by evidence such as film of apparently ecstatic crowds and acts of worship at Nazi rallies. As noted in the Introduction, the evidence about the exact motives for supporting fascism even in

Germany remains far from definitive.[87] Stress on fascism as a political religion tends to gloss over its more economic view of man, reflected in propaganda promising new consumer goods such as radios, typewriters and even cars. It is worth adding that the Social Democrats' underground reported that such developments, together with the onset of full employment by the late 1930s, was a crucial factor in consolidating support for the Nazis. Although there was a strand of military-ascetism within fascist thought, there was also a strong belief that fascism could not compete with other forms of government unless it could deliver to 'integral' man high living standards – and ones based not simply on full and stable employment. Whilst totalitarian theorists like Gentile dreamed of an ethical state, characterized by a universal new creed of nationalist-commitment, the more shrewd fascists realized that organisations like the Dopolavoro were more vital for ensuring passive conformity than mass mobilization.

3.iv. Economy

It has become a commonplace to argue that fascism lacked a clear economic vision.[88] Certainly Hitler argued for the primacy of politics over economics and pointed to the dangers of setting out specific economic policies, which would appeal to sectional groups. Nevertheless, the Nazis after 1928 developed a notable panoply of economic programmers and occupation-based organisations, which almost certainly were crucial to attracting support in sectors such as agriculture.[89] Moreover, a case can be made that after 1933 the Nazis did develop a relatively clear economic programme based on a state–private market symbiosis to achieve a stable increase in production.[90]

An important linking theme in fascist thought was a rejection of philosophical materialism. As Valois wrote: 'It's not the case, as Marx believed, that the mode of production determines moral, political and intellectual life: rather, it is the intellectual, moral and political life which determines economic formations.'[91] Fascist intellectuals saw capitalism as potentially dynamic, but also as a social solvent, prone to trade cycles and increasingly unconcerned with the nation: what was good for General Motors was not necessarily good for Germany! On the other hand, socialism with its highly redistributionist and anti-private property ethic, threatened to undermine economic creativity and to create in its place a stultifying bureaucratically planned state.

Most inter-war fascists saw corporatism as the key institutional form to resolve this dilemma. In practice, the Italian Corporate State failed to live up to the expectations of some early Fascists, especially the syndicalists who had seen it as a genuine way of shifting power towards the workers with acerbating class antagonism. By the late 1930s, the Corporations provided a forum for helping government to coordinate business activity, but they hardly challenged private business power and worker participation was essentially a sham. To the extent they can be considered in terms of an individual creator, the more right wing, social-Catholic vision of Rocco had prevailed over the syndicalists like Panunzio. The Nazis made no attempt forge a corporate state, but this does not mean that there was no interest in various forms of corporatism within the party. Gregor Strasser, for example, sought to extend pre-1933 Nazi workers organisations in this way. Gottfried Feder also wrote extensively about the representative role of corporations in the new state, claiming in 1919 that: 'The new state must therefore make a radical break ... The *House of the People* (as the first chamber) represents the political interests of the whole people, while the *Central Council* must represent the economic interests of the working population.'[92]

The various forms of fascism can be conceived as attempting to forge what some openly termed a 'Third Way' (neither capitalism nor socialism). In some ways, this involved an essentially cultural turn, epitomised by the beautification of factories programme of the KdF. Such workplace tinkering was perfectly consistent with creating a quietist labour force at a time of growing full employment to boost capitalist profits (which helps explain the lack of opposition to most Nazi policies from the business sector). This in turn helps explain why Marxists like Walter Benjamin have talked of the 'aestheticisation of politics' by fascist parties and states. The clear implication is that the underlying reality was one of manipulative exploitation in the workplace and bread and circuses more generally. But true fascists (rather than conservatives in fascist drag) sought a political and economic revolution too. This involved a centrally co-ordinated economy with the intention of radically modernising existing systems of production, distribution and exchange, and of harmonising the state and civil society around third way productive relations intended to avoid the pitfalls of both divisive market mechanisms and inefficient prescriptive state direction. This form of political economy derives its authority from the strong state (embodied in the leader), but sought to obtain its drive from a civil society embodied in the combination of a selfless nationalist working ethic tinged with consumerism.

Conclusion

In the introduction, I noted that there have been two major charges against fascist minimum approaches: First, there is the claim that they homogenise fascism, that they fail to see its contradictions, opportunism and the way it changed through time. Secondly, there has been the argument that such approaches are essentially typological abstractions and offer little or nothing by way of insight into the dynamics of concrete historical situations.

Misleading homogenisation?

Fascism was undoubtedly an ideology obsessed with propaganda, and it can be difficult to distinguish between manipulative statements and fundamental belief. At times fascism was opportunistic, and can appear contradictory in practice. However, these traits are not unique to fascism (*vide* the opportunistic changes and literally murderous disputes within post-1917 Bolshevism. Fascism never witnessed anything like the *volte face* of the 'New Economic Policy', or of world revolution turned upside down into 'Socialism in One Country', followed by mass purges). Arguing that fascism was in many ways incoherent, even nihilistic, reflects the strong tendency to focus on the brief practice of two inter-war fascist movements and regimes, rather than its more generic ideology.

The argument that fascism changed through time is also in many ways misleading. Paxton argues that fascism went through five stages: i) the initial creation of fascist movements; ii) rooting the movement in a political system; iii) the acquisition of power; iv) the exercise of power; v) the longer run radicalization or entropy of fascism.[93] The argument has at least three major problems. First, Paxton effectively has to have a working definition to identify fascist movements and regimes. As Griffin has pointedly noted, Paxton's minimum in practice seems to be remarkably close to what Griffin terms the 'new consensus'.[94] Secondly, it is widely accepted among those who have sought to build models of generic fascism that only two movements came to power largely through their own efforts, namely, Nazism and Fascism. Building a general conceptual approach where for three of the five alleged key stages N = 2 seems a strange methodology to those more attuned to social science theory. Finally, Paxton glosses over the fact that fascism was always characterised by divisions. This was not simply tensions between movements and regimes, but also within them at the personal and local level. For example, Italian Fascism in 1919 grouped together a motley crowd, including Marxists converted to nationalism like Mussolini, syndicalists, Futurists, and miscellaneous others (with many of the burgeoning rank and file typified more by a taste for violence than doctrine). During the closing months of the Salò Republic, there were splits between radicals who sought to rediscover the 'true' nature of early Fascism, genocidal anti-semites, the irretrievably corrupt, and others. And was the last of these phases entropy or radicalization?

Abstract typology?

Near the end of his life, Tim Mason confessed that the post-1960s' fashion for social over political history had failed to answer two great questions posed by Nazism: why support for Nazism was so widespread and enduring; and how could the Third Reich carry out a policy of genocide.[95]

Why fascism emerged, and why the Nazi regime in particular proved so internally bomb-proof, remain hotly contested issues. Some historians have recently reverted to relatively unicausal explanations, especially the claim that fascism was a 'political religion'. Most recent historians of Nazism have tended more towards a *Volkspartei* explanation, but this leaves open the question of why different groups turned to Nazism. The answer clearly implied by the matrix approach is that there were notably different motives for supporting fascism. Hitler's charisma undoubtedly had an effect, although it is difficult to decipher whether the impact of this was an essentially affective-quasi-religious response, or whether Hitler's personality made voters more aware of policies which could appeal in a more rational way.[96] Certainly it is important not to overlook materialistic factors in explaining fascist support. Quietist conformity, induced by fear of the more terroristic nature of the Nazi state compared to the Italian, should also not be ignored.

There has been much recent discussion of the old thesis that a crucial root of the Holocaust lay deep in Germany's alleged anti-semitism. In spite of Daniel Goldhagen's sweeping damnation of the German racial soul, most historians accept that a complex set of factors led to genocide. This includes a culture of anti-semitism, not least in the German and Austrian churches. The nature of German racial science provided important legitimation to the genocidal solution of dealing with Jews in conquered territories. Within the bureaucracy, there were many civil servants who believed they were rationally planning a better economy for a new Germany, or who were simply pursuing their own self-interest. Anti-semitic conspiracy theory, which was particularly characteristic of Nazi party officials, undoubtedly encouraged a Manichaean sense of apocalyptic war with the Jews. So too did Hitler's coterie charisma, which encouraged leading colleagues and lower officials to vie for the favour of the Führer, often radicalising policy in the process. Indeed, without the Führer there would almost certainly have been no Holocaust in the sense of mass, systematic killing. Nevertheless, when all is said and done, the Holocaust in practice almost certainly had more with what Hannah Arendt has termed the 'banality of evil' than with fanatical dreams of personal or social rebirth.

Moving on

In this presentation of the fascist matrix, limitations on space meant that the main focus was on delineating ideology rather than explaining policy. However, most of the key factors leading to the Holocaust can be gleaned from this approach. In the presentation above, the main emphasis was on trying to distil coherence from within the tensions in inter-war fascism. However, the same matrix method could have been used to highlight changes through time – though without turning these into a rigid set of stages which are even more misleading than 'static' fascist minimum approaches.

The time has come to accept that behind the opportunistic aspects of fascist movements and regimes lay a serious ideology (just like liberalism and socialism). Approached in the right way, defining generic fascism is not simply an exercise in typological analysis. Demonising the practice of fascism, especially the terror and horrors of Nazism, without understanding the different routes by which people could be attracted to fascism is a serious intellectual error.

NOTES

* I am indebted to Uwe Backes for his comments on the first draft.
1 The title of his chapter title in Thomas Childers and Jane Caplan (eds), *Reevaluating the Third Reich* (Holmes and Meier, New York, 1993).

2 For a good example of the argument that only Italian Fascism, and clearly mimetic movements, are 'Fascist', see Gilbert Allardyce, 'What Fascism Is Not. Thoughts on the Deflation of a Concept', *American History Review*, Vol. 84, No. 2, 1979. It is important to note that even before 1945, the term 'fascist' was rarely used as a form of self-ascription outside Italy, where the Fascist movement was first founded in 1919 (taking its name from the word *'fascio'*, meaning in a political context a 'union' or 'front').

3 Social historians tended to stress Germany's alleged *Sonderweg*. For a powerful critique of the *Sonderweg* thesis see David Blackbourn and Geoff Eley, *The Peculiarities of German History* (Oxford University Press, Oxford, 1984).

4 Roger Griffin (ed.), *International Fascism* (Edward Arnold, London, 1998). See also Roger Griffin, 'The Primacy of Culture: the Current Growth (or Manufacture) of Consensus within Fascist Studies', *Journal of Contemporary History*, Vol. 35, No. 1, 2002.

5 Ernst Nolte, *Three Faces of Fascism* (Mentor, New York, 1969), p. 537ff.

6 Ernst Nolte, *Die Krise des liberalen Systems und die faschstischen Bewegungen* (R. Piper and Co, Munich, 1968), p. 385, n. 64.

7 On the *'Historikerstreit'*, see Richard J. Evans, *In Hitler's Shadow. West German Historians and the Attempt to Escape from the Nazi Past* (I.B. Tauris, London, 1989). For a brief summary of Nolte's views on this debate, and relatively sympathetic criticism from a leading French historian, see François Furet and Ernst Nolte, *Fascism and Communism* (University of Nebraska Press, Lincoln, 2001).

8 Roger Griffin, *The Nature of Fascism* (Pinter, London, 1991), p. 26 (italics in the original). See also Roger Griffin (ed.), *Fascism* (Oxford University Press, Oxford, 1995), an eclectic and erudite Reader of fascist sources, which has been used widely by other scholars.

9 Stanley Payne, 'The Concept of Fascism', in Stein U. Larsen, Bernt Hagtvet and Jan P. Mykelbust (eds), *Who Were the Fascists?* (Universitetsforlaget, Bergen, 1980). See also his excellent book *Fascism: Comparison and Definition* (University of Wisconsin Press, Madison, 1980).

10 See for example: Emilio Gentile, *Le Origini dell'Ideologia Fascista (1918–25)* (Laterza, Rome, 1975), and George L. Mosse, *The Crisis of German Ideology. Intellectual Origins of the Third Reich* (Grosset and Dunlap, New York, 1964).

11 The term 'palingenesis' appears to have been first used in this context by Gentile in *Le Origini dell'Ideologia Fascista (1918–25)*, p. 205.

12 In *International Fascism* Griffin specifically cites (p. 15) as recent examples my *Fascism. A History* (Chatto and Windus, London, 1995) and Stanley Payne's *A History of Fascism, 1914–45* (University of Wisconsin Press, Madison, 1995), in which Payne moved fascism's positive ideology and goals to first place in his tripartite approach (p. 7).

13 For example, Michael Burleigh's prize-winning *The Third Reich. A New History* (Macmillan, Basingstoke, 2000) includes no reference to Griffin.

14 An interesting example is the grafting of Griffin's stress on palingenesis onto a neo-Marxist analysis, stressing the crisis of capitalism in Mark Neocleous, *Fascism* (Open University Press, Milton Keynes, 1997). See also Aristole A. Kallis, *Fascist Ideology. Territory and Expansionism in Italy and Germany, 1922–1945* (Routledge, London, 2000), where rebirth is linked to territorial aggrandizement (which was not a feature of many forms of fascism).

15 For example, Mark Antliff, 'Fascism, Modernism, and Modernity', *Art Bulletin*, Vol. LXXXIV, No. 1, 2002.

16 *Theories and Models of Fascism. A Multi-dimensional Approach* (I.B. Tauris, London, forthcoming); this book has been delayed through illness to the author. See also Alessandro Campi (ed.), *Che cos'è il fascismo? Interpretazioni e prospetitive di ricerche* (Ideazione editrice, Roma, 2003).

17 Kevin Passmore, *Fascism – a Very Short History* (Oxford University Press, Oxford, 2002), esp. p. 20ff.
18 For the classic statement of the mass society approach see Hannah Arendt, *The Origins of Totalitarianism* (André Deutsch, London, 1986).
19 Griffin was initially critical of the political religion approach, though it seems implied by his basic 'rebirth' argument.
20 Michael Freeden, 'Is Nationalism a Distinct Ideology?', *Political Studies*, Vol. 46, No. 4, 1998 argues (p. 751) that in general it is a 'thin' ideology, which fails to meet the criteria of a comprehensive ideology 'because it fails to provide its own solution to issues such as social justice and the distribution of resources'.
21 There is a common tendency to understand the term 'ideology' in terms of Marxist false consciousness or other forms of deceit. I use the term in a non-pejorative sense: see my opening chapter in Roger Eatwell and Anthony W. Wright (eds), *Contemporary Political Ideologies* (Pinter, London, 1999).
22 See especially A. James Gregor, *Italian Fascism and Developmental Dictatorship* (Princeton University Press, Princeton, 1979); and Zeev Sternhell, *Ni Droite, Ni Gauche* (Editions du Seuil, Paris, 1983). The importance of economic policy, especially corporatism, has also been argued forcefully by David Roberts, 'How Not to Think about Fascism and Ideology, Intellectual Antecedents and Historical Meaning', *Journal of Contemporary History*, Vol. 35, No. 2, 2000. See also his critique in 'Comments on Roger Griffin, "The Primacy of Culture: the Current Growth (or Manufacture) of Consensus within Fascist Studies"', *Journal of Contemporary History*, Vol. 35, No. 2, 2002.
23 Roger Eatwell, 'On Defining the "Fascist Minimum": the Centrality of Ideology', *Journal of Political Ideologies*, Vol. 1, No. 3, 1996, p. 313 [italics in the original].
24 German scholars in particular seem resistant to the ideological approach. See for example, Stefan Breuer, *Der Staat. Entstehung, Typen, Organisationsstadien* (Rowohlt, Hamburg, 1998), especially pp. 261–271. For a good brief critique see also Alexander De Grand in 'Comments on Roger Griffin, "The Primacy of Culture: the Current Growth (or Manufacture) of Consensus within Fascist Studies"', *Journal of Contemporary History*, Vol. 35, No. 2, 2002.
25 See especially Robert Paxton, 'The Five Stages of Fascism', *Journal of Modern History*, Vol. 70, No. 1, 1998.
26 Peter Merkl, *Political Violence under the Swastika* (Princeton University Press, New Jersey, 1975), especially pp. 694–5.
27 For a good collection of essays reflecting on differences with conservatism see M. Blinkhorn (ed.), *Fascists and Conservatives* (Unwin Hyman, London, 1990).
28 Georges Valois, *L'économie nouvelle* (Nouvelle Librairie, Paris, 1919), p. 15.
29 R. Eatwell, 'Towards a New Model of Generic Fascism', *Journal of Theoretical Politics*, Vol. 4, No. 2, 1992.
30 Oswald Mosley, 'The Philosophy of Fascism', *The Fascist Quarterly*, Vol. 1, 1935, p. 44.
31 For examples of important works on the Nazis as a catch-all *Volkspartei*, see Conan Fischer, *The Rise of National Socialism and the Working Class in Weimar Germany* (Berghahn, Oxford, 1996), and Detlef Mühlberger, *Hitler's Followers* (Routledge, London, 1991).
32 See R. Eatwell, 'Towards a New Model of the Rise of Right-Wing Extremism', *German Politics*, Vol. 6, No. 3, 1997. This stresses the importance of a 'three dimensional' approach which considers not just sweeping (macro) changes such as economic depression, or individual (micro) psychology such as anomie, but also the power of local-group (meso) contexts.

33 On these important cases see António Costa Pinto, *Salazar's Dictatorship and European Fascism* (Social Science Monographs, Boulder, 1995) and Stanley Payne, *Fascism in Spain, 1923–1977* (University of Wisconsin Press, Madison, 1999).

34 For the best statement of this claim see Zeev Sternhell (with Mario Sznajder and Maia Ashéri), *The Birth of Fascist Ideology* (Princeton University Press, Princeton, 1994).

35 For an interesting example of someone during this period who has openly termed himself 'fascist', see Maurice Bardèche, *Qu'est-ce que le fascisme?* (Les Sept Couleurs, Paris, 1961). Bardèche, the brother-in-law of the French literary fascist Robert Brasillach, who was executed after Liberation, sought to build on the last phase of Italian Fascism especially the Salò Republic's proclaimed new economic and political order for workers. He also admired early Peronism's attempt to create a new order for the workers in Argentina.

36 Corneliu Codreanu, *La Garde de Fer* (Editions Prometheus, Paris, 1938), p. 282.

37 Benito Mussolini, *Fascism. Doctrine and Institutions* (Ardita, Rome, 1935), pp. 25–6 and 59.

38 Although Nolte included the Action Française in his three faces of Fascism, most historians who have adopted the empathetic approach see Maurras's movement more as a form of the reactionary right. See for example, Eugen Weber, *Action Française* (Stanford University Press, Stanford, 1962).

39 Alfred Rosenberg, *The Myth of the Twentieth Century* (Noontide Press, Torrance Ca., 1982), especially p. 65.

40 Adolf Hitler, *Mein Kampf* (Hutchison, London, 1977), p. 73.

41 Ibid., p. 74.

42 A. James Gregor, *The Young Mussolini and the Intellectual Origins of Fascism* (University of California Press, Berkeley, 1979) and Richard J.B. Bosworth, *Mussolini* (Arnold, London, 2002, especially pp. 89–90.

43 Georges Valois, *D'un siècle à l'autre* (Nouvelle Librairie Nationale, Paris, 1921), especially p. 265ff.

44 From his 'Associazione Nazionalista Italiana' (1920), cited in Griffin, *Fascism*, p. 38.

45 Such conservative revolutionaries are often distinguished from Nazis, but in general their views can be fitted into the matrix set out in this paper. See Jeffrey Herf, *Reactionary Modernism. Technology, Politics and Culture in Weimar and the Third Reich* (Cambridge University Press, Cambridge, 1984).

46 Ernst Jünger, *Die Arbeiter* (1932), cited in Griffin, *Fascism*, p. 112.

47 Kevin Passmore, 'The Croix de Feu: Bonapartism, National Populism or Fascism?', *French History*, Vol. 9, No. 1, 1995.

48 Pierre Drieu La Rochelle, *Journal 1939–1945* (Gallimard, Paris, 1992).

49 See Victoria De Grazia, *How Fascism Ruled Women: Italy, 1922–1945* (University of California Press, Berkeley, 1993) and Jill Stephenson, *Women in Nazi Germany* (Longman, Harlow, 2001).

50 Cited in Michael Burleigh and Wolfgang Wippermann, *The Racial State. Germany 1933–1945* (Cambridge University Press, Cambridge, 1991), p. 242.

51 See also Martin Durham, *Women and Fascism* (Routledge, London, 1998), and especially Kevin Passmore (ed.), *Women, Gender and Fascism* (Manchester University Press, Manchester, 2003).

52 Hitler, *Mein Kampf*, p. 73.

53 Ibid., p. 299.

54 Oswald Mosley, *The Greater Britain* (BUF, London, 1932), p. 13.

55 Giovanni Papini, 'Il nostro impegno' (1914), cited in Griffin, *Fascism*, p. 23.

56 On the importance of syndicalism in Italy see David Roberts, *The Syndicalist Tradition and Italian Fascism* (Manchester University Press, Manchester, 1979).

57 See especially Benedict Anderson, *Imagined Communities* (Verso, London, 1991) and Eric Hobsbawm and Terence Ranger (eds), *The Invention of Tradition* (Cambridge University Press, Cambridge, 1985).
58 Mosley, 'The Philosophy of Fascism', p. 45.
59 Götz Ally and Susanne Heim, *Architects of Annihilation. Auschwitz and the Logic of Destruction* (Weidenfeld, London, 2003).
60 Rosenberg, *The Myth of the Twentieth Century*, p. 3.
61 Compare Daniel J. Goldhagen, *Hitler's Willing Executioners* (Little Brown, Boston, 1996) with Peter Weindling, *Health, Race and German Politics between National Unification and Nazism 1870–1945* (Cambridge University Press, Cambridge, 1993).
62 See for example, Christopher Browning, *The Path to Genocide* (Cambridge University Press, Cambridge, 1992), especially p. 169ff.
63 See for example, William. S. Allen, *The Nazi Seizure of Power* (Allen and Unwin, London, 1966).
64 Cited in Frank-Lothar Kroll, *Utopie als Ideologie. Geschichsdenken und politisches Handeln im Dritten Reich* (Ferdinand Schöningh, Paderborn, 1999), pp. 259 and 292.
65 Robert Mallett, *The Italian Navy and Fascist Expansionism, 1935–40* (Frank Cass, London, 1998).
66 Cited in Griffin, *Fascism*, p. 59. See also Aaron Gillette, *Racial Theories in Fascist Italy* (Routledge, London, 2002).
67 James Drennan (pseud. W.E.D. Allen), 'The Nazi Movement in Perspective', *Fascist Quarterly*, Vol. 1, No. 1, 1935, p. 47.
68 For instance, Degrelle paid homage to the thousands who died in the Waffen SS fighting for a truly united Europe in his book *Front de l'Est 1941–1945* (La Table Ronde, Paris, 1969): see especially the Dedication and Preface.
69 Mussolini, *Fascism. Doctrine and Institutions*, pp. 11 and 29.
70 For example, Pierre Drieu La Rochelle, *Chronique Politique, 1934–1942* (Gallimard, Paris, 1943), especially p. 104.
71 For an academic interpretation of fascism as an alternative 'activist style' thought to the dominant Western tradition of 'limited politics', see Noël O'Sullivan, *Fascism* (Dent, London, 1976).
72 For example, Hans Mommsen, 'Cumulative Radicalisation and Progressive Self-destruction as Structural Determinants of the Nazi Dictatorship', in Ian Kershaw and Moshe Lewin (eds), *Stalinism and Nazism. Dictatorships in Comparison* (Cambridge University Press, Cambridge, 1997), especially p. 76.
73 Georges Valois, *La révolution nationale* (Nouvelle Librairie Nationale, Paris, 1924), p. 165.
74 Mosley, 'The Philosophy of Fascism', p. 43.
75 Ian Kershaw, *Hitler, 1889–1936. Hubris* (Penguin Press, London, 1998), especially the Preface, and Ian Kershaw, *The 'Hitler Myth'. Image and Reality in the Third Reich* (Oxford University Press, Oxford, 1987).
76 A key theme developed in Kershaw, *Hitler, 1889–1936. Hubris*.
77 On the distinction between mass and coterie charisma, see Roger Eatwell, 'The Rebirth of Right-Wing Charisma? The Cases of Jean-Marie Le Pen and Vladimir Zhirinovsky', *Totalitarian Movements and Political Religions*, Vol. 3, No. 3, 2002.
78 See especially Emilio Gentile, 'Mussolini's Charisma', *Modern Italy*, Vol. 3, No. 2, 1998.
79 Cited in S. Payne, *Falange. A History of Spanish Fascism* (Stanford University Press, Stanford, 1962), p. 38.
80 For example, Burleigh, *The Third Reich* and Emilio Gentile, *The Sacralization of Politics in Fascist Italy* (Harvard University Press, Cambridge Ma., 1996).
81 W. Hardtwig, 'Political Religion in Modern Germany: Reflections on Nationalism, Socialism, and National Socialism', *GHI Bulletin*, Vol. 28, Spring, 2001.

82 Léon Degrelle, *Hitler pour 1000 ans* (La Table Ronde, Paris, 1969), especially pp. 158–9. According to Degrelle, Hitler once told him that if he had a son, he would have hoped that he would be just like Degrelle: Degrelle, *Front de l'Est*, p. 12.

83 A. Speer, *Inside the Third Reich* (London, Weidenfeld and Nicolson, 1970), especially pp. 148–9.

84 R. Mallett, *Mussolini and the Origins of the Second World War, 1933–1940* (Basingstoke: Palgrave, 2003), pp. 95–6.

85 Cited in Leon Volovici, *Nationalist Ideology and Anti-Semitism. The Case of Romanian Intellectuals in the 1930s* (Pergamon, Oxford, 1991), p. 85 [italics in the original].

86 D.L. Bergen, *Twisted Cross. The German Christian Movement in the Third Reich* (Chapel Hill, University of North Carolina Press, 1996). See also D. Sikkink and M. Regnerus, 'For God and the Fatherland: Protestant Symbolic Worlds and the Rise of German National Socialism', in C. Smith (ed.), *Disruptive Religion. The Force of Faith in Social Movements* (New York: Routledge, 1996).

87 Compare Griffin's stress on the affective palingenetic force of fascism in his article 'The Palingenetic Political Community: Rethinking the Legitimation of Totalitarian Regimes in Inter-War Europe', *Totalitarian Movements and Political Religions*, Vol. 3, No. 3, 2002 with the economic rational choice analysis in William Brustein, *The Logic of Evil. The Social Origins of the Nazi Party, 1925–1933* (Yale University Press, New Haven, 1996). See also the similar argument in William Brustein, '"Red Menace" and the Rise of Italian Fascism', *American Political Science Review*, Vol. 56, No. 4, 1991.

88 For example, Charles Maier, *In Search of Stability. Explorations in Historical Political Economy* (Cambridge University Press, Cambridge, 1987), especially p. 124.

89 See the primary sources in Barbara M. Lane and Leila J. Rupp (eds.), *Nazi Ideology before 1933* (Manchester University Press, Manchester, 1978), *passim*.

90 Avraham Barkai, *Nazi Economics. Ideology, Theory, and Policy* (Berg, Oxford, 1990). See also Simon Reich, *The Fruits of Fascism* (Cornell University Press, Ithaca, 1990).

91 Valois, *L'économie nouvelle*, pp. 15–16.

92 Gottfried Feder, 'The Social State' (1919), cited in Lane and Rupp, *Nazi Ideology before 1933*, p. 34.

93 Paxton, 'The Five Stages of Fascism'.

94 *International Fascism*, p. 14.

95 Tim Mason, *Social Policy in the Third Reich* (Berg, Oxford, 1993), p. 276.

96 The evidence in Merkl, *Political Violence under the Swastika*, especially p. 453, indicates that under 20 per cent of Nazi members in 1934 were charismatically oriented and that the main effect of Hitler had been to make followers aware of attractive policies.

Part II

HISTORICAL FASCISM

Cross-national comparisons

7

THE FIVE STAGES OF FASCISM*

Robert O. Paxton

The American historian Robert O. Paxton has contributed path-breaking works on the history of Vichy France (1940–1944) (1972); and the status of French Jews (Marrus and Paxton, 1981), as well as a general history of Europe in the twentieth century (1975). In this programmatic article originally published in 1998, Paxton challenges dominant approaches to generic fascism from the vantage point of comparative history. The incipient theoretical-methodological framework advanced here served as a basis for Paxton's recent book suggestively entitled The Anatomy of Fascism *(2004).*

Paxton starts by highlighting five major difficulties posed by the study of fascism: (1) the problem of timing, referring both to the unexpected emergence of fascism in interwar Europe and to its multiple and long-term intellectual and political origins; (2) the problem of mimicry of fascism by various forms of authoritarian interwar movements and regimes, which blurs the distinction between genuine fascism and the conservative or radical right; (3) the great diversity of, and "wide disparity" among, individual cases of fascism in space as well as in time, which challenge historians to spell out the relationship between generic fascism and its concrete historic articulations; (4) the ambiguous relationship between fascist doctrine and actions, which makes the task of defining the nature of fascism particularly daunting; and (5) the devaluation of the concept of fascism due to its contested character and improper scholarly usage.

In Paxton's view, these difficulties are magnified by two widespread errors of approach, namely the tendency to treat generic fascism in a static manner by focusing on defining the "fascist minimum;" and the tendency to approach fascism in isolation by disregarding the concrete social, political and cultural contexts in which it manifested itself. Together, these errors result in a catalogue of disparate portraits of fascism, making fascist study resemble a kind of "bestiary" of a limited analytical value.

In order to overcome these insufficiencies, Paxton proposes a functional approach to fascism informed by three methodological strategies: (1) to study fascism in motion, by underlying its processual character; (2) to contextualize fascism by placing it in its historical societal surroundings; and (3) to account for the "malleability" of fascism by comparing its various manifestations in time and space. Arguing against a static model of generic fascism, Paxton differentiates among five stages in the evolution of fascism: (1) the creation of fascist movements; (2) their transformation into political parties and their emergence of significant players in the existing political systems; (3) their advent to power; (4) their exercise of power; and (5) finally, their demise as a result of either "radicalization" or "entropy."

In order to understand the main features of these stages in their flux, historians of fascism need to employ different methodological tools. The first stage of fascist movements can be most fruitfully examined with the help of intellectual history and the history of ideas. These methods are, however, less useful for the later stages of fascism, since fascist parties and regimes largely ignored or betrayed their original programs and ideas. To analyse them, historians of fascism should rely heavily on comparison, understood as a type of thinking as much as an analytical method. Comparison is rewarding for understanding the second stage of fascism, allowing scholars to account for the "surrounding conditions" that shaped the transformation of fascist movements into political parties. It becomes particularly important for the third stage, that of arrival to power, which involves a double comparison: between countries where fascism managed to establish independent political regimes, namely Italy and Germany; and between Italy and Germany, on the one hand, and countries where fascism failed to gain political power, such as France or Britain, on the other hand. In the last stage of fascism, comparison is forcefully restricted to the two fascist regimes of Italy and Germany.

Paxton's article has been subject to criticism, mostly from the proponents of Weberian ideal-types models of generic fascism. Some scholars denounced the stages of fascism delineated by Paxton as an artificial and largely deterministic scheme; others see it as yet another mechanical model of fascism, with little heuristic value; finally, another group of scholars criticized Paxton for the narrow comparative sample employed (involving solely France, Italy, and Germany, punctuated by general references to the USA), and for his failure to provide a clear methodological alternative to Weberian ideal—types of generic fascism. The importance of these critical evaluations notwithstanding, it is undeniable that the insights put forward in this article have had an important impact on subsequent debates on generic fascism, challenging students of fascism to revisit the epistemological nature and methodological foundations of their analytical models. The article is particularly important for the insights it offers on the multiple uses of the comparative method for the study of fascism in its various forms of manifestation. It also inspired recent attempts to produce an alternative comparative account of fascism movements and regimes (for a relevant example, see Kallis' article, Chapter 9 in this volume). I have placed this article as the opening essay of the second part of this volume since it marks the transition from debates on generic fascism to theories of fascism and historical overviews of fascist movements and regimes.

BIBLIOGRAPHY

Marrus, Michael R. and Paxton, Robert O. (1981). *Vichy France and the Jews* (New York: Basic Books).

Paxton, Robert O. (1972). *Vichy France: Old Guard and New Order, 1940–1944* (New York: Alfred A. Knopf). New edition: (New York: Columbia University Press).

Paxton, Robert O. (1975). *Europe in the Twentieth Century* (New York: Harcourt Brace Jovanovich). New edition: (San Diego: Harcourt Brace Jovanovich).

Paxton, Robert O. (2004). *The Anatomy of Fascism* (London: Allen Lane).

*   *   *

At first sight, nothing seems easier to understand than fascism. It presents itself to us in crude, primary images: a chauvinist demagogue haranguing an ecstatic crowd; disciplined ranks of marching youths; uniform-shirted militants beating up members of some demonized minority; obsessive preoccupation with community decline, humiliation, or victimhood; and compensatory cults of unity, energy, and purity, pursued with redemptive violence.

Yet great difficulties arise as soon as one sets out to define fascism.[1] Its boundaries are ambiguous in both space and time. Do we include Stalin? Do we reach outside Europe to charismatic dictators in developing countries like Nkrumah, with his single party and official ideology of Nkrumaism, or Saddam Hussein, gigantic statues of whose own forearms raise crossed swords over a Baghdad avenue?[2] What about imperial Japan in the 1930s or the nationalist syndicalism of Juan Perón in Argentina (1946–55)? How far back in time must we go? If we choose to trace a conservative pedigree, we may reach all the way back to Joseph de Maistre, whose dark vision of violence and conspiracy in human affairs and conviction that only authority could repress human destructive instincts offer a prophetic glimpse, according to Isaiah Berlin, of twentieth-century totalitarianisms of the Left and the Right.[3] If we prefer to trace a lineage within the Left, drawing on the Enlightenment's own perception that individual liberty can undermine community, some have gone back as far as Rousseau.[4]

Even if we limit ourselves to our own century and its two most notorious cases, Nazi Germany and Fascist Italy, we find that they display profound differences. How can we lump together Mussolini and Hitler, the one surrounded by Jewish henchmen and a Jewish mistress, the other an obsessed antisemite?[5] How can we equate the militarized regimentation of Nazi Party rule with the laxity of Mussolinian Italy? Such eminent authorities as the late Renzo De Felice in Rome and Karl Dietrich Bracher of the University of Bonn have denied that German Nazism and Italian Fascism belong to the same category.[6] This article argues for their conceptual kinship, for reasons that we will develop as we proceed.[7]

Five major difficulties stand in the way of any effort to define fascism. First, a problem of timing. The fascist phenomenon was poorly understood at the beginning in part because it was unexpected. Until the end of the nineteenth century, most political thinkers believed that widening the vote would inevitably benefit democracy and socialism. Friedrich Engels, noting the rapid rise of the socialist vote in Germany and France, was sure that time and numbers were on his side. Writing the preface for a new edition in 1895 of Karl Marx's *Class Struggles in France*, he declared that "if it continues in this fashion, we will conquer the major part of the middle classes and the peasantry and will become the decisive power."[8] It took two generations before the Left understood that fascism is, after all, an authentic mass popular enthusiasm and not merely a clever manipulation of populist emotions by the reactionary Right or by capitalism in crisis.[9]

A second difficulty in defining fascism is created by mimicry. In fascism's hey-day, in the 1930s, many regimes that were not functionally fascist borrowed ele-ments of fascist decor in order to lend themselves an aura of force, vitality, and mass mobilization. They were influenced by the "magnetic field" of fascism, to employ Philippe Burrin's useful phrase.[10] But one cannot identify a fascist regime by its plumage. George Orwell understood at once that fascism is not defined by its clothing. If, some day, an authentic fascism were to succeed in England, Orwell wrote as early as 1936, it would be more soberly clad than in Germany.[11] The exotic black shirts of Sir Oswald Mosley are one explanation for the failure of the princi-pal fascist movement in England, the British Union of Fascists. What if they had worn bowler hats and carried well-furled umbrellas? The adolescent skinheads who flaunt the swastika today in parts of Europe seem so alien and marginal that they constitute a law-and-order problem (serious though that may be) rather than a recur-rence of authentic mass-based fascism, astutely decked out in the patriotic emblems of their own countries. Focusing on external symbols, which are subject to superfi-cial imitation, adds to confusion about what may legitimately be considered fascist.

This leads to the third problem with defining fascism, posed by the dauntingly wide disparity among individual cases in space and in time. They differ in space because each national variant of fascism draws its legitimacy, as we shall see, not from some universal scripture but from what it considers the most authentic ele-ments of its own community identity. Religion, for example, would certainly play a much greater role in an authentic fascism in the United States than in the first European fascisms, which were pagan for contingent historical reasons.[12] They differ in time because of the transformations and accommodations demanded of those movements that seek power. A little circle of dissident nationalist syndical-ists, such as those whom Zeev Sternhell studies, functions differently from a party in search of alliances and of complicities within the country's elites. Disparate in their symbols, decor, and even in their political tactics, fascist movements resem-ble each other mainly in their functions (a point to which we shall return).

A fourth and even more redoutable difficulty sterns from the ambiguous rela-tionship between doctrine and action in fascism. We shall have to spend much more time with this problem than with the others. As intellectuals, almost instinc-tively, we classify all the great political movements—all the "isms"—by doc-trine. It is a time-honored convention to take for granted that fascism is an "ism" like the others and so treat it as essentially a body of thought.[13] By an analogy that has gone largely unexamined, much existing scholarship treats fascism as if it were of the same nature as the great political doctrines of the long nineteenth century, like conservatism, liberalism, and socialism. This article undertakes to challenge that convention and its accompanying implicit analogy.

The great "isms" of nineteenth-century Europe—conservativism, liberalism, socialism—were associated with notable rule, characterized by deference to educated leaders, learned debates, and (even in some forms of socialism) limited popular authority. Fascism is a political practice appropriate to the mass politics of the twentieth century. Moreover, it bears a different relationship to thought than do the nineteenth-century "isms." Unlike them, fascism does not rest on formal philosophical positions with claims to universal validity. There was no "Fascist Manifesto," no founding fascist thinker. Although one can deduce from fascist language implicit Social Darwinist assumptions about human nature, the need for community and authority in human society, and the destiny of nations in history, fascism does not base its claims to validity on their truth.[14] Fascists despise thought and reason, abandon intellectual positions casually, and cast aside many intellectual fellow-travelers. They subordinate thought and reason not to faith, as did the traditional Right, but to the promptings of the blood and the historic destiny of the group. Their only moral yardstick is the prowess of the race, of the nation, of the community. They claim legitimacy by no universal standard except a Darwinian triumph of the strongest community.

Fascists deny any legitimacy to universal principles to such a point that they even neglect proselytism. Authentic fascism is not for export.[15] Particular national variants of fascism differ far more profoundly one from another in themes and symbols than do the national variants of the true "isms." The most conspicuous of these variations, one that leads some to deny the validity of the very concept of generic fascism, concerns the nature of the indispensable enemy: within Mediterranean fascisms, socialists and colonized peoples are more salient enemies than is the Jewry.[16] Drawing their slogans and their symbols from the patriotic repertory of one particular community, fascisms are radically unique in their speech and insignia. They fit badly into any system of universal intellectual principles. It is in their functions that they resemble each other.

Further, the words of fascist intellectuals—even if we accept for the moment that they constitute fundamental philosophical texts—correspond only distantly with what fascist movements do after they have power. Early fascist programs are poor guides to later fascist policy. The sweeping social changes proposed by Mussolini's first Fascist program of April 1919 (including the vote for women, the eight-hour day, heavy taxation of war profits, confiscation of church lands, and workers' participation in industrial management) stand in flagrant conflict with the macho persona of the later *Duce* and his deals with conservatives. Similarly, the hostility of the Nazi Twenty-Five Points of 1920 toward all capitalism except that of artisan producers bears little relation to the sometimes strained though powerfully effective collaboration for rearmament between German business and the Nazi regime.[17]

Sternhell responds to this line of argument by asserting that every political movement deforms its ideology under the constraints of exercising power.[18] Fascism, however (unlike Stalinism), never produces a casuistic literature devoted to demonstrating how the leader's actions correspond in some profound way to the basic scriptures. Being in accord with basic scriptures simply does not seem to matter to fascist leaders, who claim to incarnate the national destiny in their physical persons.

Feelings propel fascism more than thought does. We might call them mobilizing passions, since they function in fascist movements to recruit followers and in fascist regimes to "weld" the fascist "tribe" to its leader.[19] The following mobilizing passions are present in fascisms, though they may sometimes be articulated only implicitly:

1 The primacy of the group, toward which one has duties superior to every right, whether universal or individual.
2 The belief that one's group is a victim, a sentiment which justifies any action against the group's enemies, internal as well as external.
3 Dread of the group's decadence under the corrosive effect of individualistic and cosmopolitan liberalism.
4 Closer integration of the community within a brotherhood (*fascio*) whose unity and purity are forged by common conviction, if possible, or by exclusionary violence if necessary.
5 An enhanced sense of identity and belonging, in which the grandeur of the group reinforces individual self-esteem.
6 Authority of natural leaders (always male) throughout society, culminating in a national chieftain who alone is capable of incarnating the group's destiny.
7 The beauty of violence and of will, when they are devoted to the group's success in a Darwinian struggle.

Programs are so easily sacrificed to expediency in fascist practice that, at one point, I was tempted to reduce the role of ideology in fascism to a simple functionalism: fascists propose anything that serves to attract a crowd, solidify a mass following, or reassure their elite accomplices. That would be a gross oversimplification. Ideas count in fascism, but we must be precise about exactly when and how they count. They count more at some stages than at others. At the beginning, their promise of radical spiritual-cultural renewal and restored national community helps fascists recruit a broad and varied public, including some respectable intellectuals.[20] Early fascist ideas helped amplify the disrepute of the liberal values to which the broad middle classes had largely adhered before World War I. But it is only by distancing themselves from those elements of the early radical programs that were threatening to conservatives that certain fascist movements have been able to gain and exercise power.

In power, what seems to count is less the faithful application of the party's initial ideology than the integrating function that espousing one official ideology performs, to the exclusion of any ideas deemed alien or divisive. Much later in the fascist cycle, at the climacteric moment, under the influence of war, parts of the original radical fascist programs that do not threaten existing social or economic hierarchies (such as the Nazis' racial obsessions) may recover their ascendancy. We will return to these matters when we discuss the stages in detail. The contradictions that obscure every reading of fascist texts can be resolved, therefore, only by the study of the choices made by the fascists in their daily actions.

To illustrate this proposition, consider the two most ambiguous concepts in the fascist lexicon: revolution and modernity. Fascists like to call themselves revolutionaries, but one discovers best by their actions what they really want to change. Their revolution consists of hardening the character and purifying and energizing the community rather than making the social structure or the economic system more just or free. Fascist militants proclaim themselves anti-bourgeois; what they hate in the bourgeoisie, however, is not exploitation but softness. Sternhell has put his finger precisely on what distinguishes those revolutionaries who abandon early fascism, when it begins to reposition itself for power, from those who remain faithful to it through all its transformations. The first remain committed to a change in the socio-economic order. The faithful, by contrast, preach a moral revolution in order to create "the new fascist man."[21] Fascist "revolutionaries" believe in change in the sense used by Tancredi, scion of the decaying noble Sicilian family in Giuseppe di Lampedusa's great novel *The Leopard*: "If we want things to stay as they are, things will have to change."[22]

Similar confusions surround the fascist understanding of modernity. Hitler loved to arrive theatrically aboard a supercharged Mercedes or by airplane. It is true that he nursed the archaic dream of installing German peasant colonies in the plains of eastern Europe, but this dream could be realized only by modern weaponry. Hitler execrated the Bauhaus style; the young Mussolini, on the contrary, was attracted to aesthetic modernism.[23] It has been traditional to try to resolve these conflicts by scrutinizing fascist texts.[24] These conflicts can best be resolved, however, by examining fascist actions: all fascists seek technical and military power while simultaneously trying to escape the destabilizing social effects of the industrialization such power requires. They combine technical modernity with a system of authority and discipline intended to suppress the disorderly social consequences of industrial expansion. The meanings that fascists give to the concepts of revolution and modernity, ambiguous in the texts, become comprehensible in their concrete applications.

The fifth and final difficulty with defining fascism is caused by overuse: the word "fascist" has become the most banal of epithets. Everyone is someone's fascist. Consider Rush Limbaugh's "feminazis." A couple of summers ago, I heard a young German call Western-sponsored birth control programs in the Third World "fascist," forgetting that the Nazis and the Italian Fascists were, for once, agreed in encouraging large families—except, of course, among those considered either eugenically or racially inferior. Those people were condemned to sterilization, if not worse.[25] The term "fascist" has been so loosely used that some have proposed giving it up altogether in scholarly research.[26]

171

Nevertheless, we cannot give up in the face of these difficulties. A real phenomenon exists. Indeed, fascism is the most original political novelty of the twentieth century, no less. It successfully gathered, against all expectations, in certain modern nations that had seemed firmly planted on a path to gradually expanding democracy, a popular following around hard, violent, antiliberal and antisocialist nationalist dictatorships. Then it spread its "politics in a new key" through much of Europe, assembling all nationalists who hated the Left and found the Right inadequate.[27] We must be able to examine this phenomenon as a system. It is not enough to treat each national case individually, as if each one constitutes a category in itself. If we cannot examine fascism synthetically, we risk being unable to understand this century, or the next. We must have a word, and for lack of a better one, we must employ the word that Mussolini borrowed from the vocabulary of the Italian Left in 1919, before his movement had assumed its mature form.[28] Obliged to use the word fascism, we ought to use it well.

Unfortunately much scholarly work on fascism complicates things still further by two very widespread errors of approach. First, most authorities treat generic fascism in a static manner. With several remarkable exceptions—I think particularly of Pierre Milza and Philippe Burrin—they look for a fixed essence: the famous "fascist minimum."[29] Second, most works consider fascisms in too isolated a manner, without sufficient sustained reference to the political, social, and cultural spaces in which they navigate. Together, these two common errors of approach produce what we might call "bestiaries" of fascism. Like medieval naturalists, they present a catalog of portraits of one beast after another, each one portrayed against a bit of background scenery and identified by its external signs.[30]

We can get beyond the "bestiary" approach by adopting three quite simple historical strategies. One is to study fascism in motion, paying more attention to processes than to essences. Another is to study it contextually, spending at least as much time on the surrounding society and on fascism's allies and accomplices as on the fascist movements themselves.[31] The more actively a fascist movement participates in the political life of its country, the less one can understand it in isolation. It is ensnared in a web of reciprocal influences with allies or rivals in its country's civil society. Finally, we can put the disconcerting malleability of fascisms in time and in space to good use. That malleability is not necessarily an obstacle to understanding. It may even make understanding easier, by making comparison possible. Comparison is "a way of thinking more than a method," and it works better when we try to account for differences than when we try to amass vague resemblances.[32] Comparison works revealingly with fascisms, since every Western society has contained at least some marginal example. Their different fates across time and space in neighboring settings should help us to identify the principal factors in the varying success of specific cases, and even to isolate the constants.[33]

But one must compare what is comparable. A regime where fascism exercises power is hardly comparable to a sect of dissident intellectuals. We must distinguish the different stages of fascism in time. It has long been standard to point to the difference between movements and regimes. I believe we can usefully distinguish more stages than that, if we look clearly at the very different sociopolitical processes involved in each stage. I propose to isolate five of them:[34] (1) the initial creation of fascist movements; (2) their rooting as parties in a political system; (3) the acquisition of power; (4) the exercise of power; and, finally, in the longer term, (5) radicalization or entropy. Since different kinds of historical process are involved in each stage, moreover, we must deploy different scholarly strategies in the analysis of each.

Consider the first stage. First-stage fascism is the domain of the intellectual historian, for the process to be studied here is the emergence of new ways of looking at the world and diagnosing its ills. In the late nineteenth and early twentieth centuries, thinkers and publicists discredited reigning liberal and democratic values, not in the name of either existing alternative—conservative or socialist—but in the name of something new that promised to transcend and join them: a novel mixture of nationalism and syndicalism that had found little available space in a nineteenth-century political landscape compartmented into Left and Right (though retrospect may reveal a few maverick precedents). This first stage is the part of the fascist elephant that scholars have found most congenial as a subject; examining one limb, of course, may mislead us about the whole beast.

Comparison is of little help to us at this first stage, for all modern states have had protofascist militants and publicists since the 1914–18 war. Fascism can appear wherever democracy is sufficiently implanted to have aroused disillusion. That suggests its spatial and temporal limits: no authentic fascism before the emergence of a massively enfranchised and politically active citizenry. In order to give birth to fascism, a society must have known political liberty—for better or for worse.

But early fascisms were so ubiquitous that we can hardly attribute their origin to any one particular national intellectual history. George Mosse has fingered post-Enlightenment Germany; Sternhell, France at the turn of the century, followed by Italian disciples.[35] A body of thought that one can call "protofascist" appeared even in the United States, at the end of the nineteenth century. Brooks Adams, scion of a great New England dynasty, descendant of two presidents of the United States, lamented the moral decline of the United States as a result of the concentration of financial power.[36] Later on, in 1918, Adams believed he had found the remedy to American decline in an authoritarian regime directing a state socialism. After the First World War, the United States, too, entered the "magnetic field" of European fascisms. "Colored shirt" movements sprang up, such as the "Silver Shirts," or "S.S.," of William Dudley Pelley.[37]

But it is further back in American history that one comes upon the earliest phenomenon that seems functionally related to fascism: the Ku Klux Klan. Just after the Civil War, some former Confederate officers, fearing the vote given to African Americans by the Radical Reconstructionists in 1867, set up a militia to restore an overturned social order. The Klan constituted an alternate civic authority, parallel to the legal state, which, in its founders' eyes, no longer defended their community's legitimate interests. In its adoption of a uniform (white robe and hood), as well as its techniques of intimidation and its conviction that violence was justified in the cause of the group's destiny, the first version of the Klan in the defeated American South was a remarkable preview of the way fascist movements were to function in interwar Europe.[38] It is arguable, at least, that fascism (understood functionally) was born in the late 1860s in the American South.

Since fascisms take their first steps in reaction to claimed failings of democracy, it is not surprising that they should appear first in the most precocious democracies, the United States and France. But we come now to a paradox: it is not necessarily in the countries that generated the first fascisms that fascist systems have had, historically, the best chance of succeeding.

The second stage—rooting, in which a fascist movement becomes a party capable of acting decisively on the political scene—happens relatively rarely. At this stage, comparison becomes rewarding: one can contrast successes with failures. Success depends on certain relatively precise conditions: the weakness of a liberal state, whose inadequacies seems to condemn the nation to disorder, decline, or humiliation; and political deadlock because the Right, the heir to power but unable to continue to wield it alone, refuses to accept a growing Left as a legitimate governing partner. Some fascist leaders, in their turn, are willing to reposition their movements in alliances with these frightened conservatives, a step that pays handsomely in political power, at the cost of disaffection among some of the early antibourgeois militants.

To illustrate the issues raised by the rooting stage, consider the growth of fascism among farmers. I have been studying a peasant movement in the west of France in the 1930s, whose leader, Henry Dorgères, linked himself openly with fascism, at least at the beginning, in 1934. I chose this subject not because his Greenshirts played a major role in interwar France—they did not, except for several conspicuous crowd actions exaggerated by the press—but because it was in the countryside that German Nazism and Italian Fascism first succeeded in becoming the representatives of an important social and economic interest. The comparison between the success of rural fascism in Germany and Italy and its relative failure in France seems to me a fruitful one. It permits us to identify those aspects of the French Third Republic that made it a less propitious setting than Weimar Germany or the Italian liberal monarchy for the political rooting of the local variety of fascism.

All three of these countries experienced massive strikes of agricultural workers: east-Elbian Germany during the postwar crisis in 1919–23; the Po Valley and Apulia in Italy in 1920–21; and the big farms of northern France and the Paris Basin during the two summers of the Popular Front, in 1936 and 1937.[39] The German strikes were broken by vigilantes, armed and abetted by local army authorities, in cases in which the regular authorities were too conciliatory to suit the landowners. The Italian ones were broken by Mussolini's famous blackshirted *squadristi*, whose vigilantism filled the void left by the apparent inability of the liberal Italian state to enforce order. It was precisely in this direct action against farm-worker unions that second-stage fascism was born in Italy and even launched on the path to power, to the dismay of the first Fascists, intellectual dissidents from national syndicalism. Many militants from the first stage resigned from second-stage Fascism at this point, complaining of being transformed into "watchdogs" for the big planters.[40]

France had *squadristi*, too: Henry Dorgères's Greenshirts (*chemises vertes*), active during the great strikes of agricultural workers in the hot summers of 1936 and 1937. But the Greenshirts' role was limited to several symbolic actions in the big wheat and sugar beet farms of the north and northwest (Aisne, Somme, Seine-Maritime, Pas-de-Calais). It was the French *gendarmerie*, even with Léon Blum in power, who put down the agricultural strikes in France. The French landowners did not need the *chemises vertes*. The authority of the state and the power of the conservative farmers' organizations left hardly any space in the French country-side for the rooting of a fascist parallel power. These differences in available space and allies seem to me much more influential than any differences or resemblances in vocabulary or program among rural fascists in France, Germany, and Italy.

That is to say, the most significant differences that comparison reveals to us concern the setting as much as the character of the fascist movements themselves. This seems to be a quite fundamental principle of good comparative method (see n. 34 above). The description of fascist movements in isolation does not explain much. It leads us straight back to the bestiary or, even worse, to pruriency, as in Visconti's film *The Damned*, which invites us to leer at the decadent perversity of individual fascist thugs.[41] We learn much more if we focus our gaze on the circumstances that favor the fascists—polarization within civil society and deadlocks within the political system—and on the fascists' accomplices and allies. It is in the surrounding conditions that one must seek the differences that count, for movements that sound rather similar in their rhetoric have arrived at very different results in different national settings.

Therefore, the methods of intellectual history become much less helpful beyond the first stage in the fascist cycle. Every fascist movement that has rooted itself successfully as a major political contender, thereby approaching power, has betrayed its initial antibourgeois and anticapitalist program. The processes to be examined in later stages include the breakdown of democratic regimes and the success of fascist movements in assembling new, broad catch-all parties that attract a mass following across classes and hence seem attractive allies to conservatives looking for ways to perpetuate their shaken rule.[42] At later stages, successful fascist parties also position themselves as the most effective barriers, by persuasion or by force, to an advancing Left and prove adept at the formation, maintenance, and domination of political coalitions with conservatives. But these political successes come at the cost of the first ideological programs. Demonstrating their contempt for doctrine, successfully rooted fascist parties do not annul or amend their early programs. They simply ignore them, while acting in ways quite contrary to them. The conflicts of doctrine and practice set up by successful fascist movements on the road to power not only alienate many radical fascists of the first hour; they continue to confuse many historians who assume that analyzing programs is a sufficient tool for classifying fascisms. The confusion has been compounded by the persistence of many early fascisms that failed to navigate the turn from the first to the second and third stages and remained pure and radical, though marginal, as "national syndicalisms."[43]

A thoughtful look at the first two stages in the original fascist cycle—the creation and emergence of such movements as plausible players on the political stage—shows how much improvisation was involved in the first steps of Mussolini and Hitler. Mussolini evidently believed in 1919 that his new *Fasci di combattimento* were destined to gather discontented veterans together with other discontented nationalists, from both Left and Right, in a vast movement for profound social change. We have noted how the first Fascist program, drafted in spring 1919, mixed nationalist territorial claims with social reforms that are astonishingly radical in the light of Mussolini's later actions and macho persona. This early fascism was decisively defeated in the elections of 1919, for there was no space in Italian politics for a party that was both nationalist and Left. Mussolini would be totally forgotten today if some of his lieutenants in the provinces had not discovered different vocations—bashing Slovenes in Trieste in July 1920 and bashing socialist organizers of farm workers in the Po Valley in fall and winter 1920–21. Mussolini supported these new initiatives by the *ras*, and his movement turned into something else, thereafter prospering mightily.[44] Hitler's efforts to recruit urban and working-class voters faltered through 1928; he began assembling a mass electorate in 1929–30 when he turned his attention to recruiting rural populations afflicted by the collapse of farm prices.[45] The two apprentices learned how to be second-stage fascists by trial and error. Their adaptations to the available space undermine any effort to portray historical fascism as the consistent expression of one coherent ideology.

At the third stage, the arrival in power, comparison acquires greater bite. What characteristics distinguished Germany and Italy, where fascism took power, from countries such as France and Britain, where fascist movements were highly visible but remained marginal? We need to recall that fascism has never so far taken power by a coup d'état, deploying the weight of its militants in the street. Fascist power by coup is hardly conceivable in a modern state. Fascism cannot appeal to the street without risking a confrontation with future allies—the army and the police—without whom it will not be able to pursue its expansionist goals. Indeed, fascist coup attempts have commonly led to military dictatorship rather than to fascist power (as in Romania in December 1941).[46] Resorting to direct mass action also risks conceding advantages to fascism's principal enemy, the Left, which was still powerful in the street and workplace in interwar Europe.[47] The only route to power available to fascists passes through cooperation with conservative elites. The most important variables, therefore, are the conservative elites' willingness to work with the fascists (along with a reciprocal flexibility on the part of the fascist leaders) and the depth of the crisis that induces them to cooperate.

Neither Hitler nor Mussolini took the helm by force, even if they used force earlier to destabilize the liberal regime and later to transform their governments into dictatorships.[48] Each was invited to take office as head of government by a head of state in the legitimate exercise of his official functions, on the advice of his conservative counselors, under quite precise circumstances: a deadlock of constitutional government (produced in part by the polarization that the fascists abetted); conservative leaders who felt threatened by the loss of their capacity to keep the population under control at a moment of massive popular mobilization; an advancing Left; and conservative leaders who refused to work with that Left and who felt unable to continue to govern against the Left without further reinforcement.

Comparison with the quite varied cases where fascism flourished but failed to take power can be instructive at this third stage. In France, if fascism did not arrive in power before the defeat of 1940, the explanation is not some mysterious allergy.[49] Early fascism prospered in France, but most conservatives did not feel sufficiently threatened in the 1930s to call on it for help, and fascism was not sufficiently rooted and recentered to impose itself as a partner.[50] British fascism had little space available because the Conservative Party succeeded in ruling consensually from 1931 to 1945. Franco's military dictatorship preempted Spanish fascism, and Salazar crushed Portuguese fascism after he had copied some of its techniques of popular mobilization.[51]

The fourth stage—the exercise of power—is conditioned by the manner in which fascism arrives in power. The fascist leaders who have reached power, historically, have been condemned to govern in association with the conservative elites who had opened the gates to them. This sets up a four-way struggle for dominance among the leader, his party (whose militants clamor for jobs, perquisites, expansionist adventures, and the fulfillment of elements of the early radical program), the regular state functionaries such as police commanders and magistrates, and the traditional elites—churches, the army, the professions, and business leaders.[52] This four-way tension is what gives fascist rule its characteristic blend of febrile activism and shapelessness.[53]

The tensions within fascist rule also help us clarify the frontiers between authentic fascism and other forms of dictatorial rule. Fascist rule is unlike the exercise of power in either authoritarianism (which lacks a single party, or gives it little power) or Stalinism (which lacked traditional elites).[54] Authoritarians would prefer to leave the population demobilized, while fascists promise to win the working class back for the nation by their superior techniques of manufacturing enthusiasm.[55] Although authoritarian regimes may trample due process and individual liberties, they accept ill-defined, though real, limits to state power in favor of some private space for individuals and "organic" intermediary bodies such as local notables, economic cartels, families, and churches. Fascism claims to reduce the private sphere to nothing, though that is propaganda (which has been quite successful, moreover, even with scholars).[56] Stalin's Communist Party governed a civil society radically simplified by the Bolshevik Revolution; under Hitler, in contrast, the party, the bureaucracy, and the traditional elites jostled for power. Even if Stalin's techniques of rule often resembled those of fascism, he did not have to concern himself with concentrations of inherited autonomous social and economic power.

The exercise of power involved the same elements in Mussolini's Italy as in Nazi Germany.[57] It is the balance between the party and traditional institutions that distinguishes one case from the other. In Italy, the traditional state wound up with primacy, largely because Mussolini feared his own most militant followers, the local *ras* and their *squadristi*. In Nazi Germany, the party came to dominate, especially after the war began. This interplay between single parties and traditional elites helps us classify borderline regimes, especially if we bear in mind that the frontiers were fluid between authoritarian and fascist regimes, and they might be crossed in either direction. The Vichy regime was certainly not fascist at the outset, for it had neither a single party nor parallel institutions. As it became transformed into a police state under the pressures of war, however, parallel institutions appeared: the *Milice* or supplementary police, the "special sections" in the judiciary, the Police for Jewish Affairs.[58] Spain and Portugal, related to Vichy by style of rule as well as by sympathy, differed in that neutrality in World War II permitted them to reinforce steadily the predominance of the traditional state over these countries' small fascist movements.[59]

In the long run (the fifth stage), fascist "dual power" can evolve in either of two directions: radicalization or entropy. Mussolini's regime subsided toward routine authoritarianism after the establishment of the dictatorship in 1925–26, except during colonial campaigns. The Ethiopian War (1935–36) set off a "rivoluzione culturale" and "svolta totalitaria" in which the Fascist regime tried to shape the fascist "new man" by instituting "fascist customs," "fascist language," and racial legislation.[60] Within the sphere of colonialist action, first in Libya and then in Ethiopia, the party's arbitrary rule and policies of racial discrimination were free to set the tone.[61] The radicalism of Italian Fascism's early days reappeared at the end of the war in the phantom Republic of Salò that governed the north of Italy under German tutelage after September 1943.

Nazi Germany alone experienced full radicalization. A victorious war of extermination in the East offered almost limitless freedom of action to the "prerogative state" and its "parallel institutions," released from the remaining constraints of the "normative state," such as they were. In the "no-man's-land" of what had been Poland and the western parts of the Soviet Union they put into application their ultimate fantasies of racial cleansing.[62] Extreme radicalization remains latent in all fascisms, but the circumstances of war, and particularly of victorious wars of conquest, give it the fullest means of expression.[63]

Focus on processes and discrimination among stages—this article's principal methodological proposals—casts a clarifying light on many specialized themes in the study of fascism. Social composition, for example, evolves with successive stages. Any study that proposes a single, fixed social composition inherent in fascism is flawed.[64] It also becomes doubtful that we can identify a single unchanging fascist aesthetic that would apply to all the national cases.[65] The macho restoration of a threatened patriarchy comes close to being a universal fascist value, but Mussolini advocated female suffrage in his first program, and Hitler did not mention gender issues in his Twenty-Five Points.[66]

Having picked fascism apart, have we escaped from the nominalism of the bestiary only to fall into another nominalism of processes and stages? Where is the "fascism minimum" in all this? Has generic fascism evaporated in this analysis? It is by a functional definition of fascism that we can escape from these quandaries. Fascism is a system of political authority and social order intended to reinforce the unity, energy, and purity of communities in which liberal democracy stands accused of producing division and decline. Its complex tensions (political revolution versus social restoration, order versus aggressive expansionism, mass enthusiasm versus civic submission) are hard to understand solely by reading its propaganda. One must observe it in daily operation, using all the social sciences and not only intellectual-cultural history, and, since it is not static, one must understand it in motion, through its cycle of potential (though not inevitable) stages.

Defining fascism functionally, together with distinguishing clearly among successive stages, also helps us answer the burning question of this moment: can fascism still exist today, in spite of the humiliating defeat of Hitler and Mussolini, the declining availability of the war option in a nuclear age, the seemingly irreversible globalization of the economy, and the triumph of individualistic consumerism? After ethnic cleansing in the Balkans, the rise of exclusionary nationalisms in postcommunist Eastern Europe, the "skinhead" phenomenon in Britain, Germany, Scandinavia, and Italy, and the election of Mirko Tremaglia, a veteran of the Republic of Salò, as chairman of the Foreign Affairs Committee of the Italian Parliament during the Berlusconi government, it would be hard to answer "no" to that question.[67]

The most interesting cases today, however, are not those that imitate the exotic colored-shirt movements of an earlier generation. New functional equivalents of fascism would probably work best, as George Orwell reminded us, clad in the mainstream patriotic dress of their own place and time. An authentically popular fascism in the United States would be pious and anti-Black; in Western Europe, secular and antisemitic, or more probably, these days, anti-Islamic; in Russia and Eastern Europe, religious, antisemitic, and slavophile. It is wiser to pay attention to the functions fulfilled by new movements of an analogous type, to the circumstances that could open a space to them, and to the potential conservative elite allies ready to try to coopt them rather than look for echoes of the rhetoric, the programs, or the aesthetic preferences of the protofascists of the last fin de siècle. We may legitimately conclude, for example, that the skinheads are functional equivalents of Hitler's SA and Mussolini's *squadristi* only if important elements of the conservative elite begin to cultivate them as weapons against some internal enemy, such as immigrants.

The right questions to ask of today's neo- or protofascisms are those appropriate for the second and third stages of the fascist cycle. Are they becoming rooted as parties that represent major interests and feelings and wield major influence on the political scene? Is the economic or constitutional system in a state of blockage apparently insoluble by existing authorities? Is a rapid political mobilization threatening to escape the control of traditional elites, to the point where they would be tempted to look for tough helpers in order to stay in charge? It is by answering those kinds of questions, grounded in a proper historical understanding of the processes at work in past fascisms, and not by checking the color of the shirts or seeking traces of the rhetoric of the national-syndicalist dissidents of the opening of the twentieth century, that we may be able to recognize our own day's functional equivalents of fascism.

NOTES

* An earlier version of this paper was delivered as the Marc Bloch Lecture of the Ecole des Hautes Etudes en Sciences Sociales, Paris, on June 13, 1994. I thank members of my graduate seminars over the years, and Alice Kaplan and her students, for stimulating comments.

1 We capitalize "Fascism" when referring to the Italian party, and refer to generic fascism in the lower case. Following a period of active study of generic fascism in the 1960s and early 1970s, strongly influenced by Marxism, scholarly activity shifted after about 1975 away from generic fascism to particular cases. See Tim Mason, "Whatever Happened to Fascism?" in *Reevaluating the Third Reich*, ed. Thomas Childers and Jane Caplan (New York, 1993), pp. 253–62. Now the study of generic fascism is reappearing, in a rather traditional descriptive vein. Roger Griffin, *The Nature of Fascism* (London, 1993), and Roger Eatwell, *Fascism: A History* (London, 1996), approach fascism as a doctrine. Stanley G. Payne, *A History of Fascism, 1914–1945* (Madison, Wis., 1995), provides an encyclopedic empirical survey. Walter Laqueur, *Fascism: Past, Present, and Future* (New York, 1996), deals more fully with the present and future than with the past.

2 Samir el-Khalil, *The Monument* (Berkeley and Los Angeles, 1991). He does not evoke fascism overtly.

3 Sir Isaiah Berlin, "Joseph de Maistre and the Origins of Fascism," in *The Crooked Timber of Humanity* (New York, 1991).

4 Jacob L. Talmon, *The Origins of Totalitarian Democracy* (Boston, 1952). Talmon's student Zeev Sternhell is the preeminent scholar today of fascism's intellectual roots in a heresy of the Left, national syndicalism. See, among many works, Zeev Sternhell with Mario Sznajder and Maria Ashéri, *The Birth of Fascist Ideology: From Cultural Rebellion to Political Revolution* (Princeton, N.J., 1994).

5 The formidable Margherita Sarfatti, patron of the arts and Mussolini's official biographer, is the subject of Philip Canistraro and Brian R. Sullivan, *Mussolini's Other Woman* (New York, 1993). Mussolini's most notorious Jewish henchman was Aldo Finzi, implicated in the murder of the socialist leader Giacomo Matteotti in June 1924.

6 Renzo De Felice, *Fascism: An Informal Introduction to Its Theory and Practice: An Interview with Michael A. Ledeen* (New Brunswick, N.J., 1976), pp. 15, 55–56, 67, 94–96; Karl Dietrich Bracher, *Zeitgeschichtliche Kontroversen um Faschismus, Totalitarismus, Demokratie* (Munich, 1976), p. 20.

7 Richard Bessel, ed., *Fascist Italy and Nazi Germany: Comparisons and Contrasts* (Cambridge, 1996), the papers of a conference in honor of Tim Mason, is the latest examination of the complicated but essential conceptual unity of the two regimes.

8 Friedrich Engels, 1895 preface to Karl Marx, *Class Struggles in France (1848–50)*, in *The Marx-Engels Reader*, ed. Robert C. Tucker, 2d ed. (New York, 1978), p. 571.

9 In the 1970s, Western Marxists criticized Stalin's interpretation of fascism and found an alternate tradition in August Thalheimer, the Austro-Marxists, and Antonio Gramsci. See, e.g., Nicos Poulantzas, *Fascism and Dictatorship* (London, 1974); and Anson Rabinbach, "Toward a Marxist Theory of Fascism and National Socialism," *New German Critique*, no. 3 (Fall 1974), pp. 127–53. Wolfgang Wippermann surveys

the German case in "The Postwar German Left and Fascism," *Journal of Contemporary History* 11 (October 1976): 185–219, and in *Faschismustheorien zum Stand der Gegenwartigen Diskussion*, 5th ed. (Darmstadt, 1989).

10 Philippe Burrin, "La France dans le champ magnétique des fascismes," *Le Débat* 32 (November 1984): 52–72.

11 George Orwell, *The Road to Wigan Pier* (New York, 1961), p. 176. See also *The Lion and the Unicorn* (1941), quoted in *The Collected Essays, Journalism, and Letters of George Orwell*, ed. Sonia Orwell and Ian Angus (New York, 1968), 3:93.

12 Payne, *History* (n. 1 above), pp. 490, 518, considers fascism inherently anticlerical; religious fundamentalisms, he asserts, are more likely today to produce authoritarianism than neofascism. In practice, however, fascisms can be close to churches identified with the national cause, as in Croatia, as Payne himself shows. Laqueur, *Fascism* (n. 1 above), pp. 95, 148–51, posits a closer link between religious fundamentalism and neofascism.

13 Roger Griffin and Roger Eatwell (n. 1 above) assert vigorously that fascism is to be understood as a doctrine. The most ambitious effort is Griffin's; he overcomes the problems of variation and contradiction by paring the fascist minimum down to national regeneration. Even Payne's more narrative *History* says "reading fascist programs" is his methodological starting point (pp. 11, 472).

14 A recent brief review of these assumptions within Nazism, with an extensive bibliography, is found in Michael Burleigh and Wolfgang Wippermann, *The Racial State: Germany 1933–1945* (Cambridge, 1991), chap. 2.

15 Michael A. Ledeen, *Universal Fascism: The Theory and Practice of the Fascist International, 1928–1936* (New York, 1972), explores Mussolini's short-lived attempt to gather the other fascist movements around himself in an international organization. Hitler manifested little interest in his foreign disciples, showing notable reluctance to entrust the governance of conquered territories to Quislings like the original in Norway (out of power until 1942), Mussert in Holland, and Degrelle in Belgium. A recent study is Martin Conway, *Collaboration in Belgium: Léon Degrelle and the Rexist Movement* (New Haven, Conn., 1993).

16 Emilio Gentile, *The Sacralization of Politics in Fascist Italy*, trans. Keith Botsford (Cambridge, Mass., 1996), pp. 24–25, examines the ritual purificatory burning of captured socialist materials by the *squadristi*. For Italian Fascist racialism (more cultural than biological) directed against Libyans and Ethiopians, see n. 61 below.

17 Current authors still sometimes claim that the Nazis violated the aspirations of big business. See, for example, Payne, *History*, p. 190. In fact, most business leaders, whose negative memories of Weimar and the Depression were still fresh, swallowed their reluctance about Nazi autarky and thrived handsomely on rearmament. Peter Hayes, *Industry and Ideology: IG Farben in the Nazi Era* (Cambridge, 1987), finds an "intersection, not an identity, of interests" (p. 120). Daimler-Benz enjoyed particular favor with the regime. See Bernard P. Bellon, *Mercedes in Peace and War* (New York, 1990). The most important common interest, of course, was the emasculation of the labor movement. These issues are magisterially treated by Charles Maier, "The Economics of Fascism and Nazism," in his *In Search of Stability: Explorations in Historical Political Economy* (Cambridge, 1987), pp. 70–120.

18 Sternhell et al. (n. 4 above), p. 231, argue that actions conflict with programs no more extensively with fascism than with other political currents.

19 I draw these terms from Marc Bloch's description in summer 1943 of the two political systems then engaged in a life-and-death struggle: "the tribe that a collective passion welds to its leader is here—that is, in a republic—replaced by a community governed by laws." Marc Bloch, "Pourquoi je suis républicain," *Les Cahiers politiques*, Organe du Comité général d'études de la Résistance, no. 2 (July 1943), one of the "écrits clandestins" published in *L'Etrange défaite* (Paris, 1993), p. 215. He evoked the same distinction in *L'Etrange défaite*, p. 176: Hitlerism "remplace la persuasion par la suggestion émotive."

20 Walter L. Adamson, "Modernism and Fascism: The Politics of Culture in Italy, 1903–1922," *American Historical Review* 95 (April 1990): 359–90, holds that the principal effect of Mussolini's association with modernist intellectuals was the legitimation this lent early Fascism (p. 361). "The important issue ... is not the content of fascist ideology but the cultural sources of fascist rhetoric and of the secular-religious aura it sought to project" (p. 363).

21 Sternhell *et al.*, pp. 193, 249.

22 Giuseppe di Lampedusa, *The Leopard*, trans. Archibald Colquhoun (New York, 1950), p. 40.

23 Barbara Miller Lane, *Architecture and Politics in Germany, 1918–1945* (Cambridge, Mass., 1985); Walter L. Adamson, *Avant-garde Florence: Between Modernism and Fascism* (Cambridge, Mass., 1993).

24 Jeffrey Herf, *Reactionary Modernism* (Cambridge, 1984), tries, with great erudition, to extract the meaning of the "modern" from within fascist texts.

25 Gisela Bock, *Zwangssterilisation im Nationalsozialismus: Studien zur Rassenpolitik und Frauenpolitik* (Opladen, 1986), has transformed our understanding of Nazi family policy by underlining the antinatalist character of its programs of obligatory sterilization for foreigners, the incurably ill, Jews, and Gypsies. These antinatalist policies coexisted, however, with a natalist policy for "the master race." See Atina Grossmann, "Feminist Debates about Women and National Socialism," *Gender and History* 3 (Autumn 1991): 350–58.

26 Henry A. Turner, Jr., doubted that generic fascism is a valid or useful concept in "Fascism and Modernization," in *Reappraisals of Fascism*, ed. Henry A. Turner, Jr. (New York, 1975), pp. 132–33. Gilbert Allardyce pushed skepticism furthest in "What Fascism Is Not: Thoughts on the Deflation of a Concept," *American Historical Review* 84 (April 1979): 367–88.

27 The term is from Carl Schorske, *Fin-de-siècle Vienna* (New York, 1980), chap. 3.

28 The term *fascio* was used by syndicalists in the 1890s, as in the *fasci siciliani*; it emphasizes the solidarity of brothers in action. Pro-intervention syndicalists brought the word into the nationalist lexicon during World War I, as in the *Fasci de Difesa Nazionale* in Ferrara, to whose journal, *Il Fascio*, Mussolini contributed in 1917. The form *fascismo* seems to be Mussolini's own invention in 1919.

29 Pierre Milza, *Fascisme français: passé et présent* (Paris, 1987), presents a four-stage model of fascism; Philippe Burrin, *La Dérive fasciste* (Paris, 1986), elegantly traces the itineraries by which Jacques Doriot, Marcel Déat, and Gaston Bergery, steering between blockages and opportunities, shifted from the Left to fascism. Most recent authors seek some "fascist essence." Payne, *History*, pp. 487–95, while rejecting any monocausal or reductionist theory, presents "elements of a retrodictive theory of fascism" that apply to movements as well as to regimes; Laqueur, *Fascism*, finds fascism like pornography, in that "it is difficult—perhaps impossible—to define in an operational, legally valid way," but nevertheless presents "the essence of fascism" (pp. 6, 13–21); in *The Nature of Fascism*, Griffin proposes a "new ideal type" of fascism defined as "a genus of political ideology whose mythic core in its various permutations is a palingenetic form of populist ultranationalism" (p. 26); for Eatwell, fascism is a "coherent body of thought" (n. 1 above, p. xvii) whose "essence" is a "form of thought that preaches the need for social rebirth in order to forge a holistic-national radical Third Way" (p. 14).

30 An extreme case of this genre, Anthony Joes, *Fascism in the Contemporary World: Ideology, Evolution, Resurgence* (Boulder, Colo., 1978), includes practically every mass-based dictatorship in the developing world.

31 A superior example is Adrian Lyttleton, *The Seizure of Power: Fascism in Italy, 1919–1929*, 2d ed. (Princeton, N.J., 1987).

32 Raymond Grew, "On the Current State of Comparative Studies," in *Marc Bloch Aujourd'hui: Histoire comparée et sciences sociales*, ed. Hartmut Atsma and André Burguière (Paris, 1990), p. 331.

33 Marc Bloch, a great exponent of comparison in history, distinguished two kinds: the juxtaposition of similar phenomena in different cultures, such as feudalism in the West and in Japan: and the parallel study of "neighboring and adjacent societies" having known "change in the same direction." Marc Bloch, "Pour une histoire comparée des sociétés européennes," *Revue de Synthèse* 46 (1928): 15–50, reprinted in Marc Bloch, *Mélanges historiques*, 2 vols. (Paris, 1963), 1:16–40. This second type of historical comparison, confronting different outcomes for the same process in two neighboring regions, is the sharper tool. One thinks of the two halves of the *département* of the Sarthe, one republican and the other counterrevolutionary, compared so fruitfully by Paul Bois, *Paysans de l'ouest* (Paris, 1971); and of Maurice Agulhon's comparison of the different reception of republicanism in the early nineteenth century in two regions of the Var, one of them "virtually immobile" and the other "touched by the fever of industrial development": *La République au village* (Paris, 1979), p. 32.

34 Milza proposes four stages: a first fascism, that of marginal movements of intellectuals from both Right and Left; a second fascism, that of militant activists on the road to power; a third fascism, exercising power; and a fourth, under the pressures of war.

35 George Mosse, *The Crisis of German Ideology* (New York, 1964), and other works. Zeev Sternhell, *Le droite révolutionnaire, 1885–1914: Les origines françaises du fascisme* (Paris, 1978); Sternhell *et al.* (n. 4 above).

36 Brooks Adams, *The Law of Civilization and Decay: An Essay in History* (New York, 1895).

37 Seymour Martin Lipset and Earl Rabb, *The Politics of Unreason: Right-Wing Extremism in America, 1790–1970*, 2d ed. (New York, 1978), is a serviceable "bestiary" for the United States. Pelley is treated most fully in Leo P. Riboffo, *The Old Christian Right: The Protestant Far Right from the Great Depression to the Cold War* (Philadelphia, 1983). For a subtle discussion of how appropriate the fascist label is for the extreme right in the United States during the 1930s, see Alan Brinkley, *Voices of Protest: Huey Long, Father Coughlin, and the Great Depression* (New York, 1982), pp. 269–83.

38 David M. Chalmers, *Hooded Americanism: The First Century of the Ku Klux Klan, 1865–1965*, 3d ed. (Durham, N.C., 1987), chap. 1. Correspondences between fascism and the Klan in the 1920s are explored by Nancy Maclean, *Behind the Mask of Chivalry: The Making of the Second Klan* (New York, 1994), pp. 179–88.

39 On east-Elbian Germany, see Frieda Wunderlich, *German Farm Labor, 1810–1845* (Princeton, N.J., 1961), pp. 52, 105–8; Erich D. Kohler, "Revolutionary Pomerania, 1919–1920: A Study in Majority Socialist Agricultural Policy and Civil-Military Relations," *Central European History* 9 (September 1976): 250–93; and Martin Schumacher, *Land und Politik: Eine Untersuchung über politische Parteien und agrarische Interessen* (Düsseldorf, 1978), pp. 294–309; on Italy, see Paul Corner, *Fascism in Ferrara* (Oxford, 1976); Frank M. Snowden, *Violence and Great Estates in the South of Italy: Apulia, 1900–1922* (Cambridge, 1986); and Simona Colarizi, *Dopoguerra e fascismo in Puglia, 1919–1926* (Bari, 1971); and on France, see Robert O. Paxton, *French Peasant Fascism* (New York, 1997).

40 The disillusioned words of Barbato Gattelli, a Fascist from the movement's first days, quoted in Corner, *Ferrara*, p. 224.

41 Saul Friedländer, *Reflections of Nazism: An Essay on Kitsch and Death* (Bloomington, Ind., 1993), explores the nihilistic and erotic undercurrents within aesthetic evocations of Nazism after the 1970s.

42 It is curious how little scholarly attention has been devoted to the opening of spaces within which fascism may expand. The principal work is Juan Linz and Alfred Stepan, eds., *The Breakdown of Democratic Regimes* (Baltimore, 1978).

43 Payne, *History* (n. 1 above), describes dozens of cases. Sternhell considers that movements in opposition reveal more about fascism than regimes in power: "one is able to apprehend the true significance of the phenomenon" and "obtains a clearer understanding of fascist thought and behavior" if one studies the French movements that "never had to make the inevitable compromises." Zeev Sternhell, *Neither Left nor Right: Fascist Ideology in France* (Berkeley and Los Angeles, 1986), p. 270.

44 Local fascist leaders were called *ras* after Ethiopian chieftains, for the Ethiopians' defeat of the Italian Army at Adowa in 1896 still rankled Italian nationalists.

45 Nazi rural organizers had to overcome rural suspicions based on Point 17 of the party's Twenty-Five Points of 1920. It called for expropriation without compensation of land needed for national purposes, the abolition of ground rent, and the prohibition of speculation in land. Thomas Childers, *The Nazi Voter* (Chapel Hill, N.C., 1983), pp. 149–151, 215–21; J. E. Farquharson. "The Agrarian Policy of National Socialist Germany," in *Peasants and Lords in Modern Germany: Recent Studies in Agricultural History*, ed. Robert G. Moeller (Boston, 1986), p. 236. See, more generally, J. E. Farquharson, *The Plough and the Swastika* (Berkeley, 1976); and Anna Bramwell, *Blood and Soil: Richard Walther Darré and Hitler's "Green Party"* (Abbotsbrook, 1985).

46 Payne, among others, considers authoritarian military dictatorships the most effective barrier, historically, against fascist acquisitions of power. See Payne, *History*, pp. 250, 252, 312, 321, 326, 395, 492.

47 Interwar fascists could remember how a general strike had frustrated the Kapp Putsch in Germany in 1920.

48 Lyttelton (n. 31 above) is still best for this process in Italy. For Germany, Karl-Dietrich Bracher, Gerhard Schulz, and Wolfgang Sauer, *Die nationalsozialistische Machtergreifung*, 3 vols. (Cologne and Opladen, 1962), is still basic. The most complete analysis of the final moments is Henry A. Turner, Jr., *Hitler's Thirty Days to Power, January 1933* (Reading, Mass., 1996).

49 Serge Berstéin, "La France allérgique au fascisme," *Vingtième siècle: Revue d'histoire* 2 (April 1984): 84–94.

50 Pierre Milza (n. 29 above); Robert Soucy, *French Fascism: The First Wave, 1924–1933* (New Haven, Conn., 1986), and *French Fascism: The Second Wave, 1933–1939* (New Haven, Conn., 1995). The debate about the strength of native fascism in France turns on whether the largest movement, Col. François de La Rocque's *Parti social français*, successor to his paramilitary league, the *Croix de Feu*, dissolved in 1936, can properly be considered fascist. The positive case is made for both the league and the party by Robert Soucy and William D. Irvine, "Fascism in France and the Strange Case of the Croix de Feu," *Journal of Modern History* 63 (June 1991): 271–95. Kevin Passmore, "Boy Scoutism for Grown-Ups? Paramilitarism in the Croix de Feu and the Parti Social Français," *French Historical Studies* 19 (Fall 1995): 527–57, distinguishes between the league, which he considers fascist on behavioral more than ideological grounds, and the party, which he considers conservative. Jacques Nobécourt, *Le Colonel de La Rocque, 1885–1946, ou les pièges du nationalisme chrétien* (Paris, 1996), an exhaustive sympathetic biography, portrays La Rocque as a conservative victimized by false accusations and personal rivalries.

51 Stanley Payne, *The Franco Regime, 1936–1975* (Madison, Wis., 1987); Paul Preston, *Franco: A Biography* (New York, 1994); António Costa Pinto, *Salazar's Dictatorship and European Fascism* (Boulder, Colo., 1995). See, generally, Martin Blinkhorn, ed., *Fascists and Conservatives: The Radical Right and the Establishment in the Twentieth Century* (London, 1990).

52 Racial hygiene has recently proven a fruitful subject because it links Nazi practice to professional interests. See Michael H. Kater, *Doctors under Hitler* (Chapel Hill, N.C., 1989); Robert Jay Lifton, *The Nazi Doctors: Medical Killing and the Psychology of*

Genocide (New York, 1986). Burleigh and Wippermann (n. 14 above), p. 353, n. 1, advocate, convincingly, a more anthropologically informed study of how fascist regimes interacted with specific social groups.

53 Perspicacious contemporaries saw this compound quality of fascist rule as a "dual state," in which the "normative state" jostled for power with a "prerogative state" formed by the party's parallel organizations. See Ernst Fraenkel, *The Dual State* (New York, 1941); and Franz Neumann, *Behemoth* (New York, 1942). The compound nature of fascist rule has been conceptually refined since the 1970s by the "polyocratic" interpretation. See Martin Broszat, *Hitler's State* (London, 1981); Hans Mommsen, in many works, including *From Weimar to Auschwitz*, trans. Philip O'Connor (Cambridge, 1991); and *Der Führerstaat: Mythos und Realität*, ed. Gerhard Hirschfeld and Lothar Kettenacker (Stuttgart, 1981). For an analogous reading of Fascist Italy, see Emilio Gentile, "Le rôle du parti dans le laboratoire totalitaire italien," *Annales: Économies, sociétés, civilisations* 43 (May–June 1988): 567–91; and Philippe Burrin, "Politique et société: Les structures du pouvoir dans l'Italie fasciste et l'Allemagne nazie," *Annales: Économies, sociétés, civilisations* 43 (May–June 1988): 615–37. For "shapelessness," see Hannah Arendt, *The Origins of Totalitarianism*, 2nd ed. (New York, 1958), pp. 389–390, 395, 398, 402. She credits the term to Neumann, *Behemoth*.

54 Juan J. Linz has made the classic analysis of authoritarianism as a distinct form of rule: "An Authoritarian Regime: Spain," in *Mass Politics: Studies in Political Sociology*, ed. Erik Allard and Stein Rokkan (New York, 1970), pp. 251–83, "From Falange to Movimiento-Organización: The Spanish Single Party and the Franco Regime, 1936–1968," in *Authoritarian Politics in Modern Societies: The Dynamics of Established One-Party Systems*, ed. Samuel P. Huntington and Clement Moore (New York, 1970), "Totalitarian and Authoritarian Regimes," in *Handbook of Political Science*, ed. Fred L Greenstein and Nelson W. Polsby (Reading, Mass., 1975), vol. 3, esp. pp. 264–350. As for totalitarianism, Arendt included Stalin and excluded Mussolini, as did Carl Friedrich and Zbigniew Brzezinski, *Totalitarian Dictatorship and Autocracy* (Cambridge, Mass., 1956). By the late 1960s, the totalitarianism concept had come to seem a Cold War artifact and remains in use today mainly in popular language. See Benjamin R. Barber, "The Conceptual Foundations of Totalitarianism," in Carl J. Friedrich, Michael Curtis, and Benjamin R. Barber, *Totalitarianism in Perspective: Three Views* (London, 1969). See now Ian Kershaw and Moshe Lewin, eds., *Stalinism and Nazism: Dictatorships in Comparison* (Cambridge, 1997).

55 The borders between the two kinds of regime are blurred here, for, in practice, neither gets its wish. Faced with aroused publics, authoritarians as well as fascists may attempt to create a Durkheimian "mechanical solidarity." Paul Brooker, *The Faces of Fraternalism: Nazi Germany, Fascist Italy, and Imperial Japan* (Oxford, 1991). Fascists may achieve no more than a "superficial" and "fragile" consent. Victoria De Grazia, *The Culture of Consent: Mass Organization of Leisure in Fascist Italy* (Cambridge, 1981), p. 20 and chap. 8, "The Limits of Consent." The most meticulous study of German public opinion under Nazism, Martin Broszat's "Bavaria program," concluded that it was atomized and passive. See Ian Kershaw, *Popular Opinion and Dissent in the Third Reich: Bavaria, 1933–1945* (Oxford, 1983).

56 Robert Ley, head of the Nazi Labor Service, said that the only private individual in the Nazi state is a person asleep. Arendt believed him. See *Origins*, p. 339.

57 Alberto Aquarone, *Organizzazione dello stato totalitario* (Turin, 1965), has not been superseded. See also the articles of Gentile and Burrin cited above.

58 Michèle Cointet, *Vichy et le fascisme: Les hommes, Les structures, et les pouvoirs* (Brussels, 1987). An interesting attempt to evaluate Vichy's propaganda efforts as a failed fascist experiment is Denis Peschanski, "Vichy au singulier, Vichy au pluriel: Une tentative avortée d'encadrement de la société (1941–1942)," *Annales: Économies,*

sociétés, civilisations 43 (May–June 1988): 639–62. One may ask, with Philippe Burrin, whether an authentic fascism is compatible with foreign occupation: *La Dérive fasciste* (n. 29 above), p. 414.

59 Salazar suppressed Portuguese National Syndicalism in 1934 and downplayed the Portuguese Legion after 1939. Costa Pinto (n. 51 above), pp. 160–65, 188–90.

60 The terms are Renzo De Felice's in *Mussolini: Il Duce: Lo stato totalitario, 1936–1940* (Turin, 1981), p. 100; for this and other controversial judgments by Mussolini's principal biographer, see Borden W. Painter, "Renzo De Felice and the Historiography aof Italian Fascism," *American Historical Review* 95 (April 1990): 391–405.

61 Claudio Segrè, *The Fourth Shore: The Italian Colonization of Libya* (Chicago, 1974); Denis Mack Smith, *Mussolini's Roman Empire* (New York, 1976); Luigi Preti, "Fascist Imperialism and Racism," in *The Ax Within*, ed. Roland Sarti (New York, 1974), pp. 187–207.

62 In the debate about what drove radicalization, the artificial distinction between "intentionalists" and "functionalists" has been resolved, most effectively by Christopher Browning, in favor of an interaction between the leader's intentions and competitive harshness among subordinates who count on his approval. Browning's most recent analysis is *The Path to Genocide: Essays on Launching the Final Solution* (Cambridge, 1992).

63 Omer Bartov makes a somewhat different point about how the special conditions of the Russian campaign inured the Army as well as the SS to brutality. See *The Eastern Front, 1941–1945: German Troops and the Barbarization of Warfare* (New York, 1986), and *Hitler's Army: Soldiers, Nazis, and War in the Third Reich* (New York, 1991).

64 Stein U. Larsen, Bernt Hagtvet, and Jan Petter Myklebust, eds., *Who Were the Fascists? Social Roots of European Fascism* (Oslo, 1980), surmounts this problem better than most. Current work shies away both from class and from Hannah Arendt's classless mass, preferring to explore links with more particularly defined groups: professions (n. 53 above), clubs, fraternities, and other "intermediary bodies." See Rudy Koshar, "From *Stammtisch* to Party: Nazi Joiners and the Contradictions of Grass Roots Fascism in Weimar Germany," *Journal of Modern History* 59 (March 1987): 1–24; and, more generally, Rudy Koshar, *Social Life, Local Politics, and Nazism: Marburg, 1880–1935* (Chapel Hill, N.C., 1986).

65 Susan Sontag made an interesting effort to extract the elements of a fascist aesthetic from the work of Leni Riefenstahl: "Fascinating Fascism," in Susan Sontag, *Under the Sign of Saturn* (New York, 1980), but it may apply mainly to German culture.

66 Still basic in English is Jill Stephenson, *Women in Nazi Society* (New York, 1975); Burleigh and Wippermann (n. 14 above) have an up-to-date chapter on women in Nazi Germany and, more innovatively, one on men. George Mosse, *The Image of Man: The Creation of Modern Masculinity* (New York, 1996), culminates with Nazi Germany. Essential for Italy is Victoria De Grazia, *How Fascism Ruled Women: Italy, 1922–1945* (Berkeley and Los Angeles, 1992).

67 Payne, *History* (n. 1 above), p. 496, along with all others who consider fascism a specific doctrine born of late nineteenth-century national syndicalism, is obliged to conclude that "the same forms of fascism could not be effectively revived" after 1945.

8

FASCISTS

Michael Mann

In his book suggestively entitled Fascists *(2004), the leading sociologist Michael Mann revitalizes the tradition of comparative historical sociology in fascist studies best epitomized by the path-breaking work of Juan J. Linz. His theory of fascism is subsumed to the general sociological framework for studying power relations and networks in human societies, advanced in his magisterial work* The Sources of Social Power *(2 vols, 1986, 1993). According to the author's confession, his analysis of fascism was to be a single chapter in the third and last volume of an intended trilogy but grew into a full-size book, as a recognition of the paramount importance of fascism for understanding politics in interwar Europe. This volume—from which I have selected below a summary of the main arguments and research findings put forward in the Introduction and Conclusion—focuses on the rise of major fascist movements in Europe. More recently, Mann added another complementary volume on the deeds of fascists in power, entitled* The Dark Side of Democracy, *focusing mainly on campaigns of ethnic cleansing (2005).*

In Fascists, Mann attempts to bridge a conceptual definition of fascism with a theory of the rise and social basis of fascism as a mass movement. He criticizes the cleavage between what he calls the "idealist 'nationalist'" and the "materialist-'class'" schools in interpreting fascism—seeing it as a symptom of a more general "idealism-versus-materialism dualism" prevalent in social sciences. Mann argues that a general theory of fascism can only be built by incorporating insights from both approaches. Only then is it possible to concomitantly explain the fascists' values and programs as well as their actions and organization (2004: 5).

Following Linz's approach, Mann employed a multilayered approach to fascism, aiming to provide: (1) an ideal-type of fascist ideology; (2) a theory of the emergence and social compositions of fascist movements; and (3) a typology of political regimes and historical fascist movements in interwar Europe. First, reiterating the heuristic value of ideal-type models of generic fascism, Mann joins the scholarly debate over the fascist minimum. In a critical review, he distances himself from the existing paradigmatic models of generic fascism, criticizing them for their idealism, for overemphasis of fascists' ideas and values at the expense of their power and organization, for disembodying nationalism from its original locus, the nation-state, and for "sanitizing fascism" in the sense of obscuring its inherent drive to, and capacity of, violence and destruction (2004: 12). In an attempt to fill these major "omissions," Mann advances his own concise definition of fascism emphasizing not only its ideology but also alluding to its paramilitary organization and violent character: "fascism is the pursuit of a transcendent and cleansing nation-statism through paramilitarism" (ibid.: 13). This definition rests on five key concepts: nationalism, referring to fascists' commitment to an "organic nation;" statism, referring to the fascist cult of the state; transcendence, meaning the fascists' attempt to overcome class conflict through the creation of the new man and a corporatist organization of the society; cleansing, denoting the violent removal of the enemies of the nation; and paramilitarism, referring to both fascists' militarist values and a bottom-up type of organization.

Second, Mann develops a multi-tier comparative analytical framework for understanding the rise of fascism, approached at macro, meso and micro levels. At macro-level, his theory attempts to explain why the centre, east and south half of the European continent turned authoritarian while the northwestern half remained liberal. Mann's explanation focuses on the conjunct of post-war crises of the four sources of social power he conceptualized in his earlier work: ideological, economic, military, and political. While these crises were pan-European, the centre, east and south of the continent experienced a more severe combination of crises, which eventually led to markedly different outcomes in the two halves of the continent. In northwestern Europe, political elites successfully contained authoritarian challenges by employing a combination of repressive measures and mass integration of citizens into consolidated liberal institutions. In the other half of the continent, "panic-stricken" elites embraced authoritarianism in order to contain a highly inflated revolutionary threat from the right. Mann's taxonomy of interwar authoritarian political regimes includes the following categories: semi-authoritarian, semi-reactionary authoritarian, corporatist, and fascist. An integral member of the family of authoritarianisms, fascism went beyond "mild nation-statism" to become "the most extreme version of nationalism." In Mann's view, the rise of fascism was not a symptom of a post-liberal crisis of Western societies, but a crisis of "halfbacked attempt at liberalization amid social crisis" in unconsolidated new democracies (ibid.: 355).

At the meso-level, Mann's theory attempts to explain who the fascists were in the five countries where fascist came to dominate politics, namely Italy, Germany, Austria, Hungary and Romania, supplemented by the case of Spain, where fascists were not dominant but still played a significant role. Mann analyses the differences and similarities among these movements by means of a collection of national case studies treated in separate chapters. At the micro-level, he pays attention to the social background of fascist leaders, militants, members, collaborators of various sorts, and voters, compared to other non-fascist parties (ibid.: 26). On the basis of what the author regards as the "broadest collection of data yet presented on fascism," Mann argues that the class composition of fascist movements was highly complex and variegated. He therefore rejects the traditional Marxist class interpretation of fascism. Instead, following his thesis on the fascist attachment to the nation-state to its logical analytical implications, he identifies three core "nation-state-loving" social constituencies of fascism: those favoring paramilitarism; those favoring transcendence; and those favoring nation-statism (ibid.: 26–27).

Ultimately, Mann argues that the fascist challenge to conventional politics can be understood only by employing a long-term historical perspective. For Mann, fascism is not an anti-modernist reaction to the legacy of the Enlightenment; the political solutions it offered were not entire reactionary, but incorporated selectively certain Enlightenment principles, combining them with the turn-of-the-century "renewal of Romanticism." Fascism was an essentially modern political phenomenon, but was nevertheless part of "the dark side of modernity" (ibid.: 365). Mann treats fascism as a generic phenomenon, arguing that, while the rise of fascism as a mass phenomenon was contingent to a peculiar interwar historical constellation, certain elements of fascism might return in a new form in the future.

BIBLIOGRAPHY

Mann, Michael (1986). *The Sources of Social Power*. Vol. 1: *A History of Power from the Beginning to 1760 A.D.* (New York: Cambridge University Press).

Mann, Michael (1993). *The Sources of Social Power*. Vol. 2: *The Rise of Classes and Nation-States, 1760–1914* (New York: Cambridge University Press).

Mann, Michael (2004). *Fascists* (Cambridge: Cambridge University Press).

Mann, Michael (2005). *The Dark Side of Democracy: Explaining Ethnic Cleansing* (Cambridge: Cambridge University Press).

*   *   *

A sociology of fascist movements

Taking fascists seriously

This book seeks to explain fascism by understanding fascists – who they were, where they came from, what their motivations were, how they rose to power. I focus here on the rise of fascist movements rather than on established fascist regimes. I investigate fascists at their flood tide, in their major redoubts in interwar Europe, that is, in Austria, Germany, Hungary, Italy, Romania, and Spain. To understand fascists will require understanding fascist movements. We can understand little of individual fascists and their deeds unless we appreciate that they were joined together into distinctive power organizations. We must also understand them amid their broader twentieth-century context, in relation to general aspirations for more effective states and greater national solidarity. For fascism is neither an oddity nor merely of historical interest. Fascism has been an essential if predominantly undesirable part of modernity. At the beginning of the twenty-first century there are seven reasons still to take fascists very seriously.

(1) Fascism was not a mere sideshow in the development of modern society. Fascism spread through much of the European heartland of modernity. Alongside environmentalism, it was the major political doctrine of world-historical significance created during the twentieth century. There is a chance that something quite like it, though almost certainly under another name, will play an important role in the twenty-first century. Fascists have been at the heart of modernity.

(2) Fascism was not a movement set quite apart from other modern movements. Fascists only embraced more fervently than anyone else the central political icon of our time, the nation-state, together with its ideologies and pathologies. We are thankful that today much of the world lives under rather mild nation-states, with modest, useful powers, embodying only a fairly harmless nationalism. National government bureaucracies annoy us but they do not terrorize us – indeed, they predominantly serve our needs. Nationalism usually also appears in comforting domesticated forms. Though French people often proclaim themselves as culturally superior, Americans assert they are the freest people on Earth, and the Japanese claim a unique racial homogeneity, these highly suspect beliefs comfort themselves, amuse foreigners, and rarely harm anyone else.

Fascism represents a kind of second-level escalation beyond such "mild nation-statism." The first escalation came in two parallel forms, one concerning the nation, the other the state. Regarding the nation, aspirations for democracy became entwined with the notion of the "integral" or "organic" nation. "The people" must rule, but this people was considered as one and indivisible and so might violently exclude from itself minority ethnic groups and political "enemies" (see my forthcoming volume, *The Dark Side of Democracy*, chap. 1, for more analysis of this). Regarding the state, the early twentieth century saw the rise of a more powerful state, seen as "the bearer of a moral project," capable of achieving economic, social, and moral development.[1] In certain contexts this involved the rise of more authoritarian states. The combination of modern nationalism and statism was to turn democratic aspirations on their head, into authoritarian regimes seeking to "cleanse" minorities and opponents from the nation. Fascism, the second-level escalation, added to this combination mainly a distinctively "bottom-up" and "radical" paramilitary movement. This would overcome all opposition to the organic nation-state with violence from below, at whatever the cost. Such glorification of actual violence had emerged as a consequence of the modern "democratization" of war into one between "citizen armies." Fascism thus presented a distinctively paramilitary extreme version of nation-statism (my actual definition of fascism is given below in this chapter). It was only the most extreme version of the dominant political ideology of our era.

(3) Fascist ideology must be taken seriously, in its own terms. It must not be dismissed as crazy, contradictory, or vague. Nowadays, this is quite widely accepted. Zeev Sternhell (1986: x) has remarked that fascism had "a body of

doctrine no less solid or logically indefensible than that of any other political movement." Consequently, said George Mosse (1999: x), "only ... when we have grasped fascism from the inside out, can we truly judge its appeal and its power." Since fascists did offer plausible solutions to modern social problems, they got mass electoral support and intense emotional commitment from militants. Of course, like most political activists, fascists were diverse and opportunistic. The importance of leadership and power in fascism enhanced opportunism. Fascist leaders were empowered to do almost anything to seize power, and this could subvert other fascist values. Yet most fascists, leaders or led, believed in certain things. They were not people of peculiar character, sadists or psychopaths, or people with a "rag-bag" of half-understood dogmas and slogans flitting through their heads (or no more so than the rest of us). Fascism was a movement of high ideals, able to persuade a substantial part of two generations of young people (especially the highly educated) that it could bring about a more harmonious social order. To understand fascism, I adopt a methodology of taking fascists' values seriously. Thus each of my case-study chapters begins by explaining local fascist doctrine, followed, if possible, by an account of what ordinary fascists seem to have believed.

(4) We must take seriously the social constituency of fascist movements and ask what sorts of people were drawn to them. Few fascists were marginals or misfits. Nor were they confined to classes or other interest groups who found in fascism a "cover" for their narrow material interests. Yet there were "core fascist constituencies" among which fascist values most resonated. This is perhaps the most original part of this book, yielding a new view of fascism, and it derives from a methodology of taking fascist values seriously. For the core fascist constituency enjoyed particularly close relations to the sacred icon of fascism, the nation-state. We must reconstruct that nation-state-loving constituency in order to see what kinds of people might be tempted towards fascism.

(5) We must also take seriously fascist movements. They were hierarchical yet comradely, embodying both the leadership principle and a constraining "social cage," both of which heightened commitment, especially by single young men for whom the movement was almost a "total institution." We must also appreciate its paramilitarism, since "popular violence" was crucial to its success. Fascist movements also changed as they were tempted by two different prospects. One was to use power in more and more radical and violent ways. The other was to enjoy the fruits of power by compromising under the table with powerful traditional elites. These led toward either a hardening of fascism (as in Germany) or a softening (as in Italy, at least until the late 1930s). Fascists also experienced "careers" in the movement, which might lead them down either path. We must observe fascists in action: committing violence, trimming, pursuing careers.

(6) We must take "hardened" fascists seriously in a far more sinister sense, as the eventual perpetrators of great evil. We must not excuse or relativize this but seek to understand it. The capacity for evil is an essential human attribute, and so is our capacity to commit evil for what we believe to be moral purposes. Fascists

were especially self-deluded. We need to know more of the circumstances in which we humans do this. Though we prefer to write history and sociology as a happy, progressive, moral tale, this grotesquely distorts the reality of human experience. The twentieth century saw massive evil, not as an accident or as the resurgence of the primitive in us, but as willed, purposive, and essentially "modern" behavior. To understand fascism is to understand how people of apparently high modernizing ideals could then act to produce evil that was eventually unmitigated. However, I leave the very worst for my forthcoming book, *The Dark Side of Democracy*.

(7) We must take seriously the chance that fascists might return. If we understand the conditions that generated fascists, we can better understand whether they might return and how we might avoid this. Some of the conditions that generated fascism are still present. Organic nationalism and the adoption of paramilitary forms, committed to ethnic and political cleansing, at present move many thousands of people across the world to commit supposedly "idealistic" yet in reality murderous acts against neighbours and political opponents whom they call "enemies." This may horrify us, but it is not dismissible as a return to the "primitive" in us. Ethnic and political cleansing has been one of European civilization's main contributions to modernity; while violent paramilitarism has been distinctively twentieth-century. We must comprehend these aspects of modernity. It is rather fortunate nowadays that "statism" (the third main component of fascism after organic nationalism and paramilitarism) is greatly out of fashion, since both its historic carriers, fascism and communism, collapsed disastrously. Current cleansing regimes tend to be paramilitary and authoritarian, but pretend they are democratic; the words "fascist" and "communist" have largely become terms of imprecise abuse. Given time for a supposedly stateless neoliberalism to do similar damage to parts of the world, this rejection of the powerful state will probably fade. Then extreme statist values might be harnessed again to extreme paramilitary nationalism in movements resembling fascism – unless we can learn from the history I record here. I doubt new movements will call themselves fascist, since the word is now so abhorred. Yet some of the substance of fascism lives on.

There are two main schools of thought on fascism. A more idealist "nationalist school," which I discuss first, has focused on fascists' beliefs and doctrines, while a more materialist "class school," discussed second, has focused on its class basis and its relationship to capitalism. The debates between them constitute yet another replay of the traditional polemic between idealism and materialism in the social sciences. But since the two approaches often appear to be discussing different levels of phenomena – beliefs versus social base/functions – they frequently talk past each other. Thus we lack an acceptable general theory of fascism. Such a theory would have to build on top of both approaches, taking from each what is useful and adding what both neglect.

I have chosen not to here give the reader a heavy dose of sociological theory. But my own approach to fascism derives from a more general model of human societies that rejects the idealism-versus-materialism dualism. My earlier work identified four primary "sources of social power" in human societies: ideological, economic, military, and political.[2] Class theorists of fascism have tended to elevate economic power relations in their explanations, while nationalist theorists have emphasized ideology. Yet all four sources of social power are needed to explain most important social and historical outcomes. To attain their goals, social movements wield combinations of control over ultimate meaning systems (ideological), control over means of production and exchange (economic), control over organized physical violence (military), and control over centralized and territorial institutions of regulation (political). All four are necessary to explain fascism. Mass fascism was a response to the post-World War I ideological, economic, military, and political crises. Fascists proposed solutions to all four. Fascist organization also combined substantial ideological innovations (generally called "propaganda"), mass political electoralism, and paramilitary violence. All became highly ritualized so as to intensify emotional commitment. In attempting to seize power, fascist leaders also sought to neutralize economic, military, political, and ideological (especially church) elites. Thus any explanation of fascism must rest on the entwining of all four sources of social power, as my empirical case-study chapters demonstrate. My final chapter presents the pay-off from this model: a general explanation of fascism.

[...]

A definition of fascism

I define fascism in terms of the key values, actions, and power organizations of fascists. Most concisely, *fascism is the pursuit of a transcendent and cleansing nation-statism through paramilitarism.* This definition contains five key terms requiring further explanation. Each also contained internal tensions.

(1) *Nationalism.* As everyone recognizes, fascists had a deep and populist commitment to an "organic" or "integral" nation, and this involved an unusually strong sense of its "enemies," both abroad and (especially) at home. Fascists had a very low tolerance of ethnic or cultural diversity, since this would subvert the organic, integral unity of the nation. Aggression against enemies supposedly threatening that organic unity is the original source of fascism's extremism. Racially tinged nationalism proved even more extreme, since race is an ascribed characteristic. We are born with it, and only our death or removal can eliminate it. Thus Nazi racial nationalism proved more obsessed with "purity" and proved more deadly than Italian cultural nationalism, which generally allowed those who showed the right values and conduct to join the nation.

I view the notion of "rebirth," which Griffin saw as the key characteristic of fascism, as characteristic of nationalism more generally, including much milder nationalisms – as, for example, in Irish, Lithuanian, or Zimbabwean nationalism. Since nations are actually modern (with one or two exceptions) but nationalists claim that they are ancient, nationalists solve this paradox with a vision of a revival or rebirth of a supposedly ancient nation, but one now adapted to modern times.[3] In these cases the myth is of continuity back to the former greatness of the High Kings, the Grand Duchy, and Greater Zimbabwe – but no one supposes they would work today.

(2) *Statism*. This involved both goal and organizational form. Fascists worshiped state power. The authoritarian corporate state could supposedly solve crises and bring about social, economic, and moral development, as Gregor (1979) emphasizes. Since the state represented a nation that was viewed as being essentially organic, it needed to be authoritarian, embodying a singular, cohesive will expressed by a party elite adhering to the "leadership principle." Scholars used to emphasize the "totalitarian" quality of fascist goals and states; Burleigh (2000) and Gregor (2000) still do. Others agree that the fascist goal was "total transformation" of society, but they emphasize backsliding along the way. They see the desired fascist state as vague or contradictory, containing rival party, corporatist, and syndicalist elements, and they often note that fascism in power had a surprisingly weak state. They have detailed the factionalism and horse trading of Mussolini's regime (Lyttleton 1987) and the "polycracy" or even "chaos" of the Nazi regime (Broszat 1981; Kershaw 2000). So they rightly hesitate over the label "totalitarian." Fascist regimes, like communist ones, contained a dialectic between "movement" and "bureaucracy," between "permanent revolution" and "totalitarianism" (Mann 1997). We can also detect a tension between a more organized Italian-style syndicalism/corporatism and Nazi preference for a more "polycratic," fluid dictatorship. And in all regimes tendencies toward a singular, bureaucratic state were undercut by party and paramilitary activism and by deals with rival elites. Fascism was more totalitarian in its transformational aims than in its actual regime form.

(3) *Transcendence*. Fascists rejected conservative notions that the existing social order is essentially harmonious. They rejected liberal and social democratic notions that the conflict of interest groups is a normal feature of society. And they rejected leftist notions that harmony could be attained only by overthrowing capitalism. Fascists originated from the political right, center, and left alike and drew support from all classes (Weber 1976: 503). They attacked both capital and labor as well as the liberal democratic institutions supposedly exacerbating their strife. Fascist nation-statism would be able to "transcend" social conflict, first repressing those who fomented strife by "knocking both their heads together" and then incorporating classes and other interest groups into state corporatist institutions. The term "third way," preferred by Eatwell, seems too weak for this goal of revolutionary transformation, too capable of being appropriated by centrist politicians such as Tony Blair. It was definitely not a compromise or a mere drawing together of the best of both of them (as Eatwell says). For it did involve the supposed creation of a new man.

Fascism was partly a response to the crisis of capitalism (as materialists say), but it offered a revolutionary and supposedly achievable solution. We see below that the "core constituency" of fascist support can be understood only by taking seriously their aspirations to transcendence, for they were perfectly genuine about it. It was also the most ideologically powerful part of their appeal, for it offered a plausible, practicable vision of movement toward a better society. Transcendence was actually the central plank of fascism's electoral program. In my previous work I have argued that ideologies are at their most powerful when they offer plausible yet transcendent visions of a better world. They combine the rational with the beyond-rational.

Nonetheless, transcendence was the most problematic and the most variable of fascism's five key terms. It was never actually accomplished. In practice most fascist regimes leaned toward the established order and toward capitalism. Fascists lacked a general critique of capitalism (unlike socialists), since they ultimately lacked interest in capitalism and class. Nation and state comprised their center of gravity, not class. This alone brought them into conflict with the left rather than the right since Marxists and anarchists, not conservatives, tended to be committed to internationalism. But fascists, unlike the political left and right, could be rather pragmatic about classes – unless they saw them as enemies of the nation. Thus they attacked not capitalism per se but only particular types of profit-taking, usually by finance, or foreign or Jewish capitalists. In Romania and Hungary, where these types of capitalist dominated, this gave fascism a distinctly proletarian tone. Elsewhere fascist movements were more procapitalist. When they neared power, they encountered a special problem. Though they hoped to subordinate capitalists to their own goals, as authoritarians they believed in managerial powers yet recognized that they themselves lacked the technocratic skills to run industry. Thus they compromised with capitalists. Moreover, the German and especially the Italian fascist coups were aided by upper-class support. In power Mussolini never seemed to be correcting this pro-ruling-class bias, though Hitler was different. Had his regime lasted much longer, I doubt the Reich economy could still have been called "capitalist."

But in the short space of time allowed them, fascists did tend to backtrack from their original project of transcending class conflict. This "betrayal" is stressed by class interpretations of fascism and by others doubting the sincerity or consistency of fascist values (e.g., Paxton 1994, 1996). Yet fascists could not simply "settle down" into betrayal. All fascist movements remained riven between "radicals" and "opportunists," and this imparted an unresolvable dynamic to the movement. One form of this was especially revealed during the Nazi regime. This dynamic displaced rather than abandoned the goal of transcendence. They would transcend ethnic and class strife, but remove only ethnic enemies – since compromise proved necessary with the capitalist class enemy. This displacement of transcendent goals actually increased fascist murderousness – eventually in Italy as well as in Germany, as shown in my forthcoming book.

(4) *Cleansing*. Because opponents were seen as "enemies," they were to be removed, and the nation cleansed of them. This was fascist aggression in action. It is distressing that we have recently become familiar again with "ethnic cleansing,"

though cleansing of political enemies has been less publicized in the late twentieth century. Organic nationalists usually consider ethnic enemies the more difficult to cope with, since political identities may be changed more easily. Communists may be repressed, some killed, but if they recant, most can be admitted into the nation. Political cleansing thus often starts murderously, but eases off once the "enemy" gives in and is assimilated into the nation. Ethnic cleansing more often escalates, since the "enemy" may not be permitted to assimilate. Most fascisms entwined both ethnic and political cleansing, though to differing degrees. Even the Nazis' supposed "enemies" appeared in mixed political-ethnic garb, as in the dreaded "Judeo-Bolshevik." Movements such as Italian fascism or Spanish Nationalism identified most of their enemies in predominantly political terms. Thus the more ethnic Nazi end of the range was more murderous than the Italian.

(5) *Paramilitarism* was both a key value and the key organizational form of fascism. It was seen as "popular," welling up spontaneously from below, but it was also elitist, supposedly representing the vanguard of the nation. Brooker (1991) homes in on the comradeship of fascist movements as their defining characteristic, and they certainly viewed their battle-hardened comradeship as an exemplar of the organic nation and the new man. Violence was the key to the "radicalism" of fascism. They overturned legal forms by killings. Through it, the people would effect class transcendence, "knocking heads together." Its elitism and hierarchy would then dominate the authoritarian state that it would bring into being. In no case was a fascist movement merely a "party." Indeed, the Italian fascists were organized only into paramilitaries for many years. Fascism was always uniformed, marching, armed, dangerous, and radically destabilizing of the existing order.

What essentially distinguishes fascists from the many military and monarchical dictatorships of the world is this "bottom-up" and violent quality of its paramilitarism. It could bring popularity, both electorally and among elites. Fascists always portrayed their violence as "defensive" yet "successful" – it could roll over enemies who were the real source of violence. Not everyone believed them, but many did, and this increased their popularity, their votes, and their attractiveness to elites. Paramilitarism thus offered them a distinctive approach to electoral democracy and existing elites, both of which they actually despised. Paramilitarism must always be viewed as entwined with other two main fascist power resources: in electoral struggle and in the undermining of elites. It was paramilitarism – caging the fascists, coercing their opponents, winning the support or respect of bystanders – that enabled fascists to do far more than their mere numbers could. Thus paramilitarism was violence, but it was always a great deal more than violence. It certainly did not confer enough effective violence for fascists to stage coups if that meant taking on the state's army. Paramilitary was not the equivalent of military power. Only if fascists could neutralize military power by appealing to the soldiers themselves could fascist coups occur.

This combination of qualities obviously made fascists "revolutionary," though not in conventional left–right terms. It would be inexact to call them "revolutionaries of the right," as some have done. The combination also means that movements can be more or less fascist. We could in principle plot fascist movements (each one obviously unique) amid a five-dimensional space, though I confess that this is beyond my representational skills. It is also beyond my range here to compare fascists with communist movements in these respects, though there are some obvious similarities as well as some differences. They have been alternative, if failed, visions of modernity.

[...]

The social resonance of fascism

Very large numbers of fascists have so far appeared only amid five social settings. I start with the very broadest.

The macro-period: interwar crises of European modernity

The interwar period in Europe was the setting that threw up most of the self-avowed fascists and saw them at their high tide. My definition is intended firstly as "European-epochal," to use Eatwell's (2001) term (cf. Kallis 2000: 96), applying primarily to that period and place – though perhaps with some resonance elsewhere. The period and the continent contained four major crises: the consequences of a devastating "world," but in fact largely European, war between mass citizen armies, severe class conflict exacerbated by the Great Depression, a political crisis arising from an attempted rapid transition by many countries toward a democratic nation-state, and a cultural sense of civilizational contradiction and decay. Fascism itself recognized the importance of all four sources of social power by explicitly claiming to offer solutions to all four crises. And all four played a more specific role in weakening the capacity of elites to continue ruling in old ways.

It is nonetheless possible that fascism had different causes in each country – here generated by defeat in war, there by the Great Depression. Yet fascism was strongest where we find distinctive combinations of all four. The problem is one of degree: To what extent did each crisis – economic, military, political, and ideological – contribute to the rise of fascism? The problem is discussed more thoroughly in Chapter 2. These crises seem to have been necessary causes of fascism. Without them, no fascism. But none seems to have been an individually sufficient cause. Most countries coped with crisis without turning to organic nation-statism, let alone fascism. So this leads to a second level of analysis, and specifically to the question: Which places made these turns?

The macro-place: one-half of Europe

In the interwar period, ... virtually all of Central, Eastern, and Southern Europe embraced a family of rightist authoritarian governments, one of whose members was fascism. Only tiny minorities in the northwest of the continent sought such government. There were also fascist-leaning movements in the more economically developed countries of other continents, especially Japan, South Africa, Bolivia, Brazil, and Argentina. Here fascism had some resonance, though just how much is a matter of debate (Payne 1995: chap 10; Larsen 2001). My general view of these non-European cases is that none combined all the essential values of fascism listed above. Japan, for example, did have a highly developed nation-statism that produced the most sophisticated quasifascist economic theory in the world (Gao 1997: chaps. 2 and 3). Yet it lacked a bottom-up mass movement or paramilitary (see Brooker 1991 for comparisons between Japan and Europe). Militarism, not paramilitarism, dominated what many call Japanese "fascism." In contrast, Argentina and Brazil generated mass populist and somewhat authoritarian movements with some "radical" and statist tendencies, but these lacked cleansing nationalism. We can find theorists all over the interwar world reading Barrès, Mussolini, Hitler, and so on, adapting them to local conditions and then arriving at their own quasifascist doctrines. In India, for example, Golwalkar adapted Hitler's racial theories to his demand for a pure and organic Hindu theocratic state. Infuse the RSS Hindu paramilitary movement with such theories and the blend is quite close to Nazism (Jaffrelot 1996). But in the 1930s this movement was tiny, like almost all the other quasifascist militias and parties of the time. Only one continent came anywhere near being dominated by fascism: Europe.

Why did authoritarian nation-statism dominate one-half of Europe, liberal democracy the other half? It cannot have been some general crisis of modern society, such as the Great Depression or the defects of liberalism, for then it would have affected all of Europe, not just half of it. The difference is one that turns crucially on the behavior of political conservatives, "old regimes," and the property-owning classes. For here class does matter, profoundly, if in a rather peculiar way. Right across one-half of Europe, the upper classes turned toward more repressive regimes, believing these could protect them against the twin threats of social disorder and the political left. But this does not seem to have been very "rational" behavior. For they greatly exaggerated the threats and neglected safer means of avoiding them that were prevalent across the northwest. They overreacted, reaching for the gun too abruptly, too early. Explaining this puzzle – of class behavior that seems somewhat irrational – is one of the principal tasks of this book. Such an explanation is essential to understanding the macro-regional environment of authoritarian nation-statism in which fascism could flourish. But this cannot also explain the specific emergence of fascism, since only a few countries in this zone actually generated mass fascism, and they did not usually do so at the initiative of the upper classes.

Meso-places: the five fascist countries

Why did Italians, Germans, Austrians, Hungarians, and Romanians embrace fascism in such large numbers when most of their neighbors stopped at milder movements? It is true that quite large quasi-fascist movements later emerged in a few regions of other countries, as in the Sudetenland, Slovakia, the Ukraine, or Croatia. I examine these, but in my forthcoming book. Yet few fascists emerged in other countries and regions. Fascists did not surge only in the more economically advanced countries or in the Greater Powers of the center, east, and south (as is often argued). This argument stems from obsession with Germany and Italy. But Hungary and Romania were rather backward countries and minor powers – and so some writers argue that it is backwardness that generates fascism (e.g., Berend 1998). Yet fascism had sufficiently broad appeal – like socialism – that it could be interpreted in the light of either an advanced or a backward economy. To explain this, we must look for the commonality between these cases – and this can hardly be level of development. But this will not provide a sufficient answer. For even in these countries, only some people (minorities at that) became fascists. Who were they and why did they become fascists?

Meso-places: core fascist constituencies

Which particular social groups within these countries were most attracted to fascism? I spend many pages over several chapters examining the social backgrounds of fascist leaders, militants, members, fellow-travelers, co-conspirators and voters – compared (wherever possible) with their counterparts in other political movements. How old were fascists, were they men or women, military or civilian, urban or rural, religious or secular, economic winners or losers, and from which regions, economic sectors, and social classes did they come? I have gratefully pillaged the work of the scholars of many countries to assemble the broadest collection of data yet presented on fascists. These data suggest three core "fascist constituencies" among which the fascist values and organizations identified earlier resonated most strongly, and which therefore came to organize actual fascist movements. Of course, fascist constituencies did not come ready-made. Fascists had to discover them and then they had to work on them, organizing, persuading, bribing, coercing. Some fascists were more agile than others. Some fascist movements misperceived their constituencies, some stumbled on them almost by accident (as the Nazis stumbled on German Protestantism). Since not all fascist movements were the same, their constituencies also differed somewhat. Yet amid the variations and the accidents we can perceive the following three broad patterns of mass support. This support came from the millions who voted fascist and the thousands who joined fascist organizations. Both were critical to fascist success, though in very different ways. For the moment, however, I am not distinguishing them.

(1) *Constituencies favoring paramilitarism.* The fascist core consisted everywhere of two successive generations of young men, coming of age between World War I and the late 1930s. Their youth and idealism meant that fascist values were proclaimed as being distinctively "modern" and "moral." They were especially transmitted through two institutions socializing young men: secondary and higher education, encouraging notions of moral progress, and the armed

forces, encouraging militarism. Since the appeal was mainly to young men, it was also distinctly macho, encouraging an ethos of braggart, semi-disciplined violence, in peacetime encouraging militarism to mutate into paramilitarism. The character of fascism was set by young men socialized in institutions favorable to moralizing violence and eventually to murder. Yet the similarity of values between paramilitarism and militarism always gave fascism a capacity to appeal to armed forces themselves, not to the extent of inducing military rebellions but to the extent of generating sympathy there that at its most extreme could immobilize the army.

(2) *Constituencies favoring transcendence*. Fascism was usually neither particularly bourgeois nor particularly petty bourgeois. True, there were some class biases in Italy and perhaps also in Austria. But after 1930 there were none in Germany (if we add the SA and SS paramilitaries to the Nazi Party). These fascist coups also received some support from upper classes. But Romanian and Hungarian fascists were recruited more from proletarian than bourgeois backgrounds and received less upper-class support. Class composition was thus complex and variable. Yet there were more constant tendencies of *economic sector*. Fascists tended to come from sectors that were not in the front line of organized struggle between capital and labor. They were less likely to be workers in urban, manufacturing settings (though they were around Budapest and Bucharest because industry there was more part of the "statist" constituency). They were less likely to be small or large businessmen or their managers. Yet they were not "marginal" or "rootless." Their social location was (for the interwar period) relatively secure. But from their slightly removed vantage point they viewed class struggle with distaste, favoring a movement claiming to transcend class struggle. Of course, in most cases transcendence was not achieved, and we find tension (noted by many writers) between a more "radical" fascist base and a more "opportunist" leadership faction seeking compromise with elites. Similarly, capitalists and old regimes might also provide a more opportunistic constituency for such flawed transcendence. But if we do take fascists' beliefs seriously, then it would follow that fascism would appeal to those viewing class struggle from "outside," declaring "a plague on both your houses!"

(3) *Constituencies favoring nation-statism*. Fascists' backgrounds appeared rather heterogeneous. They tended to have had military experience, be highly educated, work in the public or service sectors and come from particular regional and religious backgrounds. For many observers, this has confirmed that fascism was a "ragbag" movement (a particularly prevalent view of the Nazis, as we see in Chapter 4). But there was a principle of unity amid these varied attributes: Fascists were at the heart of either the nation or the state. Some "nation-statist" locations were similar across countries: Soldiers and veterans above all, but also civil servants, teachers, and public sector manual workers were all disproportionately fascist in almost all the countries of mass fascism. Other characteristics varied by country. Rather distinctively, industrial development around the capitals of Hungary and especially Romania was state-assisted, which gave some

private-sector workers a more statist orientation. Religion was almost everywhere important, reinforcing organic nation-statism (except in Italy, where the Church was transnational). Evangelicals in Germany between 1925 and 1935, the Orthodox faithful and clergy in Romania, and Catholics in "Austro-Fascism" were drawn toward fascism since these religions were central to the identity of their desired nation-state. Among Germans the role of religion varied as Nazism itself changed: The perpetrators of genocide, unlike earlier Nazi voters, were disproportionately ex-Catholics (I demonstrate and seek to explain this in my forthcoming volume). In some countries fascists came more from regions that had been at the heart of the historic state or nation, but more often they came from "threatened" border territories or from refugees from "lost territories." We see below that these were all distinctively nation-statist constituencies.

Obviously, not all fascists were from these three core constituencies, nor were all inhabitants of such constituencies fascists. Nor did fascism remain unchanged in its values or characteristics. Nor were vaguely sympathetic persons taking ten minutes to register their votes the same as elites scheming for a year to do a deal with fascists. Neither were these the same as the fascist member or militant devoting enormous time and energy to the movement – perhaps even risking life. Let us consider them.

The micro-cage: fascist movements

"Fascists" were not fully formed at the moment they entered the movement. People may formally sign up for a movement and yet possess only a rudimentary knowledge of it – sympathy for a few slogans, respect for a charismatic Führer or Duce, or simply following friends who have joined. Most recruits joined the movement young, unmarried, unformed, with little adult civilian experience. On them, fascist parties and paramilitaries were especially powerful socialization agencies. These movements were proudly elitist and authoritarian, enshrining a pronounced hierarchy of rank and an extreme cult of the leader. Orders were to be obeyed, discipline to be imposed. Above all, they imposed a requirement of activism. Thus militants experienced intense emotional comradeship. Where the movement was proscribed, clandestinity tightened it. Many activists lost their jobs or went into prison or exile. Though this deterred many of the more faint-hearted, among those remaining active such constraints further tightened the movement.

So did paramilitarism. In some fascist movements (such as the early Italian or the Romanian) the paramilitary *was* the movement; in others (such as the Nazi) the paramilitaries existed alongside party institutions. The paramilitaries were time-consuming, enjoining discipline tempered by comradeship in pursuit of small group violence. Members felt strong pressures on them that were simultaneously coercive and pleasurable, since they involved physical hardship and danger, abusive discipline, intense comradeship, and a very active collective social life amounting in some cases to a cage, a virtual "total institution," in Goffman's sense of the term. Obviously, some were put off by this and many left. But for those who stayed, paramilitarism provided distinctive fascist socialization. For example, Austrian Nazis were persecuted by their government during the years 1934 to 1938. Many fled to Germany, where in the SS and its Austrian Legion they became full-time revolutionaries, "working" together, drinking together in Nazi bars, sleeping together in Nazi barracks.[5] It was from such socially caged groups that fascist leaders liked to recruit "reliable," "toughened" cadres for especially murderous tasks.

They became well prepared for violence. The one adult experience of many of the early young recruits was war. The first, or "front," generation of fascists had almost all fought in World War I; the second, or "home," generation had only been schoolboys during the war, though many had been longing to fight and now did so in the many paramilitary border skirmishing campaigns occurring around Europe in the immediate aftermath of the war. The third generation of recruits received only distorted remembrances of war from their elders, but they were plunged into extralegal street violence. By this time the longer-term members might be inured to "peacetime" violence, and they were commanding the new recruits. Moreover, successful and unpunished violence may have both a cathartic and a liberating effect on the perpetrators. It can take them beyond conventional morality and into technically illegal behavior, past points of no return, reinforcing their collective sense of being a segregated, hardened elite, beyond conventional standards of behaviour. For these young men, this was reinforced by two more conventional qualities of "gangs": the resonance of violence amid macho assertions of masculinity and the excessive consumption of inhibition-releasing alcohol. It is difficult to think of fascist paramilitaries without barroom violence. All these qualities make violence easier to repeat, once embarked on.

Careers within the fascist movement also brought material and status rewards. As the movement expanded, so did the promotion prospects and the power, the pickings, and the status. But promotion required character qualities beyond mere opportunism. Fascist elites became staffed disproportionately by experienced, "reliable," "toughened" members. Educated reliables became the "officers" of fascism, less-educated "old fighters" became the "NCOs." At most levels experienced, inured, "toughened" fascists provided an order-giving elite, able to discipline and socialize the newcomers into "normal" fascist behavior. Fascist movements had differing trajectories. The smaller movements of Northwestern Europe often rose and then declined quite quickly. When their members got the worse of street fighting, many sensibly decided to quit. But in the five major fascist countries it is impossible to understand the success of only thousands of fascists, amid the opposition/indifference of millions, without appreciating the contribution made by their extraordinary and violent activism.

Overview of the book

The above conceptual framework helps to explain fascists. I examine the social crises and the responses of elites, of the thousands who joined fascist movements, and of the millions who sympathized. The next chapter examines interwar crises, explaining the macro-level: why one half of Europe was receptive, the other half hostile. Since I believe I can answer this question, it is not necessary to examine variations among the hostile cases of North-western Europe. Instead, the following seven chapters deal with the other half of the continent in order to explain why some went more for fascism, others for other types of authoritarian rightist movements. This is the basis of my choice of six case-study countries. In Italy, Germany (which gets two chapters), and Austria, fascism dominated and rose into power unassisted. In two – Hungary and Romania – fascists became almost equal players in a kind of dialectic of death within the authoritarian family. The final country – Spain – was the most riven by struggles between democrats and authoritarians and illuminates those cases where fascism remained a subordinate member of the authoritarian family. My methodology in these case studies is almost entirely secondary analysis of other scholars' primary research – to whom I therefore owe an enormous debt of gratitude. The case studies then permit me to develop a more general explanation of fascists' rise, which is presented in my concluding chapter.

[…]

Conclusion: fascists, dead and alive

I first summarize my explanation of the rise of fascism. Then I ask whether fascism is just history or whether it may return to haunt the world again. Are all the fascists dead ones?

Dead fascists

I offered a two-part explanation of the rise of fascism. The first part concerns the forward surge of a broader family of authoritarian rightists who swept into power across one-half of interwar Europe, plus a few swaths in the rest of the world. In Europe the surge carried regimes further across the spectrum I identified in Chapter 2 [*sic*], from semi-authoritarianism to semi-reactionary and thence to corporatist. A few then went further, to fascism.

Authoritarian rightism was a response to both general problems of modernity and particular social crises left by World War I. Modernization was consciously pursued by most authoritarians: industrial growth and restructuring, more science and economic planning, more national integration, a more ambitious state, and more political mobilization of the masses. After some initial hesitation, most rightists embraced most of the modernist package while rejecting democratic mass mobilization. However, their embrace was also pressured by a series of crises – economic, military, political, and ideological – brought on or exacerbated by the war. Without these crises, and without the war itself, there would have been no major authoritarian surge, and fascism would have remained a series of sects and coteries rather than a mass movement.

Serious economic crises came at war's end and then again as the Great Depression struck in 1929. In between, in the mid-1920s, came lesser inflation crises. Yet few interwar economies were ever very buoyant. Since governments were now expected to have economic policies to ameliorate hardship, economic crises destablized governments. "Old regimes" also feared the secular economic trend of the period, since many members lived as rentiers from the profits of the least modern parts of the economy. Modernity and crisis-induced restructuring might be their nemesis. Ruling regimes, especially "old" ones, felt they had to do something.

The war produced military crisis, defeat for some, and dislocation plus sudden demobilization for all. Crisis was felt more severely in the center and east of the continent, which contained most of the defeated powers. But military crisis also endured where "revisionists" continued to challenge the terms of the peace treaties and to seek restoration of "lost territories." Embittered refugees and aggressive nationalist movements kept the pot stirred. Would revisionists triumph in Austria, Germany, and Hungary, would the many new successor regimes of the vanquished multinational empires survive, would France or Romania keep their territorial gains, would Serbia keep its Yugoslav dominance? Then military crisis became more general, as a second world war loomed and as the threat and influence of revisionist Nazi Germany grew.

The political crisis was distinct to the center, east, and south of the continent. The northwest had already stabilized liberal regimes before 1914. Its governments and electorates confronted the economic and military crises with orderly changes of government leaving unchanged the basic constitution of liberal democracy. Yet the center, east, and south were at this very time attempting a transition toward liberal democratic parliaments while leaving many old regime state powers intact. There crisis was confronted by dual states, half liberal democratic, half authoritarian. Since old regime conservatives usually controlled the executive part of the state, including its military and police, they had the option of using repression to solve crisis – reducing or overturning the power of the state's parliamentary half. Indeed, the war had enhanced the resonance of militarism, while a short postwar burst of class conflict had normalized the deployment of troops in civil strife. Yet most of the right felt that repression was no longer sufficient to maintain rule in the modern era. It was also necessary to undercut democracy with alternative ways of mobilizing the masses. Conservatives responded differently in the two halves of Europe. In the northwest the dominance of liberal institutions pushed conservatives toward building more populist political parties playing according to the rules of electoral democracy. But in the center, east, and south, conservatives launched coups by their executive half of the state linked to more mobilizing authoritarian movements. Let me emphasize: Fascism was not a crisis of liberalism, since institutionalized liberalism weathered all these crises without serious destabilization. Fascism was a product of a sudden, half-baked attempt at liberalization amid social crises.

These crises were exacerbated by an ideological crisis. On the right, though only in one half of Europe, this became a sense that modernity was desirable but dangerous, that liberalism was corrupt or disorderly, that socialism meant chaos, that secularism threatened moral absolutes – and so cumulatively that civilization needed rescuing before modernization could proceed further. So there emerged a more authoritarian rightist view of modernity, emphasizing a more top-down populist nationalism, developmental statism, order, and hierarchy. Such values began to circulate widely, especially among young moralists – middle-class youth in high schools, universities, and military academies, as well as in "established" churches that leaned toward nationalism or statism anyway. So across one-half of the more developed world occurred a conservative political offensive by the propertied classes, led by an old regime wielding state repression while sponsoring mass political parties with nationalist and statist ideologies. This insurgent authoritarian rightism was not purely reactionary (as Mayer 1981 suggests), since it wielded novel visions of modernity.

Nor was it merely a class strategy, explicable in straightforwardly functional Marxian terms. It was not even the most economically rational strategy available to the possessing classes. These had two alternative economic motives: "property defense" and "profit maximization." The early post-war burst of class struggle might threaten private property, so might some later Spanish revolutionaries, so might too close a proximity to the Soviet Union. But there was no general fundamental threat to property looming across Europe after about 1921. The revolutionary left had been defeated. Most of the rightist offensive thus occurred *after* any serious revolutionary threat from below had died away. During the relevant period no determined property defense was necessary. "Profit maximization" is more likely a motive, though it is also more complex. It is less zero-sum, since it is not necessarily the case that for one side to gain, the other must lose. It is also more difficult to calculate alternative profits. Some leftist governments and the pressures of the Great Depression led to a squeeze on profits, and it might make some short-term sense for capitalists to redress the balance by forcing labor bear more of the costs – thus to repress labor. But political elites in the countries of the northwest and beyond were devising much better strategies of profit maximization – corporate liberalism in the United States, social democratic compromise in Scandinavia, splitting the Labour Party in Britain. The first of these policies may have benefited both sides in the class war, the second certainly did, while the third probably benefited only capitalists. These were effective democratic strategies to protect the survival and profitability of capitalism – and this was the primary goal of the northwest's leading economist, Keynes.

Why were the possessing classes so hypersensitive to opposition from the left that they reached for the authoritarian gun so quickly, when neither property nor profits were much threatened? I found five reasons for their overreactions, ranging over all the sources of social power.

(1) The last decades had revealed that revolution was a real possibility in modern societies. The prospect appeared now to be receding, but property owners could not be certain of this. One version of the "security dilemma" stressed by recent political scientists suggests that people may overreact to a threat that is "life-threatening"

even if the threat has a low probability of being realized. The chance of a Bolshevik Revolution occurring in Germany after 1922 might be low, but German capitalists might overreact to leftists on the principle "better safe than sorry." For the political right, "certainty," "safety," and "order" were linked values.

(2) A particular class fraction had greater reason to fear. The property rights of agrarian landlords *were* more vulnerable. Land reform was considered desirable through much of interwar Europe; there was also some direct threat to them from below in several countries; and their hold on old regime states would probably not last much longer. For the moment, however, they still possessed unusual executive political power, especially through officer corps and ministries of the interior. *Cacique* patronage systems also still conferred on them a certain parliamentary strength in relatively backward areas. For them "certainty" of possession could be ensured through a combination of repression and disproportionate political power within the propertied classes as a whole. Why risk uncertainty when property preservation could be *guaranteed* through authoritarian rightism? Note, however, that whereas the old regime's own motivation was economically rational, that of their allies among the possessing classes was probably not. They were being led by the nose by the political and military power of the old regime, especially agrarian landlords.

(3) Some military officer corps reasoned similarly. Their caste-like autonomy, linked to the old regime, was threatened by demands for civilian control over the military by liberals and the left. Their budgets were threatened. Some officer corps were used to staging coups, others were not, but the appearance of more military-minded rightist movements seemed to offer them succor.

(4) Some churches reasoned similarly. They faced leftist secularism threatening their own property and wealth, plus their control over education, marriage, and other social practices. They were also part of the old regime and their stress on "order" and "hierarchy" also carried a more diffuse ideological power among the community of the faithful, especially in more rural areas. These possessors of ideological power favored authoritarian rightism to protect their own material and moral interests.

(5) "Order" and "threat" were not merely problems of domestic class relations but also of geopolitics. These made some ethnic, religious, or political minorities seem especially threatening because linked to foreign powers. The right characteristically fused together supposed domestic and foreign "enemies" – leftists were seen as (Russian) "Bolsheviks" and "Judeo-Bolsheviks"; foreign, finance, and Jewish capital and liberal separatists and so on were all seen as both domestic and foreign threats.

Combined, these fears worsened the overall sense of threat. As threats became more diffuse, they seemed more vaguely threatening, so the response was to "root them out," "stifle them at source." So goals were displaced away from a narrow instrumental rationality calculating about economic interest to a broader "value rationality" in the sense of Max Weber's use of the term. Order, safety, security, hierarchy, the sacred rather than the secular, national rather than class interest become the primary slogans, while the enemy was demeaned, even demonized, as the antithesis of all these values, unworthy of democratic or (in extreme cases) of humane treatment. What might have begun as the economically motivated behaviour of propertied classes was displaced through the mediation of others' sense of threat onto far more diffuse goals of nationalism and statism. Thus the propertied classes (even perhaps agrarian landlords) did not pursue the most instrumentally rational course of action. The ensuring authoritarian rightism then developed its own economic rationality by pioneering statist economic policies useful both for late development and for combating depression. But the search for order, hierarchy, and risk avoidance made most rightists lower their sights below what countries in the northwest were beginning to accomplish with increased capacity for democratic mobilization.

So though class struggle played a substantial part in the surge of the authoritarian rightist family, we must also link it in our explanation to political, military, and ideological power relations. When multiple crises generate multiple goals among collective actors who overlap and intersect in complex ways, ensuing actions rarely follow interest group rationality. This led authoritarian rightist regimes into dangerous areas that threatened their own survival. Relying on a more militarized and more sacred nation-state "threatened" by domestic-foreign enemies had dangerous consequences. It made war more likely, and modern total warfare produces far more losers than winners. Some of these regimes provoked wars with the potential to destroy them all. This actually happened in 1945. Endorsing rightist authoritarian values also made them vulnerable to being outflanked by more radical rightists.

Enter the fascists. We reach the second part of the explanation as fascists piggy-backed on top of all this. They would not have grown large without war-induced crises faced by dual states and panicking old regimes and possessing classes generating nation-statist values. Fascists did not grow large where crises came without dual states and panicking old regimes, in the northwest of the continent. Fascists were nurtured among the authoritarian rightists and continued to have close family relations with them. As in all families, their relationships could involve love or hatred. Thus the second part of the explanation involves explaining which occurred, and where.

I have emphasized that fascists were distinctive. Neither their organization nor their values allowed them to be simply a vehicle for class interests. Organizationally, they were unlike other authoritarians, for they were a "bottom-up" movement, not a top-down one. And they were driven in "radical" directions by their own core values: They believed in a paramilitary, transcendent, and cleansing nation-statism. Fascism was not committed to the existing state nor to its military arm but sought to revolutionize them, "knock class heads together," cleanse the nation of its enemies, and so transcend class and political conflict. Since they saw themselves as a "popular" movement, they were not averse to elections as a strategy of coming to power. Most fought elections vigorously, pioneering mass electoral techniques of ideological manipulation. Only in Italy, where they came very rapidly to power, was electioneering not a central part of fascist activity. Unlike the more conservative authoritarian rightists, fascists could not use the power of the state to manipulate and fix elections (until after they came to power). Though fascists did not believe in democracy, it was vital to their success.

But electoralism sat alongside a second form of popular struggle. Their activist core consisted of voluntary paramilitary formations committed to organized street violence. This had three purposes. It was "provocative," intended to produce a violent reaction from its political rivals. This would enable fascists to declare that their own violence was "self-defense." Second, it would repress enemies, since fascist paramilitarism conferred logistical superiority in street warfare, enabling them to bring "order" to the streets. It was hoped that both "self-defense" and "success" would bring more support and legitimacy to the notion that fascist "orderly violence" could end social chaos. This was then further exploited electorally. Third, paramilitarism could in the last resort launch a coup – provided the army was also immobilized (since most fascists knew that their paramilitarism was inferior to the military power of the state).

Such paramilitary activism brought distinctive recruits and distinctive values to the movement. The first cohort of recruits, without whom fascism would never have got off the ground, consisted largely of young military veterans transmitting wartime values of comradeship, hierarchy, and violence into a peacetime political movement. In this respect fascism as a mass movement would never have surged beyond being a coterie of intellectuals without World War I. Indeed, fascist activists remained cross-class gangs of young men for whom the combination of demonstrating, marching, and brawling had a special attraction. Hence they were disproportionately students, cadets, athletes, and young working-class roughnecks (who are also well represented among the perpetrators of atrocities in my forthcoming volume on ethnic cleansing). Fascism also reflected modernization impacts on young people: the liberation of young males from family discipline, and of young females from much of the burden of childbirth, the growth of organized sports, and the growth of professions requiring extensive further or higher education, especially the profession of war. Scholars of fascism (or indeed of the twentieth century in general) have paid insufficient attention to these age-cohort effects that contributed to the emergence of a general feature of the twentieth century, the cult of youth. Fascism was the first great political manifestation of this cult.

Bottom-up nationalism and statism were fascist values everywhere, drawing distinctive core constituencies of popular support. Fascism resonated especially among embittered refugees, "threatened border" regions, state employees (especially including armed forces), state-owned or state-protected industries, and churches that saw themselves as "the soul of the nation" or "the morality of the state." As class theorists have observed, fascism would not have surged without the prior surge in class conflict, and not surged so much without the Bolshevik Revolution. But it does not follow – as class theorists have argued – that fascists represented only one side in this class struggle or indeed any single class at all.

Their core constituencies reflected the appeal of the goal of transcending that struggle. Fascism tended to appeal neither to the organized working class nor to persons from the middle or upper classes who were directly confronted by organized labor. Instead, it appealed more to those on the margins of such conflict, persons of all classes and various sectors, in smaller or newer industries and the service sector, persons likely to cry "a plague on both your houses." The fascist core, especially fascist militants, rested preponderantly on macho youth receptive to paramilitarism and on social environments receptive to the message of either extreme nation-statism or class transcendence.

Nonetheless, fascist regimes did not succeed in transcending class. Since they were not actually anticapitalist, they could come to terms with the capitalist class; since they were promilitarist, they could come to terms with the armed forces; and since most of them cared little about religion, they were willing to sign concordats with powerful churches. Thus in practice, and once they neared power, fascist movements became biased on questions of class struggle. They tilted toward the capitalist class, the propertied classes more generally, and the old regime in particular. Yet, of the main fascist values, class transcendence was the one that varied most among the various national movements. Italian fascism was rather conservative and bourgeois in outcome, Romanian became decidedly proletarian.

Since big fascist movements were varied and emerged in rather varied circumstances, it is not so easy to generalize about their rise as it was for the whole family of authoritarian rightists. I first summarize their variations case by case, then move to their overall similarities.

Italian fascism rose and seized power early, in the immediate postwar years when class conflict was only just beginning to decline (and was still raging in agriculture). Thus it had a more direct class component than the other cases. There was an obvious fascist/propertied class alliance, and so Italian fascism can be partially explained in functional Marxist terms: The upper classes turned to fascists to rescue them from class revolution. But the closeness of World War I also made for a more direct military/paramilitary contribution to fascism through young male military veterans. One might almost say that paramilitarism was the means and agrarian-led class repression was the goal of Italian fascism. This would be to oversimplify, however, since paramilitarism also brought distinctive recruits and goals. Though not geared to electoralism, Italian fascism's combination of "self-defense" and success (it did destroy socialist and *populari* power) increased fascism's popularity among those valuing social order. Fascism's broader nation-statist goals were also popular and undermined the will to resist of the old regime and state executive. Geopolitical and political power relations also mattered. Since Italy had largely uncontested borders and was unthreatened from abroad, its nationalism contained little external aggression or racism inside Europe (Africa was a different story).

The Italian state was also dual, and both halves of the state were in weakened condition. This made it vulnerable to a coup. Liberal parliamentarism was not directly challenged by fascism, since fascism's sudden rise occurred between elections. But parliament had been weakened by the traditional hostility of the church and the rapidity of the transition toward full democracy. Socialists, Catholic *populari*, liberals, and conservatives were not yet socialized into the rules of the parliamentary game and failed to form the coalitions that would have best served them and democracy. But since the church had hitherto stood aside from politics and since Italy was characterized by uneven economic development, the country also lacked a homogenous old regime. Landowners, big capitalists, the army, and the church could not subvert the transition to democracy with their own conservative authoritarianism. Some were quickly driven toward the fascists (who were often their own sons). There were thus three causes of the triumph of Italian fascism: intense class struggle, postwar paramilitarism, and a weakened old regime.

German Nazism rose later, after a sustained attempt to make Weimar democracy work. Again, the condition of the old regime was extremely important. War defeat had unseated the monarchy and its loyal conservative and national liberal parties, and it had greatly shrunk the armed forces. The old regime could not now rule. As democracy faltered from 1930, conservative authoritarianism had little support outside the state executive itself.

Second, paramilitarism was again important, though its role differed from the case in Italy. Military veterans were important to the first cohort of Nazis and other populist extremists, but they needed reinforcing by later cohorts of Germans who had not fought in the war. From 1928 the Nazis were thriving on the electoral process of the republic, quite unlike Italy. This meant that their paramilitarism was more geared to gaining electoral support and rolling over its enemies in street brawling than to seizing the state.

Third, class conflict, though relevant, was not dominant. It grew during the Great Depression, but was much less severe than in the immediate postwar period and was insufficient to threaten capitalist property rights. However, there was a squeeze on profits, and one solution would be to repress labor. There was thus some complicity in the Nazi coup by the propertied classes, though much less than in Italy.

Fourth, Nazism was also a popular electoral movement, unlike Italian fascism, making two main mass appeals to the voters. The apparent "class stalemate" during the Depression made Nazi claims to class transcendence appealing, especially since the Nazi movement was the most classless in Germany. Second, its populist nation-statism thrived on Germany's geopolitical and ethnic bitterness. A Great Power resenting its loss of territories, sucked into the Central European (formerly Habsburg-centered) tensions of Germanic, Jewish, and Slav peoples, Germany had refugees, "threatened borders," and ethnic "enemies" at home and abroad. Organic cleansing nationalism had quite broad appeal. Nazism's statism was limited to Führer worship and militarism. But its nationalism was more intense and racist. Thus Nazi transcendent nation-statism was sufficiently popular to bring it to the brink of power. Its own paramilitarism and the weakness (sometimes the complicity) of the old regime took it over the top. This is a broad explanation entwining ideological, economic, military, and political power relations.

Austrian fascism was divided between two rival fascist movements. Though the monarchy and empire were gone, there was much continuity from prewar times in the institutions of parliament, the state executive, and the Catholic Church, and the old regime lived on in Christian Social governments. "Austro-fascism" and the Austrian Nazi movement both emerged as rivals out of postwar revisionist para-militaries and continued to thrive on discontents expressed through the electoral process. Both movements exploited the intensity of Austro-German antipathy toward Slavs and Jews. Austro-fascism was the less populist and radical of the two movements, being more top-down and more procapitalist. It strengthened as the mild semi-authoritarianism of the Christian Socials seemed unable to overcome Austria's class stalemate, which the Depression helped perpetuate. But the rise of Hitler next door in Germany was the decisive factor. This intensified the appeal of fascism, undermined Austro-fascism, and gave the prize to the Austrian Nazis. The paramilitaries of both parties attempted coups but got into power only with help from the military power of a state (respectively, Austria and Germany). The final result was *Anschluss* between two Nazi movements, though they had got to power in different ways, and one was vastly more powerful than the other.

Hungarian and Romanian fascisms differed substantially from the others. The two countries had fought on opposite sides in the war, Hungary emerging as a big loser, Romania as a great victor. Yet the contrast was weakened by the ensuing civil war in Hungary, which resulted in the crushing of the Hungarian left and allowed the Hungarian old regime to reemerge, if in embittered and radicalized form. Rule was by a dual state composed of the traditional executive and bureaucracy and a parliament dominated by the gentry. Yet the old regime now contained many younger radical rightists, making more populist, revisionist (i.e., demanding the return of "lost territories"), and modern appeals to the country. Romania differed somewhat. Its (mainly foreign) landed gentry had been dispossessed, but this and the great war victory allowed the monarch, bureaucracy, and army to reemerge, as a more nationalist though still corrupt regime. Thus the old regimes survived quite well in both countries, if somewhat radicalized and then destabilized by further rad-icals emerging within and around them. The political competition on the right was especially fierce within the universities and military schools and through the elec-toral process. Large fascist movements only emerged in the mid-1930s, well after the threat from the left had subsided. Thus fascists had no capitalist bias; indeed, they became rather proletarian in their composition. In both cases paramilitarism was used more as an electoral tool than to repress rivals or to seize power. An unequal dance of death ensued, in which military triumphed over paramilitary power, and radicalizing regime authoritarians triumphed over fascists. Only the chaos of the last war years allowed the fascists a brief, doomed victory.

Spanish fascism was different again. Neutral in World War I, Spain's old regime experienced the least disruption among all my case studies, and so con-servative authoritarians, not fascists, dominated. Indeed, this, and not fascism, was the most common outcome across the center, east, and south of the continent. Portugal, Bulgaria, Greece, and the Serb core of Yugoslavia resembled Spain in this respect. The new successor states of the collapsed empires – the three Baltic republics, Poland, and Albania – also moved in crisis only to reactionary or corporatist authoritarianism. Though their political regimes were not "old" but brand new, they had the power and legitimacy of being "national liberators." They, not fascists, developed veterans associations and populist parties.

The Spanish old regime did have one weak element, an unpopular monarch, and this let in the military regime of General Primo de Rivera. His failure led to the democratic Third Republic, the breakup of which did eventually produce a sizable fascist movement, complete with hastily formed paramilitaries. But these remained subordinate to the Nationalist army in the civil war and were marginalized under Franco's regime. His main props were the army, the church, and the "old" propertied classes. His regime is largely explicable in terms of my earlier general explanation of the surge of the authoritarian rightist family.

All these cases differed. To explain them required analysis attuned to local histories and social structures. Nonetheless, through the variety I perceive common forces determining the power of fascists. One potential cause actually played relatively little role: the threat from the working-class movement. This was not correlated with fascist strength. The threat was probably greatest in Spain, where there was not much fascism. The threat may have seemed substantial (though it had already peaked) in Italy; it seemed substantial though was actually more formal than real in Austria; Germany had a large but mostly moderate labor movement; Romania and Hungary had negligible lefts by the time fascism loomed – indeed, fascism itself provided their main labor movements. Fascism was to a limited and variable degree supported by the propertied classes to save themselves from labor, but this is not a very powerful general explanation of fascism.

The main attraction of fascism was the intensity of its message. This always brought committed support from mainly young people, willing to give more of their time and energy than were activists in any other political movement. Fascist militancy, always with a paramilitary component, was necessary to fascist success. By their energy and violence, the thousands could hope to both attract and defeat the millions. This militancy centered on the ability to trap young single men within comradely, hierarchical, and violent "cages." Fascist parties and paramilitaries were almost "total institutions." Fascism also attracted substantial (though not majority) electoral support, attracted by varying combinations of statism, nationalism, and class transcendence, though less by paramilitarism and cleansing. As we have seen, the first three of my five fascist characteristics had much greater plausibility in the countries that generated large fascist movements.

But the popularity of fascism was also greatly affected by the political strength and stability of old regime conservatism, which (more than liberal or social democracy) was fascism's main rival. Only weakened and factionalized old regimes let in large fascist movements. United old regimes repressed or subordinated them, weaker ones enabled fascists to find military and political organizing space. World War I provided the space for legitimate paramilitarism, initially provided by discontented war veterans. Their values were then transmitted to two further generations of recruits drawn predominantly from among young students, cadets, and workers. Democratic elections provided the second space. Fascists thrived on a three-way electoral struggle, pitting the left against a conservative/liberal center and radicalizing conservatives. Fascists could then swallow up part or all of the radical right while the center was hollowed out and the left repressed. That was how the fascists achieved electoral success.

As they said themselves, fascists were not mere "reactionaries" nor "stooges" of capitalism or anyone else. They offered solutions to the four economic, military, political, and ideological crises of early twentieth-century modernity. They propounded plausible solutions to modern capitalism's class struggles and economic crises. They transmitted the values of mass citizen warfare into paramilitarism and aggressive nationalism. They were a product of the transition of dual states toward "rule by the people," proposing a less liberal and more "organic" version of this rule. Finally, they bridged the ideological schism of modernity. On the one hand lay the tradition of the Enlightenment, "the party of humanity," that would steadily widen the sphere of reason, freedom, democratic citizenship, and rational planning in human society. On the other hand lay the modernist renewal of Romanticism: the perception that human beings also possessed sentiments, emotions, souls, and an unconscious and that modern forms of organization – crowds, mass movements, total war, mass media – might encourage these quite as much as it encouraged reason. Fascists claimed to have fused these two aspects of human and mass behavior. We may not like any of their four solutions, but we must take them seriously. Fascists were and remain part of the dark side of modernity.

So fascists were generated in large numbers by postwar crises in ideological, economic, military, and political power relations to which a transcendent nation-statist ideology spearheaded by "popular" paramilitaries offered a plausible solution. Fascism occurred only where rule was by dual states containing weakening "old regime" executives and vibrant but only half-institutionalized democratic parliaments. Dual states with more stable old regimes produced more conservative forms of authoritarianism. Fascism resulted from the process of *democratization* amid profound war-induced crises. Fascism provided a distinctly statist and militarist version of "rule by the people," the dominant political ideal of our times. Fully parliamentary regimes (in the northwest) survived all four crises with their institutions intact and fascists as small minorities.

[...]

NOTES

Chapter I

1 The notion that the twentieth century has seen the rise and fall of the state as the bearer of a moral project is the main theme of Perez-Diaz (1993).
2 The reader wishing to know more of my general theory could start with the introductory chapters of the two published volumes of my history of power in society (Mann 1986, 1993).
3 Note that Eatwell (2001) renounces the concept of "rebirth," which he had earlier used, abusing it as "philosophically banal." I deal with the rival primordial, perennial, and modern conceptions of the nation in my forthcoming book, chap. 2.
[...]

5 Homosexuality did intermittently accompany such intense male comradeship, though this remains a poorly documented aspect of fascism. It is well known that the Nazi leaders turned strongly against homosexuals in the Roehm purge of 1934. SS personnel records would sometimes note evidence of homosexuality, implying that the organization could use the member's sense of vulnerability to get him to undertake "hard" (i.e., murderous) tasks.

BIBLIOGRAPHY

Berend, I. 1998. *Decades of Crisis: Central and Eastern Europe before World War II.* Berkeley and Los Angeles: University of California Press.

Brooker, P. 1991. *The Faces of Fraternalism.* Oxford: Clarendon.

Broszat, M. 1981. *The Hitler State.* London: Longman.

Burleigh, M. 2000. *The Third Reich.* New York: Hill & Wang.

Eatwell, R. 2001. *Fascism, a History.* London; Chatto & Windus.

Gao, Bai. 1997. *Economic Ideology and Japanese Industrial Policy.* Cambridge: Cambridge University Press.

Gregor, A.J. 1979. *Italian Fascism and Developmental Dictatorship.* Princeton, NJ: Princeton University Press.

Gregor, J. 2000. "Fascism, Marxism and some considerations concerning classification." *Totalitarian Movements and Political Religions,* issue 3.2.

Jaffrelot, C. 1996. *The Hindu Nationalist Movement in India.* New York: Columbia University Press.

Kallis, A. 2000. "The 'regime-model' of fascism: A typology." *European History Quarterly* 30.

Kershaw, I. 2000. *The Nazi Dictatorship,* 4th edn. London: Edward Arnold.

Larsen, S.U. 2001. "Was there Fascism outside Europe? Diffusion from Europe and domestic impulses." In S.U. Larsen (ed), *Fascism outside Europe.* New York: Columbia University Press.

Lyttleton, A. 1987. *The Seizure of Power: Fascism in Italy, 1919–1929.* London: Weidenfeld & Nicolson.

Mann, M. 1986. *The Sources of Social Power,* vol. 1: *A History from the Beginning to 1760 AD.* New York: Cambridge University Press.

Mann, M. 1993. *The Sources of Social Power,* vol. 2: *The Rise of Classes and Nation-States, 1760–1914.* New York: Cambridge University Press.

Mann, M. 1997. "The contradictions of continuous revolutions." In I. Kershaw and M. Lewin (ed.), *Stalinism and Nazism: Dictatorship in Comparison.* Cambridge: Cambridge University Press.

Mayer, A. 1981. *The Persistence of the Old Regime.* London: Croom Helm.

Mosse, G. 1999. *The Fascist Revolution.* New York: Howard Fertig.

Paxton, R. 1994. "Radicals." *New York Review of Books,* June 23.

Paxton, R. 1996. "The uses of fascism." *New York Review of Books,* November 28.

Perez-Diaz, V. 1993. *The Return of Civil Society.* Cambridge, MA: Harvard University Press.

Sternhell, Z. 1986. *Neither Right nor Left: Fascist Ideology in France.* Berkeley, CA: University of California Press.

Weber, E. 1976. "Revolution? Counterrevolution? What revolution?" In W. Laqueur (ed.), *Fascism: A Reader's Guide.* Berkeley, CA: University of California Press.

9

THE 'REGIME-MODEL' OF FASCISM

A typology

Aristotle A. Kallis

Comparative works on fascism have focused predominantly on the nature of the fascist ideology and the national movements it generated. At the same time, the history of the fascist regimes in various European countries has remained largely under-researched, with the notable exception of the independent and long-lasting fascist regimes in Fascist Italy (1922–1943) and Nazi Germany (1933–1945). In this essay, Aristotle A. Kallis—an emerging new voice in the field of fascist studies with a research interest in theories of generic fascism (2002; 2003a; 2003b; 2004; 2009) and the comparative history of fascism in Germany and Italy (2000)—provides an original analytical framework for understanding fascism in power. Kallis acknowledges the paramount analytical importance of ideal-type models of fascist ideology for the study of interwar fascism, but argues that they are necessary but not sufficient tools for explaining fascism in power. In his view, the nature of fascist regimes was not simply defined by the main features of the fascist ideology, but by additional social and political factors, such as the nature of the fascist take-over, the domestic social support it mobilized, the nature of the political concessions ruling fascists had to make to alternative elites or centers of power in society, and their impact on the (re)formulation of the official ideology.

Building mainly on research insights advanced by Zeev Sternhell, Stanley Payne and Robert O. Paxton, Kallis pleads for a redirection of the research agenda in fascist studies from ideal-types of generic fascist ideology to constructing a regime-model of fascism in power. He argues that the ability of fascist regimes to emerge and consolidate depended on four main inter-related factors: (1) the ideology of the local fascist movement; (2) the domestic consolidation of the regime; (3) the main objectives behind policy-making; and (4) the scope of its regenerating ambitions. Kallis applies these criteria to a sample of eight case studies, which includes the two "paradigmatic" regimes of Fascist Italy and Nazi Germany but also "para-fascist" regimes in Spain, Portugal, Austria, Hungary, Romania, and Greece. Kallis excludes from his analysis the wartime "fascist puppet regime" functioning in Hungary, Romania, Croatia, Slovakia or the Ukraine, on the grounds that their main reason of existence lies in eternal factors.

After a careful and contextual analysis of the interaction of these factors and their outcomes in the eight cases under investigation, Kallis advances an ideal-type of the regime-model of fascism, having the following main components: "radical anti-system ideology, all-embracing antagonistic consolidation, radical policymaking, and the crusading spirit." Kallis cautiously points out that the aim of this model is not to provide yet another "check-list" for deciding on the gen-uinely fascist or non-fascist nature of interwar political regimes, but describes only "the end-result of a tendency towards the gradual re-organization of the authoritarian model's style and content." Instead of endorsing a rigid analytical regime-model of fascism, Kallis acknowledges that fascist regimes evolved within idiosyncratic political conditions. As a heterogeneous and negotiated outcomes, the nature of fascist regimes undercores the fluid border between authoritarian and fascist regimes in interwar Europe.

BIBLIOGRAPHY

Kallis, Aristotle A. (2000). *Fascist Ideology: Territory and Expansion in Italy and Germany (1922–1945)* (London: Routledge).

Kallis, Aristotle A. (2002). *Fascism: A Reader – Historians and Interpretations of Fascism* (London: Routledge).

Kallis, Aristotle A. (2003a). "'Fascism', 'Para-fascism' and 'Fascistization': On the Similarities of Three Conceptual Categories", *European History Quarterly*, 33: 2, 219–50.

Kallis, Aristotle A. (2003b) "To Expand or not to Expand? Territory, Generic Fascism and the Quest for an 'Ideal Fatherland'", *Journal of Contemporary History*, 38: 2, 238–260.

Kallis, Aristotle A. (2004) "Studying Fascism in Epochal and Diachronic Terms: Ideological Production, Political Experience and the Quest for 'Consensus'", *European History Quarterly*, 34: 1, 9–42.

Kallis, Arostotle A. (2009) *Genocide and Fascism: The Eliminationist Drive in Fascist Europe* (London: Routledge).

* * *

In recent years there has been a revival of interest in the nature of *generic* fascism. This renewed search for a paradigmatic model of fascism originated as a reaction to the trend of overstating specificity, of studying fascist phenomena in the *longue durée* and of using their individual differences to underscore the futility of grand theories of fascism. A large part of the blame for the discrediting of comparative approaches is borne by the erratic and often mystifying sample of the studies themselves. Lack of clarity about the nature and content of fascism resulted in a number of comparative studies, whose insufficiently justified sample of case-studies left the concept of 'fas-cism' in disarray. The 'totalitarian' approach focused on the political features of fas-cism as regime (i.e. Italy and Germany), but then subjected it to a broader definition which dovetailed with aspects of such a disparate socio-political phenomenon as communism.[1] Nolte's *Three Faces of Fascism* provided an insightful account of the ideological similarities between the Italian and German regimes, only to obfuscate his paradigm by including *Action Française* in his analysis.[2] The ideological affinities notwithstanding, the weaknesses of his generic definition are obvious. If 'fascism' is a broad *ideological* phenomenon, then why are other case-studies excluded (Austria, Britain, etc.)? If, on the other hand, 'fascism' is both ideology and action, movement and regime, then why is *Action Française* comparable to the Italian and German regimes? Even the recent account by Roger Eatwell has focused on a curious combination of two major interwar regimes (Italy, Germany) and a plethora of disparate movements (most of which achieved limited, short-lived appeal and none of which ever reached power) from two further western European countries (Britain, France). Similarly, the all-inclusive studies of the 1960s and 1970s offered insight into numerous intricate aspects of fascism, but at the same time undermined its generic value through an excessive broadening of the sample.[3] The two most elaborate recent works on generic fascism, by Roger Griffin and Stanley G. Payne,[4] have rectified to a large extent the inadequacies of previous comparative interpretations through a significantly more elaborate theoretical paradigm of fascism and a notably wider pool of case-studies. In spite of their individual methodological differences, both works rest on the presupposition that the two *dimensions* of fascism (*vertical*: fascism within long-term national history; *horizontal*: fascism as an epochal phenomenon of interwar Europe), rather than being antithetical, may jointly promote a deeper and more elaborate understanding of the nature of fascism. However, the puzzling epochal appeal of fascism, the mushrooming of movements/parties sponsoring an original or mimetic fascist ideology, and the unprecedented success of some of them in reaching power have to be carefully analysed and accounted for.[5] Recently, Robert O. Paxton has stressed the value of studying the *dynamics* of fascism's evolution 'in time': from its ideological origins to the acquisition and exercise of power. His critique of the 'static' character of 'generic' theories of fascism focuses on the fundamental difference between 'a regime where fascism exercises power' (referring particularly to Italy and Germany as the most developed expressions of fascism) and a 'sect of dissident intellectuals' (a number of fascist groups and movements which either failed to gain power or were neutralized by the political establishment).[6] In this sense, a distinction between fascist *movement* and fascist *regime* is not a question of semantics but a necessity induced by the entirely different reasons behind the occurrence of each of the two forms of fascism. In terms of its ideological crystallization, fascism may be seen as an exceptional variant of hyper-nationalism—a 'hyper-nationalism-plus' phenomenon which activated, revived or recast a set of extreme prescriptions from the reservoir of each country's radical nationalist aspirations and imagery.[7] In its epochal, horizontal dimension fascism was also motivated by a short-term, violent response to specific historic challenges—resentment from frustrated nationalist aspirations after the First World War, fear of socialist mobilization after the 1917 Bolshevik revolution, social insecurity, political crisis, etc.

However, for those cases where a regime with at least one 'fascist' component was established, the above minimum definition is inadequate. The nature of a regime is defined by a plethora of additional factors—how it was installed, who supported it, in which political direction it evolved, how competing notions of future action were negotiated and formulated into official policy, to what extent intentions were facilitated or impeded by exogenous elements. It is a truism that no 'fascist' regime in Europe was established as a result of majority popular choice. It is also a fact that no such regime was instituted in total opposition to the existing ruling political, economic and social elites. In all cases, and at least initially, fascist leaderships either headed coalition cabinets or drew their legitimacy from the support of established institutions (Head of State, church, armed forces, established political parties).[8] Everywhere the 'fascist solution' was endorsed by such powerful individuals, groups and institutions in order to strengthen the popular appeal of the existing state. This was intended to be a single remedy for two acute needs—to safeguard the state against socialist subversion and to use the principle of fascist 'charismatic' leadership as an antidote to the crisis of the liberal-parliamentary system for ensuring strong, stable government. Because of all these factors and considerations, the rationale behind installing 'fascist' regimes reflected more the elites' longing for a new type of authoritarian system rather than their endorsement of fascist ideology or—even less—a desire to see the latter's radical prescriptions translated into action. Therefore, assessing the fascist credentials of a regime involves much more than just ascertaining the 'fascist' character of the leaders' ideological beliefs and visions. This article argues that the regime-model of fascism developed in the framework of elite experimentation with new forms of the *populist authoritarian, anti-socialist* model, based on a pro-system logic of strengthening the existing political and social domestic structures. What distinguished the regime-model of fascism from conventional authoritarian systems was the ability of the fascist component to assert its political supremacy over conservative expectations, to develop its own radical momentum and to embark on the realization of its particular ideological objectives. Such ability depended on four factors—the *ideology* of the fascist component; its *domestic consolidation*; the objectives behind *policy-making*; and the *scope* of its regenerating ambitions. These criteria are applied to eight case-studies (Italy, Germany, Spain, Portugal, Greece, Austria, Hungary, Romania) in order to assess to what extent and for what reasons each of these regimes departed from the conventional authoritarian model.

The regime-model of fascism: criteria

Ideology

As with any general theory of fascism, the problem of which case-studies to include in the analysis of the regime-model of fascism has generated wide controversy. Apart from the two most obvious and generally indisputable candidates (Germany and Italy), there is a plethora of regimes which Roger Griffin has accurately described as 'para-fascist', in the sense that they comprised specific 'fascist' elements and groups with strands of conservatism, authoritarianism and indigenous nationalism.[9] In many cases (Spain, Austria, Romania, Hungary) the fascist component manifested itself in a variety of different forms, ideologies and organizations with competing programmes and aspirations. In some cases (Austria, Romania, Hungary) a para-fascist regime was established in opposition to other, more extreme fascist movements/parties or at least showed active distrust of their eventual motives. Finally, during the Second World War, fascist-style puppet regimes were introduced in a number of European countries, either as the direct result of occupation by the Axis forces (France, Hungary in 1944, Croatia) or in order to offset such a development (Yugoslavia before the Nazi invasion, Romania). The methodological postulate of this article is to exclude this last category of fascist-like regimes from its sample, as the logic behind their establishment was primarily conditioned by security considerations and not by elite-driven experiments with new forms of executive power. Instead, all other cases of regimes supported by at least one movement/party of 'fascist' character will be considered.

The first crucial factor in shaping the regime's outlook is *ideology*. Two criteria are relevant in this respect: whether the ideology of the political pillars of the regime was *radical* or *conservative*; and, in cases where the regime represented a coalition of disparate socio-political forces, which of the two elements was more dominant in the overall world-view of the regime. Here the cases of Italy and Germany are straightforward. Numerous studies on the two movements have ascertained their radical idiosyncratic ideological credentials.[10] Also, although Mussolini and Hitler came to power as heads of coalition governments, commanding the support of wide conservative and liberal groups, they succeeded in ridding themselves of this pattern of cohabitation and in gradually establishing a monocratic type of regime where the fascist component dominated the ideological physiognomy of government. In all other cases the regimes displayed a combination of conservative and fascist elements in constant interaction and sometimes conflict for the crystallization of the regime's ideological character. In Portugal the Salazar regime evolved in continuity with the Carmona military dictatorship, which had abolished the proto-liberal/parliamentary system in 1926. This continuity ensured support from conservative strata in the Portuguese society and remained unchallenged as the official political agenda of the regime. Although Salazar introduced radical social reforms in some areas (the Estado Novo/New State) and emulated 'fascist' organizational elements (militia, secret police, etc.), the *raison d'être* of the regime was the preservation of conservative and Catholic values, as well as the defence of the existing system against radical alternative conceptions of domestic organizations.[11] One of these rival alternatives was the National Syndicalist movement, headed by Preto and established in 1932. The organization, sponsoring a more extreme blend of corporatism, anti-socialism and integral nationalism, became disaffected with Salazar's timid agenda and staged an unsuccessful bid for power in 1934. Preto's coup was followed by violent suppression of the movement from which the National

Syndicalists never actually recovered.[12] Although in subsequent years Salazar accentuated his commitment to a mimetic 'fascist' model of domestic organization, this remained confined to the articulation of form and style rather than extending into the sphere of political substance. His regime remained an essentially pro-system pattern of conservative-authoritarian government whose 'fascist' elements of style were duly shed in the 1940s. The case of Spain is similar with regard to the syncretic (i.e. not purely 'fascist') basis of the regime's support but different in its balance of power between traditionalism and radicalism. The hybrid fascist organization of JONS (Juntas de Ofensiva Nacional Sindicalista), founded in 1931 and merged with the Falange in 1934 to form the Falange Española de las JONS, blended revolutionary integral nationalism and aggressive antisocialism with a traditionalist commitment to militarist and Catholic values.[13] In contrast to the fate of Preto's National Syndicalists, the organization—headed by José Antonio Primo de Rivera, son of the erstwhile Spanish dictator Miguel Primo de Rivera—sided with the Nationalist forces in 1936 and was later absorbed and diffused into the Francoist regime (under the umbrella organization Falange Española Tradicionalista y de las JONS, established in April 1937), whose ideological outlook remained deeply imbued with conservative social views, Carlist sympathies and strong Catholic values. Those initial leaders of the JONS who were opposed to the traditionalist spirit of Franco's dictatorship were either politically marginalized or arrested and placed under confinement; others gradually chose the path of political demobilization.[14]

In Greece the Metaxas regime (established in 1936) demonstrated a similar symbiosis of fascist organizational style and conservative world-view. Albeit emulating formal patterns of Italian Fascism (youth organization, neo-classicism, palingenetic/nostalgic hyper-nationalism), the Metaxas regime was co-opted by the king and the pro-monarchical bourgeois right in the framework of a system-preserving function.[15] The political agenda of the regime was dominated by the long-term aspirations and dispositions of the monarchical right-wing political elite, of which General Metaxas had long been a distinguished (though not influential) member.[16] This type of conscious co-opting may also be seen in Romania. The Iron Guard, established in 1934 by Corneliu Codreanu as the paramilitary wing of his Legion of the Archangel Michael (founded in 1927), and after its founder's assassination in 1938 headed by Horia Sima, demonstrated a peculiar mix of ultra-nationalism, antisemitism, Orthodox mysticism and mimetic fascist organizational features (youth and paramilitary organizations, street violence).[17] It was wooed into the ruling authoritarian coalition both by King Carol in 1940 and by the Antonescu regime later in the same year, creating the shortlived 'National Legionary State' (named after the Legionaries, as the members of the Iron Guard were known). However, unlike in Greece and Spain, the co-habitation between the conservative-authoritarian and the quasi-fascist component neither was continual nor originated from a long-term strategy of co-opting the Iron Guard. Hence, a pattern of inconsistent, opportunistic coopting emerged, whereby the fascist element would be exploited at crucial moments to strengthen the legitimacy of the authoritarian state but would be violently suppressed when it attempted to increase its influence on the ideology of the regime. This happened in early 1941, when Antonescu, in agreement with Hitler, disbanded the Iron Guard and substituted the Legionary State with his 'National and Social State'.[18]

The co-habitation of fascist and reactionary forces was significantly more complex in Hungary and in Austria. In spite of the co-opting of Gömbös' National Socialists by Admiral Horthy's conservative regime between 1932 and 1936, the physiognomy of the regime remained essentially traditionalist in ideology.[19] This was also manifested in the antagonistic relation between other, more revolutionary anti-system groups—Böszörmeny's Scythe Cross and Szálasi's Arrow Cross. The former reacted to the socially conservative agenda of the regime by staging an unsuccessful coup in 1936 which was violently suppressed by the authorities. The latter was significantly more influential and radical in its emulation of the National Socialist ideological model, posing a potent alternative to Horthy's conservative regime. This explains why it was consistently persecuted until 1944, when the occupation of Hungary by the Nazi forces paved the way to the seizure of power by Szálasi and the establishment of a puppet regime under the political tutelage of Germany.[20] Austria followed a similar trajectory of antagonistic pluralism of quasi-fascist organizations. The Heimwehr, a paramilitary hypernationalist organization consisting of ex-war veterans of the National Guard, emerged as a combination of mimetic Pan-German, fascist-corporatist and Christian ideological strands in 1927 under the leadership of Starhemberg. In spite of their pledge to overthrow the liberal system of government and to pursue union with Germany, the Heimwehr leadership remained essentially pliable towards the conservative political establishment and displayed a disinclination to sponsor the aggressive bid for power staged by its Styrian branch in 1931.[21] This pro-system attitude enabled the Dollfuss conservative-authoritarian regime to co-opt Starhemberg in 1933. The neutralization of the Heimwehr was completed under Schuschnigg, who succeeded the assassinated Dollfuss after the July 1934 Nazi putsch, when the regime disbanded the movement and absorbed its membership into a state-sponsored paramilitary organization (Front-Miliz) in 1936.[22] However, Austrian fascism had another, more uncompromisingly anti-system face, the DNSAP/NSDAP (Austrian National Socialists). Linked to the development of the National Socialist movement in 1918, the Austrian brand maintained its closed links with its Bavarian sister-organization after the rejection of a German–Austrian union by the victors of the First World War. It also became the main repository of support by disaffected nationalists, including radical Heimwehren, and grew considerably in the 1928–38 decade. In spite of its spectacularly unsuccessful bid for power in July 1934 and the subsequent outlawing of the organization, it fought back and co-engineered with Berlin the 1938 Anschluss.[23] It is therefore evident that the Austrian conservative establishment co-opted the more traditionalist variant of diluted fascism (Heimwehr) but remained essentially impervious both to internal models of revolutionary fascism

(National Socialists) and to external pressures (especially by Mussolini in 1933–6) for transforming the authoritarian regime into a mimetic quasi-fascist system.[24]

Consolidation

The second criterion for assessing the character of the regime-model of fascism is domestic political consolidation. This pertains to control over the official state apparatus, over the decision-making process and over other surviving (if any) antagonistic institutional poles of power within the system. In order to assess the degree of fascist consolidation in a regime, three further aspects should be appraised: the *type* of fascist consolidation (whether it was co-operative or antagonistic to existing institutions); its *degree* (limited/diffused or dynamic/allembracing); and finally its *pace* (fast track or slow). Again, Nazi Germany offers the most extreme example of fascist domestic consolidation. Apart from a short period of political cohabitation with surviving party organizations and President Hindenburg (until 1934), the Nazi leadership employed a dynamic, antagonistic and extremely fast strategy for solidifying its power. This process officially ended in 1938 with the removal of the last conservative functionaries in the government (the Economics minister, Schacht, in late 1937, the Foreign Minister, Neurath, in 1938, and the armed forces leadership—Blomberg, Fritsch and Beck—by the summer of 1938.)[25] However, Hitler's ability to rid himself of such powerful figures of the conservative establishment in such an effortless manner alludes to a highly successful prior strategy of establishing an effective monopoly of control over decision-making that had been initiated immediately after the seizure of power. The fact that this type of consolidation was intended to be entirely antithetical to the existing state structure invested the Nazi regime with a sense of extreme antagonistic dynamism and facilitated a swift transition to a monocratic (though not monolithic) fascist regime-model.[26] Fascist Italy departs from this model of consolidation in two ways. First, the establishment of the Fascist regime after the declaration of dictatorship in January 1925 did involve the gradual marginalization of traditional elite groups but did not remove a pattern of institutional co-habitation with the Head of State, King Victor Emmanuel III. This constitutional anomaly, whereby Mussolini's position as Prime Minister depended on the Crown's support or tacit approval, was maintained throughout the life span of the regime and became the mechanism for the removal of the Duce in July 1943.[27] At the same time, the Fascist regime was forced to deal with another powerful traditional repository of public loyalty, the Catholic Church. The 1929 Concordat with the Vatican produced a *modus vivendi* which, albeit antagonistic and fraught with disputes, constituted a *de facto* limitation to the regime's monocratic ambitions.[28] In this respect, the consolidation of fascism in Italy was dynamic but oscillating between co-opting and antagonism. The latter tendency was accentuated after 1935—from that point onwards the Fascist leadership accelerated the pace of consolidation and embarked on a course of increasing marginalization of alternative centres of power and neutralization of opposition by the surviving traditional institutions of the state.[29]

In all other case-studies of regime-models the pattern of consolidation pursued was either not entirely dynamic, not overtly antagonistic, or both. In Spain, as we saw, the Francoist regime diffused the influence of the real fascist element (the Falange) on the political physiognomy of the ruling bloc and chose an essentially co-operative strategy in its dealings with traditional groups and institutions (Monarchy, Church, big landowners). This should not, of course, detract from the dynamic character of the consolidation of the Francoist regime *per se*—a fact attested to by the longevity of the system, the effective neutralization of its opposition and the long-term transformation of organizational structures of the Spanish state.[30] A similar situation characterized the case of Portugal. Here, in spite of the effective removal of the true fascist component (Preto's National Syndicalists) from the ruling bloc, the Salazar regime survived the 1945 watershed, removed any credible political alternative and effected lasting modifications through the introduction of the *Estado Novo*.[31] However, the nature of fascist consolidation was significantly more precarious or complex in the rest of the case-studies. In Greece, the collusion of Metaxas with King George II and the traditionalist right ensured a co-operative pattern of consolidation which appeared dynamic in its formal aspects ('style', discourse, organization of society) but the 'fascist' component remained essentially superficial and entrenched within the framework of a conservative authoritarian regime, depending on the support of the Monarchy.[32] In Hungary and Austria there appears to be a correlation between the ideological predisposition of the fascist organizations and their participation or not in the regime-model. Gömbös' diluted, conservative variant of fascism and the Heimwehren corporatist-traditionalist mélange were accommodated in the ruling bloc, while Szálasi's more radical Arrow Cross and the Austrian National Socialists (both essentially anti-system radical forces) were ostracized and suppressed to varying degrees. However, there also seems to be a connection between ideology and type of consolidation of those fascist components that eventually reached power. The traditionalistic nature of the two former movements' ideology facilitated their co-opting but also enabled their dilution in a limited co-operative pattern of consolidation which left the essential conservative authoritarian features of the state largely unchallenged. In Romania, on the other hand, co-opting the Iron Guard into the conservative-militarist ruling bloc was bracketed by systematic persecution and repression, thus resulting in a limited and ephemeral pattern of fascist consolidation within the framework of a predominantly authoritarian regime. In fact, whenever the Iron Guard instigated activities aimed towards an antagonistic, more widespread version of fascist consolidation in the regime-model, conservative elites minimized the potential disruption through violent ostracizing strategies (as happened in 1940 and 1941).[33]

Leadership is another pivotal element of the physiognomy of a political regime. Leaders have a strong influence upon the process of policy-making, both because of their personal ideological beliefs about what is socially desirable and because of their *de facto* role as co-ordinators of the executive function of the state. In fascist movements leadership was probably the strongest element of cohesion and incarnation of 'fascist' values. Although initially performing a token role of *primus inter pares*, the fascist leadership soon rose to a level of symbolic pre-eminence, as an ideological and political elite in charge of leading the movement to power and orchestrating the process of domestic regeneration.[34] With regard to the regime-model of fascism, an important distinction has to be made between those cases where a fascist leader became head of the government (Italy, Germany, Greece), those regimes embracing the fascist component but headed by conservative figures (Spain) and those regimes coopting a less radical fascist component while ostracizing the more extreme variant (Austria, Portugal, Hungary). Again, the personal ideological beliefs of a leader determined his vision of desirable political action. However, the actual political margins for policy-making were conditional upon two additional factors—*popular legitimacy* and *attitude towards the other components/ pillars* of the regime-model.

In Italy, Germany and Greece, as already mentioned, the fascist leaders (Mussolini, Hitler, Metaxas) were co-opted by the conservative establishment to head the new executive constellation and gradually asserted their individual role in the process of policy-making. However, the Italian and German leaderships possessed two additional advantages which Metaxas could not, and did not, entertain. First, both Mussolini and Hitler could boast a high level of popular legitimacy, either as leaders of wide social movements (PNF, NSDAP) or as charismatic figures representing the 'acceptable' face of fascism.[35] Metaxas, on the other hand, was in a significantly weaker position, lacking any discernible charisma, essentially isolated from any base of popular support and deprived of any influence on traditional institutions of the state (for example, the armed forces). While all three leaders were co-opted by the conservative establishment in order to perform a system-maintaining and stabilizing function, Mussolini and Hitler championed far more radical ideologies of political/social change than Metaxas' essentially half-hearted commitment to radical reform. They could also use their carefully choreographed charismatic appeal to legitimize their antagonistic consolidation against the wishes of their initial conservative sponsors—something that Metaxas never contemplated due to his limited personal appeal. In this sense, the Greek variant of fascist regime remained entrenched in its initial function as stabilizer of the existing system and continued to rely on the political sponsorship by the conservative, pro-monarchical establishment.[36] In Spain the leadership of General Franco drew its legitimacy from the successful conclusion of the civil war against the Republican forces. Although, as we saw earlier, the Falange was absorbed in the ruling bloc, Franco's personal prestige after 1936 did not allow significant margins for alternative, more radical leadership patterns. His co-operative attitude towards conservative institutions and social groups ensured that his position as system-stabilizer would be effectively entrenched and the more radical prescriptions of other participating forces (especially of the Falange) would be diluted and neutralized by the regime.[37] In Portugal, the lack of charisma in the moderate leadership (Salazar) was compensated by its sense of continuity with previous arrangements (the Carmona dictatorship) and its promise of domestic stability in the face of destabilizing plots by both the left and other, more radical fascist components (National Syndicalists). A similar notion of continuity legitimized the choice of Antonescu in Romania (a choice of the monarchical establishment for the stabilization of the system), again in spite of the clear lack of popular legitimacy of personal charisma.[38] By contrast, the regimes in Austria and Hungary, both co-operative in their consolidation and selective in their co-opting of certain moderate fascist components at the expense of more radical organizations, were effectively reduced to an increasingly difficult task of defending the system and balancing the conflicting social claims for change. In Austria, Dollfuss and especially Schuschnigg suffered both from a distinct lack of popular appeal and from the popularity of the excluded anti-system variant of National Socialism. In Hungary, the Horthy regime was forced to deal with the increasing social support for Szálasi's radical Arrow Cross after 1935. Although the movement was carefully marginalized (and at some points ruthlessly suppressed), Horthy's regime survived until the occupation of the country in 1944 (which brought Szálasi to power) by performing a limited system-maintaining function without any departures from the long-term expectations of the Hungarian conservative establishment.[39]

It seems that there is a correlation here between the position of the fascist component in the leadership structure of the regime-model, the personal legitimacy of the leader and the policymaking character of the regime itself. In cases where the fascist group became the dominant component in an antagonistic model of consolidation (Italy, Germany), radical change was pursued to varying degrees. By contrast, co-opting moderate fascist groups in the framework of co-operative, stabilizing arrangements did not result in the pursuit of a radical, anti-system political agenda (Metaxas in Greece, Gömbös in Hungary). Finally, in those cases where the fascist component was diluted in an otherwise conservative constellation of power and under the leadership of a moderate figure, the ensuing regime-model was either unstable (Austria, Hungary) or modest in its political aspirations, performing a limited 'stabilizing' function.

Policy-making

A third crucial factor shaping the profile of a regime is the nature and long-term framework of its policy-making. The ideological worldview of the leadership determines what is perceived as both socially desirable and politically feasible for future action. However, the ability of the leaders to translate thought and ambitions into action is an extremely intricate process that is only partly defined by pure ideological intentions. Obviously, there is a correlation between the degree and type of fascist consolidation, on the one hand, and the ability of fascist ideology to permeate and shape the official state policy-making, on the other. In instances of limited-diluted and/or co-operative consolidation, as well as of inconsistent co-opting of the fascist component into the ruling bloc, the latter's

225

ability to pursue its more radical ideological prescriptions was greatly limited by the co-habitation with more conservative components. Having said that, even in cases of (near-)monocratic or all-embracing fascist consolidation, the limits of what was politically feasible were in the end defined by external factors which remained largely impervious to fascist intentions—the cohesion of the traditional elite groups, the economic and military capacity of the system, international random events and stimuli.

Unsurprisingly, the Nazi regime displays an extremely favourable combination of all the above elements—radical ideology, strong consolidation, high potential capacity of the domestic system to meet the material demands of Nazi ambitions, and auspicious random events. Notwithstanding a fairly conventional political profile until 1934, Nazi policy-making soon unfolded its radical agenda and displayed a determination to implement even the most radical traits of its long-term vision, including the elimination of 'inferior races' and a new territorial order in Europe. With regard to both these policies, external factors and resources made a substantial contribution to their implementation. A highly effective bureaucratic machinery supervised the allocation of resources for the speedy elimination of Jews and other ethnic/social groups, while the impressive performance and capacity of the German economy facilitated the approximation of the extortionate demands of rearmament for territorial expansion.[40]

In a similar vein, the Italian Fascist regime offers another example of an ideologically radical fascist party achieving a high degree of control over policy-making, albeit with some institutional limitations that formally forestalled the establishment of a monocratic regime-model. In spite, however, of such limiting factors and the much more protracted period of domestic consolidation, the Fascist regime displayed both a commitment to a more radical style of politics and an increasing ability to radicalize its political agenda. International factors (the rise of Nazism, the instability of the European system, the appeasement by western powers) facilitated or did not effectively impede the pursuit of those radical prescriptions of fascist ideology (expansion, militarization of society). The Italian regime, in common with the Nazi regime-model, demonstrated an intensely radical perception of what was socially desirable and very wide margins for what they regarded as politically feasible. However, the Italian case diverges from its German equivalent in that the limited effectiveness of the state's co-ordinating functions and the resistance of the indigenous society to the militarizing/regenerating fascist schemes (the *uomo fascista* and the *cittadino-soldato*) circumscribed the freedom of the fascist leadership to set and effectively pursue its radical agenda.[41] In the rest of the case-studies examined here, the framework of policy-making may be characterized as essentially conventional in its long-term objectives. This was the result of a combination of factors explored already—diluted radicalism in the ideology of the participating fascist movements in the regime, exclusion of the more radical fascist variants from power, limited and/or co-operative types of consolidation, and finally inauspicious external influences. While all these regimes aped organizational and stylistic aspects of either the Italian

Fascist archetype or the Nazi extreme variant,[42] their co-opting of fascist 'new' politics stayed clear of a commitment to the revolutionary, anti-system potential prescriptions of fascist ideology. Even in those cases where the leadership of a regime acknowledged the alleged 'decadence' of the existing system and called for radical reform and regenerating action, the overall framework of policy-making was largely borrowed from the conservative-authoritarian regime-model and was dominated by the long-term aspirations of its traditional social pillars. All these regimes combined a mimetic reproduction of certain 'fascist' formal aspects (militia, youth organizations, mass politics, secret police) with traditional authoritarian aspects (anti-socialism, censorship, nationalism and trans-class discourse).[43] Yet, the co-operative and/or limited type of fascist consolidation in all these cases required the preservation and defence of comprehensive continuity with past structures and policy priorities or necessitated the consent of traditional forces for any changes in the political direction of the regime. The example of the violent repression of the Iron Guard in early 1941 by Antonescu demonstrates the limiting influence of co-ordinated conservative opposition to the revolutionary designs of radical fascist movements.

Scope of change

The fourth and final criterion defining the physiognomy of the regime-model of fascism is the scope and long-term aspirations of its policy-making. As extreme and idiosyncratic variants of the hyper-nationalist tradition and imagery, all fascist regimes embarked upon the realization of their version of domestic regeneration and trans-class nationalism, thus acting as a bulwark to the expansive spirit of internationalist socialism. However, some fascist movements projected their ideological commitment to social rebirth outwards, to wider regions, to Europe and potentially to the world as a whole. This was intended to constitute a rival utopia to socialism, a form of counterbalancing the latter's appeal as the conquering creed of the twentieth century. Fascism founded its universalist ambitions on the basis of its self-perception as ethical, cultural and political elite in a social Darwinist perception of history as a struggle of cultural entities for the predominance of the fittest.[44] This version of expansive fascism was underpinned by a sense of historic responsibility and a *crusading spirit* of spreading this new 'conception of life' to territories and political units beyond the realm of its nation. Again, of course, it has to be noted that an *ideological* commitment to this type of crusade did not necessarily translate into expansive *action* by the regime-model of fascism; external factors—such as those analysed earlier—played a crucial role in encouraging, frustrating or thwarting such ideological ambitions. In this framework of analysis, the Nazi regime remains the indisputably most extreme, effective and destructive form of crusading fascism. Domestic regeneration was the first crucial step towards the restoration of the German *Volk*'s greatness. Territorial expansion along historic irredentist lines—i.e. over those lands that had historically formed the German *Lebensraum* in its most extensive version—constituted the second stage of allegedly ensuring the welfare of the German people. However, the Nazi biological perception of human society as a constant struggle of the healthy elements against alien or otherwise detrimental components remained an essentially universalist, non-state-specific ethical task. In its campaign to *eradicate* such harmful elements (seen as the only guarantee of social and cultural regeneration for the white race[45]) the Nazi genocidal machine did not limit its annihilationist designs to the extended territory of the German Reich but attempted to implement a rigid notion of race hierarchy in all conquered territories in Europe and, after the launch of Operation Barbarossa, in the Soviet Union. For the Nazi regime, the vision of 'new order' was not simply about domination and political control; it also entailed the export and imposition of an extremely unbending experiment in radical social reconstitution with unprecedented destructive implications.[46]

The Italian Fascist regime eventually rallied to the cause of a fascist crusade but followed a different trajectory and maintained a distinct version of what universal fascism would mean. In the early years of the fascist regime-model Mussolini had emphasized the domestic, purely Italian character of the fascist experiment—a quality that rendered it unsuitable for other countries. Yet, by the end of the 1920s he had made a spectacular political U-turn by declaring fascism an 'export' product. The publication of the *Doctrine of Fascism* in 1932 provided a systematization of this universalist notion: fascism, like liberalism in the eighteenth century and socialism in the nineteenth, was the only true universal doctrine of the twentieth century.[47] Initially, this commitment to international fascism was expressed in terms of a voluntary association of all kin regimes and movements in the framework of a Fascist International (the 1934 abortive Conference in Montreux). However, the outbreak of the Spanish Civil War in the summer of 1936 provided the first appropriate battleground for the ideological struggle between fascism and communism for the domination of Europe.[48] In the remaining years until the Nazi invasion of Poland in September 1939 fascist Italy displayed an increasing commitment to the aggressive agenda of the Axis alliance and a gradually radicalizing perception of the regime's long-term goals. However, in contrast to Nazism, the Italian Fascist regime remained primarily committed to its specific historic irredentist agenda of reconstituting the 'third Roman Empire' in the Mediterranean.[49] Its crusading spirit was more traditionalist in its rationale, less extended in its scope and even less rigid in its social implications for the societies of the conquered states. The genocidal campaigns in Libya during 1928–32 and the establishment of a quasi-apartheid regime in Ethiopia after 1936 reflected a fairly conventional prejudice against 'alien races', prompted by either security considerations (in Libya) or an attempt to emulate previous colonial practices of domination (in Ethiopia). There is very little evidence to suggest a rigid perception of race hierarchy for Europe similar to the Nazi notion of 'race super-state'—an assumption that is further validated by the half-hearted, inconsistent and limited implementation of the antisemitic laws after 1938. Furthermore, the crusading aspirations of the fascist regime-model were further thwarted by the limited economic/military capacity of the Italian system. Participation in the war was delayed until June 1940 due to logistical problems of preparation, it remained initially limited due to scarcity of resources and, when it acquired a more extensive character in the autumn of 1940 (in the Balkans and Africa), it was undermined in its effectiveness by similar material and organizational problems, resulting in a spectacular and swift defeat in all fronts by early 1941. Even after the rescue of the Italian war by the Nazi forces, the Italian administration of the conquered areas showed little inclination to emulate the radical social programme of the Nazi authorities in German-occupied areas.[50]

The other fascist regimes did not manifest crusading tendencies in their policy-making. In those cases where an ideological commitment to some form of expansion beyond the national territory existed, such policies were either never implemented or resulted from a conventional expansionist spirit of accumulating *irredenta* without rigid attempts to instil a new framework for social organization. Francoist Spain was a traditional nationalist regime, more intent on establishing and perpetuating domestic social stability than extending the national territory. In spite of its alleged political affinity to the Fascist and Nazi regimes, Franco's government stubbornly resisted the attempts of the two Axis leaders during 1940–1 to lure Spain into the war in return for substantial territorial compensations. Apart from his limited interest in the crusading aspects of international fascism, Franco was also aware of the extremely limited capacity of the Spanish economy and his armed forces to unleash and sustain an international war after a recent long period of infighting for the control of the country itself. These two factors explain his obstinate neutrality throughout the Second World War, as well as the inward-looking character of his regime.[51] The Metaxas regime in Greece demonstrated a similar emphasis on domestic reorganization and an even more conspicuous self-restraint with regard to its potential expansionist designs. In terms of its ideological profile, the regime's motto of a 'third Hellenic civilization' emulated the palingenetic discourse of the 'third Rome' put forward by the fascist regime in Italy. Both countries' nationalist traditions shared a similar nostalgia for past imperial glories and an emotional imagery of regeneration for future ascendancy. However, the policy-making framework of the Metaxas regime remained essentially system-preserving, tied both to the British foreign policy of avoiding war and to the political efforts of the so-called Balkan Entente to achieve enduring peace in the region.[52] Notwithstanding the traditional irredentist ambitions of Greek foreign policy in the north (northern Epirus in Albania, Cyprus, the Dodecanese, and areas on the western coast of Turkey), Metaxas remained intent on avoiding any disturbance in the region. A further restraining factor was the awareness of the structural and material shortcomings of the Greek system. The experience from the disastrous campaign against Turkey in 1920–2 had exposed the limited capacity of the Greek war machine and had resulted in a subsequent moderation of the political aims of Greek foreign policy (the abandonment of the 'Great Idea' for a Greater Greece).[53] In the 1930s, both before and during the Metaxas period, Greece—as a pro-system state—was more interested in fostering the existing status quo and defending it against growing Italian aggression (especially after the invasion of Albania in April 1939) rather than in unilaterally revising it.

Of the other case-studies discussed here, Austria offers an interesting variant of the inward-looking, system-defending type of regime. Although Austrian nationalism comprised a distinctive anti-socialist and socially regenerative discourse, it remained conspicuously devoid of any clear expansive aspirations or designs. Austrian nationalism itself lacked a definitive ideological direction and long-term vision. The creation of the Austrian state itself was the result of the dissolution of the Habsburg empire and the rejection of the claim for union with Germany by the victorious powers. In this sense, Austrian nationalism oscillated between three visibly different political rationales. There was the extreme *Gesamtdeutschland* vision, sponsored by the Austrian National Socialists and certain pan-German sectors of the Heimwehr, which had little time for the notion of Austrian independence and was intent on bringing about the absorption of Austria into a Greater Germany. There was the Habsburg, pro-monarchical legitimist variant, advocated by traditional conservative circles and by the less radical elements of the Heimwehr, which subscribed to the notion of Austrian independence as an interim stage towards the restoration of an Austrian Habsburg conservative system. Finally, there was a strong system-preserving component, epitomized by the official line of the Dollfuss–Schuschnigg regimes, which aimed to entrench the existing status quo vis-à-vis both monarchical fantasies and external assimilationist influences. This situation forced the Austrian regime to a purely defensive position, steering clear from the other two alternatives as the only available antidote to the crusading spirit of National Socialism and the threat to Austrian specificity posed by it.[54]

Conclusions: the regime-model of fascism and authoritarianism

Fascism in its generic epochal form did not evolve in an ideological and political vacuum. As an idiosyncratic and extreme variant of hyper-nationalism it was essentially rooted in (albeit not constrained by) the radical nationalist tradition of each country. In terms of its ideological production, fascism in each country recast and radicalized pre-existing radical themes, provided a new overall prescription for future action and appealed to a powerful extreme nationalist imagery in order to historicize its vision and legitimize its specificity (vertical dimension). At the same time, fascism originated as a specific form of reaction to the reality of postwar political and economic crisis in proto-liberal, unstable systems of various European countries (horizontal, epochal dimension). A generic explanation of the emergence of fascist movements may be formulated on the basis of a 'hypernationalism-plus' formula, which identifies a set of similar factors that motivated the emergence of fascist movements while taking into account relative variations in the autochthonous conditions and traditions that shaped the physiognomy of each movement. However, with regard to the regime-model of fascism, a number of other elements must be carefully analysed. Without any exception, fascist movements/parties climbed to power through the complicity of indigenous elite sectors in the framework of a conscious political experiment with more popular forms of authoritarianism. All these fascist components, even the one with the largest electoral constituency (NSDAP in Germany), initially shared executive power with certain traditional political groups and enjoyed the passive support of a wide range of social forces. In this sense, a rigid distinction between authoritarian and fascist regime-model is highly problematic—first because of this early political co-existence between the two components, and second because of their *de facto* similarities in political practice and objectives (strong state, anti-socialism, censorship, restrictions in political and social association etc.). Instead, the crucial factor is to what extent the fascist component emancipated itself from the initial predominance of its traditional conservative sponsors and to what degree it departed—once in power—from conventional forms/objectives of policy-making towards a more radical direction.

Four main criteria were employed to assess the character of a number of regimes which contained at least one 'fascist' component. *Ideology* remains a crucial determinant factor, in the sense that it set the limits of what each movement regarded as the most desirable prescription for long-term action. Especially in those countries where a multiplicity of 'fascist' movements with varying degrees of ideological extremism remained politically active (Austria, Hungary, Portugal, Spain), participation or exclusion/suppression determined to a great extent the ideological profile of the regime-model and its commitment to radical change. While in Germany, Italy and Greece the most radical 'fascist' component seized power, in the remaining countries there was a high degree of ideological dilution. In Spain, the Falange was gradually absorbed and neutralized in the more conservative Francoist regime. In Portugal the radical component (national syndicalism) was violently suppressed, while in Austria and Hungary the regime co-opted the less extreme variant (Heimwehr and National Socialists) and carefully ostracized the main anti-system force (National Socialists and Arrow Cross). In Romania the co-opting of a radical form of fascism (Iron Guard) was intermittent and short-lived, thus minimizing its ideological impact on the official regime's policy-making.

However, regimes are much more than just ideological intentions and aspirations. The formulation of policies rests on long-term perceptions of what is the most desirable course of action, but is also determined by a series of structural factors that may enhance or restrict the political freedom of a leadership to translate its ideas into action. *Domestic consolidation* is a crucial variable as it relates to the political struggle between conventional authoritarianism and radicalism (fascism) for the soul of the regime-model. Where the consolidation of the fascist component was antagonistic and all-embracing (Germany, Italy to a high extent), the margins of freedom for the fascist leaderships to promote their more extreme plans were significantly larger. By contrast, a co-operative type of consolidation resulted either in the neutralization or relative moderation of the fascist component (Austria, Spain,

Hungary). The relative strength and cohesion of the conservative authoritarian bloc is a significant factor in explaining why in some cases the antagonistic intentions of certain fascist groups were effectively thwarted (Portugal, Romania) but succeeded in overpowering the conservative opposition in other countries (Germany, Italy).

Policy-making is the qualitative criterion that provides a clear standard for judging the varying ability of the fascist components to influence the formulation of political objectives. The correlation between this factor with both domestic consolidation and ideological intentions is crucial. Those fascist groups that achieved a comprehensive, (near-)monocratic type of consolidation (Germany, Italy) generally emancipated themselves from the restraining framework of conventional policy-making and sponsored more radical activities. In co-operative or diluted models the adoption of a 'fascist' profile by the regime was restricted to aping or counterfeiting formalistic aspects of the 'fascist' *style* but did not result in a clear departure from conventional political objectives (Austria, Hungary, Spain, Portugal, Greece, Romania). Also, the co-opting of less radical fascist components (at the expense of other, more extreme forms) by authoritarian regimes ensured a more uneventful co-habitation without substantially imperilling the continuity in policy-making. Finally, the *scope* of long-term intentions depended on both the ideological nature of each movement's nationalism, the margins for anti-system action and the influence of external or random factors. In this respect, the Nazi regime departs from all other regime-models in its large-scale ideological commitment to a new universal social order, in its political determination to pursue such an ambition, and in its ability to do so extensively and effectively. The Italian Fascist regime demonstrated a comparable crusading spirit but retained the traditional focus on historic irredentism and refrained from imposing new radical models of domestic organization in the conquered areas in Europe. The rest of the regimes focused on the domestic aspects of regeneration, either as a means of defence against external threats (Austria) or because they lacked the material/structural preconditions for a form of expansive policy (Greece, Hungary). In the end, a categorical distinction between authoritarian and fascist regime-model obfuscates the complex structural and political continuities between the two models, as well as the affinities in their ideological rationale.[55] When admitted into power, the fascist movements/parties lacked a concrete political alternative vision for a totally novel form of regime. They were co-opted by traditional groups and were forced to operate within the framework of a conventional authoritarian system which entailed a combination of social forces with disparate anticipations and notions of *desirable* or *feasible* action. The varying emancipation of individual fascist components in government took the form of a gradual process of rejecting aspects of the existing system and conceptualizing new prescriptions in opposition to conventional pro-system attitudes. In this sense, an ideal-type of the regime-model of fascism [radical anti-system ideology, all-embracing antagonistic consolidation, radical policy-making, crusading spirit] does not constitute a check-list for deciding whether a regime was or was not fascist; it is only meaningful as a description of the end-result of a *tendency* towards the gradual re-organization of the authoritarian model's style and content. The Nazi regime offers the closest approximation of this model, while the Italian Fascist variety continued to oscillate between its radical ideological agenda and the restrictive structural continuities with the pre-existing composition of the system.[56] The remaining case-studies absorbed the fascist component in an essentially pro-system political structure or subjected its ideological aspirations to the needs of *Realpolitik* and adherence to pre-existing strict political choices. The epochal impact of Italian Fascism (as the archetypal fascist regime) and of German Nazism (as the most dynamic example of fascist regime-model) prompted mimetic reproductions of 'fascist' stylistic elements in many other European regimes. However, the fascist 'style' could be appropriated more easily than its substantive political implications. The crucial test was the extent to which these new constellations of power regressed into the conventional authoritarian model or developed a political momentum in the other direction, i.e. towards a new version of authoritarianism based on a radical re-ordering of social forces, forms of participation and long-term political objectives. Rather than entailing a rigid identification with any ideal-type, the regime-model of fascism evolved within idiosyncratic autochthonous political frameworks, occupying in each case varying positions between the indigenous model of conventional authoritarianism and its alternative reinterpretations by traditional or new social forces.

NOTES

1 See, amongst others, H. Arendt, *The Origins of Totalitarianism* (London 1967, 3rd edn), 461 ff; K. Friedrich, ed., *Totalitarianism* (Cambridge, MA 1954); K. Friedrich and Z.K. Brzezinski, *Totalitarian Dictatorship and Autocracy* (Cambridge, MA 1956); L. Schapiro, *Totalitarianism* (London 1973). For a recent, interesting comparison between Nazism and Stalinism see I. Kershaw and M. Lewin, eds, *Stalinism and Nazism. Dictatorships in Comparison* (Cambridge 1997).

2 E. Nolte, *Der Faschismus in seiner Epoche. Die Action Française, der Italienische Faschismus, der Nationalsozialismus* (Munich 1963), and in English translation, *Three Faces of Fascism. Italian Fascism, Action Française, National Socialism* (London 1965).

3 See, for example, S.J. Woolf, ed., *European Fascism* (London 1968), and *The Nature of Fascism* (London 1968); S.U. Larsen, B. Hagtvet and J.P. Myklebust, eds, *Who Were the Fascists? Social Roots of European Fascism* (Bergen, Oslo, Tromsø 1980); G.L. Mosse, ed., *International Fascism* (London 1979); P. Hayes, ed., *Fascism* (London 1973); Turner, 'Fascism and Modernization' in Turner, H.A. ed., *Reappraisals of Fascism* (New York 1975), 117–39.

4 R. Griffin, *The Nature of Fascism* (London and New York 1994); S.G. Payne, *A History of Fascism, 1914–45* (London 1997).

5 J.J. Linz, 'Some Notes Towards a Comparative Study of Fascism in Sociological Historical Perspective', in W. Laqueur, ed., *Fascism: A Reader's Guide. Analyses, Interpretations, Bibliography* (Harmondsworth 1979), 21 ff.; 'Political Space and Fascism as Late-Comer', in Larsen, Hagtvet and Myklebust, eds, *Who Were the Fascists?*, 153–4.

6 R.O. Paxton, 'The Five Stages of Fascism', *Journal of Modern History*, 70 (1998), 1–23 (here 11). Cf. Milza, P., *Fascisme français: passé et présent* (Paris 1987).

7 Cf. the 'nationalism-plus' formula put forward by L. Birken, *Hitler as Philosophe. Remnants of the Enlightenment in National Socialism* (Westport, CT and London 1995).

8 Cf. H. Mommsen, 'Ausnahmezustand als Herrschaftstechnik des Nationalsozialistischen-Regimes', in M. Funke, ed., *Hitler, Deutschland und die Mächte. Materialien zur Aussenpolitik des Dritten Reiches* (Düsseldorf 1977), 30–45.

9 Griffin, *Nature of Fascism*, Ch. 5.

10 For a general overview of fascist ideology see Griffin, *Nature of Fascism*, Chs 1–2; Z. Sternhell, 'Fascist Ideology', in W. Laqueur, ed., *Fascism: A Reader's Guide. Analyses, Interpretations, Bibliography* (Harmondsworth 1979), 325–406. For Fascist ideology see, among others, Griffin, *Nature of Fascism*, Ch. 3; A.J. Gregor, *The Ideology of Fascism. The Rationale of Totalitarianism* (New York 1969); E. Gentile, *Le origini dell'ideologia fascista, 1918–1925* (Rome and Bari 1975); R.J.B. Bosworth, *The Italian Dictatorship. Problems and Perspectives in the Interpretation of Mussolini and Fascism* (London and New York 1998). For Nazism see Griffin, op. cit., Ch. 4; E. Jaeckel, *Hitler's Weltanschauung. A Blueprint for Power* (Middletown, CT 1972). See also S. Saladino, 'Italy' and E. Nolte, 'Germany', both in H. Rogger and E. Weber, eds, *The European Right. A Historical Profile* (London 1965), 248–60 and 296–307 respectively.

11 P.C. Schmitter, 'The Social Origins, Economic Bases and Political Imperatives of Authoritarian Rule in Portugal', in Larsen, Hagtvet and Myklebust, eds, *Who Were the Fascists?*, 436–66. For Salazar's own explanation of his ideological beliefs see A. Oliveira Salazar, *Doctrine and Action. Internal and Foreign Policy of the New Portugal* (London 1939).

12 T. Gallagher, 'Conservatism, Dictatorship and Fascism in Portugal, 1914–45', in M. Blinkhorn, ed., *Fascists and Conservatives. The Radical Right and the Establishment in Twentieth-Century Europe* (London 1990), 157–75; P.G. Schmitter, 'The "Regime d'Exception" That Became the Rule: Forty-eight Years of Authoritarian Domination in Portugal', in I. Graham and H. Makler, eds, *Contemporary Portugal. The Revolution and its Antecedents* (Austin, TX 1979), 32–63. For a short exposition of the National Syndicalists' disagreements with the Salazar regime see Preto, 'Ersatz Fascism', translated in R. Griffin, ed., *Fascism* (Oxford and New York 1995), 194–5.

13 S.G. Payne, *Falange. A History of Spanish Fascism* (Stanford and London 1962) and 'Spain', in Rogger and Weber, eds, *European Right*, 189–96; P. Preston, 'Populism and Parasitism: the Falange and the Spanish Establishment', in Blinkhorn, ed., *Fascists and Conservatives*, 138–57. See also José Antonio Primo de Rivera, 'Total Feeling', translated in Griffin, ed., *Fascism*, 187–8.

14 H. Thomas, 'Spain', in S.J. Woolf, ed., *European Fascism* (London 1968), 296–8; M. Blinkhorn, 'Introduction: Allies, Rivals or Antagonists? Fascists and Conservatives in Modern Europe', in Blinkhorn, ed., *Fascists and Conservatives*, 1–13; Payne, 'Spain', 201 ff.

15 D. Close, 'Conservatism, Authoritarianism and Fascism in Greece, 1915–45', in Blinkhorn, ed., *Fascists and Conservatives*, 205 ff.

16 Y. Andricopoulos, 'The Power Base of Greek Authoritarianism', in Larsen, Hagtvet and Myklebust, eds, *Who Were the Fascists?*, 568–84.

17 Z. Barbu, 'Psycho-Historical and Sociological Perspectives on the Iron Guard, the Fascist Movement of Romania', in Larsen, Hagtvet and Myklebust, eds, *Who Were the Fascists?*, 382–7; and 'Romania', in Woolf, ed., *European Fascism*, 146–66; E. Weber, 'Romania', in Rogger and Weber, eds, *The European Right*, 517 ff; B. Vago, 'Fascism in Eastern Europe', in Laqueur, ed., *Fascism. A Reader's Guide*, 217–18, 222–3. See also Codreanu's own statement 'The Resurrection of the Race', in Griffin, ed., *Fascism*, 221–2.

18 F.L. Carsten, *The Rise of Fascism* (London 1967), 190–3.

19 I. Deák, 'Hungary', in *European Right*, 377–81; Griffin, *Nature of Fascism*, 127–8; Carsten, *Rise of Fascism*, 169–75.
20 P.H. Merkl, 'Comparing Fascist Movements', in Larsen, Hagtvet and Myklebust, eds, *Who Were the Fascists?*, 752–83; Deák, op. cit., 388–405; J. Erös, 'Hungary', in Woolf, ed., *European Fascism*, 111–45. For Szálasi's notion of 'Hungarism' see Griffin, ed., *Fascism*, 223–6.
21 A. Whiteside, 'Austria', in Rogger and Weber, eds, *European Right*, 334 ff; M. Kitchen, *The Coming of Austrian Fascism* (London & Montreal 1980), Ch. 3; F.L. Carsten, *Fascist Movements in Austria. From Schönerer to Hitler* (London and Beverly Hills 1979), Chs. 6, 8, 10.
22 Kitchen, op. cit., Ch. 8; Carsten, *Rise of Fascism*, 223–9; J. Lewis, 'Conservatives and Fascists in Austria, 1918–34', in Blinkhorn, ed., *Fascists and Conservatives*, 103–14; B.F. Pauley, 'Nazis and Heimwehr Fascists: the Struggle for Supremacy in Austria, 1918–1938', in Larsen, Hagtvet and Myklebust, eds, *Who Were the Fascists?*, 232–3; L. Jedlicka, 'The Austrian Heimwehr', in G.L. Mosse, ed., *International Fascism: New Thoughts and New Approaches* (London and Beverly Hills 1979), 223–40.
23 J. Gehl, *Austria, Germany and the Anschluss, 1931–1938* (London 1963); G. Botz, 'The Changing Patterns of Social Support for Austrian National Socialism (1918–1945)', in Larsen, Hagtvet and Myklebust, eds, *Who Were the Fascists?*, 202–45; Carsten, *Fascist Movements in Austria*, Ch. 14.
24 Whiteside, op. cit., 342–6.
25 J. Noakes, 'German Conservatives and the Third Reich: an Ambiguous Relationship', in Blinkhorn, ed., *Fascists and Conservatives*, 71–97; K.-J. Müller, 'The Structure and Nature of the National Conservative Opposition in Germany up to 1940', in H.W. Koch, ed., *Aspects of the Third Reich* (London 1985), 133–78; K. Deutsch, *Hitler and His Generals. The Hidden Crisis, January–June 1938* (Minneapolis 1974), 78–215.
26 K.D. Bracher, 'Stufen totalitärer Machtergreifung', *Vierteljahrshefte für Zeitgeschichte*, 4 (1956), 30–42; M. Broszat, *The Hitler State. The Foundation and Development of the Internal Structure of the Third Reich* (London and New York 1981; Griffin, *Nature of Fascism*, 107–10. For an overview of the existing literature see I. Kershaw, *The Nazi Dictatorship* (3rd edn, London 1993), Ch. 4.
27 For the role of the Savoy monarchy in the Fascist state see A. Aquarone, *L'organizzazione dello Stato Totalitario* (Turin 1965), Ch. 4; D. Mack Smith, *Italy and its Monarchy* (New Haven, CT and London 1989); M. Knox, 'Conquest, Domestic and Foreign, in Fascist Italy and Nazi Germany', *Journal of Modern History*, 56 (1984), 27 ff.
28 For the relations between state and Church in Fascist Italy see D.A. Binchy, *Church and State in Fascist Italy* (Oxford 1970); J.F. Pollard, *The Vatican and Italian Fascism, 1929–1932. A Study in Conflict* (Cambridge 1985). For the competition between the two institutions for control over education see T.M. Mazzatosta, *Il regime fascista tra educazione e propaganda (1935–1943)* (Bologna 1978).
29 R. Sarti, 'Italian Fascism: Radical Politics and Conservative Goals', in Blinkhorn, ed., *Fascists and Conservatives*, 14–30. See also the review of the existing literature in Bosworth, op. cit., Chs 5–6; Aquarone, op. cit., Chs 4–5.
30 P. Preston, 'Populism and Parasitism: the Falange and the Spanish Establishment, 1939–75', in Blinkhorn, ed., *Fascists and Conservatives*, 138–56, esp. 144 ff.; Griffin, *Nature of Fascism*, 161–2; R. Carr, *Modern Spain, 1875–1980* (Oxford 1980), Ch. 10.
31 Schmitter, 'Regime d'Exception', *passim*; *Corporatism and Public Policy in Authoritarian Portugal* (London and Beverly Hills, CA 1975), esp. 12 ff.; A.C. Costa Pinto, *Salazar's Dictatorship and European Fascism. Problems of Interpretation* (New York 1995); H. Martins, 'Portugal', in Woolf, ed., *European Fascism*, 302–36.
32 Close, op. cit., 204 ff.; Andricopoulos, op. cit., 568–82; R. Clogg, *A Short History of Modern Greece* (Cambridge 1979).

33 Weber, op. cit., 552 ff., 562 ff.
34 Linz, 'Political Space and Fascism as a Late-Comer', 169–70. See also R. Kühnl, 'Contemporary Approaches to Fascism: A Survey of Paradigms', in Larsen, Hagtvet and Myklebust, eds, *Who Were the Fascists?*, 28–9; R. Wilford, 'Fascism', in R. Eccleshall, V. Geoghegan, R. Jay, M. Kenny, I. MacKenzie and R. Wilford, eds, *Political Ideologies. An Introduction* (London and New York 1984), 194–6.
35 S. Andreski, 'Fascists as Moderates', in Larsen, Hagtvet and Myklebust, eds, *Who Were the Fascists?*, 52–5. For Mussolini's charismatic power see P. Melograni, 'The Cult of the *Duce* in Mussolini's Italy', in *International Fascism*, 73–90; E. Gentile, *Il culto del littorio. La sacralizzazione della politica nell'Italia fascista* (Rome and Bari 1993). For Hitler's charisma see J. Nyomarkay, *Charisma and Factionalism in the Nazi Party* (Minneapolis 1967); K.D. Bracher, 'The Role of Hitler: Perspectives of Interpretation', in *Fascism. A Reader's Guide*, 193–212.
36 Andricopoulos, op. cit., 574–82.
37 Payne, 'Spain', 200–5; Payne, *History of Fascism*, 252–67.
38 Gallagher, 'Portugal', 160 ff; Carsten, *Rise of Fascism*, 189–93.
39 C.W. Schum, 'The Dollfuss–Schuschnigg Regime: Fascist or Authoritarian', in Larsen, Hagtvet and Myklebust, eds, *Who Were the Fascists?*, 249–53; M. Clemenz, *Gesellschaftliche Ursprünge des Faschismus* (Frankfurt 1972), 206–32; Erös, 'Hungary', 126 ff.
40 For the importance of the racial crusading element in Nazism see M. Burleigh and W. Wippermann, *The Racial State. Germany 1933–1945* (Cambridge 1991); D. Goldhagen, *Hitler's Willing Executioners. Ordinary Germans and the Holocaust* (London 1996). For the organization of the Holocaust see C.R. Browning, *The Path to Genocide. Essays on Launching the Final Solution* (Cambridge 1992), 69–76; U. Herbert, 'Arbeit und Vernichtung. Ökonomisches Interesse und Primat der "Weltanschauung" im Nationalsozialismus', in D. Diner, ed., *Ist der Nationalsozialismus Geschichte?* (Frankfurt 1987), 198–236; and G. Aly and S. Heim, 'Die Ökonomie der "Endlösung": Menschenvernichtung und wirtschaftliche Neuordnung', *Beiträge zur nationalsozialistischen Gesundheitsund Sozialpolitik*, V: *Sozialpolitik und Judenvernichtung: Gibt es eine Ökonomie der Endlösung?* (Berlin 1987), 7–90.
41 For the two concepts of *cittadino–soldato* and *uomo novo* see M. Isnenghi, 'Il mito di potenza', in A. Del Boca, M. Legnani and M.C. Rossi, eds, *Il regime fascista. Storia e storiografia* (Rome and Bari 1995), 144–5; P.V. Canistraro, 'Mussolini's Cultural Revolution: Fascist or Nationalist?', *Journal of Contemporary History*, 7 (1972), 129 ff. For an extreme critique of the regime's organizational incapacity see D. Mack Smith, *Mussolini's Roman Empire* (London 1982), and *Mussolini* (London 1981). See also Griffin, *Nature of Fascism*, 76–82, and E.R. Tannenbaum, *The Fascist Experience. Italian Society and Culture, 1922–1945* (New York 1972).
42 See Griffin, *Nature of Fascism*, Ch. 5; Borejsza, op. cit., 359 ff.; Payne, *History of Fascism*, Ch. 5.
43 Merkl, 752–81; N. O'Sullivan, *Fascism* (London and Melbourne 1983); N. Kogan, 'Fascism as a Political System', in S.J. Woolf, ed., *The Nature of Fascism* (London 1968), 11–18.
44 H. Arendt, *The Origins of Totalitarianism* (3rd edn, London 1967). Cf. M. Neocleous, *Fascism* (London 1997), Ch. 1 and Sternhell, op. cit., 334 ff.
45 N.H. Baynes, ed., *The Speeches of Adolf Hitler. April 1922–August 1939* (London, New York, Toronto 1942), Vol. I, 668 (interview with the United Press, 27 November 1935) and 707 (speech at the 1937 Nuremberg Party Rally, 10 September 1937). For an analysis of these ideas see I. Kershaw, *Hitler, 1889–1936: Hubris* (London 1998), 50–1, 60 ff., 150–2; Goldhagen, 80–128.

46 See the selection of documentary evidence from the implementation of Nazi racial policies during the war in J. Noakes, and G. Pridham, eds, *Nazism. A Documentary Reader*, Vol. 3: *Foreign Relations and Racial Extermination* (Exeter 1988).

47 E. Susmel, and D. Susmel, eds, *Opera Omnia di Benito Mussolini* (Florence and Rome 1951–78), Vol. XXIV, 5–16 (Speech to the Quinquennial Assembly of the Regime, 10.3 1929); B. Mussolini, *Fascism: Doctrine and Institutions* (Rome 1935), reprinted in M. Oakeshott, ed., *The Social and Political Doctrines of Contemporary Europe* (New York 1949), 178–9. See also Griffin, *Nature of Fascism*, 68–71.

48 For the attempts at a 'Fascist International' see D. Veneruso, *L'Italia fascista (1922–1945)* (Bologna 1981), 165–75. For Italy's involvement in the Spanish Civil War see R. Cantalupo, *Fu la Spagna. Ambasciata presso Franco, febbraio–aprile 1937* (Milan 1948).

49 Knox, 'Conquest', 1–23; Griffin, *Nature of Fascism*, 69–76.

50 For the policies in Libya see G. Rochat, *Il colonialismo italiano* (Turin 1973), 103 ff. For the quasi-apartheid policies in Ethiopia see L. Goglia, 'Note sul razzismo coloniale fascista', *Storia Contemporanea*, 19 (1988), 1223–66. For the economic and military deficiencies of the Italian system see F. Minniti, 'Aspetti della politica fascista degli armamenti dal 1935 al 1943', in R. De Felice, ed., *L'Italia fra Tedeschi e Alleati. La politica estera fascista e la seconda guerra mondiale* (Bologna 1973), and 'Il problema degli armamenti nella preparazione militare italiana dal 1935 al 1943', *Storia Contemporanea*, 2 (1978), 1–56, M. Knox, 'Expansionist Zeal, Fighting Power, and Staying Power in the Italian and German Dictatorships', in R. Bessel, ed., *Fascist Italy and Nazi Germany. Comparisons and Contrasts* (Cambridge 1996), 115–33; J.J. Sadkovich, 'The Italo-Greek War in Context: Italian Priorities and Axis Diplomacy', *Journal of Contemporary History*, 28 (1993), 493–64, and 'Understanding Defeat: Reappraising Italy's Role in World War II', *Journal of Contemporary History*, 24 (1989), 27–61. For the implementation of the anti-Semitic legislation see J. Steinberg, *All or Nothing. The Axis and the Holocaust, 1941–42* (London 1990).

51 For Franco's negative replies to the German proposal for a joint front against the British see DGFP, D, 11, 220/207/227/246/476/491.

52 For the ideology of the Metaxas regime see Andricopoulos, op. cit., 579–80. For the regime's foreign policy see Close, op. cit., 209 ff.; Clogg, op. cit. For the attempts for Balkan co-operation in the 1930s see B.M. Janković, *The Balkans in International Relations* (Basingstoke and London 1988), 149–64.

53 M.L. Smith, *The Ionian Vision. Greece in Asia Minor* (London 1973).

54 For the various strands of Austrian nationalism see Whiteside, op. cit., 338 ff.; Griffin, *Nature of Fascism*; B. F. Pauley, *Hitler and the Forgotten Nazis. A History of Austrian National Socialism* (London 1981); Jedlicka, op. cit., 232ff.

55 Blinkhorn, op. cit., 9–13; S. G. Payne, *Fascism. Comparison and Definition* (Madison 1980), 6 ff.

56 Griffin, *Nature of Fascism*, Ch. 8.

10

HITLER AND THE UNIQUENESS
OF NAZISM*

Ian Kershaw

One of the greatest challenges faced by comparative fascist studies is to account for the profoundly racial and uniquely destructive nature of Nazism while at the same time incorporating it unequivocally within the taxonomic family of interwar fascism. In this comparatively-minded essay, Ian Kershaw, the leading scholarly authority on the history of the Third Reich, revisits the problem of the "uniqueness of Nazism." In view of the numerous similarities between Nazism and other dictatorial regimes in interwar Europe, Kershaw subscribes to the definition of Nazism as a form of fascism and totalitarianism, thus endorsing the analytical validity of these concepts. Yet, Kershaw also argues that these concepts account only for general—and in the case of totalitarianism, even superficial—similarities with other interwar movements and regimes. That is because, beyond general features, Nazism was, first and foremost, an original ideology and form of government.

Kershaw exposes the limitations of previous theories which attempted to account for the "German anomaly" either in view of deterministic long- or short-term structural conditions, such as the "Sonderweg" theory, or in terms of unilateral "single-factor explanations," such as peculiarities of the German national character, and/or Hitler's personality. Instead, building on insights advanced in his authoritative monographs on the nature of Hitler's personality and leadership (1987; 1991; 1998; 2000), Kershaw explains the uniqueness of Nazism in view of a contextual combination of structural forces (among which the most important were specific traits of the German political culture), the historical conditions of interwar Europe, and the role of Hitler's personality.

Kershaw argues that the uniqueness of Nazism is evidenced, first and foremost, by the highly destructive world war waged by Nazi Germany and its genocidal policy against the Jews. These criminal actions were a direct result of two main features that singled out the Nazi regime: its sustained "cumulative radicalization" (a concept first coined by the German historian Hans Mommsen), ultimately resulting into an unprecedented and unrivalled capacity for destruction; and the unique "leadership position" of Hitler and the type of authority he embodied. Hitler's charismatic type of authority merged with the Romantic idea of divine election of the German people into a powerful doctrine of national salvation. This doctrine resonated with the worldview of various strata of German society, paving its way to political dominance. Kershaw argues that Hitler's charismatic rule was "both different in character and more far-reaching in impact" than any other contemporary variants, including here Stalin's and Mussolini's styles of leadership. Once triumphant, Hitler's charismatic authority took hold of one of the most economically and military advanced states in Europe, transforming it into the most powerful war machine in history. The Nazi regime was consequently founded on a unique combination of "a modern state system directed by 'charismatic authority', based on ideas, frequently used by Hitler, of a 'mission' (Sendung) to bring about 'salvation' (Rettung) or 'redemption' (Erlösung)—all . . . tapping religious or quasireligious emotions." (In view of the debates included in the third part of this volume, it is important to note that, while stressing the religious or quasi-religious connotations of the Nazi doctrine of national salvation, Kershaw rejects the political religion theory as a "voguish revamping of an age-old notion," doubting its relevance for understanding the nature of totalitarian regimes.)

Kershaw's analytical framework reasserts the centrality of Hitler's personality in the evolution of the Nazi regime, while at the same time placing his actions in the context of more powerful longer-term internal and external forces that shaped the Nazi rule. Kershaw's view on the uniqueness of Hitler's charismatic form of leadership as well as his claim that "only in Germany did the striving for national renewal adopt such strongly pseudo-religious tones" invites more systematic comparative testing with similar forms of leadership in interwar Europe (for a comparison with the Iron Guard and Codreanu's leadership in Romania, see Iordachi, Chapter 14 in this volume).

BIBLIOGRAPHY

Kershaw, Ian (1987). *The "Hitler Myth": Image and Reality in the Third Reich* (Oxford: Oxford University Press).

Kershaw, Ian (1989). *The Nazi Dictatorship: Problems and Perspectives of Interpretation* (London: Arnold).

Kershaw, Ian (1991). *Hitler* (London: Longman).

Kershaw, Ian (1998). *Hitler, 1889–1936: Hubris* (London: Penguin Books).

Kershaw, Ian (2000). *Hitler, 1936–2000: Nemesis* (London: Penguin Books).

Kershaw, Ian and Lewin, Moshe, eds. (1997). *Stalinism and Nazism: Dictatorships in Comparison* (New York: Cambridge University Press).

*   *   *

There was something distinctive about nazism, even compared with other brutal dictatorships. That much seems clear. A regime responsible for the most destructive war in history, leaving upwards of 40 million people dead, that perpetrated, on behalf of the most modern, economically advanced, and culturally developed country on the continent of Europe, the worst genocide yet known to mankind, has an obvious claim to singularity. But where did the uniqueness lie? Historians, political scientists and, not least, the countless victims of the nazi regime have puzzled over this question since 1945.

One set of answers came quickly, and quite naturally, after the war to those who had fought against the nazi menace. The German militaristic, *Herrenmensch* culture that for centuries had sought dominance in central and eastern Europe was taken to be the key in this approach. A.J.P. Taylor's *The Course of German History*, written in 1944, might be seen as characteristic of its genre.[1] Its crudity was, in the circumstances, perhaps understandable. But as an explanation, it led nowhere (as could also be said of the most modern variant of the 'peculiarity of German character' interpretation in Daniel Goldhagen's controversial book, emphasizing a unique and longstanding German desire to eliminate the Jews).[2] From the German side came, unsurprisingly, a diametrically opposed position, represented in different ways by Friedrich Meinecke and Gerhard Ritter: that Germany's healthy course of development had been blown completely off track by the first world war, opening the way for the type of demagogic politics that let Hitler into power.[3] The interpretation saw nazism as part of a European problem of the degradation of politics. However, this in turn left open what was unique to Germany in producing such a radical strain of inhumane politics. Stirred by Fritz Fischer's analysis of Germany's 'quest for world power' in 1914, locating the blame for the first world war in the expansionist aims of Germany's élites,[4] and by Ralf Dahrendorf's emphasis on the essence of the 'German problem' as social and political backwardness in tandem with a rapidly advancing capitalist and industrial economy,[5] a new generation of German historians, led by Hans-Ulrich Wehler, now turned the spotlight on a 'special path' (*Sonderweg*) to modernity.[6] Defence of privilege by threatened but entrenched social and political élites provided the focus for this interpretation of the German peculiarities which saw a line of continuity running from Bismarck to Hitler. By the 1980s, however, this interpretation was itself running into a wall of criticism, beginning with the attack on 'German peculiarities' launched by Geoff Eley and David Blackbourn, who undermined much of the case that had been made for the continued dominance of pre-industrial élites and stressed instead the common features which Germany shared with other modern, capitalist economies at the time.[7] Oddly, interpretations have since that time tended to shift back in emphasis to what, if in completely different fashion, Meinecke and Ritter had been claiming so much earlier: that the first world war and its aftermath, rather than deeper continuities with Imperial Germany, explain the nazi phenomenon. Detlev Peukert, for instance, in a superb short study of the Weimar Republic, expressly rejected the *Sonderweg* argument as an explanation of nazism, stressing instead a 'crisis of classical modernity' during the first

German democracy.[8] Perhaps, it may be thought, this just reformulates the problem of German uniqueness. Perhaps, the thought lingers, the *Sonderweg* argument, or at least a strand or two of it, has been thrown out too abruptly.[9] My concern here, in any case, is not directly the *Sonderweg* debate, but the uniqueness of nazism itself, and of the dictatorship it spawned. Unavoidably, nevertheless, this raises questions about mentalities, prompting some reconsideration about what was special about Germany that led it to produce nazism.

To demonstrate uniqueness, comparison is necessary. That ought to be obvious, but seems often not to be so. Alongside those theories that looked no further than German development to explain nazism, ran, from the start, attempts to locate it in new types of political movement and organization, dating from the turmoil produced by the first world war: whether as a German form of the European-wide phenomenon of fascism, or as the German manifestation of something also found only after 1918, the growth of totalitarianism. To consider all the variants of these theories and approaches would take us far out of our way here, and would in any case not be altogether profitable.[10] So let me begin to make my position clear at this point. Both 'fascism' and 'totalitarianism' are difficult concepts to use, and have attracted much criticism, some of it justified. In addition, going back to their usage in the Cold War, they have usually been seen as opposed rather than complementary concepts. However, I see no problem in seeing nazism as a form of each of them, as long as we are looking for common features, not identity. It is not hard to find features that nazism had in common with fascist movements in other parts of Europe and elements of its rule shared with regimes generally seen as totalitarian. The forms of organization and the methods and function of mass mobilization of the NSDAP, for example, bear much resemblance to those of the Italian Fascist Party and of other fascist movements in Europe. In the case of totalitarianism, superficial similarities, at least, with the Soviet regime under Stalin can be seen in the nazi regime's revolutionary élan, its repressive apparatus, its monopolistic ideology, and its 'total claim' on the ruled. So I have no difficulty in describing German National Socialism both as a specific form of fascism and as a particular expression of totalitarianism.

Even so, comparison reveals obvious and significant differences. Race, for example, plays only a secondary role in Italian fascism. In nazism it is, of course, absolutely central. As regards totalitarianism, anything beyond the most superficial glance reveals that the structures of the one-party state, the leadership cult and, not least, the economic base of the nazi and Soviet systems are quite different. The typology is, in each case, markedly weakened. It can, of course, still be useful, depending upon the art and skill of the political scientist, historian, or sociologist involved, and can prompt valuable empirical comparative work of the kind too rarely undertaken. But when it comes to explaining the essence of the nazi phenomenon, it is less than satisfying. Whether seen as fascism, totalitarianism, or both, there is still something lacking. Martin Broszat hinted at this in the introduction to his masterpiece, *Der Staat Hitlers*, in 1969, when he indicated the difficulty of placing nazism in any typology of rule.[11] Ultimately, the singular, the unique in nazism, remains more important, if more elusive, than what it has in common with other movements or regimes.

In the eyes of the non-specialist, the ordinary layman, nazism's historic—perhaps metahistoric—significance can be summed up in two words: war and genocide. It takes us back to the self-evident initial claim to singularity with which this article began. By war, we naturally mean here the war of unparalleled barbarity that the nazis launched, especially in eastern Europe. And by genocide, we think primarily of the destruction of the European Jews, but also of the wider-ranging genocidal intent to restructure racially the whole of the European continent. Both words, war and genocide—or perhaps better: world war and murder of the Jews—automatically evoke direct association with Hitler. After all, they lay at the heart of his *Weltanschauung*, his world-view; they were in essence what he stood for. This is the obvious reason why one significant strand of historical interpretation has remained insistent that there is no need to look any further in the search for nazism's uniqueness than the personality and ideas of its leader. 'It was indeed Hitler's "Weltanschauung" and nothing else that mattered in the end', Karl-Dietrich Bracher summed up, many years ago.[12] Nazism's uniqueness was Hitler, no more and no less. Nazism was Hitlerism, pure and simple.

There was a certain easy attractiveness to the argument. At first sight, it seemed compelling. But, put at its most forthright, as so often, by Klaus Hildebrand, the thesis was bound to raise the hackles of those, prominent among them Martin Broszat and Hans Mommsen, who sought more complex reasons for the calamity wrought on Germany and Europe and found them in the internal structures and workings of nazi rule, in which Hitler's hand was often none too evident.[13] So was born the long-running, everyday story of historical folk: the debate between the 'intentionalists', who looked no further than Hitler's clear, ideological programme, systematically and logically followed through, and the 'structuralists' or 'functionalists', who pointed to an administratively chaotic regime, lacking clear planning, and stumbling from crisis to crisis in its own dynamic spiral of self-destructiveness.*

The 'Hitlerism' argument will not go away. In fact, there are some signs, amid the current preoccupation with sexuality in history (as in everything else), that the old psycho-historical interpretations are making a comeback, and in equally reductionist fashion. Hence, we have recent attempts to reduce the disaster of nazism to Hitler's alleged homosexuality, or supposed symphilis.[14] In each case, one or two bits of dubious hearsay evidence are surrounded by much inference, speculation and guesswork to come up with a case for world history shaped fatefully and decisively by Hitler's 'dark secret'. Reduced to absurdity, a rent-boy in Munich or a prostitute in Vienna thereby carries ultimate responsibility for the evils of nazism.

However, the 'structural-functionalist' argument is also weak at its core. In reducing Hitler to a 'weak dictator',[15] at times coming close, it often seemed, to underestimating him grossly, even to writing him out of the script, and in downplaying ideology into no more than a tool of propagandistic mobilization, this line

242

of interpretation left the central driving-force of nazism ultimately a mystery; the cause of the (ultimately unprovable) self-destructive dynamism hard to explain. My own work on the Third Reich since the mid-1980s, culminating in my Hitler biography, was prompted by the need to overcome this deep divide in interpretation, which was by no means as sterile as is sometimes claimed. The short analysis of Hitler's power which I wrote in 1990, and even more so the biography that followed,[16] were attempts to reassert Hitler's absolute centrality while at the same time placing the actions of even such a powerful dictator in the context of the forces, internal and external, which shaped the exercise of his power. Writing these books clarified in certain ways how I would understand the uniqueness of nazism. I will return shortly to Hitler's own role in that uniqueness.

Let us meanwhile go back to war and genocide as the hallmarks of nazism. Surprisingly, they played remarkably little part, except on the fringes, in the 'intentionalist-structuralist' debates before the 1980s. Only since then, and in good measure via the belated take-off of 'history from below' (as it was frequently called), have the war, in which nazism came of its own, and the murder of the Jews, that emanated from it, become the focus of sustained and systematic research and fully integrated into the history of the nazi regime. This research, given a massive boost through the opening of archives in the former Soviet bloc after 1990, has not simply cast much new light on decision-making processes and the escalatory genocidal phases within such a brutal war, but has also revealed ever more plainly how far the complicity and participation in the direst forms of gross inhumanity stretched.[17] This is, of course, not sufficient in itself to claim uniqueness. But it does suggest that Hitler alone, however important his role, is not enough to explain the extraordinary lurch of a society, relatively non-violent before 1914, into ever more radical brutality and such a frenzy of destruction.

The development of the nazi regime had at least two characteristics which were unusual, even in comparison with other dictatorships. One was what Hans Mommsen has dubbed 'cumulative radicalization'.[18] Normally, after the initial bloody phase following a dictator's takeover of power when there is a showdown with former opponents, the revolutionary dynamic sags. In Italy, this 'normalizing' phase begins in 1925; in Spain, not too long after the end of the Civil War. In Russia, under quite different conditions, there was a second, unbelievably awful, phase of radicalization under Stalin, after the first wave during the revolutionary turmoil then the extraordinarily violent civil war had subsided in the 1920s. But the regime's radical ideological drive gave way to boosting more conventional patriotism during the fight against the German invader, before disappearing almost entirely after Stalin's death. Radicalization, in other words, was temporary and fluctuating, rather than an intrinsic feature of the system itself. So the 'cumulative radicalization' so central to nazism is left needing an explanation.

Linked to this is the capacity for destruction—again extraordinary even for dictatorships. This destructive capacity, though present from the outset, developed over time and in phases; against internal political, then increasingly, 'racial' enemies in spring 1933, across the spring and summer of 1935, and during the summer and autumn of 1938; following this, the qualitative leap in its extension to the Poles from autumn 1939 onwards; and the unleashing of its full might in the wake of the invasion of the Soviet Union in 1941. The unceasing radicalization of the regime, and the different stages in the unfolding of its destructive capacity cannot, however, as has come to be generally recognized, be explained by Hitler's commands and actions alone. Rather, they followed countless initiatives from below, at many different levels of the regime. Invariably, these occurred within a broad ideological framework associated with Hitler's wishes and intentions. But those initiating the actions were seldom—except in the realms of foreign policy and war strategy—following direct orders from Hitler and were by no means always ideologically motivated. A whole panoply of motives was involved. What motivated the individual—ideological conviction, career advancement, power-lust, sadism and other factors—is, in fact, of secondary importance. Of primary significance is that, whatever the motivation, the actions had the function of working towards the accomplishment of the visionary goals of the regime, embodied in the person of the Führer.

We are getting closer to what we might begin to see as the unique character of nazism, and to Hitler's part in that uniqueness. A set of counter-factual propositions will underline how I see Hitler's indispensability. Let me put them this way. No Hitler: no SS-police state, untrammelled by the rule of law, and with such massive accretions of power, commencing in 1933. No Hitler: no general European war by the late 1930s. No Hitler: an alternative war strategy and no attack on the Soviet Union. No Hitler: no Holocaust, no state policy aimed at wiping out the Jews of Europe. And yet: the forces that led to the undermining of law, to expansionism and war, to the 'teutonic fury' that descended upon the Soviet Union in 1941 and to the quest for ever more radical solutions to the 'Jewish Question', were not personal creations of Hitler. Hitler's personality was, of course, a crucial component of any singularity of nazism. Who would seriously deny it? But decisive for the unending radicalism and unlimited destructive capacity of nazism was something in addition to this: the leadership position of Hitler and the type of leadership he embodied.

The bonds between Hitler and his 'following' (at different levels of regime and society) are vital here. A constant theme of my writing on Hitler and National Socialism has been to suggest that they are best grasped through Max Weber's quasi-religious concept of 'charismatic authority', in which irrational hopes and expectations of salvation are projected onto an individual, who is thereby invested with heroic qualities.[19] Hitler's 'charismatic leadership' offered the prospect of national salvation—redemption brought about by purging the impure and pernicious evil within—to rapidly expanding numbers of Germans experiencing a comprehensive crisis of social and cultural values as well as a total crisis of state and economy. Of course, manifestations of 'charismatic leadership' were far from confined to Germany in the interwar period. But Hitler's was both different in character and more far-reaching in impact than the charismatic forms seen anywhere else—something to which I will briefly return.

There was another big difference. Hitler's 'charismatic power', resting on the invocation of the politics of national salvation, was superimposed after 1933 upon the instruments of the most modern state on the European continent—upon an advanced economy (if currently crisis-ridden); upon a well-developed and efficient system of enforcement and repression (if for the time being weakened through political crisis); upon a sophisticated apparatus of state administration (if at the time its exponents were demoralized by perceived undermining of authority in a disputed and crisis-wracked democracy); and, not least, upon a modernized, professional army (if temporarily enfeebled) which was thirsting for a return to its glory days, for a chance to kick over the traces of the ignominy summed up by the name 'Versailles' and for future expansion to acquire European hegemony. Hitler's 'charismatic authority' and the promise of national salvation fitted, if not perfectly, then nevertheless extremely well, the need to unite the expectations of these varying strands of the political élite. Hitler was, we might say, the intersection point of a number of ideological traits which cumulatively, if not singly, made up the unique political culture of which these élites were a product, and which extended beyond class confines to extensive sections of German society. This political culture was not in itself nazi. But it provided the fertile ground within which nazism could flourish. Among its components were: an understanding of nationality that rested upon ethnicity (and was hence open to notions of restoration of national strength through 'ethnic cleansing'); an imperialist idea that looked not in the main to overseas colonies, but to German dominance in the ethnic mélange of eastern Europe, at the expense of the Slav population; a presumption of Germany's rightful position as a great power, accompanied by deep resentment at the country's treatment since the war and its national weakness and humiliation; and a visceral detestation of bolshevism coupled with the sense that Germany was the last bulwark in the defence of western civilization. Not the least of Hitler's contributions to the spiralling radicalism of the nazi regime after 1933 was to unleash the pent-up social and ideological forces embraced by this short catalogue of ideological traits; to open up hitherto unimaginable opportunities; to make the unthinkable seem realizable. His 'charismatic authority' set the guidelines; the bureacracy of a modern state was there to implement them. But 'charismatic authority' sits uneasily with the rules and regulations of bureacracy. The tension between the two could neither subside nor turn into a stable and permanent form of state. Allied to the underlying ideological thrust and the varied social forces which Hitler represented, this created a dynamism—intrinsically self-destructive since the charismatic regime was unable to reproduce itself—which constitutes an important component of nazism's uniqueness.

If this explosive mixture of the 'charismatic' politics of national salvation and the apparatus of a highly modern state was central to nazism's uniqueness, then it ought to be possible to distinguish the unholy combination from the differing preconditions of other dictatorships. This, however briefly and superficially, I shall try to do.

The quest for national rebirth lay, of course, at the heart of all fascist movements.[20] But only in Germany did the striving for national renewal adopt such strongly pseudo-religious tones. Even if we count the Spanish dictatorship as outrightly fascist, its national 'redemptive' element, if important, was nonetheless far weaker than that in Germany, amounting to little more than the quest for the 'true Spain' and the restoration of the values of reactionary Catholicism, together with the utter rejection of all that was modern and smacked of association with godless socialism and bolshevism. In Italy, pseudo-religious notions of national 'salvation' or 'redemption' were even weaker than in Spain, and certainly possessed little or nothing of the apocalyptic sense of being the last bulwark of western, Christian culture against the atheistic threat of Asiatic (and Jewish) bolshevism that was prevalent in Germany. Mussolini's external ambitions, too, like Franco's, were purely traditional, even if dressed in new clothes. War and imperialist expansion in Africa were intended to restore lost colonies, revenge the ignominy of Italian humiliation in 1896 at the hands of the Ethiopians, and thereby establish Italy's glory and its place in the sun as a world power, with the useful side-effect of bolstering the dictatorship within Italy through the prestige of external victories and acquisition of empire. But nothing much resembled the depth of hope placed in national salvation in Germany.

Though it is often played down in historiography these days, the extraordinarily strong fears of a threat to German culture, a profound cultural pessimism in Germany's unusually broad-based intelligentsia, widespread already before the first world war, formed one of the roots of such susceptibility. Oswald Spengler's widely-read and influential tract on the downfall of western culture, the first volume of which was published a month before the end of the war in 1918,[21] embodied feelings which, in cruder form, had been spread by a multiplicity of patriotic organizations long before the nazis appeared on the scene. In the polarized society of the Weimar Republic, the antagonism of the perceived threat of modernity to what were portrayed as traditional and true German values—a threat focused on socialism, capitalism and, not least, the representative scapegoat figure for both: the Jew—spread both at élite and popular levels. Shored up by the trauma of a lost war, a trauma arguably greater in Germany than in any other land—in a country where the hated socialism had come to power through revolution and where established religion seemed to be losing its hold—an appeal to hopes of national salvation held substantial political potential. Though other countries were also traumatized by the war, the cultural crisis, even in Italy, ran nowhere near so deep as in Germany and, in consequence, was less formative for the nature of the dictatorship. In addition, the length of the crisis and the size of the mass movement *before* the takeover of power were significant.

Only in Italy, apart from Germany, did home-grown fascism develop into a genuine mass movement before the takeover of power. By the time Mussolini was made prime minister in 1922, in the wake of Italy's postwar crisis, the Italian Fascist Party had some 322,000 members, whereas in Spain, amid quite different conditions of the mid-1930s, before the Spanish Civil War, the Falange could only muster around 10,000 members in a country of 26 million inhabitants. If these figures are a deceptive guide to the potential backing for politics of national salvation in those countries, the activist base was in both cases, quite extremely so in Spain, far more limited than it was in Germany. There, the hard core of believers in a party leader who promised national salvation as the heart of his message was already massive, with 850,000 party members and 427,000 SA men (often not members of the party itself), even before Hitler took power.

And, as elsewhere, the first world war had left, as part of its legacy, the readiness to resort to extreme violence to attain political aims. The crusading idea of national salvation, redeeming Germany from its humiliation, purging it of the enemies—political and racial—seen to be threatening its life-blood, championing the cultural fight against the threat of Slavdom, evoking notions of racial struggle to win back lost territories in eastern Europe, heralding an ultimate showdown with godless, 'Asiatic' bolshevism, tapped brilliantly into this new climate of violence. And whereas there was only a three-year period before Italian fascism gained power, after which its élan rapidly waned, the 14 years of 'latent civil war'[22] that preceded Hitler's takeover allowed the prospect of violently-accomplished national salvation to fester and spread, massively so in conditions of the complete collapse of legitimation of the Weimar Republic after 1930.

Not only the street-fighters and beer-hall brawlers in the nazi movement were attracted by the idea of violently-attained national salvation. As much recent research has shown, a new generation of intelligent, middle-class students at German universities in the early 1920s soaked up *völkisch* ideas, those of extreme racist nationalism, intrinsic to the ideas of national regeneration.[23] In this way, 'national salvation' found intellectualized form among groups which would constitute a coming élite, groups whose doctorates in law combined with a rationalized '*Neue Sachlichkeit*' (or 'new objectivity') type of approach to the 'cleansing' of the nation: the excision of its 'life-threatening diseases'. Such mentalities were carried with them, 10 or 15 years after studying, into the upper echelons of the SS and Security Police, as well as into state and party planning offices and 'think tanks'. By the early 1940s, some of these 'intellectuals' had their hands covered in blood as they led the *Einsatzgruppen* into the Soviet Union, while others were laying down plans for the racial 'cleansing' of the occupied territories of the east and the new ethnic order to be established there.[24]

That 'national salvation' involved not just internal regeneration, but a 'new order' based on the ethnic cleansing of the entire continent of Europe, also singles out National Socialism from all other forms of fascism. No small part of its uniqueness, in other words, was the combination of racial nationalism and imperialism directed not abroad, but at Europe itself. And, as already indicated, though nazism amounted to the most extreme expression of such ideas, the politics of national salvation had every prospect of blending into the cultural pessimism of neo-conservatives and the anti-democratic and revisionist-expansionist currents that prevailed among the national-conservative élites.

It is not just the force in themselves of the ideas of national rebirth that Hitler came to embody, but the fact that they arose in such a highly modern state system, which was decisive for their uniquely destructive quality. Other interwar European dictatorships, both fascist and communist, emerged in societies with less advanced economies, less sophisticated apparatus of state administration, and less modernized armies. And, apart from the Soviet Union (where policies directed at creating a sphere of influence in the Baltic and Balkans to provide a 'cordon sanitaire' against the looming German threat took concrete form only by the end of the 1930s), geopolitical aims in Europe generally stretched no further than localized irredentism. In other words: not only did the expectations of 'national salvation' invested in Hitler enjoy a mass basis—13 million nazi voters already in free elections in 1932, countless further millions to join them over the following years; not only did such ideas correspond to more 'intellectualized' notions of the defence of western culture among the upper social classes and political élites; not only did 'national salvation' involve the reconstruction on racial lines of the whole of Europe; but—something present in no other dictatorship—a highly modern state apparatus, increasingly infected by such notions, existed in Germany and was capable of turning visionary, utopian goals into practical, administrative reality.

Let us return at this point to Hitler and to the implementation of the politics of national salvation after 1933. I have been suggesting that a modern state system directed by 'charismatic authority', based on ideas, frequently used by Hitler, of a 'mission' (*Sendung*) to bring about 'salvation' (*Rettung*) or 'redemption' (*Erlösung*)—all, of course, terms tapping religious or quasi-religious emotions—was unique. (I should, perhaps, add that, in my view, this populistic exploitation of naïve 'messianic' hopes and illusions among members of a society plunged into comprehensive crisis does not mean that nazism has claim to be regarded as a 'political religion', a currently voguish revamping of an age-old notion, though no less convincing for being repeated so persistently.[25]) The singularity of the nazi form of rule was, thus, undeniably bound up with the singularity of Hitler's position of power. Though familiar enough, it is worthwhile reminding ourselves of the essence of this power.

During the course of the early 1920s, Hitler developed a pronounced sense of his 'national mission'—'messianic allures', as one ironic remark had it at the time.[26] The 'mission' can be summed up as follows: nationalize the masses; take over the state, destroy the enemy within—the 'November criminals' (meaning Jews and Marxists, much the same in his eyes); build up defences; then undertake expansion 'by the sword' to secure Germany's future in overcoming the 'shortage of land' (*Raumnot*) and acquiring new territory in the east of Europe. Towards the end of 1922, a small but growing band of fanatical followers—the initial 'charismatic community'—inspired by Mussolini's 'March on Rome', began to project their own desire for a 'heroic' national leader onto Hitler. (As early as 1920, such desires were expressed by neo-conservatives, not nazis, as the longing for a leader who, in contrast to the contemptible 'politicians' of the new Republic, would be a statesman with the qualities of the 'ruler, warrior, and high priest' rolled into one.[27]) Innumerable letters eulogizing Hitler as a national hero poured into the Landsberg fortress, where in 1924 he spent a comfortable few months of internment after his trial for high treason at Munich, which had given him new prominence and standing on the racist-nationalist Right. A book published that year waxed lyrical (and mystical) about the new hero:

> The secret of his personality resides in the fact that in it the deepest of what lies dormant in the soul of the German people has taken shape in full living features. ... That has appeared in Adolf Hitler: the living incarnation of the nation's yearning.[28]

Hitler believed this bilge. He used his time in Landsberg to describe his 'mission' in the first volume of *Mein Kampf* (which, with scant regard for catchy, publishers' titles, he had wanted to call 'Four and a Half Years of Struggle against Lies, Stupidity, and Cowardice'). He also learnt lessons from the failure of his movement in 1923. One important lesson was that a refounded nazi movement had, in contrast to the pre-*Putsch* era, to be exclusively a 'Leader Party'. From 1925 onwards, the NSDAP was gradually transformed into precisely this 'Leader Party'. Hitler became not just the organizational fulcrum of the movement, but also the sole fount of doctrinal orthodoxy. Leader and Idea (however vague the latter remained) blended into one, and by the end of the 1920s, the NSDAP had swallowed all strands of the former diverse *völkisch* movement and now possessed a monopoly on the racist-nationalist Right. In conditions of the terminal crisis of Weimar, Hitler, backed by a much more solid organization than had been the case before 1923, was in a position to stake a claim for ever-growing numbers of Germans to be the coming national 'saviour', a redeemer figure.

It is necessary to underline this development, however well-known it is in general, since, despite leadership cults elsewhere, there was actually nothing similar in the genesis of other dictatorships. The Duce cult before the 'March on Rome' had not been remotely so important or powerful within Italian fascism as had the Führer cult to the growth of German National Socialism. Mussolini was at that stage still essentially first among equals among the regional fascist leaders. The full efflorescence of the cult only came later, after 1925.[29] In Spain, the Caudillo cult attached to Franco was even more of an artificial creation, the claim to being a great national leader, apeing the Italian and German models, coming long after he had made his name and career through the army.[30] An obvious point of comparison in totalitarian theory, linking dictatorships of Left and Right, appears to be that of the Führer cult with the Stalin cult. Certainly, there was more than a casual pseudo-religious strain to the Stalin cult. Russian peasants plainly saw in 'the boss' some sort of substitute for 'father Tsar'.[31] Nonetheless, the Stalin cult was in essence a late accretion to the position which had gained Stalin his power, that of Party General Secretary in prime position to inherit Lenin's mantle. Unlike nazism, the personality cult was not intrinsic to the form of rule, as its denunciation and effective abolition after Stalin's death demonstrated. Later rulers in the

Soviet Union did not try to revamp it; the term 'charismatic leadership' does not readily trip off the lips when we think of Brezhnev or Chernenko. In contrast, the Führer cult was the indispensable basis, the irreplaceable essence and the dynamic motor of a nazi regime unthinkable without it. The 'Führer myth' was the platform for the massive expansion of Hitler's own power once the style of leadership in the party had been transferred to the running of a modern, sophisticated state. It served to integrate the party, determine the 'guidelines for action' of the movement, to sustain the focus on the visionary ideological goals, to drive on the radicalization, to maintain the ideological momentum, and, not least, to legitimate the initiatives of others 'working towards the Führer'.[32]

The core points of Hitler's ideology were few, and visionary rather than specific. But they were unchanging and unnegotiable: 'removal of the Jews' (meaning different things to different party and state agencies at different times); attaining 'living space' to secure Germany's future (a notion vague enough to encompass different strands of expansionism); race as the explanation of world history, and eternal struggle as the basic law of human existence. For Hitler personally, this was a vision demanding war to bring about national salvation through expunging the shame of the capitulation of 1918 and destroying those reponsible for it (who were in his eyes the Jews). Few Germans saw things in the way that Hitler did. But mobilization of the masses brought them closer to doing so. Here, Hitler remained the supreme motivator. Mass mobilization was never, however, as he realized from the outset, going to suffice. He needed the power of the state, the co-option of its instruments of rule, and the support of the élites who traditionally controlled them. Naturally, the conservative élites were not true believers. They did not, in the main, swallow the excesses of the Führer cult, and could even be privately contemptuous or condescending about Hitler and his movement. Beyond that, they were often disappointed with the realities of National Socialism. Even so, Hitler's new form of leadership offered them the chance, as they saw it, of sustaining their own power. Their weakness was Hitler's strength, before and after 1933. And, as we have seen, there were plenty of ideological overlaps even without complete identity. Gradually, a state administration run, like that of all modern states, on the basis of 'expedient rationality', succumbed to the irrational goals of the politics of national salvation, embodied by Hitler—a process culminating in the bureaucratically-organized and industrially-executed genocide against the Jews, premised on irrational notions of national redemption.

Not only the complicity of the old élites was needed for this process of subordination of rational principles of government and administration to the irrational goals of 'charismatic leadership'. New élites, as has already been suggested, were only too ready to exploit the unheard of opportunities offered to them in the Führer state to build up unimaginable power accretions, free of any legal or administrative shackles. The new 'technocrats of power', of the type exemplified by Reinhard Heydrich, combined ideological fanaticism with cold, ruthless, depersonified efficiency and organizational skills. They could find rationality in irrationality; could turn into practical reality the goals associated with Hitler, needing no further legitimation than recourse to the 'wish of the Führer'.[33] This was no 'banality of evil'.[34] This was the working of an ideologically-motivated élite coldly prepared to plan for the eradication of 11 million Jews (the figure laid down at the Wannsee Conference of January 1942), and for the 'resettlement' to the Siberian wastes, plainly genocidal in intent, of over 30 million, mainly Slavs, over the following 25 years. That, in such a system, they would find countless 'willing executioners' prepared to do their bit, whatever the individual motivation of those involved, goes without saying. This was, however, not on account of national character, or some long-existent, specifically German desire to eliminate the Jews. Rather, it was that the idea of racial cleansing, the core of the notion of national salvation, had become, via Hitler's leadership position, institutionalized in all aspects of organized life in the nazi state. *That* was decisive.

Unquestionably, Hitler was a unique historical personality. But the uniqueness of the nazi dictatorship cannot be reduced to that. It is explained less by Hitler's character, extraordinary as it was, than by the specific form of rule which he embodied and its corrupting effect on the instruments and mechanisms of the most advanced state in Europe. *Both* the broad acceptance of the 'project' of 'national salvation', seen as personified in Hitler, *and* the internalization of the ideological goals by a new, modern power-élite, operating alongside weakened old élites through the bureaucratic sophistication of a modern state, were necessary prerequisites for the world-historical catastrophe of the Third Reich.

NOTES

* This article was first delivered in 2002 as a Trevelyan Lecture at the University of Cambridge.

1 A.J.P. Taylor, *The Course of German History* (London 1945). 'In the course of a thousand years, the Germans have experienced everything except normality', wrote Taylor. 'Only the normal person ... has never set his stamp on German history' (paperback edn, 1961, 1). Any positive qualities in Germans were in his eyes 'synonymous with ineffectiveness': 'There were, and I daresay are, many millions of well-meaning kindly Germans; but what have they added up to politically?', he asked (viii–ix). The attack on the Soviet Union in 1941 was, for him, 'the climax, the logical conclusion of German history' (260). The long pedigree of German abnormality, and its climax in nazism, is also a theme of Rohan O'Butler, *The Roots of National Socialism* (London 1941); William Montgomery McGovern, *From Luther to Hitler. The History of Nazi-Fascist Philosophy* (London 1946); and, in essence, of William Shirer, *The Rise and Fall of the Third Reich* (New York 1960).

2 Daniel Jonah Goldhagen, *Hitler's Willing Executioners* (New York 1996).

3 Friedrich Meinecke, *Die deutsche Katastrophe* (Wiesbaden 1946); Gerhard Ritter, *Europa und die deutsche Frage. Betrachtungen über die geschichtliche Eigenart des deutschen Staatsdenkens* (Munich 1948).

4 Fritz Fischer, *Griff nach der Weltmacht* (Düsseldorf 1961).

5 Ralf Dahrendorf, *Society and Democracy in Germany* (London 1968).

6 Among Hans-Ulrich Wehler's prolific output, *Das Kaiserreich 1871–1918* (Göttingen 1973), serves as a paradigmatic expression of the thesis. He has modified, though maintained, the *Sonderweg* approach in his magisterial work, *Deutsche Gesellschaftsgeschichte, Bd.3, 1849–1914* (Munich 1995), 460–89, 1284–95. Another prominent proponent of the *Sonderweg* thesis, Jürgen Kocka, put the case succinctly in his article, 'German History

before Hitler: The Debate about the German *Sonderweg*', *Journal of Contemporary History*, 23, 1 (January 1988), 3–16.

7 David Blackbourn and Geoff Eley, *The Peculiarities of German History* (Oxford 1984).

8 Detlev J.K. Peukert, *Die Weimarer Republik. Krisenjahre der Klassischen Moderne* (Frankfurt am Main 1987), 271 for the explicit rejection of the *Sonderweg* approach.

9 On this point, Peter Pulzer, 'Special Paths or Main Roads? Making Sense of German History', Elie Kedourie Memorial Lecture, 22 May 2002 (as yet unpublished) offers some valuable reflections and insights.

10 I explored these in some detail in the second chapter of my *The Nazi Dictatorship. Problems and Perspectives of Interpretation* (4th edn, London 2000). See also my reservations about the totalitarianism concept in the essay 'Totalitarianism Revisited: Nazism and Stalinism in Comparative Perspective', *Tel Aviver Jahrbuch für deutsche Geschichte*, 23 (1994), 23–40. Among a library of works on fascism, Roger Griffin, *The Nature of Fascism* (London 1991), is outstanding in conceptualization and Stanley G. Payne, *A History of Fascism, 1914–1945* (London 1995), in typology, while Michael Mann's as yet unpublished study, *Fascists*, offers the most profound comparative analysis undertaken of the supporters of fascist movements, their motivation, and their actions. I am extremely grateful to Professor Mann for a preview of this important work and its interlinked, companion volume, *The Dark Side of Democracy: Explaining Ethnic Cleansing* (not yet published). Recent anthologies on totalitarianism, a concept revived since the fall of Soviet communism, include Eckhard Jesse (ed.), *Totalitarismus im 20. Jahrhundert. Eine Bilanz der internationalen Forschung* (2nd edn, Bonn 1999); and Enzo Traverso, *Le Totalitarisme: le XXe siècle en débat* (Paris 2001).

11 Martin Broszat, *Der Staat Hitlers* (Munich 1969), 9.

12 Karl Dietrich Bracher, 'The Role of Hitler' in Walter Laqueur (ed.), *Fascism. A Reader's Guide* (Harmondsworth 1979), 201.

13 See the directly opposed contributions of Klaus Hildebrand and Hans Mommsen in Michael Bosch (ed.), *Persönlichkeit und Struktur in der Geschichte* (Düsseldorf 1977), 55–71 and further references to the controversy in Kershaw, *The Nazi Dictatorship*, chap. 4. Martin Broszat's brilliant essay, 'Soziale Motivation und Führer-Bindung des Nationalsozialismus', *Vierteljahrshefte für Zeitgeschichte*, 18 (1970), 392–409, also amounted to a subtle assault on the 'Hitlerism' argument.

14 Lothar Machtan, *The Hidden Hitler* (London 2001), for the argument, which has encountered widespread criticism, that Hitler was a homosexual. The syphilis argument, outrightly rejected by those who have most thoroughly explored Hitler's medical history, notably Fritz Redlich, *Hitler. Diagnosis of a Destructive Prophet* (New York/Oxford 1999), and Ernst Günther Schenck, *Patient Hitler. Eine medizinische Biographie* (Düsseldorf 1989), has recently resurfaced in an investigation—the most thorough imaginable of this topic—by Deborah Hayden, to whom I am grateful for a preview of this, as yet, unpublished work.

15 A formulation which has become famous, coined by Hans Mommsen and first stated in a footnote to his *Beamtentum im Dritten Reich* (Stuttgart 1966), 98, note 26. The debate ensuing from the term is explored in my *Nazi Dictatorship*, op. cit., chap. 4.

16 Ian Kershaw, *Hitler. A Profile in Power* (London 1991, 2nd edn 2001); *Hitler, 1889–1936: Hubris* (London 1998); *Hitler, 1936–1945: Nemesis* (London 2000).

17 For a summary of the advances in research, see Ulrich Herbert (ed.), *Nationalsozialistische Vernichtungspolitik 1939–1945* (Frankfurt am Main 1998), 9–66. Much of the new research is incorporated in the excellent survey by Peter Longerich, *Politik der Vernichtung. Eine Gesamtdarstellung der nationalsozialistischen Judenverfolgung* (Munich/Zurich 1998).

18 First formulated in Hans Mommsen, 'Der Nationalsozialismus. Kumulative Radikalisierung und Selbstzerstörung des Regimes', *Meyers Enzyklopädisches Lexikon*, Bd.16 (Mannheim 1976), 785–90.

19 I first directly deployed Weber's concept to help explore the shaping of popular opinion in 'The Führer Image and Political Integration: The Popular Conception of Hitler in Bavaria during the Third Reich', in Gerhard Hirschfeld and Lothar Kettenacker (eds), *Der 'Führerstaat': Mythos und Realität. Studien zur Struktur und Politik des Dritten Reiches* (Stuttgart 1981), 133–61, 'Alltägliches und Außeralltägliches: ihre Bedeutung für die Volksmeinung 1933–1939', in Detlev Peukert and Jürgen Reulecke (eds), *Die Reihen fast geschlossen. Beiträge zur Geschichte des Alltags unterm Nationalsozialismus* (Wuppertal 1981), 273–92, and, more extensively, in *The 'Hitler Myth': Image and Reality in the Third Reich* (Oxford 1987). I deployed it more directly to examine the nature of Hitler's power in *Hitler: A Profile in Power*, op. cit., as well as in a number of essays, such as 'The Nazi State: an Exceptional State?', *New Left Review*, 176 (1989), 47–67 and '"Working towards the Führer": Reflections on the Nature of the Hitler Dictatorship', *Contemporary European History*, 2 (1993), 103–18. The concept is also used by M. Rainer Lepsius, 'Charismatic Leadership: Max Weber's Model and its Applicability to the Rule of Hitler', in Carl Friedrich Graumann and Serge Moscovici (eds), *Changing Conceptions of Leadership* (New York 1986), 53–66.

20 Griffin, in particular, has made this the focal point of his interpretation of fascism. See his *Nature of Fascism*, op. cit., 26, 32ff.

21 Oswald Spengler, *Der Untergang des Abendlandes* (Vienna/Munich 1918–22).

22 For the term, see Richard Bessel, *Germany after the First World War* (Oxford 1993), 262.

23 See, for this, especially Ulrich Herbert, '"Generation der Sachlichkeit": Die völkische Studentenbewegung der frühen zwanziger Jahre in Deutschland', in Frank Bajohr, Werner Johe and Uwe Lohalm (eds), *Zivilisation und Barbarei. Die widersprüchlichen Potentiale der Moderne* (Hamburg 1991), 115–44.

24 See the fine study by Michael Wildt, *Generation des Unbedingten. Das Führungskorps des Reichssicherheitshauptamtes* (Hamburg 2002).

25 The perception of nazism as a form of political religion, advanced as long ago as 1938 by the émigré Eric Voegelin, *Die politischen Religionen* (Vienna 1938), has recently gained a new lease of life. Among others who have found the notion attractive, Michael Burleigh adopted it, alongside 'totalitarianism', as a major conceptual prop of his interpretation in *The Third Reich. A New History* (London 2000). See also Burleigh's essay, 'National Socialism as a Political Religion', in *Totalitarian Movements and Political Religions*, 1, 2 (2000), 1–26. It has also been deployed for fascist Italy by Emilio Gentile, 'Fascism as Political Religion', *Journal of Contemporary History*, 25, 2–3 (May–June 1990), 229–51, and idem, *The Sacralisation of Politics in Fascist Italy* (Cambridge, MA 1996). See also Gentile's 'The Sacralisation of Politics: Definitions, Interpretations and Reflections on the Question of Secular Religion and Totalitarianism', in *Totalitarian Movements and Political Religions*, 1, 1 (2000), 18–55. For sharp criticism of its application to nazism, see Michael Rißmann, *Hitlers Gott. Vorsehungsglaube und Sendungsbewußtsein des deutschen Diktators* (Zurich/Munich 2001), 191–7; and Griffin, *Nature of Fascism*, op. cit., 30–2. Griffin, once critical, has, however, changed his mind and now favours the use of the concept, as can be seen in his 'Nazism's "Cleansing Hurricane" and the Metamorphosis of Fascist Studies', in W. Loh (ed.), *'Faschismus' kontrovers* (Paderborn 2002).

26 Cited in Albrecht Tyrell, *Vom 'Trommler' zum 'Führer'* (Munich 1975), 163.

27 Cited in Kurt Sontheimer, *Antidemokratisches Denken in der Weimarer Republik* (3rd edn, Munich 1992), 217.

28 Georg Schott, *Das Volksbuch vom Hitler* (Munich 1924), 18.

29 See Piero Melograni, 'The Cult of the Duce in Mussolini's Italy', *Journal of Contemporary History*, 11, 4 (October 1976), 221–37; Adrian Lyttelton, *The Seizure of Power* (London 1973), 72ff, 166–75; and, most recently the excellent political biography by R.J.B. Bosworth, *Benito Mussolini* (London 2002), chaps 6–11. It took several years before the customary mode of address and reference to Mussolini changed from Presidente to Duce and some among his old comrades never took to the 'heroic' form. See R.J.B. Bosworth, *The Italian Dictatorship: Problems and Perspectives in the Interpretation of Mussolini and Fascism* (London 1998), 62, note 14. A valuable study of the incomparably more dynamic impact of the Führer cult than the Duce cult on state administration and bureaucracy is provided by Maurizio Bach, *Die charismatischen Führerdiktaturen. Drittes Reich und italienischer Faschismus im Vergleich ihrer Herrschaftsstrukturen* (Baden-Baden 1991). Walter Rauscher, *Hitler und Mussolini. Macht, Krieg und Terror* (Graz/Vienna/Cologne 2001), provides a parallel biography of the two dictators, though offers no structural comparison.

30 See Paul Preston, *Franco. A Biography* (London 1993), 187ff.

31 See Moshe Lewin, *The Making of the Soviet System. Essays in the Social History of Interwar Russia* (London 1985), 57–71, 268–76; and also Ian Kershaw and Moshe Lewin, *Stalinism and Nazism: Dictatorships in Comparison* (Cambridge 1997), chaps 1, 4 and 5.

32 For the term, see Kershaw, *Hitler, 1889–1936: Hubris*, op. cit., 529.

33 Gerald Fleming, *Hitler und die Endlösung. 'Es ist des Führers Wunsch'* (Wiesbaden/Munich 1982), shows how frequently the phrase was invoked by those involved in the extermination of the Jews.

34 The memorable, though nonetheless misleading, concept was coined by Hannah Arendt, *Eichmann in Jerusalem: A Report on the Banality of Evil* (London 1963).

Part III

FASCISM AS TOTALITARIANISM AND POLITICAL RELIGION

11

THE SACRALISATION OF POLITICS

Definitions, interpretations and reflections on the
question of secular religion and totalitarianism

Emilio Gentile

*The past two decades have witnessed a resurgence of the scholarly interest in the
enormously complex and multifaceted relationship between religion and politics
in the modern period, with the main focus on totalitarian movements and regimes
in the twentieth century. The content of these debates has been greatly influenced
by the work of the eminent Italian historian Emilio Gentile, professor of contemporary
history at* La Sapienza *University of Rome. Following in the research path
opened in the Italian historiography by Renzo De Felice, and in a permanent dialogue
with the international debates on fascism, in numerous works published in
the Italian language since early 1970, Gentile has offered an in-depth analysis of
Italian Fascism (1990; 1996; 2003b; 2005b), supplemented by a comprehensive
view of fascism as a European-wide phenomenon (2002). He has elaborated an
innovative, complex, and systematic definition of fascism approached at three
analytical levels, as an ideology, a totalitarian movement, and a totalitarian
regime. Gentile embedded his view of fascism in a new conceptual framework
focusing on the process of sacralization of politics and the emergence of civil and
political reglions.*

*In this seminal article, Gentile summarizes his approach to one important—
although, by no means essential—aspect of his interpretation of fascism: the
emergence of totalitarian political religions. Originally published in the first programmatic
issue of the journal* Totalitarian Movements and Political Religions
*(2000), the article has been at the center of the recent interdisciplinary debates
on totalitarianism and political religions, involving not only the history of interwar
fascism but also the comparison between fascism and communism (for additional
clarifications and answers to criticism, see Gentile 2004; 2005a).*

*Building primarily on anti-fascist, Protestant and Catholic critiques of fascism
originating in interwar Europe, and on post-1945 scholarship on fascism and
totalitarianism, Gentile elaborated a comprehensive theoretical framework for*

analyzing modern secular religions (in English, see 2000; 2004; 2005a; 2006). His approach is based on the premise that modernity has been a "matrix" for new secular religions. Due to the general tendency toward secularization and the gradual waning of the influence of established religions, in the modern period, the "sacred" has been experienced in novel ways and expressed in the phenomenon of the "sacralization of politics," defined as a form of politics that "confers a sacred status on an earthly entity (nation, country, state, humanity, society, race, proletariat, history, liberty or revolution) and renders it an absolute principle of collective existence" (2004: 18–19). The sacralization of politics is rooted in the culture of the Enlightenment and has revolutionary, democratic, and nationalist origins. The process was greatly stimulated by wars and revolutionary upheavals; its first articulations appeared during the French and American Revolutions. The heydays of the phenomenon of the sacralization of politics were in the interwar period, when the experience of the Great War and the Bolshevik Revolution led to the elaboration of distinct forms of sacralized politics in the context of fascist and communist totalitarian movements and regimes.

In order to distinguish among forms of sacralized politics in democratic and totalitarian regimes, Gentile makes an analytical differentiation between civil religion, defined as a "common civic creed" based on the sacralization of a collective political entity that is not attached to a particular ideology, accepts the separation between Church and State, and tolerates the existence of traditional religious; and political religion, with an "exclusive and integralist" character, denying individual autonomy, subordinating traditional religions and eliminating rival movements. As examples of civil religions, Gentile mentions "civic creeds" developed during the American and French Revolutions, or the recent campaign of "political correctness" in the USA; the doctrine of the sacredness of the "general will" elaborated by Jean-Jacques Rousseau is considered an ambivalent example since it contained intolerant elements that place it in-between civil and political religions.

Gentile argues that totalitarian movements and regimes have the tendency to sacralize politics and create political religions. Departing critically from "classical" theoretical models put forward during the Cold War, Gentile re-defines totalitarianism as "an experiment in political domination undertaken by a revolutionary movement with an integralist conception of politics that aspires toward a monopoly of power." Its ultimate aim is the "subordination, integration and homogenization" of all individuals and their regeneration by means of an "anthropological revolution" in the spirit of the respective movement's palingenetic ideology. It is important to note that this flexible definition is centered on political movements out of which, Gentile claims, totalitarian regimes ultimately stem.

In his work, Gentile has devoted a great deal of attention to the institutional aspects of totalitarian movements and regimes at both theoretical and empirical levels (2001). In his view, the main features of totalitarian regimes are the militarization of the unique party; the concentration of power; the capillary organization of the masses; and the sacralization of politics. Totalitarian regimes achieve these goals by means of violent coercion, repression and terror; demagoguery

through propaganda and the institutionalization of the leadership cult; totalitar-
ian pedagogy along the lines of the official palingenetic ideology; and discrimi-
nation against internal or outside enemies. Gentile defines totalitarianism as an
experiment rather than a static model, a complex outcome of the continuous inter-
action of several elements: the revolutionary party, the regime, the political
religion and the "anthropological revolution" to create the "new man."

Although not the most important aspect of totalitarianism, the sacralization of
politics in the form of new political religions is nevertheless one of its distinctive and
highly "dangerous" features. The process rests on the following pillars: the procla-
mation of the primacy of a collective secular entity treated as an elect community
invested with a messianic mission; the elaboration of a code of ethical and social
commandments meant to bind together the members of the sacred community; and
the institutionalization of these bonds in a novel political liturgy. Although it intro-
duces a religious element in politics, the sacralization of politics is nevertheless dis-
tinct from traditional religions. Explicating the possible links between political
religions and established religions, Gentile argues that they can be either mimetic—
in cases where political religions adopt key elements of a traditional religion; or
syncretic—when political religions appropriate major elements of a traditional reli-
gion but insert them into their own structure of beliefs. He also points out that polit-
ical religions tend to be ephemeral—since they are inevitably worn out and
exhausted due to their inability to sustain collective mobilization.

In his own empirical research, Gentile documented the process of the formation
and institutionalization of a new "Fascist religion" in interwar Italy (1996;
2005b). This process was manifest in the search for a new "national religion" that
took place during the period of Risorgimento. *The main stages in the sacralization*
of politics and the creation of the new national religion in Fascist Italy were "the
cult of the fallen;" and the "cult of the lector"; it culminated in the fascist
"Liturgy of Collective Harmony" involving all Italians in rituals and mass demon-
strations (1996). Gentile argues that the new Fascist religion had all the "funda-
mental constituents of any religion," namely myth, faith, ritual, and communion;
it aimed at transforming the mentality, character and way of life of the Italians,
with the ultimate goal of creating the fascist "new man" (1996). More recently,
Emilio Gentile has greatly expanded the empirical scope of his analysis on the
sacralization of politics in several works devoted to the issue of civic and political
religions in the United States and in other regions of the world (2006; 2008).

BIBLIOGRAPHY

Gentile, Emilio (1990). "Fascism as Political Religion," *Journal of Contemporary History,*
25: 2/3, 229–251.
Gentile, Emilio (1996). *The Sacralization of Politics in Fascist Italy* (Cambridge, MA:
Harvard University Press).
Gentile, Emilio (2000). "The Sacralisation of Politics: Definitions, Interpretations and
Reflections on the Question of Secular Religion and Totalitarianism," *Totalitarian
Movements and Political Religions* 1: 1, 18–55.

Gentile, Emilio (2001). *La via italiana al totalitarismo: il partito el lo State nel regimo* (Roma: Carocci).

Gentile, Emilio (2002). *Fascismo: storie e interpretazione*. (Roma: Laterza).

Gentile, Emilio (2003a). *Renzo De Felice: lo storico e il personaggio* (Roma: Laterza).

Gentile, Emilio (2003b). *The Struggle for Modernity: Nationalism, Futurism, and Fascism* (Westport, CT: Praeger).

Gentile, Emilio (2004). "Fascism, Totalitarianism and Political Religion: Definitions and Critical Reflections on Criticism of an Interpretation," *Totalitarian Movements and Political Religions*, 5: 3, 326–375.

Gentile, Emilio (2005a). "Political Religion: A Concept and its Critics – A Critical Survey," *Totalitarian Movements and Political Religions*, 1: 6, 19–32.

Gentile, Emilio (2005b). *The Origins of Fascist Ideology, 1918–1925* (New York: Enigma). Originally published as *Le origini dell'ideologia fascista (1918–1925)* (Roma: Laterza, 1975).

Gentile, Emilio (2006). *Politics as Religion* (Princeton, NJ: Princeton University Press).

Gentile, Emilio (2008). *God's Democracy: American Religion after September 11* (Westport, CT: Praeger).

* * *

That the sacralisation of politics was an important aspect of the various totalitarianisms is not merely demonstrated by the historical reality of the movements in question, or by their markedly visible characteristics, dogmas, myths, rituals and symbolisms.[1] It is also confirmed by the importance given to these aspects by practically every scholar of totalitarianism during the interwar period, whatever their cultural, political and religious orientation. Indeed, most assessments broadly agree that the sacralisation of politics (variously defined as lay religion, secular religion, earthly religion, political religion, political mysticism, and political idolatry) was one of the most distinctive elements, if not the most dangerous, of the totalitarian phenomenon.[2] This process takes place when, more or less elaborately and dogmatically, a political movement confers a sacred status on an earthly entity (the nation, the country, the state, humanity, society, race, proletariat, history, liberty, or revolution) and renders it an absolute principle of collective existence, considers it the main source of values for individual and mass behaviour, and exalts it as the supreme ethical precept of public life. It thus becomes an object for veneration and dedication, even to the point of self-sacrifice.

Totalitarianism and the sacralisation of politics: guiding definitions

Totalitarianism

The term 'totalitarianism' can be taken as meaning: an *experiment in political domination* undertaken by a *revolutionary movement*, with an *integralist conception* of politics, that aspires toward a *monopoly of power* and that, after having secured power, whether by legal or illegal means, destroys or transforms the previous regime and constructs a new state based on a *single-party regime*, with the chief objective of *conquering society*. That is, it seeks the subordination, integration and homogenisation of the governed on the basis of the *integral politicisation of existence*, whether collective or individual, interpreted according to the categories, the myths and the values of a *palingenetic ideology*, institutionalised in the form of a *political religion*, that aims to shape the individual and the masses through an *anthropological revolution* in order to regenerate the human being and create the *new man*, who is dedicated in body and soul to the realisation of the revolutionary and imperialistic policies of the totalitarian party. The ultimate goal is to create a *new civilisation* along expansionist lines beyond the Nation-State.

At the point of origin of the totalitarian experiment is the revolutionary party, the principal author and protagonist, organised along militaristic and autocratic lines, and with an integralist conception of politics. The party does not permit the existence of other political parties with other ideologies, and conceives of the state, even after it has exalted its primacy, as the means of achieving its policy of expansionism, as well as its ideas for a new society. In other words, the totalitarian party, from its very early beginnings, possesses a complex system of beliefs, dogmas, myths, rituals and symbols that define the meaning and purpose of collective existence within this world, while also defining good and evil exclusively in accordance with the principles, values and objectives of the party, which it helps implement. In effect, even a party such as the Bolshevik party, which professed atheism and conducted anti-religious campaigns, constitutes a type of political sacralisation.

The totalitarian regime has its origins in the totalitarian party, which emerges as a political system based on the symbiosis between state and party, and on a power complex formed from the chief exponents of the *command hierarchy*, chosen by the *head of the party*. The head of the party dominates the entire structure of the regime with his charismatic authority.

The fundamental characteristics of the totalitarian regime are:

(a) The *militarisation of the party* by way of a rigid hierarchy whose style and mentality is based on ethics of dedication and absolute discipline.

(b) The *concentration of power* in the single party and in the figure of the *charismatic leader*.

(c) The *capillary organisation of the masses*, which involves men and women of all ages, in order to carry out the conquest of society, collective indoctrination and an anthropological revolution.

(d) The *sacralisation of politics* through the more or less explicit institution of a secular religion, that is, of a real system of beliefs, myths, dogmas and commandments that cover all of collective existence and by way of the introduction of an apparatus of rituals and festivals, in order to transform permanently the *occasional crowds* of civil events into the *liturgical masses* of the political cult.

261

In short, the totalitarian regime constitutes a laboratory wherein a revolutionary anthropological experiment takes place that aims to create a new type of human being. The chief instruments of this experiment are:

(a) *Coercion*, imposed through violence, since repression and terror are considered legitimate instruments for the affirmation, defence and diffusion of the prevailing ideology and political system.
(b) *Demagoguery* exerted through constant and all-pervasive propaganda, the mobilisation of enthusiasm, and the liturgical celebration of the cult of the party and the leader.
(c) *Totalitarian pedagogy*, carried out at high level and according to male and female role models developed according to the principles and values of a palingenetic ideology.
(d) *Discrimination against the outsider*, undertaken by way of coercive measures that range from exile from public life to physical elimination of human beings who, because of their ideas, social conditions and ethnic background, are considered *inevitable enemies* because they are regarded as undesirable by the society of the elect and, duly, incompatible with the objectives of the totalitarian experiment.

The party, the regime, the political religion and the anthropological revolution are essential elements (each of which complements the others) of the totalitarian experiment, although it should be stressed that the totalitarian nature of this experiment does not coincide separately with any of the elements taken singly, or with the methods by which it is undertaken. By defining totalitarianism as an *experiment*, rather than as a *regime*, it is intended to highlight the interconnections between its fundamental constituent parts and to emphasise that totalitarianism is a *continual process* that cannot be considered complete at any stage in its evolution. The essence of totalitarianism is to be found in the dynamic of these constituent parts and in their interconnectedness.

This suggests that the concept of 'totalitarianism' has not only an institutional significance, that is, it is not simply applicable to a system of power and a method of government (to the *regime*), but is, rather, indicative, in a broader sense, of a *political process* characterised by the *voluntary experimentalism* of the revolutionary party, whose ultimate objective is to influence the heterogeneous governed masses in such a way as to transform them into an *harmonious collective*. That is, it will transform them into a *unitary and homogenous body politic* morally united in their totalitarian religion.

The sacralisation of politics

The term 'the sacralisation of politics' means the formation of a *religious dimension in politics that is distinct from, and autonomous of, traditional religious institutions*. The sacralisation of politics takes place when politics is conceived, lived and represented through myths, rituals and symbols that demand faith in the sacralised secular entity, dedication among the community of believers, enthusiasm for action, a warlike spirit and sacrifice in order to secure its defence and its triumph. In such cases, it is possible to speak of *religions of politics* in that politics itself assumes religious characteristics.

The sacralisation of politics takes place when a political movement:

(a) Consecrates the primacy of a *collective secular entity*, placing it at the centre of a system of beliefs and myths that define the meaning and ultimate goals of social existence, and proscribe the principles that define good and evil.

(b) Incorporates this conception into a code of ethical and social commandments which bind the individual to the sacralised entity, compelling the same individual to loyalty and dedication to it.

(c) Considers its members an *elect community* and interprets political action as a *messianic function* aiming toward the fulfilment of a mission.

(d) Develops a *political liturgy* in order to worship the sacralised collective entity by way of an institutionalised cult and figures representing it, and through the mystical and symbolic portrayal of a *sacred history*, periodically relived through the ritual evocations performed by the community of the elect.

The sacralisation of politics is a modern phenomenon: it takes place when politics, after having secured its autonomy from traditional religion by secularising both culture and the state, acquires a truly religious dimension. For this reason, the sacralisation of politics should not be confused with the politicisation of traditional religions.[3] In other words, the sacralisation of politics is not a term that can be applied either to theocracy or to regimes governed by traditional religions. Accordingly, the sacralisation of politics also differs substantially from the *sacralisation of political power* within traditional society, where the holder of political power either identifies with divinity, as in the case of the pharaohs, or derives sacredness from institutionalised religion, as in the Christian monarchies.[4]

This does not imply that the sacralisation of politics has no connection with traditional religions. The relationship between the sacralisation of politics and traditional religion is, in reality, a very complex one and varies according to historical period, according to the various political movements that assume the characteristics of a secular religion, and according to the part played by traditional religion in countries where the process of the sacralisation of politics takes place.[5] Historically speaking, political religions generally incorporate elements of traditional religion, at the same time transforming and adapting them into a system of beliefs, myths and rituals.

Yet, in reality, the presence of collective myths and rituals alone does not permit one to speak of the sacralisation of politics. In order for this to take place, it is necessary that the conferring of sacred status upon a secular political entity takes place in such a way as explicitly to transform this entity into the principal controller of collective existence, and into an object of cult status and an object of dedication though the creation of celebratory rituals in which participate not *occasional crowds*, but a *liturgical mass*. The creation of civil rituals does not always suggest that a truly secular political religion has been established. For instance, this had not been the intention of the leaders of the French Third Republic, who promoted the establishment of national holidays in order to give symbolic legitimacy to the new state.[6]

Moreover, the sacralisation of politics does not necessarily lead to conflict with traditional religions, and neither does it lead to a denial of the existence of any supernatural supreme being. After all, there have been cases when the sacralisation of politics took place following a direct fusion with traditional religion, as was the case with the relationship between American *civil religion* and puritanism.[7] In other cases, as, for example, with the *political religion* of Fascism, while the movement itself had origins that were autonomous from religious tradition and anticlerical, it did not attempt to hijack traditional institutionalised religion, but, on the contrary, attempted to establish a form of symbiotic relationship with it, with the aim of incorporating it into the movement's own mythical and symbolic universe, thereby making it a component of secular religion.[8]

As regards traditional religions, it is possible to argue that the religion of politics, whether it is intended as *civil religion* or *political religion*, is:

(a) *Mimetic*, in that, whether consciously or unconsciously, it derives its system of creating beliefs and myths, its dogmas, its ethics and the structure of its liturgy from traditional religion.

(b) *Syncretic*, in that it incorporates the traditions, myths and rituals of traditional religion, transforming and adapting them to its own mythical and symbolic universe.

(c) *Ephemeral*, in the majority of historical instances, given that following a lengthy phase of vitality its capacity to instil faith and enthusiasm is easily exhausted, on the grounds that the conditions of 'collective effervescence' that created it become worn out, leading to a crisis that destroys the core political movement.

The most intense and resounding manifestation of the sacralisation of politics took place during the interwar years with the emergence of totalitarianism. However, it should be stressed that the sacralisation of politics is not identifiable with totalitarianism, and that totalitarian political religions are not the inevitable consequence of the sacralisation of politics, even if this process has clearly constituted one of the conditions that made its emergence and establishment possible. The phenomenon of the sacralisation of politics was never linear and constant, and composed of homogenous movements that all formed links in the same identical chain. Indeed, the sacralisation of politics has manifested itself in a notable variety of ways, each of which has had different origins, backgrounds, content and form. At the same time, its relationship with the prevailing historical and social environment, with the political process and with collective existence has been varied and diverse. The sacralisation of politics has been both democratic and totalitarian. Bearing all this in mind, we might conclude this first section of our analysis by highlighting the conceptual differences between democratic 'civil religion' and totalitarian 'political religion', in terms of their content and their attitude toward both traditional religion and other political movements.[9]

1. *Civil religion* is a form of sacralisation of politics that generally involves a secular entity, but at times is connected to a supernatural being conceived of as a god; it is not linked to the ideology of any particular political movement, but acknowledges the full autonomy of the individual from the collective; making use of pacific forms of propaganda, it appeals to spontaneous consensus in the observance of ethical commandments and the collective liturgy, and exists side by side with traditional religions and with the various political ideologies. It seeks to present itself as a 'civic creed' which makes the distinction between state and church clear, and which does not associate with any specific denomination.

2. *Political religion* is the sacralisation of an ideology and an integralist political movement that deifies the mythical secular entity; it does not accept coexistence with other ideologies and political movements, and sanctifies violence as a legitimate weapon in the battle against enemies of the faith and as the instrument of regeneration; it denies the autonomy of the individual and stresses the primacy of the community; it imposes a political cult and enforces obligatory observance of its commandments; toward traditional religion it adopts either a hostile attitude or attempts to establish a symbiotic relationship with it, in the sense that the political religion aims to incorporate the traditional religion into its own system of beliefs and myths, while designating to it a subordinate and auxiliary function.[10]

Clearly, historical reality demonstrates that this distinction is not always clear and precise, and it is not possible to exclude the fact that common elements exist between them. The difference between 'civil religion' and 'political religion' can appear total if we compare the USA with Nazi Germany or Fascist Italy. But even civil religion can, in certain circumstances, become transformed into a political religion, thereby becoming integralist and intolerant, as happened during the French Revolution.

This ambiguity was already inherent in the concept of civil religion developed by Rousseau, and was also present in his notion of the sacredness of the general will and the nation as a fundamental and regulating principle of the body politic. The ambiguity remained after the French Revolution applied this concept. Boissy d'Anglas pleaded for the establishment of a national religion based on the model of ancient times, '*l'époque bénie où la religion ne fessait qu'un avec l'État*', while remembering that the '*religion des anciens fut toujours politique et nationale*'.[11] Condorcet, on the other hand, accused '*la religion politique*' of '*violer la liberté dans ses droits les plus sacrés sous prétexte d'apprendre à les chérir*'.[12]

The phenomenon of the sacralisation of politics, defined in this way, appertains to the more general phenomenon of *secular religion*, a term which defines almost every form of belief, myth, ritual and symbol that confers sacred characteristics upon earthly entities and renders them the main source of inspiration for lived existence, as well as a cult object of dedication.

Secular religion: a non-existent religion, a pseudo-religion or a new religion?

Secular religion has been much studied and discussed in recent years; one need only recall the long debate on American civil religion provoked by Robert Bellah in 1967.[13] There have been various arguments against the scientific validity of the concept of 'secular religion' and its various derivatives. Moreover, real doubts have been expressed as to whether the phenomenon of 'secular religion' exists at all. Certain scholars have contested the very existence of the term, maintaining that it constitutes a type of conceptual oxymoron: in short, they argue that the term 'secular religion' is equivalent to the 'square circle'. For example, on the theme of Fascism as political religion, Roger Griffin has spoken of the 'abuse of religious concepts', even if, in his definition of generic Fascism, he has attributed, very persuasively, a fundamental significance to the role of the *palingenetic myth*, that is, a myth with strong religious connotations that constitutes a principal element in all forms of sacralised politics, as can be seen in modern revolutionary movements.[14] Others argue that defining an ideology or a political movement as a 'religion' has only metaphorical meaning. In the meantime, as regards political religion, some assessments stress that the term refers to the politicisation of institutionalised religion. Meanwhile, others believe that, in the case of political movements that make use of religious language, rituals and symbols, the term 'religion' should be avoided altogether, or that the term 'pseudo-religion' should be used. This would indicate not a political movement that became a religion, but a movement that disguised itself as a religion so as to deceive, subjugate and govern the masses. The sacralisation of politics, in these terms, amounts merely to a demagogic deception.

Gaetano Mosca, one of the founding fathers of political science, was of this opinion. At the end of the nineteenth century he provided the classic formula for a *charlatanistic* interpretation of the sacralisation of politics. In fact, for Mosca, the question of faith, symbolism and ritual within political movements amounted to a secular form of *Jesuitism* designed to deceive the masses:

> If we look closely, we can see that the devices used to entice the crowd, always and everywhere, are and continue to be greatly analogous to one another, effectively because they are able to exploit human weakness. All religions, even those that renounce the supernatural, have their own style of denunciation which they use to preach, sermonise or make speeches with; all make use of exterior pomp and ritual in order to capture the imagination; some utilise candle-lit, psalm-reciting processions, while others march behind the red flag to the sound of the Marseillaise or singing the workers' hymn.

Religions and political parties equally make profitable use of vain people by creating rank, offices and distinctions for them, and also by exploiting the simple minded, the naive and those eager to sacrifice themselves or become notorious so as to create martyrs, and once they have created martyrs, they keep the cult alive, which in turn serves to reinforce faith. ... In our times both sects and political parties are very able to create the superior man, the legendary hero, the nature of which are not up for debate. This also serves to maintain the prestige of the congregation and generates wealth and power for those cunning individuals who belong to it. ... This complex mixture of dissembling, artificiality and cunning, that is commonly known as Jesuitism, was not unique to the followers of Loyola. ... All religions and all parties which, with more or less sincere initial enthusiasm, have attempted to lead men toward a specific goal, have, more or less, used methods similar to those of the Jesuits or even worse.[15]

In conclusion, according to the above interpretation, a secular religion is a 'religion that isn't' or a 'pseudo-religion'. Therefore, considering Bolshevism, Fascism and Nazism as political religions, or maintaining that there exists an American civil religion, means that either one is the victim of a illusion or that one has confused metaphor with reality, and made improper use of the concept of religion.

Evidently, given the controversy over the existence or otherwise of secular religion, defining the concept of religion itself becomes important. A definition of religion that includes the essential reference to the existence of a supernatural god, or that exclusively recognises that this term applies to traditional institutional religion, would have every reason to deny the existence of a secular religion or of a religious dimension to politics, other than that provided for it by institutionalised religion.[16]

In any case, from this point of view, even those who maintain that a truly secular religion can exist put forward convincing arguments. The existence of such a religion could, to all intents and purposes, be plausible even without a supernatural god if one accepts the definition offered by Emile Durkheim of religion being '*un système plus ou moins complexe de mythes, de dogmes, de rites, de cérémonies*' and '*de représentations qui expriment la nature des choses sacrées, les vertus et les pouvoirs qui leur sont attribués, leur histoire, leurs rapports les unes avec les autres et avec les choses profanes*'.[17] According to this functionalist interpretation of religion, all systems of beliefs, myths and collective rituals introduced with the aim of periodically reaffirming the identity and cohesive ties of collectivised politics, party or state are manifestations of religion, or, more precisely, of civil or political religion, which would perform the same function as any other religion, namely, of legitimising organised society or political power.[18]

Equally plausible would be the existence of new types of secular religion, a theory of religion propounded, for example, by Gustave Le Bon, who views religion as the product of the need of the masses for some form of faith. In developing his theory, Le Bon argued that modern society, a place of conflict between

267

gods and religions in decline and mass aspiration toward new divinities and new beliefs, provides highly fertile ground for the emergence of new secular religions, such as socialism, which are expressions of mass religious sentiment:

> *Ce sentiment a des caractéristiques très simples: adoration d'un être suppose supérieur, crainte de la puissance magique qu'on lui suppose, soumission aveugle à ses commandements, impossibilité de discuter ses dogmes, désir de les répandre, tendance à considérer comme ennemis tous ceux qui ne les admettent pas. Qu'un tel sentiment s'applique à un Dieu invisible, à une idole de pierre ou de bois, à un héros ou à une idée politique, du moment qu'il présente les caractéristiques précédentes il reste toujours d'essence religieuse . . .. On n'est pas religieux seulement quand on adore une divinité, mais quand on met toutes les ressources de l'esprit, toutes les soumissions de la volonté, toutes les ardeurs du fanatisme au service d'une cause ou d'un être qui devient le but et le guide des pensées et des actions.*

A political religion, viewed from such a perspective, does not amount merely to a façade of power designed to manipulate the masses, but constitutes, at least in part, the spontaneous creation of the masses themselves, who are in search of new beliefs that will give meaning to their lives. Thus, they direct all their religious fervour toward a secular entity, placing all their hopes for a safe and happy world in its hands.

Lastly, the existence of a secular religion becomes even more plausible if we consider the concept of 'sacredness' developed by Rudolf Otto.[19] In fact, even the political dimension, like all human dimensions, can become a place where the individual can experience a sacred experience, as frequently occurs during times of great collective emotion such as wars or revolutions. The experience of having felt the *numinous* power as defined by Otto during the course of such events, and its subsequent identification with a secular entity, could be the basis for the formation of new secular religious beliefs. It is interesting to note that Otto's book on 'the sacred', which was influenced by his experiences during the First World War, was published in 1917 and immediately became a best-seller.

This interpretation, which we might term *numinosa* (numinous), permits the existence of a secular religion, even in the political sphere, during exceptional circumstances when events can be experienced as a manifestation of the sacred, when they can be an individual or collective experience of the *numinosa*, and can develop into beliefs and myths connected to the secular entity (the nation, the state, the revolution, or war), which then becomes perceived as a fascinating and terrifying power. Furthermore, from the earliest times violence and sacredness have had a symbiotic relationship, as indeed have religion and war.[20] As regard the direct formation of a religious dimension in politics, it is possible to note, for instance, that the first manifestations of the sacralisation of politics, in the modern sense of the term, occurred during the American and French Revolutions, from which emerged the first religions of politics. Even the political religions of the totalitarian states emerged in the wake of the Great War and the Russian Revolution.

The *numinosa* interpretation of the sacralisation of politics derives from theories of the 'metamorphosis of the sacred' in modern society. According to Mircea Eliade, the experience of the sacred is by no means alien to the consciousness of modern human beings, who have by now freed themselves from ancient religious sentiment. This liberation, argues the religious historian, is for many modern people an illusion: 'this nonreligious man descends from *homo religiosus* and, whether he likes it or not, he is also the work of religious man; his formation begins with the situations assumed by his ancestors.'[21] The modern, non-religious human rebels against this past and seeks liberation from it. Nevertheless, writes Eliade, 'he is an inheritor. He cannot utterly abolish the past, since he is himself the product of his past,' adding:

> nonreligious man in the pure state is a comparatively rare phenomenon, even in the most desacralised of modern societies. The majority of the 'irreligious' still behave religiously, even though they are not aware of the fact ... the modern man who feels and claims that he is nonreligious still retains a large stock of camouflaged myths and degenerated rituals. ... Strictly speaking, the great majority of the irreligious are not liberated from religious behaviour, from theologies and mythologies ... In short, the majority of men 'without religion' still hold to pseudo-religions and degenerated mythologies. A purely rational man is an abstraction; he is never found in real life.

Many scholars of religion agree with this argument and maintain that the modern age is not one where an irreversible process of secularisation takes place, leading to the progressive disappearance of the sacred in an ever disenchanted world. In the age of secularisation, they maintain, the sacred has demonstrated a fierce tenacity with the persistence, and often the strengthening, of traditional religious beliefs, as well as with the growth in newer sects, movements and religious cults. Moreover, it appears that the sacred has found new areas in which to manifest in the modern era, thus giving life to numerous forms of secular religion.[22]

Modernity has not eliminated the problem of religion from the consciousness of modern man. In fact, precisely because it has been a radical, overwhelming and irreversible force for change that has swept away age-old collective beliefs and age-old, powerful institutions, modernity has created crisis and disorientation – situations which have, in turn, led to the re-emergence of the religious question, even if this has led the individual to turn not to traditional religion, but to look to new religions that sacralise the human. In-depth analysis of the spiritual conditions of the early twentieth century led the Italian philosopher Benedetto Croce to affirm that the problem of modernity, at the beginning of the twentieth century, was above all a religious problem. 'The entire contemporary world is again in search of a religion.' He went on:

> Religion is born of the need for orientation as regards life and reality, of the need for a concept that defines life and reality. Without religion, or rather without this orientation, either one cannot live, or one lives unhappily with a divided and troubled soul. Certainly, it is better to have a religion that coincides with philosophical truth, than a mythological religion; but it is better to have a mythological religion than none at all. And, since no one wishes to live unhappily, everyone in their own way tries to form a religion of their own, whether knowingly or unknowingly.[23]

The experience of the sacred, in other words, has not been exhausted by traditional religions, but has found its expression in the *sacralisation of the human* through history, philosophy, art, and, not least, through politics. From this point of view, the sacralisation of politics can be interpreted as a modern manifestation of the sacred. Modernity, because of its very nature, can be a matrix for new religions. Moreover, it was the great theorist of the disenchantment of the modern world who prophesied, in 1890, that the gods had not been definitively destroyed by the modern world, but had merely returned in a different guise: '*Die alten Götter, entzaubert und daher in Gestalt unpersönlicher Mächte, entsteigen ihren Gräbern, streben nach Gewalt über unser Leben und beginnen untereinander wieder ihren ewigen Kampf.*'[24]

Victims of a nightmare?

It is probable that, as has been the case with many of the concepts used by the human sciences, the study of secular religion will not lead to the development of definitions and interpretations that will be universally accepted among scholars. It is also likely that the controversy regarding the existence, or otherwise, of a secular religion will never be resolved. Nevertheless, whether one believes in a religious dimension to politics or not, it is clear that the fanaticism of the masses, enthusiasm for myths, the cult of the leader, the dogmatic nature of ideology, implacable hatred and organised cruelty have all been tragic enough realities of contemporary history. They have had dimensions so frightful, and have been associated with ideologies, political systems, historical traditions, economic, social and geographical situations so diverse as to constitute a large and highly complex phenomenon that is, because of its specific characteristics, peculiar to the twentieth century, and particularly to the interwar period. It is necessary to enquire into the nature and significance of this phenomenon, taking careful note of its newness and its specific nature, while also taking account of the fact that history, despite its abrupt fractures and sudden changes, remains, all the same, a perpetual flow between continuity and change, and a continual pouring of the past into the present, where the new frequently takes on the form of the old, and the old is permeated by the new.

The present writer by no means excludes the existence of secular religion and the religious dimension in politics. Moreover, in their interpretation of historical manifestations of the sacralisation of politics, none of the above-mentioned concepts (the *charlatanistic*, the functionalist, the need for belief and the *numinosa*) if taken separately, help reach an understanding of the phenomenon itself. For this reason, it is perhaps inevitable that, once the existence of secular religion has been established, each of the above theories might be applied with discretion in order to analyse it within specific contexts and with specific objectives in mind.

Assuming that it exists, a political religion, like any other religion, contains *charlatanistic* aspects, fulfils a legitimising function, satisfies the religious feelings of the masses and can be a sacred experience. It is the task of the scholar to examine each of these aspects and assess the extent to which they exist in any religious manifestation. Any prejudicial judgement along the lines of a single interpretation could lead to the entire phenomenon of political religion being viewed unilaterally, and this would invariably prevent any realistic understanding of its nature from being reached.

One can legitimately regard the religious dimension of politics as simply political and go on to assert that those who disagree are the victims of an illusion, namely, of 'a religion that doesn't exist'. If this was the case, the question would remain as to why, over the past 200 years, the number of victims of this 'illusion' has risen continually and became legion during the years between the two world wars. Furthermore, in referring to victims, one does not mean the leaders and practitioners of the various political religions who, clearly, from the time of the American Revolution onward, have been numerous and who became especially powerful during the twentieth century.

By victims one means those not involved in the sacralisation of politics, who were frequently opponents and critics, and for this reason were often victimised by political religions and, thus, if victims of an illusion were also the real victims of a 'religion that doesn't exist'. The majority of these individuals were practitioners and activists from mainstream traditional religions, theologians or lay scholars of the religious phenomenon, or leaders of their respective churches. All felt great anguish in the face of the triumphant progress of totalitarian religion, all issued unheeded warnings of the consequences, all foresaw new religious wars, and ultimately despaired for the future of Christian civilisation and of humanity as a whole, being terrorised at the prospect of an apocalyptic catastrophe that would result in the triumph of the Antichrist. Many who practised Christian faiths saw in totalitarian religion a diabolic astuteness that had seen Satan transformed into God in order to conquer humanity. These views were not only held by followers of traditional religious beliefs, but also by atheists and laymen, who regarded the war against Fascism and Nazism as a religious war.

Does all this amount to a case of mass hysteria? Were all of those who viewed totalitarianism as a new religion the naive victims of an illusion, who saw religions that did not exist or were they merely individuals whose ignorance did not permit them to understand what really constituted religion, and who confused appearance with reality? In short, is the sacralisation of politics the Loch Ness monster of contemporary history?

An affirmative answer to this last question would close the debate on the sacralisation of politics. But, from the moment that the ranks of those who believed in the illusion of a non-existent religion included sceptics such as Bertrand Russell, followers of religious faith and religious doctrine such as Jacques Maritain, learned theologians such as Adolf Keller and at least one pontiff, one cannot close the debate on secular religion by hurriedly concluding that it does not exist. One would still need to explain why many individuals, religious or lay, believers and non-believers, have for two centuries believed in the existence of a secular religion that has been manifested principally in the world of politics. Eric Voegelin and Raymon Aron are generally attributed with having introduced the concepts of political religion and secular religion into contemporary political analysis.[25] Certainly, they were among the first explicitly to define these concepts. But, both the use of the two terms and their application as concepts in the analysis of contemporary political phenomena predated Voegelin and Aron. In fact, both terms had already been employed by various scholars in their interpretations of the French Revolution, nationalism, Bolshevism and Fascism.[26]

The list of victims of the illusion of a 'religion that doesn't exist' goes far back in time to well before the totalitarian era. Among these victims one may certainly include Alexander De Tocqueville, the first real scholar of the sacralisation of politics. Indeed, he had been convinced that he had, through direct experience, established the existence of a civil religion among the American people and that he had analysed its origins, nature and function.[27] Moreover, he was convinced that the French Revolution had been a political revolution which had taken place in the form of a religious upheaval and led to the creation of a new form of religion. This had so much been the case that contemporaries were frightened by the fervour of the passions it aroused, by the enthusiasm it engendered and by the extent of the conversions it inspired among the masses. It was an imperfect religion, argued Tocqueville, because it was godless, without a cult and without an afterlife. Even so, it was as capable as Islam of flooding the earth with its soldiers, its apostles and its martyrs.[28]

The sacred in politics: from the democratic to the totalitarian revolutions

The sacralisation of politics, as defined above, has revolutionary, democratic and nationalist origins. Its roots are to be found in the culture of the Enlightenment, although it went on to evolve from the mid-eighteenth century right through the nineteenth and twentieth centuries, drawing from traditional Christianity tinged with millenarian culture, which in turn combined with the latest political ideas and culminated in the emergence of a new form of sacralised politics. This was precisely what happened during the American and French Revolutions, at which points the new revolutionary culture mixed with messianic and millenarian lay religion and led to the emergence of a political and civil religion. The first elaboration of the sacralisation of politics at a theoretical level occurred when Rousseau first conceived of a civil religion. Rousseau believed it necessary to establish a civil religion within a new modern state founded on principles of popular sovereignty, and a religion that would take the place of Christianity and thus join together 'the two eagles' heads' (namely, political and religious power) in order to achieve 'political unity, without which there will never exist either a government or a state that is well founded'.[29] The need to establish a civil religion for a democratic state came from the conviction that individuals living in society 'need a religion that sustains them',[30] because a people cannot live without religion. Both the American founding fathers and the French revolutionaries shared these ideas, and aimed to put them into practice.

The two democratic revolutions were the first concrete manifestations of the sacralisation of politics. Both conferred a religious dimension upon the world of politics by interpreting revolutionary events as messianic and millenarian, and by presenting them as the beginning of a new era for humanity. Furthermore, both the American and the French Revolutions, while markedly different in their conception of the relationship with the Christian tradition and traditional religion, more or less consciously attempted to set up a civil religion. The new civil religion based on the nation drew its ritualistic, symbolic and dramatic inspiration from the two democratic revolutions; the 'new politics', as George Mosse defined it, rapidly led to the nationalist affirmations of secular religion and to the birth of mass movements.[31] Lastly, the two democratic revolutions also provided the fundamental elements that make up the permanent mythical structure of the sacralisation of politics, and this has duly remained unaltered even by the most heterogeneous ideological adaptations. Here, one refers to the apocalyptic visions of the modernists, to the myth of personal and national regeneration through politics, and to the myth of an elected people whose mission it is to bear the new religion of salvation in the world. From this mythical structure, in part based on secularised biblical archetypes, came the idea of nationalism as the first secular religion of the modern era, an idea that went on to become the most enduring, if not the most universal, manifestation of sacralised politics in the contemporary world.[32] The myth of the nation and revolutionary faith became the driving force behind the sacralisation of politics over the 200 years that followed.[33]

During the nineteenth century the sacralisation of politics developed considerably under the influence of revolutionary creeds, messianic politics, theology and secular eschatological theories such as Hegelism, Marxism and the new human religions. The nineteenth century was littered with the prophets, founders, apostles and martyrs of new lay religions that sacralised the human, history, the nation, the revolution, society, art, sex, and so on. Figures such as Saint-Simon, Comte, Michelet, Mazzini and Marx were prophets and theologians of sacralised politics. In terms of revolutionary culture, the *sanctification of violence* as a sacred instrument of regeneration also became important, and became integrated into the sacralisation of politics by revolutionary movements of both the Left and Right. But equally important was the development of the ritualistic and symbolic aspects of sacralised politics. For example, various monarchies 'invented a tradition', and, in the second half of the century, attempted to renew the sense of sacredness in their power by adapting it to democratic politics by way of ceremonies and rituals that were effectively artificial and false. In reality, this contribution toward the sacralisation of politics, having assumed this form, was somewhat limited and had only an indirect influence, given that it remained a traditional aspect of the monarchic institution. Moreover, the legitimate presence of traditional religion, however it may have been modified, imposed a limitation on the transformation of traditional sacralised power into new sacralised politics. The latter remained, essentially, a revolutionary and democratic phenomenon, and, as a consequence, was more congenial to movements challenging the traditional sacred power of the monarchy by exalting the sacredness of the nation or the people. Much closer to the idea of sacralised politics were the symbolic and ceremonial apparatus of the newer states, the national festivals and the diffusion of institutionalised symbolism through architecture, urban development and state monuments. Even in these cases, however, this did not always result in any increase in the process of sacralising politics. The lay, rationalist and individualist political culture of many within the governing elite often created an obstacle, and they often balked at the idea of establishing a new religion, even if it was a civil, national religion, fearing that it might result in the perpetuation of irrational superstition and would prevent the emancipation of the individual. Another obstacle was the incapacity to establish, or the conscious aversion to, a system of rituals and symbols, destined to transform the occasional crowds into a liturgical mass, through the use of demagogic instruments or through the imitation of those traditional religions against which lay and liberal culture had rebelled in the name of reason and liberty. If many of the leaders of liberal states deemed it necessary to educate the individual citizen on the cult of the 'national religion', the only legitimate instruments available to them were the school and the army. This explains why, despite a considerable increase in the ritual, symbolic and mythical apparatus of the nineteenth-century state, its contribution toward the sacralisation of politics was limited, although totalitarian regimes later adapted and transformed this apparatus and made use of it to establish their own political religion.

The evolution of sacralised politics received a boost with the emergence of mass movements that made considerable use of traditional religious forms and new rituals and symbols, thus giving birth to a new belief relationship between the masses and their leaders. Above all, these new movements gave a strong impetus to the creation of absolute myths around those secular entities that lay at the heart of their ideology, as well as to a sense that dedicated political militancy should absorb the militant completely, thereby becoming both a *raison d'être* and a lifestyle. It is significant that at the end of the nineteenth century sociologists began to speak of the emergence of new religions such as socialism. It was even more significant that it was the very protagonists of these movements who conceived of them as manifestations of a new secular religion, and who hoped that followers would adopt a mentality and spirit normally associated with traditional religion. Sorel and his theory on the myth of sacralised politics was, from this point of view, particularly prolific. The militants who formed part of revolutionary movements, although proclaiming their supposed atheism, readily likened their own movement to a religion so as to define their conception of politics as an integralist experience and as a force for total regeneration that would lead to the creation of a new civilisation and a new humanity. In this way, they, too, helped lay the foundations for the sacralisation of politics. Mussolini, the atheist socialist, believed in 'a religious conception of socialism'.[34] Even more categorical was Antonio Gramsci, who, in 1916, proclaimed that socialism 'is precisely that religion that must destroy Christianity. Religion in the sense that it too is a faith, that has its mystics and practitioners; and religion because it has substituted the idea of the transcendental God of the Catholics with faith in man and in his superior power as a single spiritual reality.'[35] But, at the same time, one should not undervalue the contribution, albeit indirect, that the early modernist movement made to the sacralisation of politics with their search for a new religion as a means of totally rebuilding life, a spiritual revolution, the wait for a great catastrophe that would regenerate mankind, and their invocation of the new man and the Messiah. They, too, like their revolutionary counterparts, sanctified violence as the sacred instrument for the regeneration of humanity.

At the beginning of the twentieth century, the most decisive impulse toward the sacralisation of politics was provided by the First World War, and, in various ways, the war itself generated new material for the construction of political religions of which the totalitarian movements made much use. Above all, the war contributed to the politicisation of traditional religions which, in nearly every country, offered their support in the holy war against the Antichrist and dedicated themselves to the sanctification of the nation. Each of the combatant countries proclaimed that God was on the side of its soldiers in order to help them secure victory in the name of civilisation and humanity. The war itself became interpreted as a great apocalyptic and regenerating event desired by God, thereby legitimising the use of violence in order to achieve the triumph of good. This contributed considerably to the sacralisation of the ideologies involved in the conflict. Wartime propaganda created images of the enemy as the incarnation of evil and, connected to this, also created the image of the internal enemy who had taken root within the nation, was, indeed, a part of the nation, but did not belong to it because this enemy failed to accept its sacredness and did not venerate it with absolute and loyal dedication. Moreover, the experience of mass death, witnessed for the first time by millions of men, reawakened religious sentiments and generated new forms of secular religion tied directly to the experience of the war. The symbolism of death and resurrection, dedication to the nation, the mystic qualities of blood and sacrifice, the cult of heroes and martyrs, the 'communion' offered by camaraderie, all of this led to the diffusion among the combatants of ideas of politics as a total experience, and, therefore, a religious experience that would renew all aspects of existence. The cult of the fallen was probably the most universal manifestation of the sacralisation of politics in the twentieth century. In each country that fought in the conflict, the sacredness of the nation was felt most intensely during the years of the Great War. On the other hand, the Great War, a war that had disproportionately increased the power of the state over society and the destiny of the individual, was also interpreted negatively as an expression and a consequence of a 'secular religion' that, ever since the emergence of the concept of the secular state, had deified that state as the supreme authority. As Luigi Sturzo noted in December 1918:

> The defeat of Germany revealed the practical absurdity of the concept of the pantheistic state that subjects everything to its own force, the internal and external world, man and his *raison d'être*, social forces and human relationships: in the deification of force and absolute power as a substitute for reason and the greatF purpose of the spirit.
>
> This pantheistic conception penetrated more or less all liberal and democratic civilised nations as well as the ideas that prevailed on public rights: and those that challenged the religious authority of the church denied any collective spiritual problem and substituted the church with a new secular religion, that of the absolute sovereign state, the dominating and binding force, the moral authority, the uncoercible power, the single synthesis of the collective will.[36]

Fascism and Nazism, the offspring of the war, derived the spiritual dimension of their politics primarily from the experience of war, although within the ranks of the totalitarian formations also came together various experiences of sacralised politics that already existed and had been built up for centuries, and from which the totalitarian religions drew much inspiration and welcomed with open arms. Within the realm of the sacralised politics that had been influenced by the Great War can also be included the experience of the Bolshevik Revolution, which had been nourished by Marxist eschatological vigour and by Russian millenarian traditions. However, all of this does not mean that the totalitarian religions formed part of an inevitable process. In other words, the totalitarian religions and, generally speaking, the totalitarianisms of the twentieth century are not descendants of the sacralised politics of the French Revolution, as has been stressed by various scholars: they were new political religions that emerged from the Great War and the Russian Revolution, even if they contained pre-existing currents and had been influenced by earlier experiences of the sacralisation of politics, whether ideological or practical, that had prepared the ground upon which the totalitarian religions quickly took root.

Totalitarian religions

Fascism can probably be credited with the deplorable responsibility for having been the prototype for totalitarian religions, and, therefore, for having been, in part, the model for the others. In fact, Fascism was the first political movement of the twentieth century that:

(a) Openly proclaimed itself as being a political religion, affirmed the *primacy of faith* and the *primacy of the myth* in the political militancy of the individual and the masses, and explicitly appealed to the irrational as a politically mobilising force.
(b) Brought mythical thought into power, declaring officially that this was the only form of collective political conscience suitable for the masses, who were incapable, by their very nature, of any form of self-government.
(c) Consecrated the figure of the *charismatic leader* as the interpreter of the national consciousness and the fundamental pivot of the totalitarian state.
(d) Prescribed an obligatory code of *ethical commandments* for the citizen and instituted a collective *political liturgy* in order to celebrate the *deification of the state* and the *cult of the leader*.

Various Italian democratic anti-Fascists quickly realised that there was an intrinsic connection within Fascism between the sacralisation of politics and the embryonic totalitarian party-state, as it had been defined ever since 1923. On 1 April 1923, the anti-Fascist newspaper *Il Mondo* wrote:

> A party can aspire to dominate public life, but it should never invade the individual private consciousness within which everyone has the right to seek refuge. Yet Fascism has not simply aimed to govern Italy, but has also sought to monopolise control of the Italian consciousness. Fascism is not satisfied with having power: it also wants to possess the private consciousness of each and every citizen, it wants to 'convert' all Italians ... Fascism has pretensions toward being a religion ... moreover Fascism has the supreme ambition and inhuman intransigence of a religious crusade. It will not allow happiness to the unconverted, it does not permit a way out for those who will not be baptised.

During the same period, foreign travellers who found themselves in Italy at the moment when Fascism came to power were immediately struck by its religious characteristics. In 1924, a French journalist likened the mysticism and revolutionary spirit of Fascism to Jacobinism, and made an accurate comparison between the symbols and rituals of the two revolutions. The journalist also identified the many elements both had in common with political religion, for example, rituals, symbols, and the mentality of this new *'religion civique'*.[37]

In the meantime, even if, chronologically speaking, Bolshevism preceded Fascism, and was considered to be a new religion before Fascism, it was the latter that constituted the first totalitarian experiment that showed evidence of having the characteristics of sacralised politics in the most explicit, elaborate and conscious way. While Bolshevism continued to emphasise its atheistic nature, its hatred for religion and a determination to extinguish all forms of religious belief within the new Soviet man, Bolshevism did not officially define itself as a political religion. Nor did it ever proclaim, as both Fascism and Nazism had done, that it wanted to exercise a religious type of influence over the masses, despite certain initiatives, scorned by Lenin, being taken by older disciples, such as Lunacharsky, that aimed at establishing socialism as a religion of man.[38] Nevertheless, at least to the eyes of foreign observers, Bolshevism also amounted to a political religion, not only because it had established the Lenin cult, but for the way in which it conceived of, and practised, politics.

Bolshevism was, in fact, considered to be a new religion, similar to Islam, from at least the 1920s onward. However, it is important to stress that this comparison had not been made by an anti-Communist. Bertrand Russell had proclaimed himself a Communist in 1920 when, after a journey to Bolshevik Russia, the British philosopher, showing considerable sympathy toward the new revolutionary regime, affirmed that Bolshevism was a religion similar to Islam, and judged this religious characteristic to be one of its negative aspects.[39] Neither did John Maynard Keynes prove prejudicially hostile toward the new Soviet Russia when, in 1925, he defined Leninism as a new religion. His definition is worth citing in full because it contains elements useful for an analysis of the sacralisation of politics:

> Like other new religions, Leninism derives its power not from the multitudes but from a small number of enthusiastic converts whose zeal and intolerance make each one the equal in strength of a hundred indifferentists. Like other new religions, it is led by those who can combine the new spirit, perhaps sincerely, with seeing a good deal more than their followers, politicians with at least an average dose of political cynicism, who can smile as well as frown, volatile experimentalists, released by religion from truth and mercy, but not blind to facts and experience, and open therefore to the charge (superficial and useless though it is where politicians, lay or ecclesiastical, are concerned) of hypocrisy. Like other new religions, it seems to take the color and gaiety and freedom out of everyday life and offer a drab substitute in the square wooden faces of its devotees. Like other new religions, it persecutes without justice or pity those who actively resist it. Like other new religions, it is unscrupulous. Like other new religions, it is filled with missionary ardor and ecumenical ambitions. But to say that Leninism is the faith of a persecuting and propagating minority of fanatics led by hypocrites is, after all, to say no more or less than that it *is* a religion, and not merely a party, and Lenin a Mahomet, and not a Bismarck.[40]

These early impressions of the religious characteristics of the new totalitarian movements were followed, during the 1930s, by more elaborate interpretations that could take full advantage of the increasing diffusion of the sacralisation of politics in Europe at that time. Above all, observers could analyse Nazism, which, in a new and specific way that separated it from other totalitarian movements, added a strong pagan component to the concept of sacralised politics which centred on the sacredness of blood and race. Furthermore, the specific nature of Nazism did not prevent it from being inserted in the sacralisation of politics alongside other totalitarian religions, with which it had much in common. In the identification of the aspects that separated totalitarianism from traditional forms of dictatorship or authoritarian rule, much was made of its religious aspects: the sacralisation or messianic deification of the state, the nation, the race, and the proletariat; the systematic use of symbols and collective rituals; the fanatical dedication and the implacable hatred for adversaries demonstrated by militants; the faithful enthusiasm of the masses; and the cult of the leader. It is interesting to note that in many analyses of totalitarianism in the 1930s, the religious dimension of politics was given far more significance than violence or terror, which were not considered as essential elements of totalitarianism, but, rather, as the inevitable consequences of their conception of political religion. The categories with which one explains the religious (or pseudo-religious) nature of totalitarianism are the same as those used in the analysis of secular religion. Gaetano Salvemini, for instance, offered a *charlatanistic* interpretation of the mythical and ritualistic aspects of Fascism and Communism:

> Within the modern dictatorship God occupies an uncertain place. Until now Pius XI has certified only that Mussolini has been sent 'by divine Providence'. It is possible that one day Hitler too might receive similar approval from the Holy See. One who can never aspire to such approval is the unbeliever Stalin. But even he has his bible, his source of infallible inspiration: *Das Kapital*.

> Whether or not they are cornerstones of divine inspiration, each dictator proclaims himself to be infallible. 'Mussolini is always right.' And the 'elected few' that the dictator favours from on high are as infallible as him.

> The dictator and his 'elected few' are 'the state'. ... He who is convinced that he possesses the secret of how to make man happy and virtuous and heads a party that declares him to be infallible, must always be prepared to kill. ... The dictator declares 'I am in the right, and the results of my activity will always be positive'; 'either with me or against me'; 'everything lies within the state, nothing lies outside the state, nothing lies against the state'; who opposes the state goes against the law. ... Any system under which all decisions are made on high, and where the fundamental duty and only virtue of the citizen is blind obedience, is forced to impose on its followers a more or less total intellectual abdication. It does not, therefore, appeal to the intellect and to logic but to that obscure region of the spirit of each man and woman that excludes intellect and logic. Dictators have need of myths, symbols and ceremonies in order to regiment, exalt and frighten the multitudes and suffocate their every attempt

to think. The fantastic and pompous ceremonies and mysterious rites in a strange language of the Catholic Church are masterpieces of their kind that both Fascists and Communists imitate when, by way of their mass demonstrations, they appeal to the irrational instincts of the crowd.[41]

Among anti-capitalist, non-Marxist observers, the most recurring interpretation was *functionalist*, and referred particularly to the connection between the sacralisation of politics and the need to organise the masses within a totalitarian state so as to control and mobilise it in order to achieve imperialist expansion. Paul Tillich argues that the sacralisation of politics on the part of Fascism and Nazism was undertaken in order to restore the capitalist system.[42] The concentration of power, and the conquest and control of society, were only possible if legitimised by a new concept of the world able to dominate and involve the whole human being:

> Such a world-view is religious in character and the more inclusive the claims of the state are, the more fundamental and powerful must be the myth, which is the foundation of such claims. ... When the totalitarian tendencies are more powerful, new myths are required in order to provide the basis for the struggle and for reconstruction. ... This is the totalitarian state, born out of the insecurity of historical existence during the epoch of late capitalism and designed, through national concentration, to create security and reintegration. ... It has received mystic consecration and stands, not merely as the earthly representative of God, as Hegel conceived it, but actually as God on earth.[43]

On the other hand, *numinosa* interpretations of political religion were the domain of the philosopher Adriano Tilgher, who was especially interested in the phenomenon of lay religion. He noted, in 1936, that after the First World War divine sentiment had 'focused on new subjects: the state, the country, the nation, race, class, those bodies in need of defence from mortal sin or those bodies from which much was expected':

> The post-war period witnessed one of the most prodigious eruptions of pure *numinosità* that had ever been seen in the history of the world. With our own eyes we helped give birth to new divinities. One needed to be blind and dumb to reality not to have noticed that for many, indeed very many, of our contemporaries, state, country, nation, race, class are not simply the subject of enthusiastic exaltation, but of mystic adoration, they are divine expressions because they are felt immeasurably to transcend everyday life, and as such arouse all the bipolar and ambivalent feelings that form part of the divine: love and terror, fascination and fear, and they generate an impetus for mystic adoration and dedication. ... The twentieth century promises to contribute more than one interesting chapter to the history of religious war (a chapter the nineteenth century believed closed): here is a prophesy that is in danger of being fulfilled.[44]

Increasingly, more and more interpretations associated the origins and success of totalitarian religions with a mass need for belief, which capable demagogues such as Mussolini and Hitler knew how to satisfy by making use of modern propaganda techniques. The need for belief on the part of the masses was sharpened by the traumatic experiences they had experienced in a very short space of time: the devastation wrought by the First World War, the revolutionary atmosphere of the postwar period, not to mention the devastating effects of the economic and social crisis that befell the capitalist system at the end of the 1920s. It would seem to be the case, wrote the jurist Gerhard Leibholz in 1938,[45] that 'today the powerful need to believe in and live transcendental moments' and that this found its expression in the new totalitarian states that presented themselves as new forms of religion, as 'immediate instruments of God'. This also took place in Russia, where 'the class phenomenon has been enveloped by an orthodox, mythical mass faith, that has its own distinct cult and rituals and – even if Asiatic in nature – constitutes a sort of surrogate political religion'. According to Leibholz, the totalitarian states were expressions of the era of the masses, an era dominated by the mythical and by the irrational, the means by which the masses expressed their need for faith. Totalitarianism was a development of the tendency toward 'confessional politics', as Leibholz described it in 1933 in his analysis of the destruction of German liberal democracy. The crisis in the rational, fundamental elements of parliamentary democracy led to the rebirth of metaphysical politics, of new politico-religious faiths of which both Fascism and Bolshevism were expressions.[46]

In effect, what observers opposed to totalitarian political religions found most disconcerting was the fascination and power that was emitted by irrational totalitarian myths. Irrationality and myth had become a potent political means of mobilising the masses in that they conferred upon totalitarianism the suggestive power of a new religion, and a power animated by the fanatical passion of new believers who wanted to conquer and transform the world, at the same time conquering and transforming minds. They were, therefore, determined to possess human minds and bodies and insert them within compact organisations that absorbed the individual within the masses and shaped them according to the will of new secular divinities. For the Swiss ecumenist Adolf Keller,[47] the advent of totalitarian religions such as Bolshevism, Fascism and Nazism, amounted to a *continental revolution* that threatened to destroy the moral and cultural mores of Christian civilisation in order to create a new religious civilisation based on the deification of the state, something that became embodied in the person of the *Duce*:

> The State itself has become a myth ... The State is a mythical divinity which, like God, has the right and might to lay a totalitarian claim on its subjects; to impose upon them a new philosophy, a new faith; to organise the thinking and conscience of its children ... It is not anonymous, not abstract, but gifted with personal qualities, with a mass-consciousness, a mass-will and a personal mass-responsibility for the whole world. The State in this myth acts like a superhuman giant, claiming not only obedience,

but confidence and faith such as only a personality has the right to expect. The nation is a kind of personal 'She', wooed and courted by innumerable lovers. This personifying tendency of the myth finds its strongest expression in the mysterious personal relationship of millions with a leader. A mystical personalism has got hold of the whole political and social imagination of great peoples. The leader, the Duce, is the personified nation, a superman, a messiah, a saviour.[48]

Keller immediately recognised the reality of the new totalitarian religions, and the power of their myths to provoke an inevitable mortal confrontation, an apocalyptic war, between totalitarianism and Christianity. Among the totalitarian enemies of Christian civilisation Keller included Italian Fascism, considering the concordat between Fascism and the Catholic Church to be no more than an opportunistic tactic on the part of Mussolini that left untouched the roots of future conflict. Despite the Lateran Accords, noted the Catholic jurist Marcel Prélot in 1936, there persisted a latent tension between Catholicism and Fascism, although he did not believe that Italy would ever witness the emergence of totalitarian neo-paganism, as many ardent Fascists hoped.[49]

The intrinsic connection between totalitarianism and political religion was the subject of analysis by various Italian anti-Fascists. As early as 1924, a militant of the Catholic *Partito popolare italiano* denounced the dangers posed by 'Fascist religion' that with 'its totalitarian, egocentric and all absorbing soul' aimed to transform the church into a political instrument.[50] In the years that followed, condemnations of totalitarian religion became increasingly frequent and vigorous, and explicitly attacked Nazism and Communism. Indirectly, such condemnations were also levelled at Italian Fascism by the Catholic press and by the church, which condemned the worship of the state, the deification of the nation, the cult of the leader, the exaltation of mythical thought and totalitarianism. Clearly, the presence of Catholicism in Italy acted as a brake against the conquest of society by Fascism. Yet, it was a brake that slowed, but did not halt, the ambitions of 'Fascist religion', which aimed to extend its dominion and control over body and soul; so much so that it did not satisfy the church and those Catholics that had not been seduced by the temptations of Fascism. Condemnations, nearly always indirect, against the sacralisation of politics on the part of Fascism intensified at precisely that moment when antagonism between the two religions seemed at a low ebb. *La Civiltà Cattolica* attacked ever more frequently, and with increasing vigour, the development of 'religions manipulated by man'.[51] One of the paper's frequent contributors condemned 'lay religion' founded on the cult of the nation and a mythical, political faith that humanised the divine and made divinities out of humans, and that at the same time demanded 'the total dedication of the will' toward an earthly entity and deified the nation and the state to which the individual was completely subordinated. 'In this way,' concluded the Catholic paper, 'politics becomes transformed into a lay religion that is so demanding as to expect each man to give himself entirely over to it, thereby denying him even the use of his own reason.'[52]

In the face of totalitarian religion, and especially the Nazi variant, Catholics spoke of neopaganism, idolatry, and, above all, of the deification of the state. In 1940, a Catholic university journal regarded the spread of 'sinister modern religions' as the 'final astute action of the devil' that 'conferred upon irreligion the pathos and religious fascination of revolutionary emancipation'.[53] By so doing, Catholics recognised the real existence of new forms of religion, each of which, in common with the others, were founded on the deification of man. This subsequently became translated into the deification of the state, nation, race and proletariat. The problem of totalitarian religions, according to Catholic interpretations, was only a single aspect of the much larger phenomenon of the re-emergence of paganism and idolatry which were the essence of modern lay ideas that, in all their cultural and political manifestations, denied the existence of God and deified man. The sacralisation of politics was the consequence of a single, continuous and uninterrupted process of modern man's distancing himself from God and true religion that had begun at the start of the Renaissance and with the fragmentation of Christian unity provoked by the Reformation, and continued, with devastating fury, to spread to every social and moral aspect of life through the French Revolution, liberalism, nationalism, socialism, and culminated in the totalitarian religions of Communism, Fascism and Nazism. Fascist and Communist totalitarianisms, argued Jacques Maritain in 1936, the sons of humanist idolatry and the product of the radical crisis within lay and capitalistic society, promised salvation and demanded 'of the earthly community the same Messianic love with which one should love God'.[54] Maritain insisted that totalitarianism was religious in nature, although he admitted that the totalitarian principle was, intrinsically, founded on atheism even when it professed faith in God:

> There is an atheism that declares God to be non-existent and makes an idol its God; and there is an atheism that declares that God does exist, but makes God an idol because it denies with its actions, if not with its own words, the nature and attributes of God and his glory; it invokes God but as the protector of the glory of a people or state against all others.[55]

Communism, although proclaiming itself atheistic, in reality had transformed atheism into a religion, even though it did not admit to having done so, and did not even realise it: an 'earthly religion based entirely and exclusively on achieving earthly ends', but, nevertheless, still a religion because it was as able to inspire a sense of sacredness, of faith, of dedication, of fanaticism, intransigence and intolerance as were the totalitarian religions. 'Communism is so profoundly, so substantially a religion – an earthly religion – that it ignores the fact that it is one.'[56]

Conclusions

The subject of totalitarian religions, and, more generally, the problem of the sacralisation of politics, has only in the past ten years become the focus of systematic and in-depth analysis. Consequently, it is an area that is open to contrasting ideas and interpretations. At the risk of oversimplification, one might say that even the latest interpretations follow closely in the wake of those that appeared at the same time as political movements with religious characteristics began to emerge. Did these movements merely appear to be religious or, rather, were they religious phenomena, that is, a new secular religion?

It is appropriate, in reaching conclusions, however provisional, on the sacralisation of politics and on interpretations of totalitarian religions, to tackle the question of the existence of secular religion. While brief, this analysis of the interpretations that emerged as the various totalitarian experiments got underway during the interwar period, has demonstrated the seriousness with which the religious dimension of totalitarian politics has been examined by those who did not underestimate the danger of political movements that took on the form of fanatical and integralist new religions. The question might be asked as to whether these individuals were the victims of a nightmare.

It is not easy to conclude, having absorbed the various conclusions reached on the sacralisation of politics during the interwar years, that there did not exist a religious dimension to totalitarian politics, and that all that took place can be attributed to the more concrete and prosaic motivation of material interests and unscrupulous demagoguery. While one may remain sceptical about all types of religious manifestations, and especially when one, as an historian, lives among the protagonists, witnesses and victims of totalitarian religion, it is still possible to agree with those contemporary scholars who maintained that there was a direct connection between totalitarianism and political religion, and that this connection constituted the most dangerous and deadly weapon in the totalitarian arsenal. Whether one judges totalitarianism to be a political religion or not, it remains beyond doubt that the various totalitarianisms were driven by the fanaticism of those who believed themselves to belong to an elite community; who arrogated for themselves the privilege to define the meaning and objectives of existence for millions of people; who believed themselves uniquely qualified to distinguish between good and evil; and who, consequently, acted with implacable and ruthless violence to eliminate from 'good' society those 'evil' elements that threatened and corrupted it, and prevented it from becoming a single and homogenous body politic. It is also beyond doubt that despite this, and perhaps because of it, totalitarian movements, with their myths, their rituals and their capacity to mobilise collective enthusiasm, exercised enormous powers of suggestion and attraction over both the individual and the masses. For those historians who study political religions, the fundamental question is not to ask whether the architects of totalitarian experiments were themselves true believers, whether the enthusiasm generated by their myths was genuine or manipulated, or even whether their actions amounted to a coherent translation of their ideology and faith. In the final analysis, no religion can undergo such analysis, however distant it might be from the political process and however close it might be to purity, without being immediately deemed a pseudo-religion if it contains demagogic elements and a certain incoherence between belief and behaviour. According to Raffaele Pettazzoni, an eminent scholar of religion, a religion can be true or false for a believer, 'but not for the historian, who, as an historian, does not recognise false religions or real religions, but only different religious forms within which religion develops'.[57]

The historian of political religions must study the origins, development, activities, reactions to and results of the totalitarian experiments that were undertaken in the name of politics lived and experienced as a religion. This is what I have set out to do in my studies of Fascism, while at the same time seeking to clarify the main guiding precepts and the environment within which it operates, often by taking the same path as those who lived as protagonists, witnesses or victims.

The sacralisation of politics is a complex subject, far too complex to be discussed adequately within the confines of a single article. If we link it to another, equally complex theme, totalitarianism, the risk of appearing dogmatic and summary in one's judgements and conclusions increases substantially. While aware of this risk, the present writer has aimed to define the terms of the questions raised, but has not attempted to provide definitive answers to them. The controversy over the existence, or otherwise, of the phenomenon that can be defined as 'secular religion' or 'the sacralisation of politics' is not close to being resolved. Discussing the possible existence of a religious dimension to politics is not the same as discussing the possibilities of life on Venus. Nevertheless, one should be equally prudent in analysing similar subjects, as Hans Maier and Phillip Burrin have maintained, and as I myself have realised when researching into the sacralisation of politics in Fascist Italy.[58] Moreover, the very expansion of research activity that has looked into civil religion and political religion has confirmed the need for great critical awareness when using these terms, thereby avoiding generalisation, vagueness and discrimination. At the same time, this expansion has also confirmed the value of studying modern political phenomena that demonstrate religious characteristics as a way of conceiving and practising politics.

It should be pointed out, even if it seems obvious, that viewing a political movement as a secular religion does not necessarily suggest that this constitutes the only explanation of its nature and historical significance. Political religion is one element of totalitarianism, not the principal element and not even the most important in defining its essence. It might be remembered that within the term 'political religion' it is the word 'political' that has dominated history, and should, therefore, prevail in historiographical and theoretical analysis. Drawing attention to the characteristics of totalitarianism as political religion does not signify that one will find the key to understanding the nature of totalitarianism in the sacralisation of politics. This remains a wholly open question.

At the beginning of this article we noted that all totalitarianisms, in one way or another, are incomplete, imperfect and ultimately flawed experiments. In fact, in no totalitarian system was the monopoly of power total; control over society was never total; the anthropological revolution never effectively produced a new type of human being that corresponded to the intended model; political religion never transformed the masses into a community of believers.

This evaluation does not, however, contrast with the discussion of totalitarian political religion set out in this article. Maintaining that, historically speaking, no totalitarian experiment can be defined as 'perfect' or 'complete', and that no political religion proved lasting and capable enough truly to transform enthusiasm into conviction, does not mean that totalitarianism never existed or that totalitarian religions were mere iridescent 'bars of soap'.

The laboratories where the various totalitarian experiments took place were built and came into operation during the interwar period and had the objective of transforming society, creating a new type of human being, and building a new civilisation. Certainly, no totalitarian movement brought this experiment to a successful conclusion in terms of the proscribed objectives, and none of them, even in the most favourable of circumstances, could ever have succeeded, for the simple reason that such experiments are fundamentally flawed as a result of the very objectives they hoped to achieve.

These very experiments were undertaken in real terms by individuals, driven by experimental urges, who wanted them to be successful, and regardless of the human cost. After all, the architects of these experiments considered themselves to be the possessors of the science of good and evil, and they declared that the experiment, in itself, was the good, indeed, the search for the good: however high the cost might be in human terms, it was a legitimate price to pay for achieving good. Thus, totalitarian experiments, even if they were imperfect and flawed, involved, conditioned, transformed, deformed and ended the existence of millions of human beings. In no uncertain terms, this was determined by the conviction of the principal protagonists that they were the forebears of a new humanity, the builders of a new civilisation, the interpreters of a new truth, the repositories for the discrimination between good and evil, and the masters of the destinies of those caught up in their enterprise.

Totalitarianism failed, and totalitarian religions left in their wake millions of innocent victims sacrified to fanaticism. But all this should not disguise the fact that when they were triumphant they had the power to attract and the suggestive influence of new religions. They effectively generated fanatical enthusiasm and apocalyptic terror, ferocious cruelty and implacable hatred, the hope of salvation and the sentence of death.

Acknowledgements

This article was translated by Robert Mallett and is part of a book *Le religioni della politica fra democrazie e totalitarismi* (forthcoming by Laterza, Roma Bari).

NOTES

1 For more detail on totalitarianism and the sacralisation of politics under Fascism, see E. Gentile, *Le origini dell'ideologia fascista* (Rome and Bari: 1975); *id.*, *Il mito dello Stato nuovo* (Rome and Bari: 1982); *id.*, *Storia del partito fascista, 1919–1922. Movimento e milizia* (Rome and Bari: 1989); *id.*, 'Fascism as Political Religion',

Journal of Contemporary History 25 (1990), pp.229–51; *id.*, *Il culto del Littorio. La sacralizzazione della politica nell'Italia fascista* (Rome and Bari: 1993), English translation, *The Sacralisation of Politics in Fascist Italy* (Cambridge, MA: 1996); *id.*, *La via italiana al totalitarismo. Il partito e lo Stato nel regime fascista* (Rome: 1995). For a definition of Fascism as totalitarianism and political religion, see E. Gentile, 'El fascismo y la via italiana al totalitarismo', in M. Pérez Ledesma (ed.), *Los riesgos para la democracia. Fascismo y neofascismo* (Madrid: 1997), pp. 17–35.

2 A great number of works on totalitarianism and secular religion have emerged in recent years. See: H. Maier and M Scäfer (eds.), *Totalitarismus und Politische Religionen* (Paderborn: 1997); P. Brooker, *The Faces of Fraternalism. Nazi Germany, Fascist Italy and Imperial Japan* (Oxford: 1991); D. Bosshart, *Politische Intellektualität und totalitäre Erfahrung. Haupströmungen der französischen Totalitarismuskritik* (Berlin: 1992); J. Thrower, *Marxism-Leninism of Soviet Society. God's Commissar* (Lewiston: 1992); A. Piette, *Les religiosités séculières* (Paris: 1993); H. Maier, *Politische Religionen. Die totalitären Regime und das Christentum* (Frieburg: 1995); R. Moro, 'Religione e politica nell'eta della secolarizzazione riflessioni su di un recente volume di Emilio Gentile', *Storia Contemporanea* (April 1995), pp. 255–324; A. Elorza, *La religione politica* (Donostia-San Sebastian: 1996); S. Behrenbeck, *Der Kult um die toten Helden. Nationalistiche Mythen, Riten und Symbolie, 1923 bis 1945* (Neuburg a.d. Donau: 1996); A.J. Klinghoffer, *Red Apocalypse. The Religious Evolution of Soviet Communism* (Lanham: 1996); M. Ley and J.H. Schoeps, *Der Nationalsocialismus als politische Religionen* (Bodenheim: 1997); M. Ley, *Apokalypse und Moderne. Ausätze zu politischen Religionen* (Vienna: 1997); C.E. Bärsch, *Die politische Religionen des Nazionalsozialismus* (Munich: 1998); M. Huttner, *Totalitarismus und Säkulare Religionen. Zur Frügeschichte totalitarismuskritischer Begriffs-und Theoriebildung in GroBbritannien* (Bonn: 1999).

3 See S. Amir Arjomand (ed.), *The Political Dimensions of Religion* (New York: 1993); A. Elorza, *La Religión Politica* (Donostia-San Sebastian: 1996).

4 W. Stark, *The Sociology of Religion. A Study of Christendom*, Vol. 1 (London: 1966).

5 The complexity of this relationship is discussed in J.J. Linz, 'Der religiöse Gebrauch del Politik und/oder der politische Gebrauch der Religion. Ersatz-Ideologie gegen Ersatz Religion', in H. Maier (ed.), *Totalitarismus und Politische Religionen. Konzepte des Diktaturvergleichs* (Paderborn: 1996), pp. 129–54.

6 O. Ihl, *La fête républicaine* (Paris: 1996).

7 C.L. Albanese, *Sons of the Fathers. The Civil Religion of the American Revolution* (Philadelphia: 1976).

8 E. Gentile, *Il culto del Littirio* (note 1).

9 R.C. Wimberley, 'Testing the Civil Religion Hypothesis', *Sociological Analysis 37* (1976), pp. 341–52; C. Lane, *The Rites of Rulers* (Cambridge: 1972), pp. 42–4.

10 For discussion of political religion outside the context of European totalitarianism, see D.A. Apter, 'Political Religion in the New Nations', in C. Geertz (ed.), *Old Society and New States. The Quest for Modernity in Asia and Africa* (London: 1963), pp. 57–103.

11 A. Mathiez, *La theophilanthropie et le culte décadaire (1796–1801)* (Paris: 1903), p. 23.

12 O. Ihl (note 6), p. 39.

13 R. Bellah, 'Civil Religion in America', *Daedalus* 97/1 (1967), pp. 1–21; D.R. Cutler (ed.), *The Religious Situation, 1968* (Boston: 1968); E.A. Smith (ed.), *The Religion of the Republic* (Philadelphia: 1971); R.E. Richey and D.G. Jones (eds.), *American Civil Religion* (New York: 1974); G. Gherig, *American Civil Religion. An Assessment* (1979); M.W. Hughley, *Civil Religion and Moral Order. Theoretical and Historical Dimensions* (Westport: 1983); N. Lehmann de Silva, *Religião Civil do Estado Moderno* (Brasilia: 1985); R. Schieder, *Civil Religion. Die religiöse Dimension der politischen Kultur* (Gütersloh: 1987).

14 Compare R. Griffin, *The Nature of Fascism* (Oxford: 1991), pp. 29–32. See also, *id.*, *Fascism* (Oxford: 1995); id., *International Fascism. Theories, Causes and the New Consensus* (London: 1998). For other recent studies of the political religious aspects of Fascism, see R. Eatwell, *Fascism. A History* (London: 1995); S.G. Payne, *A History of Fascism, 1919–1945* (Madison: 1995); G.L. Mosse, *The Fascist Revolution. Toward a General Theory of Fascism* (New York: 1999).

15 G. Mosca, *Elementi di scienza politica. Volume I* (Bari: 1953) pp. 283–5.

16 On this, see R. Stark and W.S. Bainbridge, *The Future of Religion. Secularisation, Revival and Cult Formation* (Berkley: 1985), pp. 3–8.

17 E. Durkheim, *Les formes élémentaires de la vie religieuse* (Paris: 1985), pp. 49–53.

18 E.J. Hobsbawm and T. Ranger (eds.), *The Invention of Tradition* (Cambridge: 1983). On the functionalist concept of secular religion, see C. Rivière, *Les liturgies politiques* (Paris: 1988).

19 R. Otto, *Das Heilige. Über das Irrationale in der Idee des Göttlichen und sein Verhältnis zum Rationalen* (Munich: 1936).

20 R. Callois, *Quatre essais de sociologie contemporaine* (Paris: 1950); R. Girard, *La violence et le sacré* (Paris: 1972); P. Crépon, *Les religions et la guerre* (Paris: 1991); E. Gentile, 'Un'apocalisse della modernità. La Grande Guerra e il Mito della Rigenerazione della politica', *Storia Contemporanea* (October 1995), pp. 733–86.

21 M. Eliade, *The Sacred and the Profane* (San Diego: 1959), p. 203ff.

22 P.E. Hammond (ed.), *The Sacred in a Secular Age* (Berkley: 1985); J.A. Beckford (ed.), *New Religious Movements and Rapid Social Change* (London: 1986); G. Filoramo, *I nuovi movimenti religiosi. Metamorfisi del sacro* (Rome and Bari: 1986); C. Rivière and A. Piette (eds.), *Nouvelles idoles, nouveaux cultes. Dérives de la sacralité* (Paris: 1990); J.J. Wunenburger (ed.), *Le sacré* (Paris: 1990); G. Kepel, *La revanche de Dieu* (Paris: 1991); G. Filoramo, *Le vie del sacro. Modernità e religione* (Turin: 1994).

23 B. Croce, 'Per la rinascita dell'idealismo, 1908', in *Cultura e vita morale* (Bari: 1953), p. 35.

24 Cited in M. Ley, *Apokalypse und Moderne Aufsätze zu politischen Religionen* (Vienna: 1997), p. 12.

25 E. Voegelin, *Die politische Religionen* (Vienna: 1938); R. Aron, 'L'avenir des religions séculaires', in *L'ages des Empires et l'avenir de la France* (Paris: 1945), pp. 287–318.

26 For various interpretations of secular religion, see the works cited in note 2.

27 A. De Tocqueville, *La Democrazia in America* (Milan: 1983).

28 A. De Tocqueville, *L'Antico regime e la Rivoluzione* (Milan: 1981), Ch. 3.

29 J-J. Rousseau, *Scritti politici, Volume II*, M. Garin (ed.) (Bari: 1971), p. 198.

30 Ibid., p. 62.

31 G.L. Mosse, *The Nationalisation of the Masses. Political Symbolism and Mass Movements in Germany from the Napoleonic Wars Through the Third Reich* (New York: 1975).

32 C.J.H. Hayes, *Nationalism: A Religion* (New York: 1960).

33 J.L. Talmon, *The Origins of Totalitarian Democracy* (London: 1952); *id.*, *Political Messianism. The Romantic Phase* (London: 1960); *id.*, *The Myth of the Nation and the Vision of Revolution* (London: 1980); J.H. Billington, *Fire in the Minds of Men. Origins of the Revolutionary Faith* (New York: 1980).

34 Mussolini cited in Gentile, *Il mito dello Stato nuovo* (note 1).

35 A. Gramsci, *Cronache torinesi 1913–1917*, S. Caprioglio (ed.) (Turin: 1980), p. 329.

36 L. Sturzo, *I discorsi politici* (Rome: 1951), p. 388.

37 R. De Nolva, 'Le mysticisme et l'esprit révolutionaire du fascisme', *Mercure de France* (1 November 1924), pp. 650–67.

38 C. Lane, *The Rites of Rulers* (Cambridge: 1981); N. Tumarkin, *Lenin Lives* (Cambridge, MA: 1983); R. Stites, *Revolutionary Dreams* (New York: 1989).
39 B. Russell, *The Practice and Theory of Bolshevism* (London: 1920).
40 J.M. Keynes, *Essays in Persuasion* (New York: 1965), p. 4.
41 G. Salvemini, 'Il mito dell'uomo-dio', *Giustizia e Libertà* (20 July 1932).
42 P. Tillich, 'The Totalitarian State and the Church', *Social Research* (November 1934), pp. 405–32.
43 Ibid., pp. 415–16.
44 A. Tilgher, *Mistiche nuove e mistiche antiche* (Rome: 1946), pp. 47–56.
45 G. Leibholz, 'Il secolo XIX e lo Stato totalitario del presente', *Rivista internazionale di filosofia del diritto* (January–February 1938), pp. 1–40.
46 G. Leibholz, *Die Auflösung der liberalen Demokratie in Deutschland und das autoritäre Staatsbild* (Munich and Leipzig: 1933).
47 A. Keller, *Church and State on the European Continent* (London: 1936).
48 Ibid., pp. 56–9.
49 M. Prélot, *L'empire fasciste* (Paris: 1936).
50 I. Giordani, *Rivolta cattolica* (Turin: 1925), pp. 72–3.
51 A. Messineo, 'Chiesa e civiltà', *La Civiltà Cattolica* I (1940), p. 181.
52 A. Messineo, 'Il culto della nazione e la fede mitica', *La Civiltà Cattolica* III (1940), p. 212.
53 M. Campo, 'Torbide religiosità moderne', *Vita e pensiero* (November 1940).
54 J. Maritain, *Umanesimo integrale* (Rome: 1946), p. 215.
55 Ibid., p. 219.
56 Ibid., p. 40.
57 R. Pettazzoni, *Italia religiosa* (Bari: 1952), p. 7.
58 P. Burrin, 'Political Religion. The Relevance of a Concept', *History and Theory* 9/1–2 (1997), pp. 321–49; H. Maier, '"Politische Religionen" – Möglichkeiten und Grenzen eines Begriffs', in H. Maier and M. Schäfer (eds.), *Totalitarismus und Politische Religionen. Konzepte des Diktaturvergleichs*, Vol. II (Paderborn: 1997), pp. 299–310.

12

CLOISTER OR CLUSTER? THE IMPLICATIONS OF EMILIO GENTILE'S ECUMENICAL THEORY OF POLITICAL RELIGION FOR THE STUDY OF EXTREMISM

Roger Griffin

The revival of the theory of political religion has stirred significant mutations in the field of fascist studies, prompting researchers to take and even change sides in the emerging interdisciplinary debate. The most relevant example in this respect is that of Roger Griffin, who—after his initial explicit rejection of the political religion theory—has become one of its most ardent and innovative proponents. Griffin's change of heart over the issue reflects not only the evolution of his scholarly view on fascism, but also the remarkable dynamism of this field of study and the radical changes it has undergone in the past two decades.

In his 1991 monograph on fascism Griffin argued for the need to neatly distinguish between religious ideology, "which affirms the primacy of the metaphysical over the secular" and political ideology, which affirms the central role played by human agency in the transformation of society. Denouncing both the "abuse of religious concepts" by theorists of the political religion approach (Voegelin 1952; Sironneau 1982; Gentile 1990), and the "uncritical application" to fascism of concepts derived from the field of comparative religions (1991: 30–31), Griffin evaluated "political religion" as a "hybrid concept" and accepted it only to the extent its usage was restricted to denoting "a useful taxonomic sub-category of political ideology" referring to the "politically militant forms of an organized and revealed religion" (ibid.: 29, 30). To political religion, Griffin counterposed yet another hybrid concept, that of "religious politics," referring to "secular policies and tactics" which are "extensively rationalized in ostensibly religious terms, but in an essentially heretical, even blasphemous, spirit from the point of view of established orthodoxy" (ibid.: 30).

In his subsequent writings, however, Griffin expanded his framework of interpreting fascism by associating to his ideal-type of the ideological mythical core of "palingenetic and populist ultra-nationalism" a set of related concepts such as totalitarianism and—in a reconsideration of his earlier position—political religion. In this programmatic article, while continuing to reject Voegelin's concept of 'gnostic politics' (1952) as "heuristically dubious," Griffin fully adopts Emilio Gentile's multi-perspective theory of political religion centered on the concept of totalitarianism, regarding it as a possible integrative theoretical framework for studying fascism. Arguing in favor of clustering as a heuristically fruitful methodological strategy able "to offset pernicious forms of reductionist and dualistic thinking" in social sciences, Griffin praises Gentile for embedding totalitarianism "into a broad web or nexus of complementary, mutually reinforcing concepts, notably palingenetic ideology, political religion and anthropological revolution." He expands on Gentile's original cluster to encompass a wider sphere of related phenomena, such as the conquest of society, political domination, the monopoly of power, social engineering and social control, propaganda, mass organizations, state terror, ideological, social, cultural, eugenic, racial or ethnic cleansing, etc. Pointing out that these concepts have been too often treated as contradictory or even incompatible, Griffin pertinently pleads for more synergy in fascist studies based on syncretic and integrative, multi-tier theoretical perspectives.

Griffin's own writings have largely followed the programmatic research agenda he advocates in this article, focusing, among other topics, on totalitarianism (2002), political religions (2005) and more recently, fascism and modernism (2007), thus rounding out his scholarly view on fascism. Since 2000, Griffin has also served as a co-editor and the main driving force behind the new journal suggestively entitled Totalitarian Movements and Political Religions, *an innovative and highly dynamic academic forum of research and debate on the topic.*

BIBLIOGRAPHY

Gentile, E. (1990). "Fascism as Political Religion," *Journal of Contemporary History*, 25: 2–3.

Griffin, Roger (1991). *The Nature of Facism* (London: Pinter).

Griffin, Roger (2002). "The Palingenetic Political Community: Rethinking the Legitimization of Totalitarian Regimes in Inter-War Europe," *Totalitarian Movements and Political Religions* 3: 3, 24–43.

Griffin, Roger ed. (2005). *Fascism, Totalitarianism and Political Religion* (London: Routledge).

Griffin, Roger (2007). *Modernism and Fascism: The Sense of a Beginning under Mussolini and Hitler* (Houndmills: Palgrave Macmillan).

Sironneau, J. P. (1982). *Secularisation et religions politiques* (The Hague: Mouton).

Voegelin, E. (1952). *The New Science of Politics* (Chicago: University of Chicago Press).

* * *

Expanding political religion's conceptual cluster

One of the outstanding merits of Gentile's cluster approach to political religion over conventional, single-point perspective ones is that each 'star' that makes up the constellation can in turn be associated with its own cluster, thus locating it in an ever widening conceptual kinship, and revealing ever more nodal points of intersection with other historical realities. Already the definitional chapter in *The Religion of Politics* has created an instructive *Verfremdungseffekt* by locating political religion within an expanded cluster definition of *totalitarianism*. If we then 'zoom in' on some of its other 'kindred components' new linkages soon emerge. Our 'portal' for this brief reconnaissance of the diverse conceptual spaces that form round political religion will be what Gentile refers to as 'the objective of conquering society'.

When political religion is associated with the attempted *conquest of society* in direct association with *political domination* and the *monopoly of power*, these in turn summon up such concepts as *social engineering* and *social control*, which in the context of inter-war totalitarianism connote the pervasive use of state *propaganda*, the regimentation of youth and leisure in *mass organisations*, and, in the case of Nazism and Stalinism, an elaborate capillary apparatus of *state terror*. They also connote not just the marginalisation, cooption, or destruction of the state and national institutions that underpinned the now superseded 'old order', but also a vast programme of ideological, social, cultural, eugenic, racial or *ethnic cleansing* intended to suppress or destroy ideological, social and/or racial enemies and remove the causes of *decadence*. In the case of Nazi Germany the radicalness of the cleansing led eventually to campaigns of systematic *genocide* waged against 'gypsies', Slav communists and Jews. The important contribution of Gentile's cluster to clearing up the many misunderstandings caused by this aspect of totalitarianism (and hence of political religion) is that it specifically links the horrific human destruction involved in these campaigns to the *revolutionary* quest to create a *new civilisation* inspired by *palingenetic myth*. This precludes seeing it as resulting from the pathological 'nihilism' either of the leader or the nation, or from some perverse attempt to resist modernity[38] or 'transcendence',[39] but rather encourages it to be understood as the product of the palingenetic logic of destruction and (attempted) creation, a dialectic that ran like a 'red thread' through every aspect of the regime.

If instead we focus on the conquest of society as the bid to install a *new state* based on a *single party*, this perspective immediately encourages us to explore political religion's relationship to five intertwined modern realities: *populist nationalism, the nation state, the centralising bureaucratic/political state, the masses* and *mass democracy*. When 'conquering society' is understood in terms of the 'integral politicisation of existence', then it highlights political religion's profound link to the partial replacement of 'legal-rational' political processes by spectacular (theatrical/liturgical) politics.[40] This in turn immediately summons up the concept of *aesthetic politics*, here used not in the Marxist sense given it by Walter

Benjamin which confined it to fascism, but as integral aspect of all totalitarian political religions once in power (including state communism). At this point it sheds its connotation of 'reaction', mass deception and revolutionary façade, and is seen instead as an expression of the project to carry out an anthropological revolution and create a populist palingenetic ethos of regeneration and renewal.

The extensive appropriation and manipulation of cultural production and the staging of a form of politics based on 'magic' or 'cultic elements'[41] is then understood from Gentile's cluster perspective, not as elaborate exercises in mass brainwashing and manipulation, but (at least in the formative phase of a regime) as the manifestation of a conscious bid by the new rulers to realise the myth of rebirth, bring about a revolution in the political, aesthetic and moral culture of the 'people', and colonise time itself, thus bringing about a *temporal revolution*.[42] At the same time the multi-nodal, interconnected nature of the cluster's concepts prevents the reduction of totalitarianism either to culture, as some critics of Gentile have implied,[43] or to ideology, a charge made against some theorists of fascism who stress the palingenetic thrust of its ideology.[44] A crucial aspect of totalitarianism's attempt at cultural transformation (but only an aspect) is illuminated by post-structuralist studies of the symbology and semiotics of collective belief in modern societies, in particular by Guattari and Deleuze's concept of '*semiotic territorialization*' in bringing about a change in political culture and social mores.[45] The dynamics of the relationship between nodes of political religion relating to 'social control' considered earlier and those implicated in 'cultural revolution' are illuminated by Gramscian theory, particularly his distinction between '*dominion*' (coercion and subjection to the cause) and '*cultural hegemony*' (persuasion and conversion to the cause).

Tracing the project of 'conquering society' back to the *palingenetic myth* that drives it forms another mini-constellation around political religion, invoking such terms as *utopianism* and *political myth* conceived as an integral component all modern political movements. As for the notion of national rebirth and the renewal of historical time itself, this immediately invokes studies of *millenarianism* (chiliasm, eschatological thought, 'gnosticism'), though the constraining effect of the cluster reinforces the need to treat modern political religions not as throw-backs to the messianic Christian movements and mystic philosophies of history of early modern Europe, but rather as manifestations of the archetypal human drive to abolish linear time especially in times of social crisis.[46] Such a line of investigation throws into relief the relevance to political religion of the concept of *charismatic politics* in the original Weberian sense which treats it both as a response to the need for political legitimacy in an age where traditional political legitimation has broken down, and as a reaction to the progressive disenchantment of the world under the impact of rationalisation.

Another star in this mini-cluster, but one that has yet to shine brightly, since it has so far been curiously neglected by scholars in the context of totalitarian politics, is the *revitalisation movement*, a concept familiar in anthropology to describe the powerful socio-cultural movements headed by a shaman and bent on the ritual regeneration of 'the world' charismatic leader that can emerge when 'pre-modern' societies are in crisis, and may continue to surface in modern guise.[47] This aspect not only links back to political religion's attempted temporal revolution and production of political liturgy, but to studies which illuminate of the dynamics of collective belief systems, new religions and the *psychology of crowds* under modern social conditions.[48] Moving in another direction it also points the enquiring mind in the direction of specialist studies (steadily proliferating since 9/11) concerned with illuminating the nexus between politics and religion, whether in the form of the politicisation of traditional religions or the sacralisation of politics to create what Tillich calls 'quasi-religions'.

Finally (though this is a matter of respecting word limits and the patience of the reader, for the cluster concept by definition precludes closure, since each component concept can form the nodal point of a large number of different clusters and the centre of its own cluster), by joining up the dots that lead from *conquering society to anthropological revolution* and a *new civilisation* we are led to another mini-cluster whose gravitational centre is the 'modern'. The first is 'modernity' itself, which, in the context of the cluster is shorn of its exclusively Enlightenment connotations. Instead, it is re-imagined in a way that makes it an integral component of the bid by totalitarian movements to use state power to integrate the people, now unfettered from the hierarchies of tradition, into a new type of society bound together through mass organisations, communal activities and shared ideology of the new age. It is a concept that opens up vistas onto a wealth of sociology in the lineage of Weber, Durkheim and Tönnies probing the new type of communal bonds that hold together society in the post-traditional age. All of these cast some light on the function of political religion in creating a new type of community to replace the atomistic 'society' that had emerged under liberal capitalism and that particularly in inter-war Europe was widely experienced as woefully inadequate to serve the material and existential needs of the majority of its citizens.

The second is modernism. Under the aegis of Gentile's cluster this highly contested concept can be understood as the manifestation in every sphere of cultural production (including political ideologies) of the striving to imagine and realise a new type of reality on the other side of the West's organic process of decadence and dissolution which so many artistically and ideologically sensitive minds of the late nineteenth century were convinced was reaching its crisis point. It was a highly diffuse longing for regeneration that incubated a plethora of movements attempting to renew history itself through the power of vision combined with symbolic, social or political action. This idea of modernism links back to the earlier theme of temporal revolution, a connection brilliantly explored in Peter Osborne's investigation of the alternative temporalities generated by the European avant-garde in the earlier twentieth century in his groundbreaking *The Politics of Time*.[49] This work establishes the subtle but important linkages between aesthetic, philosophical and political manifestations of modernism in the way the historical process is conceived, in turn casting a new light on the monographs concerning individual manifestations of the nexus between artistic modernism and totalitarianism.[50]

294

The attempt by a movement or regime to revolutionise or reawaken the 'people' and usher in a 'new dawn' (that is, an alternative modernity) necessarily involves the project of 'conquering' society through a blend of dominion and cultural hegemony, thereby producing a quasi-religion which is one of the principal manifestations of politics under modernity. Once this is realised, the accelerated excursus through the sub-clusters that form round Gentile's original 'totalitarian' model of political religion loops back upon itself, forming a conceptual mega-cluster with numerous permutations of internal linkages and a considerable potential for further growth through the accretion of new 'stars'.

NOTES

[...]

38 Michael Burleigh and Wolfgang Wippermann's otherwise excellent *The Racial State* (Cambridge: Cambridge University Press, 1991), for example, treats the Nazis' racial programme as anti-modern and leaves the relationship with the totalitarian drive of the regime to create a new civilisation obscure.

39 A central thesis of Ernst Nolte, *Der Faschismus in seiner Epoche* (Munich: Piper, 1963), p. 51; English edition *Three Faces of Fascism* (London: Weidenfeld & Nicolson, 1965).

40 George L. Mosse, *The Nationalization of the Masses* (New York: Howard Fertig, 1975), is a seminal text for exploring nationalism's transformation into a political religion in nineteenth-century Germany as a precondition for the charismatic style of Nazism, though at the time he favoured the term 'civic religion'. He uses 'civic religion' interchangeably with 'political religion' and the 'sacralization of politics' in his autobiography, *Confronting History* (Madison, WI: University of Wisconsin Press, 2000), pp. 177–8.

41 Cf. for Nazism, Klaus Vondung, *Magie und Manipulation: ideologischer Kult und politische Religion des Nationalsozialismus* (Göttingen: Vandenhoeck and Ruprecht, 1971); Michael Burleigh, 'National Socialism as a Political Religion', *Totalitarian Movements and Political Religions* 1/2 (Autumn 2000); for Fascism, seminal pieces are Emilio Gentile, 'Fascism as a Political Religion', *Journal of Contemporary History* 2/3 (1990); and *idem*, *The Sacralization of Politics in Fascist Italy* (Cambridge, MA: Harvard University Press, 1994).

42 See, for example, M. Berezin, *Making the Fascist Self* (Ithaca, NY: Cornell University Press, 1997); Richard Fenn, *The End of Time: Ritual, Religion, and the Forging of the Soul* (London: SPCK, 1997).

43 See Bosworth's attacks on Gentile's 'culturalism' in R. Bosworth, *The Italian Dictatorship: Problems and Perspectives in the Interpretation of Mussolini and Fascism* (London: Arnold, 1998); and Gentile's reply (note 4), in his contribution to the special issue of *Totalitarian Movements and Political Religions* 5/3 (Winter 2004), dedicated to the topic 'Fascism as a Totalitarian Movement'.

44 See David Renton, *Fascism* (London: Pluto Press, 1999), p. 29; cf. Michael Mann, *Fascists* (Cambridge: Cambridge University Press, 2004), p. 12.

45 For example, Malcolm Quinn, *The Swastika: Constructing the Symbol* (London and New York: Routledge, 1994). See also Roger Griffin, 'Notes Towards the Definition of Fascist Culture: The Prospects for Synergy Between Marxist and Liberal Heuristics', *Renaissance and Modern Studies* 42 (Autumn 2001).

46 The seminal works on this topic are still those of Mircea Eliade, notably *The Myth of Eternal Return* (Princeton, NJ: Princeton University Press, 1971; 1st edn. 1949).

47 Victor and Edith Turner, *Celebration: Studies in Festivity and Ritual* (Washington, DC: Smithsonian Institution Press, 1982).
48 Gustave Le Bon, *The Crowd: A Study of the Popular Mind*, 2nd edn. (Dunwoody, GA: Norman S. Berg, 1968), is still the classic text on this topic.
49 Peter Osborne, *The Politics of Time* (London: Verso, 1995).
50 Emily Braun, *Mario Sironi and Italian Modernism Art and Politics under Fascism* (Cambridge: Cambridge University Press, 2000); Igor Golomstock, *Totalitarian Art* (London, 1990).

13

NAZISM AND THE REVIVAL OF POLITICAL RELIGION THEORY

Richard Steigmann-Gall

The recent scholarly debates over the issue of political religions have stirred a new wave of research on the relationship between fascist ideology, movements and regimes, on the one hand, and the established churches and religious dogmas, on the other hand. The majority of these new works have focused preponderantly on Nazi Germany, arguably the most intriguing case of syncretism between (pseudo) religious and political values, given Hitler's highly intense but blasphemic charismatic appeal, the seemingly anti-Christian character of the NSPAD, the offensive of neo-pagan religious cults within the movement and their subversive impact over established Christian churches.

In his book entitled The Holy Reich, *Richard Steigmann-Gall challenged conventional views according to which Nazism was an atheist, pagan or anti-Christian movement, arguing instead that its anti-Semitism, anti-Marxism and anti-Liberalism "drew on Christian traditions," and that the religious views of the Nazi leadership, synthesized in their leading concept of "positive Christianity," was conceived "within a Christian frame of references" (2003: 3).*

In this essay, Steigmann-Gall questions the analytical value of the political religion theory to explain Nazism's relationship to religion. In his view, the recent revival of this theory is only reiterating arguments put forward by similar debates that took place in the interwar period, being stimulated by the politically-driven post-Cold War rejuvenation of the theory of totalitarianism. Steigmann-Gall acknowledges the strong religious components of Nazism, but rejects the argument that the Nazis intended to create an alternative 'pagan' political religion, as a "replacement faith for a de-Christianized nation." Instead, on the basis of evidence of Hitler's and other high Nazi officials' personal views on religion, he reiterates his argument that the Nazis never openly rejected the fundamentals of Christianity. While within the NSDAP there certainly existed a plurality of views on religion, the neo-pagan cults promoted by Himmler and Rosenberg remained rather marginal, never becoming official policy. Steigmann-Gall also challenges

297

the argument that the Nazi allegedly new "political religion" was responsible for National Socialism's mass appeal, charging the proponents of this view with the fallacy of favoring form and style over ideological content and social context. He argues that, instead of focusing on the ultimately misleading question of whether totalitarian regimes were or were not forms of political religions "in a phenomenological sense," it would be more rewarding to examine the concrete religious content of Nazism and its social appeal.

Steigmann-Gall concludes that Nazism cannot be characterized as a "political religion," but appears to be more a form of "religious politics," based on a variety of Christianity. This argument resonates with Roger Griffin's original view on fascism as a form of "religious politics" (1991) with the notable difference that Griffin saw Nazism as "intensely anti-Christian" (ibid.: 32) while Steigmann-Gall sees it as based on Christian precepts. Steigmann-Gall's views triggered lively controversies over the nature of the Nazism and its relationship to religion in general and to Christianity in particular (e.g. the debate in the Journal of Contemporary History, *vol. 42, January 2007, no. 1).*

BIBLIOGRAPHY

Griffin, Roger (1991). *The Nature of Fascism* (London: Pinter).
Steigmann-Gall, Richard (2003). *The Holy Reich: Nazi Conceptions of Christianity, 1919–1945* (Cambridge: Cambridge University Press).

* * *

In the last ten years, totalitarianism theory has experienced a major comeback. Whether the end of the Cold War indicates the triumph of the First World or the implosion of the Second, it has brought with it a renewed triumphalism in academic circles that would likely have pleased Hannah Arendt. Once again fascism and communism are conjoined as symptomatic of a lack of 'Western' liberal democracy in their native societies. This is evident not only in new scholarship, but in a new journal devoted solely to this subject – namely this one – and in the new *Hannah Arendt Institut für Totalitarismusforschung* in Dresden, a scholarly St Patrick committed to reviving totalitarianism theory after the collapse of social-historical Marxist historiography.[1] Directly connected with the resurgence of totalitarianism theory is a renewed interest in theories of fascism as a 'political religion'. This has been especially apparent lately in the historiography of Italian Fascism; here the political religion angle has to some degree been informed by a more innovative interest in aesthetics and identity formation.[2] By contrast, recent German scholarship has tended to be a more conventional affair of intellectual history, more inclined to re-centre the Nazi 'neo-pagans' as the locus of Nazi ideology, insisting that Himmler's or Rosenberg's attempts to create a new *Religionsersatz* to replace Christianity really were important after all.[3] In this essay, I will attempt two things: first, to survey some of the lineages of political religion scholarship, assess its theoretical and conceptual qualities, and suggest ways in which Nazism might better be understood as a 'religious politics'; second, I will turn to the historical record, to investigate exactly how the Nazis conceived their movement as potentially religious.

The complementarity of 'totalitarianism theory' and 'political religion' theory is self-evident. Totalitarianism theory, at its most elemental, suggests that the form of twentieth-century dictatorships counted more than the content; style is emphasised over substance. A militarised society, one-party state, suppression of the public sphere, a supreme leader with some degree of charisma or at least personality cult – these are the focus of attention. By contrast, the different policies these regimes pursued, their contrasting ideologies, what their societies actually looked liked – are all given secondary consideration.[4] According to totalitarianism theory, atomised 'mass man', deprived of the moral compass of *Gemeinschaft* and hurled into the anomie of *Gesellschaft*, found a *Gemeinschaft* once again, this time writ large. 'Political religion theory', by comparison, also insists on the centrality of the rootless 'mass man'. Here, the totalitarian subject suffers – especially in the German case, we are told – from a Nietzschean 'death of God', leaving him de-Christianised and therefore vulnerable to 'blind enthusiasms'. Nazism allegedly served to sacralise the collectivity once again. Like totalitarianism theory, political religion theory emphasises Nazi form (the hypnotic power of a new charismatic faith) over Nazi content (the message of that religion and to whom it appealed). Among the original representatives of this view were Eric Voegelin and Gerhard Ritter, who both argued that Nazism had been primarily a moral disease originating in the Enlightenment, and who both prescribed a simple 'return' to Christian values as the best antidote. This argument complemented the politics of conservatives like Voegelin and Ritter, by obviating the need to seek the social roots of Nazism's popularity – thereby refuting suggestions that Hitler was more than an aberration in the course of German history. This strain of argumentation was reinforced by a strong orientalising tendency in contemporary Christian apologia, whereby the rectitude of Germany's Christian culture was contrasted with an alleged 'Islamic' quality to the Nazis' political culture. This attempt to put a prophylactic around Germany, thereby casting Nazism and its historical precedents as alien infections, was particularly sneering. As Carl Jung put it in 1939: 'We do not know whether Hitler is going to found a new Islam. He is already on the way; he is like Mohammed. The emotion in Germany is Islamic, warlike and Islamic. They are all drunk with a wild man'.[5] In these varied ways, the 'moral dimension' of post-war scholarship, as Ian Kershaw calls it, served as the historical counterpart of the totalitarianism theory then being developed by political scientists like Arendt. By pointing to instances of Christian alterity to Nazism, this scholarship helped erect a potent symbol of national regeneration, the *Stunde Null* – thereby refuting those scholars of the victorious Allied powers who claimed that Nazism was a disease encompassing *all* Germans.

This was a popular argument outside of academia as well. Some of the most prominent public intellectuals of the post-war period made it part of the intellectual landscape of the post-war period. Hannah Arendt herself, the 'philosophical counterpart' to Gerhard Ritter,[6] allowed for no ambiguity when she argued:

> Nazism owes nothing to any part of the Western tradition, be it German or not, Catholic or Protestant, Christian, Greek or Roman … Ideologically speaking, Nazism begins with no traditional basis at all, and it would be better to realise the danger of this radical negation of any tradition, which was the main feature of Nazism from the beginning.[7]

The immediate post-war context for this 'moral dimension' has disappeared, but its enduring popularity is still in evidence today.

'Political religion theory', then, finds a multi-layered connection with totalitarianism theory; it is equally reliant upon, and in many ways intertwined with, theories of nationalism. For instance, George Mosse suggested almost 30 years ago that nationalism as such was literally a 'new religion', in which the secularist wine of personal charisma and racialism filled the old bottles of piety and spirituality left empty by modern apostasy.[8] Fritz Stern's study of three proto-Nazi intellectuals similarly argues that apostate academics created a Germanic religion 'which hid beneath pious allusions to … the Bible a most thoroughgoing secularisation. The religious *tone* remained, even after the religious faith and the religious canons had disappeared'.[9] These arguments presume that nationalism brought with it, and in fact was a leading cause of, secularisation. As with political religion theorists, what mattered for this school were the religious idioms, not the ideology. However, unlike many forms of secularisation theory, which suggest that modernity witnesses a decline in religiosity *per se*, the variety most associated with the literature on Nazism suggests that de-Christianisation did not lead to agnosticism or atheism, but rather left a spiritual yearning, a void waiting to be filled with another content. A recent echo of this view is found in the recent work of Michael Burleigh, who asserts that with Nazism, Christianity's 'fundamental tenets were stripped out, but the remaining diffuse religious emotionality had its uses'.[10] Amongst those arguing that Nazism was a form of Nietzschean secularisation, the most surprising was Detlev Peukert. Renowned for his unique contributions to Nazi historiography and refusal to toe party lines, Peukert nonetheless suggested:

> we view the roots of modern racism as lying in the problem of legitimation in a secularised world. A secularised world no longer provided final answers: it had no way of pointing beyond itself. Once the facade of non-transcendent everyday mythology had been shattered by crisis, the search was on for 'final solutions'.[11]

This claim is all the more surprising coming from someone whose politics were so at odds with Ritter's. Both Peukert and Ritter intersected in this case, however, in the importance they placed on the apparent de-Christianisation of Germany, and Christianity's replacement with Nazism. At the end of the day the most recent works on political religion and totalitarianism theory offer little new beyond Voegelin's earlier theories, heavily reliant as they are on complementary concepts like charisma.[12]

The many scholars who have employed political religion theory are correct in claiming to see a religious dimension in Nazism. For 'totalitarian' regimes in general, the use of physical space and prophetic language was indeed often consciously derived from religious sources. Hitler himself freely admitted that the model for Nazi night rallies came from his own Catholic upbringing.[13] There was an undeniable, highly emotionalist quality to Nazi performance, which historians generally assume supplied a growing demand in the German public for a spiritual politics. But was this the actual linchpin of Nazi social success? As descriptive as this concept is, how useful is it as a category of analysis? How far do performance and choreography go in explaining the Nazi appeal? The political religion thesis presumes the attraction to Nazism was based on emotion instead of idea, on form instead of content. Whatever the Nazi 'platform' may have been is deemed irrelevant, or at best secondary. The 'religion' of political religion theory becomes the act of believing, not *that which is believed*.

However appealing and self-contained this theory seems, it cannot sustain itself empirically. Such a focus ignores the findings of social historians who, in the last 20 years, have provided very detailed analyses of who did and did not join, or vote for, the NSDAP. To a striking degree, such analyses have demonstrated a predictability of Nazi attraction based on factors like class, region, geography and – most importantly – confession. What these studies demonstrate rather clearly is that however dramatic Hitler's display of personal charisma may have been, however emphasised by the Nazis' own propaganda, it played little if any role in actually shaping the Nazi electorate. The attraction to Nazism was instead determined by the factors that governed electoral choice between Germany's other political parties: calculated self-interest.[14] And, while functionalist interpretations have often held sway, defining that self-interest in material 'pocketbook' terms, there are provisional indications that a culturalist definition of self-interest, drawing upon intangible aspects of the Nazi appeal – like the promised renewal of morality and 'honour' – may reveal deeper insights. A culturalist interpretation would certainly take us much further towards understanding the overwhelmingly Protestant nature of the Nazi electorate than would a purely materialist interpretation.[15] Regardless of which approach is taken, the social-historical approach definitively undermines the 'political religion' presumption that their *style* earned the Nazis their electoral success. As David Blackbourn has argued, fascist ritual was successful primarily when it played to an audience receptive to the message; that is, 'where it went with the grain of particular experiences and interests'.[16] This argument has been born out by specialists of the 1933–45 period such as David Welch, who has proven Blackbourn's assertion correct *vis-à-vis* Nazi propaganda; it succeeded with those already 'converted' to the Nazi message, and largely failed to win over those who before 1933 had yet to be convinced.[17]

Nazi propaganda may have portrayed Hitler as a kind of Holy Roller, mesmerising his audience at the night rallies and 'converting' it to his cause. And the historical record is full of testimonials of Hitler's charismatic power working its magic on sceptics reluctantly dragged by friends to the rally at the Zeppelin field, only to be won over in a wave of religious fervour. But while this image of Hitler as mass hypnotist reveals a good deal about the *ambitions* of Nazi propagandists, it tells us very little about the realities of audience reception or the degree of actual social consent which the Nazis were so anxious to secure. Several studies have pointed to the Nazis' deep concern with public opinion and consensus building as a precondition for their activities.[18] Robert Gellately has demonstrated how the Gestapo, perhaps the most infamous symbol of totalitarianism in the popular imagination, was in fact heavily dependent on public participation for its success.[19] Recently Gellately has explored this theme further, demonstrating the ways in which social consensus was erected and disrupted, with little emphasis on Hitler's charisma or other quasi-religious aspects of Nazi performance.[20] The work of Nathan Stoltzfus, among others, has shown how it was possible to mount popular resistance in Nazi Germany in clear defiance of Hitler's hypnotic powers.[21] Among other things, these studies reveal that the Nazis ultimately put little store in their own charismatic gifts, their ability to 'sacralise the collectivity' through a *Religionsersatz* when attempting to form a national consensus. The Nazis knew, in other words, that their state was less than totalitarian. Significantly, some of the first studies to question the totalitarian quality of Nazi rule were examinations of churches written by non-church historians – significant because historians of church and state under Nazism were generally some of the most consistent proponents of totalitarianism theory.[22]

In spite of the findings of these scholars, 'political religion' theorists have by and large been able to carry forth with remarkably little consequence. The latest example of this is the synoptic narrative by Michael Burleigh, titled *The Third Reich: A New History*, which represents the latest and most prominent attempt, not only to resuscitate political religion theory, but also to restore it to the more influential position it once enjoyed. Recapitulating the earlier theories of Mosse and Stern, Burleigh contends that 'sacralised collectivities, such as class, nation or race, had already partly supplanted God as objects of mass enthusiasm or veneration'. He agrees with a prior generation of scholars that this political religion was 'self-consciously pagan and primitive', that in spite of its claim to be scientific, Nazism had 'one foot in the dark irrationalist world of Teutonic myth'.[23]

As self-confident as this scholarly revival seems to be at the moment, it still needs to solve the basic deep-seated problems plaguing a prior generation of 'political religion' and totalitarianism theorists. What exactly constitutes 'religion', such that both Christianity and Nazism can be considered two equally valid examples of it? By what means can we demonstrate that one form of identity – being nationalistic – must necessarily impinge upon and usurp another form of identity – being Christian? If Nazism can be seen as a religion, then cannot all politics potentially be seen in this light? Can politics be *religious* without being *religion*? As powerful as the allure of political religion theory is for a new generation of scholars, they largely leave these questions unanswered. At its most basic, political religion theory presumes a static 'zero sum' model of identity formation. The possibility that one can be national *and* religious, not national *or* religious, is not considered. Also overlooked is the historical record of nationalism in modern Europe, which frequently demonstrates not an opposition between national and religious feeling, but more often an affinity. This is seen not only in the cases of Poland and Ireland, where a structural overlap of religious and linguistic identity can be explained in geo-cultural terms, but also in countries precisely like Germany, where Christian clergy – especially Protestant – played a leading role in constructing and shaping a movement which has most often been regarded as secular.[24]

Equally unsubstantiated is the common insistence that Christianity has gone into decline in the modern age. In the last 15 years or so, a great deal of historical investigation has taken place to demonstrate the continued power and influence of Christianity in Europe, not only among an intellectual élite, but among larger social strata as well. Aside from a select number of intellectuals whose social impact has still to be measured, there is little evidence to show that German society as a whole experienced a 'Death of God' before Nazism; or more to the point, that those who were attracted to Nazism (either at the polling station or membership office) were apostate Christians. Only those who *wish* the modern era had seen the decline of Christianity – either to dissociate it from an historical record they abhor or to associate its decline with one they esteem – can any longer argue this was so.[25]

If there is indeed no 'zero sum' relationship between national and religious identity, and if the modern age has not in fact been secular in the sense of being de-Christianised, then in what sense can we still say that Nazism contained a religious dimension? Given the profoundly political character of fascism, it is less interesting – and ultimately less fruitful – to know whether it can be qualified as religion in a phenomenological sense than to identify its relationship with the extant religions that had long been part of the societies that went fascist. And here the same scholarship that valorises style can often make telling, though frequently inadvertent, references to a substantive relationship as well. Returning briefly to the historiography on Italian Fascism, we can see this reflected in Mabel Berezin's work. On the one hand, she suggests that in Fascist Italy 'everyone participated in Catholic practices that were *independent* of doctrine or belief and shaped Italian fascist and public consciousness'. The religious form is emphasised here; Berezin speaks of a 'fascist transposition' of Catholic idioms, such as the catechism, which aided the forming of Fascist political culture. On the other hand, however, Berezin points to a substantive connection to Catholicism. She speaks of ideological 'affinities', especially with regard to Fascist social theory: 'In a direct borrowing from *Rerum Novarum*, corporations, Fascist unions that encompassed the entire workforce, were the organising vehicles that concretised the state-individual relation'.[26] Berezin admittedly argues this was simply a 'borrowing' – Catholicism in her view was a pool of ideas to be siphoned off, not the ontological root of fascism *per se*. But the 'borrowing' is nonetheless comprehensive. Elsewhere Berezin points out that 'as an ideology, Fascism was anti-democratic, anti-liberal, anti-socialist, and anti-Masonic' – all components of a platform that was recognisably Catholic in certain places at certain times.

What we have is not a borrowing so much as wholesale adaptation. Rather than 'political religion', what we have is something that could be called 'religious politics', whereby a political-secular movement takes on the temporal teachings of an established religion. While a theory of 'religious politics' has yet to be developed, such a concept would place far greater emphasis on the content of a religion's message – particularly with regards to the social order – than the form of that religion's ritual. In the German case, it would emphasise the ways in which the Nazis carved out a constituency of particular religious interests. In this sense, a fruitful point of comparison would be with the Centre Party and, after the war, the Christian Democrats, both of whom undertook a type of cross-class, religious representation and hence can be classified as a religious politics, albeit of a radically different substance.[27] In the case of Nazism, the overwhelming attraction among Germany's Protestants, similarly cutting across class lines, would justifiably qualify the NSDAP as a Protestant Centre Party, fulfilling a long-held ambition to rally together a disparate Protestant electorate around an ideological *Volkspartei*.

Immediate insights are gleaned when applying the religious politics concept to historical fascism. As Berezin intimates in the Italian case, the social attraction to fascism would be explicable not through its ability to recreate religious ritual, either physical or discursive, as though the message of fascism were secondary. The key, rather, would be the ways in which fascism promised to remould state and society, and the types of social milieus regarding such a message as attractive or unattractive. In German historiography there are examples of a similar conceptual tension between style and substance. Without stating so explicitly, Burleigh suggests that Nazi *ideology*, and not just Nazi choreography, contained a religious element. While it appropriated for itself a scientistic sheen, this ideology was not just about applied biology,

> but the expression of eternal scientific laws, revealed by God and in turn invested with sacred properties ... This was politics as a biological mission, but conceived in a religious way ... Armed with his religious science, Hitler [was] God's partner in ordering and perfecting that part of mankind which concerned him.[28]

Interwoven into his analysis of Nazi political religion, Burleigh provides evidence that Nazism derived its ideology from a particular interpretation of theology. The distinction is vitally important, even if not fully drawn out in this instance. Instead of a religion with a political dimension, what we might witness in Nazism is a politics with a religious dimension.

Other scholarly voices (albeit from a distinctly functionalist rather than intentionalist standpoint) suggest that whatever the ontological sources of Nazism, at the level of ideas a 'borrowing' from Christianity similar to Italian Fascism was taking place. For example, Martin Broszat suggested that: 'A considerable part of this ideological rhetoric which the NSDAP had sucked up from all available sources, was indeed itself derived from Christian convictions'.[29] The telling expression 'sucking up' reveals a typically functionalist understanding of ideology as secondary within the Nazi movement. But Broszat opens up the possibility that more than just isolated instances of 'borrowing' from Christian tradition is taking place. It is precisely *here* where the overwhelmingly Protestant composition of the Nazi social base becomes so revealing. Instead of a political religion in which Hitler's voters rushed to the movement in a tide of emotion, might Nazism have been seen as a religious politics in which these voters dispassionately reflected on the ideological platform of Nazism, believing they saw in it a Christian platform?

Nazism cannot represent both a 'destructive mimesis of Christianity'[30] and simultaneously derive its ideology from Christian convictions. The question becomes: which was it? Did the Nazis view themselves as a replacement for Christianity, or as its restorer?

* * *

Whether the Nazis felt themselves to be a 'political religion' is best investigated by exploring the efforts of some in the movement to create a literal *Religionsersatz*. Those who uphold 'political religion theory' most strenuously usually point to 'neo-pagans' like Rosenberg and Himmler, implying that their esoteric religious ideas were hegemonic within the movement. It is then often inferred that Hitler himself subscribed to their mysticism. For instance, Philippe Burrin maintains that 'Hitler remained devoted to the idea of a religious reform of the Germans. And if he abstained from preaching this in public, it was Himmler who undertook this task by making the SS the force that was to add religious reform to political renewal'. Burrin goes further, suggesting that 'Hitler and his men ... satisfied their [religious] fascination through speculative theories that they considered scientific such as the "glaciation cosmogony"'.[31] Less well known, but equally revealing, was another attempt to turn Nazism into a religious movement by the sectarian Christian Artur Dinter. While he had no interest in Wotan or other Nordic legends, Dinter was at least as committed as the paganists to turning the party from a secular into a religious movement.

Rosenberg's paganist opus, *The Myth of the Twentieth Century*, is the most obvious attempt among the Nazis to forge a new political religion. As he wrote:

> The men of the coming age will transform the heroes' memorials and glades of remembrance into the places of pilgrimage of a new religion; there the hearts of Germans will be constantly shaped afresh in pursuit of a new myth ... Today a new faith is awakening: the myth of blood, the faith that the divine essence of mankind is to be defended through blood; the faith embodied by the fullest realisation that Nordic blood represents the mystery which has supplanted and surmounted the old sacraments.[32]

This new religion would place the highest value in the idea of racial honour: 'The idea of honour – national honour – is for us the beginning and end of all our thoughts and deeds. It can endure no equivalent centre of power of any type, neither Christian love nor freemasonic humanism nor Roman dogmatism'.[33] This Christian 'brotherhood of man' was nothing more than an attempt to allow Jew and 'Turk' to take precedence over the European. In the name of Christian love, Europe was besieged by unrest and chaos: 'Thanks to preachings on humanity and the equality of all peoples, every Jew, Negro and Mulatto can be a full citizen of a European state'.[34] When the Nordic states of Europe were overwhelmed by the Roman south, the concept of honour was overtaken by that of Christian love: 'Christianity ... did not know the idea of race and nationality, because it represented a violent fusion of different elements; it also knew nothing of the idea of honour, because in pursuance of the late Roman quest for power it subdued not only the body, but also the soul'.[35]

It is voices such as Rosenberg's and Himmler's which are invoked when historians argue that Nazism was a political religion seeking to replace Christianity. However, these voices constituted a minority within their own movement. One need look no further for proof of this than Hitler himself. Though Hitler was known for tailoring his remarks to please his audience, even in Rosenberg's presence he was less than enthusiastic about paganism. Before publishing it, Rosenberg asked Hitler for his opinion of *Mythus* (six months after receiving the manuscript, Hitler still had not read it). Hitler coolly replied: 'It is a very clever book; only I ask myself who today is likely to read and understand such a book'.[36] It was a reflection of the insecurity of Rosenberg's position that he replied by asking whether he should suppress it or even resign party office. Hitler said 'no' to both, maintaining that Rosenberg had a right to publish his book since it was his intellectual property.[37] However, on later occasions Hitler would express regret that Rosenberg had written the book in the first place. According to Albert Speer, Hitler referred to it as 'stuff nobody can understand', written by a 'narrow-minded Baltic German who thinks in horribly complicated terms ... A relapse into medieval notions!'[38] Hitler was even more dismissive in his 'Table Talk', stating privately:

> I must insist that Rosenberg's *Myth of the Twentieth Century* is not to be regarded as an expression of the official doctrine of the Party ... It is interesting to note that comparatively few of the older members of the Party are to be found among the readers of Rosenberg's book, and that the publishers had, in fact, great difficulty in disposing of the first edition.[39]

Himmler's mysticism fared no better. As Hitler told his circle of confidants: 'What nonsense! Here we have at last reached an age that has left all mysticism behind, and now he wants to start that all over again ... To think that I may some day be turned into an SS saint!' Whereas Himmler attacked Charlemagne as the subjugator of ancient pagan-Germanic tribes, Hitler declared: 'Killing all those

Saxons was not a historical crime, as Himmler thinks. Charlemagne did a good thing in subjugating Widukind and killing the Saxons out of hand. He thereby made possible the empire of the Franks and the entry of Western culture into what is now Germany'.[40] Hitler even approached Himmler himself, fully rejecting the foundation of a new religion, calling it a 'chimera'.[41] There is ample evidence that Hitler had no time for Himmler's anti-Christian neo-paganism; but even among the party's other paganists, Himmler's religious views were regarded as bizarre. Himmler unwittingly acknowledged this, warning his underlings that no polemics against such theories would be tolerated.[42] The particular obsession with 'glaciation cosmogony' was too much even for Rosenberg, who sent a circular to all NSDAP offices assuring them that 'adherence to these theories was no part of being a National Socialist'.[43]

These were admittedly private expressions. But Hitler did not spare his paganist colleagues in the party from public derision. As he wrote in *Mein Kampf*:

> The characteristic thing about these people is that they rave about old Germanic heroism, about dim prehistory, stone axes, spear and shield, but in reality are the greatest cowards that can be imagined. For the same people who brandish scholarly imitations of old German tin swords, and wear a dressed bearskin with bull's horns over their bearded heads, preach for the present nothing but struggle with spiritual weapons, and run away as fast as they can from every Communist blackjack.[44]

He disdained 'those German-*völkisch* wandering scholars whose positive accomplishment is always practically nil, but whose conceit can scarcely be excelled'.[45] Any attempt at making Nazism a religious movement came in for total reproach:

> Especially with the so-called religious reformers ... I always have the feeling that they were sent by those powers which do not want the resurrection of our people ... I shall not even speak of the unworldliness of these *völkisch* Saint Johns of the twentieth century or their ignorance of the popular soul.[46]

This last statement could have applied as equally to Artur Dinter, who sought to transform Nazism from a secular party into an explicitly religious movement. Dinter would ultimately be expelled over his growing rift with Hitler on this issue; the grounds upon which he would be removed provide us with further insight into Hitler's own thinking on religion. As this episode reveals, if Hitler believed his movement was *religious*, he entirely rejected the idea that it should be a *religion*.

Like many in the Nazi leadership, Dinter held Martin Luther in high regard, esteeming him as a nationalist figure who, among other things, had invented the German language. And among many Nazis there was an admiration for Luther's *religious* struggle as well.[47] Dinter was among them, but he took his admiration to extreme ends, going so far as to formulate a platform for 'completing' the Reformation in Germany. Luther had failed to unite all Germans under the banner of 'true' Christianity: it would now be the responsibility of the Nazi Party to complete the process. Dinter enunciated this vision in 1926 through his *197 Thesen zur Vollendung der Reformation* (197 Theses for the Completion of the Reformation), in which he declared that the only path to German political renewal was through a religious revolution. The following year in Nuremberg he established his own organisation, the Christian-Spiritual Religious Association (*Geistchristliche Religionsgemeinschaft*), and a periodical, *Das Geistchristentum* (Christianity of the Spirit).

Owing to Hitler's disinterest in his proposal, Dinter grew increasingly opposed to Hitler's leadership. In return, Hitler had Dinter expelled from the NSDAP. A few weeks after Dinter's expulsion, Hitler gave a speech in Passau:

> We are a people of different faiths, but we are one. Which faith conquers the other is not the question; rather, the question is whether Christianity stands or falls … We tolerate no one in our ranks who attacks the ideas of Christianity … in fact our movement is Christian. We are filled with a desire for Catholics and Protestants to discover one another in the deep distress of our own people.[48]

Hitler unequivocally wished to cast Nazism as a religious politics rather than a political religion; while the movement would be informed by religious ideology, it would not assume the form of a religious movement. Furthermore, Hitler contended that the religious ideology in question would be Christian – and therefore closer in content to Dinter – not anti-Christian, as the paganists had hoped.

Most of the Nazi élite joined with Hitler in rejecting these political religions, especially Rosenberg's and Himmler's paganism. As Goebbels noted in his diary, Göring complained that if Rosenberg had had his way, there would be 'only cult, *Thing*, myth, and that sort of swindle'.[49] In 1939 Göring confronted Rosenberg point blank, asking him: 'Do you believe that Christianity is coming to an end, and that later a new form created by us will come into being?' When Rosenberg said he did think this, Göring replied he would privately solicit Hitler's view.[50] No record exists of Göring asking Hitler this question, but there is little doubt Hitler would have rejected Rosenberg's contention. Goebbels's views on paganism closely matched Göring's; his estimation of Rosenberg's abilities were summarised in his reference to him as 'Almost Rosenberg': 'Rosenberg almost managed to become a scholar, a journalist, a politician – but only almost'.[51]

Hitler rejected attempts to turn Nazism into a political religion, seeing his movement instead as a religious politics – in conformity with Christian precepts, not opposed to them. In a party gathering at Munich's Bürgerbräukeller in 1922, he dealt with the question of whether one could be both antisemitic and Christian:

I say my Christian feelings point me to my Lord and Saviour as a fighter (tumultuous, prolonged applause). They point me toward the man who, once lonely and surrounded by only a few followers, recognised these Jews and called for battle against them, and who, as the true God, was not only the greatest as a sufferer but also the greatest as a warrior ... as a Christian and a human being, I read the passage which declares to us how the Lord finally rose up and seized the whip to drive the usurers, the brood of serpents and snakes, from the Temple (tumultuous applause)![52]

In this speech, delivered in front of a mostly Nazi audience, Hitler referred to Jesus as 'the true God'. He made it plain that he regarded Christ's 'struggle' as direct inspiration for his own. For Hitler, Jesus was not just one archetype among others, but, as he said on another occasion, was 'our greatest Aryan leader'.[53] While emphasising Jesus's human qualities, in this instance Hitler also alluded to his divinity. It should be pointed out that Hitler said these words publicly: what did he say behind closed doors?

At a private meeting with his confidants from the *Kampfzeit*, in which he explained why economics must be subordinate to politics, Hitler again spoke of a connection between Nazism and Christianity, one deeper than a simple 'borrowing':

Socialism is a political problem. And politics is of no concern to the economy ... Socialism is a question of attitude to life, of the ethical outlook on life of all who live together in a common ethnic or national space. Socialism is a *Weltanschauung*!

But in actual fact there is nothing new about this *Weltanschauung*. Whenever I read the New Testament Gospels and the revelations of various of the prophets ... I am astonished at all that has been made of the teachings of these divinely inspired men, especially Jesus Christ, which are so clear and unique, heightened to religiosity. *They* were the ones who created this new world view which we now call socialism, they established it, they taught it and they lived it! But the communities that called themselves Christian churches did not understand it! ... they denied Christ and betrayed him![54]

Hitler claimed that where the churches failed in their mission to instil a Christian ethic in secular society, his movement would take up the task. Hitler not only read the New Testament, but professed to be inspired by it. As a consequence, he also claimed that the substance of Nazi social theory is 'nothing new'.

Whatever Hitler's own personal religiosity – which certainly cannot be described as Christian in the conventional, ecclesiastical sense – it contained a Christian element. Until the end of his life he esteemed Christ, so much so that he decided it was necessary to rescue Christ from his own Jewishness. Even while

Hitler's anti-clericalism grew, his opinion of Jesus remained high. As he said to his confidants in October 1941: 'The Galilean, who later was called the Christ, intended something quite different. He must be regarded as a popular leader who took up his position against Jewry ... He set Himself against Jewish capitalism, and that is why the Jews liquidated Him'.[55] In Hitler's eyes, Jesus's status as an Aryan remained unquestioned: 'It is certain that Jesus was not a Jew'. However much Hitler claimed to be an enemy of organised religion, this conception of Jesus displayed a clear limit to his apostasy, and the retention of a specifically Christian dimension to his beliefs.

More than just Hitler, others in the Nazi movement exhibited a similar commitment to Christianity. One was the *Gauleiter* of East Prussia and eventual Reich Commissioner of Ukraine, Erich Koch. In addition to being *Gauleiter* Koch served in 1933 as the elected president of the provincial Protestant church synod. Contemporaries of Koch, including those against the Nazified 'German Christians', confirmed that his Christian feelings were sincere. According to the leader of the East Prussian Confessing Church, Koch spoke 'with the deepest understanding of our church' and consistently dealt with 'the central themes of Christianity'. In his post-war testimony, taken by a public prosecutor in Bielefeld in 1949, Koch would insist: 'I held the view that the Nazi idea had to develop from a basic Prussian-Protestant attitude'.[56]

This Protestant orientation among the Nazi Party élite, evident even in Hitler's estimation of Protestantism as the 'national religion' of the Germans,[57] matched the party's own heavily Protestant social base. Hans Schemm, *Gauleiter* of Bayreuth, Bavarian *Kultusminister* and head of the National Socialist Teachers' League (NSLB) further illustrates this correlation. During the *Kampfzeit*, Schemm was known for his slogan, 'Our religion is Christ, our politics Fatherland!' His speeches were designed to cast Nazism as a religious politics: as a police report stated, Schemm spoke 'like a pastor' and often ended his deliveries with the Lutheran hymn, 'A Mighty Fortress is our God'.[58] In one of these speeches, he spoke of God in Nazism's conceptual universe: 'Our confession to God is a confession of a doctrine of totality ... To give ultimate significance to the totalities of race, resistance and personality there is added the supreme totalitarian slogan of our *Volk*: "Religion and God". God is the greatest totality and extends over all else'.[59] Here Schemm makes specific reference to the 'totalitarian' nature of Nazism. But he makes it clear that the totalising claims of Nazism as a *Weltanschauung* did not preclude the possibility that such a *Weltanschauung* could have been based on a variety of Christianity. Far from conflicting loyalties, for Schemm, Christianity and Nazism went hand in hand:

> we are no theologians, no representatives of the teaching profession in this sense, put forth no theology. But we claim one thing for ourselves: that we place the great fundamental idea of Christianity in the centre of our ideology [*Ideenwelt*] – the hero and sufferer, Christ himself, stands in the *centre*.[60]

Schemm also dealt with the issue of the sanctification of racial science, which many political religion theorists consider central. In doing so, however, Schemm insisted that racialism was consistent with – indeed stemmed from – a Christian attitude. As he told a meeting of Protestant pastors:

> We want to preserve, not subvert, what God has created, just as the oak tree and the fir tree retain their difference in a forest. – Why do the trees in the forest not interbreed? – Why is there not only one type of tree [*Einheitsbaum*]? Why should our concept of race suddenly turn into the Marxist concept of a single type of human? We are accused of wanting to deify the idea of race. But since race is willed by God, we want nothing else but to keep the race pure, in order to fulfil God's law.[61]

Political religion theorists argue that the Nazis' 'theology of race' was religious but anti-Christian; however, the Nazis themselves claimed that it was Christian. Again, these were public pronouncements, and as such might be called into question. But in private, Schemm retracted none of his professions. In party correspondence regarding the sectarian Protestant League (*Evangelischer Bund*), a leading voice of politicised Protestantism seeking active political cooperation with the Nazis, Schemm stated: 'The Protestant League stands very close to the NSDAP. It is consciously German and, through moral religious energy, wants to contribute to the building up of the German people'.[62]

The racial dimension to Schemm's religion, while apparently so at odds with the message of Christianity, had in fact a rather impressive theological lineage. Within Germany, a generation of Protestant theologians had been erecting a theology of *Schöpfungsglaube*, which sanctified the *Volk* as an order of God's creation. These were not marginal eccentrics, or sycophants aping contemporary political trends, but some of the most respected Christian thinkers of the day. Their theology carried with it a message of race separation and superiority noticeable for its parallels with the efforts of contemporary American and South African theologians to erect similar theologies of race.[63] The sanctification of race qualifies Nazism not as a political religion, but as a religious politics.

We cannot here give a comprehensive overview of the religious views of all Nazis.[64] But what is clear is that, by their own account, most Nazis did not believe their movement was a political religion. Actual efforts at making Nazism a political religion were notable for their singular failure. Other Nazis not only provide evidence of the ridicule with which paganism was received, but also demonstrate how a Christian world view could be retained. Religious qualities to Nazism were certainly apparent, but there is much evidence to suggest that these qualities added up to a religious politics. Such a suggestion admittedly contravenes much of our inherited thinking about the movement and its ethos. The totalising quality of Nazism, its attempt to nestle itself into every aspect of the individual as well as the collective, certainly could argue for its 'totalitarian' nature, but hardly qualifies it as a religion. Unless, of course, we suggest that all totalitarian regimes are political religions – in which case this particular analytical device loses its ability to account for differences between systems that not only opposed liberal democracy, but also opposed each other. If the bloodiest war in Russian – and world – history is any indication, then content should take precedence over form in the investigation of the religious dimension of Nazism.

NOTES

1 Some works sponsored by this new institute include Achim Siegel (ed), *Totalitarismus-theorien nach dem Ende des Kommunismus* (Köln: Böhlau, 1998); and Klaus-Dieter Müller, Konstantin Nikischkin and Günther Wagenlehner (eds.), *Die Tragödie der Gefangenschaft in Deutschland und in der Sowjetunion 1941–1956* (Köln: Böhlau, 1998). Of course, any attempt at revival or reintroduction also brings with it a good amount of change. We do not see in the Institut a two-dimensional return to the *status quo ante* in totalitarianism scholarship *circa* 1950s–1960s, but rather an attempt to update it while retaining basic fundaments from its Cold War heydays.
2 See, for instance, Emilio Gentile, *The Sacralization of Politics in Fascist Italy* (Cambridge, MA: Harvard University Press, 1996); and Mabel Berezin, *Making the Fascist Self: The Political Culture of Interwar Italy* (Ithaca, NY: Cornell University Press, 1997).
3 Cf. Michael Ley and Julius Schoeps (eds.), *Der Nationalsozialismus als politische Religion* (Bodenheim: Philo, 1997); and Hermann Lübbe, *Heilserwartung und Terror: Politische Religionen des 20. Jahrhunderts* (Düsseldorf: Patmos, 1995).
4 See the excellent article by Ian Kershaw, 'Totalitarianism Revisited: Nazism and Stalinism in Comparative Perspective', *Tel Aviver Jahrbuch für deutsche Geschichte* 23 (1994).
5 Carl Jung, *The Collected Works of C.G. Jung* (Princeton, NJ: Princeton University Press, 1970), Vol. 10, p. 281.
6 Steven Aschheim, 'Hannah Arendt and Karl Jaspers: Friendship, Catastrophe and the Possibilities of German–Jewish Dialogue', in *idem*, *Culture and Catastrophe: Germans and Jewish Confrontations with National Socialism and Other Crises* (New York: New York University Press, 1996), p. 112.
7 Quoted in ibid., p. 112.
8 George Mosse, *The Nationalisation of the Masses* (New York: Howard Fertig, 1975).
9 Fritz Stern, *The Politics of Cultural Despair: A Study in the Rise of the Germanic Ideology* (Berkeley, CA: University of California Press, 1974), p. xxv (original emphasis). While Stern's conventional intellectual approach came under attack from a later generation of social historians, the secularisation theory underpinning it went unchallenged.
10 Michael Burleigh, *The Third Reich: A New History* (New York: Hill and Wang, 2000), p. 256.
11 Detlev Peukert, 'The Genesis of the "Final Solution" from the Spirit of Science', in Thomas Childers and Jane Caplan (eds.), *Reevaluating the Third Reich* (New York: Holmes and Maier, 1993), p. 247.
12 One of the most prolific scholars of political religion is Hans Maier, who has recently edited two invaluable volumes on the topic: Hans Maier (ed.), *'Totalitarismus' und 'politische Religionen': Konzepte des Diktaturvergleichs*, 2 vols. (Paderborn: Schöningh, 1996–97). See as well the highly theoretical analysis of Claus-Ekkehard Bärsch, *Die politische Religion des Nationalsozialismus* (Munich: Wilhelm Fink, 1999), who pays closer attention to a Christian element but claims this is confined to a discursive appropriation of tropes like the Trinity. A good introduction, emphasising

theory, is Philippe Burrin, 'Political Religion: the Relevance of a Concept', *History and Memory 9* (1997), pp. 321–49.

13 Adolf Hitler, *Mein Kampf*, trans. Ralph Manheim (Boston: Houghton Mifflin, 1962), p. 475.

14 See, for instance, Thomas Childers, *The Nazi Voter: The Social Foundations of Fascism in Germany, 1919–1933* (Chapel Hill, NC: University of North Carolina Press, 1983); Jürgen Falter, *Hitlers Wähler* (Munich: C.H. Beck, 1991); and Richard Hamilton, *Who Voted for Hitler?* (Princeton, NJ: Princeton University Press, 1982). A more recent intervention, which emphasises material considerations to the exclusion of the cultural, is William Brustein, *The Logic of Evil: The Social Origins of the Nazi Party, 1925–1933* (New Haven, CT: Yale University Press, 1996).

15 Hartmut Lehmann, 'Hitlers evangelische Wähler', in *idem, Protestantische Weltsichten: Transformationen seit dem 17. Jahrhundert* (Göttingen: Vandenhoeck and Ruprecht, 1998), pp. 130–52; Wolfram Pyta, *Dorfgemeinschaft und Parteipolitik, 1918–1933: Die Verschränkung von Milieu und Parteien in den protestantischen Landgebieten Deutschlands in der Weimarer Republik* (Düsseldorf: Droste, 1996); and Richard Steigmann-Gall, 'Apostasy or Religiosity? The Cultural Meanings of the Protestant Vote for Hitler', *Social History* 25 (2001), pp. 267–84.

16 David Blackbourn, 'The Politics of Demagogy in Imperial Germany', reprinted in idem, *Populists and Patricians: Essays in Modern German History* (London: Unwin Hyman, 1987), p. 218.

17 David Welch, *The Third Reich: Politics and Propaganda* (London: Routledge, 1993).

18 Path-breaking in this direction is Ian Kershaw, *Popular Opinion and Political Dissent in the Third Reich: Bavaria, 1933–1945* (Oxford: Oxford University Press, 1983).

19 Robert Gellately, *The Gestapo and German Society: Enforcing Racial Policy 1933–1945* (Oxford: Oxford University Press, 1990).

20 Robert Gellately, *Backing Hitler: Consent and Coercion in Nazi Germany* (Oxford: Oxford University Press, 2001).

21 Nathan Stoltzfus, *Resistance of the Heart: Intermarriage and the Rosenstrasse Protest in Nazi Germany* (New York: W.W. Norton, 1996).

22 Cf. Jeremy Noakes, 'The Oldenburg Crucifix Struggle of November 1936: A Case of Opposition in the Third Reich', in Peter Stachura (ed.), *The Shaping of the Nazi State* (London: Croom Helm, 1978).

23 Burleigh (note 10), pp. 10–12.

24 For similar observations with regard to the *Kaiserreich*, see Peter Walkenhorst, 'Nationalismus als "politische Religion"? Zur religiösen Dimension nationalistischer Ideologie im Kaiserreich', in Olaf Blaschke and Frank-Michael Kuhlemann (eds.), *Religion in Kaiserreich: Milieus – Mentalitäten – Krisen* (Gütersloh: Chr. Kaiser, 1996), pp. 503–29. Walkenhorst also provides a good summation of current work on the specifically Protestant-Christian content of 'secular' German nationalism.

25 Some of the strongest arguments for secularisation have come from committed believers. As Steve Bruce points out, this is quite relevant: 'Contrary to what one might expect from closet secularists, in their different ways [secularisation theorists] all have made it clear that they expect a secular world to be rather unpleasant … [David] Martin has a clear conservative dislike for the hedonism and liberality of the modern secular world and he adds a further reason for finding the secular world uncongenial: he is an ordained Anglican …'. See Steve Bruce (ed.), *Religion and Modernisation: Sociologists and Historians Debate the Secularisation Thesis* (Oxford: Oxford University Press, 1992), p. 2.

26 Berezin (note 2), pp. 350–1 (emphasis added), p. 60.

27 See Stathis Kalyvas, *The Rise of Christian Democracy in Europe* (Ithaca, NY: Cornell University Press, 1996), which attempts a theory of the relationship between religious

cleavage, identity and party formation. Of course Christian Democracy, while originally inimical to parliamentary democracy, parted company with totalitarianism in its gradual acceptance of liberal political form.

28 Burleigh (note 10), pp. 13–14. See as well Saul Friedländer, *Nazi Germany and the Jews* (New York: HarperCollins 1997).
29 Martin Broszat, *The Hitler State* (London: Longman, 1981), p. 224.
30 Burrin (note 12), p. 338.
31 Ibid., p. 336. Burrin relies on Brigitte Nagel, *Die Welteislehre: Ihre Geschichte und ihre Rolle im 'Dritten Reich'* (Stuttgart: GNT, 1991). See as well Jost Hermand, *Old Dreams of a New Reich: Volkish Utopias and National Socialism* (Bloomington, IN: Indiana University Press, 1992), p. 193, who maintains that Hitler subscribed to this teaching, which incidentally linked the 'flood of Genesis and the destruction of the Teutonic kingdom of Atlantis to "gravitational catastrophes" supposedly unleashed when the Earth "captured" a moon in its orbit'.
32 Alfred Rosenberg, *Der Mythus des 20. Jahrhunderts: Eine Wertung der seelisch-geistigen Gestaltenkämpfe unserer Zeit* (Munich: Hoheneichen, 1930), p. 114.
33 Ibid., p. 514.
34 Ibid., p. 203.
35 Ibid., pp. 155–6.
36 Quoted in Robert Cecil, *The Myth of the Master Race: Alfred Rosenberg and Nazi Ideology* (London: Batsford, 1972), p. 100.
37 Ibid., p. 101.
38 Albert Speer, *Inside the Third Reich* (New York: Avon, 1970), p. 96. For Goebbels's views on and relationship with Rosenberg, see ibid., pp. 122–5; and Ralf Reuth, *Goebbels* (New York: Harcourt Brace, 1993), pp. 201–5.
39 Adolf Hitler, *Hitler's Table Talk 1941–1944: His Private Conversations*, trans. Norman Cameron and R.H. Stevens, intro. Hugh Trevor-Roper (London: Weidenfeld and Nicholson, 1953), p. 422 (11 April 1942). *Mythus* was published as a private work, never becoming an official guide to Nazi thinking like *Mein Kampf*. It never received the official stamp of the NSDAP, nor did the party's official publisher publish it. Hitler occasionally considered sanctioning the book, but never did. However, *Mythus* was occasionally banned lower down the ranks of the party, for instance by the Breslau branch of the National Socialist Teachers' League (NSLB): Bundesarchiv Berlin-Lichterfelde (hereafter BAB), NS 22/410 (8 September 1935: Breslau).
40 Speer (note 38), p. 94.
41 Josef Ackermann, *Heinrich Himmler als Ideologe* (Göttingen: Musterschmidt, 1970), p. 90.
42 Hermand (note 31), p. 64.
43 Cecil (note 36), p. 119.
44 Hitler (note 13), p. 361.
45 Ibid., p. 360.
46 Ibid., pp. 361, 363. Given Hitler's utter contempt for Himmler's endless mysticism and pseudo-religious babble, not to mention Rosenberg's own rejection of it, it is extremely unlikely that Hitler approved of *Welteislehre*, as Hermand and Burrin both suggest.
47 Richard Steigmann-Gall, '*Furor Protestanticus*: Nazi Conceptions of Luther, 1919–1933', *Kirchliche Zeitgeschichte* 12 (1999), pp. 274–86.
48 BAB, NS 26/55 (27 October 1928: Passau).
49 Elke Fröhlich (ed.), *Die Tagebücher von Joseph Goebbels: Sämtliche Fragmente* (Munich: K.G. Saur, 1987), entry for 13 April 1937. *Thing* refers to the 'Thing' places, sites set up by Nordic paganists for their religious ceremonies.
50 Hans-Günther Seraphim (ed.), *Das politische Tagebuch Alfred Rosenbergs* (Göttingen: Musterschmidt, 1956), entry for 22 August 1939.

51 Alfred Krebs, *Tendenzen und Gestalten der NSDAP: Erinnerungen and die Frühzeit der Partei* (Stuttgart: Deutsche Verlags-Anstalt, 1959), p. 166.
52 *Völkischer Beobachter*, 13 April 1922.
53 Eberhard Jäckel (ed.), *Hitler: Sämtliche Aufzeichnungen 1905–1924* (Stuttgart: Deutsche Verlags-Anstalt, 1980), p. 635.
54 Henry Ashby Turner (ed.), *Hitler: Memoirs of a Confidant* (New Haven, CT: Yale University Press, 1985), pp. 139–40.
55 Hitler (note 39), p. 76 (21 October 1941).
56 *Institut für Zeitgeschichte*, MC 1 (interview of 15 July 1949).
57 Turner (note 54), pp. 19–21, 210; Seraphim (note 50), entry for 19 January 1940.
58 Franz Kühnel, *Hans Schemm, Gauleiter und Kultusminister* (Nuremberg: Stadtarchiv Nürnberg, 1985), pp. 134–5.
59 Gertrud Kahl-Furthmann (ed.), *Hans Schemm spricht: Seine Reden und sein Werk* (Bayreuth: Gauverl. Bayerische Ostmark, 1935), p. 124.
60 Walter Künneth, Werner Wilm and Hans Schemm, *Was haben wir als evangelische Christen zum Rufe des Nationalsozialismus zu sagen?* (Dresden: 1931), p. 19.
61 Ibid., pp. 19–20.
62 BAB, NS 12/638 (6 March 1931: Berlin).
63 For an exploration of *Schöpfungsglaube* and its theological origins, see Robert Ericksen, *Theologians under Hitler* (New Haven, CT: Yale University Press, 1985); and Wolfgang Tilgner, *Volksnomostheologie und Schöpfungsglaube: Ein Beitrag zur Geschichte des Kirchenkampfes* (Göttingen: Vandenhoeck and Ruprecht, 1966). On race and religion in South Africa, see T. Dunbar Moodie, *The Rise of Afrikanerdom: Power, Apartheid, and the Afrikaner Civil Religion* (Berkeley, CA: University of California Press, 1975); and Leonard Thompson, *The Political Mythology of Apartheid* (New Haven, CT: Yale University Press, 1985). For the United States, see Michael Barkun, *Religion and the Racist Right: The Origins of the Christian Identity Movement* (Chapel Hill, NC: University of North Carolina Press, 1994); and Leo Ribuffo, *The Old Christian Right: The Protestant Far Right from the Great Depression to the Cold War* (Philadelphia: Temple University Press, 1983).
64 For a broad analysis of the religious views of the Nazi élite, see Richard Steigmann-Gall, *The Holy Reich: Nazi Conceptions of Christianity, 1919–1945* (Cambridge: Cambridge University Press, 2003).

14

GOD'S CHOSEN WARRIORS

Romantic palingenesis, militarism and fascism in
modern Romania

Constantin Iordachi

The relationship between fascism and religion has remained to date one of the most debated topics in fascist studies. In addressing this controversial issue, in this study I employ as a case study the history of the Legion of the "Archangel Michael" in Romania, allegedly one of the most overtly religious and thus highly original fascist movements in interwar Europe. Elsewhere, I re-conceptualized the Legion as a charismatic-revolutionary fascist organization (2004). Building on Max Weber's theoretical framework on charismatic authority as well as on recent interdisciplinary additions and major reformulations, I employed the concept of charisma to denote not simply the leader Corneliu Zelea Codreanu's "capacity of attraction," but an explicit form of legitimizing and organizing the Legion's totalizing power. Based on an analysis of the Legion's genesis, structure and organization, social composition, and political evolution, I concluded that the movement exhibits a third major example of charismatic fascism, alongside the "paradigmatic" cases of Nazi Germany and Fascist Italy.

In the continuation of my work, in this essay I argue that the roots of the Legionary ideology are not to be found in the Eastern Christian Orthodox Church and/or dogma as a majority of historians argues, but in European Romantic historical ideologies of social palingenesis. I document the direct link between the Legionary ideology and Romantic visions of palingenesis through at least three pre-war channels: (1) the tradition of national messianism, best epitomized by Ion Heliade Rădulescu's theory of palingenesis, which redefined central Christian religious themes in the spirit of contemporary Evangelical-socialist discourses on regeneration; (2) the sacralization of politics which, having at its core the idea of sacred homeland and divine mission of the nation, aimed at binding Romania's Hohenzollern dynasty (1866–1947) more closely to the people and instilling a sense of collective mission and destiny to the national community; and (3) the conservative tradition of religious-patriotic militarism which shaped Corneliu Zelea-Codreanu's education and, through him, the nature of the Legion.

The most important dimension of continuity between Romantic nationalism and the Legionary ideology was the cult of the Wallachian Prince Michael the Brave (1595–1601) and his patron saint, the Archangel Michael, which encoded the myth of the palingenetic regeneration of the Romanian people. Revealing for the first time the origins and meaning of the cult of the Archangel Michael, the chapter concomitantly decodes the central palingenetic dimension of modern Romanian nationalism and of the Legionary ideology, and unveils their sacred roots.

I argue that the Legion was a totalitarian paramilitary organization; while inheriting major themes of palingenetic Romantic nationalism, its ideology reinterpreted them in novel forms, adapting them to the new socio-political context of interwar Romania. The Legion gave the militant spirit of the turn-of-the-century integral nationalism a revolutionary, anti-systemic orientation that was missing in its conservative-elitist variant. It merged pre-war anti-Semitism with post-1917 anti-communism into a new ideological formula, that of the "Judeo-Bolshevik" world conspiracy. It also added new elements to the conservative-elitist commitment to militarism and religious values, with deep roots in Romantic palingenetic discourses, such as the urgency of apocalyptic thinking, emphasis on expiation of sins through suffering and violent self-sacrifice, and ideas about metempsychosis linked with the cult of the ancestors, the cult of the dead and of the martyrs. Artificially separated by students of fascism from their original European context, such ideas are often "Orientalized" and treated as "Orthodox bizarreness."

On the basis of these findings, the chapter refutes the idea of an alleged exceptionalism of the Legion of the "Archangel Michael" based either on Balkan/Central European backwardness or Orthodox specificity. In doing so, it goes against the prevailing tendency to exoticize Romanian fascism as a peripheral "mutant," instead integrating it firmly within mainstream European fascism. Although it discusses a single case study, the chapter embeds it in an European context, arguing that the generic character of fascism can be properly understood only by taking into serious consideration its pan-European character, and by focusing on issues pertaining to intellectual transfers, entanglements, creative adaptation and further dissemination of fascist ideology in/from various "laboratories" of radical politics, situated in East and West alike. A central component of the intellectual background that gave birth to fascism, largely if not virtually neglected, are the Romantic discourses of palingenesis, whose importance is for the first time highlighted in this chapter.

BIBLIOGRAPHY

Iordachi, Constantin (2004). *Charisma, Politics and Violence: The Legion of the "Archangel Michael" in Interwar Romania* (Trondheim: Trondheim Studies on East European Cultures and Societies).

* * *

Our program? We want to change everything from its very foundations. The total resurrection of the country. On the ruins of the old state, sick, impotent and unjust, has to be erected the powerful structure of the new state. The New Romania. The Modern Romania.

(Codreanu 1931: 1)*

So God wanted: the germ of the renewal can grow only out of death, of suffering.

(Moța, 1936: 74-75)

Romania's interwar Legion of the Archangel Michael (also known as the Iron Guard),[1] has generally been regarded as one of the few "genuinely" religious fascist movements in interwar Europe. That is because the core of the Legionary ideology was based on religious or religion-related themes, of which the most important were the belief in God and in salvation, the expiation of sins through violent sacrifice and the cult of the martyrs. Legionary rituals were centered on rites of passage (baptism, brotherhood of the cross, marriage, oath-taking ceremonies, funerals); they employed central religious symbols, most importantly crosses and icons, and incorporated official or popular Eastern Christian Orthodox religious practices which were often officiated by priests. In view of the Legion's religiously charged language, visual symbolism, and ritual practice, as well as the massive participation of clerics in the movement, the Legion has often been singled out within the general typology of fascism as "a distinct subtype" (Payne 2006: 411–412), standing either alone or lumped together with other Central European movements under the label of clerical fascism.

Numerous students of fascism noted the religious components of the Legion, but they defined the movement in a bewildering diversity of ways, as an opportunistic pseudo-religious movement; a pre-modern religious sect; a form of clerical fascism; or a political religion. As early as 1944, the Marxist intellectual and activist Lucrețiu Pătrășcanu pointed to the charlatanic appropriation of the main tenets of the Eastern Orthodox dogma by the Legion and its masquerade-like "exploitation of the religious mysticism of the peasantry," resulting in a quasi-religious doctrine. In his view, this was a distinct feature of Romanian fascism: while German National-Socialists and Italian fascists "kept a certain distance from the dominant religions and churches," the Legion "inserted the Orthodox Christian religion into its political agitation," in both "form" and "substance" (Pătrășcanu 1944: 42, 44). This line of reasoning was continued more recently by historian Radu Ioanid, who claimed that the Legion was "one of the rare modern European political movements with a religious structure" (Ioanid 1990; 2003: 419). In line with Pătrășcanu, Ioanid argued that "Orthodox Christian spirituality underwent significant modifications within the Iron Guard mindset" and that, "despite its pronounced Orthodox character, Legionary mysticism did not signify the total assimilation of Orthodox theology," but "it is to be seen as an attempt at subordinating and transforming that theology into a political instrument" (2003: 419).

In the 1960s and 1970s, in the spirit of the then-dominant theories of modernization, pioneering scholars of Central European fascism defined the Legion as a sort of pre-modern and pre-political millennial movement, a curious revival—even if in seemingly modern garments—of similar phenomena that took place in early modern Europe, reflecting Central Europe's economic and political backwardness. Doubting its fully fascist character, Eugen Weber described the Legion as a form of "cargo cult" triggered by sudden modernization. Arguing that Codreanu's doctrine and nationalism "were of a completely different essence than that which we discover in other social movements of our time," Weber compared the Legion to Christian chiliastic movements "the West had known in the 14th and 16th century but forgotten since" (Weber 1965: 96). Zeev Barbu, most probably following Eric Hobsbawm's modernizing perspective put forward in *Primitive Rebels*, asserted that "the *legionari* constituted a psychological rather than a political group," a form of "messianic salvationist movement," symptomatic of "the transition from a religious to a political movement in a developing country" (Barbu 1968: 156, 160; 1980: 393).

In the 1980s and 1990s, historians of comparative fascism acknowledged the Legion's fascist features but still hesitated to fully locate it within mainstream European fascism. Stanley G. Payne pointed out that the Legion "is generally classified as fascist because it met the main criteria of any appropriate fascist typology, but it presented undeniably individual characteristics of its own" (1995: 280). In his view, "What made Codreanu especially different was that he became a sort of religious mystic, and though the Legion had the same general political goals as other fascist movements, its final aims were spiritual and transcendental" (ibid.: 280). For this reason, Payne defined the Legion as "a mystical kenotic form of *semi-religious fascism*," and "the only notable movement of this kind in an Orthodox country" (1980: 198–199). In a more recent article, Payne reiterated his claim that the Iron Guard politicized "a peculiar form of Romanian orthodox mysticism" in "a bizarre and extreme way" but denied that the movement created a "distinct political religion" (Payne 2005: 169; for a contrary view, see below). Similarly, pointing to its "overtly and sincerely religious" character, in a recent article Roger Eatwell defined the Legion as a form of "clerical fascism" typically developed "in highly peasant-based societies, where outside the radical Left there was little scope for parties which were not overtly religious" (2003: 154). Arguing that "increasingly during the 1930s Codreanu moved away from some of his early fascist radicalism towards an emphasis on the rebirth of a vaguely defined 'new man' and conservative mysticism," Eatwell concludes that "there are problems in unequivocally including the Iron Guard within a radical generic fascist pantheon" (ibid.: 154).

Two prominent scholars of fascism approached the religious component of the Legion from the perspective of the process of sacralizing politics, while at the same time accepting Pătrășcanu's view (via Ioanid) on the Legion's appropriation of the Orthodox dogma for political ends. The Italian historian Emilio Gentile suggested that the Iron Guard, together with the *Falange*, "may already be placed within the dimension of sacralised politics [...] because their ideology makes the sacralisation of the nation and the State evident, even if through a strongly politicised version of a traditional religion." He further argued that "movements like the Iron Guard assume, in reality, the character of a political religion in that they become the main factor of legitimation for the sacralisation of the nation, and for the nationalisation of Orthodox Christianity itself." Confronting the Iron Guard with his typology on political religions, Gentile concluded that the Legionary ideology is "a clear example" of "syncretic symbiosis between political religion and traditional religion" (2004: 361–262). A similar view was adopted by Roger Griffin. In his early writings, pointing to the "strong Orthodox Christian component in the thinking of the Iron Guard," Griffin defined the movement as a form of religious politics (1991: 30). In his latest book, Griffin argues that the Iron Guard was an expression of fascist modernism based on the sacralization of politics and the appropriation of the Christian Orthodox dogma (2007: 356).

In sum, although there seems to be an implicit consensus that the Legion had a religious "structure" or "matrix," scholars of fascism argue—from markedly different perspectives—that the Legionary ideology was either mimetic, syncretic or parasitic on the Eastern Orthodox Christianity. In a departure from this line of reasoning, this chapter reconsiders the origins and nature of the Legion's religious component and its relation to the Orthodox Church and its dogma. The study builds on Emilio Gentile's theoretical framework of the sacralization of politics, defined as a form of politics that "confers a sacred status on an earthly entity (nation, country, state, humanity, society, race, proletariat, history, liberty or revolution) and renders it an absolute principle of collective existence" (Gentile 2004: 18). Pointing to the multiple links between the process of the "sacralization" of politics that took place during the "long nineteenth century," on the one hand, and the Legionary ideology and ritual practice, on the other, I argue that the religious dimensions of the Legion originate from Romantic sources of mainstream nationalism and not from its allegedly privileged relationship to the interwar Orthodox Church and/or Orthodox theology. I contend that the Legion of the "Archangel Michael" provides a paramount example of appropriation and radical redefinition of Romantic palingenetic visions of nationalism elaborated in the first half of the nineteenth century and institutionalized in the second half of that century up to the First World War. This argument provides a striking illustration of the palingenetic core of the Legionary ideology, in line with Roger Griffin's paradigmatic definition of generic fascism as a "palingenetic form of populist ultra-nationalism" (1991: 26). However, in an attempt to potentially enhance our understanding of *the sacred components of nationalism* in general, and of fascism in particular, I depart from Griffin's usage of the term palingenesis in three ways. First, although Griffin is well aware of the etymology and history of the term palingenesis in original Romantic sources (see his discussion of Ballanche 1833, in 1991: 33), he uses the term in a generic sense, in line with present-day Italian scholars of fascism (Gentile 1975: 5; Lazzari 1984: 55), without engaging systematically with the concept's original discursive context, further elaborations and intellectual genealogies permeating the fascist ideology. Unlike

Griffin, I locate the origins of the fascist palingenetic myth in time and space by linking it to pan-European Romantic theories of palingenesis. Second, in constructing an ideal-typical analytical model of fascism, Griffin uses the term palingenesis in a metaphorical way, to refer to a universal archetype of human thinking; in doing so, he also reduces palingenesis to the myth of rebirth and regeneration, defined as the ideological core of fascism. My approach differentiates between universal ideas of rebirth and more complex, even if intimately related, Romantic *palingenetic ideologies*, defined as mystical discourses on the regeneration of society. Based on the reconceptualization of main themes of the Christian dogma, palingenetic ideologies encompass not solely the idea of regeneration, but also additional components such as the dogma of the original sin, providentialism and the idea of divine election, the idea of purification through expiation, and the myth of final resurrection. Third, Griffin accepts that "the most obvious well-head of palingenetic myth in the wider sense is religion;" yet, his approach is based on the premise that the fascist "secular palingenetic myth" does not originate from religious sources but it "is simply the expression of an archetype of the human mythopoeic faculty in secular form" (Griffin 1991: 33). I claim that fascism inherited from Romantic thinkers is a new conception of the "sacred" which can be documented by way of intellectual genealogies and affinities with theories of social palingenesis. In the Romanian context, this continuity is made evident by the fact that the palingenetic myth is the *common element* that unites Legionarism with the mainstream Romantic nationalism and not the *differentia specifica*.

The palingenetic core of the Legionary ideology permeated its myths, symbols, and rituals; it was most evident in the Legionary *historicism*, uniting the idea of divine election with that of *holy history* and *sacred territory*. While building on the legacy of Romantic visions of palingenetic nationalism, the Legionary ideology nevertheless amplified them with new elements such as mysticism, the theory of the transgression of souls, and apocalyptic thinking based on rabid anti-Semitism and anti-communism. Moreover, while pre-war palingenetic visions of nationalism were centered on the national army as a vehicle of national regeneration, the Legion appropriated the idea of the Romanians' divine mission, claiming the young generation's monopoly on the national path to salvation under the leadership of its charismatic leader, Codreanu. It also redefined militarism as paramilitary *Legionarism,* portraying itself as an earthly Christian army engaged in a great global eschatological crusade against "Judeo-communism." Most importantly, the Legion attached to the palingenetic vision of the Romanian nation an explicit *revolutionary political project*, that of building a totalitarian state through violent means. These major innovations departed from the Romantic messianic nationalism and crystallized into a novel and original ideology of *charismatic-revolutionary nationalism*. In view of these mutations, I differentiate Legionarism from earlier, Romantic versions of palingenetic nationalism, placing it instead in the camp of interwar fascist and totalitarian movements.

To illustrate the complex pattern of continuities and ruptures between the Romantic national ideology, turn of the century militarism and Legionarism, I focus on the cult of the Archangel Michael, which is generally taken as a primary proof of the movement's Christian religious character (Pătrăşcanu: 1944: 42; see also Mosse 1999: 37). I argue that, although building on a popular and wide-spread Christian cultural "code," the cult of the Archangel Michael was in fact the main axis of the process of the sacralization of politics in Romania, being organically linked with the cult of Michael the Brave elaborated by Romantic writers in the first half of the nineteenth century and subsequently institutional-ized in national ceremonies, rites, and rituals. This cult, which symbolized the fight for the political union of ethnic Romanians living in various historical provinces that made up ancient Dacia—the *idée force* of modern Romanian nationalism—found its most effective locus in elite military schools, whose edu-cational curriculum blended religion and nationalism in the ideology of patrio-tism, military glory, and messianic mission.

The study is organized into several inter-related parts. The first part provides a brief overview of pan-European Romantic ideas of regeneration, underscoring the reconceptualization of central religious themes in palingenetic theories on society and politics. It also documents the transfer and adaptation of theories of palingenesis to the Romanian context and their impact on the elaboration of the modern national ideology, focusing mainly on the emergence of the cult of Michael the Brave as a symbol of national unity. Based on representative sam-ples of Romantic historicism, I argue that Michael the Brave and his patron saint, the Archangel Michael, served as paramount symbols of the Romanians' regen-eration, whose divine, predestined, mission was to unite all ethnic Romanians in a single state. To illustrate the link between the Romantic cult of Michael the Brave, the process of sacralizing politics in the nineteenth century and the inter-war fascist ideology, the second part employs as a case study the elite military academy established in 1912 at the Dealu Monastery. An innovative pedagogical experiment in military training, this school promoted an educational program focusing on character building. I contend that the main features of the Legion's ideology, pedagogy, and ritual practice were first attempted in the military school's curriculum, being later emulated by Codreanu and adapted to interwar socio-political conditions. In the third and main part of the chapter I explore the Legion's palingenetic ideology and its sacralization of politics. Finally, on the basis of this case study, I suggest more general conclusions about the relationship between Romantic palingenesis, religion, the sacralization of politics, and the fas-cist ideology.

Reconceptualizing Christianity: from "philosophical" to "social" palingenesis

Ideas of regeneration constitute a universal archetype of human thinking, with an extraordinary long and rich tradition in various religions and cultures. During the eighteenth century, in the European context, the term "regeneration" was part of two distinct but largely interlocking theological and scientific vocabularies, being invested with two sets of meanings: (1) religious, referring either to "spiritual birth at the time of baptism" or to the renewal that would follow the Second Coming, as prophesied in the New Testament; and (2) physiological, referring to the regenerative properties of certain organisms, as argued in new scientific discourses ("Régénération," in *L'Encyclopédie*, cited in Sainson, 2001–2002: 9–25). During Romanticism, stimulated by a sense of social crisis and moral void following the upheaval of the French Revolution (Ozouf 1989: 781–791), the concept of "regeneration" permeated discourses about humanity as well, being invested with a new meaning denoting "rebirth in all its physical, moral, and, in particular, political forms" (de Baecque, 1993: 165). It soon became a "key concept" of political discourses, being accompanied by its logical corollary, the creation of the "new man" (Ozouf 1989: 790). Modeled on the behavioral model of *imitatio Christi*, the creation of the new man was conceived as a "second rebirth" and expressed by means of theological language (ibid.: 783).

In order to understand the transfer of discourses about regeneration from theology to society *via* scientific discourses about the natural world, one has to explore Romantic theories of palingenesis. The word "palingenesis," meaning renaissance, resurrection or regeneration (Lalane 1992: 729) was first introduced into modern science by the Swiss philosopher and scientist Charles Bonnet (1720–1793). In *La Palingénésie philosophique* (1769–1770), Bonnet elaborated a developmental philosophy called palingenesis, based on the idea of a series of resurrections caused by successive unfolding of "*germes de restitution*" (germs of restitution) (McCalla 1994: 423). In order to account for the manner in which the nature of living beings is transmitted and perpetuated from generation to generation, Bonnet advocated the preformationist doctrine of *emboîtement* (encasement) according to which the essence of beings is encapsulated in the germ of restitution. According to Bonnet, this transmission was not static, but was subject to evolution. To account for progress, this preformationist explanation was supplemented by the theory of palingenesis, meaning rebirth and regeneration within a preformationist structure (ibid.: 422). Bonnet argued that the earth is periodically struck by global disasters (*catastrophe générale*), as a result of which most organisms die while the survivors progress to new heights, as a result of successive acts of rebirth.

Writing at a time when the theological and scientific discourses were parts of a single unified worldview, and being himself a deeply religious spirit, Bonnet reconceptualized Christianity in the language of biological preformationism. According to Arthur McCalla, Bonnet's "philosophical palingenesis" can be defined as a form of "scientific ideology," since it employed an explanatory system specific to theology and applied it to the natural world (ibid.: 429). This scientific ideology was characterized by three main features. First, although Bonnet offered a naturalistic explanation of resurrection, his theory of palingenesis was based on a "Christian anthropology." In arguing that the locus of the soul lies in the germ of restitution, Bonnet emulated St. Paul's metaphor of the seed in discussing the resurrection,[2] reformulating it into scientific language (ibid.: 423). Second, in Bonnet's understanding, natural evolution unfolded according to a providential master plan of "revolutions of the earth" which—far from occurring at random—were coordinated by the Creator himself. Third, inspired by the theology of revelation and resurrection, his theory of palingenesis regarded *expiation* and *suffering* as the central part of the divine scenario of unfolding progress.

The theory of philosophical palingenesis was transplanted from natural sciences to the realm of historical explanation by the French writer and philosopher Pierre-Simon Ballanche (1776–1847). Published at a time of wide proliferation of Romantic metaphysical philosophies of history (ibid.: 432), Ballanche's *Essais de palingénésie sociale* (*Essays on Social Palingenesis*, 1827–1829) elaborated a highly influential theology of historical progress, expressing historical consciousness by means of Bonnet's concept of palingenesis. Ballanche adopted all the major elements of Bonnet's theological theory of natural palingenesis, such as the idea of preformationism of the human essence; the expiation of sins as the manner in which the action of palingenesis or rebirth operates; the central role played by crisis in bringing about evolution by spiritual rehabilitation; and teodical[†] concerns (ibid.: 439). Yet, in a major innovation, Ballanche shifted from natural to social palingenesis, using the term "palingenesis" to refer to the *progress of society* through the successive rehabilitation of social institutions (ibid.: 437). For Ballanche, progress was the result of acts of spiritual rehabilitation in order to overcome the original Fall that took place mainly during ages of "crisis and renewal" of human essence. These acts of redemption could occur only with the cooperation of the humans themselves, who—unlike the natural or the animal world—are able to assume their own transformation. The key action leading to spiritual rehabilitation was the expiation of sins. For Ballanche, suffering was the way to overcome the Fall and to emancipate humankind. In applying this theological explanatory system to the history of the humankind, Ballanche produced a *historical ideology*, "an explanatory system applied to human history but derived, via Bonnet, from theology" (ibid.: 439).

Popularized by Ballanche and further expanded by the republican socialist philosophers Pierre Leroux (1806–1863) and Jean Reynaud (1806–1863), *historical ideologies based on theories of palingenesis* became very influential in the first half of the nineteenth century, greatly shaping theories of social change (Sharp 2004). They were advanced, in various forms, by an astonishing variety of thinkers, ranging from liberal to traditional Catholic orientations. Romantic discourses on palingenesis were part and parcel of a more general religious revival following the French Revolution. In an attempt to cure their acute spiritual crisis, the "malaise of the soul," Romantics appealed to religion, most importantly to Catholicism. They pleaded for the transformation of society through the cultural and spiritual emancipation of the masses and their moral regeneration based on *Christian foundations* (Schenk 1969: 85). As part of a widespread Catholic traditionalist reaction against the doctrine of the French

---

[†] Teodical: related to theodicy, see below.

Enlightenment, Romantic writers re-conceptualized the Christian doctrines of revelation, providence, theodicy,[††] eschatology,[†††] and soteriology[††††] and redefined the category of the sacred (McCalla 1998: 277). In doing so, they departed from the official dogma of established churches and put forward anthropocentric forms of theology, emphasizing the emotional side of religion, the inevitable suffering of man, mysticism, ecumenism, religions' reconciliation and universal spirituality, often arguing for a return to "primitive Christianity." Unconventional versions of "transcendental Christianity" were accompanied by apocalyptic visions about the collapse of civilization, and by ideas about progress through *metempsychosis*, referring to the passing of the soul at death into another body or inanimate state. For Romantics, metempsychosis was a form of social solidarity, since it envisioned redemption and spiritual regeneration as pertaining to the community and not simply to the individual (Sharp 2004).

Arguably, the Romantic religious revival remained largely "unfulfilled" (Schenk 1969: 85). Palingenetic doctrines authored by Catholic-minded reformers developed by and large outside the established Church; although having a certain impact on the official dogma, most of them were barred by established religions, as originally happened with Bonnet's "philosophical palingenesis" (McCalla 1994: 427). Other thinkers, such as Leroux, rejected Catholicism altogether, militating for the establishment of new, more democratic religions based on the teaching of early Christianity (Bakunin 1975). These theories nevertheless impacted national Romanticism, combining deism and pantheism with the idolatry of the people (Schenk 1969: 121). Pleading for a radical transformation of society, national Romantic thinkers merged religious faith, theological worldviews, and historical-mindedness in original syntheses. By means of Romantic "prophets of the nation", the major themes of the palingenetic discourses about reforming society penetrated national ideologies, serving as the potential foundation for radical ideologies of the twentieth century, such as fascism.

National Romanticism and the regeneration of Romania

Ideas of regeneration were widespread in Romanian lands as well. In order to understand the palingenetic component of the Romanian national ideology, one

---

[††] Theodicy is a branch of theology and philosophy which attempts to reconcile the existence of evil and suffering in the world with the belief in an omnipotent and benevolent God. The term is derived from the Greek *theós* or god and díkē or justice), meaning literally "the justice of God." "Theodicy" was first coined in 1710 by the German philosopher Gottfried Leibniz (1664–1717) in *Essais de Théodicée sur la bonté de Dieu, la liberté de l'homme et l'origine du mal (Theodicic Essays on the Benevolence of God, the Free Will of Man, and the Origin of Evil)*.

[†††] Eschatology: branch of theology and philosophy dealing with the final events in the history of the world and the destiny of humanity. The term is derived from the Greek *eschatos* meaning last and *logy* meaning "the study of."

[††††] Soteriology is a branch of Christian theology that deals with salvation. The term is derived from the Greek words *sōtēr* (savior, preserver) and *sōtērion* (salvation).

needs to go back to the first half of the nineteenth century, a particularly formative period for the principalities of Moldova and Wallachia that united in 1859 to constitute modern Romania. Politically, this was a period of reassertion of the internal autonomy of the two principalities under Ottoman suzerainty, marked by the demise of the rule by appointed Ottoman Greeks from the Phanar district in Istanbul (the so-called Phanariot regime, 1711/1716–1821) and the return to the rule of native princes (1821). It was also a period of massive Westernization, characterized by rapid but uneven social and political change, and by the standardization of the Romanian language, the emergence of the first national institutions, and the formation of "public opinion." Culturally, the period was dominated by national Romanticism, defined—as everywhere else in Europe— by the discovery of popular culture and folk literature, emphasis on national values and originality, historicism, the symbolic delimitation of the national territory, and the elaboration of a pantheon of heroes.

This period of transformation was symbolically placed under the sign of national "regeneration," the word "reform" being considered unable to convey the imperious need for a thorough transformation of the society. Ideas of regeneration were expressed first and foremost in the form of *historicism*, marked by a strong interest in medieval history. Romantic writers put forward visions of palingenetic nationalism centered on the literary motives of the medieval glory of the nation, its decadence and death caused by treason, and its rebirth through heroism. Their discourses on regeneration were saturated with religious terminology and symbolism, and contributed to forging national myths of the Romanians' divine election and historical mission, providing prototypes of civil and religious values and behavioral models.

Romantic historicism was animated by *Romanianism (românism)*, centered on the idea of emancipation and political union of the Romanians through the revival of ancient Dacia. The new doctrine of national awakening of the Romanians was initiated at the end of the eighteenth century by the Greek-Catholic cultural movement generally known as *Şcoala ardeleană* (the Transylvanian School). Influenced by the ideas of the German Enlightenment, the Transylvanian School promoted historicism, bringing arguments in favor of the "pure" Latin origin of the Romanians and transforming this idea into a political weapon to alter Transylvania's constitutional framework, based at the time on the exclusion of Christian Orthodox believers from corporate social and political rights. At the beginning of the nineteenth century, its work was continued by the Banatians Damaschin Bojincă (1801–1869) and Eftimie Murgu (1805–1870), and by the Transylvanians Gheorghe Lazăr (1779–1823), and Aaron Florian (1805–1887), among others. The latter two immigrated in Wallachia and set the basis of a comprehensive program of national regeneration through education, as founders of and professors at the prestigious "Saint Sava" National College in Bucharest, the first national college in the Romanian language. Their program was continued by a new generation of Wallachian and Moldavian scholars, who acted as "apostles" of the new movement of national regeneration.

The new national consciousness in-the-making was first and foremost expressed in the creation of the national literature and history. Emphasizing the importance of studying national history, Romantic writers delimited the national territory and constructed a pantheon of heroes. They defined nationalism as the cult of the ancestors, and proposed a gallery of heroes and sites of memory emblematic for the Romanian national identity, centered mainly on the most glorious figures of the Wallachian prince, Michael the Brave (1593–1601) and of the Moldavian prince, Stephen the Great (1457–1504), the "traditional tandem" of Romanian national identity that "survived all [political] ideologies" (Boia 2001: 37). The former was soon to emerge as the central axis of Romanian nationalism and therefore deserves separate treatment.

The cult of Michael the Brave, the Unifier

In the Romantic pantheon of national heroes, Michael the Brave distinguished himself as the symbol of Romanian regeneration, for multiple reasons. First, the prince was celebrated as a highly competent military leader: in 1595, Michael successfully challenged Ottoman domination in Wallachia, scoring a brilliant victory against the Sultan's army at Călugăreni. Second, Michael was celebrated as a unifier, since he brought under his authority the principalities of Transylvania (1599–1600) and Moldova (1600), temporarily ruling over all the historical provinces inhabited by ethnic Romanians. Third, Michael's anti-Ottoman campaigns and his support of the Orthodox Church in Transylvania made him a fighter for Christianity and a defender of Orthodoxy. The prince was treacherously murdered by mercenaries on 9 August 1601 in Câmpia Turzii in Transylvania, at Habsburg orders; his body was desecrated, but his head was rescued by his faithful followers and buried at the Dealu Monastery (Cloister of the Hill) in Wallachia. Although short-lived, Michael's deeds served in the modern period as a model: the prince was hailed as Romanians' greatest medieval ruler and military commander, and as a symbol of national unity and regeneration, bringing about the restoration of ancient Dacia. His heroic but tragic death served as a Romantic symbol of the glory as well as decadence and victimization of the nation at the hands of foreigners.

The first historical portrait of Michael the Brave was depicted by Aaron Florian, who had taught since 1836 at the Wallachian St. Sava College. Convinced of the important role played by history in the awakening of national consciousness, Florian authored a monumental history of the Romanians in three volumes, published in 1835–1837. The second volume focused mainly on the personality of Michael the Brave, presented as the Romanians' most important national hero, a fighter for Christianity and exceptional military commander.

Widely disseminated at the time, Florian's Romantic portrait of Michael the Brave as an exceptional but tragic hero had a strong impact on his contemporaries. It inspired not only the writers' imagination, but also that of local princes, who, at a time of redefinition of modes of political authority and legitimization, put into practice proposals for the sacralization of politics. Eager to act as the leader of the new patriotic movement of regeneration, the Wallachian prince Gheorghe Bibescu (1842–1848) emulated the political model of Michael the Brave, presenting himself as a descendant of the illustrious prince. To emphasize the symbolic link with his glorious predecessor, during the coronation ceremony that took place in February 1843, Bibescu wore Michael's princely costume. In August 1844, Prince Bibescu went in pilgrimage to the Dealu Monastery—near Targovişte, the formal medieval capital of Wallachia—to pay his respects to Michael the Brave's grave. The account of Bibescu's visit underscores the messianic connotations of the prince's encounter with Michael's relics. As a sign of reverence, Bibescu restored the Dealu monastic complex, and exhumed Michael's skull and placed it in a glass case, which subsequently became the most important *lieu de memoirs* of the Romanian history. These incipient attempts at sacralizing politics paved the way toward the messianic cult of Michael the Brave.

Evangelical socialism and regeneration: Ion Heliade Rădulescu's theory of palingenesis

The historiographical trend initiated by Florian was to be continued by Ion Heliade Rădulescu (1802–1872). A prolific writer, editor and translator, Heliade is unanimously regarded as the most influential Romanian cultural figure of the first half of the nineteenth century. Born in Târgovişte, in a lower middle-class family, Heliade studied with Lazăr at the St. Sava College, where he was to soon become a teacher upon his professor's departure. In the 1820's, Heliade started a lucrative business as a publisher, devoting his laborious activity to the promotion of education and the development of the Romanian language through literature, translations, and journalism. Stretching several decades, his eclectic social-political and literary thought—with influences ranging from French Christian Socialists to the political thought of Giuseppe Mazzini, and from the classical literary tradition to Romanticism (Călinescu 1986: 140–142)—set the foundation of the program of national regeneration of the Romanians.

Assimilating French literary and political sources, Heliade was the first to introduce and actively use the word *palingenesis* in Romanian. He developed his own, highly elaborated, theory of palingenesis, covering all domains of existence and organically linked to his messianic vision of the Romanian nation. The essence of Heliade's theory of palingenesis was Evangelical Christianity, having at its forefront the figure of Christ. Heliade was convinced that the key to understanding the nature of the universe and the ideal organization of society was to be found in the Bible. The final goal of history was the accomplishment of the new "Evangelical man" through salvation and the establishment of the "Biblical Republic." Influenced by Romantic mystical thinkers, most importantly Aimé Martin (1781–1844), Alphonse Esquiros (1812–1876), the author of *L'Evangile du peuple* (1840), and the above-mentioned Leroux, Heliade regarded religious salvation as a collective, and not an individual, act. Although it may suffer degeneration and decadence, human society can regenerate itself though palingenesis, following the model of *imitatio Christi*. While emulating Leroux's and Ballanche's idea of the "collective man" (*l'homme collectif*), Heliade symbolically replaced humanity as the object of salvation with "the people" (Popovici 1935: 257), following in this respect Mazzini's slogan "God and the people" (Călinescu 1986: 146).

Heliade's theory of palingenesis was complemented by a philosophy of history centered on the idea of progress. While adopting Giovanni Battista Vico's (1668–1744) influential theory on the cyclical unfolding of history, Heliade replaced cyclicity with the idea of spiral evolution and explained progress through the equilibrium between antitheses, such as good/evil or spirit/matter, and regress through their confrontation. Heliade applied this philosophical principle to interpret the history of the Romanians, which he regarded, in the spirit of Romantic messianism, as the central axis of world history. In his view, the regeneration of the Romanians was part and parcel of the "palingenesis of the Orient" on the ruins of the Ottoman Empire (Popovici 1935: 240). Criticizing Catholicism, he argued that Eastern Orthodoxy in general, and the Romanians in particular, were able to contribute to European civilization by the spirit of "genuine religiosity," by restoring that vitality of "primitive communities" that in the West had been perverted by materialism (Anghelescu, 2002: XXVII). Although fully devoted to the regeneration of the Romanian nation—predestined to bring about "the universal republic or the ecumenical Cesarate, that is a single flock and a single shepherd" (Heliade, *Typograful roman,* 1870: 16–17, cited in Popovici 1935: 226)—Heliade was an essentially cosmopolitan thinker, his main unit of analysis being the mankind in its entirety. Believing that nations and nationalism are necessary but temporary stages in the evolution of humanity, Heliade supported a federative organization of Europe, under the form of "the United States of Europe" proposed by Victor Hugo.

Under the sign of the Archangel Michael, the guardian of the nation: the cult of Michael the Brave

A central piece in Heliade's grand philosophy of history was the epic poem *Mihaida*, published for the first time in 1847 (*Curier de ambe sexe*, V 1847: 37–86). In *Mihaida*, Heliade put forward a messianic vision of Romanian nationalism, establishing the symbolic link between the cult of Michael the Brave, the Romanians' saint-like historical hero, and the Archangel Michael, the archetypical model of God's warriors.

Written in the tradition of classical epic poems, the work closely emulated the highly influential baroque epic poem by Torquato Tasso, *La Gerusalemme liberata* (Jerusalem Delivered), which narrates the story of the First Crusade in which Christian armies led by the charismatic leader Godfrey of Bouillon recover

Jerusalem from Muslim occupation. Seduced by Tasso's messianic scenario, Heliade employed it in his work, adapting it nevertheless to his own philosophy of history. Heliade conceived *Mihaida* as the Romanians' national epic poem of "regeneration," centered on the figure of Michael the Brave, *the Unifier*. In order to integrate Michael's deeds into the national history of the Romanians and—more ambitiously—into that of the world, the poem starts with a short evocation of the time when "all Romanians were united, under a single sceptre," and unequivocally states their charismatic qualification of being the chosen people. After this argument, Heliade unfolds his philosophy of history according to which events follow a divine scenario. God himself reveals the meaning of the world, speaking of sacrifice and redemption, and blaming the decline of the Christians on religious schisms, fratricide wars, and the loss of the divine principle of love. Christians' decline culminated in the expansion of Ottoman Muslims in Europe. In order to invest Michael's action with universal significance, Heliade alludes to the imperious need for a new, predestined *hero of Christianity*. In a dramatic climax, he introduces the figure of Michael the Brave, the charismatic hero destined to bring salvation to the Christian world and its sacred nation, the Romanians.

Heliade continues by delineating the main stages of the charismatic scenario centered on the predestined hero, largely following Tasso's work. The Archangel Gabriel appears on Mount Caraiman and then in Târgoviște and hands to Michael the Brave the "divine decrees" of liberating the Christians from the Muslim yoke. The most dramatic moment of *Mihaida* is the hero's encounter with the archangel that occurs at midnight, in a highly Romantic setting. After ritual prayer and lighting the votive light, Michael falls asleep with his eyes fixed on the icon of Christ's redemption. During his sleep, the archangel, the messenger of God's divine will approaches to encounter the hero and give him the divine mission. Illuminated, God's chosen hero internalizes the divine mission of liberating the Christians, and gets ready for the battle. In lines full of dramatic intensity, Heliade makes the apologia of the charismatic hero: "Sublime is the man when the Divine Will's genius penetrates him and moves him well-inspired!" After detailing at length on the domestic circumstances of Michael's action, the poem ends with a suggestive parallelism between the Archangel Michael's heavenly battle against Satan, "with the fire sword, surrounded by angels," and "our Michael with the sword into his hand," among Romanian fighters. As compared to Tasso, Heliade operates here a symbolical switch, replacing Archangel Gabriel as God's messenger with Archangel Michael, a change justified not only by Michael's higher divine rank, but also by the correspondence with the hero's predestined name, Michael, "who is like God." As his divine model and patron saint, Archangel Michael inoculated the hero with "the reviving spirit of fallen peoples," enabling the prince to work toward "Divine purification."

In adopting the symbolism of Archangel Michael, Heliade followed a widespread religious culture, emulating the *Biblical tradition of angels as guardians of nations*. The Archangel Michael was one of the most popular Christian saints in the Roman Catholic as well as in the Greek Orthodox worlds, honored as

God's chosen warrior, the "Prince of Light," personal commander of the Holy War, and as a high priestly figure. Due to his multiple apocalyptic capacities and his important role in fighting the devil and in obtaining salvation and redemption, the Archangel Michael has been subject to particular adoration. Moreover, his representation was not restricted to religious symbolism; he was often employed by Romantic writers preaching charismatic or messianic forms of nationalism as the most powerful and apt protector of the chosen people. As a militant warrior, the Archangel Michael served as symbol of mass military mobilization, guaranteeing divine intervention and victory of the chosen nation against its enemies. As the glorious victor over Satan and the guide of souls to Heaven assisting in the Last Judgment, he was assimilated with the ultimate salvation and redemption of the nation.

Upon its publication, *Mihaida* was a very influential poem, inspiring numerous epic works centered on the messianic figure of Michael the Brave. Originally written for Romanian soldiers, the poem was particularly influential in the army. Heliade's grand, mystic and prophetic vision of national history, his cult of Michael the Brave and of the Archangel Michael as his patron saint became the main catalyst of Romanian national identity and a paramount symbol of *militarism*. The innovative association with the Archangel Michael was to become central to the cult of Michael the Brave, linked with a major theme in Heliade's palingenetic thought: the paramount role played by the national army as a vehicle of regeneration.

The cult of the Archangel Michael and the sacralization of politics in modern Romania

The 1859 union of Moldova and Wallachia into a single state called Romania inaugurated a new stage in the process of nation- and state-building. In order to consolidate the new nation-state "in the making," Prince Alexandru Ioan Cuza (1859–1866) initiated a process of legal and administrative unification and cultural homogenization of the two principalities. As elsewhere, the construction of a state-sponsored educational system was essential in promoting an officially endorsed model of Romanian national identity and patriotism to the national cause, disseminated through a dense network of primary schools in urban and rural areas. Equally important were new national monuments and public ceremonies as part of the process of the sacralization of politics, centered on the idea of political union of ethnic Romanians, militarism, and the cult of war heroes. The cult of Michael the Brave was central to the process of sacralizing politics, being institutionalized and invested with novel political connotations. One can distinguish three main stages in the evolution of the cult, linked with major political events: (1) 1864, in the context of the consolidation of the state union between the two principalities and the elaboration of a unified national ideology; (2) 1877–1878, during the War of Independence that resulted in the abolition of Ottoman sovereignty; and (3) the beginning of the twentieth century, marked by a strong political campaign in favor of Romania's *irredenta* war against Austria-Hungary, leading to the achievement of national unity.

The revitalization of Michael the Brave's cult during the first two stages was connected to the publication of the most ample work on the prince, *Istoria romanilor supt Mihai Vodă Viteazul* [History of the Romanians under Prince Michel the Brave] written by Nicolae Bălcescu (1817–1852), a prominent Wallachian revolutionary activist. Bălcescu began his work in 1848 but was unable to finish it by the time of his death. The manuscript was partially published in 1861–1863 in *Revista Română* and fully in 1878. The 1863 publication had a considerable influence over contemporaries. In 1864, the Minister of Education Dimitrie Bolintineanu (1825–1872) proposed the transfer of Michael's skull from Mănăstirea Dealu in Târgoviște to the church the prince built in Bucharest, in order to give Michael's tomb national exposure, a plan that remained unfulfilled due to political turmoil.

The complete publication of Bălcescu's work in 1878, during the War of Independence, had the same catalyzing effect at a time of societal mobilization for the war effort. One of the most prominent supporters of Michael's cult was the poet Mihai Eminescu (1850–1889), at the time editor of the Conservative newspaper *Timpul*. For Eminescu, the nation was the supreme social and political ideal, invested with a divine historical mission. An ardent nationalist activist, he militated for a strong state that would protect the Romanian nationality and would contain the demographic "invasion of foreigners," represented in his view mostly by the Jews. He also pleaded for the regeneration of traditional elites, the consolidation of the native middle class, and the development of state-sponsored schools in support of the national culture.

The cult of Michael the Brave was revitalized again at the turn of the century, at a time when the major irredentist movements, pleading for the achievement of national unity by annexing the neighboring provinces inhabited by ethnic Romanians, such as Austrian-Hungarian-ruled Transylvania and the Banat, gained momentum. It is important to note that the new turn-of-the-century nationalism was not a state-sponsored project, but developed as a rebellious concept against traditional politics and the existing political establishment. It rejected "bourgeois politicianism" and "materialism" and militated for an active foreign policy leading to the achievement of the national unity of all ethnic Romania by military means. The main representative of the new nationalist spirit was the League for the Cultural Unity of the Romanians, established in 1890 in Bucharest. In order to mobilize public opinion for the ideal of national unity, the League started an assiduous commemorative mania, centered on the figures of Michael the Brave and Stephen the Great, the Romanians' most illustrious rulers.

The main catalyst of the new militant nationalism and the most important animator of the cult of Michael the Brave was Nicolae Iorga (1871–1940). A prominent historian with a multifaceted but contradictory personality, Iorga captured the spirit of the turn-of-the-century national militancy in his cultural nationalism called *Semănătorism* (the Sayer) an original combination of Romantic and populist convictions. For Iorga, nationalism was "a political doctrine, a certain conception of State life and organization in the service of the nation, understood as an organic, decisive being ... Nationalism is not a sentimental, colourful background for any political faith: it is in itself a faith, and an exclusive one" (Iorga 1908: 2086).

Utilizing the writing of history as a political weapon, Iorga mobilized public opinion to achieve national union. Perpetuating the tradition inaugurated by Heliade, during the ample commemoration of three hundred years since Michael the Brave's death (1601–1901), Iorga presented the prince as a pre-destined charismatic hero, "the man sent by God three hundred years ago to unite all Romanians into a single body," so as to fulfill a divinely inspired miracle, as example for the future generations (Iorga 1901: 10). In order to continue and even out do Bălcescu's unfinished work, Iorga produced a massive, 1,500-page epic monograph on Michael the Brave, published in 1903.

Iorga was also involved in the dissemination of the cult of Michael the Brave in public ceremonies. Thanks to the League's public subscription campaign, in 1904, Michael's skull was laid in a new bronze box. Each year, on the 8th of November, the prince's skull had been taken out of the box for the religious commemoration of Archangel Michael, set on a table, together with a cross and the Gospel, and displayed in a military parade organized in his honor.

Iorga considered this achievement too modest for the prince's personality and importance. With public subscriptions, in 1913, he built a new, more imposing marble sarcophagus for Michael's skull at the Dealu Monastery. In the spirit of Heliade and Eminescu, Iorga took the charismatic cult of Michael to new heights, writing on the new tombstone of the prince:

> Here rests what crime and impiety left from the saint body of *Voievod* Michael the Brave. His soul continues to live in the soul of an entire people until the Gospels will be fulfilled, and he will finally find his saintly peace together with the blissful souls of his parents.

The idea that the achievement of Romanian national unity meant the fulfillment of the Gospels is a paramount example of the process of sacralization of politics in new public ceremonies to which history, religion, and politics fully contributed, merged as they were in the doctrine of messianic nationalism.

Militarism and palingenesis: the army as an instrument of national regeneration

A main pillar of the process of nation- and state-building in modern Romania was the national army. In the Middle Ages, Moldova and Wallachia had vigorous feudal armies. In the seventeenth century, however, the Ottomans compelled local princes to dismantle their fortifications and dismiss their armies, with the exception of a small princely guard. Local armies were re-created after the end of the Phanariot regime, under the terms of the Organic Regulations (1831/1832).

Although these small militia units were only meant to serve domestic purposes of maintaining law and order, they were regarded by the public as the main vehicles of national emancipation and regeneration. After 1859, these armies were at the forefront of the process of unification and state-building: in August 1860, a newly unified Moldovan-Wallachian army was proclaimed the first "national" institution, and benefited from a priority program of material modernization and human input.

At a time when the restricted gender and census-based political participation could not assure the integration of the peasantry into the body politics, military conscription and the discourse of patriotism proved to be the cement of the peasants' integration into the nation. Mass conscription, the regular training of reservists, and the establishment of institutions of military education spread military values throughout the Romanian society, leading to what Hans-Ulrich Wehler called, in the German context, "social militarism" (1985: 162). This process was amplified especially after the establishment of the constitutional monarchy and the enthronement of the foreign dynasty of Hohenzollern-Siegmaringen in 1866. Under the reign of prince (king after 1881) Carol I (1866–1914), military norms and patterns of conduct became increasingly important in society, in line with a more general European process of militarization (ibid.: 156). In 1872, according to a new national doctrine of "preparedness," military instruction became mandatory in primary and secondary schools. In addition to paramilitary training, the new program promoted patriotism, pride in the fatherland, and loyalty to the dynasty.

The first major test of Romania's nascent army was the 1877–1878 Russian-Ottoman war, in which the country participated in support of the Russian campaign. The war was the basis of the syncretism between militarism, religion, and patriotism (Alexandrescu 1999: 19–46). Promoted by leading politicians and writers, the official discourse valued militarism, national solidarity, and the cult of sacrifice for the fatherland. The representation of the war glorified the soldier-peasant as the national hero *par excellence*; his sacrifice for the fatherland was presented in religious language and disseminated in popular forms as the fight of good against evil, linking popular perceptions of religion and heroism with nationalism. The new patriotic literature was disseminated in schools and served as the basis of the official discourse uniting not only the throne and the altar, but also the army (ibid.).

In the decades to come, especially influential was the popularizing literature by the poet George Coşbuc (1866–1918). The son of a Greek-Catholic priest from Transylvania, Coşbuc immigrated in 1889 to Bucharest, where he engaged in highly acclaimed and influential public and artistic activity. His poetry conflated popular archetypes of fairytales (the predestined hero, the confrontation between good and bad), projecting them onto a religious background (the fight against the devil, the ultimate sacrifice as a form of salvation leading to eternal life), and united them with discourses about the nation and its messianic mission.

In its origins, the cult of the fallen soldier was thus linked with the cult of the ancestors, and the fight for salvation through sacrifice. These religious themes permeated primary schools and paramilitary education, as well as official discourses, and were to serve as the basis of the Legion's nationalism. The

Legionary ideology and practice combined a textbook version of the national history with popular patriotic poems written by Coşbuc glorifying sacrifice for the nation, and the cult of the fallen soldier with quasi-religious rites and rituals endorsed by the Orthodox Church and institutionalized in the army.

Conservatism and the militarization of youth: the Military Academy School of the Dealu Monastery (1912)

After the turn of the century, the process of militarization of society was given a new impetus in Europe, intimately connected with the widening of the franchise and the first symptoms of mass politics. In order to counter the destabilizing entry of "feminized" crowds into politics and the danger of decadence, early social psychologists such as Gustave LeBon (1841–1931) advanced plans for social and institutional reforms, recommending the consolidation of the army as an elite institution perpetuating masculine virtues (LeBon [1898] 2001: 248). In times of acute societal crisis, the army would promote "patience, firmness, spirit of sacrifice;" the doctrine of love for the fatherland would provide the nation with its "social cement" and "moral ideal" (LeBon 1910: 92).

Influential theories of crowd behavior inspired a series of conservative military reforms all over Europe, leading to an increase in militarism. Romania was part and parcel of this trend. The strength of the army grew steadily at this time, so that on the eve of the Balkan Wars (1912–1913), Romania boasted, proportionally, the largest reservist army in Europe (MacDonald 1915: 801–803). The network of military schools was also substantially enlarged, being assigned an important political-ideological role in the reform of the army.

The process of militarization did not go uncontested. Although there was a general political consensus over strengthening the army, Romania's leading Conservative and Liberal Parties had divergent attitudes toward the militarization of society, directly linked to the two parties' opposing strategies of mass mobilization in rural areas. As part of its policy of sheltered industrialization, the Liberals conducted a sustained campaign of emancipating the impoverished sharecropper peasantry and transforming it into independent farmers. They also supported the creation of a vast network of bank-cooperatives meant to undermine the economic efficiency of large landed estates, the main rivals of the Liberal Party's plans of sheltered industrialization; to consolidate a solid stratum of middle landowners as the basis for a prospective internal industrial market; and to use the dispossessed peasantry as the working force required for industrialization. In their turn, the Conservatives advocated a patriarchal organization of society based on the harmony of interests of all rural classes and the traditional dominance of the aristocracy. In order to prevent the development of domestic industry and the capitalist transformation of rural areas, they opposed the pauperization and internal migration of peasants to urban areas, imposing a ban on land transaction of poor peasants. They also defended a census-based electoral system that gave political rights only to landowners and the upper urban strata of

335

the population. In rural areas, the Conservatives relied on the army to spread the values of social discipline. To this end, in March 1906, a Conservative government passed a new law on public instructions that effectively militarized public and private schools. The agents of the conservative strategies were the military instructors, who were given generous contracts and an open mandate to shape the education of young boys. Military instruction was placed under the Ministry of War, out of the control of the Ministry of Public Education. These laws were opposed by the Liberals, who focused instead on rural schools as instruments of social transformation and on *teachers* as spiritual leaders of village communities.

Despite the opposition of the Liberal Party, the Conservatives were able to implement their agenda of social militarism in 1910–1912. Supported by leading politicians and intellectuals, the new conservative-militarist discourse promoted the militarization of youth, based on the trinity of Church–School–Army. A main proponent of the new doctrine, Simion Mehedinți (1868–1962), envisioned the creation of new elite schools to train talented individuals "predestined for church and army education" ([1910] 1923: 10). Conceived as laboratories for the creation of the new national elite, these schools were to enrol not only former aristocrats or sons of military personnel, but also peasants and lower urban classes, thus promoting the idea of social solidarity and national unity of all classes (ibid.: 10).

The new doctrine also resulted in an innovative military educational experiment linking political conservatism with militarism and religion. On 4 June 1912, a new military secondary school of "national education" was opened at the Dealu Monastery, in an impressive ceremony (Nițescu 1932). The school was to serve for decades as the country's most influential military college (1912–1948). The initiator and animator of this new military academy was the leading Conservative politician Nicolae Filipescu (1862–1916). Scion of an old *boyar* family and a large landowner, Filipescu was a staunch defender of the aristocracy's traditional privileges. Animated by an ardent nationalism, Filipescu was also a fervent supporter of Romania's military action against Austria-Hungary that would lead to the annexation of Transylvania and the achievement of national unity. To this end, as Minister of War (1910–1912), Filipescu paid particular attention to building a strong army. He also proposed the establishment of an elite military academy as means of reforming the army.

Filipescu's views on military education were influenced by the international pedagogical school known as the "new" or "progressive education" (*Éducation nouvelle*). Through a character-guidance program of "active engagement," the new pedagogy aimed at assuring a harmonious development of pupils' personality. The first modern elite schools of the new pedagogy were founded at Abbotsholme (1889) and Bedales (1893), England, by the educational reformer Cecil Reddie (1858–1932). In France, the principles of the new education were advocated by Edmond Demolins (1852–1907), director of the journal *La Science sociale,* follower of the socially conservative doctrine of sociologist Frédéric Le Play (1806–1882), and an open admirer of the English system of education—which, he thought, was the reason for England's military superiority (Demolins 1897, 1898). In 1899, Demolins established the *Ecole des Roches,* near Verneuil-sur-Avre in Normandy (Denis, 1998: 13–31). Modeled on Riddie's pedagogy and Le Play's agenda of social reformation inspired by pre-Marxist Christian socialism, the *Ecole des Roches* was meant to form the new national elite and to make possible a general reform of French society. Soon, the school developed into a prototype of the French reformed school, particularly under the long directorship of Georges Bertier (1903–1944). In the interwar period, its pedagogical philosophy was emulated by various Republican, socialist or even fascist movements; during Vichy France (1940–1944), many of its professors joined the regime's campaign of *"révolution nationale"* for regeneration and the creation of the fascist "new man" (Duval 2006: 72–74).

Filipescu adhered to the principles of the new pedagogy by way of the French model. His attempts to transplant this educational experiment in Romania materialized in the new military academy of the Dealu Monastery. The school was based on two main pedagogical principles of the "new education:" (1) its location outside urban centers; and (2) its emphasis on a well-rounded moral, physical, and intellectual education. First, in the spirit of militant Romantic nationalism, Filipescu chose as the location for the new secondary school the Dealu Monastery, the Romanians' most important realm of memory which sheltered Michael's skull, the holy relic of Romanian nationalism and the symbol of national union. Second, in order to provide "a complete—intellectual, physical and moral—education," the curriculum of the school was made up of a program of religious-national education, centered on character-building. Its main aim was to promote and inoculate core military virtues, such as courage, patriotism, and sacrifice.

The school was not simply a transplant of the French experience, but adapted it to Romania's societal context. The *Ecole des Roches* was private, secular, and civilian in orientation; the Dealu Academy was state-sponsored, military, and religiously oriented. In the spirit of the Conservative political doctrine, the military school's internal regulations combined the cult of the monarchy with religion and nationalism. Its curriculum aimed at providing pupils with a "solid patriotic education" in which "to vibrate the saint cult of the fatherland," of "honour and ardent love for glory," and "the fear of God, but only of God" (Petrescu 2002: 7). Certainly, the idea that religion should be an integral part of military training was not new at that time; however, the way it was ritualized and organically blended with nationalism made the school's curriculum very special. The daily program included prayers, meditation, Bible reading, and mandatory attendance of church services.

Created at the time of the Balkan Wars (1912–1913), one year before Romania's military involvement in the Second Balkan War (1913), the school was meant to contribute to the spirit of "national preparedness" and to keep alive the flame of messianic nationalism based on the cult of Michael the Brave. In the long run, the school was designed to create a new national elite, by recruiting physically and intellectually exceptionally endowed individuals and giving them a well-rounded education, through severe and rigorous military and civilian training, for seven years. In order to contribute to the harmonization of social interests of all classes and to eliminate class conflict, the school recruited pupils from all strata of society. The graduates were not expected to necessarily pursue military careers, but were encouraged to develop civil careers, as well.

From conservative militarism to para-military legionarism: Codreanu and the 'spirit' of the Dealu Military Academy

In the interwar years, the Dealu Military Academy continued to function as a central institution for the patriotic-militarist education of the youth under royal patronage. Its prestige was further consolidated in the 1930s when, in order to subordinate the youth to his authoritarian political plans, King Carol II (1930–1940) enrolled his son, former under-age King Michael (1927–1930), as a (honorific) pupil. One of the school's wartime graduates, Corneliu Zelea Codreanu (1899–1938), was nevertheless to appropriate the school's pedagogy and channel it into a novel, anti-establishment direction.

Codreanu was a pupil at the military school for five years, as part of the fifth promotion (1912–1919). As he recalled in his autobiography *Pentru Legionari* (For My Legionaries, 1936), the time spent at the school proved to be highly formative:

> I had had five years at the Military Academy in Mănăstirea Dealului (The Cloister on the Hill) where the head of Michael the Brave reposes, under the searching eye of Nicolae Filipescu. There, … I received a strict soldierly education and a healthy confidence in my own powers. In fact, my military education will be with me all my life. Order, discipline, hierarchy, moulded into my blood at an early age, along with the sentiment of soldierly dignity, will constitute a guiding thread for my entire future activity.

(2003: 4)

In fact, the school's influence upon Codreanu's worldview went far beyond the credit he was ready to give to it. Not only did Codreanu deeply internalize the values of militarism and messianic nationalism, but the main ideological features and forms of organization of the Legion of the Archangel Michael that he created in 1927 continued the lines of the progressive education received at Dealu. The Legion's elitist character, its principles of organization, much of its ritual language and practices, its educational pedagogy and patterns of socialization were all first institutionalized at the military school. The most important common elements are: the cult of Michael the Brave and of the Archangel Michael, organically linked with the ideas of national unity and predestination; the belief in the graduates making up a new national elite destined to save Romania, that would lead Codreanu to the creation of a new fascist elite; the sacralization of politics in rites and rituals based on the syncretism of military, religious, and nationalist symbols; and the cult of the heroes as martyrs for the national cause. The main principles in the organization of the Legion, spelled out by Codreanu in the 1933 textbook *Cărticica Şefului de cuib* (The Nest Leader's Manual) and in *Pentru legionari* emulated the organization of the Dealu Military School. Thus, following a practice implemented in the *Ecole des Roches*, pupils at the military school addressed each other with the title of "comrades," while younger pupils addressed the older ones with the title of "captain," both adopted by the Legion, as well (the latter title being appropriated by Codreanu himself and given new connotations); the official holiday of the military school was the 8th of November, the saint's day of the Archangel Michael, just as that of the Legion would be. Codreanu called the main organizational cells of the Legion "nests," just as Filipescu called the Dealu Military School a "falcons' nest," in a direct answer to Eminescu's highly militant poem *La arme* (To arms). The commemoration of the martyrs, their titles, and the permanent guard at the eternal votive light, as practised in the school, were also to play central roles in the Legionary rituals and pedagogy, constructing the charismatic community of sacrifice.

These striking similarities would allow us to contest the "originality" with which the Legion is generally credited in the academic literature, relating mainly to its name and main cult, its educational pedagogy of character building, its internal organization, its elitism and sense of mission. However, these influences should not obscure the fact that Codreanu also departed from the official ideology of the school in many respects, reinterpreting it in a manner that makes the Legion compatible with other interwar fascist movements. Indeed, as elsewhere in Europe, in Romania, many ingredients of the fascist ideology were already elaborated in the pre-war period. But it was the Great War that crystallized these ideas and provided the structural social and political conditions for their mass dissemination in novel forms of activism and organization.

The Legionary palingenetic project: salvation, metempsychosis and the cult of the ancestors

The Legion of the Archangel Michael was created in June 1927 by a nucleus of activists led by Corneliu Zelea Codreanu and Ion I. Moţa (1902–1937), as an elite organization of radical nationalists. In contrast to traditional political parties, the Legion had no political program. Instead of pursuing a concrete plan of action, the organization defined as its goal the salvation of the Romanian nation, under Codreanu's charismatic leadership and through the sacrifice of the Legionaries as the "recipients of the saving force" (Moţa 1936: 53). Later, Legionary ideologues claimed that the emphasis on salvation differentiated the Legion from both Italian fascism and German Nazism: "Fascism venerates the state, Nazism the race and the nation. Our movement strives to fulfil the destiny of the Romanian people through salvation" (Polihroniade 1933: 1).

The essence of the Legionary ideology was a kenotic vision of palingenesis centered on the idea of regeneration through sacrifice, following the model of *imitatio Christi*. To this core were associated other components of Romantic theories of palingenesis, such as Christian eschatology, metempsychosis, and the idea of ecumenical redemption of mankind, the predestination and divine mission of the Romanian people, and heroic Christianity through the expiation of sins and martyrdom. In the spirit of the ecumenism that characterized the European Romantic Evangelical revival, the Legion saw Christian salvation as the ultimate end of history. In line with Romantic visions of nationalism, the main actors and subjects of redemption were not individuals, but nations:

> The final aim is not life but resurrection. The resurrection of peoples in the name of the Saviour Jesus Christ ... There will come a time when all the peoples of the earth shall be resurrected, with all their dead and all their kings and emperors, each people having its place before God's throne. The final moment, "the resurrection from the dead," is the noblest and most sublime one toward which a people can rise.
>
> (Codreanu 2003: 315)

Codreanu envisioned the people as an entity "whose life continues beyond earth." In doing so, he articulated ideas about metempsychosis, namely the belief that the soul is an independent and immortal entity that passes from the body to an inanimate state. Ideas about metempsychosis as a form of collective solidarity and redemption were widespread during Romanticism; however, while the Romantics spoke about the universal redemption of mankind, the Legion believed in the *redemption and rebirth of the nation, as an organic entity.* Connected with the understanding of the nation as a community of kin, this belief claims that individual souls come together into a unified, collective spiritual consciousness.

In Codreanu's view, the nation possessed three main composing elements: "1. A physical and biological patrimony: her flesh and blood; 2. A material patrimony: the soil of her country and its riches; 3. A spiritual patrimony" (ibid.: 313). The nation's spiritual patrimony was made up of "her concept of God, the world and life," "her honour," and her culture, regarded as "the expression of national genius, of the blood" (ibid.: 314). For Codreanu, the national community was made up not simply of the community of interwar ethnic Romanians, but meant all past, present, and future generations:

> When we say the Romanian nation, we mean not only all Romanians living in the same territory, sharing the same past and the same future, the same dress, but all Romanians, alive and dead, who have lived on this land from the beginning of history and will live here also in the future. The nation includes: 1. All the Romanians presently alive; 2. All the souls of our dead and the tombs of our ancestors; 3. All those who will be born Romanians.
>
> (Ibid.: 2)

The Legionary metempsychosis did not involve the belief in the transmigration of souls or reincarnation, but the belief in the return of long-departed ancestors. Although cast in a Christian matrix, the Legionary metempsychosis also invoked the religion of the ancient Dacians and their leading God, Zamolxis, a former slave of Pytagoras (Eliade 1972), thus adding a neo-pagan component to the Legionary ideology. Legionaries also incorporated popular beliefs that the departed soul of a deceased person hovered round the place of burial at least for a certain period of time after death. These heterogeneous streams of thought were amalgamated into a new national doctrine of salvation and expressed in innovative forms of ritual practice.

The main axes of the Legionary ideology: the earthly and the divine

In order to assure the salvation of the nation as an organic physical, material and spiritual entity, the Legionary ideology and ritual practice encompassed two main axes originating from the process of sacralizing politics initiated in mid-nineteenth century: the cult of the Archangel Michael and the cult of the ancestral land. The first axis conferred on the Legionary ideology a transcendental dimension, linking it to the holy, or the sacred. Codreanu explicated the origins of the Legionary cult of the Archangel Michael in various ways, attributing it either to a divine revelation he had in prison or to a collective vision of the leading nucleus of activists, both inspired by an icon of the Archangel from the Văcăreşti monastery. I hereby contend that Codreanu fully internalized the charismatic scenario of Heliade's *Mihaida*, having as main components the hero's prophetic dream, the icon of the revelation, and the cult of the Archangel Michael linked with Michael the Brave's divine mission of bringing unity to the Romanian people. The Archangel Michael became the main source of the Legion's ideology and symbolism and the object of a fanatic Legionary cult; Michael's observance on 8th November was proclaimed the official celebration of the movement. A large copy of the icon which allegedly inspired his vision was proclaimed the sacred relic of the Legion and was permanently guarded by a Legionary team in the main headquarters of the movement in Iaşi. The icon was also reproduced on the cover of the Legion's official magazine; additional copies were dispersed to territorial organizations, while a miniature was worn by Codreanu himself. This led to a Legionary cult of the icon of the Archangel Michael as a symbol of divine revelation and protection: "Our Patron Saint is the Archangel Michael. We ought to have his icon in our homes, and in difficult times we should ask his help and he will never fail us" (Codreanu 2003: 248).

The second ideological axis gave the Legion an "earthly" dimension, linking it to the cult of the ancestors and of the martyrs. Codreanu claimed that, according to a "God-given law," the land is the nation's basis for existence (ibid.: 62). The cult of the ancestral land inspired the name of the official magazine of the movement, *Pământul strămoşesc* (The Ancestral Land), and was organically linked with funeral rites and rituals. In the Legionary imaginary, the national territory was symbolically marked by the graves of the Romanian national heroes: in Codreanu's words, "We are bound to this land by millions of graves." The areas inhabited by ethnic minorities were regarded as invaded territories, in violation of God's laws. The *territorialization of nationalism* was made evident by the fact that the main cover of the magazine reproduced, under the icon of the Archangel, a map of Greater Romania; the urban enclaves inhabited by non-Romanians (mainly Jews) were marked with black spots as "gangrenes" in the nation's ancestral land.

Together, the two vertical and horizontal axes of the Legionary ideology united, in a very powerful symbolism, the earthly and the divine: "Here we are with the borders of our movements firmly fixed: With one side implanted in our ancestral land, and with the other in the sky: the Archangel Michael and *The Ancestral Land*." The two axes were an expression of the Legion's *historicism*, with roots in Romantic palingenentic historical ideology: they were meant to unite the pre-Christian (Dacian), roots of the Romanian people with its Christianity and manifest destiny leading to redemption and salvation.

The fascist revolution: fighting decadence, building the totalitarian state

The Legionary palingenetic project was based on Christian visions of apocalyptic eschatology. While emulating the language and symbols of the Old Testament, as adapted and interpreted by Romantic projects of societal-religious regeneration, the Legionary eschatology also incorporated modern political themes such as anti-Semitism and anti-communism drawn from turn-of-the-century European literature and adapted to the local culture.

Following the lines set by Heliade's cyclical philosophy of history, the Legionary ideology identified two opposing trends of historical development: a descending one, leading to degeneration; and an ascending one, leading to redemption and regeneration. In Heliade's vision, the two trends alternated in a cyclical manner, their tension eventually leading to progress on a higher level. In the Legionary ideology the two trends were mutually exclusive and could prevail over each other only by means of revolution. In Legionary view, in the interwar period, mankind was at a crossroads: individuals and peoples had to choose sides in the global confrontation of good versus evil—identified with fascism vs. communism—and thus work *toward* or *against* salvation: "If the country will not be set on the path of resurrection envisioned by integral nationalism, she will choose the other path, of Communist reform" (Moţa 1936: 95).

Codreanu and Moţa used the term revolution with two distinct meanings: (1) revolution as rapture, implying chaos, destruction and the loss of traditional authority; and (2) revolution as return to tradition and the restoration of a primordial idyllic state, in line with the original meaning of the term revolution as a movement of rotation around its own axis. The first acceptance of the term revolution as chaos was exemplified by the French Revolution and its "prolongation," the 1917

Bolshevik Revolution. Codreanu condemned the "obsolete ideology of the French revolution," blaming it for being based on "false abstractions" and of resulting in the loss of traditional values, such as religious faith. But he was even more concerned with the contemporary Bolshevik Revolution, portrayed as a "devastating wave," an integral part of a universal "Judeo-Bolshevik" conspiracy. Carried onto Romanian soil by the Jews, Bolshevism threatened to develop into an "anti-Romanian revolution" aimed at "the dethronement of the king, the destruction of churches, the massacre of the officers and of hundreds of thousand of Romanians."

The Jewish attempt "to destroy the Romanian people" concentrated on the two major axes of the Legionary ideologies: the Romanian ancestral land, the material source of the nation's existence; and their religious faith, the means of transcendental communication with God. Jews' socialist atheism would sever Romanians' relation to God and the "holy," while the loss of the ancestral land to the Jews would sever Romanians' relation to their dead (Codreanu 2003: 107).

The second meaning of the term revolution was that of spiritual rebirth and regeneration, exemplified in Codreanu's and Moța's views by the Legionary revolution. The post-1918 nationalist revolt of the Romanian students was presented as "a volcanic eruption rising from the nation's depths." Students "arose to battle" walking "on the great path of our national destiny, side by side with all those who fought, suffered and died as martyrs for our land and its people" (ibid.: 54, 50). A direct continuation of the student movement, the Legion was a "great spiritual school;" its aim was to bring forth a "great spiritual revolution of the entire people," by transforming the Romanian soul. In the spirit of Romanticism, the fascist regeneration was seen as a restoration of medieval glory; but it was also a culmination of the historical development of the Romanian people: "The approaching Legionary victory will be the beginning of a great ascension and brilliance of the Romanian people in the world" (Moța 1936: 196). The Legion thus concomitantly promoted a 'regressive' and futurist political utopia based on the glorification of the Middle Ages but oriented toward forging the new man and the building of a totalitarian fascist state.

The fascist path to national salvation: forging the "new man" and the charismatic community of sacrifice

In the spirit of Romantic palingenesis, regeneration was to occur in the form of Christian salvation. Various theologies differ as to the way Christian salvation is to be obtained: from above, by action of divine grace alone; as a combined action of God and man; or as the action of man alone, without the assistance of divinity. In Legionary eschatology, salvation was the result of a struggle of God's "chosen warriors" against Satan and the infidels. Although the chosen ones enjoyed the assistance of God, through the support and guidance of the Archangel Michael, his highest messenger and Minister, salvation was neither automatic nor inevitable; it was to be the result of a gigantic struggle, a heroic crusade against materialism and atheism.

The Legionary eschatology was animated by the fear of degeneration and imminent national danger, making the action of the charismatic leader not only urgent but also indispensable. The powerful forces of decadence could be defeated only through the heroic action of a charismatic community of sacrifice. In *Cărticica Sefului de cuib,* Codreanu advanced a guide to collective salvation through sacrifice, a manual of devotion intended to assist the Legionaries in the pursuit of holiness and communion with God. He elaborated a code of conduct and a set of ideological commandments on the manner in which Legionary salvation was to be achieved. The code of conduct combined military discipline with religious asceticism. It contained nine Legionary commands (referring mainly to faith in God, self-discipline, dedication, rejection of politics, and love of Legionary death), and six fundamental rules "of discipline," "of work," "of silence," "of education," "of mutual help," and "of honor."

Proper Legionary conduct was to lead to salvation via two main paths: the creation of the new man and spiritual rebirth "from within" through sacrifice. In Codreanu's view, "The new man, or the renewed nation, presupposes a great rebirth of the soul, a great spiritual revolution of the entire person, in other words a fight against the spiritual direction of today" (1933, Point 69). The new man was to personify the national character of the nation: "All the virtues of the Romanian soul should be rejuvenated in the new man, all the qualities of our race. In the new man, we should kill all defaults or tendencies toward evil" (1933, Points 69–70).

The creation of the new fascist man was first and foremost a pedagogical endeavor. Codreanu assigned central importance to education. He conceived the Legion as a school for forging the new man in the spirit of the *nouvelle pegadogie*'s program of character building. That is why the Legion did not focus on devising new political programs, but on changing people from within:

> Our Legionary movement has the character of a great spiritual school. It tends to illuminate unknown faiths, to transform, to revolutionize the Romanian soul. Announce in all corners that the evil, the ruin, originates from the soul. The soul is the cardinal point on which we have to work at this moment. The soul of the individual and the soul of the mass ... Call the soul of the people to a new life.
>
> (2003: 2–3)

Codreanu implemented the principles of the progressive education in practice, by building a paramilitary totalitarian revolutionary movement of change based on charismatic, oath-taking authority demanding total, permanent and unconditional devotion and submission to the leader. The Legion adopted the structure, procedures, rules and training of an army. It isolated its members from the outside world, while socializing them in new values and lifestyle, thus evolving into a hierarchically-organized and self-contained social world, having its own laws, language, rites and rituals. The socialization of Legionaries started at an early age, with their enrolment in the subsection *Frățiile de Cruce* (Brotherhoods of the

Cross). The ritual of cross brotherhood initiation suggested a kind of symbolical Christian rebirth for the Legionaries, based on an Eastern Orthodox Christian tradition according to which children baptized in the same water were regarded as cross brothers (Weber 1966: 520–521). Emulating the curricula of the Dealu Military Academy, members of the Brotherhoods had to undergo training in military parades and numerous sports, such as fencing; they were also called musketeers, Alexandre Dumas's novel *The Three Musketeers* being one of their main assigned readings (*Pământul Strămoşesc*, IV, 18 May 1930, 3).

Adult members of the Legion received their Christian, national, sanitary, physical and social education within nests. To become full Legionaries, new members were subject to a probationary period of up to three years. Regular screening of membership and harsh disciplinary measures were combined with extended practical training and participation in a process of community socialization following detailed rituals.

By means of this pedagogy, forms of common socialization, and paramilitary training, the Legion evolved into a fanatical and highly disciplined totalitarian movement. It also grew into a formidable mass political force: Originally, the Legion was designed as an elite organization of a maximum of 3,000 well-chosen members. In 1937, at its political peak, and after ten years of political activism, there were 270,000 enrolled members; it also received 478,000 votes in national parliamentary elections, or the vote of circa 16 percent of the electorate.

Heroic Christianity: Legionary salvation through expiation of sins and violent self-sacrifice

The essence of the Legionary salvational formula was resurrection through the martyrdom of the chosen ones. The Legionaries' personal sacrifice was meant to redeem the Romanian nation: "Somebody has to pay with suffering the sins that crumbled the people, somebody has to redeem through pain the salvation of tomorrow" (Moţa 1936: 59). The resurrection of the nation through expiation and violent sacrifice followed the model of *imitatio Christi*: "Our Saviour could not prevail without suffering and sacrifice ... How would the Legionary be able to prevail by leading a life full of serene, cloudless days, how would he be able to prevail by leading a life begot by luck and personal satisfaction?" (ibid.: 58) The idea of expiation of sins through sacrifice stems from Bonnet's palingenetic philosophy of *emboîtement des germes*, transmitted to the Romanian context via Heliade: "So God wanted: the *germ of a renewal* (*germenul unei înnoiri*) can grow only out of death, of suffering," argued Moţa (ibid.: 74–75) employing a terminology strikingly similar to that of Bonnet. But it also incorporated behavioral models of Church martyrdom and Romantic conceptions of heroic Christianity (see Cantacuzino 1969).

The fundamental feature of the Legionary new man was his capacity for spiritual renewal through sacrifice. In attaining the superior rank of a Legionary, a member had to pass a series of initiation tests, allegorically described by Codreanu as "the mountain of suffering, the forest of wild beasts, and the marsh of desperation" (1933: Points 56–60). These tests were part of a blasphemous scenario of *imitatio Christi*: the would-be Legionary had to "receive on his shoulder the yoke of our saviour Jesus Christ" (1933: Point 56). The experience of suffering was central to the training of Legionaries. In Codreanu's view, without "the test of pain, the test of bravery, and that of faith, one cannot be a capable man, cannot be a Legionary" (1933: Point 60). He argued that "Every act of suffering is a step forward toward salvation, toward victory" (1933: Point 55).

The propensity to sacrifice led to the glorification of Legionary death as "our dearest wedding among weddings." For Moța, "Spiritual resurrection in Legionary spirit" was "a youth without spring, facing death, uprooted from personal purpose and happiness" (1936: 76). For Codreanu, Legionaries were "soldiers of other Romanian horizons," ready for apocalyptic battles or struggles, from which they were to emerge "either victorious or dead" (2003: 2).

The cult of the Legionary martyrs was thus intrinsically linked with the cult of the death. Codreanu argued: "The Legionary loves death, since his blood forges the cement of a future Legionary Romania." In addition to incorporating Christian symbolism and popular attitudes towards (self-)sacrifice, Legionary ideologues also referred to the cult of the death practiced by the Dacians/ Thracians, ancient inhabitants of the territory of Greater Romania, celebrated as ancestors of the Romanian people. The Thracians defied death and offered their bravest heroes as voluntary sacrifices to their gods, as messengers to the other world. Similarly, the Legionary martyrs were a means of communion with God: "Our dead Legionaries make the link between sky and earth. Every Legionary grave means a new root in the earth, on which the Legion is firmly grounded" (Codreanu, "Cuvânt pentru legionari," 24 June 1937, 3). Legionaries were therefore encouraged "to receive the baptism of death with the serenity of our ancestral Thracians" (2003: 2).

Legionary fanaticism led to the creation of "death squads" whose members carried out suicidal missions of assassination, thus imprinting a terrorist character on the Legion. Ion I. Moța valued self-sacrifice as the most efficient way of political combat, in a paragraph that synthesizes the self-destructive character of the movement: "The spirit of sacrifice is essential! We all dispose of the most formidable dynamite, the most irresistible instrument of fighting, more powerful than tanks and rifles: our own soot" (Moța, 1929: 207).

The Legionaries who sacrificed their life for the cause were declared "martyrs" and were proclaimed "saints" of Christianity. The most important were the three Nicadors who killed Prime Minister Duca on 29 December 1933; the ten "Decemvirs" who assassinated the former Legionary leader Mihai Stelescu for treason on 16 July 1936; Ion Moța and Vasile Marin (1904–1936), killed in January 1937 in the Spanish Civil War while fighting on Franco's side; and Codreanu and over 250 high Legionary leaders executed at King Carol's orders in November 1938. Although apparently a Christian Orthodox religious practice, the sanctification of the martyrs was in fact a major innovation of Catholic inspiration. The February 1937 funeral of Moța and Marin (1904–1936), killed in the Spanish Civil War is telling in this respect, since it was *the first attempt to sanctify martyrs in the Romanian Orthodox Church*. Backed by few high Orthodox officials, promoted by a strong press campaign, and legitimized by large popular ceremonies, this attempt was a highly successful propaganda move for the Legion. Ultimately, the Orthodox leadership resisted the pressure and officially rejected the demand of sanctification, fearing it would have a destabilizing, subversive impact upon the Church. It was only in 1955 that the Romanian Orthodox Church sanctified its first Christian martyrs, a practice that was to be resumed in the post-Communist period.

"Mad about Christ": the apostolic people of charismatic nationalism

The sacred foundations of the Legionary doctrine of national salvation challenged its ideologues to spell out the movement's relation to the Orthodox Church and its dogma. Due to overlapping themes, rituals, and even membership, this was a very difficult task that received diverse and even contradictory answers. In the following I present two prominent attempts to interpret the Legion's *charismatic nationalism* from the prism of theology: the first was developed by a lay aristocratic leader, Alexandru Cantacuzino (1901–1939); and the second by an Orthodox priest, Ilie Imbrescu (1909–1949). These discourses should not be mistaken for attempts to reconcile the Legionary ideology with the Orthodox Church and its dogma; they were explicit attempts to *subordinate* the Church to the new fascist ideology of national salvation, in the name of a higher truth. Capitalizing on the transcendental dimension of the Legion's charismatic nationalism, both authors claimed the *superiority* of the Legionary ideology over the Orthodox dogma, underscoring the Legionaries' divine mission and proposing an alternative road to collective "national salvation" through violent sacrifice. Although this path to salvation openly contradicted the position of the Orthodox Church, it was allegedly in line with God's divine will and the religious tradition of the Romanian people.

The scion of an aristocratic family imbued with a militantly nationalist, anti-communist and anti-Semitic pathos, Alexandru Cantacuzino pleaded in his writings for a new fascist theology of "heroic Christianity," leading to collective salvation through fascist combat and sacrifice for the national cause: "Legionaries have a supreme goal: the salvation of the Romanian people" (Cantacuzino 1969). The path to salvation was not the holy religious life of Orthodox monks and nuns, but the heroic fight in the service of the nation. Influenced by George Sorel (1847–1922), Cantacuzino valued violence for its positive, "purifying" effect, defining it as a "necessary sin" and a main "method of national education." Even if it went against the precepts preached by the Church, the Legionary revolutionary violence was in line with the divine, charismatic mission of redeeming the Romanian nation: "Maybe God's servants will not have the right to absolve you of your sins on earth; but trust God's grace to absolve you in the sky." While the Church was concerned with individual salvation, the Legion strove for collective salvation:

I, a Romanian soul, will be redeemed together with the souls of the Romanians, with the soul of the nation. The Romanians' sins burden me, my sins burden them. To redeem the sins of my co-nationals is the most noble but burdensome mission granted to man.

Cantacuzino was convinced that God predestined Romanians "with a mission and a destiny," in harmony with higher divine goals. In order to attain the physical and spiritual redemption of the Romanian nation and to lift the country to be among the greatest powers of Europe, he militated for the creation of the Legionary "new man," defined as a superior type of "human being" shaped by "Christian conceptions and a new philosophy of life." The new Romanian "of tomorrow" was necessarily to be anti-liberal, intolerant, and anti-Semitic, and to exhibit the militarism and *élan vital* specific to fascism movements: "The Legionary nationalism cultivates and magnifies the idea of will, of power and territorial expansion, promotes military discipline, glorifies the sacrifice and death for the common good." The specific Legionary path to redemption was the supreme sacrifice, symbolized by the graves of the nationalist fighters: "We believe in the redeeming virtue of graves." Cantacuzino's vision of the creation of the Legionary "superhuman" and the Romanian "super-nation" by virtue of divine intervention departed from the dogma of the Orthodox Church. Instead, it merged the Legion's charismatic nationalism with main Christian themes in a new doctrine of national salvation.

An even more ambitious and all-encompassing theological interpretation of the Legionary charismatic nationalism, based on the principles of love and divine revelation, was put forward by the Orthodox priest and Legionary activist Ilie Imbrescu. After studying theology in Cernowitz (BA) and Bucharest (Ph.D. candidate), in 1934, Imbrescu was ordained a priest in the historical province of Dobrogea, where he carried out an assiduous Legionary propaganda. During the brief Legionary rule (September 1940–January 1941), Imbrescu promoted an institutional reform of the Orthodox Church within the Ministry of Religious Cults. In November 1940, Imbrescu published *Biserica şi Mişcarea Legionară* (The Church and the Legionary Movement), a book he claimed was inspired by the Holy Spirit. Organized in ten chapters, corresponding to the Ten Commandments, the book constructed a gigantic charismatic scenario depicting the history of the world as an apocalyptic struggle against Satan, having at its center the Romanian people. For Imbrescu, the meaning of the world was grounded in the Gospel and centered on the figure of Jesus Christ. Nations were central theological categories: as divine creations, peoples have to subordinate their existence to the soteriologic purposefulness of redemption and resurrection. They have to work in the spirit of their nationalism toward perfection. In their endeavor, the rightful peoples are assisted by the angels of the sky to work toward God's will (Imbrescu, 1940: 195). The angels, led by the archangels, are the protectors of the faithful, transmitting Divine Grace.

Imbrescu believed that the history of mankind was at a crossroads, approaching the stage of the actual resurrection of the peoples (1940: 174). The new era was prefaced by a period of transition characterized by an apocalyptic struggle against Satan (ibid.: 183). A major battlefield of this struggle, interwar Romanian society was marked by the confrontation between two opposing forces: the young generation, inspired by the Holy Spirit and working for Christ, and therefore called charismatic (*generaţia harică*), and the old generation, made up of the patriarch and Church leadership, state bureaucrats, scholars, and the king, who had betrayed the national interest and were therefore called Satanic (*generaţia satanică*). As Missionaries of Christ, the charismatic generation followed the call of the Holy Spirit. Imbrescu backed his claim with an original theory of the divine election of the Romanians. He argued that, while the peoples in Central Europe and the Balkans were Christianized "from above" by their rulers, Romanians were "born Christian." This gift of divine providence made them the chosen people of the Gospel, "an adopted son of God," predestined to work under the protection of the archangels to save the world from Lucifer's revolt (ibid.: 197). The patron saints of the Romanian people were therefore the Archangel Michael, the defender of justice, and the Archangel Gabriel, the defender of the Divine Gift.

The charismatic generation of grace, an expression of the maturity of the Romanianness, was led to salvation by its leader, the "Captain" Codreanu. This was the reason Codreanu was attracted by an unknown, mystical power, to venerate the icon of the Archangel: "Born out of truth, Corneliu Zelea Codreanu carries the cross of being the Savior's apprentice" (ibid.: 167). Codreanu is credited with numerous charismatic capabilities, as a fighter, an annunciator, and a scholar of the divine grace: "The Captain is the greatest contemporary example of love and fight for Jesus Christ and his Book is holy water from the spring of the Holy Spirit" (ibid.: 172).

For Imbrescu, the Legionary totalitarian state was a new form of organization harmoniously combining nationalism with Orthodoxy and thus attaining a state of "national ecumenicity," "revealed to the Captain by the Holy Spirit" (ibid.: 171). The Legionary state of Romanian Christianity was "the political expression of Orthodoxy;" its goal was the resurrection of the nation. The Romanians' divine mission was that of implementing the ideal of *Orthodox nationalism*, first in Romania, and then in the entire world, thus bringing about a new era of "Christian ecumenicity." Through the Captain's action, the Romanian people were to fulfil their divine mission of being a precursor of a new historical era, a theological people, in the service of the cross, and an apostolic, missionary people, gathering peoples of the word in the "Universal Ecumenical Synod." Like St John the Baptist, precursor of Jesus Christ, so the Romanian people "is the nation that [will] fulfil the role of precursor of the new era of the unity of people" (ibid.: 186).

Cantacuzino's and Imbrescu's writings were not simply exercises in theology. Building on the long tradition of Romantic palingenetic nationalism and historicism, but also incorporating contemporary fascist references, they advanced original articulations of the ideology of *charismatic nationalism* as a new national religion of salvation. Although inserted into a Biblical matrix, the road to Legionary salvation was quite original and, from the point of view of official Orthodox dogma, undoubtedly blasphemic: it valued suffering, expiation, and—above all—the ultimate sacrifice for the cause. Although these were mainstream religious themes, the Legionary motivations, means, and goals were fundamentally different from those of the Church. First, Legionaries hailed violence as a form of social regeneration and catharsis. Second, a major form of blasphemy was the substitution of Codreanu for the Saviour; his life trajectory and actions being a form of *imitatio Christi* that took place *outside and even against* the Church. This explains why, in the long run, the charismatic ideology of the Legion was not only blasphemic from the point of view of the Church, but also ultimately competed with it (on this point, see Iordachi 2004).

Conclusion

This chapter explores the multiple intellectual genealogies of the Legionary palingenetic historical ideology of national salvation. I argue that the main ingredients of this ideology were elaborated by Romantic writers in the second quarter of the nineteenth century, were further consolidated after the establishment of the Romanian nation-state in 1859, and were given a new impetus after the turn of the century by the practices of sacralizing politics that united the church, the school, and the army around the Hohenzollern dynasty.

The foundations of this ideology of national salvation were set by Ion Heliade Rădulescu's palingenetic nationalism; its mythical core was the idea of the regeneration of the Romanian people, encoded in the cult of Michael the Brave and of his patron saint, the Archangel Michael. Heliade's political fortune was short-lived: after being a prominent leader of the 1848 revolution in Wallachia, he was forced into exile and later became a rather marginal politician in the united Romania. His literary and historical works, as well as his vision of sacralizing politics were, however, hugely influential, having a formative role on successive generations of Romanians.

In the second half of the nineteenth century, the Romanian national ideology suffered numerous mutations, triggered by major stages of nation- and state-building, such as the 1859 union of Moldova and Wallachia, and the 1877–1878 War of Independence; and by critical responses to a series of major crises, such as the "Jewish question"—referring to Romanian politicians' refusal to emancipate the Jews, the "Transylvanian question"—referring to Romania's irredentist policy of annexing the province and forgeing a unitary nation-state, and the intellectual and political ferment of the turn of the century. Corroborated by new intellectual transfers, mostly from the German and French contexts, these changes brought to the forefront a novel conception of politics "in a new key," based on an essentialist understanding of the concept of national culture, Social Darwinism and anti-Semitism, a new national militancy, and a renewed Romantic and messianic nationalism centered on the idea of national unity.

On the eve of World War I, some of these changes were captured by a new type of conservative-authoritarian nationalism. Its catalyst was the aristocratic politician Nicolae Filipescu, the initiator and director of the innovative military academy of the Dealu Monastery. While building on the main elements of Heliade's palingenetic nationalism (most importantly the cult of Michael the Brave and the Archangel Michael as symbols of divine predestination, and the army as a vehicle of regeneration and national unity), Filipescu superimposed them on traditional conservative values (such as monarchism, elitism, and a patriarchal organization of society), combined with modern political themes, such as the idea of the regeneration of the nation through the action of a youth elite educated in military-religious values according to the principles of the progressive pedagogy. Filipescu also set the conservative-military discourse on a new intellectual basis represented by the two new "prophets of the nation," the Romantic "national" poet Mihai Eminescu and the historian-politician Nicolae Iorga. In the long run, this shift obscured the intellectual origins of the ideology of national salvation in Heliade's palingenetic ideology.

Apparently, Codreanu did not implement major innovations to the Romantic doctrine of messianic nationalism. Most of the elements of the Legionary palingenetic ideology had already been elaborated in the pre-World War I period, namely the idea of divine election and the manifest destiny of the Romanians, the idea of rebirth and regeneration, its codification in the cult of Michael the Brave and his patron saint, the Archangel Michel, the cult of the martyrs, fears of degeneration centered on rabid anti-Semitism, and the central role assigned to the army and the values of militarism in the regeneration of the nation. At the level of political practice, there had already been conservative *elite* experiments in institutionalizing the palingenetic myth in new forms of education and socialization of the youth based on a combination of Romantic nationalism, religion, and militarism that provided sources of inspiration. As a specific product of an elite military school, Codreanu internalized the main tenants of Romantic nationalism and militarism, being determined to continue in interwar Romania the spirit of the Dealu Military Academy.

These lines of continuity should not conceal, however, the major innovations the Legion introduced in the Romanian national ideology and political practice. First, the Legion was successful in appropriating the palingenetic myth, portraying itself as the instrument of divine salvation and redemption. Second, the Legion reinterpreted the palingenetic myth, adapting it to the specific historical context of interwar Romania and imbuing it with a renewed apocalyptic sense of urgency, based on the alleged danger of degeneration at the hands of the "Judeo-Bolshevik" conspiracy. Third, the Legion amplified many themes that were only latently present in earlier theories of palingenesis, such as the emphasis on salvation through the expiation of sins, ideas of metempsychosis as a form of national solidarity; and mysticism based on a direct and unmediated communion with God through the vocation and actions of the charismatic leader and of the legionary martyrs. The latter was to become a defining mark of the Legion: although highly influenced by pre-Marxist Christian Socialism, for Heliade, the mystical components of palingenesis were nevertheless limited to the Evangelical foundations of his philosophical system and to religious symbols such as Annunciation, suffering, redemption and purification (Tomoiagă 1971: 56). Fifth, the Legion had an antisystemic, revolutionary character, evident in its totalitarian drive, paramilitary organization and the charismatic nature of its leadership. This was, again a major political innovation, since Heliade's palingenetic socio-political thought lacked a revolutionary dimension, opting instead for evolutionary reforms from above.

On the basis on these major innovations, I would define the Legion as a totalitarian and charismatic-revolutionary fascist organization. It was revolutionary because it had an anti-systemic orientation, it aimed at removing the "corrupt" and "decadent" political elite and replacing it with a new youth fascist elite entrusted with the mission to save Romania, under the leadership of a charismatic leader. It was totalitarian because it promoted an integral view of politics, governing all aspects in the life of its followers. The Legion exercised a new type of charismatic, oath-taking authority over its members, demanding total and unconditional devotion to the movement and the leader. It also promoted new forms of political organization and activism, militarizing the party and organizing it along the values of hierarchy and discipline, and implementing new forms of socialization and of pedagogical education aimed at the creation of the new fascist man. The Legion also attempted to build a totalitarian state by replacing the multi-party system with a single-party dictatorship, remodeling the state along corporatist lines, and advocating an ethnic understanding of citizenship and a new patriarchal organization of gender and societal relations. The Legion did not promote an overtly imperialist discourse: instead, it focused on the idea of cleansing the Romanian nation by removing ethnic aliens, targeting mostly the Jews. While the Legion's discourse on cleansing was confined to the national territory and community, the application of this principle to what they saw as the "ideal" national territory of the Romanians, coupled with the idea of removal of aliens from contested multi-ethnic territories of Greater Romania, gave the Legion's ideology an expansionist dimension, as well.

At a higher level, the Legion promoted a palingenetic historical ideology according to which the salvation and regeneration of the mankind were to be the result of a global battle of the chosen ones against the forces of decadence. On the basis of these multiple filiations, I argue that the religious components of the Legionary ideology stem neither from its allegedly privileged relation to the Orthodox Church nor from the Orthodox dogma. Instead, they stem from palingenetic discourses about society elaborated mainly by various French and Italian authors, transferred and creatively adapted to local conditions by cultural "mediators," and later institutionalized and reproduced in innovative practices of sacralizing politics. Certainly, the influence of the Orthodox Church and its dogma upon the Legionary ideology and ritual practice should be neither denied nor minimized, but can only be understood as part of a wider context. As has been pointed out in this chapter, the foundations of palingenetic discourses on regeneration were informed by the Christian-Biblical tradition, in general, and by the Catholic and

Protestant dogmas, in particular. These foundations were transferred to the Romanian context by Heliade, who also enriched them with specific Eastern Orthodox religious themes, in a peculiar syncretism. In the second half of the nineteenth century, the process of sacralizing politics initiated by Heliade was taken to a new level and became a central component of the process of nation- and state-building. The Orthodox Church actively participated in this campaign, contributing many rites and rituals to the new national ceremonies in the making; its input was amplified in the interwar period, at a time when the borders between politics and religion became even more burred. Without doubt, the Legion appropriated and adapted many Orthodox official and popular religious practices, either indirectly or by means of the numerous Orthodox priests enrolled in the movement. These multiple links and overlaps between the Legion and the Orthodox Church are very significant; they have recently been tackled by several scholars, this author included (Iordachi 2004). It is, however, essential to stress that the foundations of the Legionary ideology cannot be reduced to Orthodoxy but go back to Romantic discourses of palingenesis. The heterogeneous religious sources of Romantic palingenesis explain the *variegated* nature of the Christian as well as pre-Christian themes in the Legionary ideology symbolized by their usage of the signs of the cross and the swastika. Consider, for example, the many components of Catholic inspiration in the Legionary ideology and practice: its militancy and crusading spirit, which resembled Catholic military orders, the attempt to sanctify the martyrs of the movement, a practice without correspondence in the Orthodox Church, or Codreanu's cult of Saint Anthony of Padua, his personal patron and protector. Consider also the neo-pagan components of Legionary ideology reviving ancient Greek or Dacian beliefs in metempsychosis. Consider also the fact that, contrary to established clichés, the Legion's membership was not exclusively Orthodox, but enrolled Catholics as well as Protestants, even if in small numbers. It thus becomes evident that the Legion was not an Orthodox religious "sect" and did not profess an Eastern Orthodox religious dogma, but affirmed an ecumenical form of "heroic Christianity," which was proclaimed superior to the Orthodox Church.

The palingenetic foundations of the Legionary ideology explain its ambivalent relationship with the Orthodox Church and dogma, characterized concomitantly by intimacy and collaboration as well as by competition and conflict. The conflict is not surprising: palingenetic discourses about society have always had a difficult cohabitation with the established church; back in the mid-nineteenth century, Heliade's personalized doctrine of salvation and Biblical commentaries were openly criticized by Andrei Şaguna, the Orthodox Metropolitan of Transylvania (Moceanu 2003).

What are the implications of this case study for the debate on generic fascism? First, the study highlights the intimate link between fascism and nationalism, confirming Mosse's pertinent claim that fascist ideology was built on the "bedrock" of nationalism as a system of belief (1999). Second, it points out that, in order to understand this link, one needs to employ a *long durée* dimension of research that goes back not only to the intellectual revolt of the turn of the century, but also to the anti-Enlightenment tradition and Christian critiques of society that originate in the period following the French Revolution and the Napoleonic Wars. Third, the chapter points to the religious roots of modern nationalism, stemming from paligenetic theories on society, and incorporating major Christian themes such as the Biblical idea of divine election and predestination. Certainly, the quasi-religious character of nationalism has been noted by many scholars, Mosse included; yet, in opposition to Mosse, who treats nationalism as a "secular religion," or a substitute for traditional religion (1991). I underscore the sacred roots of nationalism and the role played by the idea of divine election in crystallizing national ideologies in the modern period.

Fourth, in order to account for the sacred core of the Legionary doctrine of national salvation I put forward the concept of *charismatic nationalism,* defined as an ideology that regards the nation as an elect community with a shared destiny living in a sacred homeland which, on the basis of a glorious past, claims a divine mission leading to salvation through sacrifice *under the guidance of a charismatic leader*. The concept of *charismatic nationalism* illuminates the nature of the "holy" or the "sacred" in nationalism, differentiating it from both established forms of traditional religions and modern secular ideologies. Charisma has a transcendental dimension, since the belief in the divine, supernatural mission depends on the belief in God as the absolute form of authority. Yet, that transcendental dimension does not qualify it as a religious phenomenon understood in conventional terms. We are dealing here with a reformulation of the concept of the "holy," or the "sacred," that originated in palingenetic discourses on society, were adopted by Romantic nationalism, redefined and amplified at the turn of the century and implemented into the political practice during the interwar period. The religious roots of nationalism prepared the ground for claims of charismatic leadership to achieve national unity and internal renewal, while the belief in the doctrine of the chosen people gave birth to an extreme form of national self-glorification. The corollaries of interwar charismatic nationalism are not simply the ideas of the "holy" community, history and territory, arguably part of any form of nationalism, *but a new way of defining the holy, which originates not from the numinous* (Otto 1923) *but from the charismatic leader*. In other words, interwar charismatic nationalism merged the idea of the holy, elected national community with that of the divine mission of the charismatic leader as a chosen prophet or saviour of the nation, and applied them to the political practice. From the point of view of a scholar of fascism, this type of religiosity, even if different from the established churches and their dogmas, deserves recognition in its own right, instead of being discarded as mere blasphemy or *ersatzreligion*.

NOTES

* All citations from Romanian are the author's translation.
1 The original name of the movement was the Legion of the "Archangel Michael," founded on 24 June 1927 in Iaşi. On 13 April 1930 Codreanu established the Iron Guard, as a political section of the movement. Soon, the Legion and the Iron Guard became interchangeable labels of the same movement. On 3 January 1931, the authorities dissolved The Legion of the "Archangel Michael"/the Iron Guard. In April 1931,

Codreanu formed the "Corneliu Codreanu Grouping," which in the 1932 national elections gained five parliamentary seats. The grouping was banned by the authorities on 9/10 December 1933. In 1935, Codreanu founded the "All for the Fatherland" Party, which took part in the national elections of December 1937, and gained 16 percent of the votes and 66 parliamentary seats. The new party was dissolved on 22 February 1938 following the establishment of a one-party system under King Carol II's personal regime. The organization is also known under the generic name the "Legionary Movement" (*Mişcarea Legionară*).

2   See 1 Corinthians 15: "But someone may ask, 'How are the dead raised? With what kind of body will they come?' How foolish! What you sow does not come to life unless it dies. When you sow, you do not plant the body that will be, but just a seed, perhaps of wheat or of something else. But God gives it a body as he has determined, and to each kind of seed he gives its own body."

BIBLIOGRAPHY

Alexandrescu, Sorin (1999). *Privind înapoi, modernitatea* (Bucharest: Univers).

Anghelescu, Mircea (2002). "Introducere," in Ion Heliade Rădulescu, *Opere,* 2 vols. (Bucharest: Univers Enciclopedic, 2002), vol. 1, I–X.

Bakunin, Jack (1975). "Pierre Leroux: A Democratic Religion for a New World," *Church History,* 44: 1, 57–72.

Bălcescu, Nicolae (1878). *Istoria românilor sub Michaiu Voda Vitézul urmată de scrieri diverse* (Bucharest: Typografia Societăţei Academice Române).

Ballanche, Pierre-Simon (1827–1829). *Essais de palingénésie sociale,* 2 vols (Paris: Imprimerie Jules Didot Ainé).

Barbu, Zeev (1968). "Rumania," in S. J. Woolf, ed., *European Fascism* (London: Weidenfeld and Nicolson), 146–166.

Barbu, Zeev (1980). "Psycho-Historical and Sociological Perspectives on the Iron Guard, the Fascist Movement of Romania," in Stein Ugelvik Larsen, Bernt Hagtvet, Jan Petter Myklebust, eds. *Who Were the Fascists: Social Roots of European Fascism* (Bergen: Universitetsforlaget; Irvington-on-Hudson: Columbia University Press, 1980), 379–394.

Boia, Lucian (2001). *History and Myth in Romanian Consciousness* (Budapest: CEU Press).

Bonnet, Charles (1769–1770). *La palingénésie philosophique, ou Idées sur l'état passé et sur l'état futur des êtres vivants: ouvrage destiné à servir de supplément aux derniers écrits de l'auteur et qui contient principalement le précis de ses recherches sur le christianisme* (Genève: Philibert et Chirol), available at: http://home.tiscalinet.ch/biografien/sources/bonnet_palingenesie.htm

Călinescu, George (1986). *Istoria literaturii române de la origini pînă în present* (Bucharest: Minerva).

Cantacuzino, Alexandru (1940). *Opere complete* (München).

Codreanu, Corneliu Zelea (1928). *Pământul Strămoşesc* (Iaşi), 15 May, II: 10, 4.

Codreanu, Corneliu Zelea (1931). "Legionari!," *Legionarii,* 11 October, II: 8, 1.

Codreanu, Corneliu Zelea (1933). *Cărticica şefului de cuib* (Bucharest: 1933).

Codreanu, Corneliu Zelea (2003). *For My Legionaries (The Iron Guard)* (York, South Carolina: Liberty Bell Publications). Original edition: *Pentru legionari,* vol. 1 (Sibiu: "Totul pentru ţară," 1936).

de Baecque, Antoine (1993). *Corps de l'Histoire: Metaphores et politique (1770–1800)* (Paris: Calmann-Levy).

Demolins, Edmond (1889). *L'Education nouvelle. L'Ecole des Roches* (Paris: O.J).

Demolins, Edmond (1897). *A quoi tient la supériorité des Anglo-Saxons?* (Paris); translated as *Anglo-Saxon Superiority: To What It Is Due?* (New York: C. Scribner's Sons, 1898).

Denis, Daniel (1998). "L'attraction ambiguë du modèle éducatif anglais dans l'œuvre d'Edmond Desmolins," *Les Etudes sociales*, 127–128: 1–2, 13–31.

Duval, Nathalie (2006). "L'Ecole des Roches, phare français au sein de la nébuleuse de l'Education nouvelle (1899–1944)," *Paedagogica Historica*, 42: 1&2, 63–75.

Eatwell, Roger (2003). "Reflections on Fascism and Religion," *Totalitarian Movements and Political Religions*, 4: 3, 145–166.

Eliade, Mircea (1972). *Zalmoxis: The Vanishing God. Comparative Studies in the Religions and Folklore of Dacia and Eastern Europe* (Chicago: University of Chicago Press).

Floru, Ion S. (1924). *Istoria românilor pentru cursul superior de liceu* (Bucharest: Socec).

Fogu, Claudio (2003). *The Historic Imaginary: Politics of History in Fascist Italy* (Toronto: University of Toronto Press).

Gentile, Emilio (1975). *Le origini dell'ideologia fascista (1918–1925)* (Rome: Laterza).

Gentile, Emilio (2004). "Fascism, Totalitarianism and Political Religion: Definitions and Critical Reflections on Criticism of an Interpretation," *Totalitarian Movements and Political Religions*, 5: 3, 326–375.

Griffin, Roger (1991). *The Nature of Fascism* (New York: St. Martin's Press).

Griffin, Roger (2007). *Modernism and Fascism: The Sense of a Beginning under Mussolini and Hitler* (Houndmills: Palgrave Macmillan).

Imbrescu, Ilie (1940). *Biserica şi mişcarea legionară* (Bucharest: Cartea Românească).

Ioanid, Radu (1990). *The Sword of the Archangel: Fascist Ideology in Romania* (Boulder, CO: East European Monographs).

Ioanid Radu (2003), "The Sacralized Politics of the Romanian Iron Guard," *Totalitarian Movements and Political Religions*, 5: 3, 419–453.

Iordachi, Constantin (2004). *Charisma, Politics and Violence: The Legion of Archangel Michael in Interwar Romania* (Trondheim: Trondheim Studies on East European Cultures and Societies).

Iorga, Nicolae (1901). *Istoria lui Mihai Viteazul pentru poporul românesc* (Bucharest: Minerva).

Iorga, Nicolae (1908). "Ce e un naţionalist," *Neamul Românesc*, 14 October.

Lalane, André (1992). *Vocabulaire technique et critique de la philosophie* (Paris: PUF).

Lazzari, G. (1984). "Linguaggio, ideologia, politica culturale del fascismo," *Movimento Operaio e Socialista* 7: 1.

LeBon, Gustave (1898). *Psychologie du socialisme* (Paris: F. Alcan); translated as *The Psychology of Socialism* (Kitchener: Batoche Books, 2001).

LeBon, Gustave (1910). *La psychologie politique et la défense sociale* (Paris: E. Flammarion).

MacDonald, Arthur (1915) "Comparative Militarism," *Publications of the American Statistical Association*, 14: 112, 801–803.

McCalla, Arthur (1994). "Palingénésie Philosophique to Palingénésie Sociale: From a Scientific Ideology to a Historical Ideology," *Journal of the History of Ideas*, 55: 3, 421–439.

McCalla, Arthur (1998). "The Structure of French Romantic Histories of Religions," *Numen*, 45: 3, 258–286.

Mehedinţi, Simion (1923). *Către noua generaţie. Biserica – Şcoala – Armata – Tineretul* (Bucharest: Socec).

Moceanu, Ovidiu (2003). *Teologie și filologie. Andrei Saguna vs. Ion Heliade Rădulescu* (Bucharest: Paralela 45).

Mosse, George L. (1991). *The Nationalization of the Masses: Political Symbolism and Mass Movements in Germany from the Napoleonic Wars through the Third Reich* (Ithaca, NY: Cornell University Press).

Mosse, George L. (1999). *The Fascist Revolution: Toward a General Theory of Fascism* (New York: Howard Fertig).

Moța, Ion I. (1929). "Spasmul și concluziile sale," in *Almanahul Societății "Petru Maior"* (Cluj: Cartea Românească).

Moța, Ion I. (1936). *Cranii de Lemn. Articole, 1922–1936* (Sibiu: Totul Pentru Țară).

Nițescu, Constantin (1932). *Mănăstirea Dealu și Liceul Militar "Nicolae Filipescu"* (Târgoviște).

Otto, Rudolf (1923). *The Idea of the Holy*, trans. John W. Harvey (Oxford: Oxford University Press).

Ozouf, Mona (1989). "Regeneration," in *A Critical Dictionary of the French Revolution*, ed. by François Furet and Mona Ozouf (Cambridge, MA: Belknap Press), 781–791.

Pătrășcanu, Lucretiu. *Sub trei dictaturi* (Bucharest: Forum, 1944).

Payne, Stanley G. (1980). *Fascism: Comparison and Definition* (Madison, WI: University of Wisconsin Press).

Payne, Stanley G. (1995). *A History of Fascism, 1914–1945* (Madison, WI: The University of Wisconsin Press).

Payne, Stanley G. (2005). "On the Heuristic Value of the Concept of Political Religion and its Application," *Totalitarian Movements and Political Religions*, 612, 163–174.

Payne, Stanley G. (2006). "The NDH State in Comparative Perspective," *Totalitarian Movements and Political Religions*, 7: 4, 409–415.

Petrescu, Ion Benone (2002). *Liceul Militar "Nicolae Filipescu" de la Mănăstirea Dealu, 1912–1940 (1948)* (Târgoviște, 2002).

Polihroniade, Mihail (1933). *Axa*, 15 January, I, 1.

Popovici, D. (1935). *Ideologia literară a lui I. Heliade Rădulescu* (Bucharest: Cartea românească).

Sainson, Katia (2001–2002). "'*Le Regénerateur de la France*'": Literary Accounts of Napoleonic Regeneration 1799–1805," *Nineteenth Century French Studies*, 30: 1 and 2, 9–25.

Schenk, H.G. (1969). *The Mind of the European Romantics: An Essay in Cultural History* (Garden City, New York: Doubleday).

Sharp, Lynn (2004). "Metempsychosis and Social Reform: The Individual and the Collective in Romantic Socialism," *French Historical Studies*, 27: 2, 349–379.

Tomoiagă, Ion (1971). *Eliade Rădulescu. Ideologia social-politică și filozofică* (Bucharest).

Weber, Eugen (1965). "Romania," in Hans Rogger and Eugen Weber, eds. *The European Right. A Historical Profile* (London: Weidenfeld & Nicholson).

Weber, Eugen (1966). "The Man of the Archangel," *Journal of Contemporary History* 1: 101–126.

Wehler, Hans-Ulrich (1985). *The German Empire, 1871–1918* (Providence, RI: Berg).

INDEX

The Routledge Companion to Modern European History since 1763
Chris Cook and John Stevenson

The Routledge Companion to Modern European History since 1763 is a compact and highly accessible work of reference. It covers a broad sweep of events since 1763, from the last days of the *ancien régime* to the ending of the Cold War, from the reshaping of Eastern Europe to the radical expansion of the European Union in 2004.

Within the broad coverage of this outstanding volume, particular attention is given to subjects such as:

- the era of the Enlightened Despots

- the Revolutionary and Napoleonic era in France, and the revolutions of 1848

- nationalism and imperialism and the retreat from Empire

- the First World War, the rise of the European dictators, the coming of the Second World War, the Holocaust, and the post-war development in Europe

- the Cold War, the Soviet Union and its break-up

- the protest and upheavals of the 1960s, as well as social issues such as the rise of the welfare state, and the changing place of women in society throughout the period.

With a fully comprehensive glossary, a biographical section, a thorough bibliography, and informative maps, this volume is the indispensable companion for all those who study modern European history.

ISBN10: 0–415–34582–0 (hbk)
ISBN13: 978–0–415–34582–8 (hbk)

ISBN10: 0–415–34583–9 (pbk)
ISBN13: 978–0–415–34583–5 (pbk)

European Dictatorships 1918–1945, 3rd Edition
Stephen J. Lee

European Dictatorships 1918–1945 surveys the extraordinary circumstances leading to, and arising from, the transformation of over half of Europe's states to dictatorships between the first and the second World Wars. From the notorious dictatorships of Mussolini, Hitler, and Stalin to less well-known states and leaders, Stephen J. Lee scrutinizes the experiences of Russia, Germany, Italy, Spain and Portugal, and Central and Eastern European states.

This third edition has been revised throughout to include recent historical research, and has expanded sections on the setting for dictatorships and comparisons between them. There are more detailed discussions of Mussolini, Hitler and the Holocaust, and an entirely new survey of Turkey. This edition also includes a completely new chapter on types of dictatorship which explores both the meaning and widely different forms it can take.

Extensively illustrated with photographs, maps, and diagrams, *European Dictatorships 1918–1945* is a clear, detailed and highly accessible analysis of the tumultuous events of early twentieth-century Europe.

ISBN10: 0–415–45484–0 (hbk)
ISBN13: 978–0–415–45484–1 (hbk)

ISBN10: 0–415–45485–9 (pbk)
ISBN13: 978–0–415–45485–8 (pbk)

Available at all good bookshops
For ordering and further information please visit:
www.routledge.com

Hitler's Germany: Origins, Interpretations, Legacies, 2nd Edition

Roderick Stackelberg

Praise for the first edition:

'This is an important new textbook on the Nazi period which is geared to intermediate and advanced undergraduates and will also interest general audiences ... this book is a real winner and deserves wide use.' *Bruce Campbell, German Studies Review*

Hitler's Germany provides a comprehensive narrative history of Nazi Germany and sets it in the wider context of nineteenth and twentieth century German history. Roderick Stackelberg analyzes how it was possible that a national culture of such creativity and achievement could generate such barbarism and destructiveness.

This second edition has been updated throughout to incorporate recent historical research and engage with current debates in the field. It includes:

- an expanded introduction focusing on the hazards of writing about Nazi Germany
- an extended analysis of fascism, totalitarianism, imperialism, and ideology
- a broadened contextualisation of anti-Semitism
- discussion of the Holocaust including the euthanasia program and the role of eugenics
- new chapters on Nazi social and economic policies and the structure of government as well as on the role of culture, the arts, education, and religion
- additional maps, tables, and a chronology
- a fully updated bibliography.

Exploring the controversies surrounding Nazism and its afterlife in historiography and historical memory, *Hitler's Germany* provides students with an interpretive framework for understanding this extraordinary episode in German and European history.

ISBN10: 0–415–37330–1 (hbk)
ISBN13: 978–0–415–37330–2 (hbk)

ISBN10: 0–415–37331–X (pbk)
ISBN13: 978–0–415–37331–9 (pbk)

Available at all good bookshops
For ordering and further information please visit:
www.routledge.com

The Routledge Companion to Central and Eastern Europe since 1919
Adrian Webb

The Routledge Companion to Central and Eastern Europe since 1919 is a compact and comprehensive reference guide to the subject area, from the Treaty of Versailles to the present day. With particular focus on the early nationalist and subsequent fascist and communist periods, Adrian Webb provides an essential guide to the events, people, and ideas which have shaped, and continue to shape, central and eastern Europe since the re-ordering of Europe at the end of the First World War.

Covering cultural, economic, political, and environmental issues, this broad-ranging and user-friendly volume explores the common heritage and collective history of the region, as well as the distinctive histories of the individual states. Key features include:

- wide-ranging political and thematic chronologies
- maps for clear visual reference
- special topics such as the economy, the environment, and culture
- full list of office holders and extensive biographies of prominent people in all fields
- glossary of specialist terms.

With a wealth of chronological, statistical, and tabular data, this handy book is an indispensable resource for all those who wish to understand the complex history of central and Eastern Europe.

ISBN10: 0–415–44563–9 (hbk)
ISBN13: 978–0–415–44563–4 (hbk)

ISBN10: 0–415–44562–0 (pbk)
ISBN13: 978–0–415–44562–7 (pbk)

Available at all good bookshops
For ordering and further information please visit:
www.routledge.com